THE WAY TO
INDEPENDENCE

Publications of the Minnesota Historical Society
Museum Exhibit Series No. 3

WOLF CHIEF (TSĔ-CA MA-TSE-ÍTSIC), GOODBIRD (TSAKAKIS-SAKIS), AND
BUFFALO BIRD WOMAN (MAXIDIWIAC)
Photographed by Gilbert Wilson, 1906 and 1913
MHS (Wilson [1903-18]:43 and MHS photo VI-30-13)

THE WAY TO
INDEPENDENCE

MEMORIES OF
A HIDATSA INDIAN FAMILY,
1840-1920

CAROLYN GILMAN

MARY JANE SCHNEIDER

WITH ESSAYS BY W. RAYMOND WOOD,
GERARD BAKER, JEFFERY R. HANSON,
AND ALAN R. WOOLWORTH

MINNESOTA HISTORICAL SOCIETY PRESS • ST. PAUL • 1987

This book is dedicated to the children of Fort Berthold Reservation.

Editor: *Ann Regan*
Designer: *Earl Gutnik*
Principal photographers: *Randy Croce and Eric Mortenson*
Typesetter: *Peregrine Publications*
Color separator: *Photo Mechanical Services, Inc. (PMSI)*
Printer: *Sexton Printing, Inc.*
Binder: *Midwest Editions, Inc.*

This book was funded, in part, by grants from the National
Endowment for the Humanities, a federal agency, and the
Northwest Area Foundation. Additional support was provided by
the Northwestern Bell Telephone Company and the Northwestern
Bell Foundation.

MINNESOTA HISTORICAL SOCIETY PRESS, ST. PAUL 55101

10 9 8 7 6 5 4 3 2 1

International Standard Book Number:
0-87351-218-9 (cloth)
0-87351-209-X (pbk.)

Library of Congress Cataloging-in-Publication Data

Gilman, Carolyn, 1954-
    The way to independence.

    (Museum exhibit series ; no.3)
    Bibliography: p.
    Includes index.
    1. Hidatsa Indians – Social life and customs – Exhibitions. 2. Hidatsa Indians – Social
conditions – Exhibitions. 3. Indians of North America – Missouri River Valley – Social life and
customs – Exhibitions. 4. Indians of North America – Missouri River Valley – Social
conditions – Exhibitions. 5. Wilson, Gilbert Livingstone, 1868-1930 – Ethnological
collections – Exhibitions. I. Schneider, Mary Jane. II. Title. III. Series.

E99.H6G55 1987   978'.00497   87-11152
ISBN 0-87351-218-9
ISBN 0-87351-209-X (pbk.)

Contents

Foreword, *Nicholas Westbrook,* vi
Introduction, *Carolyn Gilman,* viiii
THE WAY TO INDEPENDENCE, *Carolyn Gilman and Mary Jane Schneider,* 1

1.
The journey to Like-a-Fishhook Village, 4
The sounds of Like-a-Fishhook, 8
Small Ankle's earth lodge, 13
Family ties, 20
Winter, 22
The seasons of childhood, 27

2.
Corn songs, 32
A daughter's duties, 38
Gifts of skill, 43
Working with the women, 53
Feeding the family, 58

3.
Hunting like a man, 69
The promise of the buffalo, 80
Societies, 88
Lessons in leadership, 98

4.
Love and marriage, 107
Buying knowledge, 116
The birth of Goodbird, 122
White men at Like-a-Fishhook, 128
The agent and his goods, 139

5.
Ho-Washte, 144
A new language, 152
The Grass Dance, 159

6.
The journey to Independence, 181
Son of a Star's cabin, 192
Goodbird seeks his god, 196
Farming, new and old, 200

7.
Goodbird and the agent, 209
The Indian police, 214
Wolf Chief founds a store, 217
The assault on Indian culture, 222
Wolf Chief writes to Washington, 226
Going away to school, 231

8.
Ranching, 242
In the home, 252
The outside world comes closer, 264
Son of a Star dies, 274

9.
A new calling for Goodbird, 279
A new calling for Buffalo Bird Woman, 285
Wolf Chief sells the shrine, 296
Independence Day, 302
Looking forward, 312

10.
Afterwards, 314

THE HIDATSA WORLD, 319

Origins and settlements of the Hidatsa, *W. Raymond Wood,* 322
The Hidatsa religious experience, *Gerard Baker,* 328
The Hidatsa natural environment, *Jeffery R. Hanson,* 333
Contributions of the Wilsons to the study of the Hidatsa, *Alan R. Woolworth,* 340
A guide to the Wilson collections, *Mary Jane Schneider,* 348

A note to readers, 352
Bibliography, 353
Index, 363

Foreword

"There is properly no History, only Biography."
— *Ralph Waldo Emerson*, Essays, 1841

The Way to Independence catalog and exhibition appear during the centenary year of the Dawes Indian Severalty Act, one of the bleak landmarks in federal Indian policy. The intention of that act was to "civilize" Native Americans by dissolving tribes as legal entities and allotting reservation lands to individuals. Proponents expected that Indian hearts and minds would be transformed by altering the physical circumstances of Indian life: their material culture, their relationship to the land, their forms of governance. For years, American historiography has celebrated the apparent success of that policy. The Dawes Act, the history books tell us, "symbolized the final victory of the whites."

But biography illuminates a subtler story of cultural accommodation. In *The Way to Independence,* curator Carolyn Gilman traces the lives of three Hidatsa Indians: Buffalo Bird Woman, Wolf Chief, and Goodbird. Their life stories demonstrate that the changes wrought by white assimilationist policies and by the modernizing tide of an industrializing world did *not* dissolve Indian culture. Despite the outward trappings of a new world, these resilient people coped with change and fashioned for themselves their own form of cultural independence. *Things* may be in the saddle, as Emerson advised us. But they do not always ride us.

We are able to retrieve the experience of accommodation to modernization with such intimacy and depth because of the superb fieldwork of pioneering Minnesota ethnographer Gilbert L. Wilson. With the conviction that "thick description" (the approach advocated today by Clifford Geertz) was the only responsible strategy for cultural documentation, Wilson worked from 1906 to 1918 to assemble an extraordinary collection of artifacts, photographs, and field notes on the Hidatsa Indians of North Dakota. Sharing his era's apocalyptic vision of the transforming power of objects, Wilson focused on recording a "vanishing" way of life. But in the process of gathering *every* detail, Wilson also captured the Hidatsa struggle to cope with reservation life in the early twentieth century.

Wilson collected professionally for the American Museum of Natural History (AMNH) and the Museum of the American Indian, Heye Foundation; his personal collection was donated to the Minnesota Historical Society (MHS) in 1931. Now, half a century later, these collections are being presented comprehensively for the first time in an exhibition and this book, the exhibition catalog. To fill out the picture of Hidatsa cultural change at the turn of the century, Wilson's collections are supplemented with artifacts and graphics from other collections.

The Way to Independence has been a long journey indeed! Planning for the exhibit began with a small grant from the National Endowment for the Humanities. Carolyn Gilman served as curator for this undertaking. Joining the project team as research associate was Mary Jane Schneider, then chair of the Indian Studies Department at the University of North Dakota. Counseling the project team were an advisory committee of MHS collection curators and a group of specialists on Hidatsa history: Gerard Baker, a ranger with the National Park Service and himself a Mandan-Hidatsa; Jeffery R. Hanson, assistant professor of anthropology at the University of Texas at Arlington; Roy W. Meyer, professor of English at Mankato State University; W. Raymond Wood, professor of anthropology at the University of Missouri-Columbia; and Alan R. Woolworth, research fellow at the Minnesota Historical Society. During the planning year, efforts focused on collection analysis, correlating materials held at the MHS with those at the AMNH and elsewhere.

The exhibition and this catalog became reality through major grants from the National Endowment for the Humanities and the Northwest Area Foundation, with additional support from Northwestern Bell Telephone Company and the Northwestern Bell Foundation. In addition, the 3M Foundation helped to support educational programs, and the Otto Bremer Foundation underwrote a related traveling photographic exhibition. To each of these benefactors, the Minnesota Historical Society is deeply grateful. We particularly appreciate the encouragement given this project early on by Sally Yerkovich, former assistant director for general programs at the National Endowment.

A special pleasure of this project has been the opportunity to become acquainted with the Hidatsa living today on the Fort Berthold Reservation. Anson Baker, Cora Baker, Jill Gillette, Doreen Lone Fight, Alyce Spotted Bear, and Tillie Walker readily shared their knowledge of recent reservation history and gave assistance. In addition, Almeda A. Page shared her memories of her work as an educator on the reservation.

Numerous museums have generously lent artifacts

and their staffs have shared information: American Museum of Natural History: Carmen O. Collazo, Stanley A. Freed, George S. Gardner, Belinda Kaye, Judith Levinson, Anibal Rodriguez, and Sasha Stollman; State Historical Society of North Dakota: Brian Alexander, C. L. Dill, Lynea Geinert, the late Robert C. Hollow, Jr., Gerald G. Newborg, James E. Sperry, and Todd Strand; Museum of the American Indian, Heye Foundation: Nakasha Bonillia, Lee A. Callander, Mary Purdy, and James G. E. Smith; University of Colorado Museum: Terri Berman and Frederick W. Lange; Science Museum of Minnesota: Louis Casagrande and Timothy L. Ready; National Archives, Washington, D.C.: Nancy E. Allyn, Renee M. Jaussaud, and James Zeender; National Archives, Kansas City, Missouri: Nancy Hulston and Alan F. Perry; Olmsted County Historical Society: Brian Hackett. Individuals have also lent valuable materials, including Almeda Page, Mary Jane Schneider, and Deborah Swanson.

This exhibition will travel from 1989 to 1991. Staff at the host institutions have been most encouraging throughout the long gestation of exhibit and catalog. We acknowledge the enthusiastic support of James E. Sperry, State Historical Society of North Dakota; Marsha V. Gallagher, Joslyn Art Museum; and Douglas E. Evelyn and Rayna Green, National Museum of American History.

This exhibit and book were put together by a core team of dedicated workers. Carolyn Gilman, project curator, and Mary Jane Schneider, research associate, collaborated on basic research; Schneider wrote the captions for artifacts from the Wilson and Lowie collections and Gilman wrote the graphics captions and the extended narrative. Susan H. Holland managed production logistics and aided research as assistant curator. Margaret Brunner served as administrative assistant, data-base manager, and typist. Senior accountant Winslow D. Grandstrand provided caution and budgetary wisdom. Earl Gutnik has been the chief designer. John Palmer Low designed the exhibition.

No project of this scale is possible without the wholesale support of an institution and the people who comprise it, and this one is no exception. From the outset, the project had the interest and support of Minnesota Historical Society Directors Russell W. Fridley and Nina M. Archabal. Virtually every staff member aided the project at some time during the past three years. We are grateful for the special assistance of Richelle A. Anderson, Terry Carlson, Donn M.

Coddington, Diane Disse, Mary Dooley, Ellen L. Ferrari, Rhoda R. Gilman, Lila J. Goff, Kathy Hanson, Phillip A. Hutchens, Bryan Johnson, Jane A. Juhnke, Roberta Krim, Dallas R. Lindgren, Elizabeth Martin-Hinton, Tim O'Donnell, Stephen E. Osman, Thomas O'Sullivan, Maureen Otwell, Pamela Owens, Mark Schwartz, Tori E. Setterholm, R. Brad Thiel, Thomas C. Thompson, Jon L. Walstrom, John Wickre, Bonnie G. Wilson, and John J. Wood.

A major project in its own right was organizing, cataloging, and conserving the MHS artifacts used in this exhibition and catalog. That work has been ably carried out by Nancy A. Bergh, Charles O. Diesen, Jean A. Madsen, Paul R. Malcolm, Linda McShannock, Becky Plumer, Hilary Toren, and Jeff Tordoff, under the direction of Curator of Collections Marcia Anderson. Additional collections research was done by John Hiram Wilson.

Under the guidance of Jean A. Brookins, assistant director for publications and research, this book was coaxed to life by staff members of the MHS Press: Mary Burrell, Gloria Haider, Nordis Heyerdahl-Fowler, John McGuigan, Alan Ominsky, and June Sonju. Deborah Swanson prepared the bibliography. Special thanks are due catalog editor Ann Regan and catalog designer Earl Gutnik, who knew when to be patient and when to be draconian.

Randy Croce and Eric Mortenson shared the challenging task of artifact photography. Croce photographed the MHS artifacts and most of those from the State Historical Society of North Dakota; Mortenson photographed artifacts from the American Museum of Natural History and the University of Colorado at Boulder Museum. Ann Kubes worked as an intern helping to marshal information and objects during photography. In addition, each lending institution provided photographs by their own staff photographers. We appreciate the work of David Heald, P. Hollembeak, Brad Piens, and Todd Strand.

Nicholas Westbrook
Curator of Exhibits
Minnesota Historical Society

Introduction

"Is not anthropology properly a study of man himself, and is not even the material culture of primitive man chiefly valuable to us as interpreting the man himself, his philosophy, or his soul?" – Gilbert L. Wilson (Wilson 1924:130)

Few peoples have lived through such a revolution in lifeways as the Plains Indians in the late 19th and early 20th centuries. In a single generation they were catapulted from a pre-industrial, clan-oriented society into the mechanized, entrepreneurial world of turn-of-the-century America. Virtually every aspect of their society came under attack – religions, languages, kinship systems, ways of earning a living, systems of authority. For the non-Indian majority culture, straining to assimilate an influx of European immigrants and cope with the social dissolution of urbanization, conformity was the price of being an American. The scars of this traumatic era are still with us.

This book and the exhibition it is based upon chronicle the transformation of Indian society through the eyes of three members of a Hidatsa family. Their tribe, once known to whites as Gros Ventre or Minitaree, were agricultural village-dwellers, closely related to the Mandan. They were brought to the outside world's attention in the early 1800s by a series of Missouri River travelers – Lewis and Clark in 1804-05, George Catlin in 1832, Karl Bodmer and Prince Maximilian in 1834. After this short bout of celebrity the Mandan and Hidatsa disappeared from popular view. They did not, however, disappear from existence. Today they form part of the Three Affiliated Tribes (Mandan, Hidatsa, and Arikara) of Fort Berthold Reservation, North Dakota.

The family this book focuses on – Buffalo Bird Woman, her brother Wolf Chief, and her son Goodbird – were not prominent leaders or spokesmen in their lifetimes. But they were different in that their story was preserved in their own words, pictures, artifacts, and photographs. Today they can speak for the thousands of other Indian families whose stories were never recorded. From them we can still hear about the human and personal price of the Plains Indian experience – and, we might hope, learn from it.

The family's story can now be told because of their work with anthropologist Gilbert L. Wilson between 1906 and 1918. Their collaboration produced an extraordinarily well-documented collection that has been in the care of four different museums in St. Paul, Minn., and New York, N.Y., for the past 70 years. This book and exhibition partially reassembles the collection and the story it tells.

The story of Buffalo Bird Woman's family shows that the Hidatsa did not follow a one-way street toward acculturation. Their traditional society was not a static, ideal way of life that disappeared without a trace when overwhelmed by whites. The process of change was more complex than that. Individuals reacted in their own idiosyncratic ways to the pressures upon them. They developed strategies for coping with change, and for co-opting aspects of the white world to achieve continuity in their lives. They neither clung without compromise to old ways, nor accepted the new without question. Instead, they created a new culture within a culture.

When Gilbert Wilson was learning anthropology in the first decade of the 20th century, it was an axiom of the field that material culture was the key to unlocking all other aspects of culture. It was the last heyday of what is often called the "Museum Age" of anthropology, when the field was heavily focused upon chronicling craft traditions and the technological development of mankind. The fact that most anthropologists were institutionally affiliated with museums was not so much the cause of this focus as a symptom of an underlying mindset. As the factory glow of industrialism reached its height, Euro-American society was bent on material explanations – in political philosophy, in social ideology, and in history. Technology had, after all, allowed European expansion and colonization over virtually all the world and European domination of its native cultures. "You are what you manufacture" seemed to encapsulate both the history of human culture and the future destiny of the working masses.

The anthropologists of the late 19th century added to their materialism another theory characteristic of their time: evolution. Based on archaeological work in Europe and the Middle East, European scientists devised a theory of universal cultural evolution so persuasive it is still taught in grade schools today. Not surprisingly, it was based on technology. First came the Stone Age, when brutish primitives chipped rude tools from rocks. Next came the Bronze Age, when the smelting of metals allowed civilization to take a giant leap forward – particularly in the manufacture of weapons. After that came the Iron Age, leading to

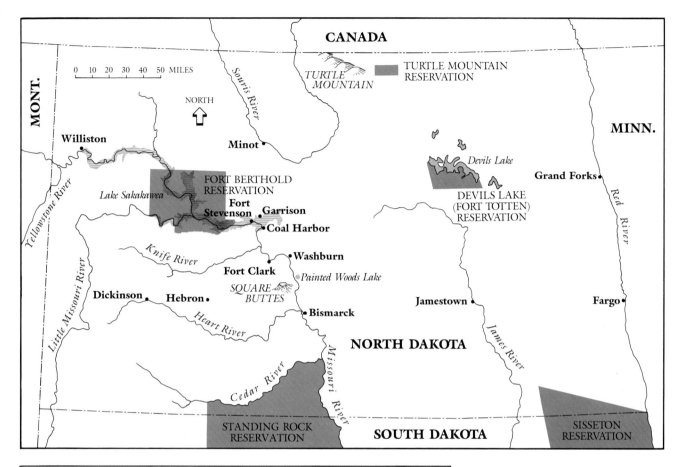

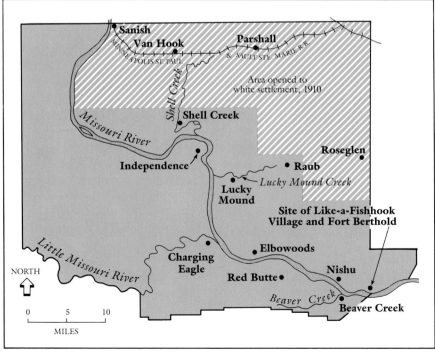

NORTH DAKOTA AND FORT
BERTHOLD RESERVATION, 1915
***Based on Cram 1907 and Meyer
1977: opp p. 192***
The shaded area in the map of North
Dakota shows the area flooded by Lake
Sakakawea, created by the Garrison
Dam in the 1950s.

medieval swords, Renaissance muskets, the steam engine, and civilization as we know it.

All cultures (so the theory went) followed the same evolutionary path from "primitive" to "advanced." European industrial civilization was the necessary culmination of the evolutionary process. It was the yardstick used to measure all other cultures and to chart their progress toward the ultimate goal. And technology formed the hatchmarks on the yardstick.

In that mysterious realm where scientific theory interacts with the public consciousness, the idea of technological evolution was simplified to the point of caricature. Technology, people began to believe, made cultures what they were – not vice versa. Gunpowder and the printing press were not merely part of the complex mix of events that was the Renaissance – they caused it. The steam engine produced Victorian England, the dynamo 20th-century America. Looking through this lens on their own history, Europeans and Euro-Americans attained an almost mystical belief in the power of their technology to effect cultural change in other groups.

Among American historians at the turn of the century, faith in the culture-altering power of technology led to a belief that the white man's superior tools had almost single-handedly shattered American Indian culture. Frederick Jackson Turner and his followers painted a portrait of the fur trade spreading across North America, causing Indians to abandon old beliefs, skills, and economic systems and to become pathetically dependent upon European goods: on receiving guns they forgot overnight how to make or use bows and arrows; when iron knives came, knives of flint were instantly discarded; the Indians' art lost aesthetic merit, their tools lost craftsmanship. Unable to manufacture, repair, or resupply their European tools, the Indians degenerated into debt and helplessness.

There were profound policy implications in this historical view of Indian culture. Government Indian policy in the late 19th and early 20th centuries was guided by a desire to "save" the tribes from their imagined dependence and cultural decline and to give them the gift of superior Euro-American civilization. To achieve this, policymakers set about systematically breaking the Indians' bonds to the tribal past in order to bring them into conformity with mainstream society. Many liberal thinkers believed such policies were merely accelerating a natural process that inevitably would have led the Indians to their own industrial civilization, given enough time.

The crusade to "civilize" the Indians was above all a campaign to redeem them with white materialism. They were given private land to awaken enterprise and dispel the old idea that land should be used as it was, not changed. The Office of Indian Affairs bombarded them with an extraordinary inventory of goods designed to impart the magical touch of civilization – plows, saws, textiles, cookware, kerosene lamps. The unspoken theory was that once the Indians' desires for such amenities were awakened, they would abandon old ways as they had abandoned flint knives, adopt the cultural baggage the artifacts represented, and embrace the role that imparted full membership in the industrial system – producer of goods.

Anthropologists of the day sometimes questioned the government's homogenizing, "one world" policies, but they seldom questioned technology's power to bring about the change. Concerned (as every generation of anthropologists has been) that Indian culture was slipping away under the onslaught of frame houses and frying pans, they rushed out to document it – by amassing museum collections of classified artifacts.

Yet even as the government pursued its assimilationist course, anthropologists were laying the groundwork for a different approach. At Columbia University in the first decade of the 20th century, a new generation of scholars under Franz Boas was discovering cultural relativism and a holistic approach to their work. Technology, they argued, had to be seen within a social context, not as a universal framework. Ethnocentric cross-cultural comparisons had to be laid aside. Boas argued that "civilization is not something absolute, but that it is relative, and that our ideas and conceptions are true only so far as our civilization goes" (Jacknis 1985:83).

Today it is a rare anthropologist indeed who argues for universal laws of cultural evolution – particularly ones based on the Euro-American experience. Yet in history books and in public policy the old attitudes linger. Aid to Third World countries often flies the banner of industrialization, on the uncritical assumption that economies develop through evolutionary stages with industrialism at the pinnacle. America continues to export technologies as cultural emissaries, scarcely questioning their ability to transmit American values. If people drink Coca-Cola and watch *Miami Vice* on their Zenith televisions powered by Westinghouse hydroelectric plants, how can they fail to love America?

And yet a look at Indian culture, which has been

subjected to a barrage of industrial technologies for over a century, might make policymakers pause. Contrary to the efforts and expectations of five generations of bureaucrats and reformers, Indian tribes have not assimilated seamlessly into majority society. They have adopted Euro-American material culture as completely as any turn-of-the-century agent might have wished; yet they remain profoundly different. They are not the same as in the 19th century, but they are still emphatically not white.

What kept Euro-American material culture from transforming the inner culture of Indian hearts and minds? Gilbert Wilson, remarkable among anthropologists of his day for his interest in what he called the "souls" of Indian people, left us some tantalizing hints. The chronicle of Buffalo Bird Woman's family, which he preserved, gives us the means to start answering the question.

If one were to page casually through a scrapbook of Buffalo Bird Woman and her family, their story would seem like a textbook case of wholesale acculturation. The family members spent many years in the traditional environs of Like-a-Fishhook Village, living in the age-old architecture of the earth lodge and supporting themselves by gardening and buffalo hunting, much as generations of their Mandan and Hidatsa ancestors had done. They participated in the ceremonial life of their community by joining age-grade societies and buying the rights to sacred bundles. Buffalo Bird Woman's brother, Wolf Chief, learned both the ceremonial and practical aspects of intertribal warfare, while she purchased the rights to make such valuable commodities as baskets and houses. The tribal economic system was based on the principle of the giveaway rather than the Euro-American principle of accumulation of property. Complex kinship systems governed family members' behavior toward others in the community. Their lives were thoroughly embedded in a traditional system of beliefs.

By 1918, however, members of Buffalo Bird Woman's family lived on 160-acre plots in a rural North Dakota community with the all-American name of Independence. They farmed with gasoline tractors and lived in frame houses. Buffalo Bird Woman now inhabited a world of cast-iron frying pans, calico dresses, and wood stoves. Wolf Chief had turned entrepreneur and supported himself by ranching and running a general store. Buffalo Bird Woman's son Goodbird was a government employee and Congregational minister.

Both the men spoke and wrote English – letters complaining to their representatives in Washington, among other things. Goodbird and Wolf Chief periodically rode the train to Chicago to market the reservation cattle.

Were these people acculturated? Their material culture says so. Their traditional technology had been largely overwhelmed by the products of the industrial world. They no longer tanned hides for clothing, or made pottery, or wove rush mats. The Indian agents at Fort Berthold Reservation thought that this alone spelled surrender, and they viewed it with approval. Year after year the agents' annual reports counted their progress by chronicling the decline of the earth lodge, blanket, and moccasin, and the rise of the frame house, suit coat, and shoe.

Only when we look more closely at the evidence do we begin to see what even the agent missed. To understand what was really going on, it is necessary to see the difference between the physical artifact and the cultural image that the artifact projects upon people's minds.

Within cultures, artifacts are powerful media of communication. For the early 20th-century white American, a plow carried connotations of yeoman self-sufficiency and industrious labor. It was the instrument that had tamed a wilderness for Thomas Jefferson's "chosen people of God." An agent simply could not see an Indian using a plow without projecting onto him the values of diligence, stability, and independence the plow evoked in the agent's own mind. But had such a process of communication in fact taken place?

One hint lies in the archaeological collections from Like-a-Fishhook Village, occupied from 1841 to the mid-1880s. The portrait of traditional life in that collection is strikingly at odds with the portrait in anthropological collections. While anthropologists selected artifacts that did not show cross-cultural contact, archaeologists generally found less biodegradable objects: metal, glass, ceramic, and other manufactured goods. Thus we learn that, though the traditional Hidatsa at Like-a-Fishhook relied on herbal and ceremonial medicine, they were also consumers of Davis's Vegetable Pain-Killer and Mexican Mustang Liniment. They hunted buffalo, but they also ate canned beef off china plates. They fetched water in heartskin bags, but they boiled it in tin coffee pots. Clearly, Euro-American technology had a firm place in Hidatsa life even in the traditional milieu of Like-a-Fishhook Village. Yet we know from documentary sources that their ceremonial, clan, and social systems flourished regardless of this technology.

In the 20th century, the proportion of traditional technology to modern is different, but it still coexists with old social and cultural systems. White architecture was well adapted to white attitudes toward privacy, the nuclear family structure, gender roles, and family ritual. Yet the evidence suggests that when frame house met Indian family, it was at least partly the architecture that changed meaning. Doors, absent in most earth lodges, were frequently left standing open – people did not knock on them. Interior partitions were either absent or arranged to leave a large meeting and sleeping room well adapted for extended family gatherings. The fire, though encased in a cast-iron stove, still formed a focal point for socialization in the center of the room. Meals were not always eaten off tables, and furnishings were lined up against outside walls instead of being used to compartmentalize the room.

Missionaries and agents at Fort Berthold Reservation encouraged the adoption of underground burial customs, equating them partly with white attitudes toward hygiene and "decency," and partly with Judeo-Christian attitudes toward the dead and the afterlife. By the early 20th century, scaffold burial among the Hidatsa was rare, yet funeral customs still showed a striking continuity in all but the physical trappings. The dying person took on much responsibility for directing the funeral. He was dressed in his finest clothes, and his clan relatives assembled to pay final respects. The family gave lavish gifts to the clan fathers and aunts for conducting the funeral and, later, for decorating the grave. Although the burial clothes were store-bought, the coffin was of wood, the grave was marked by a headstone, and the flowers were silk, the *meanings* of those artifacts were still profoundly Hidatsa. The objects of white culture, far from undermining Hidatsa belief, had become a silent means of reaffirming clan ties and the sacred obligations associated with them.

Even more abstract "artifacts" like Euro-American institutions were subject to reinterpretation in a Hidatsa setting. Wolf Chief told a vivid story from his childhood about the members of the Black Mouth Society, who were the traditional enforcers of order at Like-a-Fishhook Village. When refuse started to pile up between the earth lodges, the Black Mouths initiated a mass cleanup, enlisting the women of the village to sweep up the areas around their homes. Five decades later, the U.S. government agent called upon the Indian police – a group strikingly similar in duties and powers to the Black Mouths – to institute a reservation clean-up day. One can read between the lines of the agent's report his pleasant surprise at the success of the idea. He doubtless attributed people's ready cooperation to their increasing acceptance of the Progressive values of hygiene and cleanliness, but the truth was more complex. The police were working within the old framework of tribal organization, going with the grain of tradition instead of against it.

On a more concrete scale, the objects of industrial society often made the transition into a Hidatsa milieu. Hoes and axes were used with shortened handles to accommodate old habits of working. Patchwork quilts perpetuated an Indian aesthetic. United States flags took on ceremonial significance in dances, and Liberty Loan bonds were purchased with the enthusiasm once reserved for giveaways.

These examples suggest that changes in the tangible world were not always synchronized with changes in the inner world of the Hidatsa. New technologies or customs might be adopted, but their meanings could still remain peculiarly Hidatsa and profoundly foreign to the outside world from which the objects came. Subjected to extraordinary economic, political, and ideological pressure to conform, the Hidatsa learned to use white artifacts as allies, for the objects spoke to the authorities in a different language than they did to the Hidatsa.

The message of Buffalo Bird Woman's family for historians and anthropologists is cautionary: do not assume lightly that you can interpret the subtle nuances of another culture's lifestyle and material culture. This story gives the rest of us a glimpse of three people's courage, resilience, and humor under extraordinarily trying circumstances. I could not have worked with Buffalo Bird Woman, Wolf Chief, and Goodbird for three years without gaining tremendous affection and respect for them. The temptation has been strong to present them as better than they were, to prevent them in retrospect from making mistakes. But that would have taken away their humanness. I hope others can accept them for what they were, with all their faults as well as their virtues, and gain from their integrity as we all pursue our personal ways to independence.

Carolyn Gilman
Project Curator

THE WAY TO INDEPENDENCE

The Way to Independence

It was late July 1906 when Gilbert L. Wilson first looked across the Missouri River and saw the little settlement of Independence, North Dakota, lying below the rugged bluffs. His interest in American Indians had led him there, to a spot "practically inaccessible for a white man." Independence was in the center of the Fort Berthold Reservation, where people of the Mandan, Hidatsa, and Arikara tribes lived (Wilson 1906b:7-9; Knight 1917:5).

Wilson wanted to study Indian artifacts and how they were made. The teacher at the Independence schoolhouse led him to the home of Edward Goodbird, a local Indian man who spoke both English and Hidatsa. Wilson did not know it, but when Goodbird's family let him into their home, they were leading him on the first steps of a 12-year journey into their past.

Wilson listened as Goodbird's elderly mother, Buffalo Bird Woman, recounted memories reaching back over 65 years. He took notes as Wolf Chief, Goodbird's uncle, told stories. In Wilson's penciled notebooks, in his photograph album, and in the artifacts he collected, the family's journey through the years began to take on life.

They had traveled a complicated road to reach Independence. Buffalo Bird Woman and Wolf Chief had grown up in a traditional earth-lodge village where skilled craft work, war honors, and ceremonial societies were the stepping stones to success. But their lives changed when policies of the United States government forced the breakup of the centuries-old village life. The tribe's members were scattered onto isolated reservation farms and pressured to conform to the immigrant society around them. Their livelihood came under attack, and with it their social institutions, their religion, and their family life.

Whites wanted to pour Indians into the mold of Euro-American culture. But Buffalo Bird Woman's family had not become white. Instead, slowly and subtly, they had changed the mold. Though they might own the tools of the industrial

world, the things they made were not used in Euro-American ways. Though they might abide by the laws and institutions of the U.S. government, those institutions took on an Indian flavor. Though they might be good Christians, theirs was a new Christianity that did not turn its back on older teachings. They had coped with radical change, but never surrendered to it. Instead, they found their way to a new kind of independence.

This book, which is based on an exhibition of the collection Wilson made, gives us the chance to follow where he went. In its pages we will also meet Buffalo Bird Woman's family and share with them the memories of how they reached the town of Independence.

INDEPENDENCE FERRY
Photographed by Gilbert Wilson, 1916
MHS photo IX-43-1916

The journey to Like-a-Fishhook Village

I was born down at Knife River in the Five Villages," Buffalo Bird Woman said. "My people had had the smallpox so that they still speak of . . . the smallpox year. My birth was three years after the smallpox year. I was born in an earth lodge" (Wilson 1914b:250).

The Hidatsa, also known as Gros Ventre and Minitaree, lived by the Missouri River along with their close allies, the Mandan. Unlike many of their nomadic neighbors on the Great Plains who traveled hundreds of miles in their seasonal rounds, they farmed in the fertile valley and built fortified towns on the terraces overlooking the river. In the summertime, whole villages left the valley to hunt buffalo on the plains.

When Lewis and Clark visited the Hidatsa in 1804–05, the tribe lived at the mouth of the Knife River, in three densely settled communities containing (by one observer's estimate) over 2,000 people (Meyer 1977:34). But in 1837 smallpox struck. In one terrible year of sickness, almost half the Hidatsa and seven-eighths of the Mandan died. The remainder decided to leave the towns where so many had perished and search for a place where the timber was thicker, the soil was richer, and they could build a stronger, safer town (Meyer 1977:95, 100).

"We set out for our new home in the spring, when I was four years old," said Buffalo Bird Woman. "I remember nothing of our march thither. My mothers have told me that . . . the march was led by the older chiefs and medicine men. My grandfather was one of them. His name was Missouri River. On the pommel of his saddle hung his medicines, or sacred objects, two human skulls wrapped in a skin. They were believed to be the skulls of thunder birds, who, before they died, had changed themselves into Indians. After the chiefs, in a long line, came warriors, women, and children" (Maxidiwiac 1921:11).

The people journeyed north, following the river. Their pilgrimage ended at a hooklike bend in the Missouri, where they halted to plan a new village.

"When our tribe came . . . to build a village they camped in tipis," Wolf Chief said. "All the more important medicine men of the tribe sat in a circle and considered what design or plan they should use in laying out their village. This was seven years after the smallpox year. . . .

"At that time Missouri River owned . . . the most important shrine in the tribe. Therefore they asked Missouri River, 'Your gods are strongest. What plan do you suggest?'

"Missouri River got up and took the two skulls and went around in a wide circle, returning to the place where he had started. He said, 'We will leave a circular, open place as I have marked: thus shall we plan the village!' Then he said to Big Cloud . . . 'Your gods are strong. Where do you want your earth lodge?'

"Big Cloud answered, 'Where the shrine stands now, and facing the west. For my gods are birds, and the birds come from the west and also the thunders. And so I am sure we shall have plenty of rain. . . .'

"The next man asked to select a spot for his lodge was Has Game Stick. They said to him, 'You stand up!'

"He did so and said, 'My god is the Sunset Woman. I wish my lodge to face the sunset. Then I think the Sunset Woman will remember me. . . .'

"Then they said, 'Bad Horn, you stand and choose [a] place for your earth lodge!'

"He said, 'My gods are the bears, and bears always have the mouth of their dens toward the north. So I want to have my lodge open toward the north and so my bear gods will remember me and I will remember them and I will wish this village to stand a long time.' . . .

"They told Missouri River to stand up, and select. Missouri River took the two skulls and singing his mystery song he walked around the circle that he had marked out with his steps before, going with the sun, his right hand toward the center. . . . Three times he went around the circle and the fourth time he stopped. . . . Missouri River stood and prayed: 'My gods, you are my protectors. Give your protection to this village. . . . Do you send rains and the gardens will grow. And the children will grow up strong and healthy because my shrine is in this village.'

"Then he said to the other men: 'This now will be all. Get up and the rest of you choose sites for your lodges where you will, only keep the circle open as I have marked'" (Wilson 1911:160–62).

The village was built just as Missouri River commanded. They named it Múa-íduskupe-ḣiśeś – Like-a-Fishhook (Wilson 1913a:162).

"BIRD'S-EYE VIEW OF THE MANDAN VILLAGE, 1800 MILES ABOVE ST. LOUIS"
Painted by George Catlin, 1837-39
Oil on canvas
H. 61.2 cm, W. 73.6 cm
National Museum of American Art, Smithsonian Institution, gift of Mrs. Joseph Harrison, Jr.

White visitors to the Mandan and Hidatsa before the establishment of Like-a-Fishhook were surprised to find farms covering much of the Missouri bottomland between the American Fur Company's Fort Clark fur post and the Knife River. Riding between two of the villages on Knife River in 1806, fur trader Alexander Henry noted that "Upon each side were pleasant cultivated spots, some of which stretched up the rising ground on our left, whilst on our right they ran nearly to the Missouri. In those fields were many women and children at work, who all appeared industrious. Upon the road were passing and repassing every moment natives, afoot and on horseback, curious to examine and stare at us. Many horses were feeding in every direction beyond the plantation" (Henry and Thompson 1897, 1:344). This painting shows the Mandan village near Fort Clark, about 15 miles southeast of the area Henry described.

Mih-Tutta-Hang-Kusch, Mandan Village"
Painted by Karl Bodmer, 1834
Watercolor on paper
H. 28.6 cm, W. 42.2 cm
Joslyn Art Museum, gift of Enron Art Foundation

Prince Maximilian of Wied-Neuwied and Swiss artist Karl Bodmer spent the winter of 1833–34 at Fort Clark, near the Mandan village of Mih-Tutta-Hang-Kush southeast of Knife River. Maximilian described their first arrival by steamboat: "As we drew nearer the huts of that village, Fort Clarke, lying before it, relieved by the back-ground of the blue prairie hills, came in sight, with the gay American banner waving from the flagstaff. On a tongue of land on the left bank were four white men on horseback; Indians, in their buffalo robes, sat in groups upon the bank, and the discharge of cannon and musketry commenced to welcome us." Bodmer painted this watercolor the following winter (Bodmer 1984:284; Wied 1905-06, 22:344).

"HIDATSA VILLAGE, EARTH-COVERED LODGES, ON THE KNIFE RIVER, 1810 MILES ABOVE ST. LOUIS" (DETAIL)
Painted by George Catlin, 1832
Oil on canvas. See color page 168
H. 28.5 cm, W. 36.6 cm
National Museum of American Art, Smithsonian
Institution, gift of Mrs. Joseph Harrison, Jr.
Artist George Catlin visited the Hidatsa villages on Knife River eight years before Buffalo Bird Woman's birth. Walking along the river past the Big Hidatsa Village (shown here), he remarked upon the "garrulous groups of men, women, and children, who are wending their way along its winding shores, or dashing and plunging through its blue waves, enjoying the luxury of swimming, of which both sexes seem to be passionately fond." Catlin stayed several weeks, observing a corn ceremony and a buffalo hunt (Catlin 1841, 1:186).

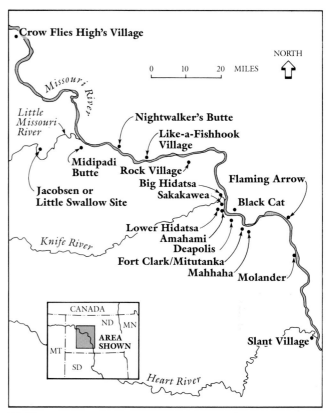

MAJOR MANDAN AND HIDATSA VILLAGE SITES ON THE MISSOURI RIVER
(Based on Wood 1986:21)
The remains of ancient Mandan and Hidatsa villages line the Missouri for over 250 miles, from below present Bismarck to above Williston. When Buffalo Bird Woman was born, the Hidatsa lived in the villages of Hidatsa, Awatixa, and Awaxawi; their sites are now known to archaeologists as Big Hidatsa, Sakakawea, and Amahami. The two Mandan settlements that were counted as part of the Five Villages are now known as Black Cat and Deapolis. The village of Mih-Tutta-Hang-Kush (or Mitutanka), adjacent to Fort Clark, was founded in 1822; it was not considered one of the Five Villages. Other sites shown here are earlier Hidatsa and Mandan villages located by archaeologists.

The sounds of Like-a-Fishhook

The Mandan and Hidatsa were town dwellers. Like people in medieval Europe, they traveled out to the fields by day and returned to the village at night. Their settlements were large: in 1849, Like-a-Fishhook Village held more people than any white settlement in the newly established Minnesota Territory.

Like-a-Fishhook, like many towns, was noisy, busy, and crowded. Sanitation was a continual problem. But it was hard to be lonely there.

A young fur trader named Henry A. Boller, who lived at Like-a-Fishhook in 1858, described the sounds of the town on a typical day. Dawn was signaled by the dogs. "The mournful howl . . . breaks the almost death-like stillness. The notes are instantly caught up by others and directly every cur in the village is taking his part with commendable energy. Commencing soft and low, the noise grows louder and deeper until it finally dies away in a prolonged wail. . . . This canine matinée rouses up the sleepers, a stir is evident in the village, and soon the curling smoke from the lodges floats in the morning air" (Boller 1959:53).

By day, the village was lively with the sounds of children playing, dogs barking, and people passing to and fro. But as the heat of noon set in, "stillness reigns supreme where a short time since resounded the stir and hum of busy life. The very dogs are quietly sleeping in the shade of the lodges. . . . The parched and

Like-a-Fishhook Village (details)
Photographed by Stanley J. Morrow, c. 1870
From stereoscopic view cards
SHSND A-1509, C-912
South Dakota photographer Stanley Morrow traveled to Like-a-Fishhook Village to make photographs in 1870, but he may have added to his album on several trips he made through the area in later years (Hurt and Lass 1956:71-76). His pictures clearly show the mix of architecture present by 1870. These photographs represent the traditional mixture of earth lodges and two-story drying scaffolds for vegetables and meat. The view at right was identified as the Hidatsa "medicine lodge."

smoking prairie fairly radiates under the intense heat of the noonday sun" (Boller 1959:61–62).

Evening was a time of activity. People swam in the Missouri, drove in the horses from the prairie, and fetched water for the evening meal. Games and races were popular, and the laughter of the onlookers echoed across the village. But as night came, "the sounds of life in the Indian camp grow fainter and fewer. . . . A woman is wailing by the dead body of her husband on one of the scaffolds. The sound is mournful in the extreme, as if her heart was broken with a grief that could not be comforted." The songs of young men courting or the drums of a society meeting might be heard. But soon "the perfect stillness that reigns over everything is broken only by the sullen, ceaseless roar of the Missouri, or the occasional whistle of an elk, borne faintly on the evening breeze" (Boller 1959:72–73).

The sounds of Like-a-Fishhook lasted only until autumn. As cold weather drew near, families closed up their houses and left to build winter cabins in the protected woods along the river where fuel was easier to find. The deserted lodges of Like-a-Fishhook "are damp and chilly, and have an earthy, sepulchral smell. Tall medicine-poles . . . rear their lofty tops like the spires and minarets of an Oriental city" (Boller 1959:208–9). But in spring the people would return, for as Buffalo Bird Woman said, "We looked upon our summer lodges . . . as our real homes" (Maxidiwiac 1921:44).

LIKE-A-FISHHOOK VILLAGE (DETAILS)
Photographed by Stanley J. Morrow, c. 1870
From stereoscopic view cards
SHSND A-3736, A-3854
Log-cabin architecture, introduced by whites, was adopted especially by the Arikara, who moved to Like-a-Fishhook after 1862. By 1872 the village held 97 log cabins and 78 earth lodges (Matthews 1877:4). The photograph at right was probably taken from a roof or bastion of Fort Berthold II, south of the village.

MAP OF LIKE-A-FISHHOOK VILLAGE
Drawn by Frederick Wilson, based on
a map by Wolf Chief and his
relative Butterfly, 1911
MHS (Wilson 1934:350)
Wolf Chief and Butterfly identified the
owners of all seventy lodges marked on
this map. "Butterfly and I cannot
recollect just where every lodge stood,"
Wolf Chief cautioned, "but we can get
them all approximately placed because
we can remember what lodges stood
behind each of the central circle's
lodges." He said the arrangement
reflected the village in about 1860
(Wilson 1911:158-64).

Like-a-Fishhook Village had
several notable landmarks:

1 The ceremonial circle. This
central open space was typical of
Mandan towns from early times. It was
here that the sacred ark stood and
public ceremonies like the Okipa (see p.
331) took place (Bowers 1965:38-39).
"The round circular open place in the
center of the village where ceremonies
were held and children played, got worn
down and the wind blew away the loose
dust," said Buffalo Bird Woman. "After
a rain, water was held here for three
days. It was at this place we got water
for mixing the earth to mend the roof
[of the earth lodge]" (Wilson 1918a:41).

2 Palisade. Like-a-Fishhook was
fortified for protection against the
Sioux. At one time it was surrounded
by a four-foot ditch and earthen
embankment surmounted by a log
palisade and bastions. People went in
and out through two hinged gates.
Every morning a bell rang as the gates
opened; women then set out for the
fields and men drove the horses out to
graze. At night, the bell again rang as
people and horses returned, and the
gates were closed (Wilson 1911:158;
Bowers 1965:40).

3 Trading posts. The first Fort
Berthold, on the north side of the
village, was built by Pierre Chouteau,
Jr., and Company (called the "American
Fur Company") when the village was

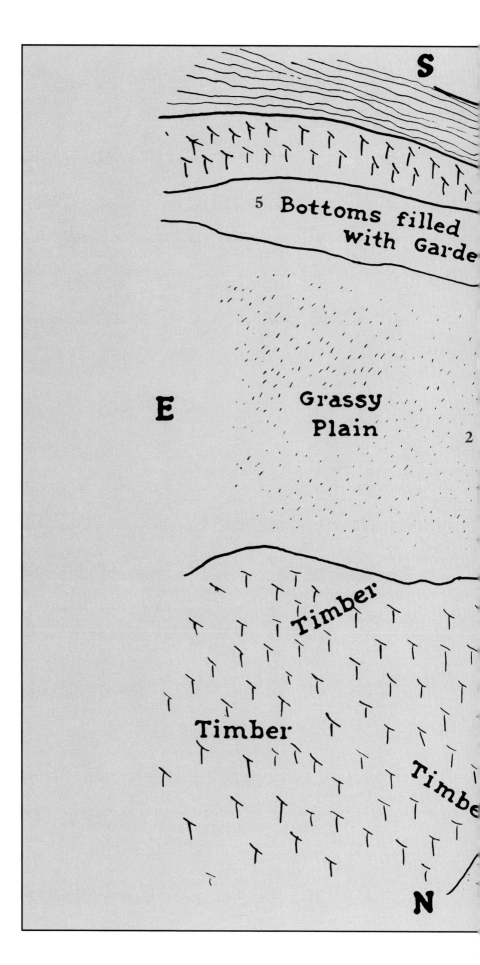

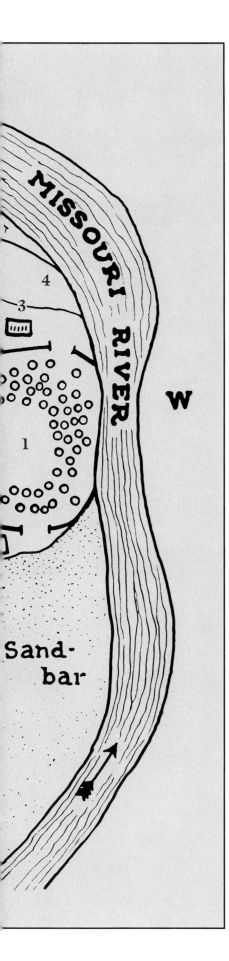

first established. Fort Atkinson, on the south, was used after 1858 by the succession of companies known as "the opposition." In 1862, the old fort burned and the larger firm moved into Fort Atkinson, renaming it Fort Berthold. It is now known to archaeologists as Fort Berthold II (Smith 1972:5, 9–10).

4 Steamboat landing. Steamboats were the main link to the outside world from the time the village was established. In the early years, only two steamboats a year plied the Missouri this far north, but by 1866 there were as many as 31 (Meyer 1977:126). The arrival of the steamboat was a gala affair, as described by fur trader Henry Boller in 1858: "All was now bustle and commotion. The Stars and Stripes were run up on the flag-staff, and . . . the *banneréts* made their appearance, painted and decked out in all the colors of the rainbow. . . . Nearer and nearer she steamed. The paddle-wheels could be distinctly heard. Then a white wreath of smoke enveloped her bows, and directly the report of a cannon was borne on the air. The salute was promptly returned, and continued until she lay at the landing within a stone's throw of the post" (Boller 1959:341).

5 Corn fields. Each family had a marked portion of the river bottomland to farm. Buffalo Bird Woman's family field was about 180 by 90 yards (Wilson 1917:24). People did not quarrel over farmland boundaries, Buffalo Bird Woman said, because "It was Indian rule to keep the garden grounds very sacred. We did not like to have disputes over them" (Wilson 1915b:458).

6 Small Ankle's earth lodge. The site of Small Ankle's lodge was probably the one Big Cloud chose when the village was first laid out, facing west in honor of the birds and thunder (Wilson 1911:159, 162). Small Ankle was Buffalo Bird Woman's father.

"INDIAN VILLAGE, FT. BERTHOLD" (DETAIL)
Photographed by O. S. Goff, 1879
From a stereoscopic view card
SHSND Col. 88-30
Almost ten years after Morrow's visit, Bismarck photographer O. S. Goff made a series of stereoscopic views of Like-a-Fishhook Village. Many of these were saved by trader and agent Daniel W. Longfellow, who donated them to the State Historical Society of North Dakota. This one is identified as the Mandan section of the town, looking northeast from the top of the trader's store. The building in the foreground is evidently part of the store.

F IRE CANOE AT FT. BERTHOLD"
Painted by William de la Montagne Cary, 1874
Oil on canvas. See color page 180
H. 62.5 cm, W. 101.5 cm
***The Thomas Gilcrease Institute of American History
     and Art 0126.1934***
William Cary painted Like-a-Fishhook Village from the point
of land just downstream. The blockhouse is that of Fort
Berthold II. Cary, a popular Western illustrator, visited Like-
a-Fishhook in 1861 and again in 1874, when he accompanied
the Northern Boundary Survey on assignment for *Harper's
Weekly* (Ladner 1984: xiii, 115).

T HE REAL SITE OF FISH HOOK VILLAGE, 1834–1886"
Painted by Martin Bears Arm, 1912
***Yellow, purple, blue, red, brown, and green paint on
     heavy canvas***
H. 220.7 cm, W. 175.3 cm
SHSND 779
"In the village, lodges were going up, some every year and
others coming down," Wolf Chief recalled (Wilson
1911:162). Martin Bears Arm's diagram of Like-a-Fishhook
may reflect a later date than Wolf Chief's, judging by the
prevalence of log cabins. The pairing of many of the cabins
with earth lodges suggests that they were used as winter
dwellings. Small Ankle's family had such a pair of seasonal
dwellings, according to Goodbird (Wilson 1913a: 156;
Goodbird 1913: fig. 42). The pattern probably became
common after about 1866, when the villagers began
staying at Like-a-Fishhook year-round (Meyer 1977: 124).

   The numbers on the diagram refer to the occupants of
the houses. Small Ankle's lodge is number 72, on the right
side of the circle. The founding date in the title is a decade
too early.

Small Ankle's earth lodge

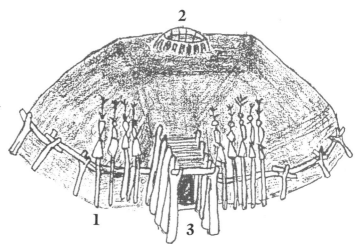

Buffalo Bird Woman grew up in the earth lodge of her father, Small Ankle. Though they called it Small Ankle's, the house actually belonged to his wives, for women built the lodges and passed them on to their daughters. Because Hidatsa husbands often went to live with their wives' families, an earth lodge usually was home to a group of related women and their husbands, brothers, and sons. So it was in Buffalo Bird Woman's home.

"We thought an earth lodge was alive and had a spirit like a human body, and that its front was like a face, with the door for mouth," said Buffalo Bird Woman (Maxidiwiac 1921:45). Small Ankle's lodge had to be treated with particular respect, for it was not just a home: it was also a community meeting place and church. In it was kept the *Maa-dúúsh* – the holy objects of the Midipadi or Waterbuster clan which Missouri River had brought from the Knife River villages. Children in most houses were allowed to climb up on the roof to play, but not in Small Ankle's. "The two Skulls of the Big Birds' Ceremony made our lodge a sacred one, and we were not permitted to lounge or sport on the roof," said Goodbird (Wilson 1913a:25).

In Small Ankle's family, people were careful to act according to rules of proper conduct. Children learned that a courteous person always entered an earth lodge counterclockwise; if he was a guest, he never sat down without being asked; if he was given food, he ate it all or took the remainder home with him; he would never pass disrespectfully before the shrine (Maxidiwiac 1921:51).

Just as there were proper actions, there were also proper places for things and people. Each member of the family had his or her own bed. At mealtimes, the cook sat to the right of the fire as one entered the lodge. Other seats around the fire were reserved for honored guests. Dishes, boats, dogs, horses, pottery, food, clothes, and tools all had places. But tidiness did not always prevail. "Whenever we had been out late to a dance or anything," said Buffalo Bird Woman, "we hung our clothes on the lazy back or else on the top of the bed, and put them away in the morning" (F. Wilson 1912b:42).

SMALL ANKLE'S EARTH LODGE
Traced by Gilbert Wilson from a drawing by Goodbird, 1913
Black carbon and pencil on tracing paper
H. 5 cm, W. 8.5 cm
MHS (Goodbird 1913:fig. 42)
Small Ankle's earth lodge had features like others in the village:

1 Votive poles. These symbols reflected the religious affiliations of the house's occupants. "Those on the right as one enters the door are votive poles to the Above Woman and Sacred Woman. Those on the left are to the Birds," Goodbird explained. "These votive poles were not all put up at once. One was erected to the Birds and to the Above Woman each year or at least at considerable intervals. . . . However, as a votive pole was never removed, but allowed to stand until it fell, a number of them came to be standing on either side of the door as the years went on" (Wilson 1913a:156).

2 Smoke hole and bullboat. The smoke hole was both a chimney and the major source of light inside. "There was always a spot in the lodge where the sun fell on the floor through the smoke hole, and this we called the 'sunbeam,'" said Wolf Chief (Wilson 1915a:72). During the day, the beam would move with the sun, tracing an arc on the earth lodge floor. People told time by the position of the sunbeam. In Small Ankle's lodge in summer, it was near the southwestern main post about nine o'clock in the morning; at noon it was centered between the two northern posts; when it neared the northeastern post, it was about five o'clock (Wilson 1913a:24).

To keep the wind from blowing down the smoke hole and making the earth lodge smoky, inverted bullboats were placed atop the roof in bad weather. They also prevented puppies from falling down the hole (Wilson 1907b:25, 1934:368).

3 Entryway. A covered walkway was the only entrance to the lodge. At the inner end was a skin door stretched on a wooden frame, hinged at the top with thongs. A buffalo-hoof rattle was attached to the door. "When the door was raised and let fall, the five hoof bells made a tinkling noise. We called these the door rattle," said Buffalo Bird Woman (Wilson 1918a:37-38).

THE INTERIOR OF THE HUT OF A MANDAN CHIEF"
Based on a watercolor by Karl Bodmer, 1833-34
Copper plate engraving on paper
H. 28 cm, W. 40.3 cm
MHS (Wied 1840—43: tableau 19)

The layout and furnishings of this house are very similar to Small Ankle's, as described by Buffalo Bird Woman and Goodbird. The artist is standing at the back of the lodge looking toward the door, which is hidden by the wooden partition. Buffalo Bird Woman's family, unlike this one, never allowed dogs into the house past the partition (F. Wilson 1912b: 33).

The next pages show objects that are like those in this earth lodge.

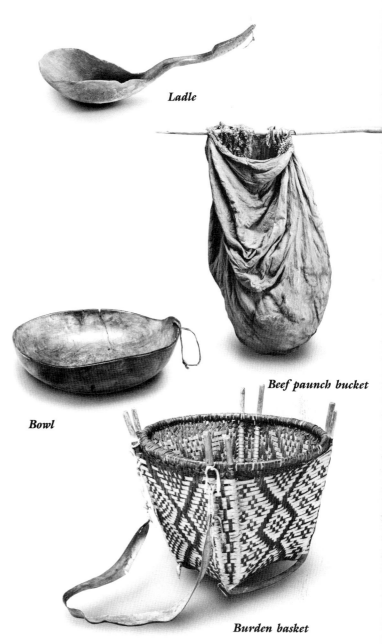

Ladle

Bowl

Beef paunch bucket

Burden basket

Mortar and pestle

Pottery vessel and stand

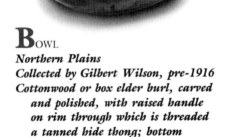

MORTAR AND PESTLE

***Hidatsa. Bought from Buffalo Bird
Woman. Made by Small Ankle,
c. 1860***

Collected by Gilbert Wilson, 1912

***Mortar of whole ash log hollowed
at one end and cracked at rim;
tied together with cloth strips.
Pestle carved of single ash piece;
handle polished, weighted end
ax-marked***

***Mortar: L. 37 cm, D. 24.2 cm.
Pestle: L. 94.5 cm***

AMNH 50.1/7330a, b

Small Ankle made this mortar by
burning out the center with hot coals.
"This mortar has been used in our
family for nearly fifty years," explained
Buffalo Bird Woman. "The last time it
was used was four years ago, since when
I have had it by me to remind me of
old times. . . .

"We had an ash pestle in the
house which we used in this mortar
until it wore out. It had been in use a
long time before. My father then went
into the woods and made another, the
one I sell you now. He made it about
40 years ago. It has worn down seven
or eight inches by use.

"The weighted end of the pestle
you note, is ax-marked. In the lodge we
habitually used to cut meat or a bone or
the like with an ax, on the weighted
end, as on a block. Hence the ax marks
usually found on a pestle" (Wilson
1912:311-12).

BOWL

Northern Plains

Collected by Gilbert Wilson, pre-1916

***Cottonwood or box elder burl, carved
and polished, with raised handle
on rim through which is threaded
a tanned hide thong; bottom
patched with piece cut from baking
powder can***

L. 32 cm, W. 25.5 cm

MHS 7059.52b

Bowls like this one were used for serving
food. They were carved from the knot
on a cottonwood or box elder tree.
Buffalo Bird Woman described how
Cedar Woman, a Hidatsa, used a knife
to shape the outside and hollow the
inside, and then scraped out the center
with a piece of steel wrapped in hide to
finish the bowl (Wilson 1916b:155).

BURDEN BASKET

***Hidatsa. Made by Buffalo Bird
Woman?***

Collected by Gilbert Wilson, pre-1918?

***Willow wood frame. Sides of dyed and
undyed willow and box elder bark
strips woven in diamond patterns.
Rawhide tumpline attached to
frame. See color page 170***

H. 47 cm, D. 45 cm

MHS 7059.61

The Arikara, Mandan, and Hidatsa
made large and small baskets of woven
willow or box elder bark. Among the
Hidatsa, basket-making was an art
practiced by only a few women,
including Buffalo Bird Woman. It is
likely that this one was made by Buffalo
Bird Woman, who, in discussing
another example of her work, described
her distinctive technique: "This basket
that I made was woven all over in
diagonal pattern such as is used on the
bottom of all the baskets that I weave. I
commonly wove the back of a basket in
one design, while the front and the two
sides were woven in another or very
similar design. Now-a-days, I sometimes
weave each side of the basket different
to show the different designs that I can
use" (Wilson 1912:240; MHS photos
III-19 to III-32 and V-56-1912 to
V-59-1912; AMNH photos 286337 to
286349).

LADLE

Northern Plains
Collected by Gilbert Wilson, pre-1918?
Rocky Mountain (Bighorn) sheep
horn, molded and carved; piece of
tanned hide threaded through hole
in tip of S-shaped handle
L. 48 cm, W. 13 cm
MHS 7059.55

This food ladle, whose carved handle is
much worn by use, was made in the
same way as other spoons and drinking
cups. Buffalo Bird Woman described the
process: "When I was a girl we used
Rocky mountain sheep horn spoons. An
old buck mountain sheep's horn made a
fine spoon. One made from the horn of
a young sheep was apt to go back to its
original shape. . . . However, we made
spoons from the horns of both buck
and ewe.

"The horn was boiled long in a
kettle, when it could be cut with a knife
like wood. It was then cut roughly into
shape, and rapidly, before it got cold.
Then it was oiled and held to the fire,
and trimmed into final shape, very
carefully.

"Spoons were of different sizes,
some big, some quite small" (Wilson
1916b:156).

POTTERY VESSEL AND STAND

Mandan. Made by Hides and Eats
Collected by Gilbert Wilson, 1911
Pot of black clay tempered with
crushed stone, decorated on rim
and body with vertical incised lines,
and flaked during firing. Stand of
willow twigs and leaves bound with
black and white cotton cloth, then
wrapped with willow bark strips
Pot: H. 13.5 cm, D. 13 cm. Stand:
D. 15 cm
AMNH 50.1/6038a, b

"Always we kept pots put away in a safe
place," Wolf Chief remembered. "This
was in the rear, near the place the
family medicines, or shrine were kept,
usually. We made ringlets of willow
bound about with bark; and into these
we set our pots, one in each ringlet. We
never set the pots on the bare ground.

"Our clay pots we considered
sacred. When a pot, set in a safe place
cracked, we knew that someone was
going to die" (Wilson 1910a:289).

This pot, along with several
others, was made for Wilson by Hides
and Eats, a Sioux woman adopted as a
child by the Mandan and living in
Independence in 1911. She was Wolf
Chief's clan aunt (Wilson 1910a:283,
289). Wilson attributed the flaking on
the surface of the pot to the poor
quality of the clay (Wilson 1910a:287).

BEEF PAUNCH BUCKET

Hidatsa. Made by Wolf Chief
Collected by Gilbert Wilson, 1908
Beef stomach with sharp willow stick
handle; three holes plugged by
piercing stomach with a stick,
twisting, then tying with twine
H. 58 cm, W. 28 cm
AMNH 50/7089

Buckets made from buffalo or beef
stomachs were used to hold the day's
water supply for the household. If the
household was very large, sometimes
more than one bucket was needed.
"When the paunch bucket was empty,"
Wolf Chief explained, "it was carried
down to the river and filled. Usually it
was brought back only about half filled
lest the membrane be broken by the
weight in the jolting that it was sure to
get as it was carried up the steep bank
of the river on someone's back. After
the half filled paunch was hung up again
in the earth lodge, it was filled quite or
nearly full with water fetched in smaller
buckets of buffalo heart skin" (Wilson
1909a:101; MHS photos III-3 to III-7).

A TWELVE POST EARTHLODGE WITH THE ROOF REMOVED"
Drawn by Frederick Wilson, 1912
MHS (Wilson 1934: fig. 27)

This sketch represents Buffalo Bird Woman's memory of her father's lodge in about 1875. Buffalo Bird Woman's description of it was transcribed by Gilbert Wilson's brother Frederick (F. Wilson 1912b: 32-44). She explained the meanings and uses of several important features inside Small Ankle's earth lodge. Goodbird's sketches of some of these are identified at right.

1 Iptsi akú topa. The four 11½-foot-tall posts which supported the roof were the center of the earth lodge. "We said the four posts were alive and we prayed always and made offerings," Buffalo Bird Woman said. "We thought the house to be sacred & the posts upheld it" (Wilson 1908a: 23; 1918a: 10, 29). It was customary to wrap a symbolic strip of cloth around each post a little above eye level (Wilson 1913a: 24; MHS photos IV-98-1911, V-61-1912).

2 Fireplace. The fire was kept in a stone-lined pit at the very center of the lodge. A drying pole, supported above it on forked uprights, held meat, wet moccasins, and other things as they dried; iron pots and sides of beef were sometimes suspended from the pole for cooking (Wilson 1913a: 24).

3 Small Ankle's bed. The bed which stood against the partition and next to the fire was used by Small Ankle and his oldest wife. "He used it as a sitting-place through the day," Goodbird recalled. "He often sat on his bed just in front of the fire-place and near under the smoke-hole plucking out his grey hairs. . . . Our people laughed at anyone who had grey hairs and teased him about it" (Wilson 1913a: 8).

4 Atuka. The place opposite the door was where honored guests were invited to sit. "When a guest entered the lodge he always came in on the right side of the door," Buffalo Bird Woman said. "'Come in,' we would say. 'Sit in the a-tu-ka,' – the honorable place back of the fire. At this place there was always a mat ready" (Wilson 1910a: 308;

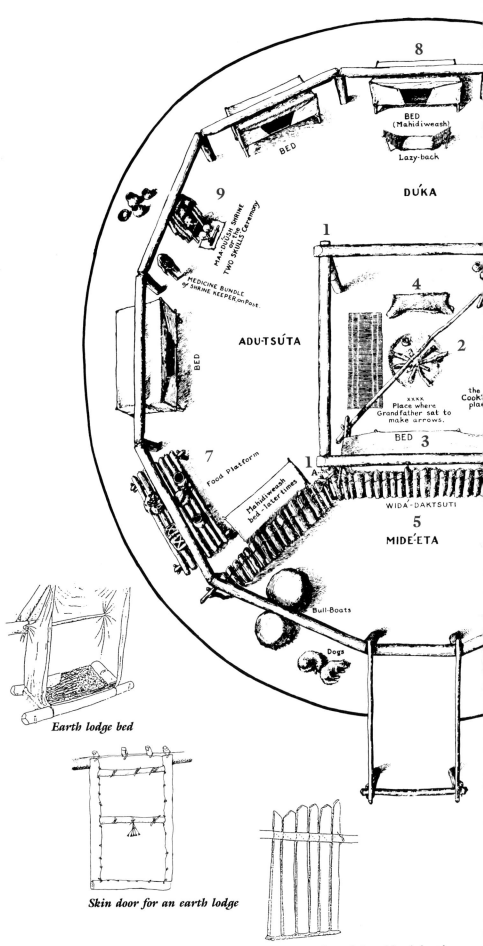

Earth lodge bed

Skin door for an earth lodge

Construction of the wida-daksuti or fire screen

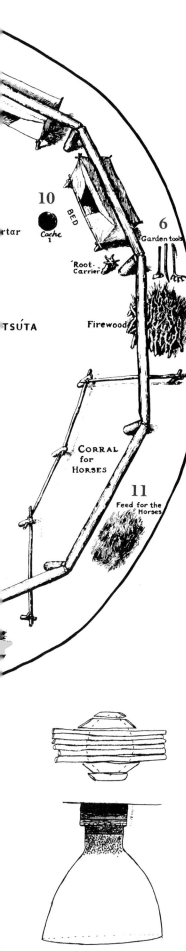

Cover and cross section of a cache pit

Matthews 1877:136). In later years, there stood a bench here made from a sawed board on blocks. "This we regarded as white man's furniture," said Goodbird (Wilson 1913a:24).

5 Widá-daksuti. Just inside the door was a wooden partition "put up to keep the wind from rushing in thru the doorway and blowing the fire about and smoking up the lodge." It was made of split logs set upright in a trench and woven together at the top with rawhide, made fast (according to Buffalo Bird Woman) "so as to keep out the dogs and boys" who might steal the food stored nearby (F. Wilson 1912b:32, 36).

6 Atuti. Around the perimeter of the lodge, twelve short pillars supported the rafters. The slanting outer walls formed a triangular space behind the pillars which was called the atuti. It was a storage space for bullboats, tent covers, firewood, and other articles (F. Wilson 1912b:32; Matthews 1877:6).

7 Food storage platform. A raised wooden platform like a table was used for storing meat and vegetables. Dishes and bowls were also kept here (Wilson 1913a:20). "Often when hunters came back we put the fresh meat here on this platform until we were ready to use or to cure it," said Buffalo Bird Woman. "Often the boys' stealing societies would raid the lodges and . . . this food was the object of the stealing societies' raids" (F. Wilson 1912b:32, 33).

8 Beds. The beds stood around the outer wall of the house, one for each person or couple. They were fitted with skin canopies decorated with the honor marks of the occupants and a buffalo-robe curtain for privacy. The curtain was "usually thrown up over the top of the bed [canopy] during the day . . . and was let down at night" (F. Wilson 1912b:35). The mattress and covers were buffalo robes, the pillows were of skin stuffed with antelope hair (Wilson 1914b:394).

9 Sacred bundles. Several of the men in the household owned personal bundles which hung from free-standing posts in the rear of the lodge. In addition, Small Ankle was keeper of the *Maa-dúush*, the ancient bundle of the Midipadi or Waterbuster clan, which was stored in an altar-like wooden shrine. The space between the shrine and the central post nearest it was holy

ground. "It was therefore not permitted to walk between the post and the Sacred Bundles. . . . If one wished to pass over to the left of the lodge, he should . . . pass between the post . . . and the fire," Goodbird said (Wilson 1913a:22; F. Wilson 1912b:41).

10 Cache pit. The family had at least four cache pits for storing dried corn and vegetables. They were bell-shaped, narrow at the top and wide at the bottom, and were covered with wooden trap doors. The largest was about seven feet deep and had to be entered with a ladder; this one, inside the house, was only about four feet deep. "We did not open the cache every day, but took out each time enough to last several days," said Buffalo Bird Woman (F. Wilson 1912b:36).

11 Corral. Only valuable riding horses were kept inside the house "when needed for work or hunt," or when weather or nearby enemies made it dangerous to leave them outside (Wilson 1913a:23).

EARTH LODGE BED
Drawn by Goodbird, 1914
Pencil on paper
H. 18.2 cm, W. 17.5 cm
AMNH (Goodbird 1914b:fig. 76)

SKIN DOOR FOR AN EARTH LODGE
Traced by Gilbert Wilson from a
*   drawing by Goodbird, 1918*
Black carbon and pencil on paper
H. 13 cm, W. 11.5 cm
MHS (Goodbird 1918:fig. 32)

CONSTRUCTION OF THE
WIDÁ-DAKSUTI OR FIRE SCREEN
Drawn by Goodbird, 1914
Pencil on paper
H. 16.2 cm, W. 12 cm
AMNH (Goodbird 1914b:fig. 75)

COVER AND CROSS SECTION OF A
CACHE PIT
Drawn by Goodbird, 1915
Black carbon and pencil on paper
Cover: H. 6.3 cm, W. 3.9 cm. Cross
*   section: H. 9.8 cm, W. 8.2 cm*
MHS (Goodbird 1915:figs. 68, 69)

Family Ties

When Buffalo Bird Woman was six, the tribe went to winter at Round Circle Place, three miles north of Like-a-Fishhook. But before the year was over they called it another name – Smallpox Winter Camp. "Many died of the disease," remembered Buffalo Bird Woman. Her own mother, Weahtee, was among the dead (Wilson 1918a:98).

Her mother's death did not leave Buffalo Bird Woman an orphan. By Hidatsa custom, a child had many mothers. Closest was the biological mother. "In speaking of his own mother who bore him, a child says, ika," Buffalo Bird Woman explained. "This word is much closer to the heart." But Buffalo Bird Woman also called her mother's sisters "ika." In addition, a female member of her father's clan was called "mother," though in this case the proper word was "hu" or "mahu" (Wilson 1911:173; Matthews 1877:156, 229). Later, when she joined a society, Buffalo Bird Woman acquired still more mothers. All had special obligations to her.

All the children of the people she called "mother" were her brothers and sisters. The clan brothers of her father were also her fathers, and his clan sisters were her clan aunts. Cousins were even more numerous. "These relations meant much to us Indians," Buffalo Bird Woman said. "Members of a clan helped one another in need; and thought the gods would punish them if they did not. Thus if my mother was in need, members of the Tsistska clan helped her; if she was hungry, they gave her food. If her child was naughty, my mother called in a Midipadi to punish him. . . . When my father died, his clan fathers and clan aunts bore him to the burial scaffold and prayed his ghost not to come back to trouble the villagers" (Wilson 1918a:665).

Even more special than her mothers was her "grandmother," Turtle. "After the death of my mother, it fell to Turtle to care for me much of the time," Buffalo Bird Woman remembered. "My grandmother used to tell me stories as she sat or worked by the lodge fire." Over the years, they developed a close and lasting relationship (Maxidiwiac 1921:35, 36).

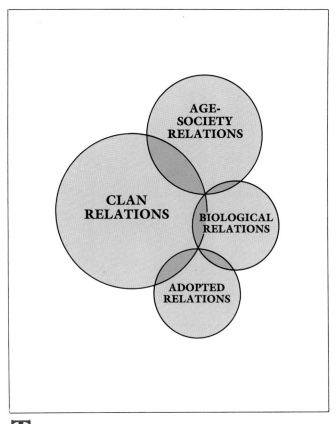

TYPES OF KINSHIP

Hidatsa people had several kinds of relationships with others in the tribe:

1. Biological relations. Family ties were reckoned very differently among the Hidatsa than among Euro-Americans. For example, Buffalo Bird Woman might address a niece, nephew, or cousin as "son" or "daughter." A relative considered distant by Europeans was often felt to be much closer among the Hidatsa (Bowers 1965:80–103).

2. Clan relations. Buffalo Bird Woman inherited her clan, the Tsistska or Prairie Chicken, through her mother. All other members of the Prairie Chicken clan were her brothers and sisters, so she could not marry them. Clan relatives were responsible for the upbringing and conduct of all younger clan members, and they were obliged to help in sacred and ceremonial situations (Bowers 1965:71).

3. Society relations. The Hidatsa had a series of social organizations known as age societies. When Buffalo Bird Woman joined a society, all the other members became her sisters. Members of other, related societies became her mothers, fathers, and daughters (Bowers 1965:93).

4. Adopted relations. Adopted relations were frequently of another tribe, and might be of any age. Adoptions were often performed through solemn ceremonies. When one of Buffalo Bird Woman's family adopted someone, she also became related to that person (Bowers 1965:91).

European Version

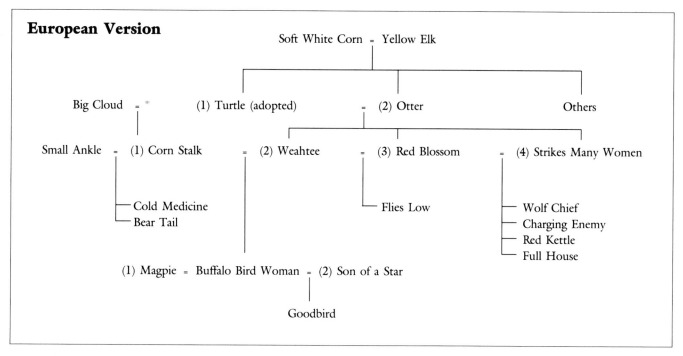

Hidatsa Version

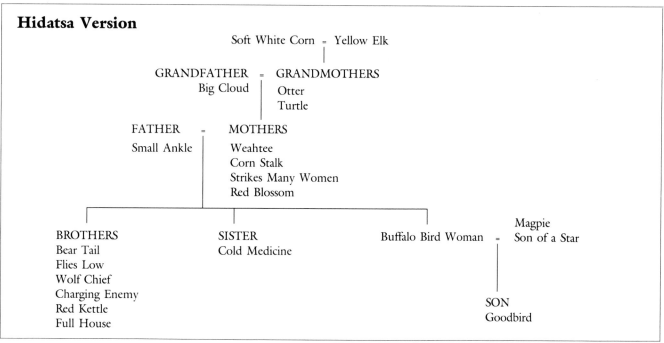

BUFFALO BIRD WOMAN'S IMMEDIATE FAMILY

Winter

"Our village at Like-a-Fishhook bend was inhabited in the summer time, and was in prairie country," said Buffalo Bird Woman. "Our fall and winter home was in the winter village which we built down in the woods along the Missouri. This was not prairie country. The ground was covered with underbrush and shaded by trees" (Wilson 1914b:362).

The trip to the winter village in fall was a time of bustle and excitement. "We gathered in all our corn, filled up all our cache pits, and prepared to transport as much of the corn as we could to our winter village. . . . Our own family had dogs with travois, and in these were carried the family dishes, pail, ax, hoe, and the like" (Wilson 1914b:346, 350).

"As each family was ready," wrote another observer, "its head led the way, followed by a train of pack and riding horses, trav[oi]s, dogs, women, and children. . . . Every one seemed to enjoy immensely the change from the staid life at the summer village" (Boller 1959:178, 184).

Before leaving, the people had chosen a winter chief whose duty it was to select the campsite and protect the people throughout the winter. Each year the leader was different, and so was the wintering place (Wilson 1914b:221).

Once they had arrived, the women set about building winter homes. These were much like their summer homes, but smaller. Large trees were felled to build the framework. "Axes were ringing in all directions," said Buffalo Bird Woman. "Here and there two women would be cutting trees near each other, and a tree would threaten to fall on one of them. The cutter could be heard crying out, 'Look out! – Look

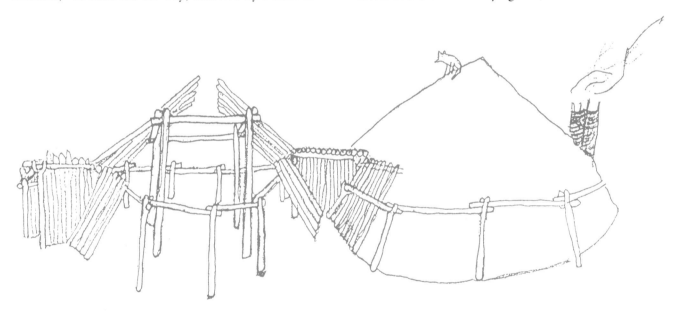

WINTER EARTH LODGE OF BIG CLOUD, UNDER CONSTRUCTION
Drawn by Goodbird with instruction from Wolf Chief, 1914
Pencil on paper
H. 7.5 cm, W. 15 cm
AMNH (Goodbird 1914b:fig. 14)
In 1857, when Wolf Chief was eight years old, his grandfather, Big Cloud, built his winter lodge at Bent Enemy Killed Village, opposite the future site of Independence. In this drawing the main lodge is under construction. The lodge on the right, called a "twin lodge," was a type of small structure often built for older people and children, since it was easier to keep warm. This particular twin lodge was built to house a white man who had married a woman of Big Cloud's family. It had a chimney of mud and sticks instead of the customary smoke hole. The two lodges were united by a covered walkway (Wilson 1914b:227, 231).

"The winter earth lodge was a somewhat rough affair," Wolf Chief said. "We built rough because we would very likely not come to the same place the following year to winter, and also it was easier. . . . Some men who had the character for being good workers helped their wives with the cutting of the logs for their lodge. Other men who were less energetic left all the work to their wives. After all it was looked upon as the woman's part to do it anyhow" (Wilson 1914b:219, 222).

out there!' Every body was busy" (Wilson 1914b:374).

Along with the excitement, winter brought dangers – cold, hunger, and storms. But none was more dreaded than illness. The Hidatsa used a wide range of medicines, from herbs to patent cures. New medicines, however, had not altered their philosophy about healing. That remained closely linked to their faith.

"As a babe I proved rather sickly," said Buffalo Bird Woman. "My father, to get me over my sickness, decided to give me a new name, and called me . . . Buffalo Bird Woman. . . . I do not know why my father chose this name to give me. Perhaps he had a dream or vision; he never told me" (Wilson 1914b:250).

One winter, sickness seemed to threaten the life of her little brother, Wolf Chief. "When I was seven years old," he later said, "it was told in camp that a man named Water Drop had come down with smallpox. . . . Water Drop died and all his family took down with the smallpox, so all our villagers ran away from that place. I had some kind of breaking out on my skin that made it

red, and my mother was much frightened, thinking I had the smallpox. My family called in my grandfather, who opened his shrine or medicine bundle and burned some pulverized cedar leaves before it. He took out some buffalo hair from the bundle and held it in the smoke of the cedar incense, then held it to my face and prayed to the gods of the sacred bundle to preserve me."

But in this crisis, a neighbor had a different idea. "A man named Rough Arm went to Fort Buford [where the Yellowstone River flows into the Missouri]," Wolf Chief said, "and got medicine and vaccinated all us children. . . .

"The next day there was a heavy fall of snow and we saw many eagles flying southward. The people . . . thought this a good omen. 'Let our sickness pass away from us!' they prayed to the eagle spirits; and it is a fact that no one took the smallpox outside of Water Drop's family" (Wilson 1914b:167-70).

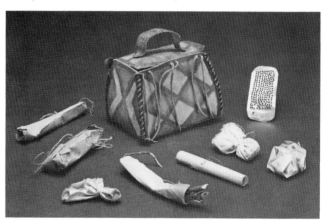

BOX WITH HERB CURES
Sioux. Bought from Iron Woman
Collected by Gilbert Wilson, 1910
Rawhide box painted in red, green, yellow, and blue
geometric designs; side seams laced with red yarn over
black fabric; handle attached to top with tanned leather
thongs. Grater made from perforated tin. Seven pieces of
root and plants wrapped in lined paper or muslin and
tied with sinew. See color page 177
Box: L. 14 cm, W. 10 cm, H. 14 cm. Grater: L. 8.5 cm,
W. 4.2 cm. Plants: L. 6.5 to 13 cm
AMNH 50.1/5466a-h
The plants in this rawhide box represent cures for earache, consumption, stomach ache, bleeding, swellings, headache, and other problems. Iron Woman, a Sioux living among the Hidatsa at Fort Berthold Reservation, said that most of the plants were powdered and steeped to make a tea (Wilson 1910a:list of items purchased, p. 1-3).

WINTER VILLAGE OF THE MINATARRES [HIDATSA]"
(DETAIL)
Based on a watercolor by Karl Bodmer, 1833–34
Copper plate engraving on paper
H. 26.3 cm, W. 32.2 cm
MHS (Wied 1840–43: tableau 26)
Although the Mandan, Hidatsa, and Arikara lived together during the summer at Like-a-Fishhook Village, the three tribes usually built separate winter villages, as they had in the days when this picture was painted. Buffalo Bird Woman's descriptions of winter villages fit this illustration well. The men in the left foreground are playing a game with what Goodbird called ice-slides (Wilson 1914b:220, 1913a:46).

STOMACH PUSHER

Hidatsa. Bought from Wolf Ghost.
Used by his parents c. 1850
Collected by Gilbert Wilson, 1909
Cedar, polished and carved with knob
on one end
L. 26 cm
AMNH 50.1/5418

Kneading the abdomen with the hands or with a wooden pusher was a common treatment for indigestion and other stomach illnesses. The knob end fits into the palm of the hand and the curved end is pushed against the abdomen while the patient lies down (AMNH photo 286453).

RATTLE

Northern Plains
Collected by Gilbert Wilson, pre-1918?
Hollow spherical head made of two
pieces of rawhide, one with fur
attached, sewn with sinew around
circumference. Hide-covered wooden
stick handle
L. 17 cm, W. 7 cm
MHS 7059.65

Songs, sometimes accompanied by rattles, were an important part of healing ceremonies. Some rattles, like the ones used in the men's societies or in the Sun Dance, were made for specific purposes. Simple ones like this, however, made by filling a rawhide bag with sand until it dried into shape, could be used for ceremonies, dances, curing, and prayers.

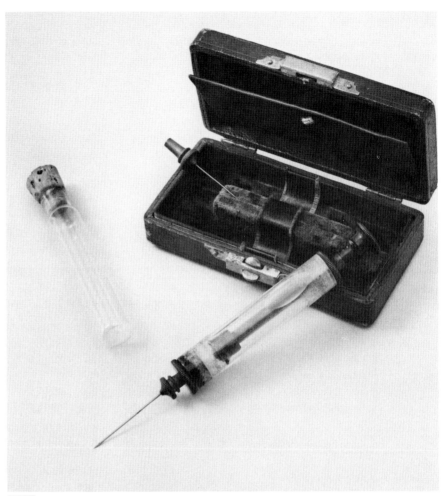

HYPODERMIC KIT

Made by F. G. Otto & Sons, New York City, patented 1873
Maroon leather case lined with velvet, containing clear glass syringe with hard
rubber plunger, needles, and clear glass vial with cork stopper
Box: L. 8.7 cm, W. 4.9 cm, H. 2.6 cm
MHS 6613.2a–e

Euro-American medicine was available to the Hidatsa throughout Buffalo Bird Woman's life, but the difficulty of transporting vaccines and equipment, together with a shortage of doctors, often made such medical care hard to get. As early as 1832, the U.S. Congress voted to make smallpox vaccination available to Indian tribes. In 1838 fur trader David D. Mitchell vaccinated two groups of Hidatsa at the American Fur Company's Fort Clark post near the Knife River villages (Chardon 1932:162, 233, 319).

In later years, doctors stationed at army posts and agencies provided European-style medicine. This hypodermic kit belonged to Dr. James B. Ferguson, a contract surgeon for the U.S. Army in Dakota Territory during the 1870s. He was stationed at a variety of posts, including Forts Totten, Seward, and Yates (Ferguson 1954:1).

PIPE

Northern Plains
Collected by Frederick Wilson, pre-1918?
Right-angle bowl of speckled pipestone with hexagonal front projection and
tobacco stains in smoking hole. Tubular wood stem with hole bored through
center, highly polished and charred from use, with carved man's head
projecting up from main stem
Bowl: L. 19 cm, H. 10.5 cm. Stem: L. 46.5 cm
MHS 9598.8a, b

The ability to cure disease and wounds was a spiritual power received in a dream or
purchased from someone with the power. Smoking a pipe was a way of honoring
and communicating with supernatural forces that might provide help. Wolf Chief's
grandmother Otter purchased a sacred bundle so she would be able to cure members
of her family. Wolf Chief's mother, who later purchased the bundle, was reluctant to
use her abilities outside the family, since different families had different sacred
practices. But Wolf Chief recalled that another family once gave his mother's sacred
bundle a pipestone pipe and requested her to examine their seriously ill daughter.
After smoking the pipe while talking to the bundle, she accepted the request and
cured the young woman (Bowers 1965:382–89).

This pipe bowl is the type used in curing ceremonies, but there is no evidence
it was ever so used.

HERB CURES

Mandan. Bought from Mrs. Foolish
*   Woman*
Collected by Gilbert Wilson, 1909
Sweetgrass braid; piece of wood; three
*   cotton print bags containing a*
*   root, twigs and leaves, and stem*
*   and root pieces*
Sweetgrass: L. 56.5 cm. Root: L. 8.5
*   cm. Bags: H. 7.2 to 10.5 cm*
AMNH 50.1/5357, 5359, 5361,
*   5362, 5363*

These plants were used (left to right) to
cure spasms, pneumonia and fever,
snakebite, bleeding, and toothache.
Although the Office of Indian Affairs
tried to prevent the use of traditional
healing techniques in the late 1800s and
early 1900s, every reservation had
people who knew cures. At Fort
Berthold in 1909, Mrs. Foolish Woman
was one of the native doctors. Goodbird
described how she had cured his child
of spasms. "She went back to her house
and in about twenty minutes returned
with the medicine. It was steeped in
water and it looked blackish. 'There,'
she said, 'Give the child one
teaspoonful. If he sweats well, it will be
enough. Cover him up and in a little
while if he don't sweat give him another
spoonful.' We did this and the child
sweat and got well" (Wilson 1909a:134).

Patent medicine bottles
Pre-1885?
Excavated at Like-a-Fishhook Village
and Fort Berthold I
Mold-blown glass with raised
lettering; light green, blue-green,
and amber
Left to right: H. 9.5 cm, D. 2.5 cm;
H. 10 cm, D. 3.8 cm; H. 12 cm,
D. 3.5 cm; H. 24.5 cm,
D. 9.5 cm.
SHSND 32ML2/12,003.1614,
12,003.2242, 12,711.430,
12,711.2239

Diseases like measles, smallpox, and whooping cough were new to the Mandan, Hidatsa, and Arikara, who had little immunity to them. Traders brought in a wide variety of patent medicines; Henry Boller noted in 1858 that his trading store at Like-a-Fishhook had "several shelves of medicine, & it looks like an apothecary shop" (1966a:167).

After 1879, the U.S. Office of Indian Affairs also purchased medical supplies and drugs from major pharmaceutical firms and shipped them to reservations for dispensing by agency physicians. These bottles, found by archaeologists at the Like-a-Fishhook site, contained (left to right) Dr. Thompson's Eye-Water (from New London, Conn.), D. S. Barnes' Mexican Mustang Liniment (New York, N.Y.), [Perry] Davis' Vegetable Pain Killer (Providence, R.I.), and Warner's Safe Kidney and Liver Cure (Rochester, N.Y.) (Smith 1972:106).

Enroute to winter camp, Indian dog sleds crossing the ice"
Painted by William de la Montagne Cary, 1874?
Oil on canvas. See color page 171
H. 52 cm, W. 90.5 cm
The Thomas Gilcrease Institute of American History and Art 0126.1855

The fort and town in this view, located only as "North Dakota," are identical in layout to Like-a-Fishhook Village and Fort Berthold I as seen from the west. The artist visited Like-a-Fishhook in 1861 and 1874. The style of dogsled is like Mandan sleds illustrated by Karl Bodmer in 1834, but the cradleboard on the woman's back is not a typical Hidatsa/Mandan style (Thwaites 1966:pl. 29; Ladner 1984:182).

The seasons of childhood

I look back upon my girlhood as the happiest time of my life," Buffalo Bird Woman said. "My little half sister was my usual playmate. . . . For playgrounds [we] had the level spaces between the lodges or the ground under the corn stage, in sunny weather; and the big, roomy floor of the earth lodge, if it rained or the weather were chill" (Maxidiwiac 1921:54-55).

Hidatsa children saw the year round with a calendar of games. In March and April the boys would find a level place where the snow had melted and play the hoop game. One team threw wooden hoops laced with rawhide into the air and the other tried to catch them on sticks. They played the game for only a few weeks, explained Buffalo Bird Woman's son Goodbird. "The rule was, that when the ice broke on the Missouri River, we should all go to the high bank over the river, and hurl our hoops into the current. We boys were taught, and we really believed it, that these hoops became dead buffaloes after they had passed out of sight around the next point of land. . . . Many dead buffaloes came floating down the Missouri in the springtime and their flesh was much valued" (Wilson 1913a:33).

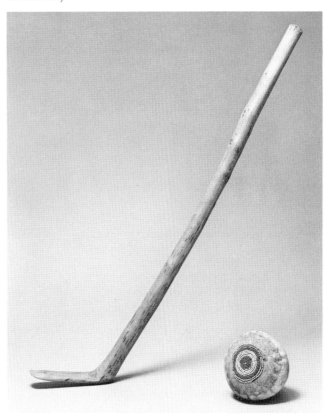

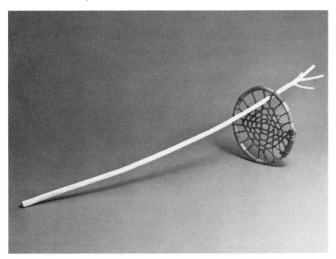

HOOP AND STICK GAME
Hidatsa style
Collected by Gilbert Wilson, pre-1918?
Hoop of willow bound with sinew and laced with rawhide; rim striped with red paint. Stick reconstructed of willow
Hoop: D. 25 cm. Stick: L. 107 cm
MHS 7059.86

The hoop and stick game was a favorite spring sport with boys. Wolf Chief was fond of the game when he was six. "If two or three of us were playing on a side we used three or four hoops. We would throw a hoop and those of the other side tried to catch it on the point of a stick with which each was armed. Then we threw another hoop. If they of the other side caught all the hoops they gave chase and tried to hit us as we ran. If they failed to catch a hoop they must surrender the uncaught hoop and another. This game was played in the spring time. The hoop that I used was made for me by my father or some old man" (Wilson 1914b:159-60; MHS photos VI-84-14 to VI-94-14).

BALL AND STICK GAME
Mandan. Made by Not-Woman and bought from her and her husband, Hairy Coat
Collected by Frederick Wilson, 1912
Ball of three pieces of tanned hide sewn together with sinew and decorated on both ends with red and blue beadwork. Stick of carved willow, curved at one end
Ball: D. 11 cm. Stick: L. 82 cm
AMNH 50.1/7321

The ball and stick game, often known as shinny, was common throughout North America. It was played by two teams of women who tried to get the ball past each other's goals. Buffalo Bird Woman recalled that girls learned to play this game at seven or eight years of age (Wilson 1911:195).

In one Hidatsa story the hero agrees to watch the unmarried women play shinny and choose a wife from among them (Beckwith 1938:188).

When the boys heard the first thunder in the spring, they knew it was time for the Ú-a-ki-hē-kē game. This was played by throwing long sticks against the ground to see who could make his bounce farthest. The winner took the losers' sticks. Half the fun was finding and decorating the sticks. They had to be just long enough, with the bark peeled off just right (Wilson 1913a:34-35).

In summer the boys fought mock battles with ammunition of mudballs. In early years, the Mandan boys fought the Hidatsa boys; but after 1862, when the Arikara moved to Like-a-Fishhook, the Mandan and Hidatsa teamed up against them. "We fought like armies, trying to take each others' positions," Goodbird said. The girls did not join in the fighting. Instead, they modeled clay figures out of mud or played a game like follow-the-leader, winding in and out among the earth lodges in a long line. Girls' ball games were popular, especially one played by teams wielding hooked sticks out on the grassy prairie (Wilson 1913a:36; Wilson 1911:194-95).

BOYS FIGHTING WITH MUDBALLS
Drawn by Goodbird, 1915
Black carbon and pencil on paper
H. 21.5 cm, W. 17.3 cm
MHS (Goodbird 1915:fig. 76)
In fighting a play battle, Goodbird explained, "each boy had a flexible willow withe about five or six feet long, like a buggy whip. A small lump of clay was squeezed on to the smaller end of this stick. In this manner the lump could be thrown to a great distance, as much as a hundred yards" (Wilson 1913a:36). Wolf Chief added, "The lump of mud hit the boy on the face or body and fell with a 'spat' and made the boy cry very often. . . . Before the mud balls reached us we could hear them 'hw-i-s-s' like a whistle for the holes made in them by the sticks caused the balls to whistle as they flew through the air. . . .

"Garter Snake was a good fighter. I remember the mud balls used to hit him but he paid no attention to them. . . . Once Garter Snake hit me quite hard at about twenty yards. The boys who were on his side were charging us and we started to run. I heard someone call out: 'Don't run away!' and I turned and saw that it was Garter Snake. At the same time a mud ball hit me in the side, stopping my breathing. 'U-r-r-r-r' I grunted but let fly a mud ball myself that caught Garter Snake right in the temple" (Wilson 1915b:430-31).

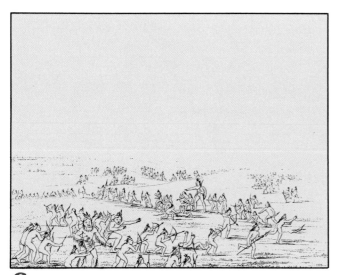

SHAM FIGHT BY MANDAN BOYS"
Based on a painting by George Catlin, 1832
MHS (Catlin 1965, 1:pl. 57)
Hidatsa and Mandan boys fought play battles from early times. George Catlin recorded the custom at the village near Fort Clark. Wolf Chief remembered learning the rudiments of warfare this way. "If the two sides were brave the fight might be long. We thus learned to handle a bow & [how to] stick to the side of our ponies. If the pony was sweaty it wasn't such a task as it might seem. This was of value later for it help[ed] us learn to avoid arrows in real warfare" (Wilson 1907c:80).

As the weather grew frosty, the girls often played inside, sitting in the yellow sunspot that fell on the floor through the smoke hole (Maxidiwiac 1921:55). But the weather sometimes warmed after harvest, and the boys of Like-a-Fishhook would go out to a sandbar on the river and build an evening bonfire of corncobs. As night fell, the boys pressed embers into mudballs and hurled them out over the river, watching the coals "glow through the air like a falling star" (Wilson 1913a:37).

In winter, girls traded their summer dolls of rush and mud for skin dolls beautifully decorated by relatives. Buffalo Bird Woman's grandmother Turtle made her one of deer skin stuffed with antelope hair. "She sewed on two white bone beads for eyes. I bit off one of these bone beads, to see if it was good to eat, I suppose. For some days my dolly was one-eyed, until my grandmother sewed on a beautiful new eye, a blue glass bead she had gotten of a trader. I thought this much better, for now my dolly had one blue eye and one white one" (Maxidiwiac 1921:22).

DOLL
Hidatsa. Made by Buffalo Bird Woman
Collected by Gilbert Wilson, 1910
Rushes woven and tied with three tanned hide thongs
L. 33 cm, W. 11 cm at top
AMNH 50.1/5503

The form of this doll, made from rushes woven into a hood at the top and folded down, imitates a baby wrapped in its bundle. Buffalo Bird Woman insisted that it did not represent a cradle: "We did not make cradles, with hoods, in old times; altho we know that other tribes did" (Wilson 1910a:305). Making the doll required two people, usually an older woman and the girl for whom the doll was intended. Wilson photographed Buffalo Bird Woman and her granddaughter making this doll (MHS photos IV-30-1910 to IV-34-1910; AMNH photos 286454 to 286458). Buffalo Bird Woman gave the doll to her granddaughter to sell to Wilson.

Throughout the year, girls and boys played separately. They learned early that their roles in life were different. Whenever Buffalo Bird Woman dressed up in her father's hunting cap, her grandmother laughed at her and said, "That is a warrior's cap. A little girl can not be a warrior" (Maxidiwiac 1921:24). Buffalo Bird Woman in turn passed her attitudes on to her son. "I did not play with little girls," Goodbird said later. "My mother would say, 'If you play with girls, you will grow up to be a woman'" (Wilson 1913a:17).

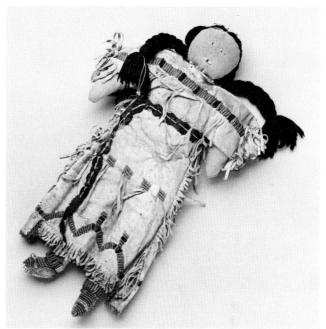

DOLL
Hidatsa or Mandan, post-1870s
Collected by Harold W. Case, post-1922
Cloth body with beaded eyes and mouth and black braided
* yarn hair. Dress of tanned hide with gold, blue, and*
* black beading. Belt of green wool with sequins.*
* Moccasins beaded in green, clear, and gold*
H. 28.5 cm, W. 18.5 cm
University of Colorado Museum at Boulder 33129, H. W.
* Case*

In the winter Indian girls played with dolls made by doting relatives out of deerskin and decorated with beads (Wilson 1911:194). This doll, collected by the Congregational minister who came to Fort Berthold Reservation in 1922, is dressed in a style characteristic of Northern Plains Indian women. Before they began sewing dresses from cloth, women wore hide dresses decorated with beadwork and fringe; wide belts with draggers, frequently decorated with metal conchos; beaded leggings; and moccasins. Even today, however, belts with draggers are worn by women who dance at powwows.

BOY SLEDDING
Drawn by Goodbird, 1915
Black carbon and pencil on paper
H. 9.8 cm, W. 9 cm
MHS (Goodbird 1915:fig. 75)

"We commonly went out in little companies to coast," Goodbird explained. "Sometimes ten would be coasting together, sometimes fifteen, and sometimes a much lesser number. Very often young men and maidens came out of the village with their sleds and coasted with us; but we smaller children always withdrew from them a little way for fear of getting hurt.

"The reason the young men came out to coast was because they wanted to be with their sweethearts" (Wilson 1914b:237).

SLED
Hidatsa style
Collected by Gilbert Wilson, pre-1918?
Five animal ribs connected on one end
*　with wood slats and tanned hide*
*　straps, at the other with tanned*
*　hide strip threaded through holes*
*　bored in bones. Hide strap for*
*　pulling sled attached to front*
L. 39 cm, W. 21.3 cm
MHS 7059.51

Sledding was a popular sport among Hidatsa boys and girls. "I was six years old when I owned my first buffalo rib sled," Goodbird recalled. "It was winter and we had gone hunting buffaloes west of the mouth of the Yellowstone. . . . At every camp that we made we children would go out with our dried hides and slide down the hills upon them. . . . After a good many buffaloes had been killed many of the boys got rib sleds that their fathers or friends made for them.

"I was quite envious of the owners of these sleds and I came to my father and said, 'Father, I want to have a rib sled also!' He promised to make me one. . . .

"My hide was not as good as a rib sled, for it did not have anything like so much speed, so I kept asking my father again and again to make me a rib sled.

"My father went out hunting buffaloes every two or three days, and the next time when he went hunting was lucky enough to make a kill. He brought in some sides of buffalo meat, and from these he cut the ribs and made me a rib sled. He took two sticks and split them and bound one stick at each end of the sled, with the ribs thrust into the split. This was an easy way of making a sled, and such a sled was the kind that was given to little boys of four or five years of age. Boys of from six to thirteen years of age were given a sled put together with sinew.

"When I found this out I was rather vexed, and I went to my father and said, 'I do not like this sled, I want to own one such as is given to larger boys.' But my father answered, 'My son, that is the best that I can do for you'" (Wilson 1914b:234-35).

TOY TRAVOIS WITH DOG

Hidatsa style
Collected by Frederick Wilson, pre-1918?
Travois of red willow twigs lashed together with wire. Harness of commercially tanned leather. Dog made of root, with twigs for legs and snout
L. 20.5 cm, W. 6 cm
MHS 9598.30

Hidatsa toys often reflected the life of grown-ups and helped children learn appropriate adult roles. The travois and dog were still used by women even after horses were available. This toy was probably made for a little Hidatsa girl by an older relative or friend.

BALL

Hidatsa style
Collected by Gilbert Wilson, pre-1918?
Four pieces of tanned hide sewn together with sinew and decorated with orange, aqua, and purple quillwork, mostly worn away. Two rawhide strips laced through hide around the center. Probably stuffed with grass
D. 17.5 cm
MHS 7059.13

According to Buffalo Bird Woman, balls were popular toys for little girls. In one game, each girl competed to bounce the ball on her toe the greatest number of times (Wilson 1911:195). Maximilian saw women in 1834 "playing with a large leathern ball, which they let fall alternately on their foot and knee, again throwing it up and catching it, and thus keeping it in motion for a length of time without letting it fall to the ground" (Wied 1905-06, 23:299). In 1916 Wilson photographed a woman as she bounced a ball on her toe 52 times (Wilson [1903-18]:266; MHS photos IX-45-1916 to IX-50-1916).

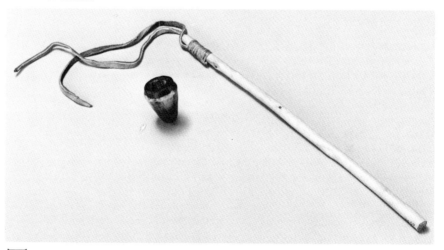

TOP AND WHIP

Hidatsa style
Collected by Gilbert Wilson, pre-1915
Top carved from cone of horn with hollow core. Tanned hide lash of whip secured to willow (?) handle with sinew
Top: L. 4.5 cm. Whip: L. 28.6 cm
MHS 1986.100.13, 7059.108a

When Wolf Chief was a boy, he and his friends "played with tops of buffalo horn. We cleaned out a circular place with a run or road, smooth or with one bad place with soft snow in it. We would whip these [tops] with a stick with 2 lashes of buckskin. The horn often had tallow in it to weight it. White children would find it hard to spin these" (Wilson 1907c:86). This whip is one of a pair acquired by Wilson; the top has no recorded provenance.

Corn songs

As a child, Buffalo Bird Woman spent many summer days out in the fields with her grandmother, Turtle. "She was an industrious woman," Buffalo Bird Woman recalled. "Often, when my mothers were busy in the earth lodge, she would go out to work in the garden, taking me with her for company. I was six years old then, I think, quite too little to help her any, but I liked to watch my grandmother work" (Wilson 1917:11).

Hoe
Hidatsa style
Collected by Gilbert Wilson, c. 1914
Buffalo shoulder bone hafted at 70° angle to ash-wood handle. Handle is split and lashed back together with sinew or rawhide. Blade secured with sinew or rawhide and plant fiber cord
Handle: L. 77 cm. Blade: L. 32 cm, W. 12.5 cm
MHS 7059.39

Before iron hoes were brought to the Hidatsa by traders, women used hoes made from the shoulder bone of a buffalo or other large animal. The bone was hafted with a short ash-wood handle. Because the handle was short, the women bent over to work. Wilson described the use of a bone hoe: "The stroke is made across the front from left to right, and right to left. This is still the custom with iron hoes, but I have noticed the women have a disposition sometimes to draw the instrument more toward the body, thus approaching our own custom. Such a stroke would have been impossible with a bone hoe. Buffalo Bird Woman in showing me how the hoe was used, would make a half dozen strokes from right to left, change to the other side with a deft motion and make a like number of strokes from left to right. The stroke was a cutting one, not a scraping one as ours often appears" (Wilson 1909a:80; MHS photos III-10 to III-15, V-46-1912, VII-1-14 to VII-3-14, VII-19-14, VII-23-14 to VII-26-14).

This hoe may be one of several made for Wilson by Wolf Chief and Butterfly to demonstrate different hafting techniques. The bone blade and hafting cord have been broken.

Turtle did things the old way. While Buffalo Bird Woman's mothers used metal hoes and axes, Turtle still broke sod with a sharpened stick and cultivated with a hoe made from the shoulder bone of a buffalo. "She always kept [the hoe] back under her bed. Sometimes we children would take it out, out of curiosity, and want to take it in the garden and try to use it. She would say, 'Leave that alone; put it back! I fear you will break it.' There were two other women in the

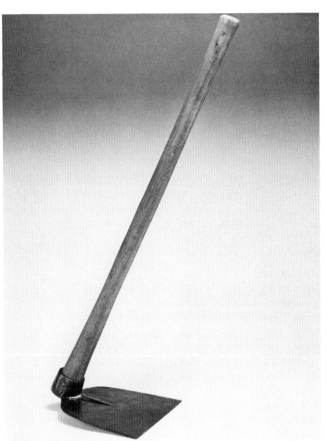

Metal hoe
Pre-1885?
Excavated at Like-a-Fishhook Village
Cast iron blade. Handle reconstructed
Blade: L. 22 cm, W. 20.5 cm. Handle: L. 88.4 cm
SHSND 32ML2/12,003.2144

Metal hoe blades replaced the bone scapular hoes used in early years, but the women shortened the handles so they could be used in the same way as bone hoes (MHS photo X-28-1918). Buffalo Bird Woman recalled that when she was a child, "Otter and my two mothers and Turtle all worked in that first field we cleared at Old Fort Berthold. Turtle alone used a digging stick; all the others used iron hoes in clearing and breaking the new ground" (Wilson 1915b:455-56).

village who had bone hoes that they still used when I was a little girl. These two and my grandmother, Turtle, were the last to use them" (Wilson 1912:208).

As she grew up, Buffalo Bird Woman learned how to grow vegetables and corn, "as every Hidatsa woman was expected to" (Wilson 1917:13). Success in farming was not just a matter of hard work. A gardener had to be kind to her corn. "We thought that the corn plants had souls, as children have souls," said Buffalo Bird Woman. "We cared for our corn in those days, as we would care for a child" (Maxidiwiac 1921:94).

As the snow was beginning to melt, while people were still in the winter village, the women's Goose Society began the year's agricultural activities. They welcomed the corn spirits back from the south with a dance and ceremonies (Maxidiwiac 1921:24). When the tribe returned to Like-a-Fishhook Village, the women cleared the fields with wood and antler rakes. First they planted sunflowers, then corn.

GOOSE SOCIETY HEADBAND
Hidatsa
Collected by Robert H. Lowie, 1910
Duck beak, iridescent green neck feathers, and skin with
*   down attached sewn onto a cloth band. Duck jaw split*
*   open to lay flat. See color page 170*
C. 54 cm
AMNH 50.1/4312
Women of the Goose Society represented the water birds who took the corn and other garden spirits to the south each fall and brought them back each spring. Every spring, before the crops were planted, the women met to dance and pray for a successful season. The women might also meet during the summer any time the crops were threatened. Wounded Face explained that "Good-furred Robe [a culture hero] started the Goose Society. He did this to help the corn to grow and make our gardens flourish. The women of this society have power to produce these results" (Wilson 1910a:202).

"We Hidatsa women were early risers in the planting season," said Buffalo Bird Woman. "It was my habit to be up before sunrise, while the air was cool, for we thought this the best time for garden work." The corn was planted in hills arranged in rows. "Planting corn . . . by hand was slow work; but by ten o'clock the morning's work was done, and I was tired and ready to go home for my breakfast and rest" (Wilson 1917:23).

As the corn sprouted, women hoed to keep down the weeds and keep in the moisture. They made scarecrows from sticks and old buffalo robes. The danger to the corn came in August, when the ears began to ripen. Then the women built a platform, or stage, in the field for girls to sit on while they sang "love-boy songs" and guarded the corn from birds,

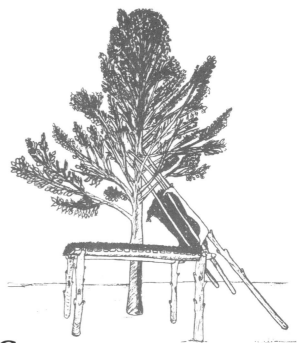

CORN WATCHERS' STAGE
Drawn by Goodbird, 1915
Black carbon and pencil on paper
H. 18 cm, W. 16 cm
MHS (Goodbird 1915:fig. 32)
Corn stages were often built under trees, and skin awnings were added for shade. They were large enough to seat two. "We went to the watchers' stage very early before sunrise or about that time and came home at sunset," said Buffalo Bird Woman. Throughout the day, the girls on the stage would sing, do quillwork, talk, and guard the ripening corn from horses and boys who would steal it. The height of the stage gave them a good view of the field (Wilson 1915b:446-54).

boys, and horses. "We thought that our growing corn liked to hear us sing, just as children like to hear their mother sing to them," said Buffalo Bird Woman (Maxidiwiac 1921:95; Wilson 1917:27).

Singing was not the only pastime on the corn stage. "The boys of the village were going about all the time trying to find the girls. . . . If there were relatives at the watchers' stage, the boys would stop and drink or eat. The boys did not try to talk to the girls but would come around smiling and try to get the girls to smile back at them. . . . If the boys came up to the stage we girls that were upon it would not say a word.

. . . If a girl was not a boy's sweetheart she never talked to him. This rule was observed at all times" (Wilson 1915b:449-50).

When harvest time came, the family held a husking feast. The day before, the women picked the corn, heaping it by the basketful in a huge pile in the center of the field. In the morning, the owner of the field notified the crier for one of the men's societies, who climbed to the roof of the society's lodge and called all the members to go husking. The young men marched out to the field together. Drawing close, they began to sing, so the women could hear them. "As the

BURDEN BASKET
Hidatsa. Made by Buffalo Bird Woman
Collected by Gilbert Wilson, 1908
Willow wood frame. Sides of dyed and undyed willow and
*   boxelder bark strips woven in diamond and cross*
*   patterns. Rawhide tumpline attached to frame*
H. 29.5 cm, D. 20.5 cm
AMNH 50/7175
"We used these baskets to bear burdens on our backs," Buffalo Bird Woman said, "but their special value was to carry the corn and vegetables of our gardens to the village, especially the corn. . . . We also carried our clay pots in these baskets when we removed from our summer to our winter village; also our other cooking utensils. In the winter we often used them to bring snow into the house, to melt for water.

"Our name for the basket is Mi-dá-hi-si, or holder" (Wilson 1912:243; MHS photo VII-40-14).

BURDEN BASKET
Hidatsa. Bought from Butterfly
Collected by Gilbert Wilson, 1916
Wooden framework covered with rawhide
H. 28 cm, D. 34 cm
AMNH 50.1/5412
Burden baskets made of rawhide were commonly used by older women. Buffalo Bird Woman explained, "We used more skin baskets in old times when buffalo skins were easy to get. We did not decorate these baskets, only scraped them bare of hair. They were made on the same kind of a frame as that upon which we weave our bark baskets; but we also made them on frames like those of the baskets which Butterfly sold you for the museum. These skin baskets were more often carried by old women. They were serviceable and could stand a great deal of use. But young women liked to use the bark baskets because they were thought to be prettier. My mother always used the skin basket but as I was a young woman she bought a bark basket for me as this was more becoming to a young girl" (Wilson 1912:256; MHS photos VII-33-14, VII-43-14).

young men passed thru the garden to some particular pile, . . . each young man would know where his sweetheart was; and as they passed her pile, that young man would yell, expecting the girl to hear his voice" (Wilson 1915b:467). The women, in turn, dressed in their best clothes. "Some girls were more popular than others," said Buffalo Bird Woman. "The young men were apt to vie with one another at the husking pile of an attractive girl" (Wilson 1917:44). Husking went on late into the night if the moon was bright, and each owner gave the workers a feast of meat and corn.

The huskers tossed most of the clean corn into a pile for threshing, but whenever they came across a particularly good ear, they set it aside to be woven into a braid. Fifty-five ears made up one braid. Buffalo Bird Woman's mothers braided about one hundred strings each year. They took them back to the village and draped them on the corn scaffolds to dry. The variegated colors of the corn braids gave the village "a gay and holiday appearance" fitting for the end of harvest (Wilson 1915b:469-70; Boller 1959:124).

"Our harvested corn lasted us in a good year until the next harvest, with a small quantity left over," said Buffalo Bird Woman. "Some families not very provident, ran short as early as in the spring. But not ours; we were more industrious" (Wilson 1915b:472).

Digging stick
Hidatsa. Made by Goodbird?
Collected by Gilbert Wilson, c. 1914
Pine wood, one end knobbed and the other end carved to a
   point; polished by use
L. 95 cm
MHS 7059.41

Digging sticks had sacred and secular uses. Women used them in gardening, digging wild plants, making post holes, and, when necessary, for self-defense. Digging sticks were also included in the Sacred Woman's bundle and in bundles associated with eagle trapping (Wilson 1918a:159, 1915a:135). This stick was probably made by Goodbird for Wilson in 1914; it appears to be the same as one illustrated in *Agriculture of the Hidatsa* (Wilson 1917:12).

Buffalo Bird Woman described some of the other uses of the pointed sticks. "Digging sticks were also used to dig up wild turnips with. . . . When one was on horseback looking for turnips, she carried her stick athwart the saddle in front of her. Her saddle bags on either side of her pony were loaded with turnips.

"A digging stick was a very useful instrument; besides its use in the garden and for digging turnips it was used for making tent pin holes, post holes, or in fact for any kind of hole and it was used as a crowbar for rolling logs" (Wilson 1912:5; MHS photos V-47-1912, VI-40-14, VI-41-14, VII-36-14 to VII-39-14, IX-59-16).

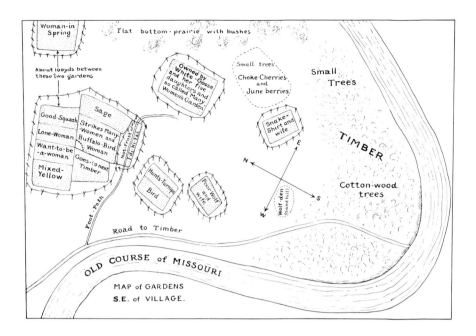

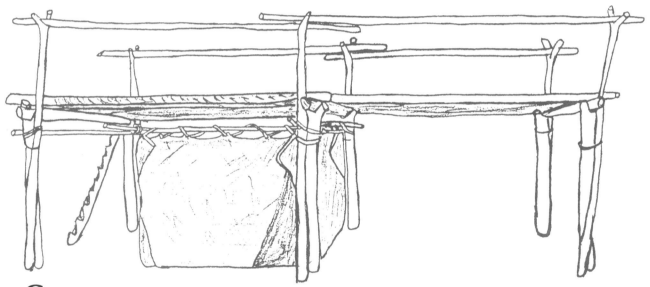

PARTIAL MAP OF THE GARDENS AT LIKE-A-FISHHOOK VILLAGE
Drawn by Frederick Wilson with instructions from Buffalo Bird Woman, 1915
Ink on cardboard
H. 23.5 cm. W. 35.3 cm
MHS (Wilson Papers)

"There were many other gardens than those represented here on the map," Buffalo Bird Woman said, but she remembered clearly only those nearest her own. All lay in the bottomlands below the bluff on which the village stood. The fields were enlarged year by year as the women broke more ground. At its largest, Buffalo Bird Woman's family field was about 3⅓ acres – twice as wide and half again as long as a football field. They also had a field on the west side of the village. All the fields were fenced to keep animals out (Wilson 1917:24, 108).

CORN THRESHING BOOTH
Drawn by Goodbird, 1915
Black carbon and pencil on paper
H. 7.2 cm, W. 18.6 cm
MHS (Goodbird 1915:fig. 30)

A two-story scaffold for drying corn, meat, and other foods adjoined virtually every house at Like-a-Fishhook Village. The upper floor was usually used for spreading out food or hanging it to dry. At harvest time a threshing booth was set up below the scaffold. Skins formed a tentlike enclosure within which the threshers would sit, beating the cobs to loosen the hard grains. Though the corn kernels flew about, the tent skins prevented any from being lost (Wilson 1917:49-52).

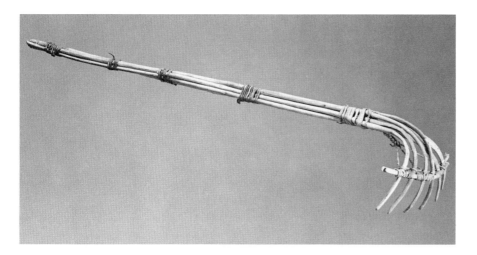

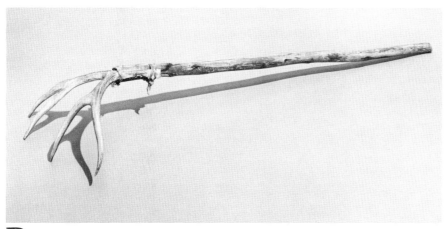

RAKE
Hidatsa
Collected by Gilbert Wilson, c. 1914
Cylindrical ash (?) handle notched to attach to a four-pronged deer antler; joint secured with rawhide
L. 128 cm
MHS 7059.43a

Wilson collected at least three antler rakes like this and photographed Wolf Chief making one (MHS photos VI-45-14 to VI-54-14). Rakes made from deer antlers were preferred to those with tines of ash because the Hidatsa believed that corn worms came from wooden rakes (Wilson 1908a:171). Deer horns were also preferred, as Wolf Chief explained, because of oral tradition: "The first that rakes are mentioned in my tribe, that I know anything of, is in the story of the Grandson. There is a little lake down near Short River. An old woman lived there, Everlasting Grandmother. There is a flat piece of ground there, five miles long by one and a half miles wide. All that flat land was Everlasting Grandmother's garden. Her servants were the deer, that thronged the near-by timber. These deer worked her garden for her. All buck deer have horns. And with their horns the deer raked up the weeds and refuse of Everlasting Grandmother's garden.

"Now deer shed their horns. Everlasting Grandmother got these shed horns and put them on sticks and so we got our first rakes. Her grandson saw what she did and afterwards taught the people how to make rakes also.

"In later times we came to make rakes of ash wood instead of horns. But we still reckon the teeth to mean the tines on a deer's antler. Sometimes deer have six, sometimes seven tines on an antler. So we made our ash rakes, some with six, some with seven teeth" (Wilson 1910a:292; F. Wilson's sketch of this rake is in Wilson 1917:14).

RAKE
Hidatsa
Collected by Gilbert Wilson, 1910
Six ash (?) saplings scraped smooth, bent, and held in a wooden cross brace lashed with rawhide strips. Handle lashed with rawhide; tines sharpened
L. 158.5 cm
AMNH 50.1/5500

The Hidatsa made rakes from ash wood bent into shape and held with thongs. These rakes imitated the older form of rakes made from deer antlers. Wolf Chief described how he made ash wood rakes: "A wooden rake should have six or seven teeth. A stick is shaved down to proper size at one end, while still green; and held over the fire with the end bent at proper angle, to make the tooth required.

"I accomplish this as follows. When the stick is well heated, I bend the tooth into shape and tie it with a raw hide thong. When all are treated thus, they are gathered into a bundle and held over a fire until dried. As each stick seems dried sufficiently, it is laid down out of the bundle.

"When all are dried, the raw hide strings are laid off.

"The various sticks are then gathered up and a small section of a stick is split for the brace that goes transversely across the teeth of the rake, to hold them in place. The two teeth of the forked piece are bound in place first. Next are bound the teeth that lie on either side. Raw hide thongs make the binding.

"Last of all the handle is bound about" (Wilson 1910a:291-92).

Wilson collected two rakes of this style for AMNH (50.1/5500, 50.2/1177) and one for himself (MHS 7059.42, 7059.129). The MHS one, which was disassembled when it came into the collection, was probably the one Wilson photographed Wolf Chief making (MHS photos VI-95-14 to VI-97-14; see also IV-55-1910).

A daughter's duties

Amother began to teach her daughter household duties at about the age of thirteen," Buffalo Bird Woman said. "The girl was taught to chop wood, hoe in the garden and embroider bead work. My mother said to me:

"'We are a family who have not one bad woman in it so you must try and not be bad.'

"She meant that I should obey my parents and marry only as my parents wished and I never met young men at night or smiled at them" (Wilson 1915b:439).

Buffalo Bird Woman had high family standards to live up to. Her mothers were all known in the village as industrious workers and neat housekeepers. Her father was considered rich.

Women's work had an important economic role in the community. By Hidatsa custom, women owned the products of their labors. Those who farmed, dressed skins, built houses, and sewed clothes made themselves and their families rich. Because men customarily did none of these things, a man needed industrious wives if he were to become prosperous. A woman who was a good worker was seen by men as a source of wealth and prestige. For a girl, work was the road to respect.

One of the first tasks Buffalo Bird Woman learned was fetching water. This was usually done three times a day: before breakfast, about noon, and just before sundown (Wilson 1913a:15). The best water came from the Missouri River, since prairie springs were too alkaline and creeks were too warm (Wilson 1912:251). As in many societies, the watering place was where women met to talk. Every day the village girls made their way down the steep bank, carrying pots, heartskin buckets, and pails. Sometimes a boy waited by the path, hoping to make a girl look at him (Maxidiwiac 1921:90-91).

Housekeeping was another daily task. Every morning Buffalo Bird Woman's mothers took brooms of buckbrush and swept out the lodge, taking particular care to keep the floor in front of the shrine clean (Wilson 1915a:55). Although there were no dressers or cupboards, the women kept the lodge tidy by putting things away in colorful bags. Often these were hung from the rafters in out-of-the-way places.

The women were responsible for cleaning the ground outside their lodge as well. But not everyone did it, and the rubbish would begin to pile up in the walkways. Then men of the Black Mouth Society took charge. The Black Mouths acted like the police of the village, enforcing laws and customs. "I remember quite

SWEEPING THE LODGE FLOOR
Drawn by Goodbird, 1914
Pencil on paper
H. 12.8 cm, W. 17.7 cm
AMNH (Goodbird 1914b:fig. 74)
"The broom was wielded with both hands," Buffalo Bird Woman explained as Goodbird made this drawing. "The sweep was from right to front, or from left to front. . . . When not in use the broom was tossed in the rear between the bed and the corral, . . . in the atuti" (Wilson 1914b:390-91).

well when I was about eight years old, seeing these Black Mouths come around ordering a clean-up," Wolf Chief recalled. "They all came together in a little crowd and went around calling: 'You women, go and clean up outside of your lodges!'

"These Black Mouths had all the lower part of their faces painted black and very often, although it was not necessary, the upper part of the face was painted red. . . .

"I was in my father's lodge when the Black Mouths came in . . . and said: 'One of you women go out and help the others clean up the village.'

"All the Black Mouths in the bunch said this, not just one and they spoke very shortly and looked severely as if to scare the women.

"Like the other women of the village, my mothers were afraid of the Black Mouths and said: 'All right, one of us will go out and clean up.' . . .

"As the Black Mouths passed, every woman came out with a basket and native-made broom and swept up the debris about her lodge into the basket. This she carried down to the bank of the Missouri and emptied it over the bank. . . . The work of cleaning up was all finished before noon but some of the women completed their work much earlier than others.

"We boys always liked to play between the lodges after the clean up for the ground was smooth and swept and it made a good place for us to play 'sticks'" (Wilson 1915a:55-59).

ENAMELWARE CUP

Pre-1885?
Excavated at Like-a-Fishhook Village
Enameled iron cup, white inside and
blue outside; metal strap handle
riveted on
H. 5.5 cm; D. 9.4 cm
SHSND 32ML2/12,003.2183
Metal cups were sold by traders and
issued by government agents. At
breakfast, remembered Wolf Chief, "The
broth in which the dried meat was
boiled was given me in a tin cup to
drink" (Wilson 1913b:440). By
Goodbird's time, the family kept
drinking water in a kettle, and "A tin
cup hung on a post near by" (Wilson
1913a:24).

This was one of several metal cups
found by archaeologists at the village
site (Smith 1972:102-4, 144).

BROOM

Hidatsa style
Collected by Gilbert Wilson, pre-1918?
Bundle of ten buckbrush stems lashed
together with tanned hide strips
L. 88.5 cm
MHS 7059.47
Buckbrush brooms were used to sweep
out the winter and summer earth
lodges, but were not needed in a tipi
unless the floor got worn down and
dirty from long use. "To make a
broom," said Buffalo Bird Woman, "I
gathered good, long plants, and laid
them side by side to be sure they were
of the same length, and bound them
together with a piece of thong so that
the stems made a handle of about
fifteen inches, enough for two hands to
grasp. We used no other kind of plant
for brooms; but we did make them
sometimes of buffalo hair." A broom
lasted about 20 days, after which it was
thrown out (Wilson 1916b:243-44,
1914b:390-91; MHS photo I-32).

STORAGE BAG

Hidatsa. Bought from Calf Woman
Collected by Gilbert Wilson, 1909
Front of deerskin, back of cowhide;
*   tanned and decorated on front with*
*   eight lines of red and blue*
*   quillwork and blue feathers. Sides*
*   beaded in white, blue, green,*
*   yellow, and red and trimmed with*
*   tassels of metal cones with red*
*   horsehair. Top flap beaded yellow,*
*   blue, green, turquoise, and red.*
*   See color page 169*
L. 55 cm, H. 35 cm
AMNH 50.1/5372
Calf Woman told Wilson that these bags
were called "round" bags (Wilson
1909a:136). They are more often called
"possible bags" because it was possible
to store so many different kinds of
things in them. Although Wilson
purchased this bag from Calf Woman, it
is likely that it was made by a Sioux
woman since it is a style common to
the Sioux.

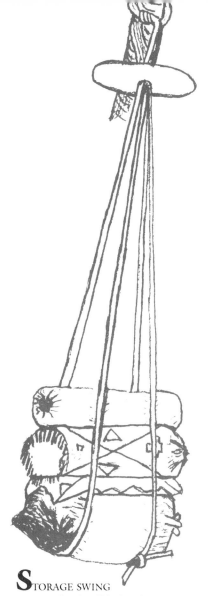

STORAGE SWING

Drawn by Goodbird, 1916
Black carbon and pencil on paper
H. 12.6 cm, W. 3.7 cm
MHS (Goodbird 1916: fig. 48)

When Goodbird drew this storage
swing, he showed it loaded with four
separate types of storage bags used by
the Hidatsa. From the bottom up, they
are a calfskin bag, an envelope-shaped
parfleche bag, a boxlike parfleche bag,
and a cylindrical bag. Buffalo Bird
Woman remembered the swing in her
father's lodge: "It hung a little behind
the left of the two rear big main posts
in the lodge and it faced the door.
There was one in every lodge but it was
not always hung just at this place. Any
convenient place between the beds and
the four big main posts could be used"
(Wilson 1916b: 147–48).

STORAGE SWING

Hidatsa. Bought from Hairy Coat,
who made it
Collected by Frederick Wilson, 1912
Single rawhide strap forming a loop
that passes through the circular
rawhide shield
Strap: L. 640 cm. Shield: D. 32 cm
AMNH 50.1/7320a, b

Parfleche bags filled with clothes were
placed in swings made of rawhide ropes
suspended from the rafters. The ropes
were run through a rawhide shield
which prevented mice from climbing
down the ropes to the bags of clothes.
The shield also helped to keep the
clothes dry if the roof should leak (F.
Wilson 1912a: [19, 21]; Wilson
1934: 394).

STORAGE BAG

Mandan. Bought from Sioux
Woman, daughter of Hides and
Eats, who thought it had been
made about 1870
Collected by Gilbert Wilson, 1910
Skin of unborn buffalo calf. Holes
sewn or tied shut with sinew and
tanned hide strips; patched
L. 59 cm, W. 40 cm
AMNH 50.1/5490

The hide of an unborn buffalo calf was
used to make storage bags for corn and
other foods. The skin was carefully
removed in one piece and turned so the
fur was inside. All but one opening was
sewn shut, and the hide was inflated,
sealed, and hung up to dry into shape.
When it was dry it was worked with the
hands to make it soft. A piece of old
tent skin was sewn to the opening, and
the bag was turned fur-side out again.
Such containers were placed on top of
the load on a pack saddle (Wilson
1913b: 537–39). Goodbird sketched
the process for Wilson (Goodbird
1913: fig. 106).

BEEF PAUNCH BUCKET
Hidatsa. Made by Strikes Many
Women, Wolf Chief's wife
Collected by Gilbert Wilson, 1908
Beef stomach sewn with sinew to
willow hoop rim; rope handle
H. 30 cm, D. 29.5 cm
AMNH 50/7087

In 1908 Wilson asked Wolf Chief to
demonstrate the different kinds of water
buckets. Wolf Chief made a large bucket
from a beef paunch and Strikes Many
Women, his wife, made a small one.
Wolf Chief explained that the small
round buckets were carried in the hand,
while the large ones were carried on the
back or on the travois. Paunch buckets
were always kept filled, because once
dried out they cracked and could not be
used. Both large and small buckets
lasted about a month if properly cared
for (Wilson 1908a:165; AMNH photos
286301, 286317 to 286321; MHS
photos III-3 to III-7).

HEART SKIN BUCKET
Hidatsa. Made by Wolf Chief
Collected by Gilbert Wilson, 1908
Beef heart membrane, sinew-sewn to
notched willow sticks; willow stick
handle attached with sinew strings
H. 24 cm, W. 14 cm
AMNH 50/7088

The membrane around a buffalo or beef
heart was similar to a plastic bag. It was
collapsible, waterproof, and strong
enough to carry water. Buffalo Bird
Woman said, "We always carried a
buffalo heart skin along to fetch
water in.

"This heart skin had another use.
Unused roasted meat was put into the
heart skin and carried along as a lunch
to be eaten on the way, or to the next
camp when the meat could be emptied
out and the heart skin made into a
water bucket again. The heart skin was a
recognized lunch bag" (Wilson
1913b:526, 1921:91).

POTTERY VESSEL AND STAND
Mandan. Made by Hides and Eats at
Gilbert Wilson's request
Collected by Gilbert Wilson, 1911
Pot of dark brown fired clay,
tempered with crushed stone,
decorated with paddle marks and
incised wavy lines. Stand of willow
(?) twigs and leaves wrapped with
orange bark strips
Pot: H. 15 cm, D. 14 cm. Stand: D.
17 cm
AMNH 50.1/6036a, b

"Water was often kept in pottery, and
generally we had several jars of water at
[the] main post . . . near the mortar,
for drinking and cooking," said Buffalo
Bird Woman. "The young girls carried
water and filled the water-jars. They
used skin (or heart skin) buckets, and
sometimes they tied rawhide around the
top of earthen jars and made handles"
(F. Wilson 1912b:38). Butterfly
remarked that a clay pot was better than
iron for holding water because
evaporation was slower. Hides and Eats
added that pots were used in the winter
to melt ice for water (Wilson 1910a:282
and list of items purchased, p. 8).

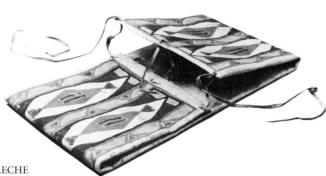

PARFLECHE
Hidatsa style
Collected by Gilbert Wilson, pre-1918?
Single piece of rawhide folded and sewn at seams with tanned hide thongs;
 geometric designs painted in red, blue, yellow, and green
L. 65 cm, W. 34.3 cm
MHS 7059.29

Parfleches, or rawhide bags, were made in many different shapes and sizes for storing food, clothes, and other household goods. Buffalo Bird Woman said, "Our clothes we put away in par fleche bags which were used only for this purpose. We never used these bags or cases to pack meat or foods in, as we wanted to keep our clothes clean. These bags were hung from loops of raw-hide or skin thongs that were fastened up over the lodge ribs. Several of these bags would hang in the same set of loops and these loops were fastened just in front of the *Atuti* stringers near the post. . . .

"There was just one bag for the man's suit and that of his wife. The war-bonnet and trail were kept in the bag, along with the clothes" (F. Wilson 1912b:42).

CARRYING AWAY RUBBISH IN A HIDE
Drawn by Goodbird, 1914
Pencil on paper
H. 10.5 cm, W. 7 cm
AMNH (Goodbird 1914b:fig. 14)

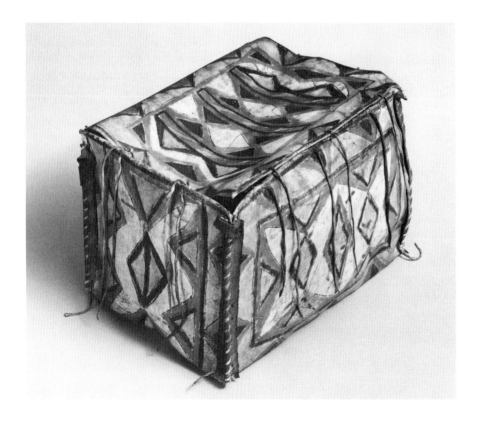

BOX
Northern Plains
Collected by Frederick Wilson,
 pre-1918?
Single piece of rawhide folded and
 sewn at seams with thongs laced
 over red wool; geometric designs
 painted in yellow, red, green, and
 blue. Top fastens with thong laces
L. 39 cm, W. 26 cm, H. 15 cm
MHS 9598.26

Boxes made of rawhide, used for storing clothes and other items, are often considered to be Sioux. Although this box's provenance is unknown, Wilson's photograph of the interior of Hairy Coat's earth lodge at Independence shows a similar box being used in a Mandan/Hidatsa setting (MHS photo V-60-1912). Wilson also purchased a pair of rawhide boxes from a Mandan, Calf Woman (AMNH 50.1/5370).

Gifts of skill

I was industrious when I was young," said Buffalo Bird Woman. "Seven robes I have worked with bird quills and two robes I have embroidered with porcupine work. I have also in my life time embroidered with porcupine quills seven buckskin coats; three of these coats were of deer skin and four of Rocky Mountain sheep" (Wilson 1910a:295, 1911:289).

She was right to be proud of her accomplishments, for just tanning a hide was a complicated process, and in her life she did hundreds. Taking a raw hide, Buffalo Bird Woman first coated it with a mixture of boiled backbone sinew, brains, and sage. Then she dried it for several days. She next soaked it, fleshed it, wrung it out, and scraped it again. She stretched it on a frame, rubbed it with a rough stone for several hours, and drew it over a rope many times. Only then was it ready to be painted or embroidered with dyed quillwork (Wilson 1916b:176-81). "Scraping the hides was hard work," she said (Wilson 1910a:295).

The effort and skill that went into making items like shirts and robes made them valued as gifts. Gifts had more complicated meanings for the Hidatsa than for whites. Gift exchanges cemented civic ties and redistributed wealth. They were a part of most social occasions, from naming a child to electing a leader. A generous gift earned the giver honor and put the recipient under obligation, so that a gift could also be a way of getting power over another person. Buffalo Bird Woman once took revenge on a man who had offended her by giving him a quilled shirt and leggings. Her generosity obliged him to give her a valuable horse in return (Lowie 1916:279).

The etiquette of gift exchange was complex. A neighbor of Buffalo Bird Woman's had to hide a quilled robe she was working on so that a visiting relative would not see it. "If he had seen that robe," she said, "he would have said, 'That is a fine robe. It is beautifully embroidered!' Then I should have said, 'Take it, it is yours now!' And he would have taken it and later on he would have given me a horse. For such is our custom. If I should not give him the robe when he admired it I should feel ashamed; and so also would he feel if he did not take it" (Wilson 1916b:182).

BUFFALO BIRD WOMAN SCRAPING HAIR OFF A HIDE
Drawn by Gilbert Wilson, 1913
Blue carbon on tracing paper
H. 6.8 cm, W. 7 cm
MHS (Goodbird 1913:fig. 102)
Buffalo Bird Woman demonstrated one method of removing hair from a hide when high-quality tanning was not needed. "A saddle blanket was put on the ground for a cushion and the skin laid upon it, fur side up. With an axe the whole surface of the skin was pounded with a scraping motion and the hair thus taken off. It was also rubbed with a stone which further cut off the stumps of hair. . . . This method of taking hair off of a hide is still used by us on this reservation" (Wilson 1913b:531-32).

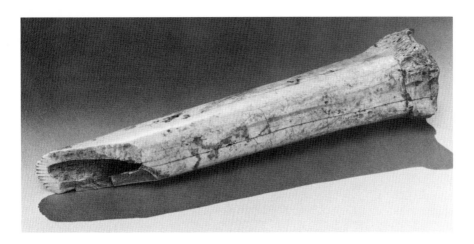

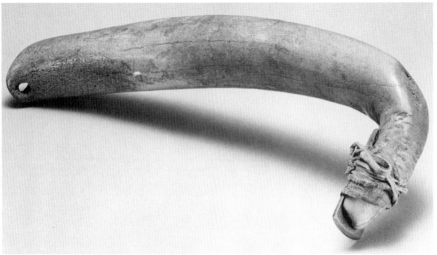

FLESHER
Hidatsa style
Collected by Gilbert Wilson, pre-1918?
Animal leg bone, split and filed to
form a serrated edge
L. 23 cm, W. 4.5 cm
MHS 7059.34e

In preparing hides, explained Buffalo Bird Woman, "We used two kinds of scrapers. The íxopi or flesher was the kind used on a green hide. The latter was thrown over a post and with the implement were removed the fleshy bits yet clinging to the inside of the hide" (Wilson 1918a:360; MHS photo VIII-64-1916). The flesher was "made from the hoof end of the shin bone of the leg of an elk. This flesher had little teeth on it. In old times the flesher I have heard was rubbed into shape and the teeth put in with a stone. But in my time this was done with a steel file. These bone fleshers were in common use in my day.

"The scrapings or fleshings removed from the green hide with these bone fleshers were boiled with the tail; or they were broiled on the coals, laid right on the live coals. . . . Next to a roast side, the scrapings of a hide tasted best" (Wilson 1914b:357).

HIDE SCRAPER
Mandan. Bought from Owl Woman
Collected by Gilbert Wilson, 1909
Carved elk horn handle. Steel blade fitted into a tanned leather pocket sewn with
sinew and tied onto handle by a thong
L. 46 cm
AMNH 50.1/5377

The second kind of scraper was the maíku, which had an elk horn handle and a stone or steel blade. It was used to scrape off hair and lumps so that the fleshed hide would all be the same thickness (Wilson 1918a:360; Hiller 1948:4–23).

FLESHER
Hidatsa. Bought from Wolf Chief
Collected by Gilbert Wilson, 1909
Breech end of an iron gun barrel,
flattened and serrated at one end
L. 21.5 cm
AMNH 50.1/5446

Fleshers made from iron or steel, often from recycled gun barrels, replaced fleshers made from animal leg bones because they kept their edge longer. The two kinds of flesher were similar in form. Wolf Chief said, "Scrapers were made each of a piece of old gun barrel about twenty inches long. I think the black-smiths did this. This iron tool was then covered with a piece of tent skin sewed around it and had a thong loop to slip over the wrist. A woman would kneel on the skin on a folded saddle blanket and as the flesh was stripped off in a wide sheet, she held this in her left hand as she worked with the flesher in her right. Some women were very fast workers, others were not" (Wilson 1918a:238; MHS photos V-19-1912, VIII-64-1916).

Fleshers much like this one were found by archaeologists at the Like-a-Fishhook site (SHSND 32ML2/12,003.985, 1100).

RIB-BONE TOOL (BEAMER?)
Hidatsa style
Collected by Gilbert Wilson, pre-1918?
Polished bone
L. 40 cm, W. 2.5 cm
MHS 7059.110
The process for tanning deer and bison hides was similar, but deer hides were too thin to be shaved with the adzelike elk horn scraper. The curved knife or beamer was used instead. It removed hair and helped to even out any lumps in the deer hide (Lowie 1922a:218).

SCYTHE BLADE
Made by E. T. Co., West Waterville, Me., c. 1900
Curved steel blade with lengthwise groove, meant to bolt onto wooden handle
L. 54 cm, W. 7 cm
MHS 1982.105.253b
Scythes were issued by the government for cutting grass to make hay, but Hidatsa women also used them in tanning hides. A shortened scythe blade, set between two handles, became a beamer for removing hair from deerhide. A woman could also tie a scythe blade to a post, with the sharp edge inward, and soften a hide by drawing it back and forth across the blade in much the same way she would have drawn it over a rawhide rope (Densmore 1918:2, pl. 4b; Wilson 1907c:34). This blade is similar to ones recovered at Like-a-Fishhook (Smith 1972:41).

WHETSTONE
Hidatsa. Bought from Little Bear's widow
Collected by Gilbert Wilson, 1909
Mottled brown-black stone
D. 6.5 cm
AMNH 50.1/5369
Small, disk-shaped flat stones were used by women to sharpen the metal blades for scraping hides. Women often carried these stones in a little bag so they would be handy when needed. Wilson observed Buffalo Bird Woman sharpening the iron blade of her hide scraper with a flat quartz stone, or sometimes "with the back of her butcher knife" (Wilson 1910a:295; MHS photo IV-38-1910).

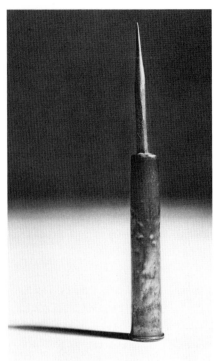

Awl
Provenance unknown
Cylindrical steel point set in a handle
*   made from a brass cartridge case*
L. 12.7 cm
SHSND 1474

Iron and steel awls were important trade goods. Some were pointed at both ends so that one end could be driven into a wooden handle. Others were already set into handles. The handle of this one was made from a used cartridge case. Similarly mounted awls were found by archaeologists at Like-a-Fishhook (Smith 1972:105). Awls were used for working hides, drilling holes in wood, tightening the weave in making baskets, and splitting bird quills for embroidery (Wilson 1911:291, 1914b:339; F. Wilson 1912c:33).

Awl
Hidatsa style
Collected by Gilbert Wilson, pre-1918?
Bone, carved to a point on one end
*   and polished*
L. 8.3 cm
MHS 7059.114a

Awls of bone, horn, or steel were used instead of needles in leatherworking. A small hole was punched in the hide with the awl and then sinew was poked through the hole. Leader commented, "In my time, we have used only steel needles to work porcupine quills. In old times I hear we used sharp elk horn awls. We wetted the end of the sinew with which we sewed, let it dry and thus made a point that would go right thru the hole punctured in the skin by the awl. Awls were also made, I have heard, from Rocky Mountain sheep horn.

"I saw the awl my mother used, when I was young; but I never saw her use it. My mother said she used it on porcupine quill work" (Wilson 1911:284).

Beads
Pre-1885?
Excavated at Fort Berthold I
White, blue, and pink glass
Wire loops: D. 7 cm
SHSND 32ML2/12,711.242, 243,
*   508, 509, 805, 1466*

Glass beads were first acquired through European trade. The earliest beads were large and scarce and so they were often used in necklaces or tied in the hair (Brasser 1972:58–60). Later, small or "seed" beads like these recovered inside the trading post at Like-a-Fishhook Village were sold by traders and distributed by government agents as part of the annuities (Schindel 1879a). They were sewn with various stitches onto clothing and accessories in designs that reflected patterns made in quills.

Sinew

Hidatsa style
Collected by Gilbert Wilson, pre-1918?
Three strips of dried sinew
L. 20 to 90 cm, W. 7 to 8 cm
MHS 7059.91a, b, c

The tendon along the backbone of a deer, bison, or other large animal provided sinew for sewing, tying, lashing, and wrapping. It was cut off in large strips and dried. When needed, a piece of the appropriate size was torn off, dampened, twisted, and smoothed for use. Fine sinew was used for thread; larger pieces were twisted to make bow strings, belts, ropes, and similar items.

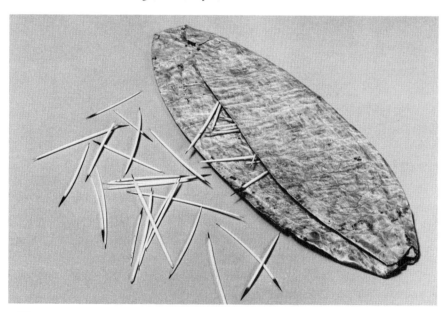

Awl Cases and Bone Awl

Hidatsa style
Collected by Gilbert Wilson, pre-1918?
Cylindrical rawhide cases with flaps
over openings and thongs for tying
to a belt. Case A (below) solidly
covered with randomly colored
beads; contains polished bone awl.
Case B (above) wrapped in red,
yellow, purple, and green plaited
quills; fringes of quill-wrapped
leather, dentalium shells, and
dyed horsehair
Bottom: L. 20 cm. Top: L. 18 cm
Awl: L. 9 cm
MHS 7059.16a, b

A slim rawhide tube covered with beads or quills in decorative patterns was used to protect the awl's sharp point. A woman hung the case from her belt so that it would be handy when she needed it.

Quill Case and Quills

Hidatsa style
Collected by Gilbert Wilson, pre-1918?
Dried animal bladder, flattened and folded in thirds, containing three
porcupine quills dyed yellow. Shown with undyed quills from a separate
collection
L. 30 cm, W. 10.5 cm
MHS 7059.19a, 1978.56.45

Animal bladders were used as cases for storing porcupine and gull quills used in embroidery. Wilson also collected several pelican beak or gullet cases (Museum of the American Indian, Heye Foundation 1/3785, 3786) and an intestine case (AMNH 50.1/5405) used to store quills. The provenance of the undyed quills is unknown.

Painting Tools

Hidatsa. Bought from Buffalo Bird Woman
Collected by Gilbert Wilson, 1910
Wood sticks, one flattened on one end, the other notched
L. 15.6 cm, 6.7 cm
AMNH 50.1/5511b, d

These are among the tools Buffalo Bird Woman used when she painted her husband's honor marks on the canopy of a model bed she made for Wilson. Tools like these were used to paint designs on robes, clothes, beds, and other items made from hide. The round stick (bottom) was used to scratch an outline of the design on the hide and the flattened stick (top) served as a brush to apply red or black paint. Bone instruments were used to cover the design with glue, or sizing, made by boiling skins. The sizing made white areas in the design, set the red paint, and helped to keep the decorated portion clean and bright (Wilson 1910a:296-97; MHS photos IV-35 to IV-41).

Woman's Bag

Northern Plains/Hidatsa style
Collected by Frederick Wilson, pre-1918?
Single piece of rawhide folded into envelope shape; seams sewn with thread and bound in green wool. Painted in green, red, yellow, and blue geometric designs outlined in dark brown
W. 34.3 cm, H. 26.2 cm
MHS 9598.24

Rawhide bags, folded at the bottom with an opening at the top, were used by women for storing tools and toiletries. Wolf Chief referred to such a bag as a woman's bag, although he used one for carrying game or his lunch. A sketch of the bag he used on an eagle hunt, "painted with a design and [having] a red flannel border," clearly shows it to be of this style (Wilson 1913a:254; Goodbird 1913:fig. 37).

Flint Carrying Case

Hidatsa. Bought from Sioux Woman, Goodbird's wife
Collected by Gilbert Wilson, 1909
Tanned hide pouch with large triangular flap beaded in black, yellow, red, blue, green, and clear seed beads; fringed edges. Three tassels of red and yellow quill-wrapped hide
L. 31.5 cm
AMNH 50.1/5393

This unusual case with a long triangular flap was used to carry flints. Women may have used the flints as whetstones to sharpen their tools, but men carried flint, steel, and tinder made from a puffball mushroom, and usually made the fire. Wilson does not provide an exact description of these cases, but artist Rudolph F. Kurz mentioned and illustrated similar bags carried by Crow Indian men in 1852 (Kurz 1937:260, pl. 26 bottom). This bag is decorated with the brightly colored beads and quills typically used by Mandan and Hidatsa craftswomen.

PIPE BAG

Hidatsa style
Collected by Frederick Wilson,
*   pre-1918?*
Tanned hide bag with scalloped rim
*   bound with red and blue seed*
*   beads; geometric designs in*
*   porcupine quillwork dyed white,*
*   black, purple, orange, red, green,*
*   maroon, and yellow, are different*
*   on front and back. Quill-wrapped*
*   leather slats and fringe*
L. 71 cm, W. 13.5 cm
MHS 9999.2

PIPE BAG

Hidatsa. Bought from Sioux Woman, Goodbird's wife
Collected by Gilbert Wilson, 1909
Tanned hide bag with scalloped rim bound with blue seed beads. Geometric
*   designs in porcupine quillwork dyed orange, green, pink, yellow, turquoise,*
*   and violet are different on front and back. Quill-wrapped leather slats and*
*   fringe. For color, see book's cover and flap, which show bag's reverse side*
L. 62 cm, W. 14.3 cm
AMNH 50. 1/5438

Pipe bags were used by men to carry pipes, tobacco, and pipe tampers. These two demonstrate the brilliant colors favored by Hidatsa craftswomen. The Fort Berthold traders carried chrome yellow and cochineal (red) dyes specifically for quillwork in the 1850s, but by 1877 the trading store stocked aniline dyes at 16 cents a bottle. These quills were probably colored with the latter (Boller 1966:157; Longfellow 1877:1).

Traditionally, commented Buffalo Bird Woman, only old men who no longer had to worry about keeping in shape for hunting and warfare did much smoking, but by the 1910s men of all ages smoked. The bags in use when her father was young were "exactly the same that we use today, ornamented with beads or quillwork; only the old men never bothered in old times to ornament their tobacco bags" (Wilson 1912:211-19). Wolf Chief noted, "Crow Flies High and High Back Bone had pipes. These were carried each in the owner's tobacco bag with his tobacco or whatever it was that he smoked. The tobacco bag was carried tied to the belt on the right side" (Wilson [1903-18]:46, 1913b:499; Goodbird 1913:fig. 75).

The AMNH pipe bag was illustrated and discussed by Robert Lowie in his monograph on Crow art (Lowie 1922b:296-97).

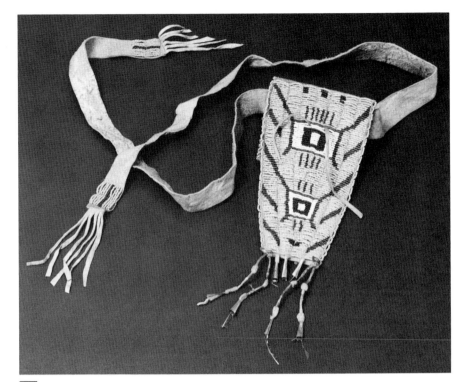

KNIFE SHEATH

Hidatsa. Bought from Otter Goes Out
Collected by Gilbert Wilson, 1910
Tanned hide, folded and sewn with
 thread; fringed with a double
 looped row of clear beads; quilled
 in yellow, pink, black, white,
 lavender, orange, and purple.
 Three beaded hide tassels and
 tanned hide tie for attaching to
 belt
L. 24.5 cm
AMNH 50.1/5497a

Both men and women carried knives in
sheaths like this. Buffalo Bird Woman,
in describing how she loaded her dog
travois in preparation for a tribal hunt
along the Yellowstone River,
remembered, "Two of the women in
the camp carried knives in their belt. I
did not do this on this journey
although I often did so. I used to go
with my husband twice a year, once in
summer and sometimes in winter on a
hunt, when I carried my knife in my
belt, but this time as I say, I put it up
in the bag on the dog travois" (Wilson
1913b:514, 562).

FLINT CARRYING CASE WITH BELT

Hidatsa style
Collected by Gilbert Wilson, pre-1918?
Small tanned hide pocket edged in pink beads, covered by a large triangular flap
 entirely beaded with yellow, white, blue, and red lazy-stitched beads. Pouch is
 sewn to tanned hide belt with fringed and beaded ends. Fringe on flap
 decorated with metal cones, red quills, and red feathers. See color page 176
Belt: L. 140 cm. Bag: L. 26.5 cm, W. 10.5 cm
MHS 7059.14

This small beaded bag for carrying flint is very similar to others collected by Wilson
in 1909 and 1911 from Sioux Woman and Owl Woman (AMNH 50.1/5393,
50.1/6023). Hidatsa garments did not have pockets, so people wore many highly
decorated bags tied to their belts or wrists. This bag kept the flint ready for
sharpening tools or starting fires.

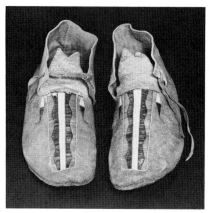

PAINTED HIDE
Northern Plains
Collected by Gilbert Wilson, pre-1918?
Tanned elk or deer hide painted in red, blue, yellow, and green. See color
page 166
L. 123 cm, W. 84 cm
MHS 7059.24

Northern Plains tribes often painted the hides used as men's robes with feather designs that symbolized war honors. Péhriska-Rúhpa, a Hidatsa man, wore a robe like this one when artist Karl Bodmer painted his portrait in 1833 (Bodmer 1984:318). Quilled and painted hides were also used as canopies that could be pulled down around a bed at night to provide privacy (Wilson 1910a:12-13).

This robe's design, commonly called the feather circle, is painted with colors more often used by the Sioux. Wilson may have purchased the robe on one of his trips to Standing Rock Reservation.

MOCCASINS
Hidatsa style
Collected by Gilbert Wilson, pre-1918?
Tanned hide uppers with separately
sewn tongue and columns of red,
yellow, and purple quillwork on
vamp, surrounded by border of
quillwork. Hard sole sewn on with
sinew. See color page 168
L. 27.5 and 27.7 cm, W. 11 and
11.4 cm
MHS 7059.6a, b

The typical Plains Indian moccasin was hard-soled, but there were several different styles in use in most tribes. The Mandan and Hidatsa made both soft-soled and hard-soled moccasins as well as simpler, heavier ones for winter use. Moccasins for special occasions were highly decorated with quillwork or beadwork in elaborate designs, while those for everyday use were less decorated or plain (Wilson 1914b:117).

While both porcupine and bird quills were used for embroidery, bird quills were preferred for moccasins. "Porcupine quill work was smoother, prettier and had a better polish," Buffalo Bird Woman said, "but bird quills were much more durable.

"Bird quills were split with the point of an awl being drawn down on either side after the vane of the feathers had been stripped off. The part used was the under side, or under half of the quill, not the upper or shiny outside.

"This in its turn was split, making two pieces. The quill strips were smoothed on the pith side by being drawn against a piece of natural brick, held under the thumb. . . .

"The Sioux, Assiniboine, Arikaras and Mandans used bird quills; I do not think the Crows did, however" (Wilson 1911:289-91).

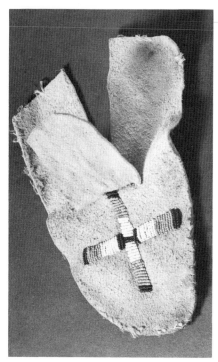

MOCCASIN TOP
Hidatsa style
Collected by Frederick Wilson,
pre-1918?
Tanned hide upper with separate
tongue sewn on with sinew;
beaded with white, blue, and
pink glass beads
L. 19 cm, W. 15 cm
MHS 9598.29
This piece of tanned hide with
beadwork in the shape of a cross was
prepared for use as a moccasin top. The
cuffs and sole were sewn on separately.

MAN'S SHIRT
Mandan. Bought from Lone Fight.
Made by Calf Woman
Collected by Gilbert Wilson, 1907
Tanned elk (?) hide, decorated with
porcupine quillwork in yellow
and purple
L. 87.6 cm, W. 44.5 cm
Museum of the American Indian,
Heye Foundation 1/3796
Although Hidatsa men generally did not
wear shirts, for special occasions or in
inclement weather they donned shirts
decorated with fringes, paint, quills,
beads, and other items. Wilson noted
two different styles of hide shirts in
1907, one with the neck cut like a cloth
shirt and the other with the older style,
V-shaped flap at the neck (Wilson
1907c:2). Wolf Chief, however, told
Wilson that the oldest style of shirt had
a square flap at the neck. "On the coat
. . . is a kind of flap or necklace as we
call it. This was of porcupine quill
work, later of beads. . . . This flap is
called ápa oda̱kapíxē, from *apa*, the
throat or better, the anterior part of the
throat of human beings, and *oda̱kapíxē*,
something that flaps or flies. . . . I have
said that in the figure this necklace or
flap is drawn square. A new fashion has
come in, making it pointed. This is
because our young men now have no
honor-marks. In old times there was
attached to this flap the black human
hair that meant that the wearer had led
a fifth war-party that had slain enemies
or he had colored horse hair attached to
it, meaning that five times he had led
war parties that had captured horses"
(Wilson 1916b:16).

   Confirmation of Wolf Chief's
statement can be found in various
sources. Bodmer's painting of Four
Bears shows a square decorated area on
the front of the shirt (1984:308).
Photographs taken by Stanley J.
Morrow in 1870 clearly illustrate the
square flap that Wolf Chief describes,
and Wilson's photographs show the men
of 1907 occasionally wearing skin shirts
with triangular flaps, but primarily cloth
shirts (Hurt and Lass 1956:71-76;
MHS photos I-47, I-48, I-61, I-69,
I-71, I-97).

Working with the women

Early in the morning, especially in winter, Buffalo Bird Woman saw her mothers take their pack straps, hitch their dogs to travois, and head to the river bottom for firewood. When a girl trained her dog to pull a travois, it meant that both of them were old enough to help with adult chores.

"I was two years older than Cold Medicine, my sister," Buffalo Bird Woman recalled. "When she and I and our two mothers went out for wood, we usually started just after breakfast, say about seven thirty o'clock in the morning and got back again about noon. Usually we went about a mile and a half to the timber from our summer village, but when we were in our winter village, of course, the wood was nearer. . . .

"When we took the travois out of the house ready to go for wood, the dogs would come around us, very glad. 'Wu, wu, wu!' they would bark, and wag their tails. Out of the three or four dogs which our family kept there was not much preference, as all of them were good working animals. . . .

"The four dogs would follow us single file. Having the travois bound upon them, they never tried to escape or run away, but whenever we stopped they would invariably lie down in the road.

"When we came to the timber, we women would cut the wood into lengths about two feet two inches long. . . . We gave to each dog a double armful of wood or a little more, for his load. We tied the load down by the two pack thongs. Besides the wood which we loaded on the travois, each woman also packed a load of wood on her back [with her packing strap]. . . .

"In returning out of the woods, my two mothers and my sister and myself would walk single file with our loads upon our backs, talking and laughing and telling funny stories. The dogs followed after us, also in single file. . . .

"We always kept wood on hand in the lodge and were careful not to let the pile get depleted. . . . If we had work in the lodge that kept us busy we might not go for five or six days, perhaps. But if we had plenty of time we might collect wood every day" (Wilson 1913a:298–302).

As Buffalo Bird Woman grew older, her diligence at household tasks earned her great respect. Hidatsa women who earned the honor could wear special ornaments testifying to their accomplishments. "If a girl was a worker and tanned hundreds of hides her aunt might give her an honor mark," Buffalo Bird Woman explained. "My aunt Sage gave me such, a maípsukaśa or woman's belt. These were broad as a man's

suspender and worked in beads. . . . One could not purchase or make such a belt; it had to be given. For working a quill decorated tent, a bracelet was given; for making a quill embroidered robe, a ring" (Wilson 1912:309).

BUFFALO BIRD WOMAN GATHERING WOOD BY BOAT
Drawn by Goodbird, 1913
Blue carbon and pencil on tracing paper
H. 6 cm, W. 16 cm
MHS (Goodbird 1913:fig. 129)
"Near Like-a-Fishhook Village [wood] was rather scarce because we sold so much of it to steam-boats," Buffalo Bird Woman said (Wilson 1913a:303). So women often walked as far as two miles upriver, carrying skin boats along to bring the wood back. "If we went for a whole day we took a lunch along, biscuits, bacon and coffee." Wilson noted that this picture of the loaded boat returning "invoked quite a laugh" from Buffalo Bird Woman when she saw it (Wilson 1913a:304–6; Goodbird 1913:fig. 129).

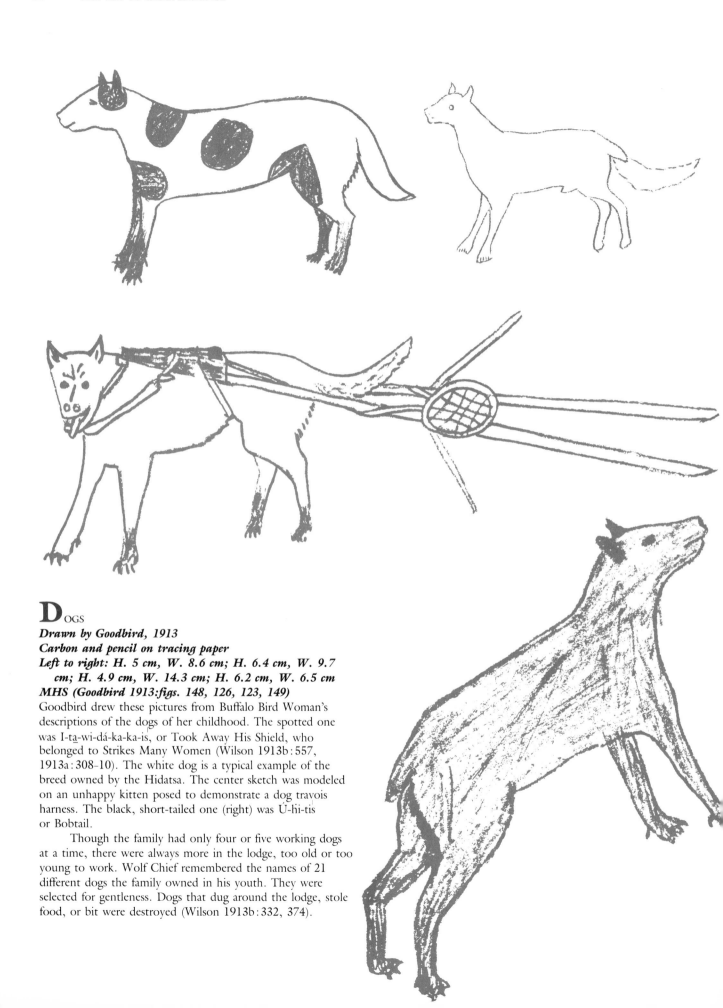

Dogs

Drawn by Goodbird, 1913
Carbon and pencil on tracing paper
Left to right: H. 5 cm, W. 8.6 cm; H. 6.4 cm, W. 9.7
*   cm; H. 4.9 cm, W. 14.3 cm; H. 6.2 cm, W. 6.5 cm*
MHS (Goodbird 1913:figs. 148, 126, 123, 149)

Goodbird drew these pictures from Buffalo Bird Woman's descriptions of the dogs of her childhood. The spotted one was I-ta-wi-dá-ka-ka-is, or Took Away His Shield, who belonged to Strikes Many Women (Wilson 1913b:557, 1913a:308–10). The white dog is a typical example of the breed owned by the Hidatsa. The center sketch was modeled on an unhappy kitten posed to demonstrate a dog travois harness. The black, short-tailed one (right) was Ú-hi-tis or Bobtail.

Though the family had only four or five working dogs at a time, there were always more in the lodge, too old or too young to work. Wolf Chief remembered the names of 21 different dogs the family owned in his youth. They were selected for gentleness. Dogs that dug around the lodge, stole food, or bit were destroyed (Wilson 1913b:332, 374).

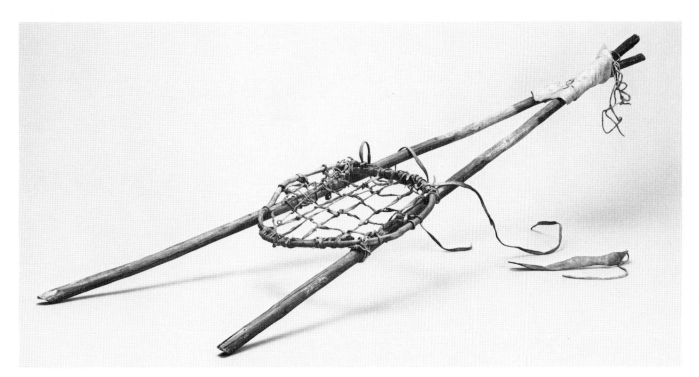

DOG TRAVOIS

Hidatsa. Bought from Butterfly
Collected by Gilbert Wilson, 1909
Wooden poles connected by a tanned hide cushion. Basket frame of bent wood laced with rawhide strips
L. 221 cm, W. 81 cm
AMNH 50.1/5414

Wolf Chief's relative Butterfly connected a new harness to an old travois frame when he sold this artifact to Wilson (MHS photos III-54 to III-60; see also XI-42-1918). The dog travois was used by the Hidatsa to transport wood and baggage. When a woman needed a new travois, she cut down two trees the right size for the poles and dried them on the drying stage. She then used a small ash sapling to make the hoop for the basket. When it was dried into a circle, the woman usually took the hoop and a wet rawhide to a man who was respected for his ability to weave travois hoops.

This man would cut the rawhide into a thong to weave the netting for the basket, which the Hidatsa always painted red. Women sometimes did this work themselves. When the weaving was done, the woman took the hoop and bound it to the travois poles. A cushion of buffalo skin with the hair left on kept the frame from rubbing against the dog's back (Wilson 1913a:316-24; MHS photos X-54-1918 to X-60-1918).

Men might take travois dogs on hunting or war parties, but women raised them, trained them, and used them most. "To train a dog," explained Buffalo Bird Woman, "we hitched the animal in the travois and called him by name. At first the dog would be afraid and would struggle and whine, but the woman would coax him and call to him and the dog would soon start to come to her. It took about four days before a dog would obey. The first three days the woman would tie a thong to the dog's neck collar and lead him. The dog would not want to come, but she would coax the dog and make him follow her. The fourth day the dog had learned his lesson and would follow his owner.

"On the first trip, a very little wood would be loaded on the dog's travois. The loads would be increased each day until the dog could carry a full load.

"Some dogs were much stronger than others and could be given a much larger load. We always knew which dog to load the heaviest" (Wilson 1913a:307).

Burden Strap

Hidatsa style
Collected by Gilbert Wilson, pre-1918?
Rawhide chest and head straps
attached to tanned hide bundle
straps by wooden pegs
Shoulder and head straps, L. 56 cm;
bundle straps, L. 188 cm
MHS 7059.48

"For the load which a woman carried on her back," recalled Buffalo Bird Woman, "she used her packing strap. It had two bands, one going across the shoulders and chest and the other across her forehead. The forehead band was used only for the purpose of resting our shoulders, as we did now and then for a short time. Then we would let the shoulder band drop and hang loose until we used it for the same purpose again" (Wilson 1913a: 299; Goodbird 1916: fig. 20).

Bracelets

Mandan. Bought from Sioux
Woman. Made by Red Stone
Collected by Gilbert Wilson, 1910
Each bracelet formed of a single piece
of iron wire, bent and polished
D. 6 cm, W. 2 cm
AMNH 50.1/5492a, b

Metal bracelets were expensive luxuries for the Mandan and Hidatsa. Wolf Chief said that "Wire used to be purchased at the trader's store and taken to Red Stone who bent it into the proper shape for bracelets. It cost a buffalo robe to get him to do this. The value of the bracelets when done was considerable – often a pony was paid for one pair. In old time, to save us from calamity we made offerings of these bracelets to the gods" (Wilson 1910a: list of items purchased, p. 8). A young woman was entitled to wear two bracelets in honor of quilling a tent cover and a young man might wear a bracelet in recognition of leading a war party (F. Wilson 1912b: 52-53).

Rings

Early 19th century
Excavated at Fort Charlotte, Minn.
Brass
D. 2 cm
MHS 362.3.294, 1131, 1359, 298, 30

Rings were popular trade items with both men and women from the 18th century on. Buffalo Bird Woman explained that a young woman often wore a ring to indicate that she had made a quill-embroidered robe. Unlike the honor belt for tanning hides, which had to be given, the ring could be purchased by the woman herself (Wilson 1912: 309). Wolf Chief recalled that when he was a young man he wore "3 or 4 brass ring[s] on fingers of both hands" (Wilson 1916c: 67). These rings are identical to ones pictured in photographs from Like-a-Fishhook Village (see SHSND photo Col. 88-20).

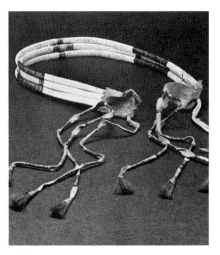

GIRL'S DRESS

Mandan. Bought from Yellow Hair. Made by Gertrude Levings, Yellow Hair's daughter
Collected by Gilbert Wilson, 1910
Tanned hide sewn with sinew. Seams fringed; neck decorated with quilled triangular flap and laces of tanned hide with metal cones and red horsehair attached. Four rows of imitation and real elk teeth attached to front by a thong which passes through holes in the leather; three rows in back. Skirt decorated with nine hide tassels, front and back. See color page 167
L. 56.5 cm, W. 68.5 cm across arms
AMNH 50.1/5487

When they reached the age of three or four, girls were given dresses modeled after those worn by their mothers. The finest dresses were those decorated with elk teeth. This garment is cut and decorated in an old style. The front always had more rows of elk teeth than the back (Wilson 1910a: list of items purchased, p. 7).

"My husband's parents gave me an elk teeth dress, with 375 elk teeth on it," remembered Buffalo Bird Woman. "Afterwards they gave me another with 600 elk teeth. Six times in my life I have owned elk teeth dresses" (Wilson 1914b: 329; Goodbird 1913: fig. 65).

In later days people came to use imitation elk teeth, many of which were made from bone by a blind man named Mason living on the Fort Berthold Reservation. Wilson collected examples and noted that they cost 50 cents each, a very high price at the time (AMNH 50.1/6907; Wilson 1912: 312).

GIRL'S BELT

Mandan. Bought from Gertrude Levings, daughter of Yellow Hair
Collected by Gilbert Wilson, 1910
Three strips of rawhide wrapped with porcupine quills dyed purple, pink, blue, yellow, and white. Belt ties of tanned hide. On each side are three tassels of tanned hide wrapped with violet quills and ending in metal cones with red horsehair attached
L. 51.5 cm, W. 2.4 cm
AMNH 50.1/5488

This belt, an imitation of a style worn by women, was made by Gertrude Levings to go with the girl's dress she made. Mrs. Levings, who learned from her mother how to make these belts, believed this to be an old style (Wilson 1910a: list of items purchased, p. 7).

Feeding the family

If a man would be chief," people at Like-a-Fishhook said, "he should be ready to feed the poor and strangers" (Maxidiwiac 1921:51). Small Ankle was a prominent man, and so his house was always open to guests at mealtimes. European visitors were surprised at the generosity of Mandan and Hidatsa leaders. "Distinguished men and chiefs of eminence are for the most part poor," one wrote, "because, in order to gain reputation and influence, they give away everything of value which they possess" (Wied 1905-06, 22:321).

Charity often came back to the giver in nonmaterial ways. "Sometimes when we brought meat home to the lodge . . . women visitors came in expecting to receive gifts of the meat," said Wolf Chief. "Among the visitors might be an old woman who was quite happy to get some meat and a dinner. . . . After this meal the old woman now contented with her stomach filled would call a boy or girl of the household to her and bless it." At other times, after a successful hunt, a man might feast his clan fathers, who then honored him in their prayers. "It has always been Indian custom so to do," said Wolf Chief. "It is a custom which we Indians much admire" (Wilson 1913b:362-64).

The food eaten at family meals changed in the years Buffalo Bird Woman was growing up. The staple meal was a succotash of pounded corn boiled with beans, served with dried, boiled meat. In early times this was supplemented with berries, squash, and wild turnips. But as store-bought food and government rations became more available, people baked wheat bread in Dutch ovens and fixed coffee by pounding the beans with an ax and boiling them in water. Canned fruit and meat were also popular. "We usually ate our boiled corn and beans out of wooden bowls," Goodbird remembered from his childhood. "Meat we more often ate from tin or iron dishes" (Wilson 1913a:11, 129).

Though the foods and dishes might change, table manners did not. Goodbird said that family meals took place three times a day. "When I was a small boy and we all lived in Small Ankle's earth lodge, I remember we always ate our meals sitting around the fire. . . .

"Strikes Many Women I remember did most of the cooking. Most of the cooking was done in a three legged kettle that we owned. When she was done cooking, and ready to serve, she would call, 'Ma-wú-tats! – We eat!' or 'Ma-du-tá-da – You (people) eat!' Then we all arose and took our places.

"Strikes Many Women had the dishes all ready

TABLEWARE
Pre-1885?
Excavated at Like-a-Fishhook Village
Stamped and cast iron. Table knife and three-tined fork have concave depression in handle; spoon handle has ridge
Table knife: L. 23.2 cm. Spoon: L. 20.8 cm. Fork: L. 18.5 cm
SHSND 32ML2/12,003.FT402, 2022, FT72
A list of annuities distributed to the people of Fort Berthold Reservation in June 1879 included table knives and forks, teaspoons, and tablespoons (Schindel 1879b). It is obvious from the numbers in the list that such items were given to each family and not to individual family members. Much of the tableware found at Like-a-Fishhook was excavated from earth lodge caches and refuse pits (Smith 1972:35-36).

and piled before her. . . . She would take the kettle off the fire and set it before her place, with the meat steaming and hot. The hot pieces of meat, she lifted out of the kettle with a sharp stick. . . .

"She had put a big wooden bowl beside her; and as she sat, she lifted all the pieces of meat out of the kettle into the wooden bowl. With a knife she then cut the pieces up into smaller size.

"The steam from the meat pile would come rushing up into her face. I remember she would blow 'Whew!' blowing the steam away as she cut off a piece of the meat with her knife; and lifting it by one corner with fingers and thumb, she laid the piece on a dish. . . .

Kettle
Pre-1885?
Excavated at Like-a-Fishhook Village
Cast iron, with three legs and an iron bail
H. 18 cm, D. 30 cm excluding bail
SHSND 32ML2/12,003.2266

When metal kettles were first introduced by the traders the Hidatsa did not like them very much. Buffalo Bird Woman recalled, "The first kettles that we got from the whites were of yellow tin; the French and the Crees also brought us some kettles that were of red tin. As long as the native [clay] pots could be gotten we of our family did not use the metal pots very much because the metal made the food taste. In my time if we went to visit any other family and they gave us food cooked in an iron pot, we knew at once because we could smell and taste it" (Wilson 1912:115).

Later, kettles became the preferred item for cooking and serving food. Different styles of kettles were frequently included in the annuity distributions made by the government.

This style was designed for use in open fireplaces. It probably once had a cover, and it may have been the kind of "Dutch oven" that Wolf Chief mentioned and Goodbird described as being used for baking bread (Wolf Chief 1881a:3; Wilson 1913a:11).

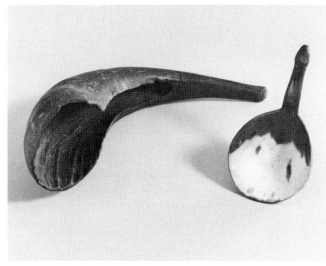

Horn Spoons
Northern Plains
Collected by Gilbert Wilson, pre-1918?
Left: hollow buffalo horn, cut open lengthwise. Right:
*   variegated cream and black horn, carved*
Left: L. 26.5 cm, W. 8.5 cm. Right: L. 13.5 cm,
*   W. 7 cm*
MHS 7059.56a, b

Traditionally, small spoons (right) were used for eating while large horn spoons (left) were used for serving food. Like modern household cutlery, spoons belonged to the family and not to individuals. After each meal, the spoons were washed and stored away on the food storage platform to the left of the lodge door (F. Wilson 1912b:37).

"We had small wooden dishes in old times and spoons of buffalo horn, Rocky-Mountain-sheep horn and mussel shells," said Buffalo Bird Woman. "When we passed the food around to any one he added broth enough in his dish and when he ate the meat he also drank the broth. All these broths we drank out of a spoon" (Wilson 1912:249).

"As Strikes Many Women filled each dish, she handed it to one of us boys, – to Full House or me, saying, 'Give this to so-and-so.' My grandmother, Strikes Many Women, served my father first because he was her son-in-law, and she thought a great deal of him. Next came Wolf Chief, then Red Kettle, Full House and Flies Low, and last, Small Ankle and his wife. . . .

"Strikes Many Women, as being the one who was serving, if the mess proved to be short for all who sat down, went without. If there was abundance, she helped herself to her share. This was Indian custom. One who served always did this, whether man or woman" (Wilson 1915b:588–92).

GOODBIRD'S FAMILY EATING
Traced by Gilbert Wilson from a drawing by
*   Goodbird, 1913*
Black carbon and pencil on tracing paper
H. 4.9 cm, W. 10.2 cm
MHS (Goodbird 1913:fig. 22)
This drawing shows Buffalo Bird Woman, her husband Son of a Star, and Goodbird eating deer or antelope meat on a hunting expedition. A husband and wife always ate together, often out of the same bowl. Wilson noted that Buffalo Bird Woman "laughed very heartily at the idea that the wife should wait on her husband like a servant" (Wilson 1910a:309). "You will notice," Goodbird said of this picture, "that I have on a vest which my mother made after white man's fashion, and it was covered over with elk teeth" (Wilson 1913a:130).

BOWL
Northern Plains
Collected by Gilbert Wilson, pre-1916
Single piece of cottonwood or box elder, carved and
*   polished. Bird head with brass tack eye carved on one*
*   rim; raised area on opposite side of rim, which has holes*
*   for missing brass tacks, represents bird's tail*
L. 31.5 cm, W. 32.7 cm, H. 12.5 cm
MHS 7059.52c
Large wooden bowls were used for serving food. Wolf Chief's family used a bowl that was "shaped something like a boat and was about twenty inches long by seventeen inches wide. The head was like a dog's head and was at one end; opposite it on the other side, was a round knob" (Wilson 1915b:518).

Frederick Wilson sketched this bowl to illustrate one of his brother's books (Wilson 1916a:94).

BOTTLES
Pre-1885?
Excavated at Like-a-Fishhook Village
Light green and blue-green mold-
blown glass; glazed crockery
Left to right: H. 13.2 cm, 21 cm, 19
cm
SHSND 32ML2/12,003.876, 956,
1392

A wide variety of bottles was found in the excavations at Like-a-Fishhook Village. Some of these appear to have been wine, beer, or condiment bottles, while others contained medicines. The presence of the bottles does not necessarily mean that Indian people were using all the products they contained. Villagers also might have collected empty bottles from traders and military men and reused them, as is suggested by the presence of reworked glass fragments in the excavations (Smith 1972:36, 42, 45, 53, 77).

The bottle at right has raised lettering saying, "J. Cairns St. Louis Mo. F.R.L."

TIN CAN
Pre-1885?
Excavated at Like-a-Fishhook Village
Tinned metal, soldered, with paper
label
H. 7.5 cm, D. 14 cm
SHSND 32ML2/12,003.FT240

The excavations at Like-a-Fishhook Village revealed a number of metal containers for food, especially for processed meats like beef or pork (Smith 1972:58). Other items shipped to the village in cans included fruit, vegetables, coffee, and spices. This can was opened on the bottom with a can opener.

LADLE
Northern Plains
Collected by Gilbert Wilson, pre-1917
Rocky Mountain (Bighorn) sheep
horn, carved and polished. Tanned
hide loop wrapped with red and
yellow porcupine quills is attached
to hole near tip of handle
L. 41.2 cm, W. 7.7 cm
MHS 9598.9

Large spoons were used as ladles to dip vegetables and broth out of the cooking pots into serving bowls. Horn implements could be used for ladles because brief immersion in hot liquid would not damage them. Buffalo Bird Woman used a horn spoon when she parboiled green corn in preparation for drying it. "When there was enough corn piled up to fill one kettle, the corn was taken up and placed in one of these two kettles. I watched the corn carefully and when it was half cooked, the ears were lifted out with a Rocky Mt. sheep horn ladle and laid on a pile of husks" (Wilson 1912:41). Frederick Wilson used this artifact as a model for a sketch (Wilson 1917:20).

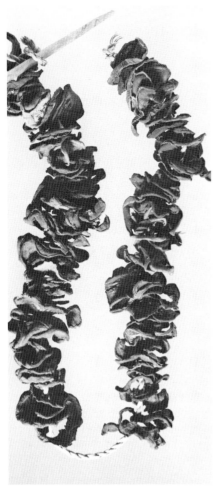

DRIED SQUASH
Hidatsa style
Collected by Gilbert Wilson, 1916
Dried squash slices strung on braided
*   beaver grass (Carex stricta) cord*
*   knotted at each end. Carved*
*   wooden needle notched for attaching*
*   cord*
String: L. 95 cm. Needle: L. 22.8 cm
MHS 7059.54a, b

In 1916 Wilson observed and
photographed Owl Woman slicing
squash for drying (Wilson 1916b:167;
MHS photos VIII-73-16 to VIII-97-16
and VII-4-14 to VII-16-14). The
circular squash slices were impaled on
willow spits and set on the drying stage
in the sun. Once dry, the squash slices
were strung on beaver grass cord using a
wooden needle. The cords of dried
squash were then stored away for
winter use.

BONE SQUASH KNIFE
Hidatsa. Made by Goodbird?
Collected by Gilbert Wilson, 1914?
Buffalo or beef scapular bone, carved
*   and sharpened*
L. 15.5 cm, W. 13 cm
MHS 7059.38

"I have seen old women use squash
knives when I was young," Buffalo Bird
Woman commented. "The squash knife
was made from the thin part of the
shoulder bone of a buffalo, never from
the shoulder bone of a deer, elk, or
bear, that I know. The bone of a cow
buffalo was best, because it was thinner.
If the squash knife was too thick, the
slices of squash were apt to break as
they were being sliced off the fruit.
Bone squash knives were used, as I
recollect, for slicing squashes and for
nothing else. . . .

"This bone squash knife that I
have had my son Goodbird make for
you is of rather dry bone. I have had
him grease it first before using" (Wilson
1914b:295-96; MHS photos VII-4-14
and VII-31-14).

In 1914 Wilson purchased a
squash knife made by Goodbird. Since
there are no other squash knives in the
Wilson collections, it is likely that this is
the same knife.

METAL SQUASH KNIFE?
Pre-1885?
Excavated at Like-a-Fishhook Village
Sheet metal cut into shape by hand;
*   top edge folded over*
L. 16.2 cm, W. 11 cm
SHSND 32ML2/12,003.165

Archaeologist James H. Howard
identified this as a beamer when it was
found in 1953, possibly because of a
similar Crow tool illustrated by Robert
Lowie (Howard 1953:fig. 13, no. 6;
Lowie 1924c:218). However, it more
closely resembles the bone knives used
for slicing squash. It was apparently
made by hand from a larger piece
of metal.

MORTAR AND PESTLE
Mandan or Hidatsa
Collected by Gilbert Wilson, pre-1913
Polished ash (?) pestle carved from a
single piece of wood. Mortar made
from a hollowed tree trunk
Pestle: L. 107 cm, D. 14 cm. Mortar:
H. 48 cm, D. 21 cm
MHS 7059.50a, b

Wooden mortars were present in every earth lodge. Usually they were sunk into the floor so that women could sit as they pounded dried corn or other foods. The pestle was held with the large end up (MHS photos VIII-32-1916, VI-64-14, VI-65-14; Wilson [1903-18]:58–59).

DRIED MEAT
Hidatsa style
Collected by Gilbert Wilson, pre-1918?
Beef
L. 9.4 to 19.2 cm
MHS 7059.60a–d

Before refrigeration, the best way to preserve meat was to slice it thin and dry it, either in the sun or over the fire. After a buffalo hunt, the men butchered the animals and brought the meat to camp where the women dried it and packed it away in parfleches. Dried meat could be eaten plain or cooked in boiling water, but the preferred way was to pound it into small pieces and cook it with corn and other vegetables. "That is the way we used to serve meat to old people," Goodbird said. "Their teeth became worn down so that they could not eat the unpounded dry meat; it hurt their gums to do so. We still follow this custom. We take this boiled dried meat and put it with fats, which we then pound up with an ax. The mess is then easier for old people to eat" (Wilson 1915b:574).

PRAIRIE TURNIPS
Hidatsa style
Collected by Gilbert Wilson, 1916
One whole prairie turnip (Psoralea
esculenta), others sliced and dried
Whole turnip: L. 16.8 cm. Slices: L.
1.8 cm to 7 cm
MHS 7059.59

Prairie turnips were an important source of food for all Plains Indians. These starchy roots, when peeled, could be eaten fresh or dried and stored indefinitely. The Hidatsa frequently dried them in slices which could be dropped into stews. Sometimes they pounded the dried slices into flour and used the flour to thicken berry puddings (Wilson 1916b:184–87, [1903–18]:57; MHS photos III-1, III-2, IX-51-1916, IX-52-1916). Prairie turnips are still harvested and used today much as they were when Buffalo Bird Woman was growing up.

HAMMER (MAUL)
Mandan or Hidatsa
Collected by Gilbert Wilson, pre-1918?
Wood handle and stone head encased
in a rawhide sheath. Attached to
back of head is a strip of white,
yellow, and red quillwork with blue
bead edging
L. 40.8 cm, W. 9 cm, H. 12.4 cm
MHS 7059.49a

Stone hammers or mauls were used to
pound up chokecherries, dried meat,
and vegetables. Buffalo Bird Woman
recalled, "In my day, the only man in
the village who made stone hammers
was Raise Heart.

"Raise Heart was a magic man and
made these stone hammers, *maopaki* is
the native name. We did not know how
he made them. When some one wanted
a stone hammer he found a suitable
stone and brought it to Raise Heart.
'Come back for it at such a time,' Raise
Heart would say. If the man came back
as directed he found the stone hammer
all worked into shape. But if he put off
coming and did not go to Raise Heart's
lodge until after the time told him, he
would find when he came that Raise
Heart had cut the stone in two! . . .

"The stone hammer was a tool
that a woman used. But very often a
woman did not want to go to Raise
Heart's lodge because he had this magic
power, and she was afraid.

"I do not know what he was paid
for making a stone hammer. He had a
large family. He was the only man in
the village who did such work" (Wilson
1916b: 218-19).

BERRY-MASHING HIDE
Northern Plains style
Collected by Gilbert Wilson, pre-1918?
Round, bowl-shaped piece of rawhide. Nine quill-wrapped thong tassels with
metal cones attached to outside edge. Six holes around edge for staking down
L. 40 cm, W. 25 cm
MHS 7059.31

Most families placed a large tanned hide under the stone anvil when berries were
being mashed to catch any berries that flew out from under the pounder. The mat
also trapped the juices so that the work area was kept clean. Some women decorated
their hides like this one. Wilson collected no descriptions of decorated berry-mashing
hides, but Wolf Chief remembered that his grandmother had made meat-pounding
mats from rawhide. "She took a piece of green hide from off a buffalo's hump or
from the hip of a buffalo bull, and cut it round, about two and a half feet in
diameter. She dug a hole in the ground about one and three quarters feet in
diameter and four inches deep. The piece of green hide was staked out over the hole
with wooden pins; and a heavy stone was laid in the center to sink the hide down
into the hole. When dry the hide was shaped with a crown something like a white
man's hat" (Wilson 1915b: 574).

BERRY CAKES
Hidatsa style. Made by Owl Woman
Collected by Gilbert Wilson, 1916
Chokecherry or Juneberry pulp, dried
into cylindrical cakes
L. 5 cm to 7 cm
MHS 7059.57

Wilson photographed Owl Woman
pounding chokecherries and making
them into dried cakes in 1916. Buffalo
Bird Woman described the process: "We
pounded the chokecherries on the stone
mortar in the lodge or out on the floor
of the corn stage. We did not like to do
so out on the ground outside the lodge
on account of the dust that got in the
cherries.

"Two or three cherries were laid
on the stone and struck smartly, then
two or three more. When enough pulp
had accumulated it was taken up in the
woman's hand and made into a ball,
and then squeezed out in lumps thru
the first finger and thumb of the right
hand by pushing with the left thumb
into the right palm.

"These lumps we dried on the
corn stage on a skin. On warm days
they dried in three days' time. But if the
weather was damp and chilly, it might
take 5 or 6 days. They were ready,
when a lump broke dry clear thru. If
the lump was put away while still soft
inside, it spoiled and smelled bad"
(Wilson 1916b:220-21; MHS photos
VIII-98-1916 to IX-2-1916).

DRIED SERVICE BERRIES
Hidatsa
Collected by Gilbert Wilson, 1916
Dried berries collected in a muslin bag
Bag: L. 49 cm, W. 31 cm
MHS 7059.58

Juneberries, also known as service berries, were picked, dried, and stored for winter
use. Buffalo Bird Woman said, "Juneberries were gathered when ripe, to be dried
and stored away for winter. The berries differed a good deal on the various trees.
Some trees bore very sweet berries, others those less sweet; and some bore large
berries, some small berries. . . .

"We gathered Juneberries, either picking them off the tree by hand, or we
broke off a laden branch and beat it with a stick, thus knocking the berries off upon
a skin. . . .

"It was . . . a common thing for a young man to help his sweetheart pick
Juneberries. A young man might send word to his sweetheart by some female
relative of his own saying, 'That young man says that when you want to go for June
berries, he wants to go along with you!' Or else he watched when she came out of
the lodge to start berrying; for it was not our custom for a young man to talk
openly with a young woman" (Wilson 1916b:210-17; MHS photos VI-73-14,
VI-74-14).

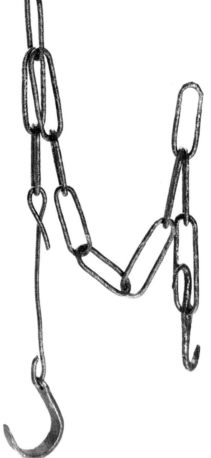

COFFEE BOILER
Pre-1885?
Excavated at Like-a-Fishhook Village
Body made from two pieces of tinned
sheet iron soldered together. Spout
and handle of metal strapping
riveted on. Decorative rings run
around the pot body. Cover missing
H. 16.5 cm, D. 15.5 cm at base
SHSND 32ML2/12,003.592

According to Wolf Chief, "When coffee
was first brought to my tribe it was
green coffee. When this green coffee was
roasted on the fire as had to be done
before it could be boiled, it made a very
strange smell. Some of the Indians,
when they smelled it put their fingers to
their noses and fled just as that day I
fled when you burned the sulphur in
my cabin to kill bed bugs" (Wilson
1914b:159).

By 1858, however, coffee was
among the three most popular items
carried in the trader's store, and trader
Henry Boller spoke of keeping a
coffee boiler constantly on the hearth for
visitors (Boller 1966a:157; 1959:65). It
is possible that coffee boilers were also
used to heat water for herbal teas,
which, said Buffalo Bird Woman, "We
never made . . . until we obtained sugar
from the whites" (Wilson 1912:249).

POTHOOK AND CHAIN
Late 19th century
Hand-wrought iron
Hook: L. 32.5 cm. Chain: L. 96 cm
MHS 64.117b, c

Logging chains were ordered by the
Office of Indian Affairs for distribution
to Indians to use with draft animals for
hauling logs. But the people at Like-a-
Fishhook found a different use for
them. A heavy chain with a hook on
the end could be hung over the fire and
cooking pots or roasting ribs could be
hung from the hook. Buffalo Bird
Woman described such an arrangement:
"This pole over the fire place was strung
over two forked posts. . . . We hung a
chain on this pole and on this chain the
kettle for the cooking. In roasting
buffalo ribs we put a skewer thru the
ribs and hung them on the chain over
the fire, swinging them back and forth
until one side was roasted, then
turned the other side" (F. Wilson
1912b:41-42; MHS photos
IV-98-1911, V-60-1912, and
IX-10-1916 to IX-12-1916).

This chain from the Grand
Portage Indian Reservation, Minn., is
similar to a fragmentary one found at
Fort Berthold II (Smith 1972:139).

STIRRING PADDLE
Mandan
Collected by Robert Lowie
Soft wood, carved
L. 50 cm, W. 5.5 cm
AMNH 50.1/4313, Lowie

"When *má-da-ka-pá* [corn meal mush]
was cooking," explained Buffalo Bird
Woman, "it had to be stirred with a
wooden paddle to prevent burning. It
was not stirred with a horn spoon,
because hot water softens and spoils a
horn object" (Wilson 1915b:473).

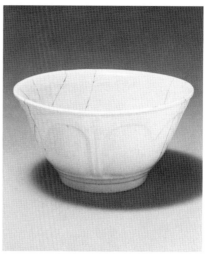

SKILLET
Pre-1885?
Excavated at Like-a-Fishhook Village
Stamped from sheet iron. Handle joined to pan with three rivets on one end; hole
*   for hanging on the other*
Pan: D. 22 cm. Handle: L. 24 cm
SHSND 32ML2/12,003.2148

Frying pans were used in Wolf Chief's childhood for parching corn. The kernels were poured into the ungreased pan and stirred with a stick until brown, then put into the mortar for pounding. The parching process apparently gave the corn more flavor (Will and Hyde 1917:158; Wilson 1913b:440).

MIXING BOWL
Pre-1885?
Excavated at Fort Berthold I
White glazed ceramic with raised
*   scallop design around outside*
H. 8.8 cm, D. 18 cm at rim
SHSND 32ML2/12,711.860

This bowl, found in many pieces and reglued by archaeologists, is among many late 19th-century ceramics found at Like-a-Fishhook Village.

A wide variety of "crockery, bowls, mugs, etc." was listed by the Fort Berthold traders in 1858 and 1877 (Boller 1966a:157; Longfellow 1877:2). The Office of Indian Affairs also purchased ironstone for distribution (USOIA 1880:422). Wolf Chief described the use of ceramic dishes when he joined the Grass Dance Society in about 1860. "We had beforehand brought many chinaware dishes into the lodge; and these had been distributed among the feasters. The feather belt wearers who distributed the meat would take out a small piece of flesh and put it into each dish, and a little broth was poured into each man's cup" (Wilson 1914b:94).

Mussel Shell Spoon

Hidatsa. Bought from Wolf Ghost
Collected by Gilbert Wilson, 1909
Mussel shell
L. 11.3 cm
AMNH 50.1/5420

As Wilson collected this item, he noted, "In the refuse heaps about the old village sites are remains of a great many of these shells. I have never found but this one in actual use today but old Indian women tell me they were commonly used as spoons and that every house wife had numbers of them as white women keep silver spoons" (Wilson 1909a:140). Buffalo Bird Woman told Wilson that mussel shells were also used to shell corn. "There was another way of shelling this half boiled corn. As before I would run a sharpened stick down the rows of kernels, loosening the grain, and they were then shelled off one row at a time with a mussel shell instead of with the thumb" (Wilson 1912:42).

Salt Shaker

Pre-1885?
Excavated at Like-a-Fishhook Village
Soldered cylinder of tinned sheet iron
***   with friction-fit top. Top perforated***
***   in six-pointed star pattern***
H. 8.5 cm, D. 5.2 cm
SHSND 32ML2/12,003.2028

The Missouri River tribes got salt from alkaline springs, burned corncobs, and trade with other tribes. They used it in cooking even before it was made available by traders and government agents; Buffalo Bird Woman's recipe for corn meal mush included "a heaping table spoon [of spring salt] to one pot of mush" (Wilson 1910:280). Later, salt was shipped to the village in 100-pound quantities and sold by the cup or distributed by the pound (USOIA 1878:332, 1880:372). Salt shakers were sold in the trader's store for 30 cents apiece in 1877 (Longfellow 1877:2).

Metal Cup

Pre-1885?
Excavated at Like-a-Fishhook Village
Cup pressed from tinned sheet iron;
***   handle of metal strapping***
***   riveted on***
H. 5 cm, D. 12 cm
SHSND 32ML2/12,003.260

In Goodbird's youth the family drank meat broth out of tin cups. Goodbird recalled his grandmother serving meals: "Strikes Many Women dipped up the broth left in the kettle after taking out the meat, into cups which she handed around. She dipped the cups directly into the kettle to get the broth. This was to drink. My father and mother had each a cup, I think; but I had none, and drank from my father's or my mother's cup" (Wilson 1915b:591).

Hunting like a man

While Buffalo Bird Woman was learning to farm, sew, and cook, her little brother Wolf Chief faced very different challenges. "I began using a bow, I think, when I was four years of age," he said. "I very often went out to hunt birds for so my father bade me do" (Wilson 1915a:60, 80). Armed with blunt arrows and snares, the village boys learned skills they would need as hunters and warriors.

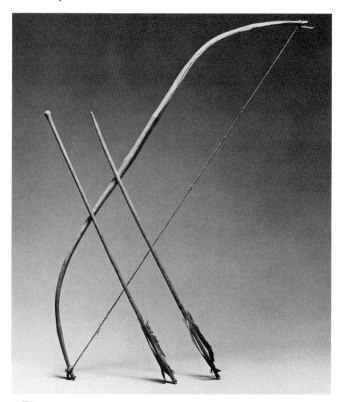

CHILD'S BOW
Hidatsa. Made by Joseph Wounded Face, age 12
Collected by Gilbert Wilson, 1911
Wooden bow nocked at each end and strung with twisted
*   sinew. Arrows have blunt (left) and pointed (right)*
*   wooden tips and feather fletching tied on with sinew*
Bow: L. 89.5 cm. Arrows: L. 62 cm
AMNH 50.1/5470a, b, b

"The first arrows that I ever used were put in my hands when I was about four years of age," said Goodbird. "The bow was made of choke cherry wood and was a little longer than the arrows. The latter were made of buck-brush shoots. . . . With such arrows I was allowed to shoot around in the lodge as they were thought too light to do any damage. . . . There were a great many mice inside our earth lodge. They would come out between the lean-to poles where they had holes. I used to shoot at them with my arrows but I never killed any that I can remember" (Wilson 1913a:15–16).

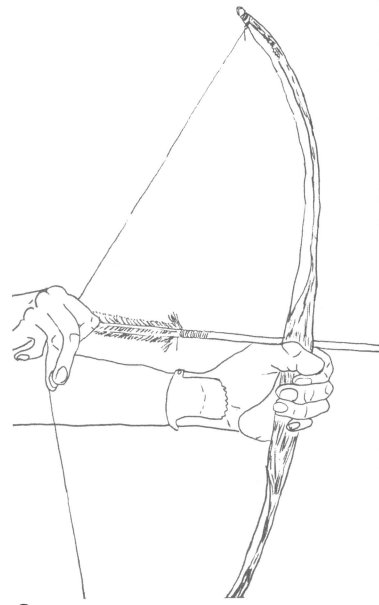

SHOOTING AN ARROW
Drawn by Goodbird, 1914-15
Black carbon and pencil on paper
H. 23.5 cm, W. 17 cm
MHS (Goodbird 1915:fig. 74)

"The ash wood bow, especially the sinew-backed ones, were . . . not ornamental but were our dependance in war and hunting," said Wolf Chief. The upper arm of a Hidatsa bow was shaved thinner than the lower arm, giving it a greater bend when the string was drawn. "Our object in making a bow thus, was to secure steadier and straighter flight for the arrow" (Wilson 1911:7-8). The archer shown here is wearing a rawhide bracer on his wrist. "A boy began using the bracer as soon as he passed from the grass arrow stage, to that of bird hunting. . . . A bracer was very necessary to a hunter. The rebound of his bow string on his naked wrist would have been very severe" (Wilson 1911:67).

"Usually we went out in the morning, returning in afternoon," Goodbird said. "Two would usually hunt together, tho often a party was made up of three, four or even five. . . . I used to go out with my uncle [Full House] who was two or three years older than myself" (Wilson 1911:102). From their companions, boys learned important lessons for successful hunting: know your prey and have the right equipment. "We knew the habits of the different kinds of birds and that each kind had its own feeding grounds where we would find them" (Wilson 1913a:27). They also learned which kinds of arrows flew best, which got lost in the grass, and which feathers were best for fletching.

Rules of generosity prevailed on hunting expeditions. "If I went in a party of three or four boys, the bird belonged, not to the one who killed it, but to the one who picked it up. And if I shot a bird, I would call out, 'Heh, – I have shot a bird. Come and find it!' And all the others would run. When an older and more skillful boy went out as partner to another, the more skillful boy might get no birds at all, because all his kill would go to his partner" (Wilson 1911:103).

As Wolf Chief grew older, his father, Small Ankle, began to teach him how to trap small game and to stalk deer and antelope. Learning to hunt was complicated, for the hunter had to make his own equipment, construct his own shelter, and find his own food. Because ammunition was expensive and scarce, the handmade bow and arrow were still everyday weapons. The hunter who could kill large game with them was thought to be hunting "like a man" (Wilson 1915b:391).

Wolf Chief learned how to hunt buffalo with a bow and arrow when he was about 16 years old. One January, his brother-in-law said to him, "I want to teach you to kill grown-up buffaloes." So they went together on a hunt.

"We found a big bunch of buffaloes and gave chase on horseback," Wolf Chief recounted. "My brother-in-law called to me to get on his left side; for as I was not yet an expert hunter I must shoot at the right side of the buffalo. . . . As we chased the herd my brother-in-law watched to see which was fattest; for he knew the signs by which he could tell. Afterwards I learned how to tell myself. . . .

"I galloped up beside a fat cow. I came up from behind and on the buffalo's right flank and made ready to shoot when about fifteen feet away.

"'No,' called my brother-in-law, 'go closer, – closer!'

"I drew closer and again made ready to shoot. My brother-in-law called out, 'Don't be afraid! It won't hurt you, – closer, closer!'

"I struck my horse's sides with my heels and came so close that the point of my arrow was not over a yard away and loosed. . . . As the arrow struck, the buffalo jumped and turned in her tracks and started back. My brother-in-law shouted to me, 'Never mind, – go on after another one!' . . . We found her afterwards on her left side, the arrow sticking in her right. She was the fattest in the bunch. . . .

"I came up with [another] one and shot when about twenty feet away. My arrow pierced about five inches. The buffalo went right on, and I followed shooting as often as I got a chance. I shot about ten arrows. They all hung in the buffalo, some sticking upright, some hanging down. The buffalo was getting enraged and when I came close she would turn on me and force me to retreat.

"My brother-in-law now came up. He laughed heartily and said, 'You are certainly making this cow suffer. What are you doing, – trying to kill her by inches? I will show you how to finish her.'

"He began to gallop around the buffalo in a circle, the buffalo turning with him and trying now and then to charge him. By and by the buffalo stood still. My brother-in-law drew in his pony and shot.

"I saw the arrow bury itself half the length of its feather. The buffalo stamped her right hind leg against the ground and ran on a little way. Then blood came pouring from her nostrils and she quivered, drew up one foot, then another, knelt down on her front legs, and sank over on her side" (Wilson 1911:79-82).

Hunting was not always fun. On one disastrous trip with his father, Wolf Chief went snowblind, almost suffocated climbing into a porcupine's den, was caught

TWO BOYS HUNTING BIRDS
Drawn by Goodbird, 1914-15
Black carbon and pencil on paper
H. 19 cm, W. 19 cm
MHS (Goodbird 1915:fig. 73)
In 1914 Gilbert Wilson asked Goodbird to draw "a few sketches of his boyhood life, leaving him to choose the subjects from a list I suggested" (Wilson 1915b:595). This is one of the sketches Goodbird drew. The boys are using blunt-headed arrows. "The time for a boy to use bird arrows was from about five years of age up to about fifteen," Goodbird said (Wilson 1913a:46).

in a sudden blizzard, and nearly froze to death. But the camaraderie he shared with his father made up for many hardships. When they returned home loaded with meat, they could expect a warm welcome. "Your son has killed a deer," Small Ankle announced to Wolf Chief's mother on one occasion. "He shot it squarely in the breast. The deer dropped dead!"

"Good," she replied. "He will be our hunter now!"

"I took my gun rod and cleaned my gun," Wolf Chief remembered, "working at this task a long time. And all the family laughed, for they thought, 'Our son is proud that he has killed a deer, and he is polishing up his gun so that every body shall know it!'" (Wilson 1915b:374).

DANCING PRAIRIE CHICKEN
Drawn by Goodbird, 1915
Black carbon and pencil on paper
H. 11.5 cm, W. 13 cm
MHS (Goodbird 1915:fig. 62)
Prairie chickens were hunted with both arrows and snares. Goodbird's familiarity with the bird is demonstrated in this picture, drawn from memory (Wilson 1915b:543).

WOLF CHIEF CARRYING A STRING OF BIRDS HOME
Drawn by Goodbird, 1915
Black carbon and pencil on paper
H. 16 cm, W. 13 cm
MHS (Goodbird 1915:fig. 7)
After a boyhood hunting expedition, "I bore the birds home in a string over my left shoulder," Wolf Chief said. "In the evening when I got home, I brought in my birds, about twenty in all. I gave them to my mother who plucked off the feathers and boiled them in a pot. . . . Birds thus brought home by boys usually went to the old people of a household as they are tender. The old people's teeth are often worn down to the gums and it was hard for them to eat anything hard" (Wilson 1915a:94, 95).

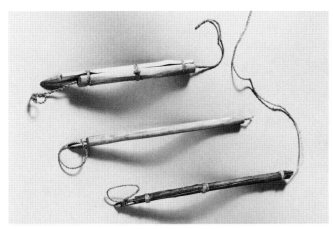

RABBIT SNARES
Hidatsa. Made by Wolf Chief, 1916
Collected by Gilbert Wilson, 1916
Willow or box elder sticks with hollow centers, notched on
*   one end. Looped sinew cord, tied to notch, passes*
*   through stick*
Sticks: L. 25 cm, 31 cm, and 34 cm
MHS 7059.69b, a, c

Rabbit snares were made and used by boys learning to hunt
and by men whenever food was needed. "We made rabbit
snares of snare plant fiber, or of sinew cord if we could not
get snare plant," Wolf Chief explained. "However, if we could
get plant fiber, we preferred to use it.

"I have caught rabbits with sinew snares. They were like
these I have made for you for the Museum and the
University. . . .

"I began snaring rabbits myself when I was about 15, I
think. We were in camp in the hills timber; hunting had not
been very good and we were hungry in the camp. I
remembered how my father made snares to catch rabbits; and
I thought I would make some snares and catch some of the
many rabbits that I saw about. I forget now, but I think that
I used four or five sinews, using box elder for snare handles
because box elder sticks have large pith cores and so are easily
hollowed out. Also I cut some large sized rose bush stems
and used them for snare handles.

"In the evening I took out the snares and looked for
places to set them. The rabbits made many trails through the
bushes. Always I put two sticks in the snow with the snare
between them. The other end of the sinew noose I tied to a
bush or small tree. . . .

"In the morning I went out and found I had caught
three rabbits. They were dead" (Wilson 1916b: 279-80; see
also Wilson 1911: 246; Goodbird 1913: figs. 145, 146,
1916: fig. 30).

Two of these snares were made by splitting a stick,
hollowing out a channel for the twine to pass through, and
binding the stick together again. The third (middle) was made
by boring a hole down the center of a stick with a hot wire.

BIRD SNARE
Traced by Gilbert Wilson from a drawing by
*   Goodbird, 1913*
Black carbon and pencil on tracing paper
H. 7.5 cm, W. 4.6 cm
MHS (Goodbird 1913: fig. 47)

The snares used to catch birds were much like rabbit snares.
"My own I used to keep behind my bed on the floor," Wolf
Chief said. "I had about ten snares and these I used to keep
tied together in a bundle" (Wilson 1915a: 87). Snares were
often set in open spaces at the edge of the woods, in snow,
or even on lodge rooftops (Wilson 1913a: 30, 31). One
method was to build a small tipi of sticks with bait inside so
that the bird entering would put its head through the loop of
the snare. The birds depicted here are a "fat-bird" (left) and a
magpie (right) (Wilson 1913a: 221).

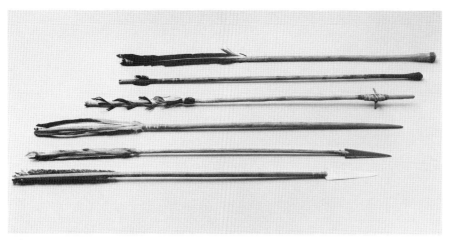

Arrows

Hidatsa. Probably made by Wolf Chief
Collected by Gilbert Wilson, pre-1918?
Juneberry(?) wood shafts variously painted in black, orange, and blue stripes, incised with lengthwise wavy grooves, and wrapped with wire or sinew. Wood, steel, and bone points. Feather fletching glued and tied on with sinew
L. 61.3 cm to 69.4 cm
MHS (top to bottom) 7059.74b, 74a, 73, 77, 75c, 76b

These arrows illustrate, top to bottom, different forms made for different purposes. The blunt-headed arrows were used by boys and men to shoot at birds and small rodents. Wolf Chief explained that the arrows with crossbars near the tip (which he called "quill and thorn points") "were used for shooting into a tree, because the arrow would come down and stick upright in the ground, and be easily found. A blunt headed arrow would fall flat and was not easily found." An arrow with spiral fletching had religious symbolism, and was the first type given to a boy learning to hunt (Wilson 1911:53, 54; see also Wilson 1913b:445).

Pointed wooden arrows were used by boys to hunt rabbits and mice (Wilson 1911:105). When metal was introduced, metal arrow points became standard, either fashioned from scrap metal or ready-made. Neither Buffalo Bird Woman (Wilson 1909a:87) nor Wolf Chief (Wilson 1918a:358) had ever seen bone arrow points, so it is likely that this arrow is made with a point collected by Wilson from one of the old village sites (Wilson 1911:52). The grooves on the shafts symbolized lightning and were made in memory of the sacred origin of arrow-making knowledge in the teachings of Burnt Arrow (Wilson 1911:44).

Wolf Chief made a set of arrows for the American Museum of Natural History (50.1/6014) that is almost identical to this set, so it is probable that he made these, too.

Arrow Shaft Straightener

Hidatsa style
Collected by Gilbert Wilson, pre-1918?
Large animal rib bone, broken on either end, with hole drilled through center
L. 12.5 cm, W. 2.75 cm
MHS 7059.115

"A good arrow could not be made in a hurry," Wolf Chief observed as he described the lengthy process. Subtle variations in weight, balance, and fletching affected the flight. One of the first steps was to smooth and firm the wooden shaft by forcing it through a hole in a bone. "Each shaft was . . . put thru the hole of a bone polisher, made from the vertebra of a buffalo's neck. The shaft was twisted about and worked around in the hole until the wood was made firm and solid. These polishers were sometimes made from buffalo ribs" (Wilson 1911:43, 44). Next, the shaft was sanded by drawing it through a sandstone abrader or, later, by using a native form of sandpaper in which ground rock was glued to cottonwood bark.

SMOOTHING STONE

Hidatsa style
Collected by Gilbert Wilson, pre-1918?
Flat piece of scoria with rounded edges
L. 4.5 cm, W. 5 cm
MHS 7059.166

Wolf Chief used pieces of scoria, a clinker produced by burning coal beds and found along the Missouri River banks, in preparing eagle feathers for arrows. The feather was split and the pulpy inner surface of the quill was scraped smooth with the stone. Feathers of other birds could be cleaned by holding one end in the mouth and scraping with a knife (Wilson 1911:45).

GLUE STICK

Hidatsa style
Collected by Gilbert Wilson, pre-1918?
Wooden stick, pointed on one end,
*   other end coated with glue*
L. 22.8 cm
MHS 7059.93

Glue was made by boiling the neck skin from a buffalo, preferably an old bull, along with various other parts such as leg tendons (Wilson 1911:107-11). After simmering for several days, the decoction was partly cooled. The glue was then scooped off the top of the kettle with a stick shaved flat on one end like a spatula to hold the congealed mass. The stick was set into the ground to dry while other glue sticks were made. When they were finished, the sticks were tied in bundles to thongs and draped over the drying pole until the glue was solid. Wolf Chief described how the glue stick was used to put feathers on arrows: "The glue stick was lifted from the feather case and a small pot of water set handily by. The glue was dipped in the water a moment; a few coals were raked from the fire and the new-wetted glue was held over them, revolved [briefly,] dipped again in the water and again revolved over the fire; and so about four times. The glue stick had now a soft coating of glue on the outside of the glue-mass; this coating was thin.

"The arrow maker takes up a feathered shaft and holds it in the left hand. With a small and very thin stick he scrapes off a little of the soft glue from the glue stick and runs it along under each feather, pressing the feather down into its new-formed glue bed by running his thumb up the feather toward the nock" (Wilson 1911:47).

STONE ANVIL

Excavated at St. Croix Access Site
*   near Stillwater, Minn.*
Granitic stone
L. 18.5 cm, W. 13 cm, H. 10 cm
MHS 504-FN-988

Stone anvils were used by women for food preparation and by men for tool making. Buffalo Bird Woman recalled, "In my father's earth lodge was a stone sunk level with the floor, which Small Ankle used for an anvil. It stood near the fireplace and between it and the rearmost of the posts from which swung the drying pole over the fire. . . . I think every lodge in the village had such an anvil.

"Upon his stone anvil my father pounded bits of metal he wished to straighten. Especially he used it for making iron arrow heads. He heated the iron in the fire red hot, laid it on the stone and cut out arrow heads with chisel and hammer. Small Ankle got his iron and chisel of the traders, as also a little pair of tongs which he used to pick up the hot iron" (Wilson 1918a:363).

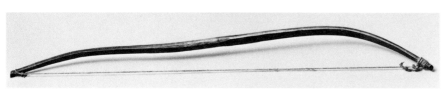

LEAD SHOT
Late 19th century
Molded lead
D. 0.2 cm to 2.7 cm
MHS 390.H184b, John Seibert;
**   1980.49.29a-e, Dr. J. C. Ferguson**
**   and Rodney C. Loehr**

Wolf Chief's father taught him how to make lead shot from bullets in order to conserve scarce ammunition. "He got some bullets; they were about as big as the end of my finger. He took a bullet and with an iron ax, he tapped the bullet until it was cylindrical in form. This he cut into three pieces with his knife, which he tapped on the back with a hammer. 'Here,' he said, 'take these pieces of lead and put them in your mouth one at a time, and chew and bite them until they are round.'

"I took one of the slugs in my mouth and bit, bit, bit it until it was round like a bullet. I did this until I had a small sack full" (Wilson 1915b:361).

Buck shot and bullets were also made by melting down small shot. "We molded our bullets in those days, in iron molds," said Wolf Chief (Wilson 1913a:245).

BOW
Hidatsa. Made by Wolf Chief
Collected by Frederick Wilson,
**   pre-1918?**
Asymmetrical ash wood bow double-
**   nocked at top and single-nocked at**
**   bottom end. Marked "H[enry]**
**   Wolf Chief" in green paint. String**
**   of twisted sinew**
L. 125 cm
MHS 9598.22

Because ammunition was scarce, the Hidatsa often used bow and arrows for hunting in order to save bullets for warfare. Wolf Chief was an accomplished bow maker and he made several examples, including this one, to demonstrate the process for Wilson. He said that ash was the best wood for bows. "Besides being a good casting wood, we prized it because in war the bow as a last resort might often have to be used as a club. An ash bow would stand a very heavy blow without breaking. As the bow would nearly always be braced when occasion arose demanding it be used as a club, the strong bow string helped break the force of the blow. It was really surprising what a heavy blow a good ash bow would stand." As late as 1915, Wolf Chief used a bow and arrows to frighten away the prairie chickens that raided his garden – but which were illegal to hunt with a gun out of season (Wilson 1915b:485).

FLINTLOCK TRADE GUN
Made by John Edward Barnett &
**   Co., London, 1850-70**
Walnut stock, once decorated with
**   brass tacks (now missing), split by**
**   a bullet hole. Butt plate and**
**   ramrod missing. Serpent side plate**
**   and ramrod pipes of brass. Steel**
**   lock still has flint in jaws of**
**   hammer. Fox in tombstone and**
**   "E.B." marks on shortened barrel**
L. 112 cm
MHS 74.33.2, Charles M. Nelson

Wolf Chief recalled the guns he and his father took on his first deer-hunting trip. "My gun was a flint lock with a barrel about two feet long. My father's was a double barreled gun, and had a larger bore than mine. 'You put in three slugs (or chewed bullets) at a load,' said my father. 'I can use five in my gun'" (Wilson 1915b:362).

But Wolf Chief had problems shooting with a flintlock. "When I shot the deer, I was kneeling on one knee. My father had warned me, 'Be sure you do not show yourself.' Crouching down then on one knee, I waited until the deer was within easy shooting distance, and raised my head and breast, pointed my gun, and fired. One eye of course must always shut when one shoots; but I think I shut both eyes! You see, my gun was a flint lock, and the powder used to flash up in the pan and nearly burn my face. I knew this from shooting ducks and geese, and I was a little afraid of the gun, which . . . I handled rather awkwardly at best" (Wilson 1915b:366).

This gun is of the type sold by the Hudson's Bay Company in the late 19th century. Traces of brass tack decorations suggest Indian ownership. The lock plate from a Barnett flintlock was found by archaeologists at Like-a-Fishhook Village (Smith 1972:81).

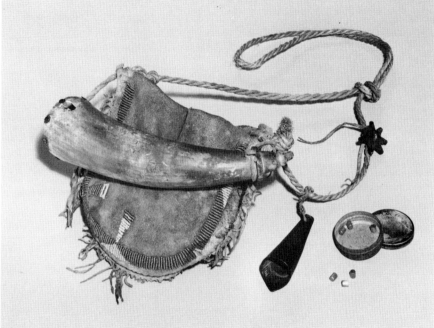

SHINGLING HATCHET
Pre-1885?
Head excavated at Fort Berthold I
Iron or steel head with octagonal
hammer on one end, notched ax
blade on the other. Handle
reconstructed
Head: L. 17 cm, W. 10 cm. Handle:
L. 33 cm
SHSND 32ML2/12,711.12
Shingling hatchets like this were used
not only for roofing but for general-
purpose wood chopping. Men on
hunting trips needed to cut trees for
firewood and for shelter. Women cut
trees for buildings and to clear land for
gardens (Wilson 1914b: 374, 1912: 2).
The head of this hatchet is corroded
from exposure.

POWDER HORN AND SHOT POUCH
Late 19th century
Tanned hide pouch sewn with thread and decorated with lazy-stitched beadwork
band in rose, yellow, and blue on one side only. Hide fringe on sides and
bottom mostly torn away. Plant fiber rope handle to which is tied a leather or
cardboard star-shaped piece, a horn measuring cup, and a powder horn
plugged at the wide end with wood nailed to horn and at the small end with
cloth. Contains a tin box of percussion caps
Pouch: L. 15 cm, W. 14 cm. Horn: L. 18.5 cm
MHS 1981.4.59a, b
Wolf Chief mentioned that his powder horn was attached to his ammunition bag.
"The powder horn was made of the horn of a three year old buffalo, as shown in
the drawing [Goodbird 1913: fig. 30]. This was a proper aged buffalo from which to
make a powder horn. One end of the horn was cut [to form] a button and the
thong from which the horn was hung was looped around the horn on either side of
this button. The greater end of the horn was plugged with a piece of cottonwood
bark, shaped to fit snug. The horn was heated and the plug driven home, when the
horn contracted. Thus, it made the plug fit snug. To make [it] more secure, a
couple of tacks were driven through the thick edge of the horn into the bark plug.
A piece of iron was twisted into an eye, and driven into the end to receive the
thong, as shown in the drawing. A pin of hard Juneberry wood was used to stop the
mouth of the powder horn. When loading the gun, I withdrew the pin with my
teeth and poured the powder out into the palm of my hand" (Wilson 1913a: 244–45).

HUNTER DRESSED FOR A
SNOWSTORM
Drawn by Goodbird, 1915
Black carbon and pencil on paper
H. 10.7 cm, W. 4 cm
MHS (Goodbird 1915: fig. 54)
The harsh North Dakota weather made
hunting hazardous, and dressing wrong
could cost a man his life. Hunters
learned to cope. An unexpected spring
blizzard once caught Small Ankle and
Wolf Chief unawares, completely
burying their tent in snow. To dig their
way out, Small Ankle covered his head
with a hood made from a saddle skin, as
shown in this sketch (Wilson
1915b: 394).

PIPE
Northern Plains
Collected by Gilbert Wilson, pre-1918?
Stem of square length of wood with burnt file decorations and hole bored through
  center. Bowl of pipestone, highly polished, with fire-blackened hole
Stem: L. 38 cm. Bowl: L. 8.8 cm, H. 6.3 cm
MHS 7059.105, 204

The Hidatsa used different styles of pipes for different occasions. Since younger men smoked only for ceremonial and religious purposes, few carried everyday pipes. The "hunter's pipe" was an exception. It was a small, undecorated, red or black stone pipe that could be easily carried in a pouch. Wilson noted that while Wolf Chief was explaining the hunter's pipe, Rabbit Head entered the cabin and, on hearing the topic of discussion, took a small pipe from his pouch. This was a hunter's pipe, although slightly larger than normal. Rabbit Head permitted Wilson to trace the outline of his pipe (Wilson 1918a:229; Goodbird 1918:fig. 22). On the basis of that sketch, this separately accessioned pipe bowl and stem have been put together to illustrate the everyday pipe.

HOE
Pre-1885?
Blade excavated at Like-a-Fishhook
  Village
Cast iron blade. Handle reconstructed
Blade: W. 20.5 cm, L. 22 cm.
  Handle: L. 88.4 cm
SHSND 32ML2/12,003.2145

Hoes were not just used for farming. Wolf Chief recounted a hunting expedition on which he and his father brought along a hoe "to scrape the snow off our camping places." It turned out to be one of their most useful implements, serving to dig a porcupine from its den and to shovel snow when their tent was buried by a blizzard (Wilson 1915b:380, 384–85, 393–94). Men also used metal hoes for digging eagle-trapping pits (Wilson 1911:264). This hoe blade was found at the site of an earth lodge in the early 1950s by Walter Plenty Chiefs.

DEER CALL
Hidatsa. Made by Wolf Chief
Collected by Gilbert Wilson, 1918
U-shaped piece of wood and thin metal
  plate, fastened together with sinew
L. 6.6 cm, W. 3.3 cm
MHS 7059.206

Hunters used bait, disguises, and calls to attract game. Wolf Chief said, "I have made a deer whistle and have given it to Mr. Wilson. It is made of a piece of wood with a blade of tin bound to it, but I think that whistles made of leaves are rather better, for those of tin are louder and harsher and sometimes alarm the deer. But they are better for antelope because they are louder" (Wilson 1918a:196).

BUTCHERED DEER
Drawn by Goodbird, 1914
Pencil on paper
Top: H. 7.7 cm, W. 13.5 cm. Bottom:
H. 7.4 cm, W. 11.1 cm
AMNH (Goodbird 1914b: figs. 56, 57)

Butchering was a skill every hunter had to learn. Small Ankle taught Wolf Chief detailed techniques of cutting up game animals (Wilson 1915b: 365-71). The cuts shown in this sketch (bottom) are, counterclockwise from upper left, the leg (saved for the marrow bone), shoulder, another leg, ham, side, backbone, and head. Which parts were taken depended upon how far the hunter was from home and whether he had a horse. To load the horse, the hunter tied the pieces in pairs so that they could be slung over the pony's back, balancing on either side. The man then rode on top (Wilson 1914b: 355-56). "Hunters could dress and cut up a deer very rapidly, some of them," Buffalo Bird Woman said. "Others were much less skillful. A good worker could dress and cut up a deer in half an hour" (Wilson 1914b: 353).

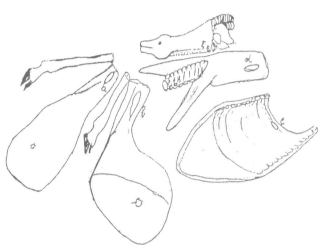

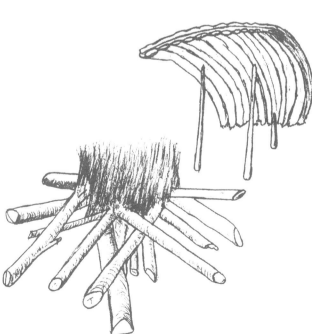

COOKING A SIDE OF RIBS
Drawn by Goodbird, 1915
Black carbon and pencil on paper
H. 13 cm, W. 11 cm
MHS (Goodbird 1915: fig. 61)

Hunters sometimes carried along corn balls, a trail food made of pounded corn meal, ground sunflower seeds, and boiled squash and beans (Wilson 1915b: 278-80). But often they depended upon killing game for food. If they had no luck they went hungry. A side of ribs was a favorite meal after a successful day's hunting. It could be roasted by hanging it over the fire or simply propping it up as shown here (Wilson 1915b: 286).

The promise of the buffalo

The buffalo, along with the hills, badlands, springs, and rivers, were first created by Only Man, one of the first two beings on the earth. To the Hidatsa, the buffalo and agriculture were the twin pillars of life (Wilson 1906b: 23-30).

The summer buffalo hunt was a communal enterprise involving the entire tribe. When word came to Like-a-Fishhook that a herd of buffalo had been sighted, the Black Mouth Society assembled to discuss the matter. "They consulted no one outside the Society," Wolf Chief said, "for the Black Mouths were just like a government. What they decided upon had to be done" (Wilson 1918a: 187). They picked a leader, usually a man who owned sacred objects or had led a successful hunt before. On one occasion when Wolf Chief was 27 years old, Black Horn was the leader.

"An old man went around the same afternoon crying: 'After three days we will start on a hunt to the

INDIANS HUNTING THE BISON"
Based on a watercolor by Karl Bodmer, 1833-34
Copper plate engraving on paper
H. 30.4 cm, W. 43.4 cm
MHS (Wied 1840-43:tableau 51)

In hunting a herd of buffalo, Hidatsa men often charged the herd in a group. Goodbird participated in such a charge on his first and only buffalo hunt. "Down came all the quirts on the flanks of the horses, making the little ponies leap forward like big cats. . . . Everyone now wanted to be first to get to the herd and kill the fattest buffalo.

"I was somewhat scared, for the horses were at break-neck speed and my pony took the bit in his mouth . . . and went over the rough, stony ground at a speed that I feared would break his neck and mine too.

"'Bang!' went a rifle. A fat cow tumbled over. 'Bang! Bang! Bang! Bang!' The herd swerved around, and started up wind as buffaloes almost invariably did when they were alarmed. . . . The herd went tearing off. Only a fast horse could overtake buffaloes" (Wilson 1913a: 134-35).

According to Wolf Chief, the transition from the bow-and-arrow hunting which Bodmer documented here and the rifle hunting of Goodbird's day was completed between about 1876 and 1879 (Wilson 1918a: 227).

Yellowstone,'" Wolf Chief recalled. "This invitation was to all the villagers who wanted to go. [They all] had a right to join the party" (Wilson 1918a:187).

"In the three days preparation we had time both to make moccasins and to get food ready," said Wolf Chief. The women parched corn and sunflower seeds and packed dried squash and beans. "We started in the forenoon, but not very early. Black Horn led the line on horseback. . . . He would trot his horse a while, then walk. Every three or four miles he would stop, and all would dismount, smoke and rest. Before an hour was gone, we would again be on the march" (Wilson 1918a:188, 199).

They traveled about 20 miles a day. When they came to a camping spot, the women built tents while the men watered and hobbled the horses. "We ate our

"LANDSCAPE WITH HERD OF BUFFALO ON THE UPPER MISSOURI" (DETAIL)
Painted by Karl Bodmer, 1833-34
Watercolor on paper. See color page 169
H. 24.4 cm, W. 31.4 cm
Joslyn Art Museum, gift of Enron Art Foundation
Many of the Mandan and Hidatsa tribes' buffalo hunting expeditions during the late 19th century took them to the rugged land west of Like-a-Fishhook, frequently on the Little Missouri and Yellowstone rivers. This scene, which probably depicts an area near the junction of the Milk and Missouri rivers, is typical of the Hidatsa hunting grounds (Bodmer 1984:207).

supper before sunset, and as the sun was going down the Black Mouths began to sing their society songs. They sat around in a circle at the camping place of Black Horn" (Wilson 1918a:189).

The rules of behavior on a hunt were more strict than in the village. The Black Mouths set the standard. "These Black Mouths were the protectors of the people. If enemies came, the Black Mouths should go to the front before all the others to defend the tribe. . . . No one could go out to hunt without asking the Black Mouths' permission. If he did, they would break his gun, or whip him, or strike him in the mouth, for they were courageous men. . . . If a young man got to acting smart, they made him behave himself" (Wilson 1918a:190-91).

Members of other societies had duties, as well. When enemies were thought to be near, the crier went around the camp summoning members of the Kit Fox Society to ride ahead of the main party. "Enemies may come," he said. "If they do be ready to fight them." Wolf Chief was happy to accept this responsibility. "I saddled my fastest horse and as I rode, called out to my friends, 'Come on, they want us to lead today.'

"Soon a number of fine looking young men came and we made a line, eighteen of us in all, and rode ahead. We sang our Society songs. . . . I was leader of the singing, for my voice was good when I was young, and I knew all the Society songs. . . . This pleased the women, and they made outcries, 'A-la-la-la-la,' meaning: 'Ah, these fine young men may die.' For if enemies came up against us, they expected us to fight even if we got killed. So we led on, and the camp followed" (Wilson 1918a:192-93).

When they were not busy scouting or guarding the party, the unmarried young men would ride along the side of the line in order to look at the girls. "They did not try to talk with the girls but would smile at them. At camp in the evening boys would often try to meet their sweethearts on the sly. We did not think it courteous to do courtship where it would attract attention" (Wilson 1918a:201).

When the group reached the area where the hunt was to take place, the leader sent out scouts while the rest of the people made camp. "About sunset the two scouts came back, galloping fast. This was a good sign, for . . . we called it 'running back,' and it meant that they had seen something." The scouts came to the leader's tent, but it was not polite for them to say at once what they had seen. Instead, two older men had the honor of asking them. If the news was good, the

WHITE BUFFALO SOCIETY HEADDRESS
*Mandan. Bought from Calf Woman. Given to her by
    Brave Woman, c. 1855*
Collected by Gilbert Wilson, 1907
*Albino buffalo skin with hawk, eagle, and other feathers.
    Ties of tanned hide*
H. 46.4 cm
*Museum of the American Indian, Heye Foundation
    1/3783*

The White Buffalo Society was composed of older women
who held ceremonies during the winter to attract buffalo to
the camp (Bowers 1965:204-7). The dance of these women,
and their distinctive headdress, was observed and described by
many of the white men who visited the Mandan and Hidatsa.
Karl Bodmer (1984:297) made several drawings and paintings
of the performances he witnessed and Boller (1959:222-28)
described the dance, although he did not completely
understand its function.

    This headdress is similar to the ones shown by Bodmer,
the major difference being in the placement of the feathers. It
is made from the hide of an albino buffalo killed by Red
Stone (Wilson [1907d]).

crier spread it around the camp (Wilson 1918a:214-15).

    On the night before the hunt, the Black Mouths
appointed a *matsë̓ akú ë̄́*, a keeper or guardsman for the
hunt. "In his charge were all the men," said Wolf
Chief. "He was responsible for all that happened, good
or bad. If enemies were killed he received honors. If
misfortune fell, he was held to blame. He must pray
that many buffaloes be killed, and indeed, on him was
laid all the success or blame of the hunt" (Wilson
1918a:217).

    In the morning, after prayers were said, the
hunters stalked the buffalo, taking care to approach
from downwind. They came in sight of the herd over a
rise. "We rode forward at a walk, slowly, and quietly
and all bunched together. When about half way, the
buffaloes sighted us, bunched themselves together and
took to flight.

    "'Ku-kats!' cried our leader. 'Now then!' and
everybody galloped forward. I had a fast black horse
and as I whipped him he fairly flew. Three of us forged
ahead of the others. The dust flew! . . .

    "I overtook the herd and looked about for the
fattest. One was a four year old, as I knew by the
horns. . . . I fired at twenty-five feet and hit a bull in
the loins. . . . The bull turned to the right in a wide
semi-circle, going slower and slower. . . . He staggered,
sank to his knees and fell over on his right side"
(Wilson 1918a:221-22).

    Other men immediately gathered round Wolf
Chief to help him butcher the buffalo. He repaid them
by giving them the skin and portions of the meat.
"This is the way we thought: the killer, he is boss. If
he wants to he keeps the hide always, but we thought
that a poor way to do. . . . To give it away was the
right thing to do and it was like winning an honor
mark. . . . If a man wanted to be good, he must not
be selfish" (Wilson 1918a:225).

    The hunt itself was soon over, but butchering and
packing the meat on the horses took a long time. "We
got back to camp about noon. Everybody in the camp
had plenty of meat to eat, and meat was boiling in the
pots at every fire" (Wilson 1918a:226).

    In winter, hunting was more hazardous. The
grassy uplands where the herds roamed provided no fuel
for campfires and no shelter from the fierce blizzards
that could sweep down without warning. So the people
used different methods: instead of going after the
buffalo, the tribe worked to bring the buffalo to them.
This was the responsibility of the women's White
Buffalo Society.

The society's four-day ritual was based upon a bargain that had been struck long ago by a Mandan man who was visited by the sacred buffalo in a dream. The buffalo spirits had promised that if their procession and ritual was faithfully performed, the ceremonies would bring on snowstorms to drive the herds into the shelter of the wooded river valleys. For years people and buffalo had each kept their side of the bargain.

"I remember when I was about five years old that the members of the White Buffalo Society used to hang their hats on a tent pole placed to the west (and south) side where the buffaloes came," remembered Good Voice, a relative of Buffalo Bird Woman. "When they hung their hats thus, the buffaloes came. . . . Thus the promise of the buffalo people came true" (Wilson 1911:179-87).

DANCE OF THE MANDAN WOMEN"
Based on a watercolor by Karl Bodmer, 1833
Copper plate engraving on paper
H. 24.4 cm, W. 32.2 cm
MHS (Wied 1840-43:vignette 28)
Bodmer's painting of the White Buffalo Society's members was most likely done during a performance for the residents of the Fort Clark fur post, and not during an actual ceremony (Wied 1905-06, 24:48-49).

LEATHER ROPE (LARIAT)
Northern Plains
Collected by Jack Rohr, 1932
Strips of tanned leather, braided.
  Loop on one end forms running
  noose
L. 1167 cm
MHS 64.139.11, Lulu Rohr
Most Indian horses were controlled by a
single rope tied around the lower jaw
and were trained to respond to knee
pressure and shifts of the rider's body
(see Goodbird 1913: figs. 137, 141).
They required no complicated bridle,
reins, or harness. Wolf Chief described
to Wilson how he made a new lariat by
softening and stretching a rawhide strap
until it was sturdy enough to be used
(Wilson 1913a: 471-72).

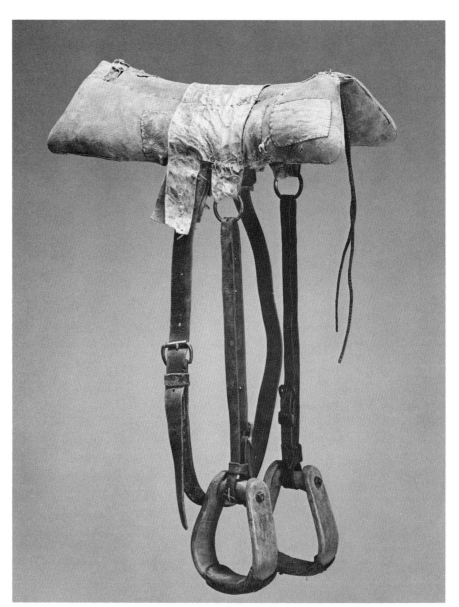

HUNTING SADDLE
Hidatsa
Collected by Gilbert Wilson, 1910
Tanned buffalo hide pad sewn with sinew, patched with rawhide, and stuffed
  with antelope hair. Commercially made harness straps attach to rawhide flaps
  with iron rings. Hand-made stirrups of wood, rawhide, and iron bolts
Pad: L. 57 cm, W. 32 cm
AMNH 50.1/5462
"Flat saddles were light to carry and were best for the buffalo chase," said Wolf
Chief. A buffalo hunting horse might be led to the hunt with its flat saddle on, but
it would only be ridden during the chase. "A flat saddle had stirrups; and leaning
with the left foot in the stirrup I could shoot my bow more strongly, for my body
in the act of shooting was not so apt to weight down on the pony's left side and so
give a signal for him to turn in. For this reason riding with [a] flat saddle was better
for buffalo hunting than riding bare back.

  "Our high pack saddles of wood or horn frame were not so good for buffalo
chasing, as they were apt to hurt the hunter's body when he bent over to shoot. . . .

  "In battle saddles were usually not used. Without a saddle to hinder him, a
warrior could better vault on and off his pony and so could better fight" (Wilson
1918a: 300-1).

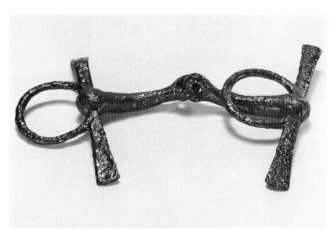

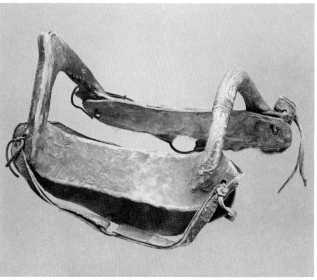

SNAFFLE BIT

Pre-1885?
Excavated at Like-a-Fishhook Village
Iron, with flared, vertical cheek pieces; hinged in center;
  right-hand ring for reins has rusted inward
H. 14.4 cm, W. 20.2 cm
SHSND 32ML2/12,003.14-9

Steel bits and other commercially made harness parts were
expensive luxuries at Like-a-Fishhook Village. Buffalo Bird
Woman recalled that the horses given for her when she
married her first husband, Magpie, "had good bridles on, with
chains hanging down from the bits. Such bridles were hard to
get in those days" (Wilson 1914b:319-20). Boller also noted
that the "heavy Spanish bit" was a status symbol in the village
(1959:68). This artifact was one of only a few horse-related
objects recovered at Like-a-Fishhook Village (Smith 1972:74,
75).

PACK SADDLE

Hidatsa. Bought from Hairy Coat. Frame made c. 1865 by
  Hairy Coat's father, No Tears, and covered by No
  Tears' wife, June Berry Blossoms
Collected by Frederick Wilson, 1912
Frame of black-tailed deer horn covered with buffalo
  rawhide sewn on with sinew. Separate pieces of rawhide
  tied on either side where saddle sits on horse's back
L. 42 cm, W. 34.5 cm, H. 21.5 cm
AMNH 50.1/7328

Pack saddles were used to carry meat home from a successful
hunt and for transporting household items when moving
camp. Hairy Coat, who owned this saddle, explained to
Frederick Wilson that a hunter did not need to fasten the
meat to the saddle because "we put a half-hide over the saddle
first, and then on this placed the meat at either end of a rawhide thong with the meat hanging about to, or a little below,
the horse's belly.

"We did not take the whole carcass but only the choice
portions. We cut out the tongue leaving the head, and took
the ribs and quarters, discarding the hoofs. The larger
portions we put on in pairs of equal weight. The small parts
first, then the quarters, and last the ribs and backbone – the
meat of one buffalo to a horse. Then we covered the meat
with the other half-hide." Dried meat was covered and the
bundle tied to the saddle. Hairy Coat added that a travois was
sometimes tied over the bundle on the saddle to keep it from
slipping. "There should be a tail piece for this saddle so that
in packing meat it would not slip, going up and down hill"
(F. Wilson 1912b:[99-100]).

PERCUSSION RIFLE
Made by H. E. Leman, Lancaster,
  Pa., 1835-60
Maple stock wrapped in rawhide with
  brass patch box, trigger guard,
  and ramrod pipes. Lock plate
  decorated with scrolls and a
  pheasant. Steel butt plate and
  short, octagonal steel barrel.
  Ramrod missing
L. 118 cm
MHS 8073.2, Major Floyd E. Eller

Wolf Chief took a short-barreled
percussion rifle with him on his first
buffalo hunt. He was much more skilled
with a bow and arrow and had difficulty
killing a buffalo when he tried to use his
gun. "I aimed my gun but I had never
used a gun and I saw the barrel shake in
my hand and I felt sure that I could not
hit the buffalo. But I rode close to the
side of the animal and fired. I guess I
hit the buffalo in the leg for he kicked.
I tried to load my gun but could not
with my horse running for I spilled my
powder. I drew up slower and loaded
my gun ramming the bullet home with
a little piece of cloth" (Wilson
1915b: 376, 390).

 The maker of this rifle was a
frequent supplier to companies trading
with Plains Indians (Russell
1967: 68-70). The donor of this gun
believed it had been picked up on the
Little Big Horn battlefield.

PERCUSSION CAP BOX
Pre-1885?
Excavated at Like-a-Fishhook Village
Soldered sheet iron box with friction-
  fit lid
D. 4 cm, H. 2.2 cm
SHSND 32ML2/12,003.1723

The percussion rifle was more
convenient than the earlier flintlock
because it did not have to be primed
with loose powder and flints. Instead,
percussion caps were used. After
graduating to a percussion gun, Wolf
Chief carried in his ammunition bag "a
small tin box of percussion caps, a small
bag of buck shot, or small bullets, and
my wads" (Wilson 1913a: 244). Instead
of commercially made wads, he
sometimes used willow bark shavings
rolled in a ball.

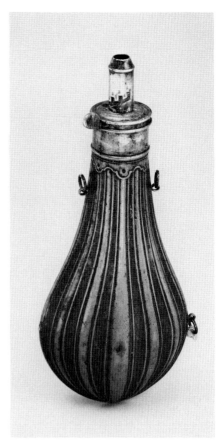

POWDER FLASK
Made by American Flask and Cap
  Co., Waterbury, Conn., c. 1865
Fluted copper body and raised throat
  decorations. Spring-loaded,
  adjustable brass charger measures
  out 2¼, 2½, and 2¾ drams. Four
  suspension rings, one of which is
  missing
L. 22.7 cm, W. 9.7 cm
MHS 6845.1, Matilda Baillif

The percussion gun Wolf Chief used on
his first buffalo hunt was muzzle-
loading, so he had to carry loose
gunpowder and balls (Wilson
1915b: 376). Although cow and buffalo
horns were popular for holding powder,
brass flasks were also sold. This one
matches a piece of a flask by the same
manufacturer that was found in
excavations at Like-a-Fishhook (Smith
1972: 88).

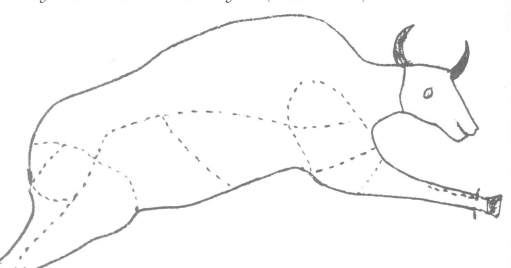

DEAD BUFFALO READY FOR BUTCHERING
Drawn by Goodbird, 1918
Pencil on paper
H. 7.5 cm, W. 14 cm
MHS (Goodbird 1918:fig. 36)
There were two ways to skin a buffalo, depending upon whether a whole skin was needed. If not, the buffalo was first positioned as shown here. "I turned the buffalo with belly to the ground and both hind legs drawn straight out behind," said Wolf Chief. "The knees were bent in front. In this position the carcass did not rock, but was firm. . . . We began at the tail and cut [the skin] straight up the middle of the back to the head. The skin was now stripped from both sides downward. While the animal was thus kneeling the various cuts of meat were stripped off the sides in regular order as our Indian custom taught us" (Wilson 1918a:222).

BUTCHER AND SKINNING KNIVES
Pre-1885?
Excavated at Like-a-Fishhook Village
Iron or steel blades riveted to wooden
*   handles*
Left: L. 19.2 cm. Right: L. 20 cm
SHSND 32ML2/12,003.277, 1946
On the buffalo hunt, men performed the butchering, a process which Wolf Chief described (Wilson 1918a:245, 253, 262), and which Goodbird later demonstrated on a cow (Wilson [1903-18]:245-49). Traders stocked distinctive styles of metal knives for butchering and skinning. These two probably looked much the same when new, but the one on the left has been sharpened so much that the blade has worn away.

DIAGRAM FOR BUTCHERING A BUFFALO
Drawn by Goodbird, 1913
Black carbon and pencil on tracing paper
H. 6.5 cm, W. 6.5 cm
MHS (Goodbird 1913:fig. 165)
A good butcher could dress a buffalo in an hour (Wilson 1918a:235). There were a number of commonly accepted cuts, including spine, shoulder, ribs, and hams (the latter subdivided into smaller cuts). Goodbird noted that this drawing was unfinished (Wilson 1913b:384).

Societies

Wolf Chief took an important step on his journey to manhood when, at 16, he bought membership in the Stone Hammer Society. Societies in the community at Like-a-Fishhook were organized according to age. "A young man bought his way into the first or lowest society at about 13 to 16 years of age," Wolf Chief explained. "As he grew older he bought his way also into the other societies in regular order, until he got very old, when he sold out" (Wilson 1911:113).

Societies were not usually considered sacred, but they were not wholly secular, either. Some had special functions: the Skunk Society performed dances of celebration when an enemy was killed; the Stone Hammers performed ritual thievery; the Black Mouths served as a tribal police; the Goose Society had power over the growth of corn. The societies and their members were linked together in ties that were much like kinship.

An individual did not buy membership in a society on his own. The sale was made only to an organized group. "There were about forty of us boys, when we bought out the Stone Hammer Society," Wolf Chief said. They ranged from about 12 to 16 years old (Wilson 1911:114–15). Large amounts of wealth changed hands at the sale of a society. When Wolf

Dance of the Mandan Indians"
Based on a watercolor by Karl Bodmer, 1832-33
Copper plate engraving on paper
H. 25.5 cm, W. 33.8 cm
MHS (Wied 1840–43: Vignette 25)
In the 1830s Bodmer and Maximilian witnessed the dance that followed the purchase of the Half-Shaved Head Society by members of the Crow Society (Lowie 1916:309-12). The purchasers were required to feast the sellers for 40 nights. Hooked sticks wrapped with wolf skins and lances wrapped in otter skins were among the symbolic equipment carried by the officers of this society. Each society had its own characteristic regalia and equipment. The Half-Shaved Head Society was originally Mandan, but the Hidatsa had adopted it by Wolf Chief's day (Lowie 1916:272).

Chief joined, the boys collected gifts from their families and "friends." "These 'friends' were the members of certain . . . other societies who naturally associated with us in society relationships," Wolf Chief explained. Members of the Lumpwood, Grass Crown, Dog, and Black Mouth societies were "friends" of the young boys (Wilson 1911:112-13).

On the appointed day, the purchasers gathered at Small Ankle's lodge. "When all was ready we borrowed a pipe and filled it ready to light. We chose one of the older of the boys to lead us and be our spokesman and proceeded to the lodge where we knew the Stone Hammers were assembled. . . . The gifts were packed in four or five bundles, each bundle borne on the back of one boy.

'Our leader . . . stood before the bundles, facing the Stone Hammers as they sat in a semicircle before him. . . . He spoke:

"'Fathers, we want to buy your songs! See all these goods. They are all that we have been able to get together. . . . Light this pipe that we may know that you accept.' . . .

"One of the Stone Hammers now arose and said . . . 'Sons, these goods are not enough. You must fetch more and put up bigger values. These cannot purchase our songs.' . . .

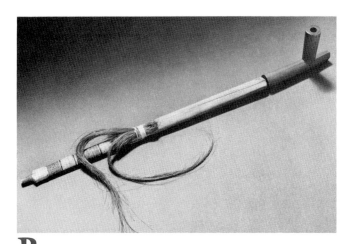

Pipe

Northern Plains
Stem collected by Gilbert Wilson, pre-1918?
Flat wood stem wrapped with braided quillwork dyed red, orange, green, and purple. Red-dyed horsehair tied on with string. Right-angle pipestone bowl with hexagonal front projection and cylindrical smoking hole, charred from use. See color page 176
Stem: L. 56.2 cm. Bowl: L. 17 cm, H. 10.3 cm
MHS 7059.102; 6333.27, Mrs. Frank C. Berry

Pipes were important ceremonial and social instruments; the Hidatsa distinguished among everyday, society, and sacred pipes. Pipes were smoked during some society performances, and a person often gained membership by presenting one to the members. There are few accurate descriptions of the pipes used by the different societies, but Poor Wolf said that the one used by officers in the Black Mouth Society had a flat stem painted red and black and decorated with quillwork and a dyed horsetail (Lowie 1916:275).

The provenance of this pipe bowl is unknown, but it is a typical Plains style.

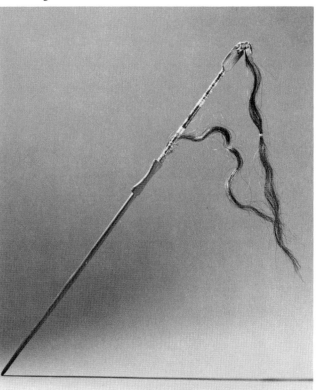

Pipe Tamper

Northern Plains
Collected by Gilbert Wilson, pre-1918?
Carved wooden stick decorated with wrapped bird quills dyed purple, red, and yellow. Dyed brown horsehair attached to handle with leather thong
L. 23.3 cm
MHS 7059.106a

Elaborately decorated sticks were used by Plains Indian men to press tobacco into their pipe bowls. Tampers were often made by wives as special gifts for their husbands (Conn 1982:145). Maximilian collected an example from the Assiniboine (Bodmer 1984:339). This is one of an identical pair collected by Wilson.

"I went to my parents and said to them, 'The fathers say that we boys have not enough. They want us to give more. So I have come to see what I can get.'

"My father said, 'Very well!' He got me a robe that he had put away for winter. I took it and went back to the society house. The others also came in with their gifts." This time the Stone Hammers were satisfied and agreed to sell (Wilson 1911:115-18, 121).

The transfer of the society took four nights. On each night, the purchasers had to bring a feast for the outgoing Stone Hammers. In return, they were taught the society songs and dances. Boys who wanted to could purchase a ceremonial stone hammer by selecting a "father," or sponsor, from among the sellers. "We all preferred to have each a stone hammer," Wolf Chief said, "but we did not consider it a serious evil to have to do without" (Wilson 1911:119).

The transfer was a public ceremony. Wolf Chief's mother was among the spectators who came to watch. The singing lasted long into the night. "As they sang, some of our 'fathers' arose and danced," Wolf Chief said. "We lads sat. Our hearts were very glad, for we thought, 'That song is going to be ours!'" (Wilson 1911:127).

By the second night, the boys were beginning to learn the songs. "We . . . began to say to one another, 'You get up! You begin to dance! You dance!' We were too bashful to get up and dance" (Wilson 1911:129). But by the third night, they no longer hesitated. One of the Stone Hammers shouted to encourage them, "'You do very well! That is the way! Do not be afraid or ashamed, but dance!'

"As dancing went on, the dancers yelled, and we boys joined in. We thought, 'We are men now! We yell just like brave men! Aï'ha! Aï'ha!'" (Wilson 1911:132).

On the fifth day, Wolf Chief received his stone hammer from the "father" he had selected. He loved it. "It had hawks' and eagle-wing feathers on it. The stone had a moon carved on one side and a star on the other. . . . To left and right of the main stick, or handle, were branch sticks, curved, having tassels of horse-hair." In exchange he gave his "father" a large brass kettle, a shotgun, a blue blanket, and a pair of beaded leggings (Wilson 1911:142, 145).

That afternoon the final ceremony took place. The boys had to wear their best clothes, with their faces painted. "Some of the boys, friends of mine, came to my father's lodge while I was painting up my face and some, who had no stone [hammer], wanted to see

CLUB
Northern Plains
Collected by Frederick Wilson, pre-1918?
Wooden handle covered with sinew-sewn rawhide wrapped
*   with fringed hide and white, green, and blue beads;*
*   purple horsehair attached to end. Quartz stone head*
*   attached with rawhide and sinew, decorated with*
*   feathers*
L. 77.2 cm
MHS 9598.6

Elaborately decorated clubs carried by members of some men's societies represented war clubs, called "stone hammers" by the Hidatsa. Though this club was probably made for a society ceremony, it is not the distinctive type used by the Stone Hammer Society. The latter had curved branches or prongs on either side of the head. When Wolf Chief joined that group, an older member told the initiates about the relationship between ceremonial stone hammers and war clubs: "The Stone Hammers are the first society; and they are the first in war, for you are now young and vigorous. Sometimes young men who want to see a vision, have a vision of a stone hammer; such a man always gets to strike an enemy with a stone hammer. For this Stone Hammer society is a very sacred organization" (Wilson 1911:138).

mine. They said, 'How pretty it is!' Others said, 'I have one just like it at home'" (Wilson 1911:146).

Soon a summons came from the Stone Hammers' lodge for all the boys to gather. "We boys said, 'Let one of us go up on the roof and make the announcement!' But we found that all were too shy to go up. At last two of the lads got up courage enough to go up on the roof. One was named Drum. He was a very droll fellow. They cried, 'Stone Hammer members, come together here!' . . .

"As we waited, we boys would say, 'Look at that one, how he is dressed!' Some of the boys were quite young, – no more than eleven years of age. These looked quite funny for they were all painted up; and they had never been painted or dressed before in gala attire. . . . We jested and laughed at each other's expense in great good humor" (Wilson 1911:147-48).

At last they left in a group for the Stone Hammers' lodge, where a large crowd had gathered. After some singing, the boys formed a procession and marched out into the open space at the center of the village. At first the spectators cried out in encouragement, "Remember you are men now! Soon war will come. You are men, to go out and fight! Dance hard! Yell always! You must show you are brave!"

But soon the yells changed. Wolf Chief said, "We could hear men calling to one another, 'Hey, you people, get sticks! Gather stones! Hit them, strike them, hurt them! Tonight they will try to steal all your good meat. Make them smart for it!'

"I tell you, we boys were good and scared!

"The whole village came into the open space, and as we danced gathered about us. We were in the center of a big crowd!

"We danced about four songs. When we got thru dancing, the ten fathers . . . called out, 'Now! Run, speed, – get into the lodge!'

"We boys broke our circle and dashed for the society lodge. The bigger boys went first, rushing thru the crowd; in their anxiety some of them knocked over some of the little fellows, who wept and cried aloud with fright. And we got hit! I got hit several times. Butterfly . . . got hit twice. The people threw small stones and sticks, heavy enough to make us smart, yet not hurt us seriously. Everybody threw at us, men, women and children, old and young.

"When we reached [the Stone Hammers'] lodge, some of the boys were weeping yet. Some were bleeding at the nose either from a fall, or from a hit on

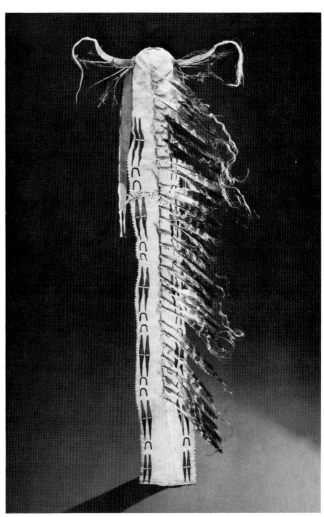

H EADDRESS
Northern Plains style
Collected by Gilbert Wilson, pre-1918?
Tanned hide hood decorated with split cow horns, beads,
*   feathers, dyed horsehair, and ribbons. Trailer of tanned*
*   hide with horsehair-tipped feathers and red and black*
*   painted designs*
L. 165 cm from crown to end of trailer
MHS 7059.4

Headdresses made with animal horns, feathers, weasel skins, otter fur, and other materials were worn by society members. The various materials represented brave exploits (Hail 1983:121-22; Lowie 1916:219-322). Each man made his headdress to reflect his own deeds, although he might then sell or give away the headdress when the society was purchased by another group of men. Although this headdress has the form of an older style, the materials suggest that it is a more recent interpretation. It is strikingly similar to one in the Great Plains Museum in Mandan, N.Dak.

the nose. We were all much excited" (Wilson 1911:152-54).

But the society was theirs.

Boys were not the only ones who joined societies. Buffalo Bird Woman joined the Skunk Society when she was 14. "When a feast was given in the society's lodge, we girls between dances, would sit together and tell stories and laugh and have a good time. . . . Some of the girls liked to dance very much; but I did not so much care. My parents were rather careful of me and I wanted to obey them. If we had a dance in the day time, I asked permission and my parents let me go; but they did not permit me to go alone when we danced at night. There were many young men that got after the girls and my parents knew it. So when I went, my mother or father went with me" (Wilson 1911:175-76).

To Wolf Chief, society membership meant more than just a social gathering. "I loved my society," he said. "I thought to myself, 'Enemies may come and take my life!' Then I would go out and sing songs of my society, perhaps all the night, so that I would be protected. I said, 'I wish to stay in this society all my life. I love it!' That is the way I felt" (Wilson 1911:114).

CRAZY DOG SOCIETY SASH
Mandan/Hidatsa
Collected by Robert Lowie, 1910
Red wool strip folded in half, to which are attached 36 eagle feathers tipped with red-dyed down and laced together with a thin rawhide strip. See color page 180
L. 229 cm, W. 35.5 cm
AMNH 50.1/4352, Lowie

This sash, worn by an officer of the Crazy Dog Society, indicated the officer's responsibility not to flee from enemies. The sash was offered only to the bravest man in the society. At first a man would refuse to accept it because it indicated his willingness to fight to the death, suggesting that he was a little crazy. The sash, however, was a mark of recognition for bravery and so the man selected as an officer would eventually accept it. He would then decorate the sash with his own honor marks (Lowie 1916:281, 307-8).

P EHRISKA-RUHPA/MENNITARRE
[HIDATSA] IN THE DOG DANSE
[SOCIETY]" (DETAIL)
*Based on a watercolor by Karl
Bodmer, 1832-33*
Copper plate engraving on paper
H. 53.2 cm, W. 37.8 cm
MHS (Wied 1840–43: tableau 23)
According to Wolf Chief and his distant
cousin Hairy Coat, the regalia of the
Dog Society was prescribed by a spirit in
a vision. It included red body paint, a
foxskin tied to the ankles, sashes of red
and black cloth, and distinctive headgear
of owl or magpie feathers. Members
carried rattles made of deer or buffalo
calf dewclaws strung on a stick.
Although from an earlier time period,
this picture closely resembles the two
men's description. The Dog Society
originated with the Hidatsa (Lowie
1916:284–90).

R ATTLE
Northern Plains
Collected by Gilbert Wilson, pre-1918?
*Wooden handle covered with tanned hide; 23 carved animal hoof rattles attached
by thongs; triangular hide flap at base of handle beaded in lazy-stitched
brown and blue glass seed beads*
L. 42 cm
MHS 7059.64a
Maximilian described the regalia worn by members of the different societies. For the
Dog Society he mentioned a headdress of feathers, "strips of red cloth hanging down
the back," and a rattle closely resembling this one. "The schischikué [rattle] of this
band is a stick, a foot or a foot and a half long to which a number of animals' hoofs
are fastened" (Wied 1905-06, 23:294).

DRUM AND DRUMSTICK
Drum: Hidatsa, bought from
Theodore Lone Fight? Drumstick:
Hidatsa style
Collected by Gilbert Wilson, pre-1918?
Wooden hoop drum held together with
nails; rawhide cover laced and
nailed over hoop; on back side, four
twisted fabric cords tied together in
center form a handle; on the cover
are traces of pink, brown, and green
paint and the penciled legend,
"Theodore Lone Fight,
Independence." Drumstick handle
of smoothed wood with cloth
wrapped around head
Drum: D. 39.3 cm, W. 10.4 cm.
Drum stick: L. 36 cm
MHS 7059.62c, b

Traditionally, society and ceremonial
music was sung to the accompaniment
of single-headed or hand-held drums like
this one. In later days, people used large
double-headed or commercial bass
drums for dancing, but the hand-held
drum is still used for special purposes.

Wolf Chief and his friends were
taught the songs of the Stone Hammer
Society when they joined. "One of the
members of the Stone Hammers, I have
forgotten his name, now arose and
spoke to us: 'Our sons, we are now
going to sing. You who want to learn,
listen to us. You must learn these songs.
When we get thru, we will go expecting
to gather here again tomorrow evening
and you must again fetch us a feast as
you have tonight. So also for the third
and fourth nights.' . . . They had two
hand drums which they brought out.
The two drummers and about seven
other singers sat now in a circle. . . . I
remember well the first song. After
every repetition all yelled and then they
sang again" (Wilson 1911:127).

The Mandan and Hidatsa
originally used several different styles of
drumstick. Karl Bodmer depicted a
rattle-headed or round-headed stick
being used in a Hidatsa scalp dance
(Bodmer 1984:311). Ethnomusicologist
Frances Densmore collected information
on that round-headed drumstick, but
she also noted that a straight stick with
a cloth-wrapped head much like this
one was used in the women's Goose
Society dance (Densmore 1918:pl. 9a,
p. 8). By the early 1900s the latter type
was commonly used in the Grass and
other dances.

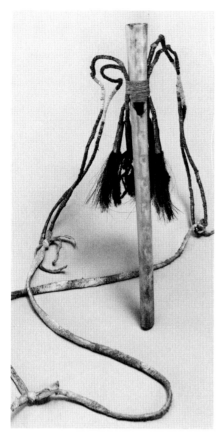

WING-BONE WHISTLE
Northern Plains
Collected by Gilbert Wilson, pre-1918?
*Bone from the wing of a large bird
with irregular sounding hole.
Tanned hide neck cord, attached
with orange painted sinew, is
wrapped with red, purple, and
yellow dyed quills. Four tassels end
in metal cones with blue yarn and
green plant fiber attached*
Whistle: L. 20.5 cm. Strap: L. 60 cm
MHS 7059.15b

Wing-bone whistles were blown by
dancers in society dances. They were
made, explained Buffalo Bird Woman,
"of wing bones of large birds, – heron,
geese, pelican, etc. for the Dog
Imitators. They were long and sounded
louder than others, and low. The
Maśuka-wadahi or Reckless Dogs used
whistles of eagles' bones, shorter, about
five inches long" (Wilson 1911:290).

Wilson mentions collecting at least
two wing-bone whistles: one he already
had in 1906, and another was given to
him in 1907 by Mrs. Foolish Woman as
an apology for having embraced him in
public (Wilson 1906b:11, 1907b:45).
It is not known which this is; it is one
of two from his collection at the MHS.

WHISTLE
Pre-1885?
Excavated at Like-a-Fishhook Village
*Metal tube, probably hand-rolled
zinc. Sinew around mouthpiece
end. Reed is missing*
L. 20.2 cm
SHSND 32ML2/12,003.FT35

Whistles were usually made from the
hollow wing bones of large birds, but
they could also be made from metal
tubes, even from gun barrels. The sinew
wrapping at one end of this whistle is
very similar to the wrappings used on
wing-bone whistles. They attached the
whistle to a cord so that it could be
hung around a dancer's neck (Smith
1972:75).

CLUB
Mandan/Hidatsa
Collected by Robert Lowie, 1910
*Carved wood wrapped with rabbit fur
and tied with red and white
printed cloth. Horsehair, hide, and
animal hair tied to the bottom; six
decoratively clipped feathers and a
plaid silk scarf tied to top. Antler
tine projects from the middle*
*L. 83 cm excluding feathers and
tassel, W. 25.5 cm*
AMNH 50.1/4359, Lowie

Mandan and Hidatsa men's societies
were closely related to warfare. Members
encouraged others to be brave and to
win war honors for the society; some
society regalia required men to stand fast
in the face of the enemy. Any man who
won honors in battle was permitted to
make an object symbolic of his success,
which could either be adopted into use
by the society or remain personal. This
club may be a personal symbol carried
by a man when he participated in the
society dances. The elaborate decoration
and the fact that the antler tine is tied
on indicates that it was made for
ceremonial use and not for warfare.
Members of the Hidatsa Black Mouth
Society and the Mandan Cheyenne
Society carried clublike objects with
metal or horn blades (Lowie 1916:276,
296).

FACE PAINT
Northern Plains
Collected by Frederick Wilson, pre-1918?
Black powder pigment and dried lichen used for yellow dye
MHS 9598.3a, b

Different colors of face paint symbolized different events.
Black was worn for celebrations. "To paint the face a man
would pound up a little bit of charcoal fine or crush it with
his thumb and drop it in his left palm," Wolf Chief said.
"Then he put a little bone grease in the charcoal, stirred it
around with the fingers of his right hand and rubbed it over
his face and hands. Sometimes we used to rub it over our
hair, and the shoulders of our shirts.

"A very few, when enemies had been killed, would
paint their face red instead of black; and some of these also
would rub the red paint over their hair and shoulders"
(Wilson 1914b:196).

Red and yellow were worn for everyday occasions or
whenever a person wanted to look especially attractive. Buffalo
Bird Woman said, "Young men in olden times usually
provided themselves with a light red paint and a yellow paint.
Older men did not care for the yellow paint but just used the
red" (Wilson 1914b:23).

White clay was worn in ceremonial situations and on
those occasions when the wearer needed spiritual protection
(Wilson 1913a:13).

The pigments shown here would have been used in a
base of fat from the back of a buffalo, marrow from the leg
bones, or bone grease (Wilson 1914b:196).

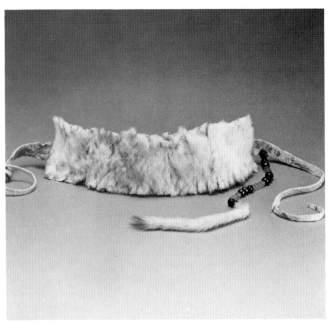

HEADDRESS
Hidatsa
Collected by Robert Lowie, 1911
Tanned weasel skin strip sewn to two tanned hide ties and
a string of black and yellow faceted beads ending in a
weasel tail
L. 79 cm, W. 6.5 cm
AMNH 50.1/6011, Lowie

Members of the men's Lumpwood Society carried carved
wood sticks representing buffaloes and other animals. Their
regalia also included headdresses of weasel skin strips decorated
with beads and caps of bear gut with hawk feathers (Lowie
1916:261). Other articles worn or carried during a
performance were based on individual visions or the official
position of the member. Lowie collected this example of the
weasel skin ornament when he visited Fort Berthold
Reservation in 1911.

KIT FOX SOCIETY RATTLE
Mandan/Hidatsa
Collected by Robert Lowie, 1910
Tin can filled with pebbles attached to
a wooden handle wrapped with red
wool cloth and white string.
Decorating the handle are a piece
of white-haired pelt, feathers,
horsehair both plain and dyed,
ermine tails, and dyed down
Stick: L. 49 cm. Overall: L. 83 cm
AMNH 50.1/4343, Lowie

Fur-wrapped staffs and ornate rattles
were insignia for Kit Fox Society
officers. Wolf Chief recalled that the
rattles were originally made of rawhide,
but by the time he joined the society,
tin cans filled with pebbles and
decorated with horsetails had replaced
the earlier forms (Lowie 1916:255).
Other societies also used rattles made
of metal cans. Baking powder cans were
particularly popular and remained so
into the 1980s.

HORSE SOCIETY RATTLE
Mandan. Made by Little Bear
Collected by Robert Lowie, 1910
Horsehide dried into a sphere and painted green, then filled with seeds or sand.
Sphere decorated around circumference with a red wool strip to which black
feathers are sewn with sinew. At top of rattle are sewn six blue feathers and
two eagle feathers. Handle of wood wrapped with cotton cloth covered with red
wool bound on with a quill-wrapped hide strip. Triangular red wool trailer
has six eagle feathers tied on with black thread
L. 100 cm overall
AMNH 50.1/4333, Lowie

Society membership provided social experiences outside the family and clan groups.
Traditionally, the societies also helped to prepare men for leadership, but cessation of
warfare and the prohibition of ceremonies necessitated changes. The Horse Society,
for which this rattle was an emblem, was one of the new societies adopted by the
Mandan after about 1890 (Bowers 1965:295). In the 1980s, societies provided
assistance to needy families and sponsored powwows and other events.

Lessons in leadership

I t was spring and some snow still lingered on the sides of the hills when Wolf Chief got his first chance to go to war. He was 16 years old. Everyone in the village knew that Wolf Eyes, whom Wolf Chief called "grandfather," was going to lead a war party, for he had hung his medicine bundle on a tall pole outside his lodge. "One evening I was over at his earth lodge," said Wolf Chief, "and he said to me, 'Kuahawi, I am going on a war party and I want you to go along also'" (Wilson 1914b:111-13).

The Hidatsa did not go to war just to conquer other tribes for land or wealth. Instead, war was a very personal test of a man's integrity and spiritual power. Often, the riskiest way of winning was the best, for it tested a man's faith to the limit. War was extremely dangerous. Of 40 boys who joined the Stone Hammer Society with Wolf Chief, nearly one in five was killed in war before reaching the age of 30 (Wilson 1911:157).

Wolf Chief knew that his father would not want him to go with the war party, for he was young and had never fasted for a vision that might give him protection. The risk did not concern Wolf Chief, for he knew his grandfather to be "a powerful mystery man" who could extend protection to those in his party (Wilson 1914b:114). "I did not return to my father's lodge until it was dark, and all had gone to bed," Wolf Chief said. "I made no noise as I came in the lodge for I wanted to get my things and be off.

"I walked very quietly across the floor and got my moccasins and my father's as well, for I thought I should need them. I also got my gun and powder horn, but thinking there was not enough powder in it, I slipped over to my father's powder horn and was pouring out the powder into my own horn when my father awoke. 'Who is that?' he cried. 'Is that you Kuahawi? What are you doing with my powder horn? Are you going on Wolf Eyes' war party? I do not want you to go!'

"'No,' I answered, 'Wolf Eyes wants merely to borrow my gun and some powder and I am getting them for him!'

"'All right,' said my father, and said nothing more. . . .

"I got back to Wolf Eyes' lodge . . . some time after night fall. I found about thirty men in his lodge. It was very dark within. However I made my way to the place where Wolf Eyes sat and said to him, 'Grandfather, you must get away at once, or my father will suspect that I am going on the war party. . . .'

"'We will start just as soon as this pipe is smoked

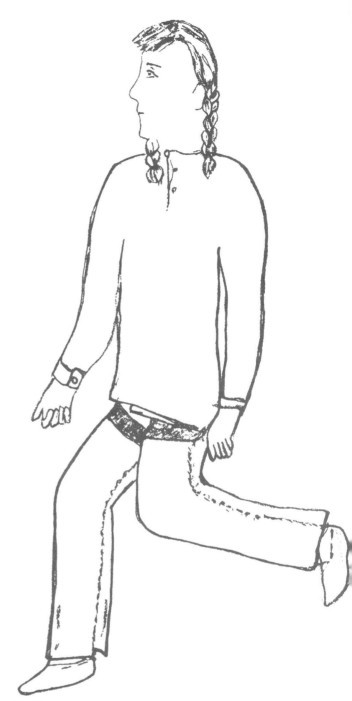

WOLF CHIEF ON HIS FIRST WAR PARTY
Drawn by Goodbird with instructions from Wolf Chief
Pencil on paper
H. 14.5 cm, W. 7.6 cm
AMNH (Goodbird 1914b:fig. 34)
This sketch illustrates how Wolf Chief dressed on Wolf Eyes' war party. Beneath what is shown, he wore a breech clout, belt, and knife. His shirt was of white calico with stripes, made by his mother to open "at the throat like a white man's shirt." His leggings were of heavy white wool or "blanket cloth." On his wrist was a bracer. He explained, "It happened that I had been out hunting birds the day I left the village, with my bow and arrows; and I had not taken off my bracer, and therefore went off wearing it." Over these clothes he wore a skin robe with a belt and his gun (Wilson 1914b:153-56).

out,' said Wolf Eyes (Wilson 1914b:115–18).

Wolf Chief soon learned that war was interwoven with ceremony at every step. The men would not leave until they had sat in the dark lodge and smoked. "There was a little fire in the fire place," Wolf Chief remembered, "but it had died down. The night was cloudy, indeed it looked as if it might storm. . . . Every thing was quiet and still. . . .

"The pipe was passed around, and Wolf Eyes offered it to me. But I did not take it because my father did not permit me to smoke, as I was still but a boy. . . .

"But Wolf Eyes said to me, 'Smoke! I have prayed to the spirits, and it will be well for you to smoke!' So I took the pipe, put it to my mouth and drew, but the fire in the bowl had already gone out. Wolf Eyes however, took the pipe from me, (saying, 'Good!' as he did so) and he thrust out the ashes and put up the pipe in his tobacco bag. . . .

WOLF EYES DRESSED FOR A WAR PARTY
Drawn by Goodbird with instructions from Wolf
  Chief, 1914
Pencil and watercolor on paper
H. 18.2 cm, W. 14.5 cm
AMNH (Goodbird 1914b:fig. 23)
When Wolf Eyes, leader of Wolf Chief's first war party, set out, he carried his sacred bundle on a stick over his left arm. "When he came into camp, he would thrust the stick into the ground, the hawk's head at its top," Wolf Chief remembered. In this sketch, he carries his gun in a fringed leather case on his back. "The gun was borne stock-up, and thrust upward over the left shoulder. In case of attack the right hand seized the stock and jerked case and all over the head, when the case would fall off at once." The robe Wolf Eyes wears belted around the middle was a typical garment: "Some of the warriors had robes with the fur on as here, some had tanned skins, and some had blankets," said Wolf Chief. The head covering was made of white sheeting or handkerchief, and could be tied under the chin or around the head, turban-style. "Such a head covering kept the head warm and made us think of the wolves that we imitated; but it had another use, especially when worn by spies. The spy would creep up behind a hill and peer over to see if any enemy was in sight. The covering of grey-white cloth over his black hair made it much less likely that the enemy would notice him against the sky line" (Wilson 1914b:121, 123–24).

DOORWAY OF WOLF EYES PREPARING FOR WAR
Drawn by Goodbird with instructions from Wolf
  Chief, 1914
Pencil and watercolor on paper
H. 13.5 cm, W. 11.4 cm
AMNH (Goodbird 1914b:fig. 22)
"When a man put his sacred objects outside his lodge in this way," said Wolf Chief, "it meant 'I want all the gods to know that I am going on a war party, so that they will give me protection.' It was also a notice to the people that he was forming a war party and was an invitation to the young men of the village to join it" (Wilson 1914b:113).

"Having put up the pipe, Wolf Eyes arose, saying, 'O young men, I must go and pray to my gods. When I come back I will lead you forth; do you then follow me!' . . .

"We walked thru the village and left it, taking an easterly direction. Wolf Eyes went ahead, the rest of us following bunched together in a group, and talking together, some half whispering, some in a very low tone" (Wilson 1914b:118–22).

Members of the war party were said to represent wolves, so they wore white handkerchiefs on their heads and called one another by special names like "Old Wolf" and "Young Wolf." The young boy acted as camp tender; he gathered firewood and fetched water. At their first camp, the men sat around the fire singing "sweet heart songs" and telling of their past war records. As they sang, a brave young Mandan named Son of a Star rose to dance, wearing an eagle feather bonnet with sleigh bells attached. "His dance meant 'I want to die,'" said Wolf Chief; "he would expose himself with reckless bravery whenever necessary, and would conquer or die. . . .

"But Wolf Eyes was alarmed when he saw Son of a Star dancing. 'Hold!' he cried, to the singers, 'don't sing any more. Stop!'

"They did so, and Wolf Eyes said to Son of a Star: 'We all know you are a brave man, but I do not want you to die! I cannot get the honor marks I want, if you die on this war party!'

"Son of a Star had stopped dancing when the singing ceased. 'Very well,' he said. 'I will come back, since you want me to live!'" (Wilson 1914b:132–33).

They traveled northeast about 30 miles a day, toward the country of the Devils Lake Sioux. They hunted as little as possible, for fear of drawing unfriendly attention by their gunshots. They camped by lakes, lying close to one another so each sleeper could be roused silently by a push.

On the foggy morning when they arrived in enemy territory, Wolf Eyes called the group together to appoint eight young men to the honorable post of spy. For the spies' leader, he chose a man who had fasted and sacrificed for a vision. After prayers, the spies set off.

The party waited until afternoon, when they saw the spies returning, running fast. "As the spies came up they cried, 'We saw a Sioux but failed to kill him. And we have discovered a Sioux camp, eight tepees on the side of a hill, and probably many more beyond. There is no time to lose, – what shall we do?'

RIFLE
Made by Winchester Repeating Arms Co., New Haven, Conn., 1891
Model 1873, .32-caliber lever-action repeating rifle with walnut stock, iron frame, and round, smooth-bore barrel
L. 109.4 cm
MHS 63.168, Karl G. Parchert
When he reached adulthood, Wolf Chief used a Winchester .44-caliber repeating rifle for hunting and warfare. He explained that on a hunting trip, "Every man slept with his gun under his head with a bit of the blanket over it for a pillow. . . . My gun lay with the barrel pointed to the left as I lay on my back. This was done so that if I was aroused in the night by enemies, I could seize the barrel of the gun as I got up" (Wilson 1914b:121, 125–26).

This gun is similar to, but smaller than, Wolf Chief's. Its provenance is unknown. Cartridges from Model 1873 Winchesters like this were excavated at Like-a-Fishhook Village (Smith 1972:81).

"We asked our leader. 'This my mystery object,' cried Wolf Eyes, 'has deceived me!'" Knowing that they were probably outnumbered and the enemy was warned, Wolf Eyes decided to return home (Wilson 1914b: 133-48).

"So we started off again," Wolf Chief said. "We would run about two miles and then walk for about a quarter of a mile, then run again. . . . We ran all that night, guiding ourselves by the stars. . . . It was just sunrise when we caught sight of our village, and we reached it soon after.

"I estimate that we ran fifty miles that night, and the evening previous."

HEART SKIN BUCKET
Hidatsa. Made by Wolf Chief
Collected by Gilbert Wilson, 1916
Beef heart membrane sewn with sinew to a wooden rim;
willow stick handle with bands of bark removed;
braided sinew string
Stick: L. 49.4 cm. Bucket: L. 16 cm, D. 10.5 cm
MHS 7059.67a

This is the type of heart skin bucket used on a war party by the young man who fetched drinking water for the others. Wolf Chief explained the rings in the bark thus: "In old times a young man marked on the handle of his heart-skin bucket the honors that he had won as a spy. . . . Now the handle of this bucket which I have just made you represents nine honors. There are as you see, four bark stripes and five peeled stripes, representing that the maker either spied out enemies or else spied out the tents [camp] of enemies nine times. . . . I have ten spy honor-marks which I have a right to use" (Wilson 1916b: 58-59).

WOLF CHIEF ACTING AS WATER-CARRIER
Drawn by Goodbird, 1914
Pencil on paper
H. 13.8 cm, W. 12.8 cm
AMNH (Goodbird 1914b: fig. 29)

One of the honorable posts a young war party member could attain was that of "worker," whose duty was to fetch drinking water. "Only a spry, active lad was chosen," Wolf Chief said (Wilson 1909a: 103). He himself held the post on his first war party. He remembered, "They appointed Scattered Village to make the bucket. . . . 'My son,' he said, 'receive now your bucket. Begin your labors now, and go fetch water in your bucket. All the members of the Rough Wood Society are here sitting in a line. Do you begin at that end of the line and give water to drink out of your bucket, and then pass to the next in the line. But if any one doesn't volunteer to tell you that he has been on a war party and spied out enemies, then you will know that he has never done so. Do you then give that one a rousing thump on the back and empty your bucket over him!'" Wolf Chief followed these instructions, giving the two inexperienced party members a "resounding whack on the back. . . . As I did this all the others laughed and cried out 'Hyih! Hyih!' and rolled over on the ground with laughter." Goodbird drew this sketch of the event, which Wolf Chief thought was "very good" (Wilson 1914b: 129-31).

"The people were sorry when they heard our story. 'Wolf Eyes' medicines gave him that enemy; but for some reason they took back their gift,' they said. No one laughed however, or made sport of us for having failed.

"But when I came back to my father's lodge, he laughed. 'I know you have just gotten back from that war party,' he said. 'I know you hid from me and escaped. Did you not steal my moccasins?'

"'Yes,' I answered.

"'What have you done with them?'

"'Here they are,' I said, 'I did not wear them!'

"My father took the moccasins and smiled.

"Soon after this Wolf Eyes came into our lodge. 'My grandson Kuahawi,' he said, 'is a very good boy.' And he told my father how he had made me water carrier, and how when we thought enemies pursued us, I had run all evening and all the night. . . .

"I felt rather proud. I felt I was ahead of all the boys of my size. None of them made any comments to me – perhaps they felt a little shame that none of them had been on a war party.

"But my mother said, 'You foolish boy, why did you not ask your father? Had you come to him in the right way he would have let you go, and he would have let you have some of his mystery things.'

"She brought me some succotash and some boiled dried green corn. I ate a lot of both!" (Wilson 1914b:148-50).

As he grew older, Wolf Chief learned that there was a very serious side to war. Before a young man could risk his life, he had to earn supernatural protection by fasting and sacrificing for a vision. In the winter when he was 17, a clan father encouraged Wolf Chief to seek a vision. Every night for the next four months, the young man went out into the woods to pray. At the end, he had a dream that made him confident he would some day lead a war party (Wilson 1916b:62-66).

It was not until he was 23 that Wolf Chief asked his father's help to prepare an expedition to steal horses from the Sioux. He told Small Ankle of his vision, then said, "'You must tell me what a leader should do.' . . .

"'All right,' said my father. . . . [He] then sent all of the family out of the lodge. 'Go out,' he said, 'I want to teach my son how to be a leader'" (Wilson 1916b:68-69).

The lessons Small Ankle taught had little to do with tactics or command and much to do with religion.

There were songs and ceremonies, ways of divining the future, and proper care for sacred objects. True leadership, Wolf Chief learned, lay not so much in a man's own abilities as in his ability to call upon higher powers for aid. If enemies were killed or horses stolen, the leader's gods were strong, and he would receive the credit. But if men were killed or horses lamed, the leader's gods had deserted him, and he would receive the blame.

Wolf Chief was successful in war. As his record grew, he earned the praise of the community in many ways. Returning warriors were sometimes paraded through town on horseback, or given new names or the privilege of holding a ceremonial giveaway. They also earned the right to wear honor marks – symbols of achievement emblazoned on clothes, tent covers, and tools. Through a complicated system of counting coups, young men could compare their achievements and the risks they had overcome.

Immemorial custom surrounded all aspects of a warrior's life. In a thoughtful moment years later, Wolf Chief reflected that the training of young men was "like driving a wagon along a deeply rutted road. There was no way to get anywhere but by going forward in the same path as others had done before – a person could make no progress backing up, and the depth of the ruts prevented him from taking a different course" (Bowers 1965:220).

"We went out & underwent hard things so we get to be called leaders," said Black Hawk, a neighbor of Wolf Chief's, "as white men go out to earn lots of money & get to be called leaders" (Wilson 1908a:101).

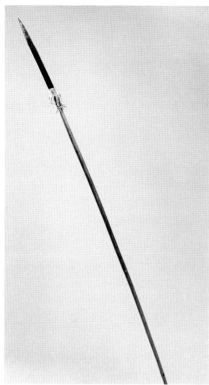

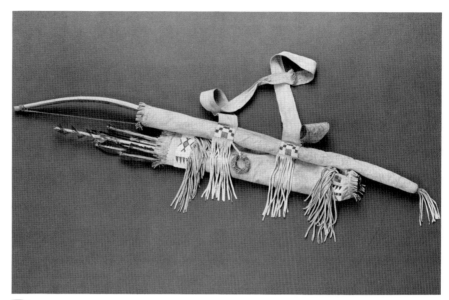

LANCE
Northern Plains
Collected by Gilbert Wilson, pre-1918?
Round ash (?) shaft with bayonet-
shaped steel or iron blade inserted
in shaft and secured with sinew-
sewn rawhide covered with yellow
paint. Decorated with tanned hide
strips beaded in red and blue
L. 196 cm
MHS 7059.81

"I have heard that in olden days before we obtained horses, we Hidatsas fought with lances as well as with bows and arrows and shields," Wolf Chief recalled. "After we got ponies, we fought with lances on horseback. . . .

"In my life time lance heads were made of steel. . . .

"Guns were coming into use in my youth and I never saw war club or lance used in actual battle" (Wilson 1918a : 173, 177).

Once abandoned as weapons, lances became objects carried in society dances. Buffalo Bird Woman recalled that some members of the Fox, Raven Imitator, Enemy-Imitates-Woman, and Reckless Dog societies carried lances, some with blades and some without (F. Wilson 1912b : 45). Society lances seem to have been decorated, many with feathers, furs, and beads (Lowie 1916 : 225-354).

BOW AND ARROW SET
Hidatsa. Bow made by Wolf Chief
Collected by Gilbert Wilson, 1911
Bow of chokecherry wood with sinew string, signed "H.W.C." (Henry Wolf
Chief) in green paint. Tanned hide bow case and quiver decorated with hide
fringes and panels of white, yellow, green, blue, and gold beads in geometric
patterns. Wood arrow shafts with wood and metal points and feather
fletching. Rawhide bracer and extra bowstring attached to bow case.
See color page 173
Bow: L. 129 cm. Bow case: L. 99 cm
AMNH 50.1/6014a–l

Wilson photographed the entire process of making this bow and case, from cutting the wood and hide to final use (MHS photos IV-99-1911 to V-14-1911, AMNH photos 288288 to 288305). Wolf Chief demonstrated how the bow case was worn – horizontally across the back with the strap passing over both shoulders and across the chest – until it was ready for use, when it was slipped under one arm. The bracer tied to the bow case was used to protect the wrist when drawing the bow.

The Hidatsa recognized the qualities of different bow shapes and different kinds of wood, including ash, chokecherry, plum, cedar, and elm. Until guns and ammunition were made available in sufficient quality and quantity to meet their hunting and defensive needs, bows and arrows continued to be preferred. "This bow that I am making for you," explained Wolf Chief, "is not as heavy as they were often made in old times, when their use as clubs was more often kept in mind. But this bow is quite strong enough for either war or buffalo hunting" (Wilson 1911 : 5; Hamilton 1982 : 99).

PROTECTIVE FEATHER

Hidatsa. Bought from Wolf Chief, who used it in warfare
Collected by Frederick Wilson, 1908
Eagle feather connected to the remnants of a second feather
by a tanned hide strip
L. 22.5 cm, W. 9.5 cm
AMNH 50/7095

Men who successfully sought visions were often told by their
spiritual protectors to make symbols of their visions to be
used for specific purposes. Such symbols, which often took
the form of feathers, could also be given to others to extend
spiritual protection to them. Wolf Chief remembered receiving
at least three separate bundles of protective feathers. The first
came from his grandfather. "When my grandfather Big Cloud
was dying, I came and sat beside his bed. He opened his
medicine bag & took out a bunch of feathers & told me how
when a young man he went out [in the] hills to fast & find
his god. He dreamed he saw [a] bunch [of] feathers like this
hanging in the sky. . . . He gave me the medicine because I
was a young man and he wanted me to be brave & successful.
He also told my mother to teach me all about the bird
mystery song – which he heard the day he saw the feather. In
preparing for a battle he put the feather bunch on and sang
the song.

"One winter after he died – about July, some enemies
spying around the village were seen. . . . I took my medicine
out and tied [it] on [the] mane of [my] horse . . . because my
grandfather told me – if the horse [is] slow, tie on horse's
mane. If fast – put on my own head. The birds would help
the slow horse out fly all the others" (Wilson 1907b:62-63).

On this occasion and many others, Wolf Chief was
successful in war. A second protective feather was given him
by his society "father," Deer's Head, when Wolf Chief joined
the Stone Hammer Society (Wilson 1911:144). Later, when
Wolf Chief had a close call with an enemy and managed to
escape only because the smoke from the guns covered him,
his father gave him this eagle feather. "As the eagle was sacred
to him, he gave me this eagle's feather that I might keep it
sacred and it would protect me from danger" (F. Wilson
1912b:[102]).

MODEL BED

Hidatsa. Made by Buffalo Bird Woman, 1910
Collected by Gilbert Wilson, 1910
Tanned hide canopy folded and tied over a wooden frame.
Canopy incised and painted brown and red. Two model
robes, one undecorated; other made from dark leather
embroidered in blue, lavendar, violet, orange, and pink
quills, with ten quilled tassels down center
Bed: H. 53.5 cm, L. 43 cm, W. 34 cm. Undecorated robe:
L. 44 cm, W. 30 cm. Quilled robe: L. 51 cm, W. 28
cm
AMNH 50.1/5479a–c

Many of the decorations used by the Hidatsa were actually
symbols reflecting an individual's war honors. Inside the earth
lodge, the bed curtains were often painted with a man's honor
marks. Buffalo Bird Woman made this model and decorated it
with her husband Son of a Star's honor marks. According to
the complex Hidatsa system of honor symbols, the
appropriate mark was determined by the position of the
person gaining the honor, the type of honor, and the
circumstances. Beginning at the top right, the marks refer to
Son of a Star's record for spying out the enemy. The pipe
symbols at top left represent the times Son of a Star led a war
party. The marks on the right side refer to a time he was
wounded and had a horse wounded under him, and the
marks on the left side are for the times he struck the enemy
(Wilson 1910a:295-304; MHS photos IV-35-1910 to
IV-41-1910).

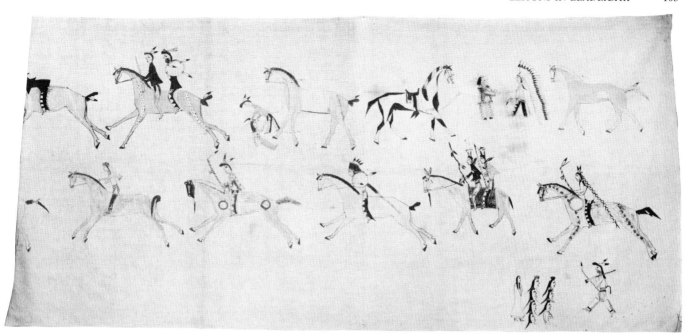

PAINTING (DETAIL)
Northern Plains
Collected by Gilbert Wilson, pre-1918?
Paint on muslin
L. 269 cm, W. 88 cm
MHS 7059.27

Warriors painted the stories of their exploits on buffalo robes. In later times it was impossible to get robes suitable for such purposes and so men painted their stories on muslin or in ledger books supplied by traders, Army men, and others (Ewers 1939:42-45). Since most of the representations are symbols rather than exact depictions of events, the painter must explain the drawing. This painting represents the exploits of an unknown individual, possibly Sioux or Hidatsa.

HORSETAILS
Hidatsa style
Collected by Gilbert Wilson, pre-1918?
Horsetails dyed red and green; undyed
L. 53 cm, 59 cm, and 48 cm
MHS 7059.219, 218a, b

Colored horsehair was used as an honor mark by the Hidatsa. Wolf Chief explained how a man earned the right to wear it: "For the fifth time a war-leader [or any member of his party] captured horses (on separate parties) he hung white or colored horse hair on his neck flap. I never saw it but have heard that in old times when there were many wars, that a sixth capture was marked by tying white or colored horse hair on the robe, but I never saw this myself" (Wilson 1916b:20, 30).

LEGGINGS
Mandan. Made by Leader; belonged to her husband, Lance Owner. Marks
   painted by Wolf Ghost, a Hidatsa, and Wounded Face, a Mandan
Collected by Gilbert Wilson, 1911
Tanned hide sewn with sinew, painted in red and brown, and decorated with
   white, purple, blue, and orange quillwork. Fringed at seams, top, and
   bottom. See color page 172
L. 85.5 cm
AMNH 50.1/6017b, a

Only men who had won honor marks were permitted to paint them on clothing and other objects. If a man had not won the kind of marks he wanted on his clothes, he hired others to paint them. Thus when Lance Owner wanted to decorate his leggings, he had Wolf Ghost paint the legging shown on the left and Wounded Face paint the one on the right, each man drawing the honor marks indicating his first strike on the enemy. Lance Owner explained that the painting on the left legging "means exactly the same as the honor marks on the right legging, only this [on the right] is the Mandan way; the other is Hidatsa." Leader and Lance Owner debated whether Wolf Ghost had put too much on his legging, since all the marks referred to the same honor (Wilson 1911:283-88).

"SCALP DANCE OF THE MINATARRES [HIDATSA]"
Based on a sketch by Karl Bodmer, 1834
Copper plate engraving on paper
H. 30.1 cm, W. 43.7 cm
MHS (Wied 1840–43 : tableau 27)

The celebration that followed the return of a successful war party gave women a chance to participate in the honor. Only particular women's societies had the right to rejoice, including the Older Women's Society and the Skunk Society. Buffalo Bird Woman remembered being a member of the latter society: "When an enemy was killed all we girls who were members got ready to have a good time. We painted our faces black, with grease and pounded charcoal; a white stripe ran from the tip of the nose straight up the forehead to the hair. An eagle's feather hung from the back of the head, from the spot where a man's scalp lock would have hung. . . .

"The society then, with faces painted, . . . went out into the village and sang and danced in an open place. Then they would go to another place and do so again. And so four times, they danced and sang" (Wilson 1911 : 174-75).

Wolf Chief also described a nighttime dance following a war victory when he was a child. "The women made a big circle around the fire, with about ten or a dozen men making a smaller circle within. Of this inner circle of men five had hand drums and two had rattles. Two old men, Guts and Big Cloud, had each a pole with a piece of the Sioux's scalp upon it. . . . I and about a dozen little boys stood admiringly about Big Cloud; or we sometimes ran around and stood about Guts. Sometimes we would dance around one of the old men, and he would chase us away" (Wilson 1914b : 189-90).

This print was based on sketches made by Bodmer, probably at Fort Clark in February of 1834, when a group of Hidatsa came to perform the dance for the men at the trading post (Wied 1905-06, 24 : 67).

Love and marriage

Being young and ready for love could be both hard and easy in Like-a-Fishhook Village. On the one hand, there were many rules of decorum that young people had to obey. Courting was supposed to be a private thing, and sweethearts were embarrassed to be seen talking or looking at each other in public. On the other hand, there were plenty of opportunities to notice members of the opposite sex.

"In old times," Goodbird said, "the young men sat on the house top most all the time just finely dressed and singing chants and they did this just to get the girls." In her own tart way, Buffalo Bird Woman agreed. "Young men dressed up and made themselves look nice so as to be admired by the girls. And they hardly did anything else" (Wilson 1907b:25; 1914b:376).

But when she was young, Buffalo Bird Woman herself did not object to dressing up and looking pretty. "I painted [my face] every day by habit then," she said, "red all over the face, but deeper and heavier on the cheeks" (Wilson 1914b:332). She also paid attention to perfumes and scents. "Every man and woman had regard for perfumery. When a young man or woman went out, you could smell him or her quite a way off" (Wilson 1910a:299).

There were two ways of getting married. One was casual. "A young woman met a young man evenings and talked with him; and sometimes in a short time, sometimes in several months, they went off together and were considered married." But the other way was formal and ceremonial. Like many other social interactions, it included a symbolic exchange of goods.

COSMETIC KIT
Hidatsa/Mandan
Collected by Gilbert Wilson, pre-1918?
Buckskin bag with rounded corners and flap closure; decorated with horizontal lines of wrapped purple and yellow quillwork and four metal tinklers with orange horsehair. Brush of porcupine skin mounted on a wooden handle. Checked gray and white cotton bag contains plant shavings, possibly for paint
Skin bag: H. 22 cm, W. 24 cm. Brush: L. 22 cm. Cloth bag: L. 16 cm
MHS 7059.12a, b, c

Buffalo Bird Woman described the kit carried by her second husband as being like this one. "My husband, Son of a Star, carried a small bag, with awl, scissors, and sinew thread. His paint bag he carried inside this bag" (Wilson 1914b:24). When originally accessioned, this bag also contained sinew, paint, and a mirror. Porcupine tails with the quills removed were used by both men and women to brush their hair.

PERFUME
Hidatsa
Collected by Gilbert Wilson, 1910
*About ten flowering stems of horse mint (*monarda fistulosa*), dried*
W. 10 cm
AMNH 50.1/5483

Sweetgrass was the most common form of plant used as a perfume, but there were others. "I have told you," said Buffalo Bird Woman, "how young men put braids of sweet grass on the under side of their fans. I have seen Horse Mint used for the same purpose, – bound on fans so that every wave of the fan brought some of the scent" (Wilson 1916b:208).

For this reason it was called "buying a wife." "Girls who were thus bought as wives were those who had parents to look after them," said Buffalo Bird Woman. "[They] were not foolish and nobody monkeyed with them. These were the kind of young women who were bought" (Wilson 1914b:331–32). Buffalo Bird Woman was such a young woman when she was 16.

"In our village at Like-a-Fishhook Bend there lived a Crow Indian who had a stepson named Magpie. This

Crow Indian's name was Hanging Stone or Mi-i-xḗ -xēc. . . . One morning, after breakfast, and before noon, Hanging Stone came into our lodge. He walked up to my father and put his right hand on my father's head and said:

"'I want you to believe what I say. I wish my boy to live in your good family. We are poor, but I wish you to help us and be willing to do as I ask.'

"He stepped over to each of my two mothers and did likewise, speaking the same words to each of them.

"Neither my father nor my two mothers said anything, and I did not know what all this meant. Hanging Stone did not sit down, nor did he say anything more. When he had gone my father sat for a while, facing the fire; then he said, 'My daughters are too young yet. When they are old enough for them to marry, I shall then be willing; but not now.'

"In the evening Hanging Stone and his wives and some other relatives brought four horses and three good guns to our lodge. The horses had good bridles on, with chains hanging down from the bits. Such bridles were hard to get in those days. On each horse was also a blanket and calico like a saddle. . . .

"Hanging Stone, after he had tied the horses, came into the lodge and said to my father: 'I have brought you four horses and three guns.'

"'No,' said my father, 'I am going to refuse: I do not think that my daughters are old enough to marry.'

"Hanging Stone went away but did not take back the four horses. My father, however, sent some young men to lead the horses back to Hanging Stone's home.

"Two days after this, in the evening, Hanging Stone came again to our lodge. As before, he brought

MIRROR AND PAINT BAGS
Hidatsa. Bought from Lance Owner
Collected by Gilbert Wilson, 1909
Mirror of silvered glass with decoratively etched edges, broken from a larger piece and set with five nails into a frame carved from a single piece of cottonwood. Through a hole in the handle is tied a tanned hide thong attached to two sinew-sewn hide bags holding red pigment
Mirror: H. 16.3 cm, W. 9.2 cm. Bags: L. 15 cm, W. 7.5 cm
AMNH 50.1/5409

Men and women commonly painted their faces, hands, and the parts in their hair. Although paint could be made from local materials, Buffalo Bird Woman preferred "Venetian red, that white man's paint, . . . for it washes off easily" (Wilson 1910a:297). Mirrors, also introduced by traders, made it easier to apply the paint correctly. Lance Owner said that he had had this mirror for many years (Wilson 1909a:138).

Buffalo Bird Woman commented, "I painted every morning. The reason that I painted so often was because the wind and air made our faces dark – tanned them as you would say. We Indian women painted so that our complexions would not get dark." The young men were also "rather particular about their toilet. . . . Son of a Star carried his paint in a paint bag. In olden times the husband carried a paint bag and every morning painted his face, as did his wife and children also. In those good times everybody in the village appeared with faces handsomely painted. In these days we no longer follow this custom, and, although living, we walk about with our unpainted faces looking just like ghosts" (Wilson 1914b:22–24).

four horses and the guns and gifts back to us. But two of the four horses which he had brought before he had rejected, and in their place he now brought two good hunting horses. Now hunting horses at that time were very expensive and very hard to get. A higher value was set upon them because anyone who had one of these swifter horses could easily hunt buffaloes and have lots of meat. . . .

"After Hanging Stone had gone my father said to his two wives, 'What do you think about it?'

"'We won't say anything,' they answered. 'You do as you think best.'

"'I know this young man Magpie,' my father said. 'He is a very kind young man. I have refused the gifts once, but I see that he wants my daughters very badly. I think that we had better agree.'

"Then my father said to me, 'My daughter, I have tried to raise you right. I have hunted and worked hard to give you and your younger sister food to eat. Now I want you to take my advice. You are old enough to marry: I want you to take this young man for your husband. I want you to try to love him. Don't think to yourself, "I am a pretty nice girl – and he is an old man," – do not try to make him angry.'

"I did not answer 'No' or 'Yes,' for I thought, 'If my father wishes me to do thus, why, that is the best thing for me to do.' And so I agreed to it. . . .

"My father and mothers now spent six days collecting food for a feast. . . . At the end of six days we were all ready to go to Hanging Stone's lodge. After breakfast my father took a feather war bonnet and a weasel skin cap, placing the first on my younger sister's head and the weasel skin bonnet on my own head. He took the weasel skin bonnet from his bag that hung on the wall of our earth lodge near his bed. The weasel skin cap and the feather bonnet were each of the same value, and either was worth a horse.

"We now marched to Hanging Stone's lodge. My sister and I walked together. . . . Behind us came our relatives, leading three horses. . . . Five pails of cooked food were brought by our women relatives. . . .

"Hanging Stone was sitting on his bed. I went up to the old man and took off my weasel skin cap and put it on his head. My sister took off her feather war bonnet and placed it on the head of Hanging Stone's wife.

"The man who was going to be our husband was sitting on his bed. My sister and I went over and seated ourselves on the earth floor near by. The kettles of feast foods had been set near the fireplace. . . . Magpie's

family sent his mother to notify their relatives, and the members of the husband's [clan]. This was the Awaxe ná-wa-i-ta [clan]. 'My son's marriage feast is at hand,' she said, 'and we call you to come and eat.'

"So all these invited people came and everyone of them brought a gift – a woman's skin fancy work, women's leggings, women's belts, a blanket, calico, or something else of this kind – and in the evening two women fetched home these gifts to our lodge, and piled them on the floor near my mother. . . . Red Blossom, I remember . . . distributed the gifts to our relatives who had helped us to give the feast, – to our women relatives, of course, I mean. . . .

"My sister and I ate some of the pemmican, and what was left my sister put in the fold of her robe under her left arm to take home. We rose as soon as we had eaten and went home.

"We remained at home for several days; neither I nor my sister going near Magpie. . . .

"My mother Red Blossom fixed our bridal bed, an old-fashioned one: she fixed it very nicely. She helped me to put a lazy-back before it.

"All was now ready, and my father fetched to the lodge one newly obtained horse. It was an American horse; a big horse, not a pony; a sorrel. Its name was

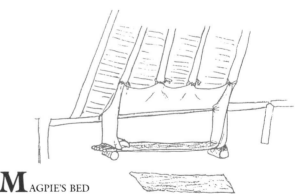

MAGPIE'S BED
Drawn by Goodbird, 1914
Pencil on paper
H. 11.5 cm, W. 15.2 cm
AMNH (Goodbird 1914b : fig. 45)
This sketch shows the corner of Hanging Stone's lodge where Magpie sat when Buffalo Bird Woman's relatives came to feast him at the time of their marriage. "When my sister and I and our mothers and our relatives went to Magpie's lodge, Bird Woman [Hanging Stone's wife] said nothing to my mothers or aunts; but to my sister and me she said, 'My granddaughters, sit there!' and she pointed to a buffalo robe lying all flat and ready, fur side up, as a place for us to sit" (Wilson 1914b : 333).

Charlie. My father had paid sixty hides for it. My father tied this horse just outdoors, to our corn stage.

"My mother Red Blossom then said to me and my sister, 'Go and call your husband. Go both of you and sit, one on his right side and the other on his left, and say "We want to call you to come to our lodge." Do not be ashamed but go boldly and never fear.'

"So my sister and I went slowly and shyly about noon to Magpie's lodge. I went ahead, my sister following. . . . Magpie was sitting on the edge of the bed. No one said anything as we entered, as is quite in keeping with Indian custom. My sister and I went over to Magpie's bed and sat down. I myself took the pillow end and my sister the foot end of the bed. Neither of us said anything.

"Magpie himself was the first to speak.

"'What have you come here for?' he asked, looking at each of us and laughing. We too smiled and laughed, hanging our heads down, and I said, 'We have come to call you.'

"'All right!' he said; and myself and sister arose and went out and returned to our lodge. I went ahead as before, and my sister followed me, although sometimes we walked together. Magpie did not go with us but followed a few minutes afterwards. . . .

"Before Magpie came, Red Blossom had talked with me. 'My daughter,' she said, 'your father has given you to this young man. A young woman should be willing always; for what her parents say, that is the right thing for a girl to do. That is the right way to be married. You should do as your father says.'

"We had cooked dried meat and bone grease and my father had instructed me to say to my husband, 'That is your horse that is outside.'

"So when Magpie came and was sitting by me eating, I said to him 'That is your horse that is tied to the corn stage outside.'

"And so Magpie came to live with us in our lodge; for such was our custom. . . . Thus I was married, and as we thought, in the proper way" (Wilson 1914b:318–29).

Wolf Chief's experiences were very different. He was as adventurous as his sister was shy. But his first sweetheart nearly broke his heart.

"It was down at Like-a-Fishhook Village, and I was 18," he said. "One morning in the latter part of June . . . I went down to the river. Goes Back to Big Bunch was just coming up the bank with a bucket of water in her right hand. There was no other girl with her, – she was alone. . . .

"I looked at Goes Back to Big Bunch and smiled. She smiled back, and kind of laughed.

"'What are you laughing at?' I asked.

"'Why do you laugh?' she answered.

"'I didn't,' I said.

"'Yes, you did,' answered the girl.

"I passed her, not trying to touch her; but I thought to myself, 'I think that girl likes me.' And it was quite a comfort to me to think I was a fine looking young man!

"I resolved to go to her lodge in the evening and try if I could 'catch her,' as we Hidatsas said.

"A little after dark I went to her lodge, and took my station in the entrance way. . . . I confess, I felt rather scared as I stood there; and my heart went beating faster. I listened with my ears, as I heard those within talking, talking. I was eager to hear that girl's voice.

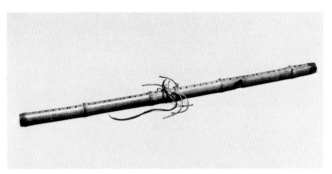

FLUTE
Tribe unknown
Collected by Gilbert Wilson, date unknown
Hollow reed with carved reed hole and burned decorations resembling stops; two fabric ribbons wrapped around center
L. 69 cm
MHS 7059.30

The flutes usually used by Plains Indian men in courting or ceremonies were really elaborate whistles, some carved in the shape of birds' heads or decorated with animal figures. The player blew air past a reed made of quill or other material, held in the sound hole with pitch. Flutes like this one were probably designed to look like flutes introduced by non-Indians, although this one works in the same way as the earlier flutes. Wolf Chief recalled that his father had had a flute made of reddish cane. "When I was twenty-three years old, my father gave me his whistle. When I was young, as I was then, and went to see a girl, I carried this whistle on my arm. Sometimes I stood on the earth lodge, all decked and painted, and having this whistle. At night I would go around blowing this whistle" (Wilson 1910a:209-10).

"At last I heard a woman's voice, calling the girl by name, say, 'Come, let us go outside. . . .'

"I shrunk back in the lodge entrance, covering my face with my robe. I feared the girl's mother . . . might scold me. The mother came out first, walking straight ahead, and not seeing me apparently, as the entrance way was quite dark. The girl followed, and they went without the porch.

"Soon they came back and the mother stopped just outside the porch; I heard her say to the girl . . .

'I am going in. When you come in also, I will bar the door.' The mother then went into the lodge, passing me but again not seeing me.

"I now ran outside myself. . . . I was so scared I could not swallow the water in my mouth. And I could not breathe regularly, – I choked up. I came close to her and she saw me. I showed my face from under my blanket. 'Why did you laugh today?' I said; that was all I could think to say.

"'I didn't laugh; you did!' she answered.

"'No, you laughed first,' I said.

"I went forward and threw my blanket about her and put my arms around her neck. She put her arms around me, over my breast. . . . So we stood there, teasing each other about which of us laughed first. Finally she said, 'My mother will be coming out if I do not go in. You come tomorrow night.'

"I put my arms around her again and kissed her when I left her. I felt as light as I could be; and I was so glad! I went home and went to bed, but I could not sleep, I was so excited.

LOVE CHARM
Hidatsa? Bought from Mike Bassett, who made it
Collected by Gilbert Wilson, 1909
Elk horn smoothed with a knife. A strip of faded beige
*   cloth is tied through two holes drilled in the base.*
*   Remnants of yellow and red paint on horn*
L. 13 cm
AMNH 50.1/5341
Certain animals like deer, elk, and antelope were believed to have the power to attract women. If a young man dreamed about such an animal he took this to mean that he should make a charm symbolic of the animal and that when he wore it, the animal would help him attract young women. Mike Bassett had a dream in which he saw a man with an elk horn ornament on his head and a long wood whistle in his hand. Bassett then duplicated the ornament and wore it in his hair. "It is a love charm," noted Wilson, "and has been quite efficacious according to its owner" (Wilson 1909a:128).

WOLF CHIEF "CATCHING" HIS FIRST SWEETHEART
Drawn by Goodbird with instructions from Wolf
*   Chief, 1915*
Black carbon and pencil on paper
H. 7.8 cm, W. 4.2 cm
MHS (Goodbird 1915:fig. 23)

"The lodge of Goes Back to Big Bunch was not far from that of my parents. Early the next morning I got up and went up on the roof. She also got up early and came out of her lodge door and looked over to where I was, and smiled. She went in again; but I felt as if I wanted to sit up there on the roof all day, and just look for her to come out again! . . .

"Evening came, and I was very eager to go to my sweetheart's lodge again. I was so eager that I got there, all dressed up, a little before dark, – as I should not have done. People passing by stared at me – anyway I felt they did. Finally it got darker, and I took my station in the entrance way. . . .

"I kept my ears open. From within the lodge I could hear a sound as if those within were eating parched corn. 'They are eating their evening meal,' I thought.

"Then someone came to the door. I looked. It was the girl, and going to her I 'caught her,' that is threw my blanket over her.

"'What have you come out for,' I said.

"'I was looking if you were around,' she answered. 'My mother is eating now, and I knew it was my only time I could come out alone.'

"We talked for quite a time and then she said, 'I must go in. My mother knows nothing of what you and I do and I am afraid she will scold me!' So I let her go, and ran away myself, very light hearted.

"I now went down to my sweetheart's lodge quite often. And I watched her lodge day and night! . . . Sometimes in the evening when I met her, we would sit on the ground near her door for a little while, – never very long, for her mother kept too sharp a watch. 'What are you doing over there? – come back!' she would sometimes call, and the girl would go, fearing a whipping.

"Mothers were afraid that a daughter might run away with a young man, and be foolish; and for this reason a mother would call a girl in, if she was meeting a young man. . . .

"All that summer I coaxed the girl to marry me. She was willing enough, but wanted me to give horses

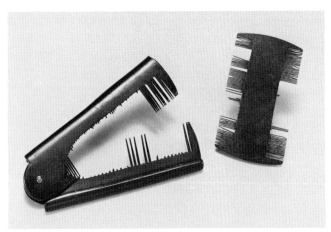

Combs
Made by I. R. Comb Co., post-1851
Excavated at Fort Berthold I
Hard, black molded rubber and copper hinge pin
Left: L. 18.1 cm, W. 2.7 cm unfolded. Right: L. 6.9 cm,
*   W. 4 cm*
SHSND 32ML2/12,711.1552, 401

Henry Boller, trader at Like-a-Fishhook Village in 1858, stocked "combs enough to clear out all the heads in the country" (Boller 1966a:157; Longfellow 1877:11). Combs were also distributed as annuity items. In February 1879, 88 fine combs and 86 coarse combs were distributed at Fort Berthold Reservation (Schindel 1879a). The comb on the right is stamped, "I.R. Comb Co. Goodyears/Patent May 5, 1851." The folding comb on the left says, "IRC Co. Goodyear 1851." The patent referred to is for the process of hardening rubber (Smith 1972:107).

Tweezers
Pre-1885?
Excavated at Like-a-Fishhook Village
Sheet iron (left) and milled sheet brass (right), bent
*   into shape*
Left: 5.6 cm, W. 1.7 cm. Right: L. 5.5 cm, W. 3.5 cm
SHSND 32ML2/12,003.1184, 1191

Tweezers were used by Indian men to pull out facial hairs. This style of metal tweezers duplicated an older form made from elk horn (Wilson 1909a:157). Most, like these, were apparently made locally from scrap metal. Another style was made from a wire coil or spring. The popularity of metal tweezers is suggested by their presence at both Fort Berthold II and at Like-a-Fishhook Village (Smith 1972:76, 152).

for her. . . . I did not want to give those horses. I was still a very young man, and was rather ashamed to give many horses for her, tho when we met we kissed, and talked a long time. I thought I could coax her to come with me without the horses. . . .

"Summer soon went, and fall came. Then I heard that Small Bull wanted to marry my sweetheart, and that her parents were willing. I heard my mother telling this to my aunt. . . .

"I never spent so long a day in my life as that day that followed my hearing this news. My body shook as I heard my mother's words, and at meal time I had no appetite and could not eat! I thought evening would never come. I was so eager to see her just once more.

"After the evening meal, about dark, I went over to her lodge, and watched, and soon she came out, and I met her. We went aside near the lodge.

"'I hear you are going to marry Small Bull!' I said. 'Is that so?'

"'Yes,' she answered, 'but it is no will of mine. My parents wish it. They have said to me, "That love-boy of yours does not want to give any horses for you. But this good young man's relatives will give four horses, two good ones, and two poor ones." So I have consented, for you would not give any horses for me!' . . .

"The next day my sweetheart was married. I saw the four horses led thru the village by Many Growths, Small Bull's mother. . . . That night I lay in my bed, and could not keep the tears from coming out upon my cheeks. I did not go to bed in the evening for a long time. . . . I went over to Hairy Coat's lodge where met the Rough Woods, and where many older men were telling stories, and listened to them a long time. I had to leave at last, and go home and to bed. . . .

"I got in my bed. I gazed up thru the smoke hole. The night was cloudy, and only a very little, dim light shone from the sky. But if my eyes were on the smoke hole, my heart was with that girl. I could see her yet, her hair yellowish, her face light. It seemed to me I was still standing with her, my blanket over her head, my arms around her neck, and her arms around my waist.

"But even after she was married, whenever by chance I met her in the village, I smiled at her; and as she always smiled back at me, I knew that she still thought of me. . . .

"About a year after her marriage, it happened one day that she was going out to her garden. . . . I determined to meet that girl once more; and in about half an hour I went over to the woods near the garden. . . . At last I saw her look my way; and I held up my hand palm out and called softly, 'Come!' . . .

"Pretty soon Goes Back to Big Bunch left her work and went to the woods . . . where I was. I put my arms around her and kissed her and said, 'I have been lonesome all the fall and winter!'

"'That also has been true of me,' she answered. 'I did not like that young man, my husband, but my parents compelled me to marry him!'

"'Well,' I said, 'let us hide. We can run away and go to my lodge and be married.'

"'All right,' she said, 'I am willing.'

"'Then,' I said, 'if you are willing, let me use you now; and it will be for a sign that you care for me.'

"'I am afraid you want to deceive me,' she said.

"'No,' I answered, 'I only want a sign that you are in earnest.'

"So I pushed her over and used her like a wife. . . .

"But I never married her. I just fooled her with my words.

"I never 'caught her' again. But I had used her, and so had gotten pay for the tears I had dropped" (Wilson 1915b:398–410).

Wolf Chief never lost his appetite for flirtation. By the end of his life, he had had 26 wives (Wilson 1915b:410). Buffalo Bird Woman, on the other hand, stayed with her first husband, Magpie, for 13 years until his death of tuberculosis. "I remained a widow the next summer and winter following," she said; but all that time she knew that a brave young Mandan named Son of a Star was interested in her. "Every time I saw him, he smiled and looked at me with a pleasant face and one night he tried to catch me; but I ran away." But Son of a Star was persistent, and at last caught her. "I am going to marry you!" he told her; "My people have put up four horses for me."

"I told my mothers and my father," said Buffalo Bird Woman, "and they agreed with me, for the four horses; so I married this second time" (Wilson 1914b:396, 399). The marriage lasted the rest of her life.

Rings

Pre-1885?
Excavated at Like-a-Fishhook Village
Brass and copper
D. 1.8 to 2.2 cm
SHSND 32ML2/12003.1470,
*   unnumbered, 1761, 2584*

Rings were worn by men, women, and children. Often several were worn on each hand. Wolf Chief wore "3 or 4 brass ring[s] on fingers of both hands" when he started to attend school (Wilson 1916c:67). When he posed for photographer O. S. Goff in 1879, he wore a ring on every finger.

Wolf Chief

Photographed by O. S. Goff, 1879
From a stereoscopic view card
SHSND Col. 88-20

Wolf Chief described how he dressed when he first went courting: "I was a fine looking young man. I wore a switch in my hair. I painted my face red and I had a bead necklace with round shells hanging down on my breast. I also wore brass armlets, and had a shirt of white sheeting with the edges all trimmed with red cloth where it opened at the neck, and . . . red fringe hanging down. I had leggings of blue black cloth, and a blue blanket. But my moccasins were plain" (Wilson 1915b:398). He was thirty years old when this photograph was taken.

Detail of arm bands, p. 115

ARM BANDS
Pre-1885?
Excavated at Like-a-Fishhook Village
Left: iron band with eight horizontal
   ridges around circumference and
   hatchmarks on one rim. Middle:
   brass with seven horizontal ridges.
   Right: corrugated sheet copper
Left to right: D. 6 cm, 7.2 cm, 5.3
   cm
SHSND 32ML2/12,003.1759, 1290,
   1450

Both beaded and metal arm bands were
popular with young men who wanted
to look their best to impress young
women. Silver arm bands were also
worn by men who danced at powwows
in the 1980s.

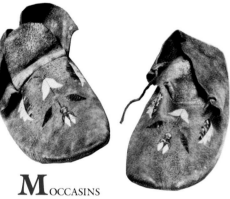

MOCCASINS
Northern Plains
Collected by Frederick Wilson, pre-1918?
Uppers of a single piece of tanned hide with separate sinew-
   sewn tongue and hard soles. Pink, purple, orange, and
   green floral quillwork on the vamp. Tanned hide ties
   attached to cuff of one moccasin
L. 24 cm, W. 10 cm
MHS 9598.27d

Plains Indian moccasins, especially those preserved in museum
collections, were often elaborately decorated with quills or
beadwork. Bodmer's paintings of Mandan and Hidatsa men
also show them wearing highly decorated moccasins (Bodmer
1984:299, 300, 306-8, 315-18), but Wolf Chief recalled that
his moccasins were often plain (Wilson 1915b:398). Floral
quillwork was common among Northern Plains tribes. The
Wilsons collected several examples from the Hidatsa.

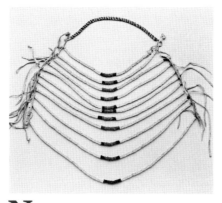

NECKLACE
Northern Plains style
Collected by Harold W. Case
Ten tiered strands composed of a
   fabric cord wrapped with white,
   red, and blue glass seed beads
   strung on a thread. On sides, the
   strands are attached to vertical
   rawhide strips by tanned hide cords
   which form a fringe. Half of the
   neck cord is composed of yellow and
   blue seed beads
L. 60 cm, W. 24 cm
University of Colorado Museum at
   Boulder 33257

This type of necklace, sometimes known
as a "Crow necklace," was popular dress
attire for men throughout the Northern
Plains in the late 19th century (Ewers et
al. 1985:145). The collector of this
necklace was a Congregational
missionary at Fort Berthold Reservation.

BLANKET
Made c. 1898
Blue-grey wool with single dark blue
   stripe at each end and frayed edges
L. 200 cm, W. 166 cm
MHS 64.98.1, Marion Klosterman

Blankets superceded the buffalo robe as
standard outerwear. In the late 1870s,
"Mackinac" blankets colored black,
white, red, blue, and green were
stocked by traders and distributed as
gifts and annuities by the agent
(Longfellow 1877:12, 17; USOIA
1878:348). Red, white, or blue were
the preferred colors. Worn-out blankets
were often cut up for other uses and
very small fragments were used as
decoration on dresses, coats, leggings,
and other items.

   This army issue blanket of the
1884 pattern is the kind of military
surplus item often distributed to Indian
tribes. On at least one occasion Wolf
Chief noted wearing "all-wool soldiers'
blankets instead of robes" (Wilson
1915a:121).

Buying knowledge

After Buffalo Bird Woman was married, her father gave her some advice. "My daughter," he said, "you are married, you must stay home and try to be a good worker; you will sometimes not want to do your work; you will think it is too hard but stand up, go forward and see if you can not do it any way" (Wilson 1915b:439).

Buffalo Bird Woman never disappointed her father. In fact, she was ambitious to achieve more than the honor connected to household chores. She wanted to become a skilled craftswoman.

Among the Hidatsa, there were two kinds of knowledge: ordinary hearsay knowledge and ancient or sacred knowledge (Wilson 1910a:254). The latter could not be passed along casually; it had to be purchased from a teacher. Many skilled crafts were sacred knowledge. "If one did it [a craft] who had no right he or some of his friends would get hurt," said Buffalo Bird Woman (Wilson 1908b:123).

Among the sacred crafts were basketmaking, pottery making, tipi making, and house construction. Buffalo Bird Woman purchased the rights to all but pottery. She was proudest of her right to construct houses, which earned her great respect. "Not many women in the village had the sacred right to trim the four big posts and beams. My mother Red Blossom was one. Has Much Sweet Grass was another. Sage was a third. . . . My right to superintend the raising [of the house] was a gift from my mother, who got the right from an old woman. I gave my mother a whole suit for the right. Every body knew this & I could refuse none. I got many robes thus" (Wilson 1914b:379, 1908a:23).

Buffalo Bird Woman also learned crafts, like mat weaving, that were not sacred but merely difficult. "Any one who wanted to learn could go to a mat maker and learn," she said, "but it was not easy work, and not very many cared" (Wilson 1910a:307, 311). An industrious mat maker could trade mats for other valuable things, but she could never sell the knowledge, for people did not respect it in the same way. Even prices depended not so much on difficulty of the work as on sacredness. "When one came to do a sacred thing, he got of course a good price," Wolf Chief said. "When my sister Buffalo Bird Woman was called in to put up the four central posts of an earth lodge, or to cut the skins for a tent cover, and prayed, then she got a good price" (Wilson 1911:348). But her mat weaving skills became so rusty that she scarcely remembered them by 1910 (Wilson 1910a:312).

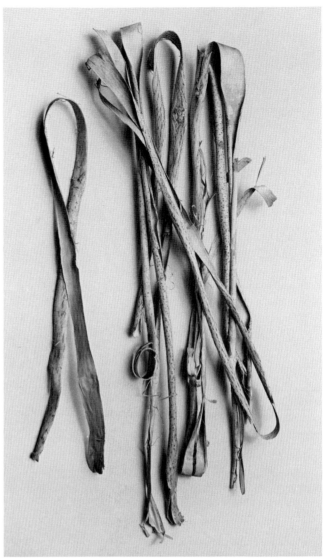

BARK
Hidatsa. Made by Buffalo Bird Woman
Collected by Gilbert Wilson, 1908
Bark from peach-leaved willow (Salix amygdaloides
Anders), dried and cut into strips
Average L. 140 cm
AMNH 50/7098c

"Baskets are usually made of two kinds of bark," explained Buffalo Bird Woman, "box elder and maxoxica willow. The box elder bark is of a very light yellow, almost white, but the maxoxica willow bark was dyed black. This bark is yellowish-brown before being dyed. . . .

"Maxoxica willow bark is tough and strong. Box elder bark is softer and works easier. We used, and indeed now use, box elder bark on the sides of the basket, but for the bottom of the basket we used the stronger willow bark, for which reason the bottom of a Hidatsa basket is usually black" (Wilson 1916b:253-55).

Buffalo Bird Woman demonstrated the process of stripping, soaking, cutting, and dyeing the bark for Wilson (MHS photos III-19 to III-32). These samples show the willow bark before being dyed.

BASKET FRAME
Hidatsa. Made by Buffalo Bird Woman
Collected by Gilbert Wilson, 1908
Willow saplings stripped of bark, bent, and tied into place
with sinew and tanned hide strips
H. 28 cm, D. 29.5 cm
AMNH 50/7096

Making a frame was the first step in basket construction. "Basket frames were made as I have said of maxoxica willow and also of the trunks of young diamond willows or midáhátsi popokci," Buffalo Bird Woman said (Wilson 1916b:253). This unfinished frame was probably made to demonstrate the process for Wilson (AMNH photos 286337 to 286349; MHS photos V-56-1912 to V-59-1912).

BASKET
Hidatsa. Made by Buffalo Bird Woman
Collected by Frederick Wilson, 1912
Willow wood frame; box elder and willow bark strips
woven in a diamond pattern; tanned hide carrying
strap attached to frame
H. 37.6 cm, D. 37 cm
MHS 9598.17

Buffalo Bird Woman taught Frederick Wilson how to make baskets and he recorded the process. Later, under her guidance, he attempted to duplicate the procedure (MHS 9598.18). "Basket makers would not let others see how they worked," Buffalo Bird Woman explained, "because if another wanted to learn how to make baskets she should pay a good price for being taught. All basket makers did thus. They would not teach another how to make baskets without being paid. Another reason why I did not want people to watch me at my work was because they asked me questions. These questions would bother me so that I was apt to make a mistake with the splints; so that I did not like to have people around when I worked. . . .

"When I was working at making a basket and some one hung around and watched me in order to learn how I did it, I would work so fast that she could not see how it was done, because I didn't want her to learn.

"That is why there are so few basket makers on the reservation. They do not want to pay to learn and we do not want to teach them when they don't want to pay for it" (Wilson 1912:242; MHS photos V-56-1912 to V-59-1912).

Mat

Hidatsa. Made by Buffalo Bird Woman
Collected by Gilbert Wilson, 1910
Rushes with rawhide warp
L. 214 cm, W. 73.5 cm
AMNH 50.1/5505

Rush mats were used on the floor of the earth lodge. Buffalo
Bird Woman described the uses of mats and made one for
Gilbert Wilson while he photographed the process (MHS
IV-56-1910 to IV-61-1910, VIII-44-1916 to VIII-55-1916).
"We learned to make rush mats from Arikaras. They had
learned it from the Pawnees. Our tribe had learned the art
long before my life time. I do not know how long ago it was
when the art of making mats was taught to our tribe. I began
making mats when I was twenty years old [c. 1859].

"The Hidatsa and Mandans no longer make these mats,
and the art is almost forgotten. I do not think we have made
mats for forty years. . . .

"In any lodge there would be one or two rush
mats. . . . Mats were never hung up on the wall, they were
always laid on the floor.

"Our moccasins had smooth soles and did not injure
the mats when we walked over them. We left the mat on the
floor all the time. We moved it a little when we swept"
(Wilson 1910a: 307-9).

Buffalo Bird Woman was at first reluctant to make this
mat because she had nearly forgotten the process. She noted
that the rushes she used were too green and might not last
(Wilson 1910a: 311).

Pottery Vessel and Tool

Mandan. Bought from Hides and Eats, who made them
Collected by Gilbert Wilson, 1910
Pot of fired brown clay with incised marks on rim; tool of
**   cottonwood bark**
Pot: H. 14.5 cm, D. 16 cm. Tool: L. 13 cm
AMNH 50.1/5510a-c

Hides and Eats, a Sioux woman captured and adopted by the
Mandans as a little girl, was one of the few women at Fort
Berthold Reservation who still knew how to make clay pots in
the early 1900s. The clay, tempered with crushed rock, was
formed into the desired shape and then hammered with a
wooden paddle to firm and thin the walls. For firing, the pots
were covered with coals made by burning dry bark; then they
were coated with liquid made from boiling pounded corn.
According to Buffalo Bird Woman, the best pots were those
with the thinnest walls because they lasted the longest (Wilson
1910a: 272-82). By the time Wilson visited the reservation,
no women were able to make the large, very thin-walled pots
used in the 19th century, and so Wilson's collections include
only small ones.

Hides and Eats told Wilson, who had hired her to
make this pot while he recorded the process, "This is the first
time I ever made a clay pot in the house. Those that taught
me gave me this rule, that I work away from others. I only
get pay here from these white men; yet as I work, many
people come in and watch. For that reason I have always
gone among the hills when I work" (Wilson 1910a: 286;
MHS photos IV-42 to IV-44, IV-67-1911, IV-68-1911).

POTTERY PADDLE
Hidatsa
Collected by Gilbert Wilson, pre-1918?
Cottonwood bark with 13 horizontal
  grooves cut in paddle surface
L. 25.4 cm, W. 4.3 cm
MHS 7059.123

Cottonwood paddles with grooves or cross hatches were used to beat the walls of pottery vessels to make them thin and strong. The designs on the paddle were impressed into the clay, where they might be left as decoration or smoothed off. Buffalo Bird Woman explained, "The beater was cut (on the side of the bark that is nearest the wood of the tree) in grooves that the rough surface might further knead the moist clay when beating it. . . . This beating of the sides of the pot was important because by it the pot was beaten to a desirable thickness and the clay was also made firmer" (Wilson 1910a:276).

Wilson collected pottery paddles with grooves running both vertically (AMNH 50.1/5493) and horizontally.

ROBE
Hidatsa. Made by Buffalo Bird Woman with help from Goodbird and
  William Hale
Collected by Gilbert Wilson, 1911
Cowhide painted in red and black
L. 132 cm, W. 135 cm
AMNH 50.1/6013

Buffalo Bird Woman decorated this robe with a design used by her mother. She worked the pattern out on a board and then Goodbird and William Hale painted it on the robe (Wilson 1911:1, 3). These robes with geometric designs were worn by women of most of the Northern Plains tribes. Wilson photographed both the process and several people modeling the completed robe (MHS photos IV-76-1911 to IV-85-1911).

STANDS FOR POTTERY VESSELS
Hidatsa/Mandan style
Collected by Gilbert Wilson, pre-1918?
Willow twigs wrapped with willow
  bark
Left: D. 16.5 cm. Right: D. 14.5 cm
MHS 7059.122a, b

"When putting [a pot] on the fire," said Buffalo Bird Woman, "the woman would work a hole in the ashes to fit the bottom of the pot, so that there was no danger of the pot falling over. When her pots were not in use she would set them aside in bark ringlets" (Wilson 1910a:282).

Building an Earth Lodge

Drawn by Goodbird with instructions from Buffalo Bird Woman, 1914
Pencil on paper
Upper left to lower right: H. 12.4 cm, W. 15 cm; H. 15.6 cm, W. 16.5 cm; H. 10.7 cm, W. 12.5 cm; H. 9.3 cm, W. 15.8 cm
AMNH (Goodbird 1914b:figs. 61, 66, 70, and 80)

House building was heavy work that took many laborers, yet certain parts of the job could only be done by a woman who had purchased the right. In her role as house builder, Buffalo Bird Woman did all the measuring and planning, supervised the work, and cut the notches where beams had to fit together. This series of drawings illustrates various aspects of the job.

The women selected, cut, and hauled the lumber for making the lodge (above). It took up to four women to carry the big central beams, but the shorter beams and rafters could be carried by one woman, either with a burden strap or on her back, as shown here. "We were about three days bringing in the timbers that were to make the lodge," Buffalo Bird Woman said in describing the construction of a smaller winter lodge, "but we also did other work in these three days. We also cleared off the piece of ground that was to be the site of our lodge" (Wilson 1914b:377).

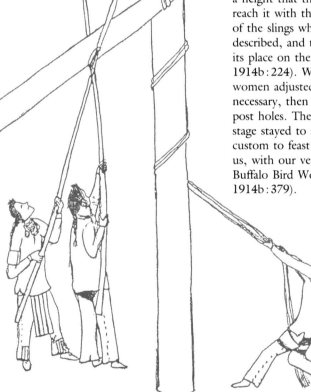

The raising of the tall central posts was done by a group of men (below). The women had already measured and notched the posts and dug the post holes. The men erected the uprights, wedging them temporarily in place. They then "used slings made of two poles, crossed, and with the ends united by a short thong, to raise the beams. A rope or lariat was tied to one end of the beam; the free end of the rope was now thrown over the fork of a post and one or two men pulled at the rope, while the others lifted at the beam. When the end was raised to such a height that the men could no longer reach it with their hands they made use of the slings which I have just described, and the beam was pushed to its place on the posts" (Wilson 1914b:224). With the beams raised, the women adjusted the uprights as necessary, then filled in and packed the post holes. The men who helped at this stage stayed to supper: "It was our custom to feast those who thus helped us, with our very best foods," said Buffalo Bird Woman (Wilson 1914b:379).

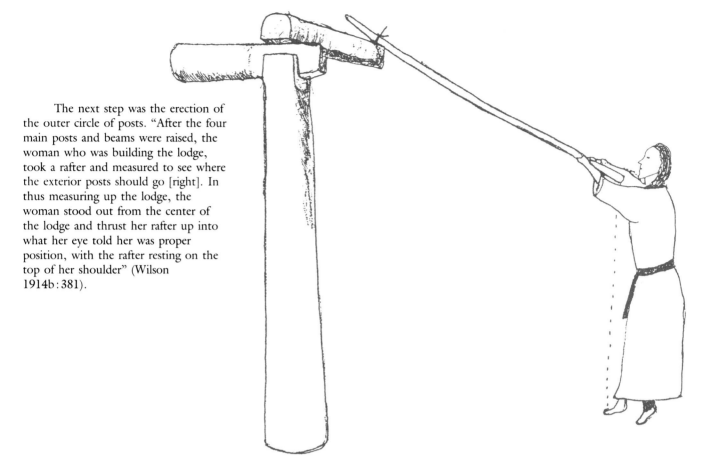

The next step was the erection of the outer circle of posts. "After the four main posts and beams were raised, the woman who was building the lodge, took a rafter and measured to see where the exterior posts should go [right]. In thus measuring up the lodge, the woman stood out from the center of the lodge and thrust her rafter up into what her eye told her was proper position, with the rafter resting on the top of her shoulder" (Wilson 1914b:381).

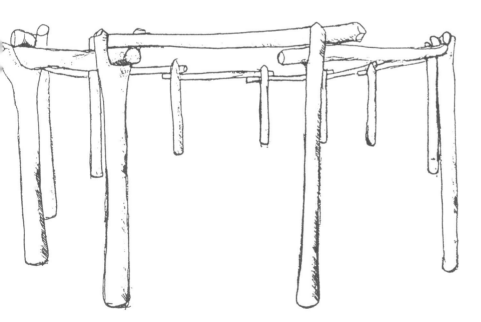

"Measurements being all made, and places marked by the woman's heel so no mistake could be made, the holes were dug for the exterior posts and they were raised in place and the stringers or beams laid on them [left]" (Wilson 1914b:384). For simplicity, Goodbird left the four central posts out of this sketch. It depicts the construction of a winter lodge; in a summer lodge the uprights were trimmed off at the top instead of forked (Wilson 1908b:15).

With the frame up, the rafters were measured, cut, and laid; then the house was walled with poles or puncheons and roofed with willow, grass, and earth (Wilson 1914b:385-87). "These were our old houses," Buffalo Bird Woman said. "When we used them we were healthy and there were many children and old people" (Wilson 1908a:17).

The birth of Goodbird

Buffalo Bird Woman was 30 years old in 1869 when her first and only child was born. It was the autumn of the year after she married Son of a Star, the season when the tribe usually moved into a winter village. But not this year. "For seven years we people at Like-a-Fishhook Village had seen no buffalo herds," she said, "but we had heard that there were some far up the Missouri River, so the whole village, Mandans and Hidatsas both, made ready to start." Buffalo Bird Woman then knew that her child would be born in what is now Montana, far from Like-a-Fishhook (Wilson 1913b:514, 1910a:244).

"Birth was always considered to be a serious thing by us," said Wolf Chief. "An expectant mother commonly asked a sacred society to pray that the child might be born right; and if this event came as desired, the reward promised to the society was always given. Either a women's or a men's society might be asked to pray thus" (Wilson 1914b:164).

"When a birth was expected," said Buffalo Bird Woman, "we of course got ready for it in the earth lodge. Two sticks or posts were driven into the earth floor, about three feet high and about two and a half feet apart, at the place the bed was to be. This bed we made of dry grass which we fetched in for the purpose and covered with a buffalo robe. The bed was four or six inches thick and the woman knelt on it, grasping the two posts in her hands; she did this to support herself. . . .

"There were women in the tribe that acted as midwives. When a woman knew she was to be a mother, she notified one of these midwives when to expect to be called. When the pains began, the midwife was summoned and hurried to the scene. . . . There might also be a medicine man present, for if the family could, they often sent for one. This medicine man sang mystery songs, and might even give medicine to the woman in labor. Songs and medicine were both designed to influence a normal birth. The medicine man bought the right to his profession, from others who owned it. There were several *ceremonies* that we believed aided women in labor, the River ceremony, the Corn ceremony, the Buffaloes' ceremony, the Wolves' ceremony, were among these.

"Those present at the birth talked only in whispers and everything was kept as quiet as possible. Quiet was also enjoined for ten days after the birth" (Wilson 1910a:245–47).

Despite all precautions, Buffalo Bird Woman knew that "Accidents sometimes happened at birth. . . . If the mother died at birth-bed, some relative who happened to be suckling a babe, took the little orphan" (Wilson 1910a:244, 247).

But she had good cause to be confident. Her mother, Strikes Many Women, was owner of the River Ceremony, and her father, Small Ankle, owned a sacred bundle with more than ordinary supernatural power.

The birth came during the journey west. The tribe had camped for the night on a sandbar by the confluence of the Yellowstone and Missouri rivers. "I remember that the moon was in the last quarter . . . a thin half circle, shaped like a bow. . . . It was known to everyone in the tent that I was to give birth to a child, so all went away to neighbors, except myself, my father Small Ankle, and Strikes Many Women. My husband Son of a Star went to stay with his brother Red Stone. The moon came up and the child was born a little before sun up.

"Son of a Star, my husband, was in a tent near by, and heard the cry of the child. Afterwards he said to me, 'I was very happy when I heard the cry of the babe'" (Wilson 1913b:529).

The next morning the tribe went on to cross the ice-clogged Missouri. "Our family crossed in the bull

"JUNCTION OF THE YELLOWSTONE AND THE MISSOURI"
Based on a watercolor by Karl Bodmer, 1833
Copper plate engraving on paper
H. 30.3 cm, W. 43.2 cm
MHS (Wied 1840–43:tableau 29)
The spot where Goodbird was born looked like this thirty-six years prior to that event. The extensive sandbars where the tribe camped can be seen in the background.

boat that belonged to Small Ankle, and which we had fetched along. My husband Son of a Star helped me in the crossing. . . . Usually a bull boat was paddled by a woman, but in this case my husband paddled while I held our babe" (Wilson 1913b:533-34, 1913a:1).

Ten days later, the new baby was named. "A child's name was given him as a kind of prayer," Buffalo Bird Woman said (Maxidiwiac 1921:8). Normally, a family called in "some older person, a friend of the family or a Medicine Man, or someone that we

esteemed" to name the child in exchange for a gift. In this case, there was no one the family esteemed more than the baby's grandfather. Small Ankle took the baby in his arms and said, "His name shall be Tsakáka-sakis." It meant good bird (Wilson 1913b:584).

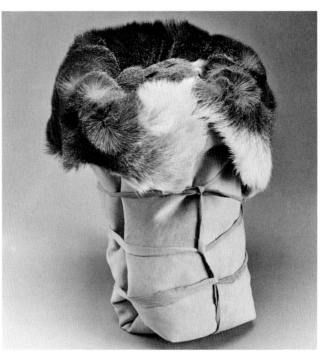

CRADLE BUNDLE
Reproduction, 1986
Tanned deer hide folded and tied with tanned hide strips
H. 53 cm, D. 36 cm

Buffalo Bird Woman described how a baby was wrapped in its cradle bundle. "A finely dressed buffalo calf skin was first laid down on the floor, fur up. The skin was so laid that the head of the skin would be at the babe's feet. Over this first skin would be laid a second, of like size, but an older or less valuable skin than the first one; it also lay fur up." Warmed sand was then placed in the bottom of another skin that had been folded and sewn to form a sack. "The babe was now laid on its back and a small skin, for breech clout, was passed between the legs, and its ends drawn up and made to rest on the stomach and back, respectively. A broad band, with the fur side next the skin, was passed under the babe's arms and around the babe's body. This band was never absent. . . . The babe being now wrapped with the band and his buttocks protected with clout or cattail down, he was dropped into the sack with his feet resting on [a] small skin that covered the warm sand. The sack, enclosing the babe, was then laid down on the two calf robes or skins . . . and these robes were folded. . . . Last of all the binding thong was passed around the bundle" (Wilson 1910a:250-53; Goodbird 1913:fig. 100).

MIDWIFE'S MEDICINE
Mandan/Hidatsa
Collected by Robert H. Lowie, 1910
Outer wrapping of red and white printed fabric; inside is
***   a rattlesnake neckbone wrapped in striped cloth***
Outer wrapping: L. 24 cm, W. 18 cm. Neckbone: L. 3.7
***   cm, W. 2 cm***
AMNH 50.1/4308

Plains Indians believed that snakes and other animals had the ability to cure diseases or to help people stay healthy. Among the Hidatsa, a midwife purchased both the right to practice and knowledge of the medicines from another midwife. Buffalo Bird Woman explained, "When suffering took hold on a woman and she was about to become a mother, she took medicine. She was soon delivered, without a great deal of pain. Different ones in our tribe knew different medicines that they sold to others. These medicines given a woman in labor were not always the same" (Wilson 1910a:244). Wolf Chief's mother, Strikes Many Women, owned the River Ceremonies, which gave power to officiate at births. When she died, she passed the ceremonies on to Buffalo Bird Woman (Wilson 1910a:24).

"It was a severe winter," Goodbird later explained, telling what his mother had said to him. "The weather was cold. But in spite of my youth, I was well taken care of, for my mother was a careful nurse" (Wilson 1913a:4).

The first three months of the child's life were spent tied in his cradle bundle. "Occasionally," said Buffalo Bird Woman, "in the day time the cradle wrappings were loosened to rest the child for a little time; or his arms might also be freed for a little time, and for the same purpose.

CATTAIL DOWN
Grown in Minnesota, 1986
Down: D. 15 cm. Cattails: L. 60.6 cm
Cattail down was gathered by men for insulating and diapering babies on journeys during cold weather. "One application lasted two or three days," explained Buffalo Bird Woman. "I would apply say ten cattails in the morning we started on the journey. At noon or eve the child perhaps would cry and I knew it was uncomfortable. I would open his bundle and remove the wetted part which would be made into a kind of ball, for the down would ball up with the wetting. But I would not put in any more down. But at the end of two or three days I had taken out so much of the down that I now had to replace with some more of the down.

"Cattail down was used only on journeys in cold weather. I never knew it to be used in the earth lodge where indeed it was unnecessary. Its use was essentially for warmth. . . . On such a journey, we carried along always an extra supply in a sack, in the whole heads. I would pull the down off the heads when needed" (Wilson 1916b:321–22).

"About the end of the third month a child began to sit up and move about. The cradle wrappings were now removed. . . . At night the babe was carefully wrapped about the loins and lower part of the body during this period. A discarded skin or piece of old tent cover was commonly used and a second piece was placed under the child to catch the night moistures" (Wilson 1911:189).

In the long winter nights, Buffalo Bird Woman often sang her child to sleep. "There were many such childrens' songs, so used. Often the words were improvised by the singer. A child went to bed early, soon after night fall.

"Our custom of singing every night to children made them familiar with our nursery songs, so that they did not forget them when they grew up. . . . [One] song is of two words, and we patted the child as we sang it. The words are, A-ho, i-lo, a-ho! We sang it to a droning, soft tune" (Wilson 1911:193, 192).

When spring came, the tribe gathered the hides and meat of the buffaloes they had killed and returned down the Missouri by bullboat. On the way, they nearly had a tragic accident. "When we left our winter camp in the west," recalled Buffalo Bird Woman, "grass was growing and the snow had disappeared from the ground, but now as we came down the Missouri a snow storm came up. It was terribly windy and as we rounded the bend at the Little Missouri River the water became very rough and the waves made our boats see-saw up and down, in a way that frightened us all. . . .

"The boat which my husband and myself paddled had two others in tow, each of them loaded with hides and meat, and . . . in the middle boat, the one immediately behind ours, was Flies Low, my younger brother, holding my infant son Goodbird. . . .

"Now when the storm came up we turned toward shore. . . . Suddenly, my husband stopped paddling and leaned over the side of the boat. He leaned over so far that I was nearly pitched over upon his side. A bull boat is a tub-like craft, rather clumsy, and is easily upset. . . .

"Then I saw what was the matter. My baby Goodbird had fallen into the water, and my husband had just caught him and was taking him into our boat. . . .

"I do not remember now whether Flies Low made any outcry when he dropped the infant into the river or not, but I recollect that my husband, as he leaned over the boat, cried out, 'He has dropped the child!'

"'I-ná!' I cried, an exclamation of alarm. But I had enough presence of mind not to drop my paddle. We could not have gotten to shore without our paddles. . . .

"Goodbird was crying lustily when we drew him out of the water but was not choking or strangling. I do not think that his face got into the water at all. . . .

"We came to shore without any further mishap and camped there in two tents. A wet rain began to fall. . . . I did not scold Flies Low. 'I am not to blame,' he said. 'I tried to hold the baby but that boat seemed to turn up side down and the baby fell out of my arms.'

"We knew this was true, so we said no unkind words to him" (Wilson 1913b:589-92).

As a boy, Goodbird sometimes proved hard to handle. When he was little, it was enough to frighten him with tales of the owl who carried off bad children. But even when he grew older, his mother was gentle with him. "A boy that was punished too often was apt to get reckless and not listen to his parents. But that was not a good way to train a child. It was better to talk with him and be patient, and tell him to be

good. . . . But if a boy was persistently bad to his parents or made himself objectionable, crying all the time and refusing to stop, because he wanted something; or if the child was obdurate or disobeyed or got saucy, the parents might call in one of the same [clan] and say, 'Brother, take your bad [clan] brother down to the river and throw him in!'

"This the other would pretend to do, frightening the child who would cry out, 'Don't, I will be good!'" (Wilson 1911:201-2).

The clan relation who took on much of the responsibility for disciplining Goodbird was Flies Low. Later, Goodbird remembered clearly how his uncle got his attention. "Once, in the winter time, I was quite peevish, and fought my mother, striking her with my hand and weeping and stubbornly refusing to be quiet. At last my mother cried, 'Apatíp' – 'Dip in water!' My mother's brother, Flies Low, answered, 'All right,' and picked me up with my legs over his shoulder and thrust me, head and shoulder, into a pail of water. I broke away from him screaming, but he caught me and put me in again. The water choked me and I came up gasping, thinking I was going to die. My mother and

BUFFALO BIRD WOMAN AND SON OF A STAR IN A BULLBOAT
Drawn by Goodbird, 1914
Pencil on paper
H. 13.4 cm, W. 22.7 cm
AMNH (Goodbird 1914b:fig. 37)
After the accident in which the infant Goodbird nearly drowned, Buffalo Bird Woman's family stopped to hunt buffalo and rearrange their boats. Goodbird drew this sketch to show how they continued on down the river (Wilson 1914b:16, 1924:254).

father and Wolf Chief were looking on. 'Stop crying,' cried Flies Low. I did so, fearing to be ducked again, and he let me go. My mother took me and said, 'My son, stop crying. If you are bad, I will call your brother again,' and she put me to bed" (Wilson 1913a:18-19).

Like all parents, Goodbird's mother and father had many ambitions for their child. Son of a Star, whose bravery in war had won him many honors, hoped some day to see his son follow in his footsteps. "My father was an experienced warrior," Goodbird said. "[He] had a fine eagle-feather war bonnet. This he kept hanging up in his lodge. 'If enemies come against our village,' he said, 'my son shall have this bonnet to wear when he goes out against them'" (Wilson 1913a:38-39).

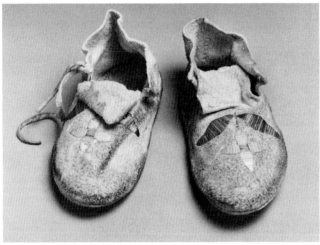

CHILD'S MOCCASINS
Mandan/Hidatsa
Collected by Gilbert Wilson, pre-1918?
Tanned hide uppers decorated with pink and green floral
  quillwork. Hard soles and separate tongue sewn on with
  sinew
L. 12 cm, W. 5.5 cm
MHS 7059.6c, d
Children did not begin to wear clothing regularly until they were three or four years of age, but all children were given clothing for wear on special occasions. These baby moccasins may have been such a gift. "At the end of the first year," Buffalo Bird Woman recalled, "a little girl had moccasins and woman's leggings added to her dress. A great deal of pride was often shown in the workmanship of the leggings and moccasins. The moccasins had each one stripe of quill work down the upper and the leggings had a horizontal strip running around them. Only the better families did this, however, owing to the expense" (Wilson 1911:189-90).

But the enemies Goodbird was destined to face were far different from those Son of a Star foresaw. The boy would never wear the war bonnet in battle. His honors were to be won on a far different field.

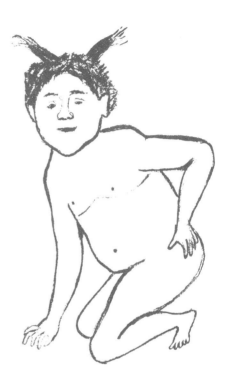

CHILD WITH OWL HAIRCUT
Drawn by Goodbird, 1914
Pencil and watercolor on paper H. 8.5 cm, W. 6.3 cm
AMNH (Goodbird 1914b:fig. 17)
"When a child, boy or girl, was two years old," said Buffalo Bird Woman, "we cut the hair off short, leaving only a tuft of hair on either side of the head like the horns of an owl." Thousands of years ago, she explained, an owl had told the people to do this, saying, "This you shall do so that they may look like owls, and I will make your children grow up strong and healthy. Also when a child of this age gets foolish and weeps, the mother must say, 'The owl will come and get you!' This will frighten the child and he will stop being foolish and will obey you!" (Wilson 1911:191).

Buffalo Bird Woman followed this advice. Goodbird testified, "I was afraid of owls. Someone in the lodge might cry out, 'The owl is coming,' and another would say, 'hun, hun,' and when I heard this I would be afraid and would hide under my grandfather's robe, which I pulled over my face as I clung to him" (Wilson 1913a:17).

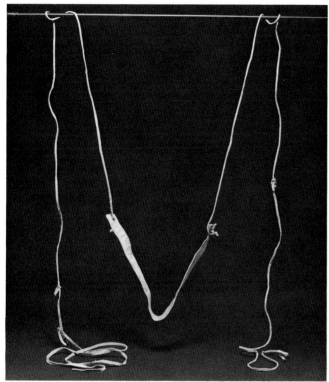

CARRYING-STRAP SWING
Mandan/Hidatsa. Bought from Little Bear's widow
Collected by Gilbert Wilson, 1909
Rawhide strap pierced at each end for attachment of two
 rawhide thongs tied to cottonwood pegs
Strap: L. 68 cm. Thongs: L. 240 cm, 312 cm
AMNH 50.1/5368

Goodbird often told how he used his mother's carrying strap
to make a swing. "The drying stage had one other use that we
children thought was pretty good. When I was a little boy I
used to love to swing under the stage on my mother's
carrying strap. A carrying strap of old style had two bands,
though later we came to use a carrying strap with only one
band, the shorter one being discarded" (Wilson 1912:202–3,
1913a:23; Goodbird 1916:fig. 20).

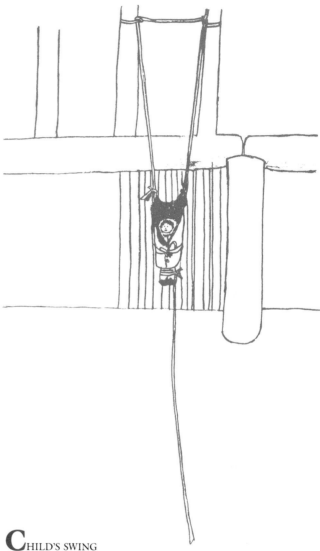

CHILD'S SWING
Drawn by Goodbird, 1916
Black carbon and pencil on paper
H. 21 cm, W. 16 cm
MHS (Goodbird 1916:fig. 47)

From the time a child was ten days old to the time it could
walk, a mother often kept it in a swing made from a buffalo
calf skin pouch, hung from the rafters of the earth lodge. A
rope tied to the bottom of the pouch "trailed to the fire
place where the mother could pull the rope and swing the
child. . . . It was like a mother's helper and took the place of
a woman caring for the baby. Every lodge where there was a
baby had one of these."

    This sketch shows the swing of White Neck, one of
Wolf Chief's children. Buffalo Bird Woman noted that "When
Goodbird was born I had one by my bed" (Wilson
1916b:145).

White men at Like-a-Fishhook

hites had lived at Like-a-Fishhook since the village was first founded. In fact, some of Wolf Chief's earliest memories were of white men. When he was a very small child his grandfather, Big Cloud, took him to visit a white man in his lodge. "Big Cloud said to me, 'Sit down!' and I did so on a board. The white man gave my grandfather some biscuits, and he also gave me a piece which I ate. I liked the biscuit and thought it was good. It was the first time I ever ate bread" (Wilson 1914b:166).

Later, other white men came to live with the tribe. Most familiar were the "Big Knives," or Frenchmen, who came from the north. "They said *sacr-r-e-e!* whenever they got angry," Wolf Chief explained wryly (Wilson 1911:87). Another nation of white men came from the east and were "quite dark, almost as dark as Indians": the Ic-pa-mi-di-ŏ-di, also known as Africans (Wilson 1914b:157). And then there were people like Wild White Man, a lone hunter so named by the Hidatsa because he seemed like an "animal that is unclaimed by any owner." He had wandered north to Like-a-Fishhook from the Black Hills and married one of Wolf Chief's relatives (Wilson 1914b:174).

"THE TRADING POST"
Painted by William de la Montagne Cary, 1870s
Oil on canvas
H. 42.5 cm, W. 46 cm
The Thomas Gilcrease Institute of American History and Art 0126.1800
The trading posts at Like-a-Fishhook were kept stocked by the periodic arrival of steamboats, at first run by the fur companies themselves, and later by independent operators (Kurz 1937:65). Steamboats also provided transportation for Indians between the villages along the Missouri and purchased cut firewood from tribal members. When artist and trader Rudolph F. Kurz arrived at Like-a-Fishhook, goods for the trading post were merely piled on the riverbank, as shown here. "Commodities consigned to this post were already disembarked when I received the message to take my luggage and go ashore. The steamer departed. I remained on guard near the wares until they were taken in a two-wheeled cart to the fort. At a little distance off, shy children peered curiously from behind piles of merchandise and made comments on the strangers" (Kurz 1937:73).

The location shown in this painting is not recorded, but the layout of the village resembles Like-a-Fishhook.

Most of the whites at Like-a-Fishhook in the early years came to trade. Such men usually obeyed the rules and customs of the community. Their square, stockaded log forts – one of which was called Fort Berthold after a St. Louis fur company manager – were always open for people to shop or just pass the time of day. They provided a market for furs, buffalo robes, wood, farm produce, and craft work. In exchange, they sold imported food, hardware, and textiles.

Starting in 1864, a new type of white man arrived: soldiers of the United States Infantry. These also were welcomed by the tribe, for their mission was to protect the village against raids by the Sioux. Hidatsa relations with the Sioux had been deteriorating for years, until by the 1860s a state of open war existed. Like-a-Fishhook was like a fortified camp under siege (Meyer 1977:107).

The soldiers stayed for three years, then moved 14 miles east to build a new fort called Fort Stevenson. They were replaced at Like-a-Fishhook by the Indian agent, who was yet another kind of white man.

None of these three types of white men thought much of the others. To Agent Samuel Latta, the traders were degenerate swindlers, and "This old American Fur Company (so called) is the most corrupt institution ever tolerated in our country." But fur trader Charles Larpenteur had no use for agents, whom he branded as lazy drunkards. "Major Latta was a pretty fair kind of a man, but the less said of him the better. He came up

OLD BLOCK HOUSE AT FORT BERTHOLD"
Photographed by O. S. Goff, 1879
From a stereoscopic view card
MHS (Wilson [1903–18]:268)
This fort on the south side of Like-a-Fishhook Village was originally called Fort Atkinson but was renamed Fort Berthold II after the first fort of that name was burned by the Sioux in 1862 (Meyer 1977:119; see also p. 11). By 1876 the blockhouse and some log cabins were all that survived of the fort; one of the rooms was used as a council room by the Indians and as a Sunday school by the missionaries (Hall 1896).

TRADERS DEPARTING FROM FT. BERTHOLD"
Painted by Rudolph Friederich Kurz, post-1851
Watercolor on paper
H. 38 cm, W. 52 cm
The Thomas Gilcrease Institute of American History and
*   Art 0226.1351*
Kurz, a romantic Swiss artist, worked as a clerk at the first Fort Berthold post in 1851, recording his impressions in numerous sketches and a journal. He found Like-a-Fishhook to be a "village of 80 clay huts surrounded by palisades and frequented by billiard players, idle lookers-on, horse traders, and Indian women engaged in daily tasks. . . . This fort, they say, is always alive with Indians, except in winter." His own accommodations in the fort were less than pleasant: "A dark room, lighted only by a tiny window, the panes of which seem never to have been washed. A large fireplace and two wooden bedsteads, which I found upon closer inspection to be inhabited by bedbugs" (Kurz 1937:73).

to Fort Union, put the annuities out on the bar, and next day was off. . . . All the Indian agents were of the same material." Colonel Philippe Régis de Trobriand, army commander at Fort Stevenson, also cared little for the agents. "The Indians . . . are pillaged, plundered, and oppressed without mercy by the government agents," he wrote (Meyer 1977:108, 119; Larpenteur 1898:418-19).

Though they disagreed about each other, these white men all assumed that they were better than the Indians. To them, there was an immense gulf between "civilized" and "uncivilized" ways of life – and civilization was, by definition, the manners and customs of Europe and European America. But, though they looked down on it, the traders and soldiers did not find it in their interest to change the Indian way of life.

FORT BERTHOLD II
Photographed by Stanley J. Morrow, c. 1870
From a stereoscopic view card
SHSND A-372

The fort, shown here from one of the two blockhouses, was the center of much mercantile and social activity. Because there were often two competing traders in the village, sellers had to get out word about their wares. "A crier used to go around the village crying, 'Buy powder! Buy powder!'" Wolf Chief said (Wilson 1915b:362). Despite this, Wolf Chief complained that "the trader didn't keep very much" in stock (Wilson 1916c:61).

FIRE STEEL (STRIKE-A-LIGHT)
Hidatsa style
Collected by Gilbert Wilson, pre-1914
Steel file reforged into oval shape,
*   with tanned hide cord attached*
L. 10 cm, W. 4.2 cm
MHS 7059.220

When matches were not available, fires were made by striking a piece of flint against a piece of steel. The spark produced was caught in a piece of dry tinder and tenderly nursed into a flame. Steels were important trade items, but they were often produced locally from metal bars or files. Buffalo Bird Woman remembered how her father carried flint and steel. "Every man had a flint case and also carried a steel made like a ring from an old file. This steel he used to make fire and for sharpening his knife also" (Wilson 1916b: 312). This artifact is nearly identical to one found in excavations at Like-a-Fishhook (SHSND 12,003.2177).

CLAY PIPE
1850s
Excavated at Fort Snelling, Minn.
White clay, molded and kiln fired;
*   broken in three pieces and mended*
L. 12 cm
MHS 310.172.7, 172, 188.1

Pipes and tobacco were common trade goods at many Missouri River trading posts, but the Hidatsa claimed not to make much use of them. Wolf Chief said that young men did not carry pipes. "The older men, however, did. We younger men did not care much for smoking. Indeed, we were afraid. In olden days young men did not smoke much. Now-a-days they smoke a great deal and burn their lungs" (Wilson 1918a: 228). Wolf Chief also recalled what happened when his father tried to smoke chewing tobacco distributed by the agent. "'I do not like this kind,' he said, 'it makes my head ache'" (Wilson 1915a: 73). Numerous fragments of factory-made clay pipes like this one were excavated at Like-a-Fishhook Village (Smith 1972: 77, 78). However, photographs taken by Wilson after 1908 show men still smoking the traditional long-stemmed pipestone pipes rather than trade pipes (MHS photo III-7).

QUILL PRESSER AND TWEEZERS
Hidatsa. Bought from Wolf Ghost
Collected by Gilbert Wilson, 1909
Quill presser of iron bar bent and
*   flattened at ends, with incised*
*   hatchmarks. Tweezers of a bent*
*   sheet-iron strip with three punched*
*   holes*
Presser: L. 19.5 cm. Tweezers: L.
*   18.5 cm*
AMNH 50.1/5419b, c

Wilson bought these items from Wolf Ghost as part of a set of tools kept in a bag made from the skin of an unborn Rocky Mountain sheep. Quill pressers or flatteners were used to smooth the quillwork after it was complete. Metal quill pressers were modeled after ones of bone or horn (Wilson 1906b: 14). Pressers were not used to flatten the quills before they were attached to the hide; a woman prepared quills for use by holding a few in her mouth and drawing them out between her teeth (Conn 1982: 138).

Tweezers made of bent metal or metal coils were used by Indian men to pull out facial hairs. Wolf Ghost kept for his own use another pair of tweezers made of brass (Wilson 1909a: 157). Similar tweezers of brass were uncovered at Like-a-Fishhook Village (Smith 1972: 76).

Sleigh Bells

Pre-1885?
Excavated at Like-a-Fishhook Village
Cast brass with incised designs; one bell has a piece of commercially tanned
  leather harness strap attached
D. 4.5 cm to 2.5 cm
SHSND 32ML2/12,003.1264, 2054, FT129, FT372, 255

Sleigh bells were, and are, worn by men dancers. When the Hidatsa bought the Grass Dance from the Devils Lake Sioux, Wolf Chief described the outfits they received (Wilson 1914b:83). "The outfits consisted of head dresses, sleigh bells for the garters, otter skins for the head, armlets of bead work, yarn belts, and the like." Wilson's photographs of dancers in 1908 and 1909 show many men with sleigh bells on their garters, belts, bandoliers, and other ornaments (MHS photos I-61, I-63, III-69).

Hawk Bells

Pre-1885?
Excavated at Like-a-Fishhook Village
Two-piece, hollow brass with loops on
  back and sound holes in front
D. 2 cm
SHSND 32ML2/12,003.unnumbered

Hawk bells and the larger sleigh bells were popular trade items. In 1858 Boller listed hawk bells in the inventory of his trading store (Boller 1966a:157). They were attached to clothing, especially dance costumes, to make a jingling sound. These three still ring.

Metal Projectile Points

Pre-1885?
Excavated at Like-a-Fishhook Village
Cut from sheet iron
L. 15.1 cm, 9 cm, and 7.7 cm
SHSND 32ML2/12,003.2178, FT284,
  1460

Metal arrow points could be purchased ready-made or fabricated from sheet metal or scrap. Even after guns were introduced, arrows tipped with metal points were preferred. Wolf Chief explained why he took bow and arrows on his first buffalo hunt in about 1866. "My father had a muzzle-loading flint lock and I had a short barreled percussion rifle and my bow and arrows. My bow was of elm wood and in my quiver were eighteen iron headed arrows and four bird arrows all with blunt heads. I hoped to kill buffalo with my bows and arrows. At this time arrows were still used; we used our guns to fight our enemies and we killed deer and antelopes also with our guns, but powder was scarce" (Wilson 1915b:376-77).

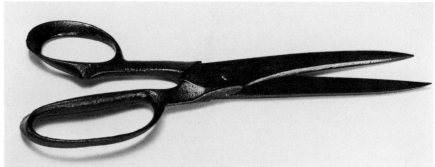

SCISSORS
Pre-1885?
Excavated at Like-a-Fishhook Village
Iron or steel; screw hinge still pivots
L. 24.7 cm
SHSND 32ML2/12,003.2269
Hidatsa women found traders' scissors useful in cutting materials for sewing, basketry, and other household tasks, as well as for cutting children's hair (Wilson 1914b:245). Buffalo Bird Woman cut her basket splints with scissors and also showed Frederick Wilson how the splints were folded, scored, and cut with a knife before scissors were available (F. Wilson 1912b:[63-64]).

BEADS
Pre-1885?
Excavated at Fort Berthold I
*Mandrel-wound, faceted, and seed
    beads of blue, red, white, and
    black glass*
D. 0.2 cm to 1.1 cm
SHSND 32ML2/12,711.112, 1607
Traders at Like-a-Fishhook carried beads of "all sizes and kinds in profusion" (Boller 1966a:157), probably including esoteric varieties called by names like pigeon egg, barleycorn, snake, and agate beads (Smith 1972:77). The large ones were used for hair ornaments and necklaces, the small "seed" beads for embroidery. Buffalo Bird Woman remembered beading a coat for her husband, Son of a Star. "My husband wanted [a coat] made for him after the pattern of the coats you saw the soldiers wear. He wanted the long kind, he said. I measured a soldier's coat that reached down to his knees and made the coat for Son of a Star. On the breast I worked bead work and put bands around the wrist. It had pockets on each side" (Wilson 1913b:480; Goodbird 1913:fig. 62).

BALE TAG
Pre-1885?
Excavated at Like-a-Fishhook Village
*Sheet brass, die-stamped with the
    number "1274" and punched at
    one corner*
2.5 cm square
SHSND 32ML2/12,003.1902
Several metal tags were found in excavations at Like-a-Fishhook, Fort Berthold I, and Fort Berthold II. They were probably attached to bales of robes shipped out by steamboat or to bundles of merchandise shipped in (Smith 1972:105, 147).

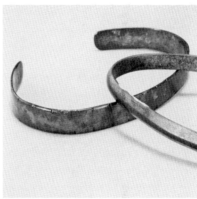

BRACELETS
Pre-1885?
Excavated at Like-a-Fishhook Village
*Left: flat brass strip decorated with
    hatchmarks. Right: brass with
    ridge down center*
D. 6.2 cm, 7.1 cm
*SHSND 32ML2/12,003.unnumbered,
    FT208*
Once the Hidatsa wore bracelets made from deer bone, but when the trader brought in metal, people learned to make bracelets by bending wire or cutting metal bands into shape. When Wolf Chief went to school he wore "brass wristlets marked with [a] knife and brass wire on my arm" (Wilson 1916c:67; Smith 1972:76).

Office of C. W. Darling,
DEALER IN
GEN'L MERCHANDISE.
Fort Berthold, D. T. May 1877
Received in apparent good condition on board the Steamer
to be delivered to the N. P. R. R. Co. at their warehouse at Bismarck D.T. the following named property

Marked	Articles	Weight
J. W. Raymond St. Paul Minn. Care Coster & Penner	24 Bales Deer Skins	Rates contract J. C. Barr
	9 " Antelope "	
	6 " Buffalo Robes	
	1 " Mountain Sheep Skin	
	1 Sack Sundry Skins	
	2 Bundles Elk Skins	
	2 Sax Beaver Skins	
	1 " Kit Fox "	
	1 " Badger	
	1 Bundle Red Fox	
	1 " Wolf Skins	
more or less	315 Cow Hides 12 calf skins	
	244 Wolf " 1 Bear "	

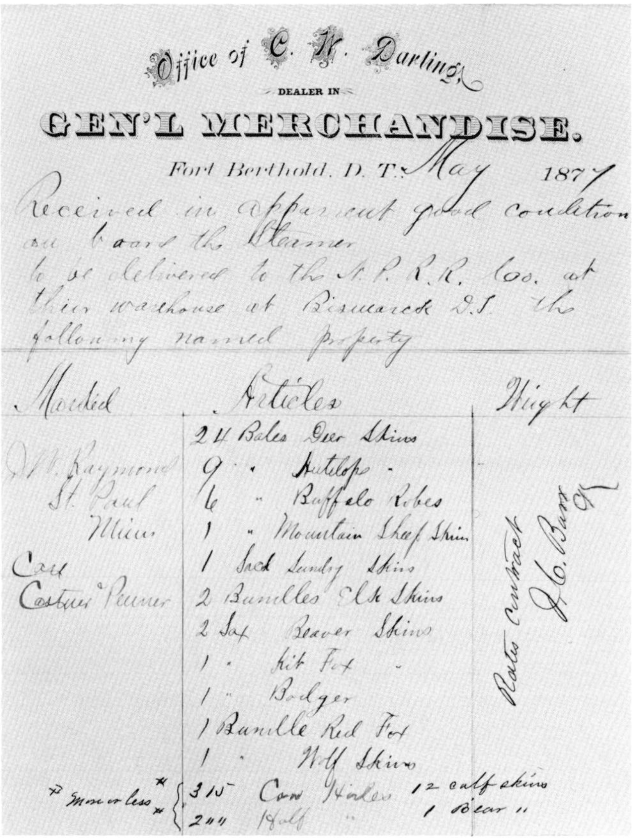

BILL OF LADING
1877
Black ink on printed stationery
L. 25.2 cm, W. 20.1 cm
SHSND (D. W. Longfellow Papers)
In the 1870s skins and furs sold to the trader by the people of Like-a-Fishhook were shipped out by steamboat to Bismarck. From there they went east via the Northern Pacific Railroad. This cargo list was probably compiled by Daniel W. Longfellow, manager of the store in 1877.

Butterfly	29 60	Howard Manlan	15 48
Black Horn	19 98	Tall Bear	16 96
Womans Ghost	27 52	Eagle	37 64
Little Bear	30 76	Lone Buffalo	27 80
Scattered Village	12 32	Big Black	24 52
Bear Chief	9 92	Siggings	17 36
Lying Down	16 00	Sitting Bull	5 92
Sick Hawk	80 76	Whistling Bear	5 96
Hawk	77 04	Hard Horn	82 68
Star	30 64	Blue Bird	38 78
Sharp Horn	33 74	Elk	19 80
Jumping Bear	4 64	Man Chief	22 74
White Man	17 43	Ree Chief	6 88
Man that pulls his hair	15 58	Little Bull	13 22
Grey Bear	[illegible] 29	Two Chiefs	6 44
Foolish Wolf	4 58	P. Beauchamp	6 04
Buffalo Paunch	14 76	White Flag	13 1[illegible]
Son of the Star Ree	6 20	Bear Wolf	6 28
Son of the Star G. V.	56 26	Bulls Head	8 28
Bad Coat	10 82	Man that looks around	11 32
Afraid to be Chief	13 38	Red Bear	15 88
Stinking Face	5 20	Two Bulls	23 16
Wolf Chief	128 36	Big Head	6 58
Strike the Enemy	22 16	Scabby Elk	4 40
Dance Flag	58 84	On the Ground Bear	7 32
Bears Eye	6 32	Yellow Horse	5 84
Crows Breast	34 56	He Hawk	5 48
Short Bull	11 32	Red Horse	7 86
Paint	15 84	Belly Up	9 21

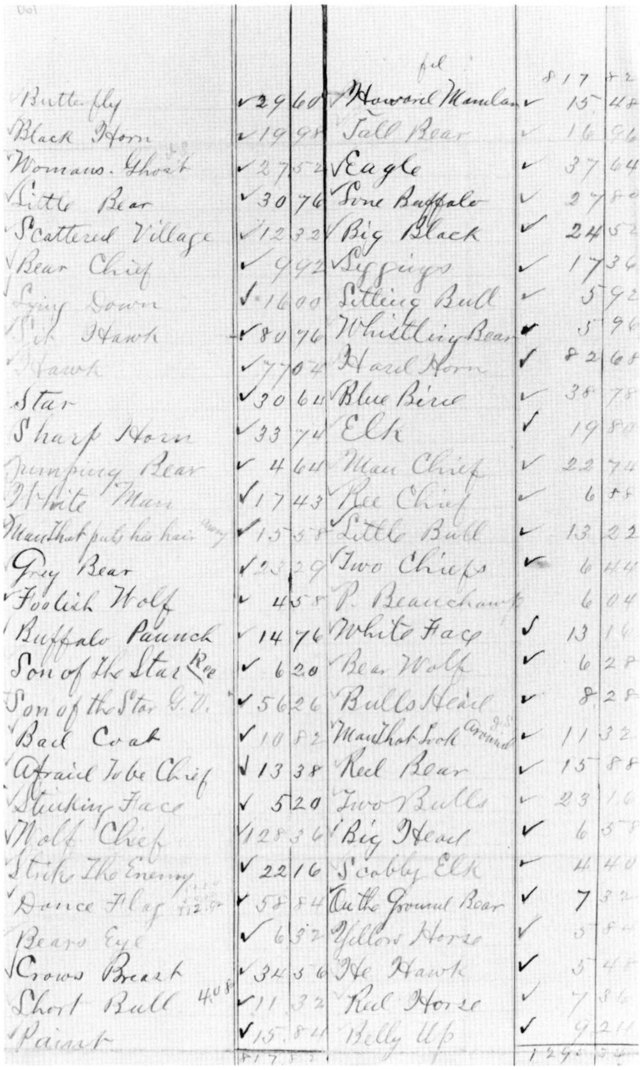

LIST OF DEBTS
Written by Daniel W. Longfellow, [1877]
Black ink on lined ledger paper
L. 31.6 cm, W. 19.4 cm
SHSND (D. W. Longfellow Papers)
Like many other 19th-century businessmen, Indian traders operated largely on a credit basis, keeping careful accounts. In 1876, when Daniel W. Longfellow arrived as manager of the store at Like-a-Fishhook, it was operated as a branch of J. W. Raymond's Bismarck store (Longfellow 1938:8). This undated manuscript is preserved in an 1876-77 collection. It lists Buffalo Bird Woman's husband as "Son of the Star G. V." (for Gros Ventre) to distinguish him from the Arikara of the same name. Wolf Chief has the largest debt on the list.

TRADER'S STORE, FT. BERTHOLD, DAKOTA TERRITORY"
Photographed by F. Jay Haynes, 1880
From a stereoscopic negative
Montana Historical Society H-346
When F. Jay Haynes, official photographer for the Northern
Pacific Railway, came through Like-a-Fishhook Village in
1880, he caught Wolf Chief standing (third from right) in
front of the trader's store. Wolf Chief later sent part of the
stereoscopic view card to the commissioner of Indian affairs,
identifying himself in the picture (Nolan 1983:12, 38; Wolf
Chief 1882a).

MILITARY COAT
Made 1861-65
Army infantry officer's nine-button frock coat made of
black wool with gilt buttons, quilted lining, and
nonregulation black velvet collar. Shoulder straps for a
captain made of gold bullion on blue wool
Coat: L. 98 cm, W. 42 cm at shoulders. Shoulder straps:
L. 11.4 cm, W. 4.6 cm
MHS 6643.1, Louie Banwart; 1985.68.167a, b
In the three years of Fort Berthold's occupation by the
military, four different units were assigned there: the Sixth
Iowa Cavalry and three separate companies of U.S. Infantry.
After 1867, two full companies of infantry manned Fort
Stevenson. They used Civil War-style uniforms like this one
until a redesign in 1872. Nevertheless, issued clothing varied
greatly from post to post in the West. At Fort Stevenson,
morale was maintained by full-dress ceremonies and daily drills
and inspections (Chappell 1972:14; Steffen 1978:color pl. 6;
Mattison 1951:71). But since much of the officers' time was
taken up supervising routine duties like "cutting of trees,
escorting of trains, making of adobe, and guarding of cattle,"
dress uniforms like this were not daily wear (Trobriand
1951:44).

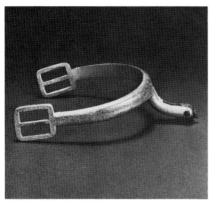

SPUR
Pre-1885?
Excavated at Like-a-Fishhook Village
Brass frame with broken iron rowel;
strap for attachment to boot
missing
L. 12.5 cm, W. 8.3 cm
SHSND 32ML2/12,003.FT149
Spurs issued to the cavalry were
strapped onto the boot. This one
resembles the standard form of spur
used from the 1850s through the 1880s
(Steffen 1978:86, 110, 183-84).

ARMY UNIFORM BUTTONS
Made by Scoville Manufacturing Co.,
Waterbury, Conn., 1854-84
Excavated at Like-a-Fishhook Village
Two-piece, dome-shaped, hollow brass
with loops on back and embossed
eagle and shield design on front
D. 2 cm
SHSND 32ML2/12,003.FT245,
FT157, FT157
The military garrisons at Forts Berthold
and Stevenson, far from their
administrative center, saw little action,
but the commanders tried to keep up
the standards of dress and armament.
These buttons are the "General Service
Pattern" used on enlisted men's
uniforms. They were worn on the
fatigue or sack coat, on overcoats, and
on various types of dress coats (Smith
1972:88).

MILITARY CARBINE
Made by Springfield Armory, 1873-76
Springfield Model 1873, .45-70
caliber "trap-door" carbine with
walnut stock, iron mountings,
cylindrical barrel, flip-up folding
rear sight, and saddle ring on left
side. An eagle is stamped on the
lock plate. Stock, breech block, rear
sight, and trigger have all been
replaced
L. 104.8 cm
MHS 72.53.2, Minnesota Veterans
Home
During the Civil War, dozens of
different makes of guns were purchased
for military use. Afterwards these guns
continued to be used, although the
Spencer repeating rifle quickly became
the favorite. In 1870, however, the
army settled on the Springfield
breechloading carbine, which, with
modifications, was the first of many
such guns to be issued during the next
twenty years. Parts from Springfield
carbines like this one were found by
archaeologists at Like-a-Fishhook Village
(Butler 1971:174-93; Smith 1959:233,
1972:81).

HORSE BIT
Pre-1885?
Excavated at Fort Berthold I
Iron curb bit with straight cheek pieces and curved port
L. 14.9 cm, W. 13.6 cm
SHSND 32ML2/12,711.1003
Like-a-Fishhook Village not only housed a company of cavalry
in 1864, but it was also on major routes to Forts Benton and
Buford in Montana (Mattison 1951:57). "Troops were
constantly traveling back and forth, sometimes in large
numbers that required great wagon trains drawn by mules," a
resident at the agency recalled (Walker 1953:39). This bit
may have been associated with the military traffic, although it
is not a typical military curb bit, most of which had double-
curved lower cheek pieces (Steffen 1978:59-60, 183).

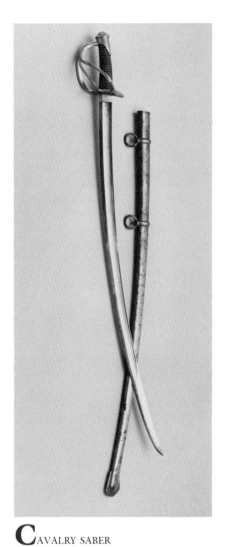

MILITARY SASH
Made in 1860s
Crimson silk net with tassels on each end
L. 139.4 cm, W. 9.2 cm
SHSND 12,051

This sash was worn by Andrew N. Canfield, first lieutenant in the 13th U.S. Infantry, stationed at Fort Berthold starting in June 1866 (Mattison 1951:56). It is the type worn by commissioned officers of most ranks and branches between 1851 and 1872. Canfield would have worn it over his frock coat and under his sword belt, wrapped twice around his waist and tied at his left hip with the tassels hanging down his left side.

CANTEEN
Made 1860s
Excavated at Like-a-Fishhook Village
Tinned sheet iron, stamped and
*   soldered into a pill shape with a*
*   pewter mouthpiece and three tinned*
*   brackets for straps added*
W. 20.5 cm, H. 22.5 cm
SHSND 32ML2/12,003.FT361

The U.S. Army experimented with several types of canteens before adopting the familiar cloth-covered tin model. This one is a style manufactured during the Civil War. It was probably originally covered with gray or blue cloth (Smith 1972:88; Steffen 1978:33, 47).

CAVALRY SABER
Made by Ames Manufacturing Co.,
*   Chicopee, Mass., 1857*
Model 1840 saber with curved, single-
*   edged steel blade, brass hilt, and*
*   grips wrapped in leather and brass*
*   wire. Iron scabbard with two*
*   suspension rings*
L. 105.5 cm
MHS 6229.3a, b, E. R. Haseltine

This saber is identical to one whose remains were excavated at Like-a-Fishhook Village (SHSND 32ML2/12,003.1418; Smith 1972:88). It belonged to General Charles P. Adams, who served in expeditions against the Sioux in 1864-66. Sabers were regularly issued to members of the cavalry, although they were little used on the Plains. A photograph of the Hidatsa leader Crow Flies High shows him wearing a saber very similar to this one; the model was called a "wristbreaker" because it was so heavy (Steffen 1978:65, 70; Meyer 1977:opp. p. 77).

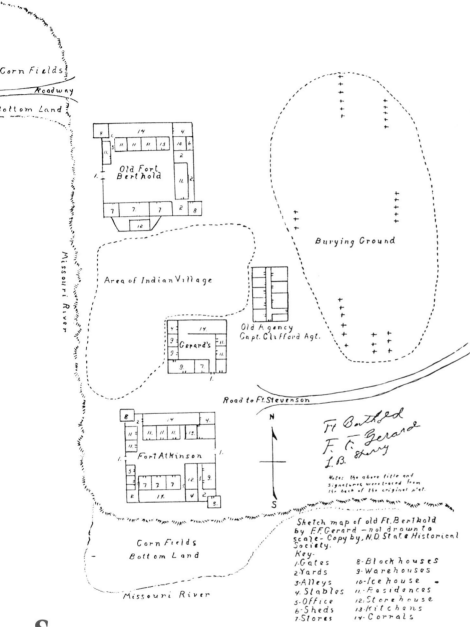

"SKETCH MAP OF OLD FT. BERTHOLD"
Redrawn from a map by Frederic F. Gerard and Lyman B. Sperry, c. 1871
SHSND (Van Ostrand 1942–43:236)

By the 1870s Like-a-Fishhook was becoming surrounded by buildings erected for the use of fur traders and agents; their view of the relative importance of Indian versus white architecture is captured in this map. Not all the buildings shown here existed simultaneously, nor are their sizes and relationships entirely accurate. Gerard was a long-time trader at Like-a-Fishhook, and Sperry was agent in 1873-74. The "Capt. Clifford" referred to on the map was Walter Clifford, agent from 1869 to 1871 (Meyer 1977:116, 119). The original of this map is in the State Historical Society of North Dakota.

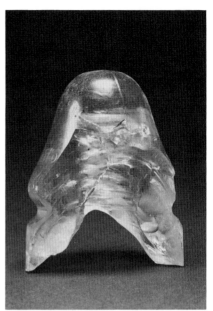

TELEGRAPH INSULATOR FRAGMENT
Pre-1885?
Excavated at Like-a-Fishhook Village
Blue molded glass with threaded hole
*   for attaching to posts; raised*
*   lettering says, "CAUVET," "...*
*   ROOKFIEL ...," "FULTO ...,"*
*   and "NY"*
H. 9 cm, D. 7 cm
SHSND 32ML2/12,003.1821

Between 1876 and 1879, trader Daniel W. Longfellow purchased a mail-order, battery-run telegraph kit to connect the village with the school about a mile and a half away (Longfellow 1953:11-12). By 1879 a telegraph office was installed at nearby Fort Stevenson (Smith 1959:214). Shortly after, the mission school at Like-a-Fishhook was connected to the fort, and the Indian agency began to use the telegraph to send urgent messages to the main office in Washington, D.C.

The agent and his goods

The Hidatsa tribe's relationship with the U.S. government began in 1851, when Wolf Chief was only a year and a half old. He knew the story well. "They got word from Washington from the Great Father that each tribe should [send] delegates to a place in [the] south at White River to a council. Our chief Four Bears chose 4 good young men as chiefs to take along to the council. . . . The Commissioner said he wanted the Indians all to stop fighting & be friends. Any tribe entering this agreement, [the] Government would offer $50,000 a year in goods & provisions. These will be issued thus for 25 years. But if any tribes continue their fighting others, they will receive nothing and their share be given to the peaceful ones.

"We still have the copy of this agreement at Mrs. Foolish Woman's. This treaty I saw, on skin written with ink & where folded [the] letters in [the] crease [are] worn out & can't be read." The whites knew this agreement as the Fort Laramie Treaty (Wilson 1916c:62-63; Meyer 1977:103).

FORT BERTHOLD/JUIN 1868"
Drawn by Col. Philippe Régis de Trobriand, 1868
Pencil on paper
H. 29.5 cm, W. 45 cm
SHSND

Wolf Chief remembered steamboats leaving "a lot of freight from the government . . . piled up outside of the village" (Wilson 1916c:64). When this sketch was made, the steamboat *War Eagle* had just delivered annuities of "flour, biscuits, pork, plows, wagons, a forge, iron, farm tools, and implements" to Like-a-Fishhook Village, and the steamboat landing was still full of supplies being carried uphill by wagon. The artist came to the area in 1867 as U.S. Army commander for the Department of Dakota's Middle District, headquartered at Fort Stevenson. The year he drew this sketch, a permanent agency was established at the village (Trobriand 1951:xviii, 300-2).

Soon after the treaty was signed, the payments started arriving. "A big steamboat came and brought a lot of freight from the government," Wolf Chief said. "Then the Mandans & Hidatsas had a big gathering together outside [the] village and the pile of freights [was] divided half to each tribe. . . . Thus things continued about 15 years. . . . The last steamboat came & brought provisions and a captain that built a house and started an agency. This was when I was 23 years old" (Wilson 1916c:64).

The agent was the U.S. government's representative to the Mandan, Hidatsa, and Arikara, who were treated as a single group and would later be given the official name of the Three Affiliated Tribes. The agent embodied an aspect of white culture different from that of the traders and military men who had come before him. His was a subculture of paper, of rules and regulations. Unlike other whites, he did not come to blend into Hidatsa society – he came to change it. His charge was to "civilize" the tribes.

The agent's greatest source of power was his control over the annuities, or payments for the land and rights surrendered by the tribes in treaties. Annuities were not paid in cash, but in "issue goods."

Issue goods played more than just a utilitarian role. For government policy makers, issue goods were silent missionaries for the Euro-American way of life. Most whites of the era thought that once Indian tribes became accustomed to Euro-American technology, they would forget their own ways and become dependent upon the products of eastern farms and factories. Once they dressed like whites, ate like whites, and used white tools, they would *be* like whites.

The Hidatsa also knew that goods had power, but not in the way the agents thought. In their system, the exchange of goods cemented social ties and hierarchies. Prominent people gave away gifts for power, honor, and prestige. But when the government started holding ceremonial giveaways, old social structures were threatened. This flood of issue goods did not come from the generosity of the tribe's leading families. It did not spring, as wealth always had, from a woman's skill, or a hunter's courage, or favorable dreams. The leading men petitioned the government to let them distribute issue goods through traditional channels, but the agents refused. So every biscuit, knife, and coffee grinder flouted age-old systems (Meyer 1977:121).

Some issue goods came in the twice-yearly shipments by steamboat. Wolf Chief remembered "much clothing, blankets of all kinds, suits, dress goods & provisions" coming this way (Wilson 1916c:64). But there were also rations, issued every other Saturday (Hall [1881-86]:236). "A ration consisted of seven pounds of beef, seven pounds of flour, four ounces of coffee, one-half pound of sugar, one-half pound of soap, four ounces of salt and one pound of bacon," Goodbird said. "We Indians thought that these rations would go on being issued to us forever. 'The government will take care of us and feed us for all times,' we said. We thought that the government was very kind to us and would help us after the buffaloes were gone" (Wilson 1913a:55-56).

ISSUING ANNUITIES TO THE THREE NATIONS, FORT BERTHOLD, DAKOTA"
Photographed by Stanley J. Morrow, 1872
From a stereoscopic view card
W. H. Over State Museum, Vermillion, S.Dak., photo 167

The arrival and distribution of the annuities was often a grand ceremonial occasion. In this photograph taken at Like-a-Fishhook, the goods are piled on the prairie and the people sit in several circles around them. Trader Henry Boller cynically described such an occasion in 1859: "The Agent held the usual council, gave the usual stereotyped advice to love their Great Father and their enemies, . . . and the council broke up, without the Indians having a very exalted opinion of the Agent, or his ability" (Boller 1959:343).

FORT BERTHOLD AGENCY
Photographed by O. S. Goff, 1879
From a stereoscopic view card
SHSND Col. 88-27

The agency at Like-a-Fishhook came to be a small town in itself. The first agency was located in buildings connected to the trading post. These burned in 1874, and the agency was rebuilt a mile and a half downstream from the village (Mattison 1955:34). James Walker, who lived at the later agency as a child, described it as "a quadrangle enclosed by a solid plank stockade seven or eight feet in height. There were two principal gates, one forming an east and the other a west entrance. The residences were five in number, ranged along the south side of the quadrangle, facing the river." The residences housed the agent, the blacksmith, the doctor, the assistant farmer, and the clerk. On the north side of the quadrangle was a granary and machine shed, a "vast storehouse," and a "commodious" mess house. Outside the complex lay a blacksmith shop, a carpenter shop, a horse barn, a combination grist and saw mill, and a large cow barn. This photograph seems to be taken from the southeast (Walker 1953:30-31).

SUPPLY CHECK
Issued by Agent E. H. Alden,
1876-78
Black ink on pink card
L. 4 cm, W. 6.7 cm
NA (Ellis 1879)

Agents were instructed to teach Indians the value of labor and to issue goods only to Indian men who worked. Rather than pay cash to Indians who provided goods and services to the agency, the agents issued supply checks like this, which could be redeemed for goods at the agency store. Since not all men could be employed and since Indian people believed the rations and annuities were owed them in exchange for the land and hunting rights they had given up, the method was controversial. In 1879 the agent wrote that he intended to drop the system in favor of payment in cash and a more general distribution of goods (Ellis 1879).

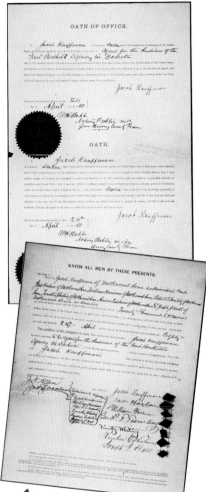

AGENT'S BOND AND OATH
Submitted by Jacob Kauffman, 1880
Brown-black ink and red seals on
form printed on blue paper
L. 33.5 cm, W. 26 cm; L. 40.8 cm,
W. 26 cm
NA (Kauffman 1880a)

The job of agent was frequently a political appointment, and no training was offered. To ensure against mismanagement, the Office of Indian Affairs demanded that each new agent post a $20,000 bond to be refunded upon retirement if there was no evidence of fraud. An agent also took a loyalty oath and an oath of office stating that he would carry out orders received from the president, the secretary of the interior, the commissioner of Indian affairs, and his supervisor. Jacob Kauffman was agent at Fort Berthold Reservation from 1880 to 1884 (Meyer 1977:117).

KNIFE

Issued by the U.S. government, 1850s?
Collected by Harold Case, post-1922
Iron blade, sharpened to an awl-like
point; two-piece wooden handle
attached with five rivets
L. 28.7 cm, W. 3.7 cm
University of Colorado Museum at
Boulder 33242, Case

Since issue goods had to be transported
up the Missouri River by boat, the first
issues were generally small items that
were easily packed yet desired by
Indians. This knife was identified as
"first issue" by the collector, a long-time
missionary at Fort Berthold Reservation.
The first issue goods paid to the
Mandan and Hidatsa arrived in the
1850s as a result of their signing the
1851 Fort Laramie Treaty (Meyer
1977:103). Even before knives were
issued by the government, the Hidatsa
were acquiring them by trade with fur
companies and other tribes. Wolf Chief
recalled, "I think it was about 120 years
ago that Chippewa half breeds brought
many iron axes, and big butcher knives
with deer horn handles, which our
people bought. White men had come to
us before, but did not sell us much"
(Wilson 1918a:356-57).

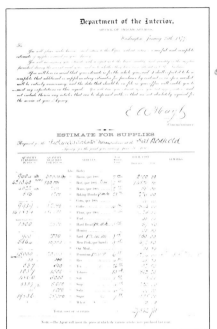

ESTIMATE FOR SUPPLIES

Submitted by Agent E. H. Alden,
1879
Brown-black ink on lined paper
L. 35.6 cm, W. 21.9 cm
NA (Alden 1879)

The agent began the task of issuing
goods by filling out forms requesting
certain items for the following year.
Food and clothing made up the
overwhelming majority of issue goods.
The food issued was often different from
what the Hidatsa were accustomed to.
"At first we didn't like the new foods,"
Wolf Chief said, "but when we ate what
was sweet and good we kept eating and
have done so ever since" (Wilson
1916c:65). Though the agent requested
particular items, the main office in
Washington decided what and how
much would be sent. The people in the
field were often unhappy with
the results.

COFFEE GRINDER

Issued by the U.S. government at Fort
Yates, Standing Rock Reservation,
c. 1877
Wooden base with drawer; cast iron
handle and grinding mechanism
L. 16.5 cm, W. 16.5 cm, H. 22.9 cm
SHSND 4405

Tools that bridged the gap between
European and Indian domestic customs
were a small but important category of
issue goods. The Hidatsa were fond of
coffee, but they had to improvise ways
to prepare it. "We made coffee by
putting it into a skin and pounding
it fine with an axe, and then
boiling it," Goodbird explained
(Wilson 1913a:129). The remains of
several coffee grinders were found in
excavations at Like-a-Fishhook (Smith
1972:80).

(FILES AND RECORDS.)

Department of the Interior,

OFFICE OF INDIAN AFFAIRS,

Washington, November 15, 1878.

The especial attention of Officers of the Indian service is called to the following instructions relating to official correspondence:

1. Communications will be folded in three equal folds parallel with lines of writing, indorsement to be placed upon *middle* fold of the *last* sheet of the communication, leaving blank space of one and one-half inch at the top for Bureau Stamp and "File Mark." (See form on back of this circular.)

2. The indorsement should state: 1st. The official name of agency, its location, and date of the communication. 2d. Name of writer and designation of his official position. 3d. Brief, or indorsement, which should be short, yet sufficiently explicit to convey a clear idea of the contents of the communication. Loose sheets or jackets for this indorsement must not be used.

3. White paper, letter-sheet size, should be used in official communications.

4. All inclosures to communications, except regular Quarterly Returns, must be briefed, and numbered in the order in which they are to be read, and their number stated at bottom of indorsement. The various pages of a letter are not, however, to be considered as inclosures.

5. Only black ink should be used—pale ink of any kind discarded.

6. Special care should be used in taking press copies of letters, to avoid blurring and indistinctness.

7. Replies to communications from this Office must refer to their date, and initials and numbers found in upper left-hand corner of the same.

8. But one subject will be embraced or referred to in any one communication; when several are forwarded in any one mail they may be inclosed in one envelope.

E A Hayt

Commissioner.

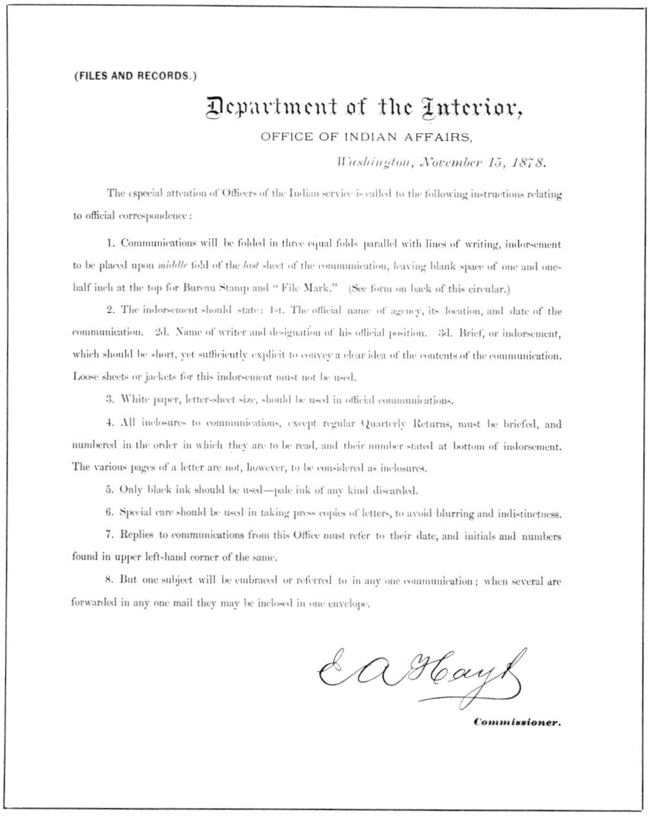

CIRCULAR ON HOW TO FOLD AND ADDRESS LETTERS

Issued by Commissioner E. A. Hayt, 1878
Printed in black ink on paper
L. 26 cm, W. 20.3 cm
NA (Hayt 1878)

The U.S. Office of Indian Affairs was a vast bureaucracy that tried to standardize the government's dealings with a myriad of contrasting cultural groups. The central office in Washington communicated with its agents in the field by means of printed circulars like this one, which specified the color of ink, the size of paper, and the method of folding that the agent should use in every letter sent to headquarters.

[5–276.]

UNITED STATES INDIAN SERVICE,

Fort Berthold Agency,

31st December, 1879.

THE COMMISSIONER OF INDIAN AFFAIRS:

Sir:

Please furnish, for official use at this Agency, during the six months ending June 30th, 1880*, the following-named blanks.*

Very respectfully,

William Courtenay

Acting *U. S. Indian Agent.*

QUANTITY.	No.	TITLE OF BLANK.	QUANTITY.	No.	TITLE OF BLANK.
	1–002	Bonds, (Contractors'.)		5–212 (a)	Receipts—Supplies—Contract. (Flour & Grain.)
	1–006	Oath of Disinterestedness.		5–212 (b)	" Open Market. (Flour and Grain.)
	1–007	Abstract of Proposals.	20	5–240	Proposed Changes in Employés.
20	5–001	Abstract A to Property Return. (Articles Purchased.)	20	5–242	Quarterly Reports of Employés.
20	5–002	Abstract B to Property Return. (Received from Contractors.)	20	5–245	Reports Indian Police, Proposed Changes.
20	5–003	Abstract C to Property Return. (Received from other sources.)	50	5–248	Monthly Report of Physician.
20	5–004	Abstract D to Property Return. (Articles issued to Indians.)	50	5–249	" " " Schools.
20	5–005	Abstract E to Property Return. (Sold to Employés.)	50	5–250	Weekly Supply Reports.
20	5–006 (a)	Abstract F to Property Return. (Expended in Service.)	10	5–276	Requisitions for Blanks and Blank Books.
50	5–006 (b)	Extra sheets for Abstract F.	50	5–300	Weekly Statements of Funds.
50	5–007	" " " Abstracts A, B, C, D, and E.	10	5–301	Monthly " " "
20	5–010	Abstract of Disbursements.	20	5–305	Quarterly " " Rec'pts & Disbursem'ts.
2	5–037	General Instructions for Governm't of Agents.		5–310 (a)	Vouchers—Abs't D, Prop'y Return, Form No. 1.
	5–080	Contracts for Beef.		5–310 (b)	" " " " 2.
	5–082	" " Goods and Supplies.		5–310 (c)	" " " " 3.
10	5–084	" " Miscellaneous.		5–310 (d)	" " " " 4.
	5–086	" " Transportation.	10	5–315 (a)	" " F, Account of Sales of Public Property.
	5–092	Estimates of Funds.		5–315 (b)	Vouchers—Abs't F, Issues to Boarding Schools.
	5–094	" " Supplies—Medical.		5–320	" Advertising.
20	5–097 (a)	" " " &c.		5–322 (a)	Annuity Pay-Rolls, Form No. 1.
50	5–097 (b)	Extra sheets for Estimates of Supplies.	30	5–322 (b)	" " " 2.
10	5–098	Estimates for Stationery.	30	5–322 (c)	" " " 3.
20	5–115	Accounts-Current.		5–326	Invoices of Medical Supplies.
	5–119	Bills of Lading.	20	5–330 (a)	Monthly Receipt Roll. (Regular.)
20	5–134	Certificates of Inspection.		5–330 (b)	Pay-Rolls of Irregular Employés.
30	5–138	Descriptive List of Employés.		5–335 (a)	Vouchers—Miscellaneous—Long.
10	5–140	Descriptive Statement of Governm't Buildings.		5–335 (b)	" " (Extra Sheet.)
20	5–155 (a)	Property Returns.		5–335 (c)	" " Short.
50	5–155 (b)	Extra Sheets for Property Return.		5–338	" Contract.
	5–155 (c)	Property Returns—Medical.		5–340 (a)	" Purchases—Open Market.
500	5–160	Ration-Checks.		5–340 (b)	" " " (Certified.)
	5–176	Weighers' Certificates.			Cash Books.
10	5–210	Receipts—Beef.	2		Sub-Voucher Books.

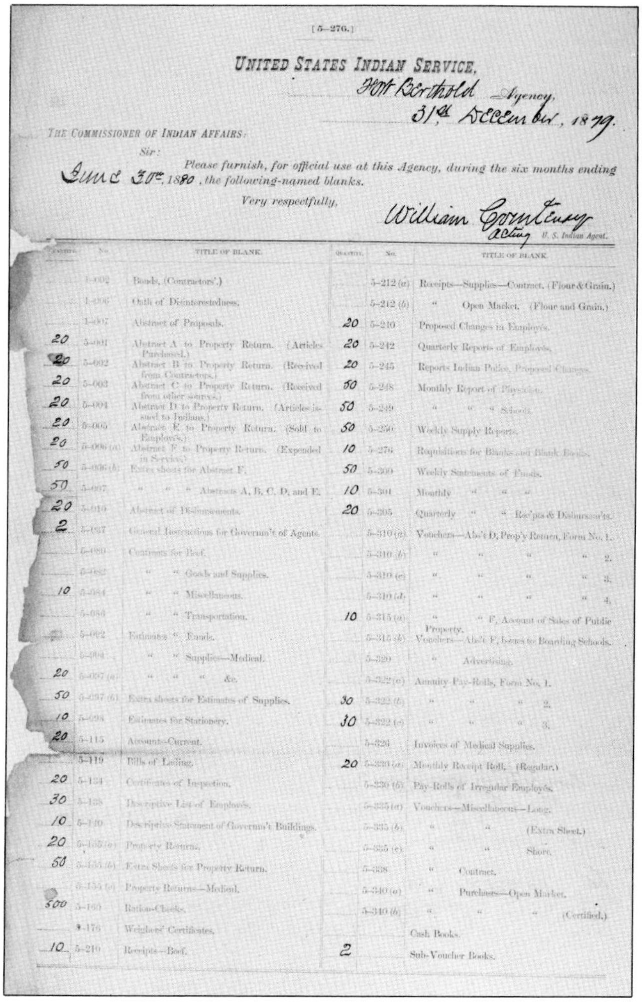

FORM TO ORDER FORMS

Submitted by Acting Agent William Courtenay, 1879
Black ink on form printed in purple ink
L. 35.6 cm, W. 23.5 cm
NA (Courtenay 1879c)

Paperwork was a formidable part of the agent's job. Every item received at the agency had to be accounted for, and there were forms for almost every possibility. In addition, the agent was required to make weekly, monthly, and quarterly financial reports on the proper forms. Any decision made by the agent had to be approved or disapproved in writing by the Washington, D.C., office, and so reams of stationery and telegraph forms were also required. Forms could only be ordered twice a year, on January 1 and July 1.

Ho-Washte

A white man who would have a profound influence on Goodbird's life arrived at Like-a-Fishhook in 1876 when Goodbird was seven years old. "Mr. Hall came as missionary," he said. "He came from the Santee Siouxs and could talk the Dakota language. He had a song that he sang which began, 'Ho-waste.' So we named him Ho-Washte, or Good Voice, as the words mean. He was a good singer and used to sing in the village even before he knew our language.

"Mr. Hall's wife came with him, and they built a five-room house and later on, a church house also. . . . Every Saturday, Mr. Hall would go around to the village people and invite them to come to the church services the next day. He would shake hands with them as he invited them to the services. Later on, Poor Wolf acted as his crier and would go around the village on Saturday evening and invite the people. He would call out, 'Ho-Washte, Ho-Washte, – Come you people tomorrow and sit for him!' He meant by this, for the people to come to church service and sit on chairs.

"Mr. Hall would preach to us at the church services. . . . Sometimes I went to these services but not very regularly. He used to draw pictures from the Bible on the blackboard. . . . Sometimes he would say, 'Thirty years ago I saw the light.' I thought that he meant by this that he had seen a vision, as our people had a custom of going out among the hills and fasting until they saw a vision. However, I did not think very much of the gods at this time for I was too young" (Wilson 1913a:47, 50, 51).

Charles L. Hall was a Congregationalist who came to Like-a-Fishhook with twin goals: to "civilize" and to Christianize the Mandan, Hidatsa, and Arikara. Unlike the soldiers and agents, his commitment to the community was to be life-long. He and his wife Emma brought with them a New England heritage full of both idealism and prejudices. To Emma, the Indian village seemed "horribly squallid, equal to some tenement houses I have seen." Yet she added, "The people are more civilized than I could expect. They have nice farms – hundreds of acres. The men work, but only begin to dress in citizen's clothes. Some get a hat on, others a coat, and others shoes; but few get two pieces on at a time. Not a one has cut his hair" (Hall [1881-86]:18).

The message of the missionaries was sometimes paradoxical. They came as missionaries not just for a religion, but for the Euro-American way of life. In fact, they thought Christianity and culture were inseparable.

To attract converts, they created a little island of Victorian life in their mission, half a mile from the village. There, backed by the silent testimony of Oriental rugs and lace curtains, they hoped by friendship to encourage the Indians to follow the white man's way of speech, dress, and worship.

Their dual purpose sometimes created confusing conflicts. Christianity encouraged the virtues of charity and generosity. But the Hidatsa carried those virtues to an extreme that was incompatible with Yankee values of thrift and self-reliance. The missionaries found themselves encouraging the Hidatsa "to change from the old way of dependence on the common food supply to the individual family taking care of their own needs. They still have that generosity, which comes to

CHARLES L. HALL FAMILY
1890s
Collected by Harold Case
SHSND Col. 41-406
Missionary Charles L. Hall is shown here with his second wife, Susan Webb Hall, and their children Evan and Deborah. He was originally a New York architect who came to Like-a-Fishhook Village under the auspices of the American Board of Commissioners for Foreign Missions. Susan, like Hall's first wife, Emma Calhoun Hall, started her mission work at Alfred L. Riggs's mission to the Sioux in Santee, Nebr. This photograph was probably taken in the "parsonage," Hall's house near Like-a-Fishhook, which was moved to Elbowoods in 1902. Hall lived on the Fort Berthold Reservation until his death in 1940 (Missions Council 1947:3, 5; Hall 1937a, 1937g).

them from the old [customs]. And this fact hinders the progress of many. . . . The less thrifty impose on the thrifty. . . . They are a generous people and they feel their responsibility toward their brother. But the mission work is gradually overcoming this" (Case 1932:1-2).

A number of people from the village became interested in the Halls' religion of forgiveness and redemption. Congregations of 15 or 20 were not unusual at Sunday services (Wilson 1913a:90). But culture was still a barrier between the Hidatsa and the new faith.

"Dr. Hall required that when people became Christians, all their traditions must be left behind," wrote a colleague. "The Indian men must cut off their long braids. The religious dances must cease. The beautiful ceremonial robes must be burned. This confused and saddened many of the people" (Missions Council 1947:5). "The new must take the place of the old," Hall wrote sternly. "There must be no compromise. It must be 'unconditional surrender,' if Christ's way is to remain pure" (Meyer 1977:127).

The Halls had no converts for 11 years. One of their first was Poor Wolf, an elder who had been strongly drawn to religion all his life. His conversion was not without its costs. Poor Wolf expressed his anguish at Christianity's severe demands. "What will I have to do to belong to God's people?" he said to Hall. "Many years ago I gave up fighting, stealing horses, and other bad deeds. I have obeyed the white man's laws as far as I know them. . . . Must I give up the old Indian songs, which are a part of the life of our people? Must I give up the charms that I have carried on my body for years and which I believe have defended me from demons? My body is tattooed to show my allegiance to various spirits. How can I cut these out of my flesh?" (Hall and Hall n.d.:8).

For the members of Goodbird's family, the price was too high. "[Mr. Hall] seemed to be against all my Indian customs," Wolf Chief said. "Sometimes he would say, 'I want you to believe in Christ & join the Church.' But I said, well, let me try, let me wait. But I knew I was not able to stand against all the things asked of one. . . . I was afraid to join in for I had shrines and I loved them & if I joined [the] church I would have to not pray to them" (Wilson 1916c:97). Son of a Star had similar feelings. "My father thought the Christian way was a very good way," said Goodbird, "although he never became a Christian himself. He had purchased membership into some of our sacred

ceremonies and had done everything which Indian custom required for leading an ideal Indian life. He always remained true to his beliefs and would not desert his gods" (Wilson 1913a:112).

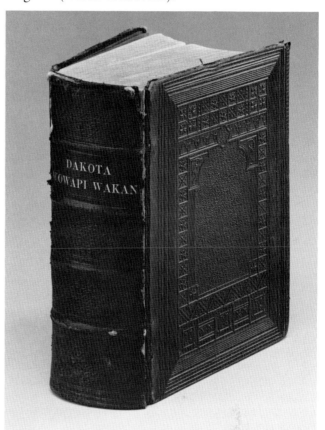

DAKOTA WOWAPI WAKAN: THE HOLY BIBLE IN THE LANGUAGE OF THE DAKOTAS
Printed by American Bible Society, New York, 1883
Embossed black leather cover with gilt title on spine;
***   interior printed in black on white paper***
H. 18.4 cm, W. 15.2 cm
MHS BS345.DZ/1883
The missionaries at Like-a-Fishhook owed their training to the missionary families founded by Stephen R. Riggs and Thomas S. Williamson, who translated a large body of Christian literature (including this Bible) into Dakota. Emma Calhoun worked with Riggs's son Alfred L. Riggs at Santee, Nebr., and with John P. Williamson, son of Thomas, at Yankton Agency, S.Dak. She met Charles L. Hall at the latter mission and married him.

Dakota served as a common tongue for sermons, hymns, and Bible readings in the days before the Halls learned the local languages. Since the Bible was never fully translated into Hidatsa, Mandan, or Arikara, Hidatsa Christians used Dakota Bibles (Hall 1937a; Case and Case 1977:54).

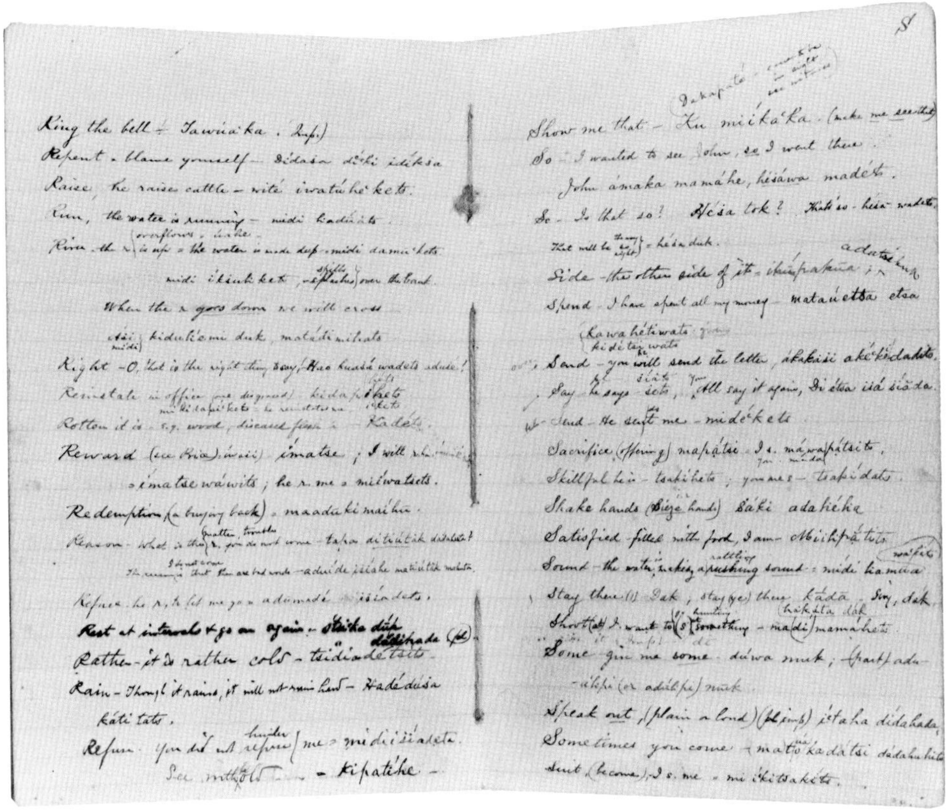

Ho waśte, ho waśte,

On Jesus yatan miye:

Ho wankan, ho wankan,

 Nina ḣin yeyam:

Woyatan wankantkiya,

Jesus Christ cajeyatam;

Ho wankan, ho wankan,

 On Jesus ẏatan.

Wośice, wośice,

On wanna mata hehan,

Jesus hi, Jesus hi,

 Qa hehan wani:

Towaśte kin on econ,

Nimaye kte ḣin heon;

Wopida, wopida,

 Ohinni yuha.

Ho miye, ho miye,

Heciya unyanpi kte,

Nicopi, nicopi,

 Wohanpi wakan.

Jesus Christ iye wohan,

Qa ekta unkicopi,

Najin po, najin po,

 Jesus en u po.

GROS VENTRES (HIDATSA) PHRASES"
Written by Charles L. Hall, post-1882
Ink on blue lined paper; black leather cover
H. 16.9 cm, W. 10.5 cm
SHSND (Hall Papers)

The three languages spoken at Like-a-Fishhook were not mutually comprehensible. Hidatsa and Mandan were both Siouan languages; Arikara was a Caddoan language. Hall took extensive notes on Hidatsa in this notebook. In 1879 his wife Emma wrote that "Mr. Hall has given his attention to learning the Ree [Arikara] language, the most difficult of the three. He has succeeded in getting several songs translated, the twenty-third Psalm, the ten commandments, and the story of the prodigal son. These are all doing good work" (Schneider 1986:37-40; Case and Case 1977:52). By 1883, Hall was fluent enough to correspond in Hidatsa (Hall 1883).

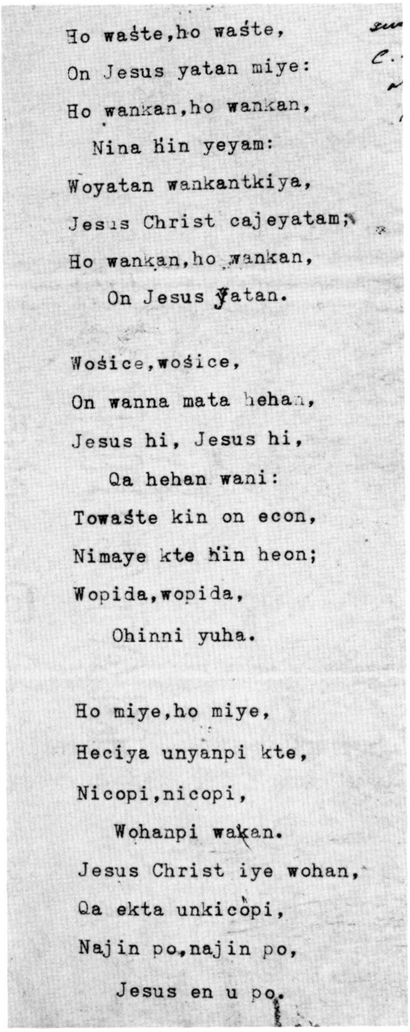

HO WASTE"
Written by John P. Williamson,
 transcribed c. 1913
Typescript on paper
H. 21.5 cm, W. 14 cm
MHS (Wilson 1913a: endsheet)

When the Halls first arrived at Like-a-Fishhook, Charles remembered, "Our first singing was from the Dakota (or Sioux) hymn book. This was a strange performance to these Indians, and the young men guyed [teased] us. Afterwards they greeted us at a distance on the prairie by shouting the first words of the hymn we had attempted to sing. These fortunately chanced to be Ho Washte, and meant Good Voice. The voice of one crying in the wilderness, we told them was the meaning" (Hall 1923?:10). In the 1980s, Congregationalists on Fort Berthold Reservation were still called Ho Washte.

 These Dakota lyrics, to be sung to the tune of "Sweetly Sing," were probably given to Wilson by Hall.

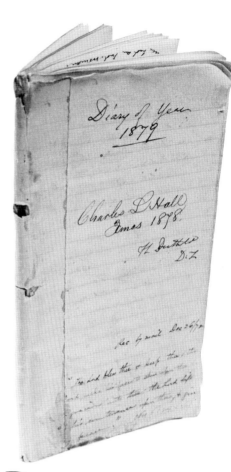

HYMNS AND SCRIPTURE SELECTIONS
IN THE MANDAN LANGUAGE; NIKUTATI
ISATAU NATCITCITU (I AM THE BREAD
OF LIFE)
Printed by Santee Normal Training
School Press, Santee, Nebr., 1905
and 1924
Printed in black ink on paper; stapled
paper cover
H. 13.3 cm, W. 8.9 cm; H. 13.5 cm,
W. 9 cm
MHS PM1701.Z71b/1905,
PM636.Z7/1924

One of the major goals of the
missionary was to translate Bible
passages, hymns, and other elements of
the church service into native languages.
These pamphlets, printed under Hall's
supervision, present Bible passages and
songs such as "Rock of Ages" and "Joy
to the World" in Mandan and Arikara.
The Mandan translations were done by
LeRoy Holding Eagle. Hall and
Goodbird also worked on Hidatsa
translations, which were printed in a
similar pamphlet (see p. 283).

IAPI OAYE/THE WORD CARRIER
Published by the Dakota Mission,
Santee Agency, Nebr., Dec. 1882
Printed paper
H. 39.6 cm, W. 26.8 cm
MHS PM1021/f.A1I11.S

This bilingual Dakota/English
newspaper was founded by missionary
John P. Williamson in 1871 to reach
the Dakota in their own language. Over
the years it provided communication
among Congregational and Presbyterian
missions to the Plains Indians,
publicized the efforts of the missionaries
to the outside world, provided reading
material for mission schools, and
published letters and essays by Indian
students. Missionaries at Fort Berthold
frequently sent the *Word Carrier* newsy
columns about activities on the
reservation. Since students from Fort
Berthold attended the Santee mission
school as early as 1873, the newspaper
provided a way for them to maintain
contact with friends and relatives at
home (Hall n.d.: 3).

DIARY
Written by Charles Hall, 1879
Ink on blue lined paper; cover missing
H. 16 cm, W. 8.5 cm
SHSND (Hall Papers)

Missionaries often kept records of their
work to be used in annual reports, in
letters to sponsoring agencies, and to
chart the progress of the church's work.
Hall later published many of his early
experiences at Fort Berthold in fund-
raising pamphlets.

PARSONAGE, FT. BERTHOLD"
Photographed by O. S. Goff, 1879
From a stereoscopic view card
SHSND Col. 88-36

Three years after their arrival at Like-a-Fishhook, the
missionaries had erected the complex of buildings shown here.
The house was first. "The Indians called it the house with
eyes because of the windows all around," wrote Hall. "They
seemed to think that windows were to look into. They came
and spread their blankets over the panes and looked in" (Hall
1937b). According to Hall, the house was the hub of
continual activity. Women and children came to sew together,
make bread, brew cough syrup, and learn to read. Young men
came to attend school.

INTERIOR OF COLTON COTTAGE
1890s?
Collected by Harold Case
SHSND Col. 41-433, 365

One of the main goals of the missionaries at Like-a-Fishhook
was to introduce young people to a Euro-American cultural
milieu. For that purpose they set up several "cottages," or
boardinghouses, overseen by matrons, where children could
be immersed in white society while only half a mile from their
earth lodge homes. "We are called a 'home school,'" Hall
wrote. "We work on the principle that the nearer a school is
like a home the better. Therefore the limitation of the
numbers; also the breaking up into three cottages with
separate matrons; also the providing of those things that can
be provided in a well-to-do home and the omission of those
things that are not found in the middle-class country homes
in North Dakota" (Hall 1900:316).

This photograph shows one of the "sitting rooms"
where students socialized. In addition to academic and
vocational training, the missionaries tried to arouse in students
an aesthetic "taste for flowers and trees. . . . Our efforts to
give material and spiritual beauty to our surroundings helped
to lead the whole community" (Hall 1937f).

PLAYING CARDS
Russell and Morgan Printing Co., Cincinnati, Ohio, c. 1900
Printed paper with blue and white backs showing bicycling cherubs
H. 8.8 cm, W. 6.3 cm
MHS 1986.100.8a-yy

Card games were among the new pastimes taught to children at the mission school. In 1888 the children played "Boston," a card game like whist (*Word Carrier* 1888a). Boys also played card games at Colton Cottage (see photo at left).

KEROSENE LAMP
Base maker unknown, chimney by Macbeth Co., Pittsburgh, Pa.; 1870-1920
Iron base has octagonal foot, decorated with molded floral reliefs and bolted to fluted iron column. Pressed glass reservoir, brass burner, and glass chimney with beaded top
H. 47 cm, D. 15 cm
MHS 9654.6, Mrs. P. N. Hamm, 72.60.4, Folsom House

In order to give Indian students an illustration of middle-class Euro-American life styles, the missionaries built and furnished a modern house with materials shipped upriver from Bismarck. Students lived with the Halls in the early years; later they stayed in similar buildings run like homes. "The school aims to be a model farm-home for the pupils and for the people who have just begun to make such homes for themselves . . . on the reservation," Hall wrote. "Here the pupils will learn what is taught in common school, and also learn how to farm and garden in a profitable way. Here they will get a spiritual strength to live above debasing influences." The home was furnished with drapes, lamps, tables, chairs, books, and other necessities (Hall 1888a).

W OMEN'S SEWING MEETING
1897
Collected by Harold Case
SHSND Col. 41-401

The weekly sewing meeting was one of the most popular
activities sponsored by the missionaries. Susan Hall (standing,
third from left) described one held in the mission house: "By
one the room is generally full, yes, crowded, so that in
passing around among them one has to stumble quite often
over feet which have no place to retreat. We do not pretend
to offer chairs to all. The floor holds as many without chairs
as with. . . . Here the women sit patiently to be given work
at or a little after two o'clock. . . . Hidatsas, Mandans and
Rees [Arikara] all meet together, although generally the two
first mentioned tribes are on one side of the room and the
last on the other. . . . Our fifteen [school] boys have learned,
when sewing day comes, to bring forth every article that
needs repairing in any way. . . . The women often have a
laugh over the variety of work I have for them, and I
sometimes think it is one attraction of the meeting. After
sewing about two hours, the thimbles and needles are
gathered up, the names taken, . . . and each ones' desire
discovered, tea, sugar or coffee. . . . Some tell me in Hidatsa,
some in Ree, others in English, and Dakota. They often try
to puzzle me, and will ask in fun for things they know they
cannot have. . . . I often wish I could understand their jokes,
although I have no doubt they are often upon me, or white
people's ways. . . . The faces of these women go with me all
the week, and I can pray for them with far more zeal for the
afternoon spent with them" (Hall 1937g).

Shown standing next to Mrs. Hall is Mrs. Howlingwolf;
sitting are Maude Gillette, Miss Field, Mrs. Whitewolf, and
Susie Enemy, a little girl (Case and Case 1977:50).

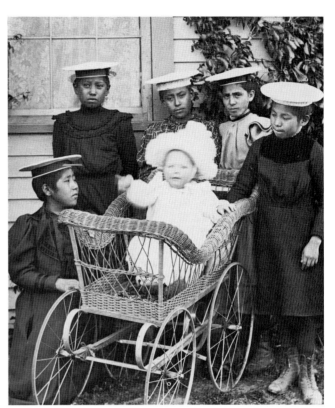

M ISSION GIRLS
1890s?
Collected by Harold Case
SHSND Col. 41-378

The missionaries made a particular effort to reach the children
of Like-a-Fishhook, who were initially so shy that "they
would run and hide when one approached." The Halls' first
baby was, in Charles's words, a "passport to many hearts. . . .
The missionary got out the new baby-carriage and put Harry
in it. He prominaded among the lodges. Soon children
crowded into closer contact than was advisable. . . . White
Shield, the old Ree chief, said: 'If you feed the children they
will come to school, like flies to syrup.' His advice was taken
and a Friday dinner, a la White Man, was provided. This was
as attractive as ice cream cones and lolly-pops" (Hall 1937b).
Later, children boarded at the mission school, dressing in
clothes provided by the missionaries. The baby in this
photograph is unidentified.

RATTLE
Hidatsa. Bought from Wolf Chief
Collected by Gilbert Wilson, 1913-15
Cone-shaped rawhide rattle; handle of willow twigs wrapped with fiber.
   Painted red
L. 26.3 cm, W. 11.7 cm
MHS 7059.66
This mushroom-shaped rattle may have been created by Wolf Chief to illustrate the construction of similar sacred rattles used in the Hidatsa Sun Dance and in ceremonies relating to eagle catching. In 1913 Wilson photographed Wolf Chief with two rattles identical to this in front of a model Sun Dance lodge (MHS photo V-99-1913; see also Wilson 1915a:246, 1915c). A similar mushroom-shaped rattle was photographed by Frances Densmore (1923:pl. 9d).

TATTOOING INSTRUMENTS
Hidatsa. Bought from Hairy Coat
Collected by Frederick Wilson, 1912
Cottonwood cylinder with four pointed
   metal blades; pointed wooden stick
   with yellow and black feather
   attached with sinew; two pointed
   wooden sticks with rattles made by
   folding a bird quill over and filling
   it with sand or pebbles; yellow and
   black feather
Cylinder: L. 5 cm, D. 3.4 cm. Sticks
   and feather: L. 18 cm, 11 cm,
   11.8 cm, and 8.3 cm
AMNH 50.2/3591a–e
Poor Wolf was tattooed by Road Maker when he was a young man. As Road Maker cut his skin with the tin blades, a singer sang and shook rattles. "Road Maker would strike with the tattooer at each beat of the rattles in the song," recalled Hairy Coat, who watched as a boy. "Kinnikinnek charcoal . . . made into a powder [was] put into quills from which it was dropped into the wounds. . . . It took about a year to do the whole design" (F. Wilson 1912b:[86-88]).

Poor Wolf thought his tattoos were an obstacle to his conversion to Christianity. In 1910, Gilbert Wilson and Robert Lowie made a study of them, taking photographs and making drawings of the marks (Wilson 1910a:cover letter, p. 2). Hairy Coat, who described the process, made these replicas of the instruments used.

POOR WOLF
Painted by Frederick N. Wilson, 1911
From a photographic print
MHS (Wilson [1903–18]:157)
This portrait shows Poor Wolf in his 89th year. Born about 1820, Poor Wolf had lived through the smallpox epidemic of 1837. He was drawn to Christianity in the 1880s by his daughters, Otter and Miriam. His conversion apparently influenced Wolf Chief, whom he exhorted to "Persevere in the way of God" (Hall and Hall n.d.:10).

A new language

By 1877 there were two schools at Like-a-Fishhook Village – one run by the government, one by the mission. To recruit students, the missionary visited families in the village. "Send your children to my school and I will teach them the English language," he would say (Wilson 1913a:51).

Not everyone thought it was a good idea. "Many of the old people laughed at anyone who wished to learn the English language," Goodbird said. "They said, 'You want to forsake your Indian ways and be a white man.' But there were a good many in the village who wanted to learn English, nevertheless" (Wilson 1913a:50-51).

Small Ankle was one who saw advantages in knowing English. He said to his sons, "I want you boys to go to school & learn English, how to write, to read and to count in arithmetic. If you learn English it will help you when lots of white men come out here" (Wilson 1916c:50). Both Goodbird and Wolf Chief took his advice.

Goodbird was eight years old when he started going to school. "My teachers were Miss Pickens and Miss Ward," he said. "I would go to school in the morning and come home to dinner at noon. Sometimes I went back in the afternoon." He found English a hard language to learn. Classroom etiquette was not easy, either. "I was rather afraid of my teacher. When her back was turned, we boys were pretty apt to talk, and she would turn around and come down to us boys who had been talking and give us each a spat on the head with a book; but it did not hurt very much" (Wilson 1913a:47, 50).

MISSION SCHOOL
Photographed by C. B. Brown, Minot
SHSND Col. 88-3
Students stood in front of one of the school buildings erected by Congregational missionaries at Like-a-Fishhook Village. The building was later moved to Elbowoods.

Wolf Chief followed a different course. During the winter when he was 29, he went to a friend, a white man named Fred Huber who had married into the tribe. "'My friend,' I said, 'I want to learn English. I want you to teach me how to write & read. And we will begin arithmetic first & count up to ten. I will keep you in my house. And when the government issues clothing I will give you all for I don't use this white man's dress anyway – I dress in a different way.'

"'I don't believe you,' said that white man. 'Your age is too old to learn the things taught at school – too hard to learn to write & read.'

"'That might be,' I said, 'but I want to learn'" (Wilson 1916c:51).

Huber first sent Wolf Chief to the trader's store to buy supplies: lead pencils, paper, and candles so they could study at night. Wolf Chief had no money, but he knew the store would take deer and antelope skins. As he watched the trader weighing up the skins, he was acutely aware that his ignorance of figures made him dependent on the trader's dubious honesty.

They started Wolf Chief's education that night. Using an old box for a table, Huber wrote down the numbers from one through ten. "Then he said, 'Say *one*' and I repeated it. Then 'two' and I went on up to ten. 'Now say it yourself.' So I began 'one, two, three,' but got no further.

"'Try again,' said Mr. Huber. I tried & got to *three* but I couldn't pronounce plainly. 'Put your tongue so,' said Mr. Huber – I did so & tried. I worked on till far into night & got as far as to say one, two, three up to ten but I couldn't remember the figures – except one which was easy. I said the names just like singing them. . . .

"Next morn[ing] after breakfast we sat at our box desk & had further study. 'Now I will teach you a, b, c,' he said. 'All these letters mixed up this way mean words and if you can read all these you can read books.' So he wrote on the paper with a lead pencil and read it & I followed, a, b, c, and sounded it and at the end he came to z. But I couldn't get it. And to this day I can't say z. . . .

"It was hard. I was 3 weeks before I learned the abc's all thru. I read them pretty well only that z was hard. 'Here!' Mr. Huber would say – 'Look at my mouth, watch my tongue!' . . .

"Next Mr. Huber wrote 'A man. A woman, dog, horse, child, boy.' I think 13 different animals & man. This took us a long time. Even after I got to understand what the words meant I found it hard to pronounce. My lips and tongue couldn't do like a white man's. This used to make me laugh & Mr. Huber would get mad. 'If you laugh & don't pay attention you will never learn.' He always showed me his tongue & lips – how he opened and closed them. If any one came into the cabin, I would be ashamed & not want to read. . . .

"March came. I learned every month, from November on to March. And on days we studied, Mr. H. put [down the] figures of the day of the month on which we studied. This also I learned."

By June, Wolf Chief had learned to write as well as read. Huber was pleased. "You are [a] smart fellow," he said. "I want you to go to school – if you can go 10 years you will know all about books and arithmetic. Then you will be a big chief & [the] government [will] put you in [the] agent's place & you will lead your people & issue rations & write letters and go to Washington" (Wilson 1916c:52-60).

This promise was appealing, and in the fall of 1880 Wolf Chief did as Huber suggested. But he soon found that learning at school was different

SCHOOL BELL
Late 19th century
Cast brass with iron clapper and turned wooden handle bolted to bell. Handle is stamped "1864"
L. 21 cm, D. 11.5 cm
MHS 8962.12, Mrs. David F. Swenson

The sound of the school bell called Indian boys and girls into the classroom and signaled the different activities of the day. Wolf Chief remembered, "I kept the key after school & got up early & after breakfast [went] and built a fire & rung the bell. I did this without pay just to help the teacher" (Wilson 1916c:68).

from learning at home. Here he had to contend not just with a strange language, but with strange customs as well.

"I was 30 years old," Wolf Chief said of his first year in school. "The first teacher I had was a lady. . . . I was married & dressed as our custom. I painted my face red, long hair braided, wore switches & bead necklace over my breast & round pearl shells on either breast & I wore blanket and shirt of white sheeting, leggings of blanket cloth and moccasins. . . .

"Sometimes there was just no one but myself & teacher & I learned fast. I could sing from a hymn book pretty good. My teacher was kind & I liked her because she taught me fast. . . . Sometimes I came every day and she sat beside me & we talked. . . . I wanted to make her my sweetheart for I thought she sat close to me for that. Lots of times she put her arm on my shoulder & I thought she liked me. . . .

"My teacher taught me the organ but it was very hard. She would place her hands on the keys and I would do likewise. I put my fingers on the keys but my hands were painted red and when I took them away the white keys were red. My teacher took her handkerchief and wiped them off. . . .

"The next day I learned again, and I got red on the keys again. She got mad & cross, and wiped off the keys & said, 'Why do you paint up your face & hands that way?'

"I arose & went to my desk, but she seemed awful mad. Then I stood up and walked to the door and started home.

"'Stop, stop,' she said, 'Come back.' And she pointed to the desk.

"I came back & sat down, & thought it all right. I was not a child and if she got mad I wanted to leave" (Wilson 1916c:65-68).

Despite misunderstandings, Wolf Chief persisted. He liked the idea that education would gain him respect in the white man's world, even on a day-to-day level. "When Indians come to a white man's store for bacon," he gave an example, "and think [the white] man cannot understand them they make signs like a flat curled up nose for pig & go unh-unh – grunting. But when I go to a store I say 'bacon' and get it right away" (Wilson 1916c:73).

But even more important, he saw education as an alternative route to power and honor. The way to power in his own culture was harder. "When we Indians want to be chief one goes out & fasts 2 days & nights and goes without food & water and often

tortures & makes [him]self suffer. . . . All this hard work to be chief.

"But this school way is hard but no suffering. . . . It will be hard to sit in a house, but I think I can do [it], and I [want] to be a chief" (Wilson 1916c:60).

Goodbird had no such ambitions, but he also kept going to school. When he was about 12, the military post at Fort Stevenson was vacated and the government established a boarding school there. "The officers came and wanted my parents to sign a paper to permit me to go to the Fort Stevenson school, but my parents said, 'No. We have a school here. Let him attend the missionary school'" (Wilson 1913a:50).

As he learned to read books, Goodbird came to a troubling conclusion: the truth taught in school was not always the truth his parents lived by. One such dilemma came when he first studied geography.

"My people believed that the world was flat and surrounded by seas. My people also thought that the sky was a thin covering like a blanket or a sheet of paper. In my geography I learned that the earth was round, and that the sky that we see surrounds it all, everywhere. There was a story, a myth, that is told in my tribe about Itsikamahidish climbing the sky; that he and the Sun sang a song that brought the sky down close to the earth so that they could mount it. When now I learned that the earth was round, that the sky surrounded it, I knew that the story about the Sun and Itsikamahidish could not be true, so I began to have my faith shaken in my people's beliefs" (Wilson 1913a:90).

Confused, he went to ask his elders which of the two truths to believe. "'This world is round,' I said. But they answered, 'It is not true. That is white man's teaching and they are foolish. This world is flat.' Especially my relative Butterfly would say, 'That is foolish talk. This world is flat'" (Wilson 1913a:112).

The teachers at the mission school were just as convinced of their beliefs as Goodbird's family. Neither side thought there was any room in the world for the other's beliefs. In the end, Goodbird had to decide for himself.

HIDATSA CONCEPT OF THE SUN
Drawn by Goodbird, 1913
Black carbon and pencil on tracing paper
H. 17.3 cm, W. 14 cm
MHS (Goodbird 1913:fig. 43)
Goodbird made this drawing to illustrate how he pictured the sun before learning Euro-American concepts at school. He explained that "The Sun is painted red and light shines from all parts of his body" (Goodbird 1913:fig. 43).

TEXTBOOKS
Published 1875-83
Printed paper, cardboard covers, cloth
*   bindings repaired with binding*
*   tape*
Left to right: L. 18.2 cm, W. 12 cm;
*   L. 27 cm, W. 20.2 cm; L. 18.4*
*   cm, W. 13.3 cm*
MHS 1986.100.10, 11, textbook
*   collection*
The teachers at the mission school received textbooks from supporters and bought others that fit their needs. We do not know the exact books Goodbird used, but texts by Charles Sanders and the Sheldon textbook publishing company were among 23 dozen books ordered by Acting Agent William Courtenay in 1879 (Courtenay 1879b).

Shown here are Charles W. Sanders, *Sanders' Union Speller* (New York and Chicago: Ivison, Blakeman, Taylor & Co., 1878); William Swinton, *Elementary Course in Geography* (New York and Chicago: Ivison, Blakeman, Taylor & Co., 1875); and M. French Swarthout and M. A. Farnham, *Sheldon's Graded Examples in Arithmetic* (New York and Chicago: Sheldon & Co., 1883).

Slate

c. 1900
Two wood-framed slates edged with felt bound on with
brown fabric cord laced through holes in frame. Laces
hinge slates together along one side
Folded L. 27.2 cm, W. 19.7 cm
MHS 1978.79.51, John Dobie Estate

Slates were commonly used in schools on and off the
reservation. Children practiced writing on these erasable
surfaces rather than using more expensive paper and ink. In
1879 William Courtenay ordered four dozen medium-sized
slates to be used in the schools on the reservation (Courtenay
1879b). Numerous fragments of machine-cut, beveled slate
were found by archaeologists at Like-a-Fishhook Village
(Smith 1972:144; NMNH 32ML2/430241, 430430, and
430971).

Slate Pencils

Late 19th century
Wooden pencil case with notched and inlaid sliding cover,
containing one lead pencil and four slate pencils
Case: L. 23 cm, W. 4.7 cm. Pencils: L. 6 to 17.2 cm
MHS 63.57.19a-g, Mrs. George R. Becker

School slates were written on with soft, pointed stone
"pencils." The writing was erased with a sponge. Slates were
used in both the government and mission schools. Fragments
of slate pencils like these were found by archaeologists at
Like-a-Fishhook Village (Smith 1972:144; NMNH
32ML2/430431, 430918, 430970).

Pencils

Maker and date unknown
Top: graphite encased in hexagonal wood sheath. Bottom:
square blue crayon pencil with round cedar sheath
L. 13 cm and 10.4 cm
MHS 1986.100.6, 7

When Wolf Chief hired Fred Huber to teach him to read and
write, he bought paper and pencils from W. B. Shaw's trading
store at Like-a-Fishhook Village (Wilson 1916c:52). Writing
materials were also imported by the agents and missionaries.
The pencils available on the reservation appear to have been
those called "draftsman's" or "carpenter's" pencils today. They
had thick, square leads in round wood sheaths. Pencil stubs
and leads like these were found by archaeologists at Like-a-
Fishhook Village (Smith 1972:145-47; NMNH
32ML2/430675, 430699).

Paper

Late 19th century
Blue and white paper ruled in blue and red ink
Back: L. 30 cm, W. 18.5 cm. Front: L. 32.5 cm,
   W. 19.8 cm
Private collection

The agency and school were supplied with paper by the main office in Washington, but for others paper was expensive. When Wolf Chief set out to learn English, he "bought paper piled 4 inches high or breadth of my hand and 5 lead pencils & about 20 candles" from the trader (Wilson 1916c:52). His letters to Washington were written on a variety of paper sizes and qualities, including lined school paper, paper apparently torn from a notebook, and agency stationery.

Inkwell

Pre-1885?
Excavated at Like-a-Fishhook Village
Clear glass, molded with ridges
   around base, shoulder, and lip.
   Paper label reads "Carter's Fast-
   Drying Ink"
H. 6 cm, D. 5 cm
SHSND 32ML2/12,003.1522

This inkwell was found in one of the houses in the Mandan/Hidatsa section of Like-a-Fishhook Village. The almost complete label suggests that the bottle was relatively new when it was discarded (Smith 1972:48, 79).

Pen

Made by E. Faber Co., late 19th
   century
Varnished wood handle with a
   tarnished metal nib holder and
   bronze-finish nib
L. 18.7 cm
MHS 1986.100.5

Writing pens with replaceable steel nibs were first carried to the Three Tribes by explorers and traders' clerks who recorded business transactions in record books. Agents and missionaries also wrote with such tools, so it is not surprising that Indian people learned to use them, too. Wolf Chief habitually wrote with pen and ink.

"Washington great Father
President Garfield
                    Issued every thing
you mine will sell   Wagon many $.
I did not like   No $ . . great Father
I Will sell   I can not wagon great Father
president Garfield him talk. I hear.
Wagon sell think   I did not like No. $
President Garfield. you tell. J Kauffman
all Wagon 80 $. I hear and Glad I think
tell me. Major Kauffman I hears
President Garfield J Kauffman. two will
sell like, all President Garfield talk
Major Kauffman issue Wagon sell I cannot.
Great Father you talk I hear I like. Talk cannot
you paper I did not recive I did not like
White man talk half I know and I White half
I can and you paper. recive I like I am sure
President Garfield Issued. sell I cannot
and I tell you   see Examine Good —.
Now great Father talk all I hear Good
all. and I am glad Gros Ventres all and
Gros Ventres all to be White man I think
great Father talk I hear I like.
you paper   recive   can not —
                    Washington great Father
Whiteman Good all school sher and
Examine all issue, sell. I did not like
Fort Berthold. White paper me Wolf Chief

LETTER
Written by Wolf Chief, 1881
Pen on paper
L. 31.4 cm, W. 20.3 cm
NA (Wolf Chief 1881c)

In his second year at school, Wolf Chief decided to demonstrate his ability to write by sending a letter to the president. "I asked my teacher to give me the name of [the] president. He wrote it out. And I went home and I wrote and asked for a wagon. [I said] that there were plenty of wagons at [the] agency but not issued" (Wilson 1916c:66).

This is the letter he wrote. It reached the White House and was forwarded to the Office of Indian Affairs, which sent it back to the agent at Fort Berthold for interpretation. Agent Jacob Kauffman's three-page response explained that Wolf Chief "has made some progress in his studies, and feels greatly elated over his ability to write, he also possesses a degree of pardonable egotism in being able to write to the 'Great Father'" (Kauffman 1881:1).

Wolf Chief addressed his letter to James A. Garfield. "The president was killed before my letter reached [the] Postoffice," he said. Nevertheless, "After a long time I got an answer saying '[The] President did not see your letter but he is dead. We are sorry he did not see it. He would have been glad that an Indian boy has learned to write. We too are glad & understand what you mean. We are also writing [a] letter to your agent asking [that] he issue you a wagon.'" Wolf Chief felt that his letter had received a response and he was encouraged to write more (Wilson 1916c:66).

Although Wolf Chief remembered this as his first letter, he had actually written a previous one to President Rutherford B. Hayes (Wolf Chief 1881a).

The Grass Dance

Goodbird's school days came at a time when relative peace had been established between Plains tribes. It was not an unmixed blessing. Men whose energies had been focused on war for years suddenly found themselves without a clear-cut way to achieve recognition. Often, they turned to art and ceremony, sparking a renaissance of cultural activity. Exchange between tribes flourished as never before. It laid the groundwork for a sense of shared Indian heritage that crossed tribal lines.

New arts and institutions appeared at Like-a-Fishhook during the 1870s. "In those days we often had big dances in the village and fine times," Goodbird said. "I am sorry to say that I played hookey sometimes. . . . If I knew there was going to be a big dance I would sometimes hide in the village instead of going to school, so that I could be present and enjoy the good time. The next time my teacher would ask me, 'Where were you yesterday?' and I would tell her, 'I went to see the dance.' My parents scolded me for this but they never whipped me" (Wilson 1913a:48-49).

The most important of the movements that swept across the Plains to Like-a-Fishhook was called the Grass Dance. One year early in the 1870s, a party of Hidatsa went to visit the Santee Sioux living at Devils Lake near the Canadian border. There they witnessed a new ceremony. "We want to buy that dance from you," they said. So a group of Santees came to Like-a-Fishhook to negotiate the purchase (Wilson 1914b:38).

Son of a Star, Goodbird's father, was one of about 30 men who got together to buy the Grass Dance. They formed the Big Grass Dance Society. Later, some younger men who had not been included in the original purchase decided to buy the dance as well; they set up the Night Grass Dance Society. Wolf Chief was a member of the second group (Wilson 1914b:38, 65).

The meaning of the Grass Dance was different to every tribe that adopted it. For the Ojibway, who called it the Drum Dance, the most important element was the sacred drum played during the ceremonies. The Sioux added the feature of a dog-meat feast. But among the Hidatsa, the Grass Dance symbolized the life of a warrior. For them, its name referred to the grass a warrior carried in his belt for tinder (Vennum 1982:51-75; Wilson 1914b:37).

The version of the Grass Dance celebrated at Like-a-Fishhook resembled an age society ceremony. There were a number of officers. Most important was the keeper of the drum. "The drum keeper was carefully

SMALL ANKLE IN GRASS DANCE COSTUME
Drawn by Goodbird, 1914
Pencil and purple, green, red, and yellow watercolors
  on paper
H. 19 cm, W. 9 cm
AMNH (Goodbird 1914b:fig. 12)

Goodbird said that this was "a sketch I have made from memory of my grandfather Small Ankle, in Grass Dance dress. I have showed this sketch to my mother and she pronounces it accurate in colors and design of dress and painting. The four feathers attached to the little model of a gun in wood, mean that he has four strikes to his credit; the gun, that he had been wounded by a gun shot. He wears a round headdress [of porcupine and deer tail]. The white band in his hair just above his forehead is made with white clay" (Wilson 1914b:48-49). The diagonal stripes on his leggings are also honor marks.

chosen and had always to be a good man," said Goodbird. "His lodge was open day and night to the members of the society. He had always a pile of tobacco and two pipes ready for use; and he bought coal oil for a lamp to burn at night. And there was food in his house always for any who wanted to eat.

"The drum hung on the wall of the keeper's lodge. And it was a rule of the society, that if at a dance any one struck it except the keeper, he must give the society a feast as a forfeit" (Wilson 1914b:39).

Next came the four drumstick carriers, who opened the dance by striking a drum with their ceremonial beaded sticks, each one in turn. "It was the rule that each of these drumstick carriers must give away something to a [clan] father or to some old person, at each of these big dances." Both Goodbird and Wolf Chief were appointed to this post (Wilson 1914b:42, 76, 1913a:38).

There were four officers who wore feather trails or bustles, one of whom had to be a warrior wounded in battle; his feathers were dyed red. At the beginning of the dance, a song was sung in their honor and they performed a dance. They also distributed food at the ceremonial dog-meat feast, and the owner of the red trail closed the ceremony with a dance performed to the Quitting Song (Wilson 1914b:43, 85, 94, 107-8).

Two pipe bearers kept the company supplied with tobacco and matches. Another officer owned a special skewer to pluck meat from the feast kettle and symbolically "feed" the other officers and the feather trails. A crier summoned people to the ceremony. There were four women singers, a flag man to keep and raise the Stars and Stripes, and two "whippers," whose duty was to keep the dancers lively. "Sometimes in the dance, the whipper finding that the dancers were lazy or sluggish, would call out, 'Here, I give a horse to so-and-so my [clan] father! Now I am going to whip you hard to make you dance!' Everyone grew afraid then, for the whipper thus bought the right to beat the dancers as he would . . . and no one dared get angry because he had paid for the privilege." Besides their tools of office, all the officers wore costumes of "head dresses, sleigh bells for the garters, otter skins for the head, armlets of bead work, yarn belts, and the like" (Wilson 1914b:44-45, 62-64, 83).

The Grass Dance ritual often lasted all afternoon. "The old men sang glad songs and all were joyous," said Wolf Chief. "If anyone had given presents they called aloud his name and all sang his praises. Everybody had good times." The high point came when, after a feast of

dog meat, four old warriors rose to "dance against the dog head," which symbolized the enemy. Each one pantomimed how he received his wound, then gave a speech and distributed gifts (Wilson 1914b:87, 99).

GRASS DANCER
Drawn by Goodbird, 1914
Pencil and watercolor on paper. See color page 175
H. 18.5 cm, W. 17 cm
AMNH (Goodbird 1914b:fig. 5)
Goodbird drew this sketch of one of the feather trail wearers in the Grass Dance. "The pattern of the body painting is not distinctive of the Grass Dance," he explained. "It was just a very common pattern used by young men when I was a boy" (Wilson 1914b:45). The dancer wears a porcupine and deer-tail roach, a hair pipe necklace, armbands made of nickel and brass, a belt of leather studded with brass tacks, garters with sleigh bells and quill-wrapped rawhide slats, and dogskin moccasins. The feather trail or bustle he wears, sometimes called the "crow belt," is made from eagle feathers mounted on wool, or as Goodbird called it, "Indian cloth, which was quite expensive then, of a red, or deep blue, or black dye" (Wissler 1916:862; Wilson 1914b:47). He carries "a stick or skewer to lift food by, in a feast, as for example out of the pot, – a kind of one-tined eating fork so to speak." The skewer was used to perform a ceremonial "feeding" of the feather trails and the Grass Dance officers (Wilson 1914b:49).

Dancing was an important part of the ceremony. "We young men who had not yet won any honor marks were all dressed up very elegantly," said Wolf Chief, "and we danced about very fast and quickly and nimbly. Those who had been in war and had honor marks . . . marched about here and there with a quick marching step, going through the pantomime of their war experience. Thus one would hold up a little wooden model of a gun. Another would pretend to shoot; another would take the little wooden gun from one who brandished such, or would pretend to scalp him, provided, however, the latter were a [clan] brother or else a brother in law. . . .

"We danced very often in our Grass Dance Society, and each time that we had a formal dance horses and other valuable presents were given away.

"I have myself in my life given away many valuable gifts; among them ten war bonnets and a great many horses. I do not believe there is any one on this Reservation who has given away as many horses as I" (Wilson 1914b:106-7, 109).

But even though the men of the family embraced the Grass Dance enthusiastically, Buffalo Bird Woman remained skeptical of the new Sioux fad. "I quit dancing early," she said. "I did not care much for dancing anyway and I have no interest in dances brought in from foreign tribes. . . .

"Our tribe bought these new songs and thought them better, but I did not think them so" (Wilson 1911:178).

HEADDRESS
Hidatsa. Bought from Ben Benson
Collected by Gilbert Wilson, 1907
Porcupine guard hair dyed green, yellow, and red, woven and sewn into base
L. 27 cm
Museum of the American Indian, Heye Foundation 1/3791

This kind of headdress, called a roach, was part of the Grass Dance regalia. Wolf Chief said, "The headdress was of deer tail of the white-tailed deer, and porcupine bristles, or moose bristles. Only this one kind of headdress was given. Of the seventy Hidatsas and Mandans that were initiated into the dance not every one received this headdress, only a portion of them; but what proportion of them received the headdress I do not know" (Wilson 1914b:46, 84).

DANCE GARTERS
Northern Plains style
Rawhide slats wrapped with quills dyed orange, purple, red, and blue, sewn with thread onto a beige fabric backing. Red wool borders top and bottom, the latter cut to make a fringe. Strips of tanned hide at corners for tying garters to leg
Left: W. 32 cm, H. 22.8 cm. Right: W. 33.5 cm, H. 23.5 cm
MHS 8034.32, C. B. Lyons

Garters and belts, often trimmed with quillwork and sleigh bells, were worn as part of dance outfits, and Wolf Chief mentioned them as part of the officers' uniforms when he joined the Grass Dance (Wilson 1914b:81). Goodbird's illustrations of Grass Dance costumes both show garters worn just below the knees (Goodbird 1914:figs. 5, 12).

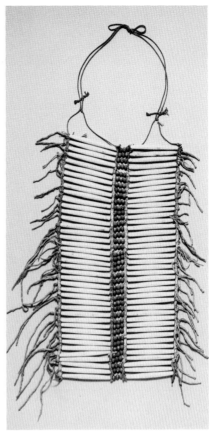

GRASS DANCE DRUMSTICK
Mandan / Hidatsa
Collected by Robert Lowie, 1910
Wooden handle covered with red and white patterned calico over which a single
*   strand of blue and white beads has been wrapped. On one end is a triangular*
*   flap beaded in blue, black, red, and yellow, with a tanned hide fringe with*
*   two eagle feathers attached. To the other end are attached green and yellow*
*   ribbons, red feathers, and yellow and blue horsehair*
L. 71.5 cm
AMNH 50.1/4341, Lowie

This decorated drumstick was carried by an officer in the Grass Dance. Its use was
ceremonial rather than practical. Wolf Chief remembered how he learned his duties
as a drumstick carrier. "The Sioux now called out, 'You men who have been elected
to be drumstick carriers, come and take your places by the drum.'

"I and the other drumstick men came forward and stood beside the drum.
One of the Sioux now addressed us.

"'We will now teach you the duties of the drumstick carriers. At every dance
you are to strike the drum once with the knotted end of the drumstick, and each
one of you as he strikes shall give away a present to some person of his selection.
This ceremony of striking the drum opens the dance.'

"Obeying these instructions I and the other drumstick carriers each struck the
drum, and I gave the shirt that I was wearing to one of my [clan] fathers.

"The drumstick was long: about two and a half feet; and was covered with
beads, sometimes feathers or weasel skins were tied to it." Goodbird added that the
beads were customarily blue and white (Wilson 1914b:41, 84-85).

HAIRPIPE NECKLACE
Northern Plains
Collected by R. Fiksdel, pre-1931
Two rows each of 41 tubular bone
*   beads strung horizontally on flour*
*   sack rag twisted and stretched*
*   between vertical strips of leather.*
*   Faceted, rose-colored glass beads*
*   form a row down the middle. Neck*
*   strap and fringe of cloth string*
L. 42 cm, W. 22 cm
Science Museum of Minnesota A61-8,
*   Reiff Collection*

Hairpipes, long thin beads made from
animal bone, were thus named because
they were originally worn in the hair.
At first they were rare and costly, but
they became more common after a
manufacturer in Chicago found a way to
mass-produce them from the leg bones
of slaughtered cattle. On the Plains,
they were made into tiered necklaces or
breastplates worn by both men and
women. The standard man's hairpipe
necklace reached from neck to waist.
The woman's breastplate reached below
her waist, sometimes to her ankles.
Goodbird illustrated a hairpipe necklace
as part of the Grass Dancer's costume
(Goodbird 1914b:fig. 5; see also MHS
photo II-3; Ewers 1957).

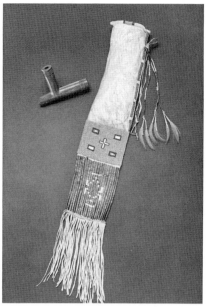

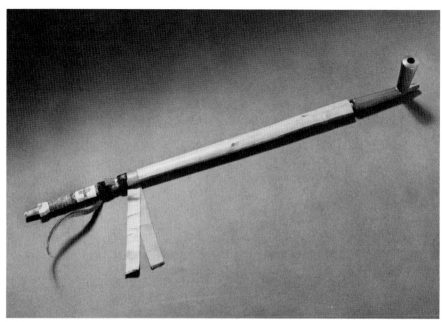

PIPE

Stem: Northern Plains. Bowl: from Fort Clark, N.Dak.
Stem collected by Gilbert Wilson. Bowl collected by Frederick Wilson, pre-1918?
Flat stem of wood with hole bored through center, wrapped with red, white, and
purple braided quillwork; decorated with two fur strips, red horsehair, yellow
silk thread, and red satin ribbon. Elbow-shaped bowl of catlinite with short
front projection and fire-blackened smoke hole
Stem: L. 71.2 cm. Bowl: L. 15.7 cm, H. 10.1 cm
MHS 7059.103a, 9598.4

The pipes used in the Grass Dance and other ceremonies had flat stems decorated
with quillwork and horsehair. Originally these decorations reflected the honor marks
of the owner, but later they came to be accepted as generic decorations. The
ceremonial pipe bearers' duty, said Goodbird, was "to keep these pipes filled and
hand them around to be smoked. Some one in the company would say, 'Pipe filler,
fill the pipe for us!' . . . The pipe filler [then] would fill his pipe and bring it to the
one asking for it together with matches for lighting it, for these were commonly used
in my time" (Wilson 1914b:44).

PIPE BOWL AND PIPE BAG

Sioux. Bought from Butterfly,
Hidatsa, who was given it by Long
Fox, a Montana Sioux
Collected by Gilbert Wilson, 1909
Elbow-shaped catlinite pipe bowl with
tapered front projection and
circular ridges carved around bowl
and base. Bag of tanned hide with
beaded rim and quill-wrapped
tassels ending in tinklers and pink
horsehair. Panel at base of bag of
blue, white, yellow, pink, and
green beadwork, below which are
quill-wrapped slats with a red,
white, and purple geometric design,
ending in a long hide fringe
Bowl: L. 17 cm, H. 10.4 cm. Bag: L.
85 cm
AMNH 50.1/5350a, b

The Grass Dance and other Indian
cultural movements of the late 19th
century provided a forum for intertribal
exchange, which often took the form
of gift-giving and adoption ceremonies.
Long Fox, who made this pipe and
bag, gave it to Butterfly to
commemorate their adoptive in-law
relationship (Wilson 1909a:131).
Catlinite or pipestone was mined in
Minnesota and carried or traded to
people farther west. Like other gift
pipes, this one was presented in the
decorated bag in which it and the
tobacco were carried. The stem of the
pipe is missing; its bowl closely
resembles a Grass Dance pipe bowl
illustrated by Goodbird (Goodbird
1914b:fig. 4).

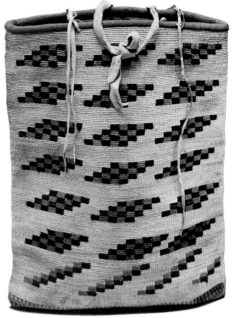

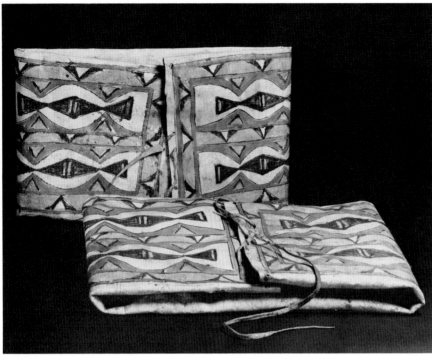

PAIR OF PARFLECHES
*Sioux. Bought from Wounded Face, Mandan, who got them from a Standing
   Rock Sioux*
Collected by Gilbert Wilson, 1910
Rawhide painted red, blue, and yellow
L. 59 cm, W. 33.5 cm
AMNH 50.1/5476, 5477

Hidatsa relations with the Sioux were complex. Even during the years of outright
war between the tribes, commerce and personal friendships continued. About the
same time the Hidatsa received the Grass Dance from the Devils Lake Sioux to the
north, Wolf Chief went on a war party against the Standing Rock Sioux to the
south. "The government had given a big reservation to the Sioux at Standing Rock,"
he explained, "but the land was not theirs but ours, and for that reason we went
down and fought those Sioux" (Wilson 1914b:56).

Unfortunately, Wilson did not record the circumstances under which
Wounded Face acquired this pair of parfleches from a Standing Rock Sioux. These
rawhide bags, used for storing meat, clothes, and other items, were often given as
gifts; a particularly generous family would fill the parfleches before giving them away.
Sioux women often decorated their parfleches with bright geometric designs.

CORN HUSK BAG
*Nez Percé style. Bought from Mrs.
   Foolish Woman, Mandan.
   Brought to Fort Berthold by
   visiting Crow Indians*
Collected by Gilbert Wilson, 1909
*Corn husk fiber interwoven with red,
   black, green, and blue wool yarn
   in geometric patterns. Rim bound
   with red wool. Tanned hide
   handle*
H. 41 cm, W. 31.3 cm
AMNH 50.1/5364

Corn husk bags, woven by the Nez
Percé and other western tribes, were
brought to Like-a-Fishhook Village by
the Crow Indians (Wilson 1909a:135),
who were closely related to the
Hidatsa. The Crow acted as middlemen
in trades and gift exchanges among
these tribes. The interchanges traveled
in both directions; the Crow bought
the Grass Dance from the Hidatsa in
the 1870s (Wissler 1916:868).

DRUM AND DRUMSTICK
See page 310

PAINTED HIDE
See page 51

GIRL'S DRESS
See page 57

GEORGE CATLIN, "HIDATSA VILLAGE, EARTH-COVERED LODGES"
See page 7

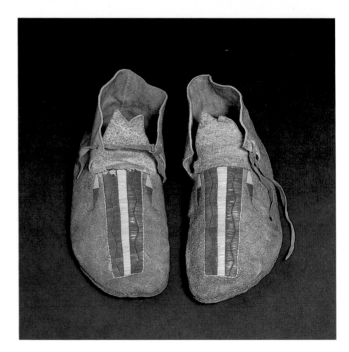

MOCCASINS
See page 51

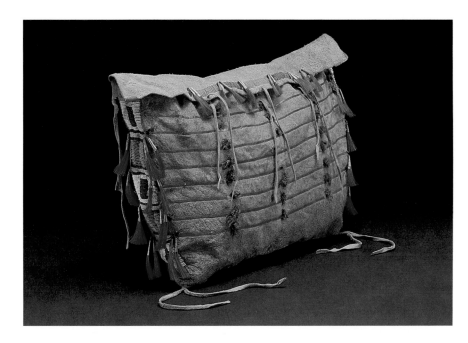

STORAGE BAG
See page 39

KARL BODMER, "LANDSCAPE WITH
HERD OF BUFFALO ON THE UPPER
MISSOURI"
See page 81

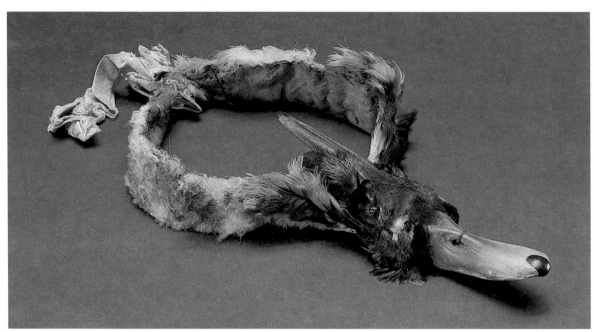

GOOSE SOCIETY HEADBAND
See page 33

BURDEN BASKET
See page 16

QUILT
See page 256

WILLIAM DE LA MONTAGNE CARY, "ENROUTE TO WINTER CAMP, INDIAN DOG
SLEDS CROSSING ICE"
See page 26

LEGGINGS
See page 105

JULIAN SCOTT, "PORTRAIT OF
GOOD BIRD"
See page 196

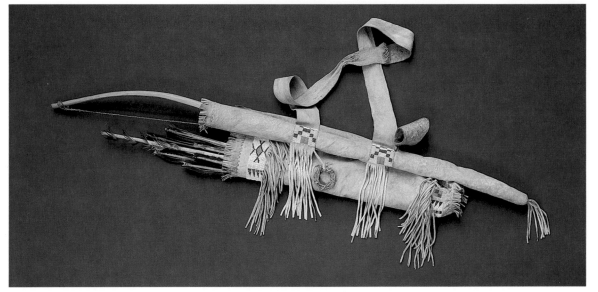

BOW AND ARROW SET
See page 103

HEADDRESS
See page 306

HEADDRESS
See page 307

Yellow horse hair

Headdress of deer hair + porcupine

Horse hair single hide

Eagle plumes

whole eagle tail

bands of quill work

grass wrists

Belt of leather brass nails

ribbons sewed together

dark blue cloth

quill work

dog skin

GRASS DANCER
See page 160

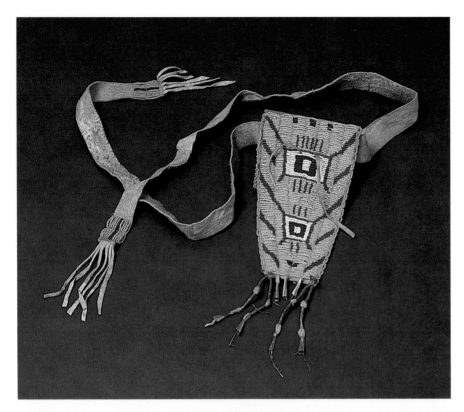

FLINT CARRYING CASE WITH BELT
See page 50

PIPE
See page 89

FREDERICK WILSON, "INTERIOR OF AN EARTH LODGE"
See page 300

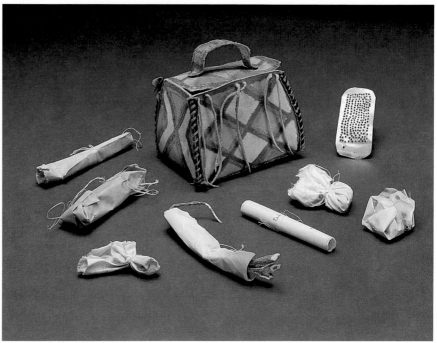

BOX WITH HERB CURES
See page 23

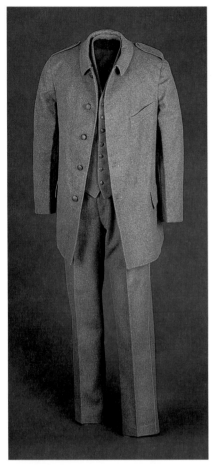

INDIAN POLICEMAN'S UNIFORM
See page 216

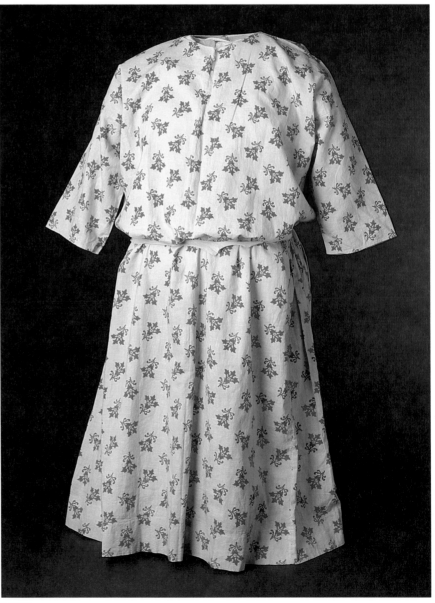

DRESS
See page 257

STORE MERCHANDISE
See page 220

CRAZY DOG SOCIETY SASH
See page 92

WILLIAM DE LA MONTAGNE CARY, "FIRE CANOE AT FT. BERTHOLD"
See page 12

The journey to Independence

The Grass Dance drums still rang over Like-a-Fishhook when news started coming from the east that would change the lives of Buffalo Bird Woman's family forever.

The United States government had changed its policy toward Indians. Up to 1870, Indian reservations had been seen as separate nations within the nation, to be owned and used according to tribal, not European, custom. The government treated tribes like foreign countries, not like other ethnic groups. But by the 1880s, this no longer satisfied most white Americans. They wanted nothing less than total assimilation – the seamless blending of Indians into mainstream American society, until they ceased to exist as separate groups.

Policy toward Indians closely reflected other events in the eastern United States. In the 1880s, development and progress were the watchwords in the country's newspapers and corporate offices. The frontier was disappearing. Railroads spanned the continent. The people in power believed in self-reliance, achievement, and prosperity.

But there was also fear in the air: fear of people who were different. Hundreds of new languages and customs were coming to the New World along with a tide of immigrants. Many Americans feared that the country would splinter apart if its people could not all blend together into a common culture. Minorities would have to break their ties to the past in order to participate in the great American experiment, the "new phase of Aryan civilization" that was spreading irresistibly across the West (Hoxie 1984:25).

Indian reservations stood in the way of those who wanted to develop Western land and incorporate its native people into the American melting pot. As one writer put it, reservations were "islands, and about them a sea of civilization, vast and irresistible, surges" (Hoxie 1984:12). In this atmosphere of siege, the government made a crucial decision: reservations had to be abolished.

The dismantling of reservations was to be accomplished through a policy called *allotment*. Under its provisions, reservation land would no longer belong to the tribe as a whole, but would be parceled out among individual Indians. Each head of a family would receive 160 acres. "Surplus" land left over would be sold off to whites. Once an Indian received a deed to his land, he became eligible for full citizenship in the United States of America, including the right to vote and pay taxes. The government took responsibility for "giving to the Indian Anglo-Saxon civilization" in exchange for the land he would lose (Hoxie 1984:24).

The architects of allotment had an almost mystical faith in the power of private property to spark a revolution in Indian life. "It is impossible to overestimate the influence of property in the civilization of mankind," one anthropologist wrote. Congressman Henry Dawes, the author of the Allotment Act, measured civilization in material property. To be civilized was to "wear civilized clothes, . . . cultivate the ground, live in houses, ride in Studebaker wagons, send [one's] children to school, drink whisky, [and] own property." Reformers like Dawes felt that once Indians

SMALL ANKLE AND SONS
c. 1882
Collected by Gilbert Wilson
MHS (Wilson [1903-18]:268)
The circumstances under which this studio portrait was taken are unknown. Standing are Charging Enemy and Red Kettle; seated are Wolf Chief and Small Ankle. Small Ankle died in 1888 (Wilson 1913b:555).

received deeds to their own land, they would abandon tribal ties and become self-sufficient entrepreneurs. The economy-minded government would then be saved the expense of treaty payments. "Ownership of lands . . . should be looked forward to as the ultimate settlement of our Indian problems," a policy maker wrote (Hoxie 1984:19, 42, 24).

Allotment came early to Like-a-Fishhook Village. At the agency, staff members disapproved of life in the congested village, where old traditions flourished. One agent wrote that "Unless the Indians are removed some *distance* from their village, the tribal organization broken up, and they are deprived of the means, and the opportunities for dances, and ceremonies, by scattering them out on farms, it will in my judgment, be impossible to civilize and render them self-supporting" (Courtenay 1879a).

"What the agent wanted was to make us farmers," Goodbird said. "He wanted to scatter us all over the reservation so that we would each have an allotment for a farm. . . . The agent had said to us, 'You people had better leave the village and take up claims. You should choose your claims where there is good land.' About one-third of the village people took up his advice" (Wilson 1913a:52-53).

The people started leaving Like-a-Fishhook in about 1885. Before long, they were scattered for 50 miles up and down the Missouri. The Arikara took up claims in the eastern part of the reservation, forming the small community of Nishu. The Mandans congregated south of the river, around the villages of Red Butte and Charging Eagle. And the Hidatsa lived to the north at Lucky Mound, Independence, and Shell Creek (Hall 1937n; Meyer 1977:192; see map p. ix).

In June of Goodbird's 16th year his family left the village for good. "We crossed the Missouri in a bullboat," he said. "With a monkey wrench we took our wagon apart, taking off the wheels and unlocking or unbolting every part that we were able. These parts we loaded in the bullboat, swimming our horses over the river" (Wilson 1913a:53).

"They wanted to be independent," missionary Charles Hall later wrote of the group of four or five families that went with Goodbird's. They traveled upstream 40 miles from the village, to where a tall hill stood alone above a sharp curve in the river. "The Hidatsas called it Awatahesh, that is the hill by itself," the missionary said. "So considering the character of the people, as well as the landscape, we called the place Independence" (Hall 1937q).

Wolf Chief was among the last to leave the old village (Gifford 1886:1). He chose his allotment in a way the policy makers in Washington never foresaw. Years before, when fasting for a vision, he had dreamed of standing on the lone hill called Awatahesh. Hearing a voice that cried, "A boat comes," he had walked over to a big stone and looked down toward the river, where a steamboat was coming up the stream. Following the dream, he built his cabin on the crest of Independence Hill.

Years later, Wolf Chief reflected on his choice. "Often I walk to that very same big stone which you

WOLF CHIEF AND FAMILY
c. 1882
Collected by Gilbert Wilson
MHS (Wilson [1903-18]:268)
From left to right, these are Female Coyote, Frank Wolf Chief, and Wolf Chief. Frank was the longest-lived of Wolf Chief's children. He died in 1902, while at college in Fargo (Wolf Chief 1905:2; Watkins 1902).

see out there in front of my cabin and from that stone I have seen many steamboats coming up the river, so all that I saw in that dream has come true. I have prospered here and am a hale old man, though my former wife died here and my children, but then they never had this dream. Perhaps it was God who gave me that dream. I do not know. I only know that all that I saw in that dream has come true" (Wilson 1916b:64).

The move to allotments meant the breakup of a communal way of life that had been the Hidatsa tradition for as far back as memory reached. In its place was put a uniquely American settlement pattern: a surveyed gridwork of square plots. True to Yankee ideals of self-reliance, allotments isolated each nuclear family on its own farmstead. At Like-a-Fishhook, Goodbird remembered, "four or five families lived in one large earth lodge, but now we built each family a cabin for themselves" (Wilson 1913a:52).

It was an isolated way of life. "Older Indians, who came from Like-a-Fishhook Village, find their life on allotments rather lonesome," Goodbird said. "Cabins are often two or three miles apart and the old men cannot amuse themselves with books, for they cannot read. In old times, Indians often met in big dances; but pagan ceremonies are used in these dances, and Mr. Hall does not like the Christian Indians to go to them" (Goodbird 1914a:71). At Like-a-Fishhook, agents and missionaries had tried unsuccessfully to break up societies, clans, and religious organizations, the framework of Hidatsa social life. But where they had failed, it seemed as if the sheer vastness of the North Dakota plains might succeed.

As the people left Like-a-Fishhook, the agent had the old earth lodges destroyed to prevent anyone coming back (Meyer 1977:135). Gradually, the village crumbled away. "Rings of dirt where the lodges used to stand, half-filled cache holes all covered with weeds, – these are all that remain," the missionary wrote. But the village still held a spot in the people's hearts. They came back now and then to walk over the site that held so much of their past, tracing the outlines of old houses. "We feel as though we had come to a great river," one man said as he looked at the empty village site. "And the way over is not plain" (Hall 1937n).

"VIEW OVER THE INDIAN VILLAGE"
1887
AMNH 15979
The lodges at Like-a-Fishook were being dismantled when this photograph was taken in July 1887.

BULLBOAT
Mandan. Made by Owl Woman and Many Growths
Collected by Gilbert Wilson, 1916
Cowhide stretched hair side out over a frame of wooden rods tied with tanned
*   hide and cotton strips*
H. 55 cm, D. 138 cm
Science Museum of Minnesota A76:2:399

Bullboats, so called because the largest were made from buffalo bull hides, were
made by stretching a hide over a framework of pliable wood. The boats were almost
round and the best ones were flat on the bottom for stability. Goodbird explained,
"A bullboat is usually paddled by one person, kneeling, (or sometimes sitting,) in the
forward part of the boat and dipping the paddle directly before. In old times the
bullboat was rather a woman's craft, tho men used it also. Often a war party would
float in a bullboat by night, down into the enemy's country, steal horses and ride
back, abandoning the boat.

"A bullboat is sometimes paddled by two persons, one on either side, as in a
canoe.

"A bullboat should be built so that the covering hide runs length wise with
the bottommost ribs of the frame. This avoids friction against the water by the ribs.

"The boat should be paddled so that the tail of the hide is behind, so the hair
will not rise and make friction against the water" (Wilson 1911:278, 1914b:19-22;
Goodbird 1914b:fig. 37; MHS photos II-13 to II-29, II-94, II-95, IV-86-1911 to
IV-94-1911, V-19-1912 to V-31-1912, and VIII-57-1916 to VIII-67-1916).

Wagon

Late 19th century
Freight wagon with wooden box once painted red, wooden wheels with iron rims,
*   cast iron hubs, fittings, and brake mechanism; some wrought iron repairs.*
*   Seat from a separate wagon*
L. 365 cm, W. 172.5 cm, H. 136 cm
Olmsted County Historical Society 09130

Wagons were among the earliest and most popular of issue goods. "Our wagons were issued to us by the government," Buffalo Bird Woman said. "Fifteen were issued the first summer and fifteen the next summer, and pretty soon everyone in the village was using them. We often borrowed wagons, one from another. . . . The first wagon owned in the tribe was owned by Had Many Antelopes. My father hired him with a pair of pantaloons to bring in the corn from our gardens for one year. He fetched three wagon loads from my own garden" (Wilson 1913a : 324, 1912 : 159).

The wagon owned by Buffalo Bird Woman's family during their move to Independence was likely a "Studebaker" made by the Moline Wagon Company of Illinois, since 31 such wagons were issued to "deserving" Indians in August, 1880 (Gardner 1880; Kauffman 1880b).

Monkey Wrench

Made by [Pennsyl?]vania Wrench
*   Co., Meadville, Pa., early 20th*
*   century*
Iron with adjustable lower jaw moved
*   by turning a hexagonal nut on a*
*   threaded stem*
L. 30 cm, W. 7 cm
MHS 1986.100.12

The wrench Goodbird's family used to take their wagon apart to cross the Missouri must have looked like this. By the time the family moved, wrenches and other tools were common among the Three Tribes.

MAP OF INDEPENDENCE
Compiled from township survey maps for T149-150N, R91W, in RG 75, "Indian Plats," Vol. 58, Map Dept., NA; and FB, Farm Records, Dept. of Interior, p. 54, NA, Kansas City

The community of Independence had several notable landmarks:

1 School. In 1895 the government established Day School No. 2 at Independence (Meyer 1977:148). In 1918, the day schools on the reservation taught up to third grade. Many of the inhabitants of the Independence area lived too far from the school for their children to walk each day, so consistent attendance was difficult. In addition to the children's classes, the day school teachers were expected to "assist the Indians to a very large degree in farming and stock raising, holding meetings at their schools for the purpose of stimulating interest." As a result, the day school was a center of community activity (Jermark 1918:11; Knight 1917:14).

2 Church. In early days, the Congregational Indians at Independence met in a log house; in 1910 they built a frame chapel. It was a good place to see old friends. "That our Christian Indians may meet socially now and then, we now observe many white men's holidays," Goodbird said. "At such times, we make our chapel the meeting place. In August, we hold a Young Men's Christian Convention, when families come from miles around, to camp in tents around the chapel. At Christmas, we have feasting and giving of presents; and our chapel is so crowded that many have to stand without, and look through the windows" (Wilson 1910b:9; Goodbird 1914a:71).

3 Store. Wolf Chief opened a general store adjoining his house; it became a major meeting place.

4 Issue house. Since the agency was across the river and 40 miles away, it was impossible for residents of Independence to get there every other week to collect rations. Therefore, the

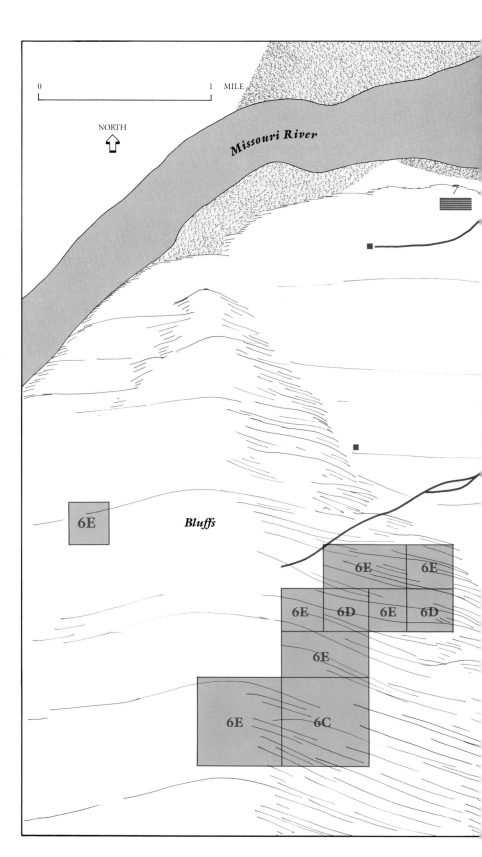

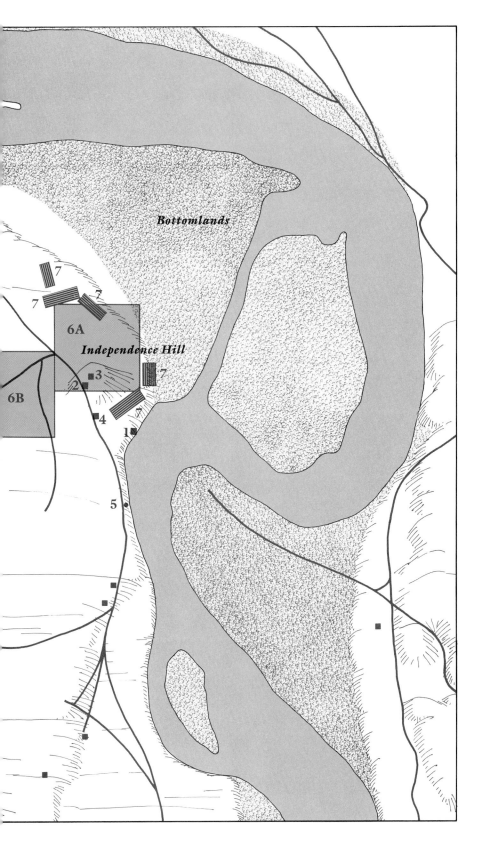

government erected a frame house for issuing rations. Goodbird and his family later moved into the old issue house.

5 Ferry. In winter, the people of Independence drove sleighs or walked across the iced-over river; but in summer they operated their own oar-powered ferry. Across the river was a north-south road that connected the communities of Elbowoods, Lucky Mound, and Shell Creek.

6 Allotments. Although the Hidatsa moved onto farms in the 1880s, they did not receive legal title to their land until surveyors came through in the 1890s (Meyer 1977:137-38). The government judged that 160 acres was ample for a farm, as was true in the eastern United States. Land was parceled out on a first-come, first-served basis, with children often receiving small plots in the hilly range country away from the river after all the choice spots near the river were taken. Members of Goodbird's family were luckier than many, because their allotments were relatively clustered; families with scattered allotments could not pool their land. In later years the original allotments were "fractionated" as the land was split up among large families.

The allotments shown here belonged to: **A**, Son of a Star; **B**, Wolf Chief; **C**, Goodbird; **D**, Buffalo Bird Woman; **E**, Goodbird's children.

7 Fields. At Like-a-Fishhook, farming had taken place in the fertile bottomlands along the river. The agents, on the other hand, encouraged the Hidatsa to farm on the level bench lands between the river bottom and the bluffs. Whites typically thought the wide-open plains of North Dakota had only to be developed to become productive. Because of this, they tried to get the Hidatsa to orient their lives away from the river and toward the "undeveloped" uplands.

STEAMBOAT ON THE MISSOURI
Photographed by Gilbert Wilson, 1915
MHS photo VII-90-15
This photograph was probably taken from Independence, not far from Wolf Chief's house.

MISSOURI RIVER VALLEY
Photographed by Gilbert Wilson, 1908
MHS photo III-9
The contrast between the low, wooded bottomlands and the dry, sandy uplands can be seen in this view from Hawk's Nest Bluff. The bottomlands provided wood, plants, game, and farm land for the Hidatsa.

SADDLE BUTTE
Photographed by Gilbert Wilson, 1915
MHS photo IV-15
This prominent landmark a few miles south of Independence is typical of the rugged badlands formations in the western part of Fort Berthold Reservation. The arid uplands away from the river were virtually useless for agriculture.

INDEPENDENCE DAY SCHOOL
1933
NA (File 40205/1933, FB 800, CCF, USOIA, RG 75)
The original log school building (foreground) had been
demoted to a stable by the time this picture was taken. It was
replaced by a new frame structure (background).

OLD ISSUE HOUSE, INDEPENDENCE
1890s?
Collected by Harold Case
SHSND Col. 41-368

MEETING HOUSE AND DWELLING, INDEPENDENCE
1897
Collected by Harold Case
SHSND Col. 41-431
The Congregational mission established a branch at Independence in the 1890s. In the early years, religious gatherings were held in
the building on the left. The building at right was a dwelling, probably for the mission worker, who at this time was Elizabeth
Kehoe (Kehoe 1896; Hall 1897).

Independence in Winter
1904
Collected by Harold Case
From a cracked glass plate negative
SHSND Col. 41-400

Winter weather was more severe at Independence on the exposed bench land than in the sheltered bottomland where the Hidatsa had traditionally wintered. In 1893 the agent told of one storm that lasted three days; "during a great part of the time the thermometer registered 50 degrees below zero." Much livestock perished because people could not find their barns during the storm (Murphy 1893b).

Scenes at Independence
Photographed by Gilbert Wilson, 1914-18
MHS photos VI-57-14, X-47-1918, and VIII-38-1916

These unidentified scenes preserve the flavor of life at Independence. They show: top, a child standing by a fire where meat is being smoked; right, a girl fetching water from the river; bottom, a girl harvesting beans. As at Like-a-Fishhook, women descended the steep riverbank several times a day for water, but they fetched it in galvanized metal pails.

Son of a Star's cabin

For a month after arriving at Independence, Goodbird's family camped in a tipi while they built a house. In former times, construction would have been Buffalo Bird Woman's responsibility. But here, building a house was no longer sacred, and no longer a woman's job. The four central posts that Buffalo Bird Woman knew how to measure, cut, and pray over were gone. The floor plan was not circular, but square as a township grid. And the men were the ones who directed the action.

"My father built our cabin with my mother's help and mine," Goodbird said. "Our tools were an axe, shovel, spade, hoe, plow, saw, hammer and hatchet. My father cut down the trees to make the logs for our cabin. He hitched our team to the logs and dragged them one by one to the wagon, on which they were loaded. As these logs were cut, they were trimmed of their branches. The bark was peeled off and they were hauled on the wagon to the place that was to be the site of the cabin. We cut, as I remember, forty logs, ten for each side; and one big log for the ridge pole, one foot in diameter. The cabin was about eight and one-half feet high. The logs were notched at the ends so that they would lock into one another. Rafters were cut, four inches in diameter, and then laid on the ridge pole for the roof. On these were laid willows, grass and sod. . . . My mother plastered the cracks with mud" (Wilson 1913a:53-55).

In many ways, Son of a Star's new house seemed exactly like a white settler's cabin. It was a secular space, unlike the sacred earth lodge. It had glass windows, a hard dirt floor, and an iron stove. If it was like most other Hidatsa homes of the period, the main room was furnished with low benches that ran around the outside walls and two bedsteads made of unplaned wood. In earth lodges, all family activities happened in the same large room, but cabins had a partition that divided the house into men's and women's spaces. The women's room was, according to one observer, "kitchen, pantry, store-room, women's living and sleeping room, nursery, etc., combined" (Hall 1888b).

But there were subtle things that made the house different from a white man's. Although many families cooked on a stove instead of an open fire, they still left a smoke hole in the roof instead of windows (Meyer 1977:124). Unlike whites, who placed their stoves against the wall, Hidatsa families often put the stove in the center of the main room, where the earth lodge fireplace had been. And standards of behavior were still different. Simply having board doors did not mean using them as white people did. In most Hidatsa homes, the door stood open all day; and if a visitor found the door closed, he did not knock, but waited outside until the host noticed him (Hall 1888b, 1937l). Inside, there were still certain places for seats: women on one side, men on the other, and the place of honor opposite the door (Hall 1937k).

But perhaps most meaningful was what Son of a Star did when he finished building his new log cabin. On the roof over the door he placed a buffalo skull, symbol of the Wolf Ceremony into which he had been initiated. A new architecture could not alter his pride in that (Wilson 1913a:55).

SON OF A STAR'S CABIN
Drawn by Goodbird, 1913
Blue carbon and black ink on tracing paper
H. 5.4 cm, W. 16 cm
MHS (Goodbird 1913:fig. 10)
Son of a Star's cabin at Independence faced south, with Goodbird's bed on the east side and his parents' on the west (Wilson 1913a:54). Most homes of the time had a main room that measured about 20 feet square and a second one half that size (Hall 1888b). This house, unlike some others, appears to have a stovepipe chimney.

CABIN INTERIOR
Photographed by Gilbert Wilson, 1914
MHS photos VI-81-14 and VI-82-14
Although this up-to-date cabin with board floors, curtains, and whitewashed walls is unidentified, it may have been Goodbird's. Chairs had replaced the earlier benches, but they were still placed around the outside walls. The stove was in the center of the room. The family, in the midst of a meal, sat with women on the right and men on the left.

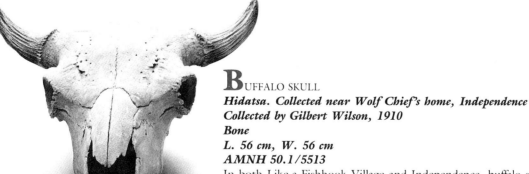

BUFFALO SKULL
Hidatsa. Collected near Wolf Chief's home, Independence
Collected by Gilbert Wilson, 1910
Bone
L. 56 cm, W. 56 cm
AMNH 50.1/5513
In both Like-a-Fishhook Village and Independence, buffalo skulls were placed on roof tops to indicate that an inhabitant had purchased membership in a religious ceremony. The number of skulls indicated the number of ceremonies represented in the home. The buffalo skull remained on Son of a Star's roof to the end of his life (Wilson [1903-18]:61).

FELLING AX
Head made by Reser(?) and Co., Chicago, late 19th century
Wedge-shaped iron head with rectangular, reinforced poll, flared sides, and oval
* eye. Handle reconstructed*
L. 90 cm, W. 13 cm
MHS 1982.105.34

The first step in building a log house was felling and notching the trees, a task either a man or woman might perform. "My wife helped me," Wolf Chief said of building his cabin. "We worked the same. Sometimes she used the ax and sometimes I" (Wilson 1916c:53). Wolf Chief commented on how the old men talked about life before the introduction of metal tools: "'In olden times,' these old men used to say, 'we led a harder life than now. If we had not worked mighty hard, we would have died out. It was hard work to build earth lodges with stone axes, and hunt with flint arrow heads. Now that we have iron, and steel arrow points, life is much easier for us'" (Wilson 1918a:354–55).

HAMMER
c. 1880
Cast steel head with round face and
* wedge-shaped peen. Wooden handle*
* inserted through oval eye and*
* secured with nails pounded into top*
L. 32 cm, W. 13 cm
MHS 6774, Mrs. Theodore Ungerman

Although house construction was traditionally a Hidatsa woman's job, agents issued construction tools to men in order to encourage them to take over this role. Buffalo Bird Woman voiced approval of the new technology, but did not comment on the social roles it implied: "In old times and even when I was young, it was hard for us to get tools; and house building of any kind was hard work. Now we can build a house of any shape we wish, and tools are easy to get. In this respect our new way of living is better than the old" (Wilson 1918a:375).

This wagon maker's hammer could be used for either metal or woodworking.

NAILS
19th century
Square-sided, flat-headed, tapered
* cut nails*
L. 3 cm to 12 cm
MHS 9925, Vern Klossner

Traditional Hidatsa building techniques did not require nails, but Wolf Chief used them when he built a wooden door for his log cabin. "We had a door for the cabin with hinges of rawhide. Door made of planks – two boards I got of the agency at either side & these I split with an ax in the middle. Used nails I pounded in with a stone – got of agency issue." Goodbird's sketch of the door shows the two boards nailed top and bottom to the split planks (Wilson 1916c:54, 55).

CROSSCUT SAW
Made by H. Disston & Sons,
* Philadelphia, early 20th century*
Skewback hand saw with small-toothed
* metal blade fastened with four*
* brass rivets to a wooden handle*
L. 16 cm, W. 13 cm
MHS 1982.105.53

The Hidatsa got board lumber at the agency sawmill for making doors and furniture, and the agency carpenter taught the use of woodworking tools. In 1879 the agent wrote, "In the beginning of the present summer an issue of a number of carpenter's and blacksmith's tools and farming implements was made and a good many of the Indians have made for themselves doors, bedsteads, stables, corrals and hay and wood racks, etc." (Wilson 1913a:73; USOIA 1879:30).

GOODBIRD'S CABIN
Photographed by Gilbert Wilson, 1906
MHS (Wilson [1903-18]:65)
This photograph illustrates a somewhat later construction technique, in which the logs were squared off and the eaves finished with boards. As late as 1915, sod roofs were "an institution of rural North Dakota" used by both whites and Indians, according to a government worker (Michael 1915:cover sheet). At right is a corral.

EARTH LODGE
Photographed by Gilbert Wilson, 1908
MHS photo III-36
Earth lodge architecture did not disappear at Independence; it was often used for stables and summer kitchens. The structures, however, were not as carefully built as before. Goodbird said, "Our own family's first barn was just four forked posts sunk two feet in the ground with stringers in the forks, and poles the size of corral poles leaned against these stringers; then willows, hay and dirt to cover all. . . . The door of this barn was made of planks that were issued to us by the government sawmill" (Wilson 1913a:72-73). This earth lodge belonged to White Woman, a resident of Independence.

Goodbird seeks his god

Independence was a good name for the family's new home for more than one reason. To whites, the name expressed the residents' spirit of self-help. But for many Indians, there was a more important independence than the economic kind: independence from the agency, the mission, and other aspects of the encroaching white world.

"The first effect of our coming to Independence was to send me back to old ways," Goodbird said. "I was not under the influence of the missionaries as I had been." In this situation, he began to turn again to his own people's religion (Wilson 1913a:56, 104).

Years before, when he had been a child living in Like-a-Fishhook Village, Goodbird had gone with his father Son of a Star to witness a Sun Dance. One aspect of the ceremony was a ritual self-sacrifice. "I saw Turtle No Head with his breast pierced and thongs tied to skewers in the wounds, and these fastened by a lariat to a forked post. The women were crying, 'A-la-la-la-la-lá' while the old men looked on and cried out, 'Good! That's the way a man should do! That's doing a man's part! You should go through much suffering here, and then you will win many honor marks. A man should always be willing to suffer in order to find his god!'

"I was much stirred by what I saw, and by the applause of the old men. My father was with me as I looked at the dancers; and when we returned home I said to him, 'Father, when I get big I am going into the Sun Dance and do like Turtle No Head.'

"'Good!' he said, laughing" (Wilson 1913a:103–4).

"We Indians did not torture ourselves for amusement by any means," Goodbird explained. "A man tortured himself because he thought it was necessary to have the protection of the gods if he would lead a prosperous life, and there was no way to get an answer from the gods but by torturing one's self, and praying to the spirits until one of them answered in a dream or a vision.

"If we saw an old man, very poor, with no possessions, going around begging for something to eat, we would say, 'That man's body is just like a woman's. He has never cut his flesh nor tortured himself, nor suffered in any way. If he had tortured himself and made himself suffer much, and found his gods, he would be welcome everywhere and be made much of, and have plenty to eat and would not be poor, because his gods would take care of him'" (Wilson 1913a:110–11).

When he was 16, Goodbird spent much time hunting around his family's home. "It was a wild country around Independence Point at that time. There were many deer and antelopes and there were no roads, and the bluffs over the river were quite high . . . and the waters were here deep, swift, and dangerous. We Indians thought that the gods inhabited wild and dangerous places. As I came here and looked down at the deep waters over the high bluff, I thought of the promise I had made to my father years before, at the

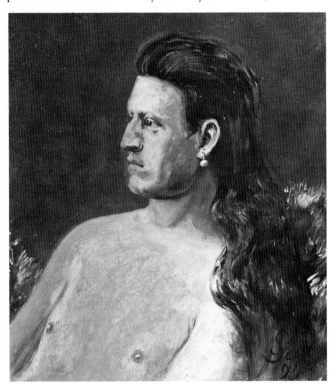

"PORTRAIT OF GOOD BIRD"
Painted by Julian Scott, 1891
Oil on board. See color page 173
H. 28.3 cm, W. 23.3 cm
MHS AV1985.33

This, the earliest known picture of Goodbird, shows him a few years after he performed his vision quest. It was painted by Julian Scott, a Vermont-born artist and illustrator. Scott and four other artists were hired in 1890 by the Department of the Interior as "Special Agents" to record information on the condition of Indians in America for the 1890 census. Scott spent three years painting Western tribes. This picture, published as a chromolithograph in the Census Office's 1894 volume, *Report on Indians Taxed and Indians Not Taxed*, was labeled, "Good Bird. A Mandan, Twenty Years of Age, Son of 'Son of the Star.' – North Dakota, 1891" (U.S. Census Office 1894:opp. p. 422; Appleton 1985:29; Samuels 1976:431). Goodbird, who was in fact 22 years old in 1891, was Mandan on his father's side.

Sun Dance; that I too would suffer in order to find my god. I went out into the thicket and cut two skewers of Juneberry wood and in the evening I said to my father, 'Father, I want to suspend myself on the face of the high bluff yonder, there over the deep waters. . . .'

"'Good!' said my father, so I stripped to my moccasins and clout and painted my body all over with white clay in order to humble myself. . . .

"My father went out and got a man named Crow. While he was gone I took a long rawhide rope, and a stout stick for a post, and an axe, and came to the high, steep place of the bank that overhung the river, and waited for them. They came at last, and I dropped down on one knee while my father pinched together the skin of my breast, and Crow, having taken an arrow, wetted the iron head and thrust it through the flesh of my breast as my father held it. He now did likewise to my other breast. I felt little, if any pain, for my heart was hardened to it by excitement, I think.

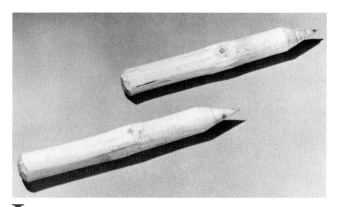

JUNEBERRY WOOD SKEWERS
Reproduction, 1986
Juneberry wood
L. 10.3 cm

WHITE PAINT
Collected by Gilbert Wilson, 1909
Clay
Largest piece L. 7 cm, W. 4 cm, H. 3 cm
AMNH 50.1/5452
This clay, found on a hill near Independence, was used as body paint when a man wanted to humble himself. Goodbird said, "Men painted themselves red for any joyful occasion, like a dance or a feast, and they painted themselves black when they wanted to rejoice over a dead enemy. To paint one's self with white clay meant that you had nothing to rejoice over and that you wanted the gods to come and comfort you. The fasters in each ceremony painted themselves in white clay and laid aside all their fine clothing" (Wilson 1913a:105).

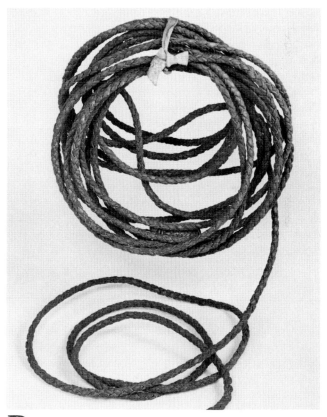

ROPE
Southwestern U.S.
Collected by Ben (?) Wittick, late 19th century
Braided leather
L. 1592 cm
Science Museum of Minnesota A63:27:53

"With the axe, my father and his friend drove the post into the ground and to it tied one end of the rawhide rope. The other end of the rope ended in two thongs, each of which was looped at the extremity over one of the skewers on either side of my breast. . . .

"I slid down the steep bank until the thong was drawn tight. Then my father cried, 'Loosen your hands from the rope. You must not touch it now but show the gods that you are willing to suffer. If you catch hold of the rope, it will show that you are not willing to bear the pain!'

"I let go of the rope and swung upon the skewers all night until near morning, my hands behind my back. . . . My father went back home with his friend, but before he left he said, 'Stay here just as long as you can. But when you cannot stand the suffering any longer, take off the rope and come home.'

"Toward morning I began to feel greatly exhausted although the actual pain was not nearly so great as one might think it would be, but I had had no sleep all night. . . . I climbed up the bank to the ground above, and went back home. It was a little before morning when I got there. I was so weary and exhausted that I threw myself down and went to sleep almost at once. But I did not get any dream or vision so all my pains came to nothing, for it was in a dream or vision that the gods answered one. . . .

"The following year in the fall, I again made myself suffer, hoping to find my god as we Indians say. . . . One dark night, my father and I went out among the high hills that lie along the Missouri River, a mile or two back from the stream. It looked dangerous out there and lonely, and I thought surely that I would now find my god. . . .

"We went up to the top of a hill and drove a stout stick for a post, into the ground. It was a cold night, with a few snow flakes falling. My father gathered together the skin of my breast and thrust an arrow through, as Crow had done, a year before. . . . My father now left me and I began to circle around the post straining at the thong that was bound to the skewers at my breast. . . . It was very lonely up there in the dark, with the snow falling around me. Ordinarily, I was afraid of ghosts at night and not very fond of the dark, but it was so lonely out there on that hill that I would have been glad to have any ghost come to me, just to keep me company. I ran around and around that post but I didn't fall in any faint, just ran around and shivered with the cold and pain. No vision came to me. . . .

"My father made no remarks the next morning, but he seemed to think that the reason I had received no vision was because I had not yet suffered enough.

"I did not feel greatly concerned over my failure to see a vision because I expected to undergo the same suffering at some future time when I got a little older.

"But before I had opportunity to do so, the government stopped all the Sun Dances and voluntary torture of this kind. My father did not like the government's interference at all. He thought that the government was oppressing the Indians when they stopped these customs which were a part of our religion. However, he said very little about it, although I know that was the way he felt about it. He always held that the government was wrong in stopping any of the old Indian customs.

"But I was glad of it, for I could not help thinking that in the matter of torture, the Indian way was a pretty hard one for a young fellow to travel" (Wilson 1913a:104-9).

Goodbird at the site of his vision quest
Photographed by Gilbert Wilson, 1913
MHS photo VI-29-13
Years later, Goodbird posed on the spot where he went to find his god. He held a bullboat paddle with honor marks and an elk horn bow.

IRON-HEADED ARROW
Hidatsa. Probably made by Wolf
*   Chief*
Collected by Gilbert Wilson, pre-1918?
Juneberry (?) wood shaft incised with
*   wavy lines; black stripe painted*
*   near nock. Sheet iron point inserted*
*   in slot and tied with sinew. Feather*
*   fletching now deteriorated*
L. 66 cm
MHS 7059.75b

Goodbird's father and his friend Crow
used an arrow to pierce Goodbird's skin
when he sought his vision (Wilson
1913a:105). Wolf Chief explained that
the three wavy lines on the shaft
symbolized Adapȫzis̄ or Burnt Arrow, a
figure in Hidatsa mythology who came
to earth as an arrow. "He used these
three lines and called them lightenings;
we made them likewise because he
taught us" (Wilson 1911:44).

GOODBIRD ON HIS VISION QUEST
Drawn by Goodbird, 1913
Pencil on tracing paper
H. 22.7 cm, W. 17.7 cm
MHS (Goodbird 1913:fig. 19)

Goodbird drew this to show how he sought a vision. "The bank at this point was
quite steep and the earth was loose, so that the weight of my body was chiefly
thrown upon the skewers at my breast," he said (Wilson 1913a:106).

Farming, new and old

At the same time Goodbird was seeking his god, another interest was growing in his life. "The government furnished each family with a plow and seed to plant flax, wheat and oats," he said. "We planted our fields and took our crops to Hebron, eighty miles away, the grain being loaded in sacks. It took two days to make the trip to Hebron. Our family took over about four loads in as many trips. We got seventy-five cents a bushel for our flax, sixty cents a bushel for our wheat, and twenty-five cents a bushel for our oats. Every load that we took over to Hebron, yielded us about twenty dollars. . . .

"I was now seventeen years old . . . and able to help my father, and got very much interested in farming. For this reason perhaps, I gradually forgot my earnest promise to my father, that I would some day suffer in a Sun Dance, and became quite reconciled to the government's orders" (Wilson 1913a:109-10).

Goodbird and Son of a Star farmed in ways that were different from what Buffalo Bird Woman had done at Like-a-Fishhook. The crops were not planted in the river bottom and hand-tended by women. Instead, the men used horse- and steam-powered machinery to break the prairie sod on the bench land between the river and the bluffs. The crops were not used by the family, but sold for cash. The trip to the Northern Pacific Railway at Hebron showed the family's new dependence upon the grain markets and shippers in the outside world.

PLOWING AND SEEDING ON FORT BERTHOLD RESERVATION
Photographed by J. J. Pankratz, c. 1910
NA 75-PA-8-8
Fort Berthold Reservation received some of the most up-to-date farm machinery available, and also some of the biggest. In 1916 the agent reported that the agency owned "one gasoline engine and separator, one steam engine and separator, seven or eight binders, mowing machines, gang plows etc." (Jermark 1916:1). The next year, a 40-80 Reeves traction engine, an International separator, and a set of six stubble plows were bought for use at Independence, but they proved to be too big (Knight 1917). The caption on this picture noted that the outfit could disk, seed, and drag 150 acres in 24 hours.

But just as agriculture had been full of symbolism for Buffalo Bird Woman, so this new kind of agriculture was symbolic to whites. Ever since Thomas Jefferson had written that "those who labor in the earth are the chosen people of God," Americans had held the yeoman farmer as an ideal to measure themselves by. In addition to instilling Christian values, agriculture taught the "self denial, thrift and economy" that the government wanted to impress upon Indian people. Thus it became the government's purpose, regardless of tribe or place, to "convert [the Indians] into prosperous farmers" (Jefferson 1955:164-65; Hall 1937p; [Hauke] 1910; Leupp 1907:3).

Unfortunately, the North Dakota environment

was against them. Even before the three tribes of Fort Berthold Reservation got their allotments, their agent was having grave doubts about encouraging them to depend on farming. "Insufficient rainfall, hot scorching winds, and early frosts, have contributed to make western North Dakota a colossal failure," he wrote to his supervisors in Washington. "50% of the farmers in North Dakota, experience the greatest difficulty in going on from year to year. . . . 80% of the farms and 'proved up' claims are covered by mortgages to their full aggregate value. . . . It was a grand mistake to attempt to make farmers exclusively, of these Indians" (Murphy 1893a:1-2).

Despite this and other warnings, bureaucrats in Washington continued to send the tribe's land payments in the form of seed grain and farm machinery and to encourage agents to promote agriculture. As machinery stripped away the stable prairie grasses, the delicate soil beneath was exposed to the dry wind in a cycle that would eventually turn the Great Plains into the Dustbowl of the 1930s. And still the dismal news kept coming. "Spring rains amounted to little or nothing," the agent reported in 1901. "Seed failed to sprout in many cases or where it did appear above ground the tender shoots were killed by late frosts. The rainfall for April was nothing, May .47 of an inch and June 4.02 inches. On June 7, a frost killed or blighted everything above ground. . . . Such conditions make it uphill work to keep these people interested in agriculture" (Richards 1901a:163-64).

By 1911 officials began to think that the Fort Berthold Indians could not succeed at agriculture. "A lack of industry on their part was not the cause of their failure," the agent said. "They failed for the same reasons that almost every white farmer in western North Dakota failed. This is not a farming country, the seasons are too short, the soil is not fit to do dry-farming on and there is not sufficient moisture for doing any other kind of farming. There are not a half dozen white farmers in this county who have made a success of farming. How, then, can it be expected that the Indians should be successful?" That year the reservation farming supervisor concluded that future efforts at farming should be confined to "corn, potatoes, and garden vegetables" – the exact kinds of crops that the Hidatsa had raised before whites tried to change their methods of agriculture (Hoffman 1911b:2; Davis 1911:4).

If they had asked Buffalo Bird Woman, she could have told them as much. Throughout the years when her menfolk struggled with their reapers and threshers, she continued to plant a garden as she had always done, and it throve. "The government has changed our old way of cultivating corn and vegetables and has brought many new kinds of vegetables and showed us how to use them," she said. "The government also came and broke up prairie ground and had us plant corn in it, but these fields on the prairie up near the hills get dry very quickly and the ground is hard and difficult to work. I do not think that the new way is so good as the old way of keeping our gardens down in the timber" (Wilson 1912:144).

She had proof. When the agent organized a reservation agricultural fair, hoping to encourage the Indians to take pride in farming, she entered some corn in the contests. "The corn which I sent down to the fair took the first prize," she said. "I raised this corn on new ground. This ground was plowed, but aside from that was cultivated with a hoe, exactly as in old times" (Wilson 1912:75).

CORNFIELD
1908
Collected by Harold Case
SHSND Col. 41-377
In contrast to Hidatsa harvesting techniques, which left the corn stalks in the field, whites cut the stalks off for use as silage. This field may have been at the agency's model farm in Elbowoods.

PRIZE WINNERS AT THE INDIAN FAIR, ELBOWOODS, N. DAK."
1911
SHSND C20
A reservation agricultural fair was established in 1911, as a speaker from the Office of Indian Affairs told those attending, in order "to bring together the best of your crops, the best of the stock, the best of the needlework, cooking, housekeeping, the best in keeping your tepees, together with an exhibition of the progress you are making on the reservation" (Abbott 1911:4). Privately, the Indian Office acknowledged that "the primary object of the Indian fair is to break up the Indians' habit of visiting other reservations and holding meetings and councils of their own" ([Hauke] 1910).

Buffalo Bird Woman took first place in the corn-growing competition, but she does not appear to be in this picture. Assistant Commissioner F. H. Abbott wanted to make the picture "part of an exhibit that I have there in my office in Washington so that every visitor who comes from all over the country may see the pictures of the Indians of the Fort Berthold reservation who took part and helped to make a success of this annual fair" (Abbott 1911:7). By the 1920s residents of Fort Berthold Reservation were taking prizes in the State Corn Show and competing in the State Fair (*Word Carrier* 1927a, 1927b).

HARVESTING GRAIN
Photographed by Fred O. Olson, 1910
SHSND E-337

Like many farmers, the people of Independence shared their machinery. "We had only one reaper to do the work of harvesting the grain and we tied up the sheaves with twine," Goodbird said. "When haying time came, . . . we had but one mowing machine for every three or four men. We would let one man use it for three days and then he must pass it on to the next man. Afterwards a machine was furnished to each family" (Wilson 1913a:70-71). Horse-, steam-, and gasoline-powered threshing machines were borrowed from the agency; the people later pooled their resources to buy their own tractor and threshing machine (Baker 1985).

This photograph was taken near Roseglen, a white community on Fort Berthold Reservation.

PLOWING
Early 20th century
Collected by Harold Case, post-1922
SHSND Col. 41-197

When they first moved to Independence, "The people were quite willing to break their ground, having some experience in plowing at old Fort Berthold," Goodbird said. By 1912 plowing was almost universal. Indeed, the tough prairie sod could not be broken by hand; it required special breaking plows. Goodbird noted that plowshares frequently grew dull and had to be taken back to the agency for sharpening (Wilson 1913a:70, 1912:258). This photograph is part of an undated, unidentified collection of reservation scenes assembled by missionary Harold Case.

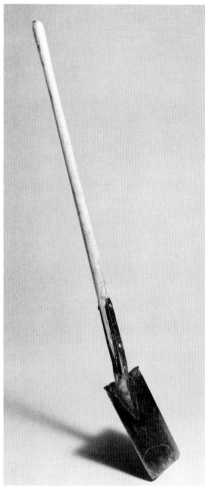

Spade
20th century
Forged No. 2 square blade with welded handle socket and foot pads on top edge. Straight hardwood handle has been replaced
L. 127 cm, W. 18.2 cm
MHS 75.48.2, Minnesota Veterans' Home

Most large acreages were broken by agency plowing teams, but smaller plots could be turned over with spades or with the old-fashioned digging stick that some women preferred. Agent L. B. Sperry reported in 1875 that he had "Issued to the most industrious and deserving Indians . . . a number of hoes, shovels, spades, picks, rakes, scythes, axes, grindstones and kindred farm-implements." They were used, among other things, for gardening and for digging up earth and sod to make cabin roofs. The Office of Indian Affairs regularly purchased long-handled No. 2 shovels with both round and square blades for reservation use (USOIA 1875:241, 1889:672, 1900:370).

Seed Packages and Catalog
Seed packages printed by Genesee Valley Lithograph Co., Rochester, N.Y., 1915. Catalog printed by Northrup, King & Co., Minneapolis, Minn., 1902
Seed packages of green, blue, yellow, and black lithograph on paper, folded and glued. Catalog of black ink on paper, bound with stapled orange, yellow, and black printed paper cover
Seed packages: L. 11.2 to 11.8 cm, W. 6.5 to 8.2 cm. Catalog: H. 24.9 cm, W. 17.5 cm
Private collection; MHS (Northrup King Papers)

The government gave Indian farmers seeds to encourage them to plant crops for sale as well as home gardens. "They issued new kinds of seeds to us, oats and wheat," said Buffalo Bird Woman, "and showed us how to plant them. They made us plant these seeds in these plowed fields. They also plowed up a big garden in the bottom land and showed us how to plant potatoes. . . . These potatoes we Indians did not like at first, because they smelled strong. Sometimes we dug up these potatoes and took them into our earth lodges and when the cold came in the winter the potatoes frosted and spoiled; so we did not care very much for them and often left them in the ground, not bothering even to dig them.

"Also the government issued seeds for new kinds of vegetables, watermelons, big squashes, onions, turnips and the like. We tried to eat some of these vegetables and did not like them and so let them stand in the field" (Wilson 1912:144-45).

The seed packages shown here contained "Kentucky Wonder" beans, squash, "Bloomsdale" spinach, and parsley packed for a New York seed dealer. Northrup, King & Co., whose catalog is shown, was a Minneapolis company that specialized in seeds adapted to a northern climate.

OIL CAN

Made by Radbill Oil Co.,
Philadelphia, Pa., early 20th
century
Two-gallon metal oil can painted red,
white, and blue, for Penn-Rad
Motor Oil
L. 17 cm, W. 24 cm, H. 24 cm
MHS 1976.2.221, Harkin Store
Goodbird maintained the agricultural
machinery for the Independence district.
"I carried around machine oil with me
to oil the machines for the Indians," he
said (Wilson 1913a:71). A can similar
to this one, but made for Standard Oil,
was found by archaeologists at Fort
Berthold II (Smith 1972:142).

HAYFORK

c. 1900
Three-pronged iron head and round
oak handle. Handle stamped
"Quality-Value-Utility/True
Temper/For over 100 Years" and
"Fire Hardened/Resists Weather
& Wear"
L. 181 cm, W. 17 cm
MHS 70.65.5, Mrs. V. W. Okey
Even at Like-a-Fishhook Village, Indian
men earned money by providing hay for
agency animals (Kauffman 1881:2).
Later, each man had to cut and store
enough hay to feed his cattle and horses
through the winter. Hay was cut with a
scythe, piled onto wagons, and
unloaded into the barns with pitchforks
like this one (Wilson 1913a:70).

GRAIN BAGS

Late 19th century
Three-ply cotton plain-weave with
faded brown vertical stripes,
stamped "Massopust" on one side
and "Stark Mills-Seamless-A" on
the other. Holes patched with
cotton muslin
L. 107 to 108 cm, W. 46 to 47 cm
MHS 1976.2.324, 325, Harkin Store
Goodbird and his father hauled their
grain to market in bags similar to these.

Hoe

Pre-1885?
Excavated at Like-a-Fishhook Village
Cast iron blade. Handle reconstructed
Blade: L. 24.5 cm, W. 10 cm.
*   Handle: L. 88.2 cm*
SHSND 32ML2/12,003.1215

By the 1890s metal hoes, the innovative tools of Buffalo Bird Woman's childhood, were a sign of conservatism. They were used to cultivate fields by hand rather than by machine. The handles were cut short so that women could bend over and use the stroke they were accustomed to (MHS photo X-28-1918).

The blade of this hoe has been narrowed, possibly to shape it like a bone hoe (Smith 1972:101).

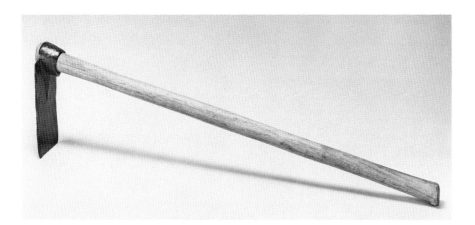

Drying prairie turnips

Photographed by Gilbert Wilson, 1916
MHS photo IX-19-1916

Prairie turnips were still gathered by women using digging sticks. Owl Woman held a braid of whole turnips; sliced ones were spread out on the canvas behind her.

Working in the field

Photographed by Gilbert Wilson, 1912
MHS photo V-46-1912

Here a woman – probably Sioux Woman, Goodbird's wife – hoed the squash plants in her garden at Independence. She was demonstrating the use of a bone hoe which had been obsolete for more than half a century; metal hoes, however, were held and used in much the same way.

Vegetables

Grown by Fred Schneider, 1986
Corn braid: L. 74 cm, W. 24.5 cm. Squash: H. 18 cm, W. 21 cm. Melons: H.
*   12 to 19 cm, W. 11.5 to 15 cm*

Even after the introduction of mechanical farming methods and new crops, many
Hidatsa women continued to plant gardens with the same crops they had always
used. Along with wild fruits and vegetables, these crops provided a balanced diet that
was familiar (Wilson 1912:145, 146). Shown here are, left to right, a braid of
Mandan red sweet corn, Mandan Banquet (winter) squash, Hidatsa pole beans, and
Arikara melons. Seeds for traditional varieties were preserved by anthropologists
Alfred W. Bowers, Melvin R. Gilmore, Oscar H. Will, and George F. Will, working
in the early to mid-20th century. These plants were grown from such preserved
seeds.

Braid of Prairie Turnips

Harvested 1986
Peeled prairie turnips (Psoralea
*   esculenta) with stems braided*
*   together*
L. 30 cm

Prairie turnips, starchy roots that grow
wild on the plains, were eaten by
residents of Independence at the turn of
the century. They are still used by
Plains tribes today.

Burden Basket

Hidatsa or Mandan
Collected by Gilbert Wilson, 1916
Bent willow frame; willow and box
*   elder bark strips woven in diamond*
*   and chevron patterns. Rawhide*
*   tumpline attached through two*
*   circular leather pieces*
H. 34 cm, D. 38 cm
Science Museum of Minnesota
*   A76:2:410*

Baskets made of woven bark or hide-
covered willow frames continued to be
used for harvesting corn, squash, and
beans by the women who maintained
traditional gardens. Because the baskets
were of a familiar size, women could
measure crops by the basket load as they
had always done. "Burden baskets were
very useful," Buffalo Bird Woman said.
"We carried all our vegetables from the
gardens to the lodges in baskets and also
we used baskets for carrying stones and
earth and ice. In old days we had no
wagons and so carried our vegetables to
the lodge in baskets. Also we gathered
all kinds of cherries or berries in baskets.

   "I remember the baskets that were
made when I was a little girl were still
being used years afterwards" (Wilson
1916b:256-57; MHS photos
VII-33-14, VII-40-14, VII-43-14).

Husking corn
Photographed by Gilbert Wilson, 1909
MHS photo III-97

Husking was still a social event at Independence, even though the scattered settlement pattern made it hard for people to get together. Here, women are braiding the best ears. In the husking season, women could also get work from nearby white farmers. Buffalo Bird Woman said, "Last year a white man hired me to gather the corn in his field and husk it; and I kept all the green ears for myself, for that is my custom. I do not know whether that white man liked it or not. It may be he thought I was stealing that green corn; but I was following the custom that I learned of my tribe.

"I am an Indian; if a white man hires me to do work for him, he must expect that I will follow Indian custom" (Wilson 1917:44).

Drying corn
Photographed by Gilbert Wilson, 1909
AMNH photo 286444

Corn, hauled back from the field by wagon, was spread on the corn stage to dry just as at Like-a-Fishhook Village. The braided strings were hung from the railing.

Goodbird and the agent

Goodbird's enthusiasm for farming did not go unnoticed at the U.S. government agency across the river. One day in 1895, William H. Clapp, the agent, called Goodbird into his office. "I have been told that you are becoming a good farmer," he said. "I want to appoint you to the position of government farmer in this reservation. Your district shall be that part of the reservation from the Little Missouri River down to your home at Independence. Will you do it?"

"I will take it and see if I can do it," Goodbird said (Wilson 1913a:69; USOIA 1895:547).

Goodbird soon learned that the job was not an easy one, for he was caught between two systems. As a government employee, he had to represent Euro-American values. But no government order could free him from older obligations to family, clan, and tribe.

The agent's first orders let Goodbird know what was in store for him. "You are to measure out to each able-bodied man, ten acres to be tilled. If he is lazy and does not attend to its cultivation properly, you report the matter to me and I will have a policeman go out and bring him in. You are also to tell the people that they must put up two wagon-loads of hay for each head of cattle that they own."

"So I now went from cabin to cabin telling the people the agent's orders," Goodbird said. "When haying time came, I went around counting the stacks and keeping the Indians at work. . . . I also inspected the Indians' gardens, and saw that they were kept clean. I urged them to keep the weeds down in May and June. Some of the Indians who went away visiting or elsewhere and forsook their gardens, I reported to the agent" (Wilson 1913a:70-71).

Goodbird's orders showed how the agent's role had changed since the 1870s. Instead of being an ambassador to the tribe, the agent was now more like a benign feudal lord trying to guide the Indians to civilization and citizenship. He walked a slippery road between a mountainous bureaucracy and a chasm of cultural differences.

The agent's mission was strongly tied to the work ethic. "The chief duty of an agent," said a 1904 handbook, "is to induce his Indians to labor in civilized pursuits" (USOIA 1904b:99). In the agent's world, labor was the morally uplifting way to civilization, and he had a clear idea of what "labor" meant. Trapping, hunting, and harvesting wild plants were not *work* as the agent defined it. Indians who chose such ways to earn their livings were guilty of "laziness and thriftlessness." "At times," lamented one agent, "it has been impossible to get some of these Indians to haul freight, to mine coal, or to perform any other arduous labor although the cash was waiting for them when the work was completed" (Richards 1901a:171). The agents did not realize that the kinds of manual labor they found honorable could be pointless or even degrading from the Hidatsa viewpoint. It sometimes seemed to the Indians as if thrift and ambition were the English words for greed and selfishness.

As the agent struggled with a cultural gap on one side, he faced bureaucratic barriers on the other. For the civil servants at the Office of Indian Affairs on the East Coast, the agent was low man in the pecking

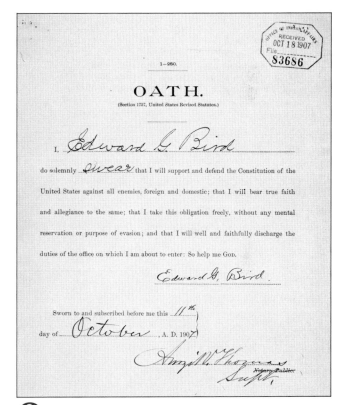

OATH OF OFFICE
Written by Goodbird and Amzi Thomas, 1907
Brown ink on printed letterhead
L. 25.4 cm, W. 20.5 cm
NA (Goodbird 1907)
All employees of the Office of Indian Affairs had to take a loyalty oath, and those in responsible positions had to post bond. Goodbird, who took the name Edward as a schoolboy, signed this oath of office in 1907 before helping with that year's roundup. He was first hired as assistant farmer in 1895 (Goodbird 1914a:42; USOIA 1895:547).

order. Every decision he made – from hiring a secretary to buying coal to heat his office – meant filling out endless forms, vouchers, and reports. All the paperwork had to go back to Washington, and it might take months for the office to respond.

But on the reservation, the agent was boss. He controlled the Indians' land. Most Indians did not actually own their allotments; instead, the government

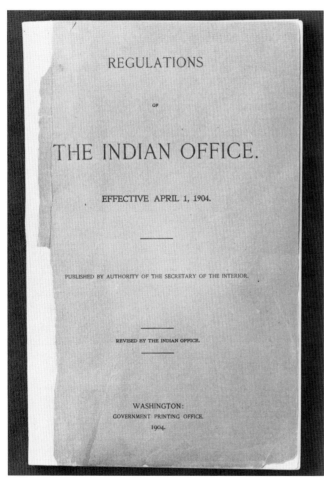

REGULATIONS OF THE INDIAN OFFICE
1904
Black ink on paper with green paper cover
H. 22.8 cm, W. 14.6 cm
MHS (USOIA 1904)
Agents had to keep track of rules and regulations of the Indian Office as well as various acts of Congress and court decisions. The agent's handbook covered such subjects as employee supervision, contracting and purchasing, accounting methods, proper forms to fill out, record keeping, and administration of Indian lands.

acted as trustee to protect them from unscrupulous speculators. To actually receive a deed to his land, an Indian had to prove he was "competent" – that is, that he understood and lived by white laws and customs. Until he did, no one could buy, rent, or take away his land without the government's permission. Though the system was meant to protect, it also encumbered. As late as 1911, Wolf Chief spent months getting permission from the agent, character references from the missionary, and approval from the Office of Indian Affairs in Washington to dispose of 11 acres of his land (Wolf Chief 1911a).

The agent had other sources of power. He administered the tribe's income from the government. Money from reservation land sales often did not go to individuals but was spent by the government "in the Indians' interest." The agent also had authority over public health, law enforcement, education, and trade. If he was a feudal lord, the agency was his castle. In 1896 the Fort Berthold agency contained a commissary where rations were issued, two licensed general stores, a boarding school, half a dozen houses for agency employees, a hospital, an office building, a harness shop, a blacksmith shop, a sawmill, and a gristmill (Ilsley 1896b).

Like the missionaries, the agent often found himself in a paradoxical position. Though he strove to foster the Yankee virtue of self-reliance and the concept of private property, his own powers had a way of nipping these ideas in the bud. Because the tribes of Fort Berthold knew little about animal husbandry at first, the agent took on management of their herds. Soon the agent had an armlock on commerce. "We were not allowed to kill our cattle without a permit from the agent," Goodbird said (Wilson 1913a:74). Nor were they allowed to buy or sell. In 1904, when Wolf Chief dared to purchase six steers from his neighbors at Independence "without any authority from this office," the agent furiously recommended he be punished and the stock be forfeited to the government (Thomas 1904). "The Indian should have a free hand to dispose of his goods," another agent wrote, "but not before the [agent] has sanctioned the sale" (Hoffman 1910:2).

Wolf Chief claimed that the reservation had never had a good agent (Wolf Chief 1889b). It was no wonder. Smothered in paperwork, agents strove for contradictory goals – to help the Indians so they would no longer need help and to control them so they could become independent.

```
                              5-105

          (This application should be made out by the applicant)

                    APPLICATION FOR A PATENT IN FEE
                    ────────────────────────────

      Fort Berthold
      _____ Agency.

      I,      Henry Wolf Chief
                                    _____, make application
   for a patent in fee covering   Eleven and 1/2 (11 1/2) acres
                                          (All or part)
   of my allotment No.      588      , described as follows:   Beginning at
   the stake 12 chains South of the 1/4 corner between Sections 34 and
   35 in Township 150 N. of Range 91 West of the Fifth Prin. Meridian in
   North Dakota, thence south 8 chains, thence west 11 chains, thence
   north 16 chains, thence east 4 chains, thence south 8 chains, thence
   east 7 chains to the point of the beginning, containing eleven and
   1/2 (11 1/2) acres

      As evidence of my competency to care for my affairs, the fol-

   lowing facts are submitted:

   Age?   62 years   Degree of blood?   Full   . Married or single?
   Married
                     Did you attend school?  If so, where and how long?
   No.

                               No.
   Do you use intoxicants? _____
   Are you in good physical condition?   Yes.

   What is the value of the land covered by your application? _____
        About $1.00 per acre.

   Does your application cover your own allotment or inherited land?
   My own allotment.

                                                       A part
   Does your application cover all or a part of your land? _____
   Do you cultivate your land?   Yes, about 40 acres

   Are you self-supporting?  If so, how is your self support obtained?
   Yes. By farming and conducting a small store.

                                                 No.
   Have you accumulated any property?  If so, what? _____

                                                       5-2543
```

APPLICATION FOR A PATENT IN FEE
Written by Wolf Chief, 1911
Typewritten on a printed form
H. 26.5 cm, W. 20 cm
NA, Kansas City (Wolf Chief 1911a)

When Wolf Chief wanted to give 11 acres of his land to the Congregational Church for a chapel and graveyard, the federal government in Washington refused to let him. Despite the fact that Wolf Chief had been supporting himself by farming, ranching, and keeping a store for 19 years, he was technically a ward of the government. Like many others, Wolf Chief had to find a way to outwit the system. Goodbird explained, "The government did not allow him to give [the land] to us. They asked him, 'What do you want to give that land away for?' Then he wanted to give five acres, but the government wrote and said, 'No, you may sell the land, but you cannot give it away.' Wolf Chief then said, 'Well, I will sell the church the ten acres and charge them only one dollar an acre.' So we bought it of him and he gave the money back to us. One dollar an acre is the lowest sum that the government will allow us to sell land for" (Wilson 1913a:123).

FORT BERTHOLD AGENCY, ELBOWOODS
1890s?
Collected by Charles Hall
SHSND, Hall Collection

After Like-a-Fishhook Village was abandoned, the agency was moved west to a more centralized location that came to be known as Elbowoods. The buildings shown here are probably the residences of agency employees. "They are all painted a light brown with red roofs," a mission worker wrote in 1896. "That of the Agent has a very pretty veranda on the south, which gives such a pleasant finish to a home, especially where there are no trees to afford the least shade" (Ilsley 1896b).

Elbowoods was also the site of two missions, Congregational and Catholic, both of which operated boarding schools.

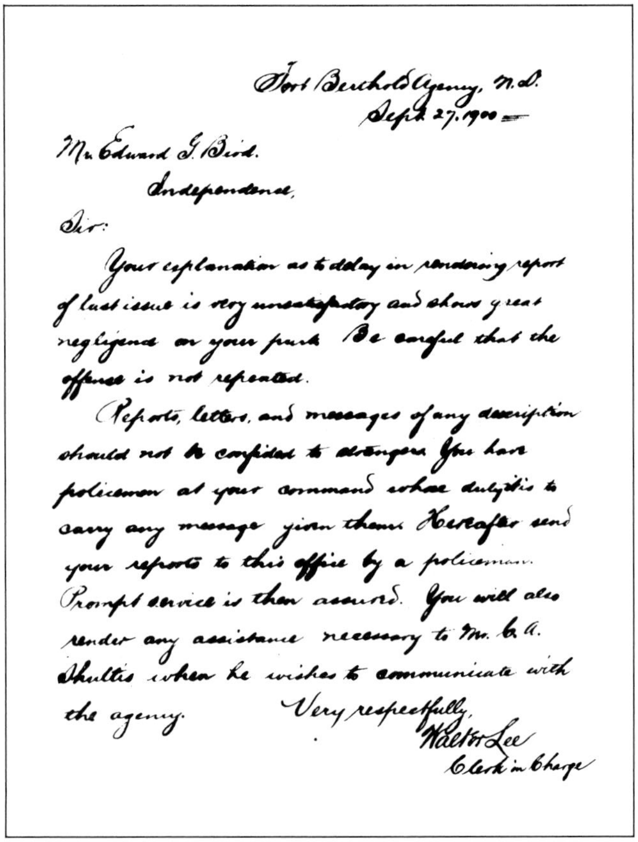

Fort Berthold Agency, N.D.
Sept. 27, 1900

Mr. Edward G. Bird.
    Independence,
Sir:
    Your explanation as to delay in rendering report of last issue is very unsatisfactory and shows great negligence on your part. Be careful that the offense is not repeated.

    Reports, letters, and messages of any description should not be confided to strangers. You have policemen at your command whose duty is to carry any message from them. Hereafter send your reports to this office by a policeman. Prompt service is then assured. You will also render any assistance necessary to Mr. C. A. Shultis when he wishes to communicate with the agency.   Very respectfully,
                        Walter Lee
                        Clerk in Charge

LETTER
Written by Walter Lee, 1900
Sepia letterpress copy on paper
H. 29.2 cm, W. 22.9 cm
NA, Kansas City (Lee 1900)
Late reports drew stinging rebukes from the agency employees Goodbird worked with. Because the agency was 40 miles away by boat and wagon, prompt communication was a problem.

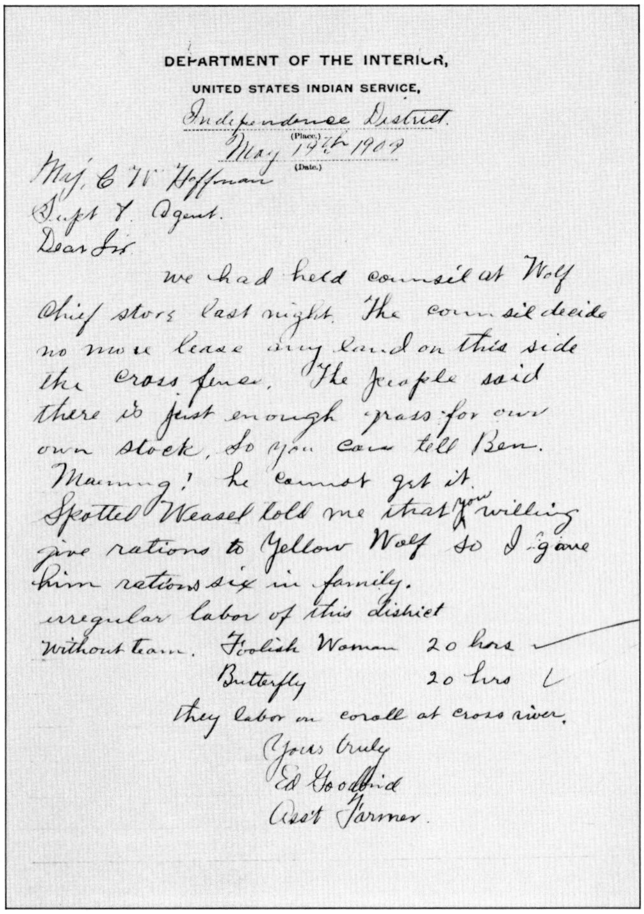

DEPARTMENT OF THE INTERIOR,
UNITED STATES INDIAN SERVICE,
Independence District.
(Place.)
May 14th 1909
(Date.)

Maj. C. W. Hoffman
Supt. & Agent.
Dear Sir
            we had held counsil at Wolf Chief store last night. The counsil decide no more lease any land on this side the cross fence. The people said there is just enough grass for our own stock. So you can tell Ben. Manning! he cannot get it. Spotted Weasel told me that you willing give rations to Yellow Wolf so I gave him rations six in family.
irregular labor of this district without team. Foolish Woman 20 hrs
                Butterfly   20 hrs
            they labor on corall at cross river.
                        Yours truly
                        Ed Goodbird
                        Ass't Farmer.

LETTER
Written by Goodbird, 1909
Ink on printed letterhead
H. 26 cm, W. 18.5 cm
NA, Kansas City (Goodbird 1909b)
Goodbird's ability to read and write English, as well as his job, made him a mediator for neighbors and sometimes placed him in the middle of disagreements over proper use of reservation land. In this letter, he had to inform his employer of an unwelcome decision made by the people of Independence.

ISSUING RATIONS"
Early 1890s?
Collected by Harold Case
SHSND Col. 41–465

Government officials saw rations as a stopgap measure to tide the tribes over until they could support themselves. By the late 1890s only the elderly and infirm still drew rations. It was always a controversial system. Senators in Washington opposed spending "millions of dollars to support these people in unproductive idleness," and even the Hidatsa's agent wanted to "compel them to labor or accept the alternative of starvation" (Hoxie 1985:77; Meyer 1977:128). Members of the tribe, on the other hand, saw the rations as something they were entitled to under treaties and agreements with the government. This picture was probably taken at Elbowoods.

RATION TICKETS
Hidatsa, 1903–04
Manila cardboard printed in ink
L. 9.7 cm, W. 4.8 cm
SHSND 603

"For the first ten years after we left old Fort Berthold, every Indian on the reservation drew rations," Goodbird said. As assistant farmer, Goodbird was appointed to issue rations at Independence. "I issued to about two hundred people each two weeks," he said (Wilson 1913a:72). The Office of Indian Affairs printed standardized ration tickets for use on all Indian reservations. When the agent issued articles to the Indians, he either punched out a number or crossed it out with a pen. The card was the Indian's record of what he had received (U.S. Census Office 1894:opp. p. 76). These tickets were used for issuing beef. They belonged to four residents of Independence: Thad Mason, Sioux Woman, Coyote Necklace, and Hairy Coat. Goodbird was probably the issuing agent. Rations were discontinued about 1916 (Meyer 1977:172).

The Indian police

In Like-a-Fishhook Village, law enforcement had been the province of the Black Mouth Society. Composed of mature men, proven in war, this society had absolute authority in matters that concerned the whole community.

But the U.S. government did not acknowledge the power of the Black Mouths, and the Black Mouths' ancient customs did not include enforcing laws made by white legislatures. So the government instituted another system of law and order on the reservation. The Office of Indian Affairs made the laws, the agent was chief of police, and Indian officers made up the police force.

When Wolf Chief first heard of the Indian police, it seemed like a short cut to power. He accurately foresaw that the new police force would undermine traditional systems of authority. An ambitious young man would not have to accumulate prestige slowly, in customary ways, over the years. He could achieve prominence quickly by cooperating with the agent.

"I worked with [the] agent," Wolf Chief said. "The agent liked me. Other Indians sometimes opposed me. . . . My other friends laughed at me & said – Look at him – he wants to be like white man. He [is] foolish. . . . Then they got in trouble with the agent and came to me for help" (Wilson 1907c:73-74).

Wolf Chief was a policeman for eight months. He was given a gray uniform to wear and he earned five dollars a month. But one day the agent told him to go

A GROUP OF INDIAN POLICEMEN OF NORTH DAKOTA"
Photographed by Fred Olsen, c. 1905?
SHSND A5346
This group of Fort Berthold police are, right to left, Young Snake, Foolish Bear, Ben Benson, Clair Everett, James Eagle, Percy Baker, Burton Bell, Jim Baker, and Hunts Along. Their duties, in addition to keeping the peace, included helping the government farmers, keeping white ranchers' cattle off the reservation, and recovering Indian cattle that strayed onto white men's land (Richards 1901a:160). They also ran errands for the agent. By 1918, the police force was decentralized, with each of six privates located in a different district of the reservation (Jermark 1918:3).

into a root cellar where the potatoes raised by the Indians were stored and select a bag of the best to sell to a visiting steamboat. "I did so," Wolf Chief said, "but was afraid, saying, 'These belong to the Indians.'

"So I went to [the] agent & said, 'Major, these belong to Indians. I am afraid you steal!'" Furious at the accusation, the agent fired Wolf Chief and took away his uniform. "I went back home without any thing on – but [my] shirt. I went back home ashamed" (Wilson 1907c: 74).

But Wolf Chief had been right. Not long after, an inspector from Washington came to Fort Berthold Reservation. Wolf Chief told his story.

The inspector asked the agent if it were true. "It is true," the agent said. "Indians every spring have to throw away some potatoes so I sold some."

"Yes," said Wolf Chief, "he sold about 50 bushels for 50¢ [a] bushel."

"What have you done with [the] money?" the inspector demanded.

"[It is] in my pocket yet," the agent said.

"Well keep it," the inspector said, "but you lose your place."

Wolf Chief was vindicated, but he never again trusted an agent to help him get ahead in the world (Wilson 1907c: 76).

By the time Goodbird had grown old enough to attract the agent's attention, allotment and the pressure to conform to Euro-American ways had taken a toll upon the Hidatsa age societies. The Black Mouths were no longer an active institution, but a strange transformation had begun to overtake the Indian police force.

"I was nineteen years old when Major Murphy, who was agent at the old Fort Berthold agency, called me to his office," said Goodbird. "He had been agent about three years. 'I want you to be a government policeman,' he said to me.

"'I am only a boy,' I said. 'The police have to arrest men. I am not old enough.'

"'That's all right,' he said, 'I will send others along when an arrest has to be made, but I need an interpreter to talk to the Indians.'

"I left him without pledging myself and came home and told my father. 'You were right,' my father said. 'You are not old enough to be a policeman'" (Wilson 1913a: 68).

The agent didn't know it, but Son of a Star was right. The authority of the police was not based on United States law nearly so much as the agent thought.

It was based on the fact that the police were an association of mature, proven men – much as the Black Mouths had been before them.

"The police . . . control those who are inclined to violate the law more by moral than physical force," one agent wrote. "Practically no difficulty is experienced in keeping order among the Indians" (Richards 1901a: 160; [Jermark] 1918: 3, 8). The effectiveness of the system seems to have surprised some agents. But even more mysterious was the result when the agent enlisted the policemen to enforce a reservation "clean-up day." He was astonished at how readily people obeyed the policemen's orders to clean up their yards. Little did he know that older customs had percolated into new institutions like water seeping slowly into the ground.

INDIAN POLICEMAN'S BADGE
Made by Williamson Stamp Co., Minneapolis, Minn.
Five-pointed star in a circle, stamped from silver-colored
*   metal. "U.S. Indian Police" stamped on rim. Pin*
*   on back*
D. 8 cm
SHSND 9131
The Indian police at Fort Berthold were organized and outfitted in a pseudo-military style, much like white law enforcers. The ranks of captain, lieutenant, sergeant, and private were distinguished by the style of the hats and badges (Murphy 1891c). This badge was worn at the Standing Rock Sioux Reservation in southern North Dakota.

INDIAN POLICEMAN'S UNIFORM
Standing Rock Reservation, N.Dak.
Gray wool coat, vest, and trousers.
Coat has shoulder straps with red
stars, black buttons reading "U.S.
Indian Service," and three pockets.
Vest has brown silk back and blue
wool lining. Trousers have
suspender buttons on waistband
and red piping on legs. See color
page 178
Coat: L. 90 cm, W. 50 cm across
shoulders. Vest: L. 65 cm,
W. 38.5 cm. Trousers: L. 113 cm,
W. 49.5 cm
SHSND 2015

Uniforms for Indian police were standardized across the nation. When a man was appointed to the force, the agent sent his measurements to Washington for a uniform (Murphy 1891c). This suit was worn by Thomas Frosted on the Sioux reservation south of Fort Berthold.

"**D**ESCRIPTIVE STATEMENT OF PROPOSED CHANGES IN THE INDIAN POLICE FORCE" (DETAIL)
Written by Agent John S. Murphy, 1891
Pencil and ink on printed form, stamped in purple ink
L. 25.7 cm, W. 40.6 cm
NA (Murphy 1891a)

Despite Goodbird's refusal to join the Indian police, the agent enrolled him. Since all changes in the force had to be approved by the Office of Indian Affairs, the agent sent this form to Washington showing Goodbird's appointment and his pay of $10 a month. Goodbird was surprised when, two months after he had declined to become a policeman, the agent called him in and wanted to pay him.

"'But I refused to be a policeman. I am only a boy,' I answered.

"'Oh, take the money,' said the agent. 'I took your name and enrolled you. You take the money home and I will try to get someone in your place.' So I took the money" (Wilson 1913a:69). On September 14, 1891, Murphy sent in another of these forms to show that Goodbird resigned (Murphy 1891b).

INDIAN POLICEMAN'S BUTTON
1894
Halftone print
**MHS (U.S. Census Office 1894:opp.
p. 76)**

The U.S. government never lost a chance to impress white values upon Indians. The brass buttons designed by the Office of Indian Affairs for police uniforms showed a man plowing surrounded by the words, "God helps those who help themselves."

Wolf Chief founds a store

Wolf Chief was an entrepreneur at heart. He had never been satisfied with the way traders operated on the reservation. After moving to Independence, he decided to do something about it.

In December 1889 the hunting was good and Wolf Chief had a supply of deer and antelope hides to sell. He loaded the hides onto a bobsled and set out for the town of Coal Harbor, 100 miles downriver. He knew of a man named George L. Robinson who ran a general store there.

"When I got in [the] store, Robinson was glad to see me," he said. "He weighed out my hides & I traded. I bought one barrel brown sugar."

"That costs lots of money," Robinson warned. "Your hides won't pay for that, but I will trust you [with] $100 & when you sell you collect & pay me."

"So I got [a] barrel sugar, some coffee, & tobacco & calico, soda crackers, & other things. But I brought back my sleigh loaded."

The road back passed through nearly every community on the reservation. Wherever he stopped, people wanted to buy goods from him. At Fort Stevenson he sold candy to the children in the boarding school. At Armstrong, so many people wanted to buy sugar that Wolf Chief had to flee before he sold out. It was the same at Elbowoods. "People had no store, but a white man's," he explained. "Lots of people wanted sugar and coffee. Of that barrel I had hardly any left. Everyone who had money came out. The people got money by selling wood & coal at [the] agency.

"I bought a lot of hides at Elbowoods, deer & antelope. . . . When I got back home at Independence [I] had little sugar left."

Two weeks later, he had 31 hides and $80 to take back to Coal Harbor. When he got there, Robinson said, "I'm glad to see you. You gots lots of hides!"

"He led one horse & I [the] other to [a] barn. Then he went in a corner where was oats in [a] little closet & called me. I went in there & he opened a sack & took out a bottle & drank himself & said, 'Drink some – you know what it is!' I said, 'Yes, I know. I drank before.' It was whiskey. He said, 'Drink some more.' I said, 'I have enough.' I didn't want to get dizzy for I wanted to trade hides there.

"When we got back in [the] store he weighed the hides & figured out – it was $19. . . . 'I will pay what I owe you,' I said. He opened his book, & I paid him. 'Now buy what you want' he said, 'All you need. Next time you come bring another sled – you can take two loads home – you can manage them.'

"I then began selecting calicoes. And I bought bright colors – red, pink, blue, white. . . .

"'All these are different prices,' [Robinson said.] 'This [is] 8¢ yd. – this 10 – this 15. You want all? And agree on price? There is 320 yds.'

"'All right,' I said. And I bought . . . mittens and socks and blue flannels & 2 sacks of coffee & [a] barrel of sugar. . . .

"'How is trade?' asked Robinson.

"'Good,' I said. 'I was afraid I would sell out before I got back.'

"'Good,' he said" (Wilson 1916c:75-80).

Wolf Chief learned the storekeeping trade quickly. Robinson told him how to mark up his prices. "I sold

INTERIOR OF WOLF CHIEF'S STORE
Photographed by Gilbert Wilson, 1909
MHS photo IV-22
According to one of the mission workers, Wolf Chief's store was "a model of cleanliness and order" (Case n.d.). This photograph shows Wolf Chief waiting on Ada M. Wilson, Gilbert's wife.

the 8¢ [a] yard calicoes at 12½¢,' he said, "and so [I] got more money than I had before." His main problem was that his customers had little cash; they "have no money but buy Goods in the Store and are not able to let me have my money [for] about a year or two." The fact that the agent forbade them to exchange cattle aggravated the problem, but custom made the system work over the long run. "Indian law is always keep [your] promise and I usually got my money," Wolf Chief said (Wilson 1916c: 81, 83-84; Wolf Chief 1894).

The biggest problem Wolf Chief had was with the law. Because there had been many abuses of the Indian trade in the past, the government strictly regulated business on the reservation. A white storekeeper had to have a license from the Office of Indian Affairs and post a $10,000 bond. The kinds of goods that could be sold were strictly limited. This protectionist law meant that the Indians could only do business with stores approved by the agent. One unlicensed lumber dealer near Fort Berthold Reservation complained at having to turn Indian customers away. "They can not see into it why they have not as good a right to buy lumber [at this store] as the white man," he said (Stoelting 1909: 3).

Since Wolf Chief was an Indian, many of the regulations were not meant to apply to him. He quickly ran afoul of them, nonetheless. Early on, many of his neighbors, lacking cash, wanted to pay by bartering the clothing issued to them by the government. But when Wolf Chief took the clothes to Robinson, he found he had broken the law.

"'What's these?' Robinson said, opening two boxes. 'Issue,' I said. 'Unh-hunh,' he said. After a bit he said, 'Come upstairs.' Then he took me upstairs and showed me in a book [a] law that no white or Indian on [a] reservation could buy or sell issue [goods]. 'I did not know that,' I said. 'Well,' he said, 'I will take these & sell them 1 piece at a time, when no one is around & sell out for you. I can't put [them] in the store'" (Wilson 1916c:82-83).

But worse was the trouble that erupted when the agent found out what Wolf Chief was up to. The first hint of trouble came one day when Wolf Chief arrived at Robinson's.

"The agent's brother was here & wanted . . . to keep store on [the] reservation," Robinson told him. "I went to find out what his prices [are so] you can sell under. They will camp here tonight." Soon eight men with six sleds full of goods showed up at Robinson's door. "They talked with Robinson a long time," Wolf Chief said. "When he was thru, he came up & said,

'Those men are going to sell some things pretty cheap. I have charged you a big price – but I will change the price so you can [under]sell them.

"'This man wanted to sell 2½ lbs. coffee for [a] dollar. In that case you can sell [at] 25¢ [a] lb. for yours. They will sell 6 lbs. for [a] dollar [of] sugar. You sell 8 lbs. for [a] dollar. . . . If I don't make [a] fair price next time you tell [me] & I'll fix it.'"

On the way home, Wolf Chief stopped at the agency to warm up. The agent, John S. Murphy, asked him if he had seen anyone else on the road. Wolf Chief described the group of eight men.

"They are going to open a store here," said the agent. "I will fix their price, & yours too, so both [are] alike."

"All right," Wolf Chief said.

"Tell me your price."

WOLF CHIEF'S STORE AND CABIN
Photographed by Gilbert Wilson, 1907
MHS photo II-57
"I have three cabins standing in a row," Wolf Chief said in 1915. "In one I keep my little trading store; the second is my family's sitting room and the place where my wife and I and our three children sleep; the third is a kitchen with a cot in one corner, where my sister [Buffalo Bird Woman] sleeps" (Wilson 1909-18:83, 1915b:587). In 1911, his store burned, but he kept trading in spite of this setback (Wolf Chief 1911b).

"No," Wolf Chief said. "I am in a hurry and those white men got lots of money. If they sell cheap, I [will] quit [my] store."

A few days later, a policeman knocked on Wolf Chief's door. "Our agent wants to see you," he said.

"What for?" Wolf Chief asked.

"About your store. That white man asks high prices. Some people say you sell cheap. He wants you [to] come down right away."

When Wolf Chief reached the agency, the agent sent for the new storekeeper. "I want to see you both," he said. "If you will, I will mark your prices so you sell at one price to Indians."

"That's a good plan," the storekeeper said.

The interpreter turned to Wolf Chief. "What [do] you think about it? You want him [to] mark your price & count your money?"

"No," said Wolf Chief. "I can count my own money."

The agent said, "You make a mistake to refuse. This man agree[s] to work with you. You say you [will] quit before long. I want you to keep your store. This man will not undersell you. . . . I want to show you what he has."

So the agent took Wolf Chief into the warehouse to see how many goods the competition had. But Wolf Chief saw that the Indians' issue goods and the trader's stock were all piled in the same building, and it made him suspicious.

"This man will sell [to] you cheap for your store," the agent reasoned. "It is far to Robinson's."

"I don't know," Wolf Chief said.

The agent was getting impatient. "I have authority to run any store on this Res[ervation]," he said. "If you don't do as I think best I will stop your store. . . . Now this [is my] last word . . . do you want to run your store or I run it for you?"

"I want you to run it for me," Wolf Chief retorted. "I want you to issue [goods] to me & I sell [them] to Indians just like you do for this man."

"Why do you say that?" the agent demanded. "[Because] that man piles his goods here?"

"Because . . . I could easily take issue goods & sell [them] to Indians for all is piled in [the] same store."

"Well," the agent said, "we have [had] quite a talk & [are] both kind of mad – we better put [it] off till some other time" (Wilson 1916c:82-87).

But that was not the end of it. In February 1890 the agent fired off a letter to Washington about Wolf Chief's store. He said that Wolf Chief was "one of

those Indians made vicious, by bad white influence and association, so common on the western frontier." His goods were "beads, spangles, gaudy prints and other useless and barbarian trinkets – goods that should be relegated to the past and not allowed on the reservation, if we are to civilize these Indians." On top of it all, he said Wolf Chief's prices were "exorbitant" (Murphy 1890a).

Not to be outdone, Wolf Chief also wrote to Washington. "The present Agent John S. Murphy bothered me in every way to keep me from keeping a Store," he said. "He did not do a single act that will encourage me in this. . . . I think it's [an] honorable way of making my living, but all to my discouragement. . . . I wish you sent me a coppy of Reservation laws so that I will read it and be not troublesome to my agent and to this office" (Wolf Chief 1890a).

The agent went after George Robinson next. He demanded that Robinson furnish him with an invoice so he could monitor Wolf Chief's purchases and the prices he paid (Murphy 1890b).

The dispute raged until Washington sent out an inspector. In the end, Wolf Chief agreed to sell no cartridges or liquor, and he stayed in business. The agent's brother had his store closed down (Wolf Chief 1894; Wilson 1916c:88).

OUTSIDE OF WOLF CHIEF'S STORE
Photographed by Gilbert Wilson, 1908
MHS photo III-7
Wolf Chief's store, like many rural markets, was a place where people gathered to pass the time of day. Here, Goodbird (left) and Wolf Chief (right) sit on Wolf Chief's front step with a neighbor, probably Butterfly.

Spring scale

Early 20th century

Cylindrical metal body encasing a coiled spring; hooks at top and bottom for hanging scale and pan or item to be weighed; flat brass front marked from 0 to 24 pounds in one-pound increments; metal pointer indicating weight. Stamped "American/Improved/Spring Balance/Warranted"

L. 22 cm, W. 4 cm

MHS 61.94.9, Sylvia Gottwerth

On his first trip to Coal Harbor, Wolf Chief bought a scale to use in his store. "It had a kind of pan on the bottom & a spring and when you held it up it had a kind of finger that pointed out the number of pounds. I could read the figures pretty well but all the way from Coal Harbor home my mind was on that scale – thinking about it.

"I used this by putting it around my neck like a necklace. I wanted to learn this scale and I would push it and watch it spring down. I tied my handkerchief around [my] neck & had [the] scales tied to it" (Wilson 1916c:76).

This scale, which is missing its pan, is probably the kind Wolf Chief used.

Store merchandise

Late 19th and early 20th century

Clockwise from top (all MHS): fabric (reproduction), scale (1982.11.18), dyes (74.88), starch box (67.252.14), socks (1978.73.280a–e, 1978.73.581a–g), soap box (1980.65.23), biscuit crate (1980.65.24), sardine can (63.104.7), tea tin (1982.35.2), cracker tin (9714.1), soap tin (1981.41.33), apricot crate (1982.105.212), lard can (9370.64), wet keg (8879.119a), flour bin (1983.19.3a, b), barrel (1981.11.22). See color page 179

This assemblage of goods represents the kinds of items Wolf Chief stocked in his store, as suggested by photographs and surviving invoices. On the left are four barrels that could have held (counterclockwise from bottom left) liquids like syrup or molasses, lard, sugar or coffee beans, and flour. The two bolts of cotton cloth at top match dress cloth worn by reservation women in photographs by Gilbert Wilson (MHS photos IV-40-1910, IX-24-1916; see also SHSND artifact 847); bolts of cloth can also be seen on the shelf behind Wolf Chief in photographs of his store (MHS photos IV-22 and IV-23). Shown below the cloth are some of the types of canned goods Wolf Chief purchased from O. J. Rued in 1910: sardines, tea, soap, and crackers. They rest on a crate for canned fruit, which, along with dried fruit, seems to have been one of his best-selling items. He purchased apricots, peaches, pears, prunes, raisins, and dried apples in 1910. At the right are boxes of dye, knit socks, and crates for Swift's Pride Soap and Works' Northland Biscuits; the latter two products were sold on the reservation (MHS photos IV-23, VII-56-15, IV-51-1910; Wilson [1903-18]:59). Other items which could have been shown include shoes, hats, overalls, corned beef, cookies, candy, tobacco, and baking powder (Wacker 1910; Rued 1910).

HENRY WOLF CHIEF
GENERAL MERCHANDISE
INDEPENDENCE

Letterhead
1927
Ink on printed stationery
NA, Kansas City (Wolf Chief 1927)
Wolf Chief, like other merchants in his area, had stationery printed with his business name and address. The letterhead served him for both correspondence and accounting. It is not know when he took the name of Henry; he often signed letters as "Wolf C. Chief."

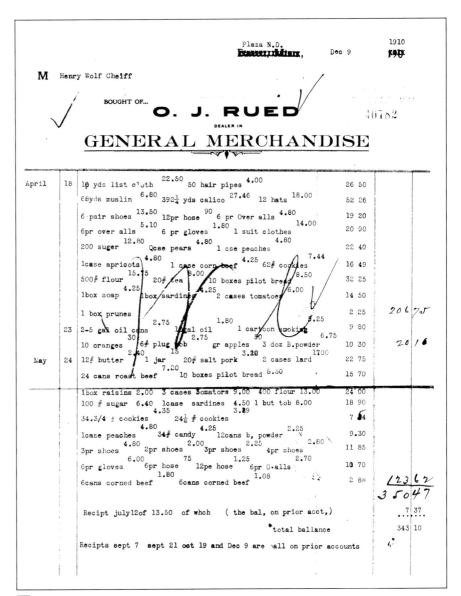

Invoice for Merchandise
Written by O. J. Rued, 1910
Purple typescript and red pencil on printed form
H. 27.9 cm, W. 21.6 cm
NA, Kansas City (Rued 1910)
This bill for purchases during April and May of 1910 shows how quickly things sold in Wolf Chief's store. In April he bought sugar, peaches, tomatoes, shoes, overalls, flour, and cookies, which he had to restock about a month later.

The assault on Indian culture

The U.S. government had assumed control of Indian property, law enforcement, and commerce for one goal – so that Indian culture would cease to exist. Without the barrier of their separate ways, Indians could blend into majority society. "As soon as the Indian is capable of transacting his own business and of taking care of his property," wrote the Commissioner of Indian Affairs, "the ties which bind him to his tribe in the communal sense should be severed" (Leupp 1907:2).

But communal ties were only too real upon the reservation. The arts, customs, and beliefs that Indians shared made them *different*. And so the government launched an offensive war against those beliefs.

At Fort Berthold the first target was religion. The ceremony called the Sun Dance by the whites was outlawed. Persons found guilty of participating in it, or in any other "heathenish rites and customs," had their rations withheld; for a second offense they were imprisoned. The practice of traditional medicine was punishable by ten days in jail (USOIA 1904b:102-3). Age societies were banned, and traditional music discouraged.

Marriage and morality, which had been a personal and family matter, now became a legal one. "Polygamy has disappeared with other dark practices," the agent declared in 1901. Men with more than one wife were "compelled to set aside all but one woman," and arrested if they failed to do so (Richards 1901a:169). Wolf Chief struggled to adapt. "I was a young man that the young women liked years ago, and was married many times. But afterwards, when I learned white customs and became a Christian I did not do such things" (Wilson 1910a:237-38).

Divorces, violations of morality laws, and breaches of the peace were taken to the Court of Indian Offenses. The judges of the court were selected by the agent from among the more acculturated elders of the Indian community. In 1899 Wolf Chief became a judge. "If I found a man having two wives, I took one away," he said. "If a young man got to running after another man's wife, I put him in the guard house. . . . I do all [the] best I can because it [is] too hard for my tribe to keep [the] white man's way. Often the police bring young people. I talk to them & tell them about white ways & [what] it [is] best to do. Often I just say . . . you [are] young, don't do that, but if you do again you [will] go in [the] guard house" (Wolf Chief 1899; Wilson 1910a:237, 1907c:87-88).

Because it was at gatherings and dances that Indian customs were shared and passed on to younger generations, the agents did what they could to curtail free association. Visits to other reservations were governed by strict rules. Indians were forbidden to leave their reservation without the agent's consent (USOIA 1904b:103-4). Even within the reservation, the law reached into people's social lives. There were few opportunities to socialize on the isolated allotments, so it became the custom to hold dances where old songs were sung, costumes worn, and giveaways held. But the agent viewed such activities with alarm. "It only creates in them a desire to become worthless with their heathen notions, which seems to destroy or poison their mind, and lose all their ambition, to exert their mental and physical faculties to live better. . . . They

VOTIVE POLES
Photographed by Gilbert Wilson, 1908
MHS photo III-16
Despite government efforts to suppress traditional religion, people living in isolated places like Independence held to their own beliefs. These votive poles, similar to the ones erected outside lodges in Like-a-Fishhook Village, stood by Calf Woman's log cabin.

can have some other enjoyment, which does not fill their mind with too many Indian notions" (Hoffman 1909).

The missionary supported the agent. "Mr. Hall . . . is very much against our old dances," Goodbird said. "If he did not stand against these things, and would allow Christians to dance some, I think he would get nearly everybody on this reservation [into the church]" (Wilson 1913a:148).

A delegation of Arikaras took the issue all the way to Washington. "It is the only pleasure the old Indians have," they told the Commissioner of Indian Affairs. "The Almighty put us on this earth to live, and he gave us the pleasure and fun to have in this world, too. I think the Almighty wants the pleasure, and I think there should be no one try to take the pleasure away from Him" (Red Bear et al. 1911:1, 6).

Yet even in issues of culture the message of the whites was strangely mixed. In 1913 a delegation of Hidatsas went to Washington in connection with a land claims case. A newspaper reported that the commissioner of Indian affairs asked the Indians to "dress up in their old Indian regalia and attend the ceremony of the dedication of the site for the Indian monument at New York." At this, Joseph Packineau of Elbowoods stood up and declared that "twenty years ago the commissioner had started out to civilize him, had made him wear the white man's clothes and adopt his customs, and that after this lapse of time he did not care to put on the regalia and paint his face to become a spectacle at the dedication. . . . This rather stumped the commissioner and other officials" (*Garrison Times* 1913:1).

Laws could do away with the outward symbols and practices of Indian culture, but they could not abolish belief. In secret, many people still kept their sacred bundles. Though the societies ceased to meet, they still lived in people's minds. To the end of her life Buffalo Bird Woman considered herself a society member. "All these old dances are now done away," she said. But "I am still a member of the third society, the Enemy Woman Society" (Wilson 1911:178). "I [do not] like white men's laws," she said. "I do not understand them nor know how to make them rule my life" (Wilson 1918a:375). With a firm will, she held to the customs and morality she had always known.

INDIAN DANCE
Photographed by Gilbert Wilson, 1907
MHS photo I-61
The dances that the agents were trying to abolish were the descendants of ceremonies like the Grass Dance and the ancestors of today's powwows. The dance shown here was sanctioned by the agent. It was held at Elbowoods in a dance arbor set up for the purpose.

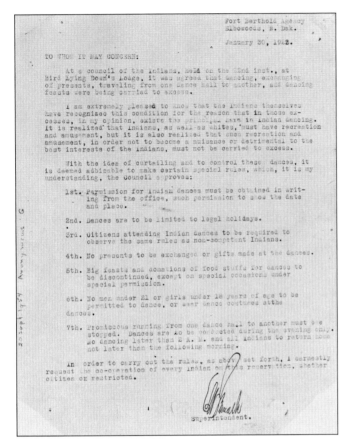

CIRCULAR REGARDING DANCES

Written by Ernest Jermark, 1922
Typescript and ink on paper
H. 26.5 cm, W. 20 cm
SHSND (Jermark 1922)

In this circular to all reservation residents, the agent sets out strict rules governing dances. Like the many circulars that preceded it, this one probably had little effect. Indian agents continued to discourage traditional practices until 1934, when Commissioner of Indian Affairs John Collier reversed the government's policy and directed that Indian traditions should be encouraged and revived whenever possible (Meyer 1977:194).

PETITION FOR PERMISSION TO SING SONGS

Written by residents of Fort Berthold Reservation, 1913
Black typescript, black ink, and pencil on lined paper
H. 31.8 cm, W. 20.3 cm
NA (Sitting Bear et al. 1913)

Because traditional Indian social and religious practices were banned, the people of Fort Berthold had to petition the Office of Indian Affairs for permission to teach songs to their children and visiting anthropologists. The petition was approved, provided that the singers did not indulge in "practices which tend to retard the moral, social and industrial welfare of the participants." Those practices were listed as dancing, Indian medicine, and giveaways (Abbott 1913a; Jermark 1913).

SACRED ARK OF THE MANDAN
Photographed by Gilbert Wilson, 1909
MHS photo IV-8

The Ark of the First Man, which commemorated the near-destruction of humankind in flood, had been a feature of Mandan villages since time immemorial (see painting p. 5). At Like-a-Fishhook Village it was set up in the central plaza (Bowers 1950:111-13; see p. 12). Allotment eliminated the village plaza, but the ark was still kept up in the early 20th century by the group led by Crow's Heart, who lived near the Little Missouri River, south of Independence (Wilson 1910a: cover letter, p. 3). A delegation from Fort Berthold to Washington in 1911 pleaded for religious toleration: "They have different ways of their own doings everywhere, and we have our way of our own doings. We have our own religion and you have your own religion. You have your own God and we have our own God. We don't know your God. We don't know how to satisfy your creator, but we know how to satisfy our own creator and we must do it that way" (Enemy Heart in Red Bear et al. 1911).

MARRIAGE LICENSE
Issued for Charles Goodbird and Nellie Old Mouse, 1902
Ink on printed form
H. 33 cm, W. 20.3 cm
NA, Kansas City (Hall 1902)

When Goodbird's son Charles wanted to marry, the procedure was very different from what Buffalo Bird Woman had known. "Marriages according to the old Indian customs are not permitted," wrote the agent in 1901. "All persons desiring to marry are required to procure a license from the agent and to be married by the agent, a clergyman or magistrate" (Richards 1901a:169-70). The intricate legal requirements and the marriage rituals often required some coaching. Missionary Charles Hall, who performed Charles Goodbird's marriage, described presiding at another wedding where "I told them (in private) what to say and do, how to stand and which hand to hold and when to say: 'I do'. I gave the girl the big bouquet and showed her just how to hold it. They did as told perfectly and composedly" (Hall 1937k).

Wolf Chief writes to Washington

Wolf Chief was fed up. There were a lot of things he did not like about the way the government was running things on the reservation. From the example of other Plains tribes, he knew that armed rebellion was a futile way to try to settle disputes with the whites. So he decided to use the white man's weapon – the written word. He began writing letters.

His career as a correspondent was launched one day in about 1880 when Crow's Paunch, Had Many Antelopes, and John Smith came to his house. They asked him, "Can you write a letter to Washington? If you can we want you to do this. We would like to go to Washington to see the president & tell him all that we need here. If you know the president's name or can write we want to know."

"I think I can do it," Wolf Chief said.

So he wrote what they wanted.

"If you can say this do it too," the men said. "We are hungry. [The] buffaloes [are] gone. We want more rations."

"No," John Smith said. "If you write you are hungry, they will say go to [the] agent. He can issue what you want."

"If that is so don't write it," the others said.

Crow's Paunch said, "Tell them we are good people. We never killed white man. [We are] always kind to them."

"Don't do that," Wolf Chief suggested, "or they will think there has been trouble here."

When they had agreed on what to say, Wolf Chief sent the letter off. He soon received an answer: the Office of Indian Affairs would not pay the men's way to Washington, but it promised to send an inspector to Fort Berthold Reservation. Wolf Chief called the three men to his house, fed them supper, and then told them what the letter said.

They were very impressed.

Had Many Antelopes said, "I hear[d] this boy wrote a letter to Washington before, and all the village [did] not believe it. But now I know it. He is Indian but does white man's work."

Even Wolf Chief's father Small Ankle approved. He said to his other sons, "You see your elder brother goes to school as you don't. Now he understands English. You don't. I wish you would study & learn to write & read & speak English" (Wilson 1916c:70-73).

That was only the beginning. Wolf Chief continued to send messages to the outside world, writing over 100 letters to the Office of Indian Affairs

WOLF CHIEF (DETAIL)
Photographed by Gilbert Wilson, 1908
MHS photo III-4

by 1906. He wrote to newspapers and magazines. He wrote to his congressman. He wrote to the president. Nothing stopped him.

It drove the agents to distraction. "There is no tribe or band of Indians on this reservation who have given me . . . as much trouble as 'Wolf Chief' whose character is that of a troublesome, meddlesome and dissatisfied Indian," one agent complained. He had an "evil influence" over "a certain class of our Indians viz. those who oppose everything." Another agent answered a query from Washington, "This letter is simply Wolf Chief's annual eruption. He has contracted the letter writing habit and cannot be suppressed" (Gifford 1885, Gifford 1886; Richards 1901b).

The problem was that Wolf Chief's letters often got results. Letters from Indians were unusual at the

Office of Indian Affairs, and Wolf Chief's got the civil servants' attention. Although they eventually met the regular arrival of his letters with skepticism or annoyance, each change of administration brought him new attention. The agent who gave Wolf Chief such trouble over his store complained furiously that "one letter from one poor, 'lone' Indian has an effect upon the Department that five lucid letters and reports from me had not. This seems truly 'passing strange'" (Murphy 1891d).

It did not seem strange to Wolf Chief. He had legitimate complaints. In the early years, his most frequent subject was the reservation trader's prices and how "My agent and the trader love each other" (Wolf Chief 1882b). Later he became concerned about hunger on the reservation and the insufficiency of the rations. "The children cried yesterday because the agent they did not give out any sugar. They are in trouble indeed – and the flour they give is eaten up in two days" (Wolf Chief 1884). After 1888, he repeatedly pointed out the government's failure to make promised payments on land sold by the tribe. He wanted the agency moved. He was worried about crop failures and the poor repair of the reservation boarding school. He wanted a ferry and a day school at Independence. He did not like the fact that white ranchers trespassed on the reservation. "Why do you not regard our rights?" he asked (Wolf Chief 1891c).

But not all his letters were complaints. He knew how ignorant the Washington bureaucrats were about reservation life, so he filled them in on local news. "I have plowed and sown, this spring, about sixteen (16) acres of Wheat and some other vegetables but most of it are the former," he wrote in 1889. "I have very [few] plow ponies and have no ox but I done my work by borrowing from my good friends a york [yoke] of oxes. I have a small team of ponies and they can not plow New ground, neither can they draw my harvester when harvest come[s]" (Wolf Chief 1889a). Some of the news was more discouraging. "We all thought we would have a big crop last Fall. But the frost came and now we have no crop [at] all. And we do not know what we will do this winter for food. Now I [write] to you for I want you to know how we are fixed for this winter, and we all wish you would give us more food, so we would [not] starve this winter" (Wolf Chief 1888b).

He knew his correspondence campaign did not win him friends at the agency. "My Chief [the agent] says I am bad bec[a]use I write," he said early on (Wolf Chief 1882b). Years later, the story was the same. "I want to hear from you because the Agent don't lik[e] me and speaks to me in hard words" (Wolf Chief 1890b). "Agent Murphy . . . says we have No right to say anything that He had everything to say," he charged (Wolf Chief 1892).

But Wolf Chief was not about to keep quiet, nor would he counsel others to. In 1898 the Office of Indian Affairs received its first letter from his son Frank (F. Wolf Chief 1898). It looked like the tradition was going to continue.

INKWELL
Pre-1885?
Excavated at Like-a-Fishhook Village
Cylindrical, molded body of clear glass with wide neck
H. 3.1 cm, D. 2.5 cm
SHSND 32ML2/12,003.2241
As Indian children returned from boarding school, writing skills grew more common on the reservation. Although he occasionally got someone else to take down letters for him, Wolf Chief wrote the great majority of his letters in his own hand, using ink or pencil.

PEN
Made by E. Faber Co., c. 1900
Tapered black wood pen holder and steel nib
L. 19 cm
MHS 67.122.49, Miss E. G. Cockburn

Fort Berthold, Dakota Terry.
April 7th 1888.

Hon. J. D. C. Atkins
Commissioner of Indian Affairs
Washington, D.C.

My Dear Sir

I want to tell you that last year we were very glad to see Hon. J. V. Wright, Chas. S. Larrabee, & D. Danick[?] on Dece. 15th 1886. They told us the Great fathers desires for us. We liked what they said, & agree to it. We believe that they told us the truth, & we all write our names. We think that all of the officers in Washington are good men, & we thank you for what you have done for us. The Commissioners said they wanted us to have $(80,000) eighty thousand dollars a year for 10 years & each one to have 160 acres of land. Now we want to have the $(80,000) this year. I belong to the Mandans. The Mandans are a good people. We listen to what the President says, & do nothing foolish nor do we harm the Whites. We have always been friends to the Whites. We are poor, but we want to go to Washington and see your face and talk with you. We want to know the ways of the Great fathers. We would like to shake hands with the new Great father and with all the Great Chief in Washington. We believe all are true men. Dear sir, when you see this letter please help us. We are Now making houses on both sides of the Missouri river. We think it is a nice place to live. We are not skilful in building large houses. We cannot do it alone. We want to be like the White people in all our ways. We want this to do something more. We want to have Cows like you people, so please help us. Our little children very [sick] from hungry because in a few days all the flour given is eaten up; & we cannot lift a plow because we are weak, and people die from hungry and sickness. And. Now. My Dear father Commissioner Atkins. When you get this letter Please write to me very soon at once, and Washington My all good friends Shall not be [for]gotten.

Respectfully yours
Mr. Wolf C. Chief

LETTER
Written by Wolf Chief, 1888
Black ink on lined paper
L. 31.4 cm, W. 20.3 cm
NA (Wolf Chief 1888a)

Wolf Chief reminds the commissioner about an agreement reached between his tribe and the U.S. government over a year earlier. The government had not paid money promised for the sale of part of the Fort Berthold Reservation, as Wolf Chief notes – in fact, Congress had not yet ratified the agreement. Wolf Chief paints a bleak portrait of life on the reservation.

It is not clear why Wolf Chief calls himself a Mandan.

Fort Berthold Agency, N.D.
February 17th, 1891

Dear Great Father and
Gen. T. J. Morgan Commissioner of Indian Affairs
Washington, D.C.

My Dear Friends,
           Dear Sir,
        I received your letter dated Jany 17th And I was very
glad to hear that I can trade in Indian Country without
license. But I am sorry that I can not sell any fixed
ammunitions. I believe every body in this reservation wished to
have me sell cartridges not that we want to fight anybody but
because we use them in hunting. You need not be fraid of us.
We are taking up White mans ways. We dont hunt all the
time neither most the time, but we [do] some farming hay
making, setting [selling] dry bones cutting wood and all that.
but in such time as this when we can not plough, make hay
sell wood and bones and the rations cut down we need some
thing to make our living somehow then are [our] antelop, deer
and other games we can hunt and make part of our livin.
        I am sure that you have a very poor knowledge of the
Indians in this reservation. If I take you to visit an Indian
family of a husban, wife and child on Sunday evening next day
after rations day we see now that he get fifteen pounds of flour
and few ounces of each coffee and sugar for forteen day. Do you
think they will not consume them till at the end of forteen
days? We cannot, and no one can, you know that we can not
get living in no way but hunting, and we depend upon rations
but they are very little indeed. you know that you can not live
on 5 lbs of beef and flour for 14 day, and work every-day. I
would not asked you this if we can find some week [work] to
make our living. Tak[e] Whites the rations all fair long as we
can [find] some work to help along. Please consider the matter
not in the interest of any White-men, but in the interest of the
Indians of this reservation. I rather think that the section 31
applies only to the license traders.
        Please I want to hear form [from] you soon. today we
Mandan have come all together and we want you all Great
Chief in Washington to help us. And the Washington all Big
Chief Shall not be forgotten.
                Please Very soon write me
                Very truly you friends
                    Mr. Wolf C. Chief
Mandan, Crow B[r]east, Little Bear, Red Shield, Many
Crow, Bear heart, not good, Short Bull, Running Wiles, Ded
Drum, good Bunch, Charging Enemy, Bear Tail, Two Chief,
White fingernail, Mandan Son Star

LETTER
Written by Wolf Chief, 1891
Brown ink on lined paper
L. 31.8 cm, W. 20.5 cm
NA (Wolf Chief 1891a)
Wolf Chief complains about the dilemma that is trapping his
people: the Indian Office is cutting down rations but refusing
to let reservation storekeepers sell ammunition so that the
Indians can hunt for food. The "Section 31" he refers to was
probably the passage in the Office of Indian Affairs regulations
that restricted the goods traders could carry (USOIA
1904:96).

United States Indian Service,
Elbowoods, P.O. Agency,
Independence, N. Dak.
February 3th, 1895

Hon. Hake Smith Secretary of the Interior
at Washington D.C.

My Dear Friend,

I was very much Pleased to hear to [from] My Chief Hake Smith and also very thankful for your nice Picture. I have framed it nice and hung it up in my room where the people can see it. Many of the men have seen it Now and I told them that was their Grandfather at Washington. They say by your looks you seem to be a very good kind man.

And. Now. My Dear Great Father, and Secretary Hake Smith Sir. I am going to tell you something. Please help me. It is a month Now since I wrote to the Commissioner at Washington and thought I would hear from them by this time but have not yet. I wrote and told them that I am trying to be like a White man and am learning the best I can I told also that I have obeyed them and sent my little ones to school to learn. I thought it would help me [?] to keep a Small Store so I began it in Dece 20 1889. But it is very slow because the Pleople have no money but get Goods in the Store. I wrote to the Commissioner and asked them to help me and talk about it for me for I want to take their cattle instead of money for they have no money at all. Then I asked them what I would trad[e] in my Store. I have land for my own Now and I thought maybe it might be right for me to sell anything. So I told them to let me know everything about it whether I would sell anything or not. The law was not to sell cartridges so I did not sell those things but last year I ask my agent to let me have the permission to sell cartriges and he told me to so I am selling cartridges in my store. I wrote all these things and sent it to the Commissioner to help me, and I am very anxious to hear from them soon and like to know soon what they say about it.

I also wrote to Commissioner Armstrong and told a little about it. I told him that the police mans here get goods [at] my store and dont let me have my money about a year or two and I tolds my Chief to help me but he said He is not able to help me. The police mans buy stuff at issue house and when the money is given to them for their earnings Then my agent is able to take the money from the police mans for what they get at the issue house, but is not able to help me to have the money from his police mans. I tolds these things about it to Commissioner Armstrong.

Please when you get this my letter let me hear very soon.

Very truly your friend
Wolf C. Chief

LETTER

Written by Wolf Chief, 1895
Brown ink on printed letterhead
L. 26.7 cm, W. 20.3 cm
NA (Wolf Chief 1895)

Wolf Chief has three problems. Cash is scarce at Independence, but the Indian Office regulations forbid him to accept cattle in payment for goods sold at his store. He asks the commissioner to permit him to barter with his neighbors. Moreover, since he has been allotted land, he is uncertain how his changed legal status affects the trade regulations he must obey. He is also having problems collecting payment from Indian policemen who have purchased goods at his store.

Going away to school

As he watched his children grow, Wolf Chief found his deepest feelings and beliefs pitted against each other. He was ambitious for his children, and he believed strongly in the value of education. But an Indian in the 1880s and 1890s who sought an education for his children had to give them up to a hostile system whose explicit goal was to turn children against their parents' ways.

The government's efforts had made inroads on Indian culture, but there was still one formidable obstacle to wholesale assimilation: family ties. Boarding schools were the government's answer. They were cheaper than establishing many little schools to serve the scattered communities created by allotment. In addition, boarding schools separated children from the influence of their parents and plunged them headfirst into Euro-American culture.

The Indian education system was part of a larger movement in education during the late 19th century. Then, as now, Americans often turned to schools to solve social problems. In the 1890s cultural diversity was seen as a problem. Social reformers felt that a well-controlled education would give all Americans the same

opportunities and values. New laws required all children to attend school. Standardized teacher training and textbooks ensured that ideas would be taught in the same way across the nation (Weibe 1967:57, 157).

Indian boarding schools had existed since the 1870s, and the children of Fort Berthold were among the first to attend. In 1878, 13 children left Like-a-Fishhook Village for the Hampton Institute in faraway Virginia. Later, others went to privately run schools like the Carlisle Indian School in Pennsylvania and the Santee Normal Training School in Nebraska (Meyer 1977:145). But most children got their first taste of boarding school when the government turned the old army fort 14 miles east of Like-a-Fishhook into a school.

The Fort Stevenson school was controversial from the beginning. "For some reason the Indians have formed a great dislike for the Fort Stevenson School which is met on every hand," the agent reported in 1886. "I purpose using my best endeavors to have them send their children without resorting to force." He was, however, willing to resort to depriving parents of their ration cards until they gave in (Gifford 1886:4).

FORT STEVENSON BOARDING SCHOOL
Late 1880s
National Anthropological Archives, Smithsonian Institution, Records of the River Basin Surveys 32ML1-L116
Fort Stevenson was turned into a boarding school in 1883 (Meyer 1977:143). The buildings had a military quality even after they were converted. Barracks became dormitories, and the mess hall became a dining room.

Attendance at the Fort Stevenson school grew from 36 when it opened to 106 in 1888. There were complaints early on that the school was overcrowded (Meyer 1977:143-44).

The reasons for the Indians' dislike of the school were not hard to understand. "The government school at Stevenson is not fit to fill it with children for it is dangerous," Wolf Chief wrote to the commissioner of Indian affairs. "No good White man will keep childern in such Bad and dangerous buildings. At a little blow of wind the houses might fall down, killing every child. You know that we love our childern. I like the School and the supt. very much and I wished that the school houses be removed. . . . Therefore I earnestly ask you to built a new govern. school-house inside the reserve and in the middle of our settlement" (Wolf Chief 1889b, 1891b). His warnings were well founded. Children were crowded three to a bed in the unsanitary old buildings, where disease flourished. In 1894 the dilapidated school buildings finally burned down (Meyer 1977:143-44).

Wolf Chief also feared that the agent would start enrolling children in schools "contrarie to the parents will" (Wolf Chief 1889b). This concern, too, was justified. The government's tactics grew more forceful through the years. In 1893 a mandatory school attendance law was passed and the Indian police were ordered to enforce it. Policemen apparently disliked such orders, as officials criticized them for lacking "the moral courage to take the children against the protest of the parents" (USOIA Superintendent 1893:23).

But the hardest fear to overcome was that of being separated from children for months, sometimes years. It was winter, about 1889, when the superintendent of the Fort Stevenson school first came to Independence to take the children away. He went to Wolf Chief first. He said, "I understand you wrote to Washington & that you got an answer & that you [want] to send your children to school."

Wolf Chief sent out word around the community, and the parents gathered at his house. He gave them a meal of antelope and deer meat, and they sat on the benches around his main room. He then rose to address them. "This man is Sup't. of Ft. Stevenson school and he wants you to send your children to school," Wolf Chief said. "I think he is right. I want you to send your children to school.

"I knew the gov[ernment] wanted to teach our children to write & read & I think we ought to have it. I want you to be willing to do this. If you don't maybe there will be trouble and they will put you in jail."

When Wolf Chief was done, Has Red Shield rose. "I want to send my boy to school because Wolf Chief says it is [the] right way and everything will come out all right. I want to put him in school. . . . He may die

any place. He may die down there, or here – any way I will send him down."

Standing Bear then said, "Well I think I will send my brother."

Butterfly said, "I will send my daughter to school."

Plain Color said, "I will send my grandson."

Good Worker said, "Yes I will send my boy. He is about 8 years [old]."

"And I," said Wolf Chief, "I am the man who started to get you to send your children. I will send mine. He is only six but he will be a man & he needs English and an education."

The day of parting was a hard one. When the children were assembled, the superintendent "got many blankets and wrapped them up carefully & crossed on [the] ice on [the] Missouri River. And the people waited and many of the people wept. Men and women both. The parents & sisters & brothers [all] wept" (Wilson 1916c:98-100).

MATRON'S ROOM, ELBOWOODS MISSION SCHOOL
1903
Collected by Harold Case
SHSND Col. 41–472

At the mission school, both before and after its move from Fort Berthold to Elbowoods, boys and girls lived separately in homelike "cottages" overseen by matrons who supervised domestic duties, home discipline, and recreation. Through example, the matrons taught children the most modern tastes in keeping and decorating a house (Field 1896; Powell 1896).

The scene was repeated many times all across Fort Berthold Reservation. The missionary was often present. "Could Eastern friends, or rather unbelievers in the Indian, see how these fathers and mothers cling to their children, they would never doubt they had warm hearts, tender affections, and souls worth saving," he wrote (Hall 1888c).

When the children arrived at school, they found a world very different from that they were accustomed to. Indian languages were strictly forbidden, as were Indian dress, song, and customs. "The white people's ways were so strange to us," one student wrote; "when we go home . . . we would tell them to our friends and make them laugh" (Montclair 1888). Half the day was spent learning reading, writing, mathematics, history, geography, and other academic subjects. The other half was devoted to vocational training. Girls were sent to the laundry to wash and to the kitchen to cook and clean. They ironed and sewed the clothes for themselves and the other students. Meanwhile, the boys learned trades like farming, harness making, shoemaking, blacksmithing, and carpentry. They raised the school's food, shod its horses, and repaired its furniture and buildings (Richards 1901a:162).

Student labor was used to save government money and to give Indian children "respect and even love for work." But the method could have drawbacks. "Many schools use the children chiefly as helping hands," an 1894 government report charged (USOIA Superintendent 1894:9, 11).

The evening was supposed to be devoted to "the pleasures of home." As at the old mission school near Like-a-Fishhook, this meant parlor games and songs, magic lantern shows, and "social entertainments of an elevating and cheering character." The object was to teach children "the desire to seek a broader education and, subsequently, a happier and richer life away from the reservation" (USOIA Superintendent 1896:9, 10).

In addition to the government school, there were mission schools on the reservation run under government contract by the Catholic and Congregational churches. The Congregational mission school was a happy compromise for many families, for the children were allowed to return home for weekends under the philosophy that "to train the children is the best way to train the parents" (Hall 1937p).

Returning home from school was sometimes as hard as leaving had been. "Children were taken out of all the old customs and conditions and in a year or two trained into new," the missionary wrote. Then "they were sent back to face the old, from which they had been entirely severed" (Hall 1937n). They frequently found that their new skills were useless on the reservation. "When they return home, they are soon discouraged," wrote one agent. "As an example, a returned boarding school girl, who thought, it would be nice to show her mother, how to make [yeast] bread, she took [a] hundred pounds [of] flour dumped it into [the] washtub, and before she finished set down [on] the dirt floor and cried, because she found her parents did not have the same materials in the house, that she had been accustom[ed] to use at the school" (Hoffman 1909b:2).

For all the government's optimistic rhetoric, the boarding schools did not have the intended effect. Children who were separated from their families, isolated from their culture, and put to hard work did not joyfully accept the new system. Indian solidarity flourished in the hostile environment of the schools. When the children returned, it was not to reject their parents' ways.

In the mid-1890s, the government began to give in to the arguments of the Fort Berthold people for local schools. A day school was established at Independence in 1895. Here, children learned by day and returned home each night. The people of Independence were satisfied. "It is a very hard thing for us to have to let our children be taken from us and sent away to school where we cannot see them," Buffalo Bird Woman said. She was not sure about the things young people learned at boarding schools, anyway. "In old days," she said, "mothers watched their daughters very carefully; and girls did not give birth to babies before marriage. But after schools were started on this reservation, then our daughters began to have babies before marriage, for they now learned English ways" (Wilson 1918a:375; 1915b:450).

SCHOOL DESK

Early 20th century
Cast iron frame with open scrollwork
and the words "The Elgin" and "Z"
on sides; feet have holes for screwing
to floor. Swiveling wooden seat and
fixed writing surface with pencil
groove and hole for inkwell
L. 87 cm, W. 60.5 cm, H. 81.5 cm
MHS, Michael Pedersen

The desks used at the Fort Stevenson
boarding school were made by the
Sterling School Furniture Company;
they had cast-iron frames and wooden
seats and surfaces much like this one
(Smith 1960:214). They were used
during the half-day devoted to academic
subjects. This desk was purchased in
Yankton, S.Dak.

BOY'S CLOTHES

1890–1900
Cotton ticking shirt with white stripes
on faded blue ground, long sleeves
with button cuffs, back yoke, and
tab front with three glass buttons.
Suspenders of blue, green, and
white striped elastic, white leather
belt loops, and brass gripper buckles
for adjustment. Knee pants of
plain-weave, natural-colored linen
with hidden button fly front, side
pockets, bone and shell suspender
buttons, and adjustable buckled
strap at back of waist. Shoes of
black patent leather with metal
eyelets for laces, stacked heel with
rubber base, and white cotton
lining
Shirt: L. 69.5 cm, W. 35 cm.
Suspenders: L. 101 cm. Pants: L.
64.5 cm. Shoes: L. 25.5 cm, W.
8.5 cm
MHS 65.45.4, Florence Greene;
69.120.2, Irene Larson; 8258.10,
Mrs. L. E. Breckenridge Estate;
63.178.2a, b, Ramona Englebrecht

In traditional Hidatsa society, children
did not wear clothes until they grew to
be three to six years old (Kurz
1937:89). Schools and agents did all
they could to change this custom.
Boarding schools provided students with
clothes similar to these and taught girls
how to wash, iron, and mend them.
Clothes were also provided as part of
annuities until at least 1902 (Meyer
1977:171). One field matron reported
that "A number of women have been
given assistance in making new
garments, but more stress has been
placed upon repairing or making over
old garments otherwise cast to one side.
Some of the young women have done
very well in making trousers for little
boys and skirts for little girls out of such
garments. . . . I would make a grateful
mention of the timely help from an
eastern society of an unsolicited barrel of
warm clothing at Christmas" (USOIA
1909:6).

According to the missionary,
young people had accepted changed
styles of dress by the turn of the
century, and the men were "getting
particular about white collars and bright
ties and fancy socks and tan shoes"
(Hall 1937k).

TEXTBOOKS
1879–95
Printed paper, cardboard covers, cloth
  bindings
Left to right: H. 18.7 cm, W. 13 cm;
  H. 31.5 cm, W. 26 cm; H. 19 cm,
  W. 13.1 cm
MHS textbook collection
Texts were purchased by the Office of
Indian Affairs in Washington for
reservation schools across the country.
They were standard titles also used in
non-Indian schools. These are three of
the books specified for purchase in 1895
(USOIA 1895:914). The curriculum in
the mission school was similar to that in
government schools. A mission teacher
described a typical class: one group
learned long division while another
received a practical lesson in
bookkeeping. A third struggled to read
a passage from Sir Walter Scott's *The
Lady of the Lake* (Brickett 1896).
      Shown here are *McGuffey's Fourth
Eclectic Reader* (Cincinnati and New
York: Van Antwerp, Bragg & Co.,
1879); Alex Everett Frye, *Complete
Geography* (Boston and London: Ginn &
Co., 1895); and D. H. Montgomery,
The Beginner's American History (Boston:
Ginn & Co., 1894).

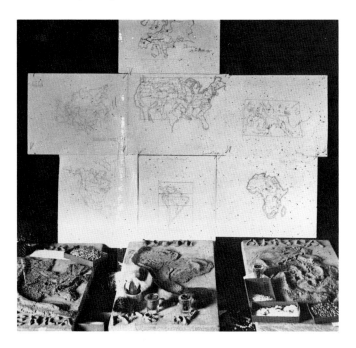

SCHOOL PROJECTS
1897
Collected by Harold Case
SHSND Col. 41–421
Progressive educational methods were introduced into the
Indian schools at the same time they were sweeping through
the rest of American public schools. Turn-of-the-century
educators wanted to teach abstract ideas through concrete
activities. "At every step the pupil is not merely a learner, but
also a doer," was the maxim (USOIA Superintendent
1894:14). These geography projects are examples of "object
teaching," by which students learned through modeling and
drawing. They were probably created in the Congregational
mission school at Elbowoods.

Egg Beater
Made by Holt Co., c. 1900
Sheet tin whips turned by cast-iron
*   gear mechanism with wooden*
*   handle*
L. 27.5 cm
MHS 1978.26.12

Teachers, field matrons, and missionaries worked to introduce the girls of Fort Berthold to a new diet requiring different cooking techniques. The use of eggs in cooking was a new concept to Indian women, as were the necessary beating, whipping, and measuring. Said one matron, "Whenever opportunity presented itself instruction in practical, plain but wholesome cookery, has been given, such as how to make soup-stock, vegetable soups, cooking of cabbage, potatoes, green tomatoes, macaroni, rice, eggs, etc., in various ways, while lessons were also given on pastry, pies and cake, and the necessity of thoroughly cleaning fresh and dried fruits before serving and cooking was emphasized" (USOIA 1909:6).

Washboard
Early 20th century
Horizontally fluted brass scrubbing
*   surface mounted in wooden frame*
*   with legs, and ledge for laundry*
*   soap. Brand name "Brass Prince"*
*   painted on frame in faded red and*
*   black*
H. 59.5 cm, W. 31.5 cm
MHS 65.78.76, Magdalene Wagner

Female students were given instruction in using modern laundry equipment at school. The superintendent of the Fort Stevenson boarding school described the laundry as "a pattern of neatness and dispatch. Here hundreds of garments are carefully washed and ironed each week. Four medium-sized boys, two each fore and afternoon, assist in running the washing machines, which helps to lighten the work of the girls in this department" (USOIA 1891:577).

But for most Indian households, washing machines were an unattainable luxury; instead, women used washboards like this one (Wilson [1903-18]:58-59; MHS photo X-72-1918). In 1909 the field matron had to supply laundry soap for women who could not afford to buy it for doing the family laundry (USOIA 1909:6).

Muffin Pan
Late 19th century
Eleven shallow cast-iron cups welded together in three rows; stamped "Favorite
*   Ware" on bottom*
L. 27.5 cm, W. 20 cm, H. 2.5 cm
MHS 70.137, Betty Ratzlaff

A muffin pan almost identical to this was found by archaeologists at the site of the Fort Stevenson school (Smith 1960:pl. 53). It may have been used in baking lessons given by school matrons. Since breads were unknown in the traditional Hidatsa diet, many families did not use flour, and girls could not learn to bake from their mothers.

BACK SAW
Early 20th century
Sheet metal blade, wooden handle attached with two brass screws and
   stamped "U.S."
L. 39 cm, W. 11 cm
MHS 1976.2.178, Harkin Store

Mechanical skills like carpentry were part of the curriculum at boarding schools. The superintendent of the Fort Berthold Reservation schools reported that "The engine room has been supplied with carpenter, shoe, and harness repairing tools, and when the boys were not otherwise employed they have been required to repair woodwork, shoes, and harness, and to manufacture ax handles, under the instruction of the engineer, who is a good all-around mechanic" (USOIA 1904a: 274). Fragments of several saws were found by archaeologists at Fort Stevenson (Smith 1960: 224).

HORSESHOE
c. 1900
Wrought iron, pierced for eight nails,
   with toe and heel calks
L. 16.5 cm, W. 14 cm
MHS 64.183.14ii, Mrs. Rudolph A.
   Kunz, Sr.

Most Indian boarding schools included a blacksmith shop where boys learned the ironworking skills needed by self-sufficient farmers. At Fort Stevenson, boys performed "the hundred and one little things in iron repairs needed about such a place as this" (USOIA 1889: 352). Unfortunately, skills like shoeing horses were fast becoming outmoded on the mechanized farms of the 20th century. A number of horse, mule, and ox shoes were found by archaeologists at Fort Stevenson (Smith 1960: 224).

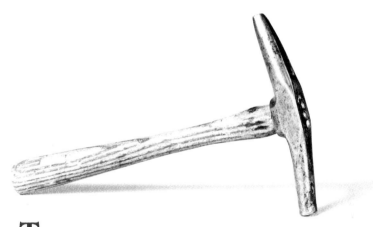

TACK HAMMER
Made by R. Robertson, Mass., 1890-1900
Cast steel head with smooth face and claw; hardwood handle
L. 25 cm, W. 14.2 cm
MHS 66.74.6, Carolyne Sawyer

At Fort Stevenson, boys could learn carpentry, shoemaking, harnessmaking, tailoring, farming, and ranching – although critics contended that none of them were taught in enough detail for a boy to be master of the trade (Meyer 1977: 147). The school superintendent reported that the carpentry class had performed "a great deal of repairing . . . on the buildings. . . . The old picket fence in front of the buildings has been replaced by a new one, and many articles have been made, such as wardrobes and lounges for the rooms, pegging-jacks or horses for the shop, a wheelbarrow for barn use, and many other necessary and convenient articles" (USOIA 1889: 352). Tack hammers like this could be used in shoe and furniture making. Part of one was found by archaeologists at Fort Stevenson (Smith 1960: 224).

TOY CRADLE BUNDLE WITH CHINA DOLL

Hidatsa
Collected by Gilbert Wilson, c. 1915
Black cloth bundle with hood made of
*   hide decorated with red, yellow,*
*   and blue quillwork; tufts of yellow*
*   feathers; fringed flap at back.*
*   Lined with gray cloth. China doll*
*   has moveable arms*
L. 9.5 cm, W. 3.5 cm
MHS 7059.10

Some children's toys still reflected
traditional life. Hidatsa babies were not
placed in the stiff baby carriers used by
other Plains tribes, but were tightly
wrapped in hides, sometimes
ornamented with quillwork (Goodbird
1916:fig. 27). Cradle bundles were still
used at the turn of the century, but
they appear to have been made from
cloth (MHS photo IV-77).

This toy was probably made for
anthropologist Robert H. Lowie. In a
1915 letter to Clark Wissler at the
American Museum of Natural History,
Wilson said that he had a doll and some
other items ordered by Lowie. Because
there is no record that any of the items
were sent to the AMNH, it is likely
that this is the doll he mentioned
(Wilson 1915c).

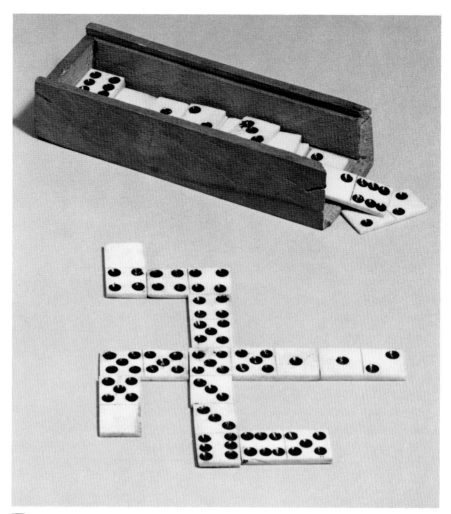

DOMINOES

19th century
Set of double-six dominoes made of bone with indented spots painted black, kept
*   in a wooden box missing its sliding top and one side*
Each domino L. 3.7 cm, W. 1.8 cm
MHS 7520.13, Minneapolis Home for Children and Aged Women

The Hidatsa probably first learned the game of dominoes from traders; playing pieces
made from bison or beef ribs suggest that Indians made sets modeled after
commercially produced ones. Dominoes closely resembling these were excavated by
archaeologists at both Fort Stevenson and Like-a-Fishhook Village (Smith
1972:71-72, 1960:227).

BOYS PLAYING THROW-STICK
Photographed by Gilbert Wilson, 1909
MHS photo III-78

Vacation-time activities at the turn of the century included a mixture of non-Indian and Hidatsa games. A mission worker described children playing "either in the playroom with their toys and dolls, plying needles to make doll dresses; or on the ice with their sled and whipping tops; or, if the day be warm and pleasant, making little mud houses in the sand" (Field 1896). Tobogganing was still popular, although the new sleds were made of barrel staves instead of buffalo ribs. In spring, "Foot ball has already begun on the dry hill-top in the campus. While the game of skipping-sticks will soon send wooden missiles over the yard" (Powell 1896). Here, boys at Independence compete in the ancient game of darting sticks against the ground (Wilson 1909a:95).

TOYS
Hidatsa. Made by Joseph Wounded Face
Collected by Gilbert Wilson, 1910
Wagon of commercially cut board with wheels of baking powder can lids nailed on. Hand-carved figurine of cottonwood with white and blue yarn wrapped around waist and neck. Hand-carved cottonwood boats have nails at prow for pulling; larger one has rough bark exterior
Wagon: L. 29.5 cm, W. 18.6 cm. Figurine: H. 14.5 cm. Small boat: L. 22 cm, W. 6.3 cm. Large boat: L. 28 cm, W. 10.5 cm
AMNH 50.1/5470c, d, f, g

Commercially made toys were expensive luxuries in reservation households, so most children made their own toys and games. Twelve-year-old Joseph Wounded Face, who lived at Independence, made these. Wilson wrote that he lived "in rather an isolated part of the reservation and Joseph seldom or never sees white children and has had no toys that I can discover to model after. . . . I have purchased this specimen, or rather these specimens of the child-passage from the old to the new. . . . The boats are skiff-fashion, like those now superseding the bullboat" (Wilson 1910a:cover letter, p. 5).

CHILDREN OF INDEPENDENCE
Photographed by Gilbert Wilson,
1910–18
MHS photos VII-47-1915,
VII-94-1915, VI-21-1913,
IX-22-1916

Ranching

The Hidatsa had a story about how cattle came to be. Only Man and First Creator, the first two beings on earth, split up the job of creation. They made the river and the plains and the badlands. To populate them, First Creator made the buffalo. But Only Man picked up a dead wolf and created a white man and the spotted cows the white man raised. When First Creator saw what Only Man had done he said, "You are foolish to make these things." The white men were "a queer kind of men, – they will always be greedy!" And the spotted cows all had short hair, too short to protect them from the winter. "That is so," said Only Man; and so he opened a hole in the earth and sent all the spotted cattle down underground. "But," he said, "when [the] buffalo are all gone they will come again and cover this earth as buffaloes [did]" (Beckwith 1937:16-17; Wilson 1906b:29-30).

And that is what happened.

Although the spotted cattle were a second-best solution, the Hidatsa came to be grateful for Only Man's gift. The dry, rugged range land where the buffalo had flourished was perfect for raising cattle. Where the white man's agriculture had failed the tribe, ranching succeeded.

The government first issued cattle to the Hidatsa in 1891. "At first they issued one cow to each family," said Goodbird. "At the time I began farming there were about thirty-five head of cattle in the herd which we kept at Independence. These cattle we had to feed through the winter. We saw that every farmer had a barn for their cattle. . . .

"All the cattle of the Indians at Independence were let run out on the prairie. There was at that time no fence around the reservation, which was quite large, over eight hundred thousand acres. . . . Every cow and steer was branded. My brand was the letters SU on the right shoulder. All the [Hidatsa] cattle were branded on the right thigh and the Arikara cattle on the left thigh" (Murphy 1893a:3; Wilson 1913a:72-73).

There were problems to overcome before the raising of livestock took hold. For one thing, Hidatsa customs were not geared to the profit motive. "We Indians have a custom," said Goodbird, "that when we kill an animal we send a present to our friends. When I slaughter a steer, I send ten pounds to Wolf Chief and ten pounds to each of the other families of my friends in Independence. In this way half the steer is gone to my friends, but when my friends kill a steer they do likewise, and always remember me.

Cowboys
Photographed by Gilbert Wilson, 1916
MHS photo IX-25-1916
Many Hidatsas earned their living as cowboys. According to Goodbird, the cattle owners of Independence hired herders "who camped all summer and guarded the cattle at ten cents a head for about four months." Indian and white cowboys used the same styles of work clothing and tools (Wilson 1913a:75).

"But this custom of ours makes it so that it does not pay to keep pigs or do a great deal that white men want us to do. It is hard for us to break our Indian customs. . . . I kept a pig last year and fed it a good deal of corn and worked hard so as to keep it, but when I killed it in the fall, the pig's meat lasted me and my family only four days. . . . I would keep pigs but what is the use of raising pigs when our custom makes us give away the meat?" (Wilson 1913a:154).

Even more crucial was the problem of land. Ranching required much more land than farming, and the 160-acre allotments were woefully inadequate. The unallotted range away from the river became crucial to the Indians' self-sufficiency. Yet the government intended to sell off that land to white settlers. In 1909 a special agent strongly recommended that this step not be taken. "The ability of these Indians to develop the stock raising industry depends upon their keeping a considerable range," he said. But a communally owned cattle range undermined the government's zeal for private property. Anything that "would involve the continuance of that communal system" was looked on as "a backward step" by the Office of Indian Affairs (Allen 1909:3; Leupp 1907:2).

Despite these hurdles, the residents of Independence generally took to ranching. The work had a seasonal rhythm based on the natural cycles of weather and breeding. In the spring the men rounded up the herd to brand and castrate the new calves. Then they left the cattle alone on the range until about July 10, when the bulls were put in with the herd. During summer the Indians cut and stored hay to feed the cattle in winter. In August or early September, a second roundup was held. More branding and castrating was done, and grown cattle were chosen to be shipped away to market (Goodall 1912:1-2).

A roundup, like a buffalo hunt, involved the whole community. Families camped in tents near the roundup grounds. The younger men then left to find the cattle. "We rode on horseback," Goodbird said, "and surrounded the herd in a long line with our ponies. . . . We Indians drove our cattle to the edge of a high, steep bank over the Missouri River." The older men waited on the hills, smoking their pipes, to spy the herders coming back. When they were seen, their horses glistening with sweat, the cry would go up, "Here they come!"

The cattle were penned in a corral against the cliff. Then, said Goodbird, "the agent appointed a man to brand the calves. The branding iron was heated in a fire and the calves were roped by the neck by a man who went in with a lariat, on foot. We did not rope from horseback at that time. . . . The brand was the same as the mother's, in order to establish the right owner" (Wilson 1913a:74; Baker 1984).

After fall roundup the cattle were sent to market. At first the people of Independence sold to local ranchers, but later they realized they could get a better price by taking the cattle east to St. Paul or Chicago. Accordingly, yearly cattle-selling trips became the custom. In 1900 Wolf Chief was selected by his neighbors to make the journey. It was his first taste of the big city.

"Myself & Water Chief, Henry Bad Gun, Louis Baker, & Frank Packineau . . . gathered up steers & fat cows between here & [the] Little Missouri," Wolf Chief said. "This was my district – everybody wanted me to go, & wanted me to bring money back. . . . I drew no pay for taking [the] cattle. . . . Our custom is not to charge one another" (Wilson 1916c:88, 90).

They drove the cattle to the railroad stockyard at Hebron, N.Dak., where the stock commissioner counted the cattle and charged them five cents a head for shipping. Then they loaded the cattle onto the train. The men rode in the caboose, sleeping on bare board shelves that served for bunks. A German livestock dealer from Hebron named Charlie Weigel went along to translate for them (Van Dersal 1902:45-46).

"We expected to find [the] price when we came to St. Paul," Wolf Chief said. "We reached St. Paul & crossed [the] Mississippi on [a] high bridge & came to [the] stockyards in So. St. Paul. Got in about noon." But when they arrived, Charlie Weigel found out that the price for cattle was higher in Chicago. So the men decided to go on.

ROUNDUP CAMP
Photographed by Gilbert Wilson, 1915
MHS photo VIII-1-15
In 1915 the people of Independence corralled their cattle in a fenced pen out on the range, rather than against the cliff. The families camped in tents nearby.

The Hidatsa called the train má'ti aku tidía, or "boat that runs." After leaving St. Paul, "There was a bad hill there and our train got stuck. . . . We stopped [a] little while till another engine came & pushed us up. Then he went awful fast. Weigel said, '[The] road is good here [and the] engineer will go fast.' It was awful fast, kind of dangerous & pretty near we went off our seats."

They got into Chicago at about 9:00 A.M. The "day was kind of smoky – whether air is that way in town I [do] not know. . . . They turned our cattle in [at the] stockyard again & [we] went to [a] hotel. . . .

"We had fine visiting that day. [We] went to [the] stockyard of Swift & Co. They showed us . . . [the] room where they killed pigs. [A] man had chains in his arms, snapped [them] on [the] leg of [the] pig and fastened [it] to a wheel, and a man cut [the pig's] throat, [the] next take off [the] hair. So each one did something [to the] pig sliding along till all done & ready for packing" (Wilson 1916c: 88-91).

Another big attraction was Lake Michigan. "I asked and I heard [the] lake was 60 miles [in width]. I couldn't see any hills on [the] other side but saw steamboats.

Prosperous and influential Indians of the Ft. Berthold Reservation"
1913
SHSND (Hall Papers)
This photograph was taken in Chicago on September 4, 1913, when these men were delivering 48 carloads of cattle to Clay, Robinson & Company, their livestock commission merchant. It was probably Wolf Chief's second trip. They are, front row: Wolf Chief, "Mr. Hall" (perhaps a son of Charles), John Goodall (superintendent of livestock for the Office of Indian Affairs), Tom Smith, and Francis Charging; back row: James Baker, Crosby Beaks, Edgar Crows Heart, Louis Baker, and Foolish Woman. All the men in the picture were from Independence except Hall and Goodall (Case and Case 1977: 223).

"We . . . watched [the] water come up & go down & come up again. We never saw the Missouri do that. We thought also in this city they haul water from this lake. Afterward we learned a big ditch took all the bad water and ran it in the lake so we didn't try to drink the lake water" (Wilson 1916c:94).

There were less pleasant sights, as well. "Back of a hotel in Chicago they threw old foods that they did not want any more on their tables. I saw some poor women, dirty and in rags, take off the covers of the cans, and they took out the food to eat. I said to myself, 'These poor white women must be hungry,' and I did not understand how this could be in Chicago where there was so much food. If an Indian man is hungry, no matter what he has done or how foolish he has acted, we will always give him food. That is our custom. There are many white customs which I do not understand and which puzzle me very much" (Wilson 1915a:28-29).

The men could not sell their cattle on the same day they arrived, but they decided to see where the cattle were being kept. "We went in & walked around a kind of fence. Lots of corrals there. We saw lots of cattle all mixed. We found few of our own. We were scared, thinking now we would lose some of our cattle.

"We got back to [the] hotel in eve[ning]. Had supper & Weigel told us, 'All go [out] in [a] bunch. That's best, for you fellows might get lost.' That scared us too, for we don't know city customs.

"He said, 'You must not go to any bad house – they will take your money & might kill you!'" (Wilson 1916c:91-92).

They slept that night in the hotel. "In the morning I heard a bell ring and I thought it must be time for breakfast. I arose and, as was my custom, prepared to bathe. I had on my breech clout as we Indians wear and took a sheet from the bed and went down and washed my face. Other men were there and they looked at me and seemed curious. I had no moccasins on but I had the sheet and breech clout on. While I was washing, the owner of the hotel came and asked me:

"'Why don't you put your clothes on?'

"'Because it is too hot,' I answered.

"He went away not looking pleased but said no more. Then I went into the dining room and men and

VIEW NORTHEAST IN CHICAGO UNION STOCKYARDS
c. 1910
Chicago Historical Society ICHi-20065
Train tracks from all over the west carried cattle into Chicago at the turn of the century. Wolf Chief's train came in over tracks like these. He noted Chicago's "smoky" air (Wilson 1916c:91).

TRANSIT HOUSE, CHICAGO
Photographed by J. W. Taylor, c. 1910
Chicago Historical Society ICHi-04088
There is no record of which Chicago hotel Wolf Chief stayed in, but it must have been similar to this one. He said that it was a "high building" with a "big dining room" and "lots of white men." When Wolf Chief's party entered, "They gave each a key first & led us to our rooms." For 25 cents the travelers could get a bath in a "big tub" with spigots for "hot or cold water on [the] wall" (Wilson 1916c:91, 94).

women were eating their breakfast. I sat with the sheet draped about my waist but with my shoulders bare and I noticed that all the people stared at me and seemed curious, but I did not care; that was my custom for I was an Indian and I followed Indian custom. They could think what they chose. After I ate, I went upstairs and put on my white men's clothes.

"Now I should like to ask you, Mr. Wilson, why those people looked at me. If you are on our reservation and you follow your custom we think that is all right and if you choose to follow our custom we think that is all right also. When I was in Chicago I followed my Indian custom and I do not see why any white man could find fault with me" (Wilson 1915a:27-28).

After breakfast, they went back to the stockyards. They "Found lots of cowboys there & they . . . told us to cut out our cattle. We worked all day at this, hard to do too, [for] the cowboys didn't help us much [and] we were afoot."

They slept at the hotel again that night. The next morning they went to the livestock commission merchant's office and he paid them for their cattle. Wolf Chief insisted that the checks be made out to the individual cattle owners, not to the agent. He got $2,000 for his own cattle. The "Commissioner gave [me the] checks in [a] big envelope & sealed it. 'Don't lose this, for there is lots of money here.'"

"I won't lose it unless I lose my life," Wolf Chief replied (Wilson 1916c:92-93, 89).

On the way back, they stopped for three days in St. Paul to talk to a government commissioner about some late treaty payments. Later, as he sat in the hotel restaurant, Wolf Chief thought to himself how he was surrounded by "Lots of people [in] fine clothes. . . . They had big rooms, big houses, and lots of foods & I thought of home and our cabins & how we lived & dressed & I wondered if we would ever live in big houses & have fine clothes. There were so many white people – and [they] lived so well. These white people I thought must have more power or are different people from mine. All [the] time I was eating I thought this.

"Girl waiters waited on us and I thought they had sweet faces & nice clothes. I wished they were [at] home, & I would get after one as my wife or sweetheart. But I knew customs were different [here]. But at home if I were young, I would.

"We had beef steak every meal & eggs, & I thought to myself: Well, I learned these white people's ways. I will put on fine shoes and underclothes & [a]

good watch & hat & hair cut and I am just like one of those rich men in [the] city.

"When I got back I distributed [the] money, & gave [out the] checks. I gave a feast when I did so and distributed the money. The people were all glad" (Wilson 1916c:95-96).

Trips like Wolf Chief's grew more common as ranching became the mainstay of the reservation's economy. "Cattle raising by the Indians has proved pretty successful," Goodbird said in 1913. "Members of my own family now own about thirty head of cattle and I own, in addition to these, fifteen horses. Our Indians here at Independence own about three hundred head of cattle." By 1915, the Indian-owned livestock on the reservation numbered 2,596 cattle and 3,274 horses. The Hidatsa were finding their way to a new prosperity (Wilson 1913a:90; Michael 1915:2).

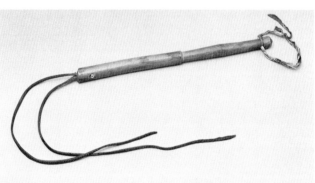

QUIRT
Northern Plains
Collected by Frederick Wilson, pre-1918?
Carved wooden handle with hole bored in base for a hanging strap of leather. At other end two leather lashes are inserted in a hole and secured with two brass tacks
Handle: L. 44 cm. Lashes: L. 58 cm
MHS 9598.10

Some traditional riding equipment changed little after the transition to ranching. Wolf Chief recalled the quirt he carried when herding horses as a young man: "I carried a quirt of willow wood. Sometimes I bore this in my hand, sometimes I thrust it into my belt. It had two lashes of raw hide. It was not painted. I never whipped my horse with it. My father once had a vision and gave me this quirt to carry as a sacred object because of what he had seen in this vision. . . .

"If I had been attacked by enemies and was in danger of being captured and wanted to escape, I would have whipped my horse with this quirt; but I would then have expected the quirt to have supernatural power and that it would make my horse go fast" (Wilson 1913b:447).

Hat

*Made by Hamley & Co., Pendleton,
Ore., c. 1940*
*"Ten-gallon"-type gray felt hat with
grosgrain ribbon sewn around brim
and inner hatband of leather with
gold stamped label. Outer hatband
of woven horsehair colored black,
cream, reddish orange, and green*
L. 41 cm, W. 38 cm, H. 14 cm
*MHS 66.205.24, Mark Severance
Estate*

The wide-brimmed, high-crowned hats
worn by western ranchers were quickly
adopted by Indians. The hats were
designed to provide protection from the
sun while keeping the head cool.
Wilson's photographs suggest that
Indians at Fort Berthold wore the
crown undented, unlike many non-
Indians (MHS photos IX-25-1916,
VIII-5-15, IX-91-1918). The maker of
this hatband is unknown, but woven
and braided horsehair items like it were
made by Joe Packineau of Elbowoods
and probably by others on Fort
Berthold Reservation (SHSND 12412).

Bandana

Pre-1930s
*Cotton square printed in red, white,
and brown*
L. 53 cm, W. 49 cm
MHS 7829.32b, Mary H. Folwell

For years the government purchased
thousands of "turkey red handkerchiefs"
and distributed them to Indians
(USOIA 1889:614, 1894:900). Besides
providing a touch of color, a bandana
kept the sun off the neck, served as a
handkerchief or towel, and could be
torn into strips if necessary for string.
Their use on Fort Berthold Reservation
is well documented in photographs
(Wilson [1903-18]:63; MHS photos
VI-21-13, VII-99-15).

Chaps

c. 1890
*Legs of white sheepskin lined with light-colored leather and white cotton canvas.
Waistband of tooled brown leather, laced together at center front and
fastened in back with nickeled iron buckle*
L. 72 cm, W. 81 cm around waist
MHS 66.195.1, Elizabeth Turpin

Chaps, tough leather leggings worn over trousers, were not very common on the
Northern Plains until fancy ones decorated with silver-colored conchos or made with
Angora goat hair became popular (Rickey 1976:46-48). Wilson photographed Fort
Berthold youngsters wearing Angora chaps (MHS photos VI-38-13, IX-22-1916).

Boots

Early 20th century
Western-style black leather boots with
stacked leather heels and bootstraps
at top of reinforced side seams;
decorated with stitched designs
L. 28.2 cm, W. 9.8 cm, H. 48 cm
MHS 69.102.2a, b, William
Westphal

Boots and shoes were symbolically
important to Indian agents because they
represented a change from the
traditional moccasins; nevertheless,
moccasins were still worn long after
other aspects of traditional clothing had
disappeared. Early in the 20th century
both styles of footwear were used on
the Fort Berthold Reservation. Wolf
Chief, for example, sold shoes in his
store, but he is shown in photographs
wearing moccasins (Rued 1910; MHS
photos III-4, VII-72-15). The tall riding
or cowboy boot, shown in a number of
Wilson's photographs of younger men
(VIII-2-15, IX-91-1918), became
popular with Indian stockmen because it
protected their feet on rough terrain,
while the tall heel prevented the boot
from slipping in the stirrup.

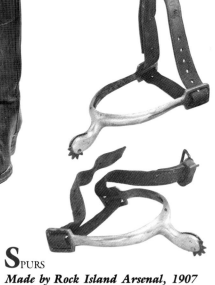

Spurs

Made by Rock Island Arsenal, 1907
Brass frames, iron rowels, and buckles
on leather straps that pass around
boot at instep
L. 13.5 cm, W. 9 cm
MHS 66.195.4a, b, Elizabeth Turpin

These army regulation jack spurs were
worn by cowboy Charles Parsons, who,
like others, re-used old army equipment.
Indian men also learned to use spurs
from the example of the military.
Wilson's photographs show cowboys
wearing spurs during roundup (MHS
photo VIII-3-15).

Bridle

Made by Rock Island Arsenal, 1903
Brown leather with brass rosettes and
buckles; nickeled steel riding bit
Reins: L. 155 cm. Bit: H. 16.5 cm,
W. 14 cm. Bridle: L. 52 cm
MHS 7174.1, Theodore Bernier

This U.S. cavalry bridle is similar to the
plain, utilitarian bridles used on the Fort
Berthold Reservation (MHS photos
IX-25-1916, VI-36-13, VIII-2-15,
VIII-9-15). The Office of Indian Affairs
distributed some bridles to Indians who
owned horses, but Indian ranchers
purchased many more for their own use
(USOIA 1895:930, 1913:363). The
government, emphasizing farming over
ranching, distributed much more horse
equipment for use with wagons than
for riding.

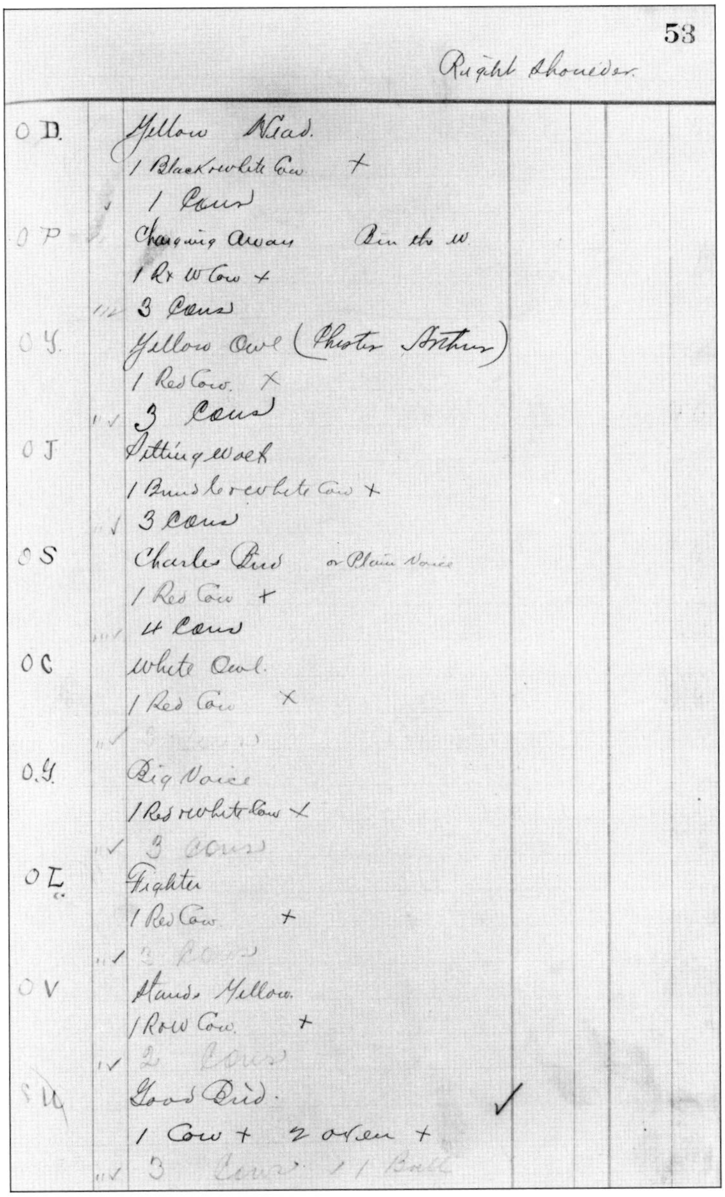

53

Right Shoulder.

O D.	*Yellow Head.*	
	1 Black & white Cow	+
	1 Cow	
O P.	*Charging Away*	*Run the W*
	1 R & W Cow	+
	3 Cows	
O Y.	*Yellow Owl (Chester Arthur)*	
	1 Red Cow	X
	3 Cows	
O J.	*Sitting Wolf*	
	1 Brindle & white Cow	+
	3 Cows	
O S	*Charles Bird* or Plain Voice	
	1 Red Cow	+
	4 Cows	
O C	*White Owl.*	
	1 Red Cow	X
O Y.	*Big Voice*	
	1 Red & white Cow	+
	3 Cows	
O L	*Fighter*	
	1 Red Cow	+
O V	*Stands Yellow*	
	1 Roan Cow	+
	2 Cows	
S U	*Good Bird.*	
	1 Cow + 2 oxen	+
	3 Cows 1 1 Bull	

BRANDING IRON
Fort Berthold Reservation,
1897–1918?
Wrought iron handle of rectangular
bar stock; branding surface reading
"3" riveted to handle
L. 105.4 cm, W. 10.8 cm
SHSND 6806

Cattle purchased by the government to start Indian herds were branded "ID" for Indian Department or "USIS" for United States Indian Service. These animals remained government property and could not be sold or slaughtered without permission (USOIA 1904b:76; see also SHSND 6808). As the herds increased, cattle were marked with brands identifying individual Indian owners. This branding iron from Fort Berthold may have been used for the latter purpose.

RECORD OF BRANDS – INDIAN STOCK"
Written by agency employees, 1917–19
Hard covers with black book cloth and
red leather corners and spine; label
on front. White ledger paper with
red and blue lines; hand-written in
black and red ink
H. 34.9 cm, W. 22.2 cm
NA, Kansas City (Fort Berthold
Agency 1917–19)

When the government first issued cattle to the Indians of Fort Berthold in 1891, the agent assigned each owner a brand, creating them by combining letters of the alphabet (Murphy 1893a:3). The brands were then recorded in this book. Wolf Chief received the JL brand and Goodbird was given SU. Later, when Indian ranchers began registering their brands according to the regulations of the state livestock commission, Wolf Chief personalized his brand by changing it to WC.

WOLF CHIEF'S BRAND
1902
MHS (Van Dersal 1902:44)
Brands were registered annually by county so that cattle could be easily identified. Samuel Van Dersal of Bismarck published a directory of ranchers in North Dakota as a service to cattlemen. This brand for Wolf Chief was listed under Mercer County.

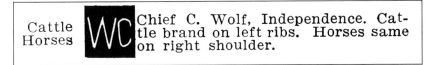

Cattle Horses   WC   Chief C. Wolf, Independence. Cattle brand on left ribs. Horses same on right shoulder.

Haying

Photographed by Gilbert Wilson, 1914
MHS photo VI-75-14

Because the North Dakota winters were long and severe, a rancher had to cut and store three tons of hay for every head of cattle he owned (Hoffman 1909b). The Hidatsa used the grasses that grew naturally in the river bottomlands and stream gullies.

Branding

Photographed by Gilbert Wilson, 1915
MHS photo VIII-4-15

Goodbird described how the branding was done: "The lariat was thrown over the calf's head and then another noose was easily slipped over the calf's hind legs so that the animal fell. The lariat was then taken from the calf's neck and noosed over its fore legs. The fore legs and hind legs were then held extended apart, while the brand was being applied" (Wilson 1913a:74).

DRYING MEAT
Photographed by Gilbert Wilson, 1910
MHS photo IV-52-1910
To keep meat from spoiling, it was dried in the sun on a scaffold. The Hidatsa custom of giving away freshly butchered meat also ensured that the food would be used before it spoiled.

WATCHING THE ROUNDUP
Photographed by Gilbert Wilson, 1915
MHS photo VIII-12-15
Women lined the fence where the cattle were penned to watch the branding in 1915. Even the children were dressed in their finest clothes.

In the home

While the men were learning to be farmers and ranchers, Buffalo Bird Woman was adjusting to new tools and new rules in her domain as well. Foods and food preparation had undergone radical changes. To the old diet of meat and garden vegetables were added innovations like dairy products, eggs, and grain. The Hidatsa had mixed feelings about the new variety of foods. Goodbird reported that "My parents had learned to use milk from the white men. We were very fond of it. We had cream in our coffee, and made biscuits with it. Sometimes we made butter." But Buffalo Bird Woman's reaction was less positive. "I do not know much of white man's foods," she said. "I was given some canned sweet potatoes once and I thought it was some kind of squash. A friend of mine given some of those sweet potatoes and not tasting them, thought it was some bone grease" (Wilson 1913a:73, 1915b:464).

With the new foods came new methods of preparation. Buffalo Bird Woman had learned the techniques of cooking over an open fire from her mothers, but there was no one to pass her knowledge on to, for, she noted, "my son's wife cooks by a stove" (Maxidiwiac 1921:175). Stove cookery introduced baking and frying to the Hidatsa cook's repertoire. The cook's knowledge of the new foods, however, did not always keep pace. "In old days," said Wolf Chief, "when a buffalo was killed, our women knew how to cook every part. But our women cannot make things like rice, potatoes, wheat, and oats, into good-tasting foods. And this I think very bad for sick people. An Indian woman's baby gets sick. The reservation doctor is maybe thirty miles away. That Indian woman gets scared. She does not know what to do. She remembers that when she feels tired, she drinks coffee, and it makes her feel good. So she makes a big pot of coffee, and gives it to that baby. Maybe that is why so many babies die on this reservation." Buffalo Bird Woman laid the blame on the food, not the preparation. "In old times . . . we did not have to buy food with money, and the new food that white men have brought us, and their diseases, cause our people to die. In old days we did not thus die" (Wilson 1926:88, 1918a:375).

Clothing had changed, too. Gone were the days when Buffalo Bird Woman could win prestige by embroidering a quilled shirt for a man to display his honor marks. In the white man's world, praise was reserved for the women's sewing society that met to create utilitarian underwear, coats, and aprons (Dawson 1901:5). Textiles might seem easier to sew and wash,

BUFFALO BIRD WOMAN
Photographed by Gilbert Wilson, 1910
MHS photo IV-35-1910
Though Buffalo Bird Woman wore a calico dress in later years, she still dressed in leggings and moccasins. Here she was trimming sticks for making a model bed (see p. 104).

but only if a woman had the knowledge. "In olden days," said Wolf Chief, "we dressed in skins, which we could clean with white clay. Now our clothes are of cloth, and we do not know how to care for them. Many of our women own washtubs, and know how to use soap; but it is hard for them to heat water in our cold winters. Our cabins are small; our women cannot take their tubs out of doors in the biting wind, when the ice is four feet thick on the Missouri; and if they wash the clothes in the cabin, the air gets full of steam while the water that splashes on the floor freezes. Then the door is opened to let out the steam and the room gets cold. . . . Our children thus catch cold, and have lung sickness" (Wilson 1926:87).

Buffalo Bird Woman had high standards of household management, but they were not the standards of the white world. In the eastern United States, people had discovered the doctrine of hygiene and were following it with the zeal of the newly converted. To introduce the concepts of sanitary housekeeping to Indian reservations, the government created the office of field matron and filled it, in many cases, with Indian women educated at boarding schools. The matrons were the government's representatives to Indian homes and kitchens.

The houses on the reservation in 1911 reflected the incomes of the owners, and the field matrons could see little to praise about them. "They are of logs," wrote one, "mud-chinked and mud-roofed, with dirt floors, except in occasional instances. When it rains, the roofs leak; a succession of storms weakens the mud in the chinks, so that the sides also leak. There are few windows and doors; light and ventilation are entirely insufficient. The dirt floors make it impossible to keep a clean house, let alone a sanitary one. Where the men spit on the floor, and the babies roll on it and where it must be dampened often to keep the dust from rising, it requires no imagination to conceive that housekeeping is a difficult art" (Newton 1911:5).

The field matrons aspired to a life in which fancy stitchery, wholesome reading, and good works were women's ideals. To change the reservation woman's world, they used encouragement and peer pressure. An association called the Circle of the King's Daughters was organized among young Indian women returned from boarding school. "Our motto was 'The people had a mind to work,'" said a member. "Our work was to clean two homes a week. . . . Some of us wash the clothes which were dirty and some do the cleaning and cooking. We made some biscuits and cooked some rice

FIELD MATRON ANNA DAWSON AS MINNEHAHA
Photographed by McCormick, Boston, pre-1901
SHSND Col. 88-19
Anna Dawson, an Arikara woman, was "one of the best educated Indian women I have ever met," according to a government inspector. She got her education at the Hampton Institute in Hampton, Va., the normal school in Framingham, Mass., and a domestic science course in Boston. She taught at the Santee Normal Training School, in Santee, Nebr., for several years, then returned to Fort Berthold as a field matron, where she wrote idealistically of "awakening" her people "to new ideals of home." She was dressed here in an improbable Indian costume to portray the heroine of Longfellow's *Hiawatha* for an East-Coast photographer (Newton 1911:2-3; Dawson 1901:6).

and after we get through with the work which we were doing, we had a supper, and after supper we just had only a little prayer meeting in the house which we had just cleaned" (Bear 1896). They also called upon the sick and, when there was nothing more pressing, made "some pillow covers, [crocheting] and knitting." They "tried to do a little reading of [a] wholesome sort" and went on "trips to gather flowers" to decorate graves. "It is a comforting pleasure to feel, that we can depend upon these young women for help and sympathy in this work of uplifting our people," a field matron wrote (Dawson 1901:4).

The young women felt that their home visits to spread "uplifting" standards were having an effect. "Though all the homes, do not look as well kept, as one would like to see them, yet when there is a rush and hurry because we are coming, to put them into better order, or a woman comes running out to meet us at the door, confessing and apologizing for the ill appearance of her house, we feel pleased and encouraged to see that they do wish to reform" (Dawson 1901:5).

It is impossible to tell what Buffalo Bird Woman thought of the eager young women who spread the new gospel of women's work. Their assumption of the role of teachers to their people disrupted the traditional path that knowledge had always followed – from grandmother to granddaughter. To the field matrons, Buffalo Bird Woman's immense store of traditional knowledge meant nothing. Their school learning devalued her own hard-earned knowledge.

There were no young buyers now for the sacred skills Buffalo Bird Woman had paid to learn. The system that had given her economic power was gone, and in its place was one that gave value only to work that produced money. She had grown old in a world where gadgets and grocery stores had replaced grandmothers.

Women in Plain and Fancy Dress
Photographed by Gilbert Wilson, 1918
MHS photos IX-83-1918, IX-87-1918
Two unidentified young women made a quick cultural transformation for the camera, changing from the clothes of the boarding school to the clothes of the Indian dance. The dance dresses themselves show a change in style: they were made from calico with ribbon and rick-rack appliqué; sequins replaced elk teeth as decoration on the bodice; and elaborate hair-pipe breastplates reflected the easy availability of these mass-manufactured decorations. The woman on the left wore canvas sneakers.

CHINA

Cup and saucer: made by Alfred Meakin, Tunstall, England, late 19th century. Plate: maker unknown, c. 1900

Cup and saucer of white Royal Ironstone China with tea leaf pattern in brown lustre. Plate of plain white ironstone

Cup: H. 7.5 cm, D. 8.5 cm. Saucer: D. 15.5 cm. Plate: D. 23 cm

MHS 65.56.1m, q, Myra M. Murray; 66.130.2, Carolyne Sawyer

Ceramic dinnerware was available to the Hidatsa from at least the 1850s, and probably earlier (Boller 1966a:157). Fragments of ironstone china were frequently found by archaeologists at Like-a-Fishhook Village, including some made by Alfred Meakin, the maker of this cup and saucer (SHSND 32ML2/12,711.1809). Field matrons noted that in most homes "the family . . . ate off of tables. Much of the kitchenware was good." All the same, they encouraged women to spend "less for calicos to satisfy the new longings for better dishes and new furniture for the home" (Newton 1911:6; Dawson 1901:6). Wolf Chief implied that the whites' passion for washing dishes had at least some basis in elitism. "Christ himself when He ate did not say, 'I am God's Son, therefore I want clean foods and clean dishes,'" he said (Wilson 1914b:316).

WOMEN MAKING FRY BREAD
Photographed by Gilbert Wilson, 1915
MHS photo VIII-8-15

While the men branded cattle, these women in the roundup camp prepared coffee and fry bread. The origin of fry bread is unknown, though today it is popular with Indian tribes across the country. Frying was not one of the cooking techniques Buffalo Bird Woman remembered from her childhood, but it was common by at least 1906 (Wilson 1913a:122). Goodbird described making bread on a hunting trip in the 1880s by simply mixing water with flour and spreading the dough on the coals of his campfire (Wilson 1913a:61-62). Here, the women had rolled out the dough (usually made from flour, water, baking powder, and salt) and were preparing to cut off pieces to fry in fat. The frying pan and coffee boiler rested on a grill over a fire pit while the coffee grinder sat nearby.

QUILT

Made by Marie Young Bear, Mandaree, N.Dak., 1985
Front of cotton patchwork starburst design in maroon,
yellow, gold, orange, and red on a blue ground with red
edging. Back of cotton printed in circus motifs. Quilted
in concentric circle patterns. See color page 171
L. 103 cm, W. 100 cm
Mary Jane Schneider

Missionary wives are credited with teaching Indian women
how to quilt. In about 1885, when Goodbird's family moved
to Independence, he noted that his bedding consisted of "a
straw mattress, with blankets, quilts and one buffalo robe for
covering" (Wilson 1913a:54). Later, women at the sewing
meetings sponsored by the field matrons sewed and tied "a
number of quilts . . . which also found a ready market"
(Dawson 1901:5; AMNH photo 288284).

The craft of patchwork developed in uniquely Indian
ways. This pattern, sometimes called "Indian Star," is
reminiscent of feather circle designs used on painted robes in
earlier generations. Today quilts are frequently given as gifts.
This one was made for a child. The town of Mandaree, where
it was made, is the closest present-day town to the site of
Independence.

LAUNDRY BOILER

Early 20th century
Tinned sheet iron sides and bottom, with turned wooden
handles mounted on metal brackets riveted to sides. Two
rust spots on bottom show use over stove burners
L. 66 cm, W. 30.5 cm, H. 34 cm
MHS 1986.100.9

Cleanliness was of great concern to the Indian agents and field
matrons, but the facilities for doing laundry were limited at
best. The government distributed washboards, washtubs,
clotheslines, and pounds of soap, but water had to be hauled
from the river by pail and heated in a tub like this one, set
over a stove. A teacher at the Fort Stevenson school noted
that the North Dakota water was so hard that soda had to be
added to get any lather (USOIA 1885:32). Although Wilson's
photos show no laundry drying in the western sun, they do
show laundry tubs being used for tables, cisterns, and storage
bins (MHS photos V-2-1911, X-73-1918, IV-35-1910).

HOUSE DRESS

Made by Barmon's, Buffalo, [N.Y.?],
c. 1915
White cotton with black pin-stripes.
Bodice has turned-down collar,
three-quarter-length set-in sleeves,
front button placket closure with
eight shell buttons, and vertical
tucks from shoulder to waist. Full-
length skirt sewn to bodice at
adjustable waist line
L. 137 cm
MHS 69.95.20, Mr. and Mrs.
Edward Briese

Two styles of women's dress coexisted
on Fort Berthold Reservation in the
early 20th century: dresses influenced by
store-bought styles like this one, and
less tailored, hand-sewn dresses worn by
older women. Girls were taught in
school how to sew and care for clothes.
In 1889 the girls at the Fort Stevenson
school sewed 621 articles of clothing
and mended from 2,000 to 2,500
(USOIA 1889:352). Dresses made from
pin-striped ticking cloth, similar to but
heavier than this, had been worn since
the 1850s (Kurz 1937:80; SHSND 847).

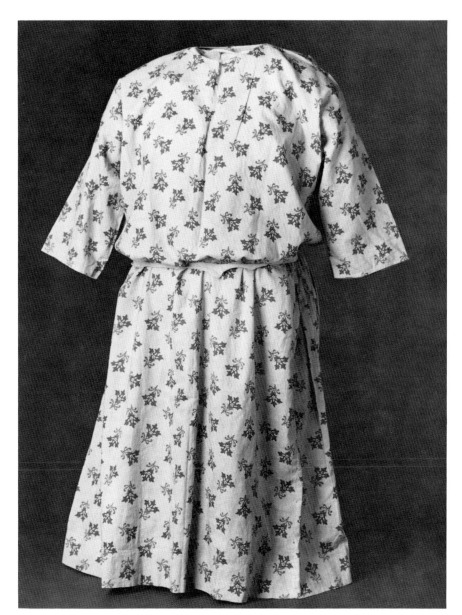

DRESS

Late 19th century
Tan cotton with red and purple stylized floral print. Square bodice with
triangular gussets from waist to arm, shell button at neck, and short, set-in
sleeves. Wide waist seam into which skirt is gathered on sides. Full skirt with
gussets down sides. See color page 178
L. 106.5 cm, W. 61 cm
SHSND 9969

This dress, collected on Fort Berthold Reservation in the 19th century, may have
been made short for use with leggings. Wilson's photographs show older women
wearing loosely fitting dresses like this, usually drawn in at the waist (MHS photos
IV-38-1910, IX-24-1916). Although this one was machine-stitched, a similar one in
the collection of the State Historical Society of North Dakota was sewn by hand
(SHSND 847). As early as 1879, the agency distributed fabrics such as wool, cotton,
calico, and gingham along with needles and thread so that women could make
dresses for themselves and their daughters (Schindel 1879a).

Ax

Early 20th century
Single-bitted iron head with beveled
*   blade and dented poll. Handle*
*   reconstructed*
Head: L. 17.8 cm, W. 11.4 cm.
*   Handle: L. 90.5 cm*
MHS FH 2945, Aino Johnson

"Iron axes make the work of our
women easier," Wolf Chief said (Wilson
1926:88). In fact, axes were so
important to the Hidatsa that assorted
sizes and shapes of them were included
in annuities (USOIA 1900:404). Wilson
saw single-bitted axes like this being
used by women for chopping wood,
antler, and bone (MHS photos
IV-37-1910, VI-49-14, VIII-58-1916).
Wilson, commenting on the axes used
to crush bones for bone grease, noted
that "The handle of the ax is shortened
to a trifle over two feet, as is not
uncommon among these people,
presumably because it is so often used
by the women while working in a
kneeling position" (Wilson 1910a:354).

Enamelware Basin

Early 20th century
Mottled pale blue and white enameled steel with flat bottom, flared sides, and
*   black rolled rim. Two handles attached below rim with rivets*
H. 8.5 cm, D. 29.5 cm
MHS 1986.100.3

Basins like this one were often used for serving and processing food (MHS photos
III-2, VI-82-14, Wilson [1903-18]:58). They were inexpensive and readily available
through mail order or rural stores, as well as through the agency. Wolf Chief recalled
that when he built a log cabin one winter, he and his wife used a "big tin dish &
water pail to throw up earth from [the] wagon bed" to make the sod roof (Wilson
1916c:54).

Pail

c. 1900
Cylinder of tin with rolled top edge
*   and one side seam; bail attached to*
*   two brackets riveted to sides of pail*
H. 16 cm, D. 17.5 cm
MHS 1982.105.58a

Tin lard pails like this are among the
most frequently seen cooking utensils in
Wilson's photographs (MHS photos
IV-48-1910, IV-53-1910, IV-97-1911).
The Hidatsa used tin pails at least as
early as 1876, when Wolf Chief
described their use on a buffalo hunt
(Wilson 1918a:195). Pails were also
used to carry foods eaten at feasts,
especially the Grass Dance (Bowers
1965:402; Weitzner 1979:253).
Examples were found in excavations at
Like-a-Fishhook Village (Smith
1972:144).

COFFEE GRINDER
c. 1900
*Wooden box with door in base
containing round tin cup for
catching grindings. Cast iron
hopper with swing-out cover
decorated with floral relief,
surmounted by cast iron crank with
turned wooden handle*
L. 15.3 cm, W. 15 cm, H. 23.5 cm
MHS 64.24.1a, b, Myrna Anderson

When coffee beans were first sold on
Fort Berthold Reservation, they did not
come roasted or ground. Instead of
roasting the coffee, the Hidatsa at first
parched it like corn by stirring it in a
hot pan. "When it was parched," said
Wolf Chief, "we put it in a corn mortar
and pounded it fine and boiled it in a
copper kettle . . . and drank the coffee
liquor with the sugar. The grounds that
were left behind we dried carefully,
parched them a second time in a pan,
and boiled again. This, the second
boiling, tasted almost as good as the
first. We did so then, because coffee was
so expensive" (Wilson 1911:88). Coffee
mills like this were better suited to the
job of grinding (see MHS photos
VIII-8-1915, IX-21-1916).

CHURN
Early 20th century
*Oak barrel with iron bands resting on wooden double trestle stand. Barrel is
rotated by an iron crank. Top and bottom of barrel painted red; top has
removable cover with pivoting latch*
Barrel: L. 39 cm, D. 31.5 cm. Stand: L. 56 cm, W. 49 cm, H. 61.5 cm
MHS 9926, John Stauffer

Milk, butter, cheese, and other dairy products were not a part of the Hidatsa diet
until the government introduced dairy cattle, but they became popular in some
households. Goodbird spoke of making butter, so his family must have had a churn
(Wilson 1913a:73). Others on Fort Berthold Reservation remembered using hand-
cranked cream separators (Baker 1984).

FRYING PAN
c. 1920
*One-piece cast-iron pan with two
pouring lips and teardrop-shaped
cutout in handle. Stamped on
bottom "Wagner/Sidney/O"*
H. 5.5 cm, D. 24.5 cm
*MHS 66.43.43, Mr. and Mrs.
Walter G. E. Adams*

Although parts of frying pans were
excavated at Like-a-Fishhook Village,
where they had been distributed as
annuities, Wolf Chief's and Buffalo Bird
Woman's remarks suggest that they were
used more for parching corn than for
frying with grease (Smith 1972:102,
144; Wilson 1916b:78). Later, fried
foods like fry bread became popular;
they remain so today.

TEAKETTLE
*Made by Terstegge, Gohmann & Co.,
New Albany, Ind., 1883*
*Cast iron. Flat, hinged cover has
scalloped design at edge and
maker's name in raised lettering.
Handle of flat metal strapping.
Spout marked with raised "7"*
L. 28 cm, W. 20 cm, H. 17 cm
MHS 75.87.84, Ray E. Wilkins

This kettle demonstrates the transition
from open fire to stove cookery. The
round-bottomed pots best for heating
water on an open fire were replaced by
ones with flat bottoms or, like this one,
with bottoms indented for fitting into
burners on wood stoves. By the late
19th century the Office of Indian Affairs
was ordering cooking stoves complete
with kettles, frying pans, cooking pots,
steamers, coffee boilers, teakettles, and
baking pans. Cooking stoves were
available for distribution at Fort
Berthold in 1894, and they can be seen
in use in Wilson's photographs (USOIA
1894:814; MHS photo IX-21-1916).

COFFEEPOT
Early 20th century
*Blue and white enameled metal with
attached spout, corrugated black
enameled handle, bail handle, and
fitted gray metal lid with wooden
knob*
H. 31 cm, D. 25.7 cm
MHS 1986.100.4a, b

Coffee was prepared in pots like this by
simply boiling the ground beans over a
stove. Coffee boilers were used with
both stoves and grills (MHS photos
VIII-8-1915, IX-21-1916).

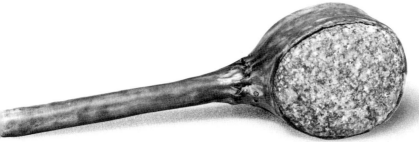

HAMMER (MAUL)
Hidatsa or Mandan
Collected by Gilbert Wilson, pre-1918?
Granite head, wooden handle encased
***   in rawhide***
L. 24 cm, W. 6.5 cm
MHS 7059.49b

Wolf Chief stated that stone hammers
were sometimes preferable to metal tools
because they did a better job of crushing
bones for marrow (Wilson 1918b: 355).
Stone tools were still being used in the
20th century (MHS photos IV-48-1910,
VIII-100-1916).

STONE ANVIL
Excavated at St. Croix Access Site,
***   Minn.***
Light brown granitic rock
L. 20.4 cm, W. 17.5 cm, H. 7.8 cm
MHS 504 FN 1138

Stone anvils continued to be used with
stone hammers for pounding food well
into the 20th century. Their use had
changed little from earlier times. "In
every lodge was kept such a stone all
the time," said Buffalo Bird Woman.
"Sometimes when not in use it was laid
over the mouth of the corn mortar and
kept the dust out of the mortar, and
protected it from dogs. This stone had
three uses. We pounded chokecherries
on it. We pounded dried meat on it to
make it fine for pemmican and for
eating. Old people especially had to
have dried meat pounded fine for them.
Also we used the stone to break bones
on for boiling for bone grease" (Wilson
1916b: 220).

MAKING CHOKECHERRY BALLS
Photographed by Gilbert Wilson, 1916
MHS photo VIII-100-1916

Owl Woman formed chokecherry pulp into a ball before drying it. Older women of
Independence still used stone mallets and anvils for such jobs as crushing
chokecherries, pounding dried meat (MHS photo IV-48-1910), and breaking bones
apart for the marrow.

CHANGE PURSE

Fort Berthold Reservation
Collected by Harold Case, post-1922
Tanned hide bag with hide fringe
around edges, strap for hanging,
and flap closed with two thong ties
and decorated with red beaded
edging. Beadwork pattern laid out
in blue ink, then filled in with
orange, blue, and green beads.
Sewn with thread
H. 12.5 cm, W. 13.5 cm
University of Colorado Museum at
Boulder 33,073

Indian people had traditionally used
small bags tied to the belt in place of
pockets, so it is not surprising that they
began making small bags to hold cash
when they began to use money.
Missionaries and schoolteachers, hoping
that a handicrafts industry would
develop Indian self-sufficiency,
encouraged Hidatsa women to apply
traditional sewing techniques to new,
salable items. Examples of craft work
from various reservation schools were
displayed at exhibitions held around the
country (USOIA 1903:243, 380-81).

BEADED BELT

Fort Berthold Reservation
Collected by Harold Case, post-1922
Commercially tanned leather belt with metal clasp, studded with brass tacks and
lazy-stitched with sinew in pink, blue, white, and red beads
L. 104 cm, W. 3.8 cm
University of Colorado Museum at Boulder 33,111

The growth of tourism and the popularity of western clothing styles provided a
market for items like this belt. In 1903 the superintendent of the Browning Boarding
School at Elbowoods noted, "We have been able to employ an Indian woman to
teach the native industries to quite a number of our girls, and samples of this work
have been sent to the Boston Indian exhibit, held by the Indian Office in connection
with the National Educational Association" (USOIA 1903:236). Beaded belts were
also popular with Indian men.

NAPKIN RINGS

Fort Berthold Reservation
Collected by Harold Case, post-1922
Tanned hide circles lined with pink
cotton fabric sewn on with thread.
Floral beadwork in green, blue,
and red
H. 5.5 cm, D. 5 cm
University of Colorado Museum at
Boulder 33,215a, b

The creation of items that fit into a
Victorian lifestyle reflected both the
aspirations of boarding schools for their
students and the pragmatic demands of
the market for Indian souvenirs. The
beadwork pattern used here is virtually
indistinguishable from post-1900
patterns used by other Northern Plains
and Woodland tribes.

INTERIOR OF AN EARTH LODGE
Photographed by Gilbert Wilson, 1911
MHS photo IV-67-1911

Some residents of Independence still chose to live in earth lodges in the early 20th century. Hairy Coat and his wife, shown here making pots, were such a couple. She sat in front of the partition between the fire and the door.

INTERIOR OF A LOG CABIN
Photographed by Gilbert Wilson, 1906
MHS (Wilson [1903–18]:58)

Although the agency had a mill for grinding corn meal, women continued to use mortars and pestles to pound their corn for cooking. Here Mrs. James Baker demonstrated the use of a corn mortar in Wolf Chief's cabin. A washboard hung on the wall.

The outside world comes closer

Scarcely more than 50 years after the Hidatsa had first started to use the wheel, automobiles came to the reservation. In the span of one lifetime, the people had adapted to centuries' worth of change – and the pace was accelerating.

By the turn of the century, two transcontinental railroads framed the Hidatsa homeland – the Great Northern to the north, the Northern Pacific to the south. The river, so long the lifeline to the outside world, no longer churned with steamboats; roads crossed the prairie between new towns like Washburn, Garrison, and Minot. Even Independence was no longer quite so isolated. A telephone line reached it in 1910. A modern ferry boat linked it to the east bank. Before long, a highway bridge would cross the river at Elbowoods (Hoffman 1907-12; Meyer 1977:174, 246).

In 1911 a commissioner from the Office of Indian Affairs happily told a gathering of Fort Berthold Indians that "In two or three years all the land that is now grass land in the Northern part of the reservation will be covered with homes of white people and the little towns that are now merely small villages will be developed into small cities right here at your door, and there will be railroads running within two or three

hours drive from the home of every Indian on this reservation" (Abbott 1911:5).

If he expected his audience to cheer at his rosy vision of the future, he was disappointed. The Hidatsa, Mandan, and Arikara knew that the "progress" that brought them closer to the outside world also brought tremendous pressure to give up their land. White settlers moving into North Dakota disliked the sight of the reservation lying "undeveloped." The tribes' land base had been dwindling for decades, but the early 20th century brought the most wrenching sacrifices for them.

The government's policy said that, once each Indian had received an allotment, the "surplus" reservation land would be opened for sale to whites. The long-run intention was to make reservation boundaries nothing more than a legal relic; whites and Indians would blend together as neighbors.

But the Indians did not see the unallotted land as "surplus." "The Almighty placed us on this earth and he gave it to us so we call it this mother earth that was ours since way back," said Enemy Heart, an Arikara spokesman. "It is the only ground we have, the ground we have lived on since way back. So we look up to it as our savior" (Red Bear et al. 1911:3-4).

MAIN STREET LOOKING NORTH, GARRISON"
1920s?
SHSND A-5906
The town of Garrison grew up on the Missouri downriver from the reservation, near the old site of Fort Stevenson. Its original site was wiped out with the building of the Garrison Dam in the 1950s.

In 1901 the agent reported that the Fort Berthold Indians wanted "to hold the unallotted portion of their reservation for grazing and hay lands. They say the area is none too large for their herds" (Richards 1901a:166). There was also the younger generation to think of. After years of decline, the tribes' population began increasing again in the early 20th century, and those children would need land, too.

Despite all these arguments, the government sent a commissioner to negotiate for the sale of the northeast portion of the reservation. The tribes were adamantly opposed. "Away back in the olden times we did not know how to make treaties with the Government," said Sitting Bear, an Arikara, "but now we begin to know the value of our land." Nevertheless, in an intense, week-long council, the commissioner convinced them that the land would probably be taken anyway, and it was in their interest to sell for a good price.

The land was opened to white settlement in 1910. A branch line of the Minneapolis, St. Paul and Sault Ste. Marie Railroad – the Soo Line – was built into it, and the towns of Parshall, Van Hook, and Sanish sprang up almost overnight. But it hurt the Indian people to know that the land was gone. "They have got us now to our homes," said Enemy Heart. "That is the only thing we have now to protect. The land has been taken away and we have only to defend our homes. The line has come close" (Meyer 1977:160-65; Red Bear et al. 1911:8).

The land was slipping from their control in other ways, as well. White ranchers and farmers who wanted to use Indian land and could not buy it resorted to leasing it. Agents usually favored this practice, since it put the land to use and brought income to the tribe. But the Indians wanted to use the land for their own herds. When the agent overruled them, their only recourse was to appeal to Washington "to ask you to inform us, If we have any rights or not about the permit" (Crows Heart et al. 1908). The answer was frequently no. On one occasion, although the reservation Business Committee and the tribal elders all agreed to oppose a lease, the agent recommended to Washington that "their action in the matter should be disregarded" (Jermark 1914:2-3). Wolf Chief and Goodbird earned the wrath of at least one agent for organizing meetings to protest leasing (Thomas 1903). "Our money makes us many troubles," said Wolf Chief. "I tell Indians we must be stockmen. Buy cows now with this money to stock our grass instead of leasing it to white stockmen.

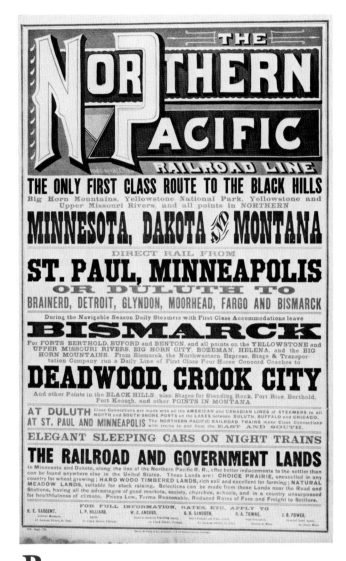

RAILROAD ADVERTISEMENT
Printed by Rand, McNally & Co., Chicago, for the
Northern Pacific Railway, 1879
Red and blue ink on beige card stock
H. 56.2 cm, W. 35.8 cm
MHS

Railroads were the conduits of immigration to the Plains. In order to encourage railroad construction, the U.S. government subsidized the companies with vast land grants near the tracks, which the railroads then sold to incoming settlers. Advertisements like this enticed settlers to travel west and buy railroad land. A large portion of the Fort Berthold Reservation was given to the Northern Pacific Railway Company in 1880 (Meyer 1977:113). Aided by railroads, the population of North Dakota increased more than 1,000 per cent between 1878 and 1890 (Robinson 1966:134).

. . . White men want to keep our grass lands and want to sell us cars which we don't need, so we won't have any money to stock our land. So that they may keep our grass lands" (Wolf Chief 1931).

But the growing incursion of the outside world had advantages, as well. Jobs, once scarce, grew easier to find and more attractive to Indian men. In 1908, Indians from Fort Berthold constructed roads, repaired bridges, cut and hauled telephone poles, built fences for the Soo Line, and did a large amount of freight hauling. They mined and hauled coal, with which the area was abundantly supplied. They gathered and sold buffalo bones for making fertilizer, and they marketed their wheat to nearby mills (Thomas 1908:3; Meyer 1977:150, 153). Local newspapers, rodeos, and circuses lent variety to life. Although Wolf Chief grumbled about the younger generation's love affair with the auto, faster transportation cut down the isolation of allotment life.

Clinics at the agency and mission gave reservation dwellers easier access to modern health care. In 1896 the mission health workers delivered babies, treated trachoma and pneumonia, dressed assorted burns, cuts, and sores, pulled teeth, and gave instruction on hygiene (Creighton 1896). The agency physician treated more serious ailments. But not everyone welcomed such innovations. "The Almighty . . . gave us medicine to cure us and heal up ourselves," said Red Bear, an Arikara spokesman. "Our medicine has been proven in the generations gone. We used that medicine . . . and it healed us, and that is why we try to keep this medicine, because we have proved it among ourselves. You white men think there is something wrong with this medicine, but we know it is right. Doctors come to our reservation now, and are using white man's medicines and all that, and it is supposed that they want the Indian medicine cut off; but still these old people want to use their old medicine" (Red Bear et al. 1911:2).

With towns nearby, the people of Fort Berthold had more exposure to politics. The government granted citizenship to Indians when they received titles to their allotments, and people at Fort Berthold started to vote almost at once. By 1902 they were electing each other delegates to the Republican county conventions. Soon the missionary, unconscious of the irony of the situation, could declare that "our Fort Berthold Indians are law abiding citizens and are beginning to take part in government of, by and for the people" (Meyer 1977:155, 176; Hall 1937k).

TRAIN WITH ROTARY SNOW PLOW
1906
Collected by Gilbert Wilson
MHS (Wilson [1903-18]:71)
The Great Northern tracks that ran north of the Fort Berthold Reservation were kept open in winter with plows like this one, shown near Langdon, N.Dak.

Washburn
c. 1897
SHSND Col. 32 ML-6-6

Washburn was the seat of McLean County, which included much of the eastern portion of the reservation. Fort Berthold residents shopped and did legal business there, like filing lawsuits and buying marriage licenses.

Johann Jacobs Family, Van Hook
1915
SHSND Col. 32 MN 12-10

The white settlers who moved into the newly opened reservation land often lived no more luxuriously than their Indian neighbors. The missionary described two separate waves of settlement on the reservation, which he characterized by ethnic stereotypes. The first was composed of "white Americans" who "came with their machinery, tearing up the prairie to raise great crops of wheat . . . with the idea of speedily making fortunes without great labor, exploiting the land. Some made a great deal of money at first, others lost a great deal, leaving the land weedy and exhausted." The second wave of settlement was composed of "Russians, Germans, Scandinavians and other Europeans who were used to hard toil. . . . They worked in a safer and more intelligent way, developing their homesteads, living frugally, and were able by degrees to build up homes" (Hall 1937n). The Jacobs family probably belonged to the latter group.

AUTO WRENCH
*Made by Ford Motor Co., early 20th
 century*
*Curved iron bar with socket on one
 end, open jaws on the other, and
 "Ford" in relief on handle*
L. 25.9 cm, W. 4.6 cm
SHSND 81.78.8
This wrench was made for use on a
Model T Ford.

TELEPHONE
*Made by Chicago Telephone Supply
 Co., Elkhart, Ind., early 20th
 century*
*Magneto wall telephone in
 rectangular wooden case with
 binged front, hand crank on right
 side, metal Y-shaped receiver hook
 on left, and black bakelite receiver
 connected with fabric-wrapped
 cord. On front of case are two
 metal bells, adjustable mouthpiece,
 and wooden shelf*
L. 36 cm, W. 32 cm, H. 56 cm
*MHS 67.230.1, Mr. and Mrs. Harry
 D. Ayer Estate*
In 1910 a telephone line was strung
across the river to Independence and a
telephone was installed in the school. It
was used for emergencies, like
summoning the minister to attend a sick
child (Hoffman 1907-12). This model
of telephone was frequently used in
rural areas in the early 20th century.

OIL CAN
Made by Marshall Oil Co., c. 1925
*One-gallon tin container with screw
 cap, spout, and swivel handle on
 top. Painted label in yellow, green,
 and red*
L. 20 cm, W. 7.5 cm, H. 26 cm
MHS 1982.105.92
Since mechanics were not common in
the remote areas of North Dakota, early
drivers learned to do their own
maintenance and repairs. Toward the
end of his life, Goodbird used a car to
visit the Congregational churches around
the reservation. The mission helped pay
his gas and oil expenses, which came to
four cents a mile ([Case?] 1936:3, Case
1925a:2).

LICENSE PLATE
1911
*Steel sheet with four slots for
 mounting vertically. Lettering
 painted in gold on black*
L. 24.1 cm, W. 7.6 cm
SHSND 11676
With new transportation methods came
new kinds of government control over
Indian life. A car, unlike a wagon,
needed a license like this one from the
state of North Dakota.

P ARKING LOT
Early 1930s
Collected by Harold Case
SHSND Col. 41-72

The occasion that drew this crowd of cars was probably a rodeo or powwow. North Dakotans owned cars at a far higher rate than people in the rest of the country – one for every 3.7 persons in the 1930s. The automobile changed settlement patterns, the location of towns, and social life. One historian compared its effect on the mobility of rural North Dakotans to the impact of the horse on Plains tribes 150 years earlier (Robinson 1966:379).

G AS STATION
Collected by Harold Case, post-1922?
SHSND Col. 41-98

Automobiles were used on the Fort Berthold Reservation at least as early as 1909 (Hoffman 1907-12), but they probably were not common until some years later. In 1931 Wolf Chief criticized his neighbors for spending money to buy cars instead of livestock. "I don't like cars," he wrote. "Cars give no dinner" (Wolf Chief 1931).

THE FAIR

Ladies' Tailored Suits

Just received, Fifty of the Season's Newest Styles in Strictly Tailored Suits made expressly for us in New York City. Many new Ideas and Kinks never shown in the earlier suits.   :-:   :-:
New Cloths, New Patterns, all the Popular Shades, Wisteria, Rose, Browns, Blues and Teas.   :-: :-: :-:

THE PRICES
$9.75 $11.50 $15.00 $19.50

You'll wonder how we can sell them so cheap. You will admit that they would sell just as readily for $20.00, $25.00, $30.00, $35.00. We are satisfisd to sell them at a reasonable profit.   :-:   :-:   :-:
We are also showing some very special values in Ladies' Skirts, Waists and Petticoats.   :-   :-:   :-:

Headquarters for
LADIES' WEARING APPAREL

Spring Styles In

Our spring line of Gents' clothing has arrived, and if you wish to see nifty and up-to-date patterns in the latest styles, we shall be glad to show them to you if you will step in.

Gents Furnishing Dept.

Hats. Caps. Ties, Dress Shirts of all kinds.   The place to buy your goods is

THE GARRISON MERCANTILE CO.

City Meat-market

Garrison, N. Dak.

Our reputation and growth is builded upon cleanliness, fresh meats and honest weight. Fish and Game in season. Highest price for hides. A big stock of cured and salted meats

THEODORE DUBBS

NEWSPAPER ADVERTISEMENTS
Printed 1897-1913
SHSND
Local towns brought the consumer culture of the early 20th century to the Indians' doorstep. These advertisements, showing the variety of shops and goods available within a day's ride of the reservation, were published in the *Garrison Times* and the *Minot Daily News.*

DOCTOR
Post-1930?
Collected by Harold Case
SHSND Col. 41-267

Health care was available at the agency from the late 19th century, but it was not until 1930 that the reservation got a hospital at Elbowoods, where this photograph was probably taken. The new hospital mainly served for emergencies and births; when times were good, people tended to go to Bismarck and Minot for more serious health problems. "Now it is quite popular to go to the hospital," the missionary declared in 1937. All the same, traditional medicine was still practiced (Hall 1937m; Meyer 1977:182, 200).

The hospital was flooded out in the 1950s and never replaced. In the 1980s, there was still no hospital on the reservation.

CARNIVAL GROUNDS
Collected by Harold Case, post-1922?
SHSND Col. 41-74

"A one horse dog circus came here today & the Goodbird clan all pulled up & came over to see it," Gilbert Wilson wrote in 1918 from Van Hook, a town about 12 miles north of Independence (Wilson 1918b). This carnival was probably similar to that one.

FOUR BEARS BRIDGE
1934
Collected by Harold Case
SHSND Col. 41-124

The building of a bridge between Elbowoods and the south shore of the Missouri in 1934 was the culmination of years of lobbying by local residents. It was named after the two prominent leaders named Four Bears, one of whom was Mandan, the other Hidatsa. The bridge was later moved to New Town, where it is still in use (Case and Case 1977:196-99).

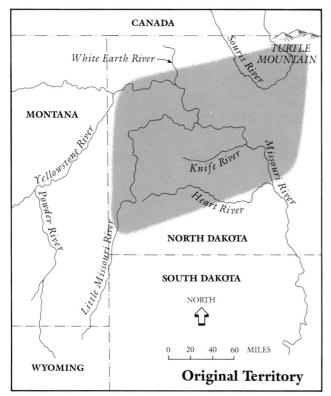
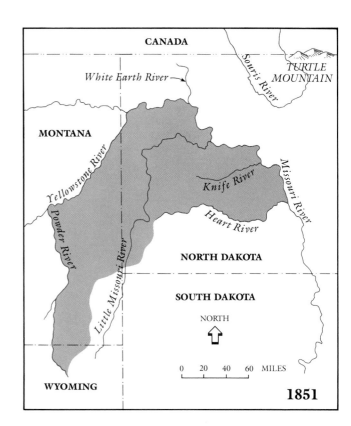

F ORT BERTHOLD RESERVATION, 1851-1910
Based on Bowers 1965:12, Meyer 1977:opp. p. 112

Original territory. In Buffalo Bird Woman's childhood, the Hidatsa had felt free to use land between the Souris River on the Canadian border, the Turtle River on the east, the Heart River on the south, and the Yellowstone River on the west. But in 1851 their world began to shrink.

1851. In the Fort Laramie Treaty, the government defined the Hidatsa homeland as the triangle between the Yellowstone River, the Heart River, and the Missouri. This left out the northeastern part of the Hidatsa's land – including Like-a-Fishhook Village – but the area contained 12.6 million acres.

1870. When Goodbird was one year old, Fort Berthold Reservation was established. The boundaries were smaller than those in the Fort Laramie Treaty. Neither Congress nor the Hidatsa ever agreed to the change. The land was owned communally by the tribe; as a member, Goodbird still had a heritage of about 7.8 million acres.

1880. The Northern Pacific Railroad wanted to put a line through the southern part of Fort Berthold Reservation, and it needed land along the track to sell to incoming white farmers. The government lopped off the southern half of the reservation and added some land north of the Missouri instead. Neither Congress nor the Hidatsa ever agreed to the change. Goodbird's heritage was now about 1.2 million acres.

1891. The General Allotment Act of 1887 introduced a different pattern of land holding – private land ownership – to the reservation. Goodbird's heritage dwindled to 160 acres plus whatever land the Hidatsa, Mandan, and Arikara still held in common. His wife and children received smaller amounts. In 1891, Congress authorized the sale of two-thirds of the reservation as "surplus" land. In exchange, the three tribes were to receive $800,000, which mostly went for support of the agency, schools, and mission.

1910. Through the first decade of the 20th century the tribes of Fort Berthold fought off attempts to sell more of their land. At last, in 1910, the land on the northeastern corner of the reservation was sold to white settlers, although in the Indians' view (later confirmed by the courts) the land still remained within the reservation boundaries. "By and by," said Bear's Ghost, "we will not have enough left to sit on" (Abbott 1911:28).

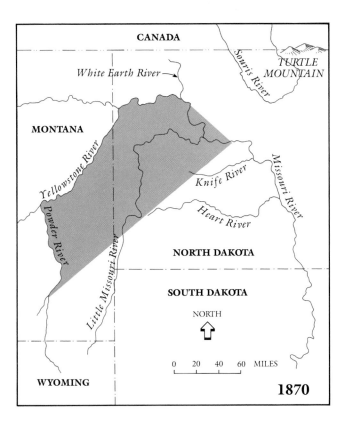

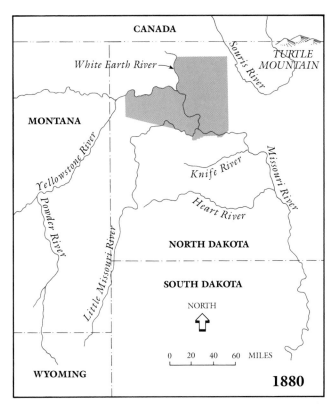

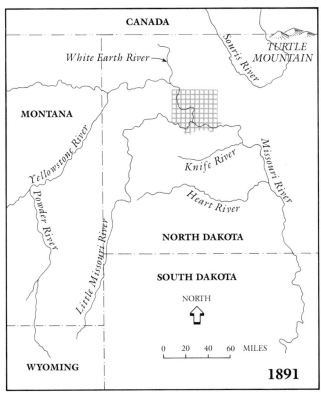

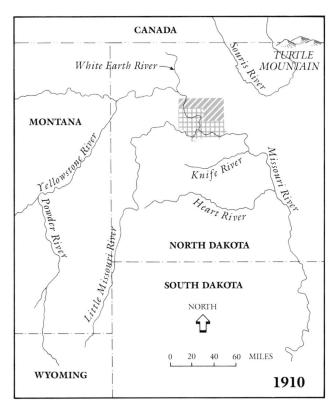

Son of a Star dies

Goodbird always thought of his father, Son of a Star, as a man who "had done everything which Indian custom required for leading an ideal Indian life." He had been a warrior and hunter, and had purchased the rights to sacred ceremonies. But as he grew old, he was struck with a crippling disease. Unable to walk, he dressed in his best quilled shirt, leggings, and moccasins to have his photograph taken in the summer of 1906. A few months later, he was dead. "He always remained true to his beliefs and would not desert his gods," said Goodbird (Case 1925a; Wilson 1906b:68, 1913a:112).

If Son of a Star had died 30 years earlier at Like-a-Fishhook Village, his family would have expressed their grief according to Hidatsa customs. Members of the dead person's father's clan, not the immediate family, were the crucial actors in traditional funeral rites. "When someone had died . . . the [clan] fathers and [clan] aunts brought rich clothing and dressed the body," said Wolf Chief. They also "brought a good many presents of rich clothing and laid them down in a pile beside the dead man. This clothing was afterwards taken by the wife and children of the dead man.

"Meanwhile the relatives of the dead man brought many rich gifts [which] were afterwards divided up" among the clan members.

"In this way both sides made gifts. . . . Sometimes when families had a death they neglected to do this duty, and then all the people in the tribe talked against them. . . .

"In the burial field the [clan] fathers and [clan] aunts made a kind of platform. When the time for burial came [they] put the body in a blanket or robe, and a few of them, catching hold of the edges of the blanket, brought the dead man to the burial field. . . . When they had put the body on the burial scaffold, [they] paused and talked to it. 'My son,' they would say, 'I wish you to go to the Ghost Land right away. Do not remain here, or try to harm anyone in the village, but go at once to the Ghost Land. . . .'

"If they talked thus to the dead body, [they] knew that the spirit would always obey them. But if any other person than the [clan] aunts and [clan] fathers buried the body and spoke thus to the dead man his spirit would not go away" (Wilson 1914b:71-74).

By 1906 the Hidatsa felt tremendous pressure to give up their old practices and instead "observe the civilized custom of conducting funerals" (Dawson 1901:4). Missionaries urged that the dead be buried in caskets and graves instead of on scaffolds and in robes.

The undertaker was supposed to dress the body and the clergyman to deliver the speeches at the graveside instead of the clan relatives.

Most Hidatsa accepted the outward trappings of white custom. When the Indians used coffins and underground burials, the missionaries thought that they accepted the Christian and cultural meanings of those artifacts. Yet the ways of expressing respect for the dead

SON OF A STAR WITH GOODBIRD AND BUFFALO BIRD WOMAN
Photographed by Gilbert Wilson, 1906
MHS (Wilson [1903-18]:43)
Son of a Star's clothing in this photograph is like a graphic biography. The two eagle feathers in his hair symbolize the two times he struck coup fighting against the Sioux. Marks on his leggings give the circumstances of the same events. His moccasins are embroidered with designs telling of the times he and his horses were wounded. Since Hidatsa people frequently set aside their best suit of clothing for their burial, it is probable that these are the clothes in which Son of a Star was dressed at death.

"The old man is quite feeble, 76 years [of] age, and can hardly walk," Gilbert Wilson wrote when he took this picture. "These were the first pictures I believe the old people ever had taken" (Wilson 1906b:68-69).

remained uniquely Hidatsa. When a sick man was dying, his relatives dressed him in his best clothes. He appointed a committee to make and bring in the coffin as he would have asked someone to "bring the robe" in former times. After death, clan relatives brought calicoes, blankets, beadwork, saddles, and other valuables, while the family gave away the dead man's possessions, "even to the cattle and horses" (Bowers 1965:168-72; [Case? 1930s]:1-2).

Even the most Christian ways of honoring the dead underwent a subtle tranformation in Hidatsa hands. In the 1880s, the missions started to promote observance of Decoration Day (now called Memorial Day). Students at the mission school were sent to gather flowers, then "formed in line and marched a round about way bearing their few flowers to our little Christian grave yard" (*Word Carrier* 1888b:24). The custom caught on, and by the early 20th century Decoration Day was one of the major holidays of the year for the people of Independence.

"We have been observing Decoration Day for about five years," Goodbird said in 1913. "All our people come to the church house and camp in a circle. Last year we had about ten tents. Sometimes two or three families would be in one tent. All our Independence friends came, and also some from Shell Creek and from the Little Missouri.

"We made a booth just outside of the church house, making it as we did our old time booths of stringers on forked poles, and small trees, cut with the leaves on them, leaned against the stringers. We gathered in this booth at about ten o'clock. We have always asked the school teacher to begin the exercises by telling us how Decoration Day began. We did thus last year, and we had songs and some national hymns. Then we had speeches. . . . We had the chiefs of the leading Dance Societies present. They were Rabbit Head, Chief of the Grass Dance Society, and Wounded Face, who says he is a member of the Sun Ceremony. . . .

"At noon we had dinner and in the afternoon we all got flowers in our hands and every family who had anyone dead in the cemetery near our church house, got a [clan] father or a [clan] aunt of the deceased, to go out and decorate the dead one's grave. The [clan] father or [clan] aunt would then go out and clean the grave, pulling out all the weeds and removing any stones or chips or anything. The relatives of the dead person paid the [clan] father or [clan] aunt for doing this. . . .

"At two o'clock in the afternoon we made a procession and marched to the cemetery. The procession was led by two old scouts, Black Chest and High Eagle. The two scouts carried a big flag with them, High Eagle being a bearer of it. We followed them, the men going first, two by two, and the women and children following. We marched clear around the graveyard, and sang some hymns. Then I made a speech.

"'All you relatives and friends, I want to make a speech to you. It seems sad to our hearts to come here, and yet, we are glad because we come to remember our loved ones at their graves. So gladness and sorrow are both in our hearts.

"'These warrior men whom you see, have fought against our enemies. They fought because they wanted to save us from our enemies, so that today we are not captives but free. Some of the brave men who fought to save us, have died for this country. Also, you good people here, some of your loved ones have died and are here in this graveyard. Many of these loved ones did not die fighting against the enemy, yet they too were brave warriors against evil and temptation. Now they are gone from us. But they are in a new world – the Ghost Land. They are with God. I am sure they will find themselves in a good, safe, comfortable place. Now come forward all those who want to set up flowers on the graves'" (Wilson 1913a:144-47).

Some older Indians found the new attitudes toward burial amusing. When Catholic missionaries tried to convert Francis Porcupine by telling him that he would be comfortably buried in their cemetery with a fence around it, he said wryly, "How nice it would be to be buried inside your grave yard. I could sit up in my grave and admire that pretty iron fence" (Hall 1937m). Wolf Chief also had his opinion: "White people seem to want to make a grave to be just like a home for the dead man." But, he added diplomatically, "I think that is a pretty good custom" (Wilson 1914b:74).

Moccasin

Hidatsa. Made by Sioux Woman
Collected by Gilbert Wilson, 1910
Rawhide sole, tanned hide upper sewn with sinew and
*   decorated with orange, blue, and purple quillwork on*
*   instep*
L. 25.5 cm, W. 14 cm
AMNH 50.1/5506b

This replica of one of Son of a Star's moccasins was made after
his death by Sioux Woman, Goodbird's wife, who followed
Buffalo Bird Woman's directions. It is like one of the
moccasins he wore in his 1906 photograph. The designs – his
honor marks – meant that three horses were wounded under
him in battle. The other moccasin, now missing, had other
designs symbolizing the three times he himself was wounded
(Wilson 1906b:69).

Carrying a Body to Burial

Drawn by Goodbird, 1914
Pencil on paper
H. 10.9 cm, W. 10.5 cm
AMNH (Goodbird 1914b:fig. 41)

"Four persons commonly held the edge of the robe or blanket
holding the body," Wolf Chief said, "but if the dead man was
very heavy they called in two or three others to help of their
own [clan] or tribe." Only clan relatives from the father's side
bore the body. Goodbird noted he had never seen a body
carried in a robe to burial: "In my time it was always carried
thither in a wagon" (Wilson 1914b:72-73).

Scaffold Burial

Late 19th century?
Collected by Harold Case
SHSND Col. 41-364

The Hidatsa used both burial scaffolds and shallow, board-
lined graves. Which method of burial was used depended
upon the individual family's traditions. Each village had its
own burial grounds. Scaffolds were stridently opposed by
government officials (Bowers 1965:169-70; Meyer 1977:145).
They survived only into the late 19th or early 20th century,
when this picture was probably taken (Densmore 1923:6).

CALICO, QUILT, AND BLANKET
Calico: reproduction, 1986. Quilt: made in Defiance, Ohio, c. 1890. Blanket: made early 20th century
Printed cotton calico with small yellow, blue, and white flowers on red ground. Cotton quilt pieced in "bear's paw" pattern in red and green on white ground. Plaid wool blanket with broken twill weave in brown, blue, and white
Calico: L. 420 cm, W. 112 cm. Quilt: 212 cm square. Blanket: L. 177 cm, W. 154 cm
MHS 8975.23, Mrs. John Horatio Benton; 65.89.4, Dr. and Mrs. Walter E. Jones

Textiles were some of the most appropriate gifts to exchange with clan relatives at a funeral or on Decoration Day. In 1913 Goodbird said, "To prepare the grave of our little daughter, and pluck the weeds from it, Mrs. Goodbird and myself paid to Howard Mandan, one quilt, one blanket, and three calicoes, and to Many Growths, we paid one shawl and four calicoes. Each calico had from seven to ten yards in it" (Wilson 1913a:147). Gift giving in honor of a deceased family member is still an important tradition among the Hidatsa and other tribes.

The patterns of these artifacts are similar to those shown in photographs from Fort Berthold Reservation. Wolf Chief noted that he purchased brightly colored red, pink, blue, and white calicoes for his store, and small floral prints can be seen in photographs of dresses worn by women at Independence (Wilson 1916c:79; MHS photos X-52-1918, VII-56-15, IV-77). Most early quilt patterns shown on the reservation were geometric pieced work (Case and Case 1977:53; AMNH photo 288284). Plaid blankets and shawls were not only used for bedding but were also worn by women, wrapped around the legs like a skirt (MHS photo VIII-64-1916) or around the shoulders and over the head (Case and Case 1977:57; SHSND Col. 41-465).

SILK FLOWERS
Reproduction, 1986
L. 15.5 to 66.5 cm
Placing flowers on graves at Decoration Day was originally a white tradition, but the Hidatsa made it their own by paying clan relatives to perform the ritual. In 1913 Goodbird noted that "Sometimes when the season is favorable, we are able to gather flowers to put on the graves, but this year the season was late and no flowers were out, so we bought artificial silk flowers from the stores in the nearby towns" (Wilson 1913a:145-46).

BUFFALO BIRD WOMAN AND SIOUX WOMAN
Photographed by Gilbert Wilson, 1908
MHS photo III-1

Hidatsa women often mourned their husbands by cutting their hair short and
wearing it loose, as Buffalo Bird Woman wore hers in this photograph. It is possible
she was still in mourning for Son of a Star. Wolf Chief explained that "Some Indian
wives, when their husbands had died, made themselves suffer for their dead ones.
Often a wife would cut off the first joint of her little finger with a knife or axe or
some other tool, or would cut off her hair" (Wilson 1914b:70; Bowers 1965:172).
A 1926 photograph of Buffalo Bird Woman (SHSND B191) shows that she at some
time cut off the tip of one little finger. Since she was married twice, there is no way
of telling when she did this.

The two women peeled prairie turnips in this photograph.

A new calling for Goodbird

Goodbird came from a profoundly religious family. In his youth he had sought, and failed, to find a vision to guide him through life. By the time he was a man, the missions and agency had put the spiritual expressions of his culture beyond his reach. After 1903, when the government eliminated his job of assistant farmer for the Independence district, he began to turn toward the only spiritual path still open to him: the Christian church.

Goodbird had been casually connected to the Congregational church since his days at school. "After we came down to Independence, I could not attend the church meetings at old Fort Berthold very well, but Mr. Hall used to come down and hold meetings," he said. "Sometimes these meetings were in my house or in the school house, after it was built. Very often I interpreted for him. . . . The missionary would speak in English and I would translate into Hidatsa, which all the Mandans also understood. I did not receive pay for interpreting in this way, except the thanks of the missionary. But I learned a great deal more about the Bible" (Wilson 1913a:113-14).

Yet there was a strong strain of skepticism in him. "I was not a very strong Christian. I could not keep the Ten Commandments very well because I did not believe all that the missionaries and the preachers told me. I did not want to trust anybody, nor what they said, unless I saw it and proved it for myself. I did not want to take anything on faith, but wanted to prove it first" (Wilson 1913a:118).

When he was 35 years old, Goodbird attended a prayer meeting organized by some Christian Indians. "We would like you to join the church," they said to him. "We would like you to speak and tell us what is in your mind."

Goodbird rose and spoke. "I have gone to the missionary school and I know a good many of your Christian ways and have gone to church a good deal, and I love to read the Bible for I can read it pretty well. . . . I have not yet been baptized, although I have tried to lead a life like a Christian. But I am now willing to be baptized."

Sitting Crow cried, "Good! I am glad that Goodbird is favorable to this meeting. I will tell Mr. Hall!"

"So the next Sunday," said Goodbird, "I went down with Hollis Montclair, who also wanted to unite with the church, and with my family. I had my sons, Alfred and Charley, baptized at the same time also."

Goodbird's decision was not based on any rejection of his tribe's old beliefs; he reassured himself that "The old people of my tribe have never talked much against the Christian way. Neither my grandfather nor his two wives were at all opposed to the Christians. . . .

"I looked at it thus: while I thought of myself as one of the Christians of the reservation, and went to church and was a friend of the missionaries, I did not really know God, and I did not use God's way very

GOODBIRD IN THE OLD INDEPENDENCE CHAPEL
1907
Collected by Harold Case
SHSND Col. 41-450
Goodbird stood at the pulpit of the original Independence chapel, a log building. It became a social hall when replaced by the new chapel in 1910 (Case and Case 1977:294).

well. When my friends asked me, 'Why are you not baptized and take a stand as a Christian?' I thought that they were right; that I could not go back and use the Indian way any more, and that as soon as I found God, I must join the church.

"I thought also that this Indian life and these Indian customs of ours cannot long continue. I could see that white men's ways and their ways of thinking about God were becoming stronger; Christian ways are being recognized on this reservation, and they are going to prevail, I thought. When I was baptized, I thought to myself, 'Now I am traveling the new way'" (Wilson 1913a: 114-15, 118).

"When I came back to Independence I cannot say that my life was much different," he said. He continued to go to church meetings and interpret for the missionaries. "I did not get better all at once, but at least I kept up my attendance at the church and I grew a little better from year to year" (Wilson 1913a: 115, 118).

The missionaries were more impressed with Goodbird than he was with himself. In October 1904, Robert Hall, the son of the original missionary, made him an offer: "They want an assistant missionary at the [Independence] station and my father and I have talked it over, and we think that you would make a good assistant. We want to appoint you to that place."

Goodbird agreed at once. "I knew that the people on this part of the reservation needed somebody to explain the gospel to them, and that I could read English and could speak their language. . . . Since then we have not had a white assistant to visit us very much. Every Sunday I have preached to the Christians in the Hidatsa language. I do not preach a sermon, but explain the Sunday-School lesson to them. Indians do not care much for sermons such as white people are accustomed to. We do not have the Bible in our own language and none of the old people can read English. For this reason we like the Sunday-School lesson because it explains to us what the Bible tells, which most of my people cannot read for themselves" (Wilson 1913a: 119, 116).

The church became Goodbird's new vocation. In 1925, in a packed church at Independence, he was formally ordained as a Congregational minister – the first Indian on his reservation to be so honored. He preached his ordination sermon in the Hidatsa language. "He holds the love and respect of all," said the missionary ([Case?] 1936: 3; Case [1925b]).

In his Christianity, Goodbird achieved a synthesis of white and Hidatsa values. His beliefs were like himself: kind-hearted and forgiving. Translating from English to Hidatsa was not the only challenge he faced, for his neighbors tended to expect from the Christian church the same sorts of benefits that societies and sacred ceremonies had once offered. "Sometimes Indians have joined the church, not fully understanding the way, and their reasons are not just what white people are accustomed to hear. Perhaps one will say, 'I want to be a Christian because I have sickness and perhaps God will help me so that I will get well.'

"Others will say, 'I want to join the church because I believe Jesus Christ will save me to be a spirit with Him.' They mean by this, that they think Jesus Christ will take them to live with Him when they die. . . .

"Some of the Indians who used to be quite strong Christians, have gone back to old ways again. Frank White Calf did so because the Christian people did not help him to become a policeman. 'I wanted to be a policeman,' he said, 'and the Christian people did not help me. When I asked them to help me to get the position they kept putting me off. Christian people should stick together and help one another.'

"Our old Indian customs made us Indians very clannish. Relatives worked for one another, and members of the same [clan] helped each other. It is hard for Indians to understand why Christians should not work for them and to get them positions if they become Christian" (Wilson 1913a: 119-21).

Wolf Chief, perhaps influenced by Goodbird, also decided to join the Christian church. "His idea about the Christian way is this," said Goodbird: "'I have traveled very faithfully the way of the Indian gods, but they never helped me, and I never got any aid from them. . . . Now I am going to see if God will not help me. If God will help me so that I have plenty, and if God gives me a long life, I am sure his way will be best, and when I die, God will give me a new life with Him in the Spirit'" (Wilson 1913a: 120).

Wolf Chief played an important role in one of the greatest accomplishments of Goodbird's ministry to the Independence community: the building of the new chapel in 1910. The project was initiated and carried through entirely by the Indians. "Wolf Chief and Tom Smith started the movement," Goodbird said. "A council was called in Wolf Chief's house. A number of men came, with their wives. . . . Wolf Chief made a speech to us, 'We Christian people should have a house to worship in. We should try to raise money for a church house where we can go and worship.' Tom Smith also made a speech and said the same thing.

"It was an evening in December when we met. We ate together. We had fried bread, tea, pie and tomato soup. Each family fetched along something to eat.

"After our supper, we started to raise money. Mrs. White Calf gave five dollars. Charging Enemy, Wolf Chief's brother, although not a Christian, gave a pony. Others promised, some ten dollars, some fifteen, some twenty-five dollars. . . . They appointed me as treasurer to look after the funds. We wrote to Water Chief's Dance Society and asked them if they would give a donation toward our church house. They gave us something. . . .

"When our money amounted to about three hundred and fifty dollars, we began buying lumber.

"Wolf Chief gave us ten acres of land for our church house. . . . Wolf Chief said that he did not want us only to have a little piece of land around the church house. He said that when he went among the white people he saw that they had a piece of land around their houses, and we should be ashamed not to have a piece of land around God's house. . . .

"We Indians raised altogether about one thousand dollars for our church house. When we dedicated it, Arthur Mandan played the clarinet and a young white woman sang for us. Mr. Gilbert Wilson preached the sermon, and his brother played the organ. Dr. [Robert] Lowie was present and gave five dollars. We asked the

INDEPENDENCE CHAPEL
Photographed by Gilbert Wilson, 1913
MHS photo V-78-13
The frame chapel at Independence was built in 1910 entirely through the donations and labor of the Indian congregation. In the steeple hung the bell which had rung from the first schoolhouse and chapel at Like-a-Fishhook Village (Hall 1937q). The church still stands on Fort Berthold Reservation, although it was moved from its original location in the 1950s.

people to subscribe on the debt, and raised eighty-one dollars, and all this money was paid in" (Wilson 1913a:122–25).

The spirit of giving was very much alive at Independence throughout the year, but never so much as at Christmas. It was the one time of year when white custom approved of traditional Indian gift giving. In old times at Like-a-Fishhook Village, sacred ceremonies had often called for a giveaway. At such times, the hosts would stretch a rawhide rope around the earth lodge and load it with brightly colored gift robes and blankets. Often a feast of meat and corn accompanied the giveaway (F. Wilson 1912b:36).

The missionaries, on the other hand, decorated their house with paper chains, cut-out stars, and evergreen boughs. They hung their gifts upon a tree instead of on a rope. Their holiday feast menu leaned toward sandwiches, cookies, apples, candy, peanuts, and coffee (Ilsley 1896).

At Independence, the two traditions blended. "At Christmas time, we held a Christmas Tree service at our church house," Goodbird said. "Christ said, 'When you give to my brethren, you give to me,' so we think it a good thing to give presents at Christmas time, for it is the one day in the year we are taught to give.

"We often stretch a rope across the front of the chapel and our gifts are then laid over the rope. Sometimes the rope has been piled so full of gifts that it breaks. We have singing and recitations just as in white men's churches, and then we have something to eat, a kind of feast. Our little church house is full of Indians at our Christmas services" (Wilson 1913a:147–48). The tree they chose to decorate was a cedar, the same kind of sacred evergreen that had been planted outside Mandan ceremonial lodges since time immemorial (Hall 1937q; Bowers 1965:38, 39).

As they learned first-hand about Christianity, some Hidatsa began to think it was not as antithetical to old traditions as the missionaries once said. The doctrine of charity appealed to many people above all. "I have myself in my life given away many valuable gifts," said Wolf Chief, "among them ten war bonnets and a great many horses. I do not believe there is any one on this Reservation who has given away as many horses as I. . . . I have changed my ways and become Christian, but that one way I have not changed. When poor people and hungry old people come for food, I cannot refuse them. I am sure that Jesus fed people when He was on earth. Also I cannot take money with me to Heaven. If I did not look at things in this way, I would feel that I had lost a great deal of money by feeding old people" (Wilson 1914b:109, 1913b:364).

But to Goodbird the reward of Christianity was much more personal. "I feel that I have been growing closer to God all the time and that I am much closer to God than I used to be," he said in 1913. "I do not think that Jesus is so very far from me" (Wilson 1913a:119).

I NDIAN PREACHERS
1920s?
SHSND B198
These men prominent in the Congregational church at Fort Berthold Reservation were, back row left to right: Little Owl, Mandan, from Twin Buttes; Enemy, Arikara, from Elbowoods; Wolf Chief; front row, left to right: Goodbird; Whitebull or Rev. Robert Lincoln, Arikara, from Nueta; and Howling Wolf, Arikara (Case and Case 1977:169).

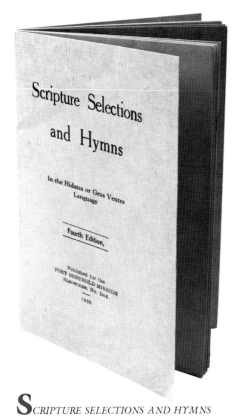

SCRIPTURE SELECTIONS AND HYMNS

**Published for the Fort Berthold
Mission by Santee Normal
Training School Press, Santee,
Nebr., 1926**
**Printed in black ink on paper; stapled
paper cover**
H. 13.3 cm, W. 8.9 cm
SHSND (Hall Papers)

This pamphlet, first published in 1911,
was a collaborative effort of Goodbird
and missionary Charles Hall. Goodbird's
son Benjamin also contributed to the
fourth edition. It presents Bible passages
and hymns in Hidatsa translation.
Goodbird may have used the pamphlet
in services at Independence. "We have a
very few hymns that have been
translated into the Hidatsa language," he
said. "If there are any white people
present, we ask them to sing the same
hymn in English, while we sing it in
our own language" (Wilson 1913a: 117).
Among the hymns translated here are
"Nearer My God to Thee," "Rock of
Ages," and "The Doxology."

POSTER

Early 20th century?
**Color lithograph in black, yellow,
pink, blue, red, and green ink on
paper; framed in oak with painted
grain**
L. 44.8 cm, W. 34.5 cm
Private collection

Large, brightly colored posters with
religious messages were evidently
distributed by missionaries on Fort
Berthold Reservation, since photographs
of the inside of Goodbird's home show
them decorating the walls (MHS photos
III-2, IV-41-1910). The Independence
church was also decorated with such
posters (SHSND Col. 41-450; MHS
photo V-77-13). Poster themes included
"The Raising of Lazarus," "The Laborers
in the Vineyard," and "The Brazen
Serpent." Home decorations were fairly
scarce; some Indian families decorated
their walls with pictures cut from
magazines (Ilsley 1896).

SUNDAY SCHOOL CARDS

**Some published by Harris, Jones &
Co., Providence, R.I., 1908–13,
or David C. Cook Publishing Co.,
Elgin and Chicago, Ill., 1913;
others unidentified**
Multicolored ink on white cardboard
L. 10.2 cm, W. 7.3 cm
SHSND 15587

The Sunday school at the
Congregational mission in Elbowoods
used cards like these to teach Bible
lessons. One week in 1895, the school
had 46 pupils divided into five groups.
"We placed the chairs in semicircles,"
said one missionary. "I looked on and
counted and took names, and felt proud
of my teachers. . . . I enjoyed it. We
have some Pilgrim picture cards, now
back numbers, perhaps ten of a kind. I
gave them out in divisions, and told the
story of the picture, and they took
them home. They were interested"
(Ilsley 1895).

This collection of cards includes
Little Pilgrim Lesson Pictures, Little
Bible Lesson Pictures, and Westminster
Lesson Cards. The cards were issued
quarterly and mailed to subscribers.

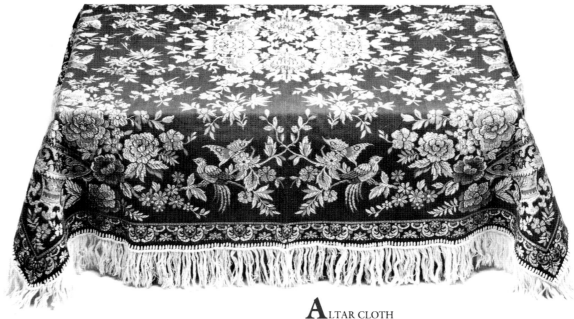

ALTAR CLOTH
20th century
Black fabric with floral pattern in metallic gold, pink,
orange, blue, and aqua thread. Gray yarn fringe added
on all sides
L. 122.5 cm, W. 116 cm excluding fringe
Private collection

The Independence church was furnished with simple, readily available materials. A floral rug or shawl served as a covering for a table, making it into an altar or pulpit. An organ, chairs, blackboard, and posters completed the furnishings (MHS photo V- 77-13; SHSND Col. 41-450).

GOODBIRD IN THE NEW INDEPENDENCE CHAPEL
Photographed by Gilbert Wilson, 1913
MHS photo V-77-13

Gilbert Wilson was present at the dedication of the new chapel. He preached a sermon, donated $20 to the building fund, and wrote of the "dandy speech" Wolf Chief made the following Sunday (Wilson 1910b:10). Three years later, he took this photograph of Goodbird at his new pulpit.

A new calling for Buffalo Bird Woman

In the summer of 1906, Buffalo Bird Woman found on her doorstep a blond, bespectacled scholar in a tweed cap and puttees. Unlike the agents and field matrons, Gilbert Wilson had come to the reservation because of an insatiable curiosity for recording the skills and customs of old times. To him, Buffalo Bird Woman's storehouse of knowledge was a priceless treasure. To her, the anthropologist presented a way of passing on her knowledge to future generations. She ended up adopting him, both literally and figuratively. In the next 12 years their collaboration would produce books and monographs that were a lasting monument to her teaching skill, memory, and exacting accuracy.

Wilson was the same age as Goodbird, and like Goodbird, he was looking for another career. Born in Ohio, he had tried his hand early in life at making money in real estate, only to end up impoverished and heavily in debt (Wilson 1907b:39, 1913c:2). He then turned to the ministry. But no sooner was he established in a parish than his boyhood interest in Indians took over. Along with his brother Frederick, and later with his wife Ada, Gilbert began to take summer leaves from his pastoral work in Minnesota to visit reservations under the sponsorship and guidance of the American Museum of Natural History. As his professionalism grew, he decided to "major in one chief subject . . . each summer" in his work with Buffalo Bird Woman and her family. Eventually, he turned his studies into a doctoral degree in anthropology from the University of Minnesota (Wilson 1916d:3).

It was Charles Hall, the missionary, who had suggested to Wilson that he take up his studies at Independence. In his diary, Wilson recorded his first day there. "There are . . . quite a number of Indians living hereabouts – Mandans and Gros Ventres [Hidatsa], the latter I think in majority. They have the usual Indian cabins floored with wood, erected by the Government, but there are many fine tepees used as summer dwellings. At Miss [Jessie] McKenzie's advice I called on Wolf Chief, Gros Ventre trader and chief and leader of the Indians hereabouts and made formal application to piquet our horses here. He was quite good natured and courteous." The next day he went to see Goodbird, recommended to him as "thoroly reliable. . . . He is a member of the church here and speaks English pretty well." They got along, and a few days later Goodbird took Wilson to see his parents (Wilson 1906b:7-9).

Wilson found Buffalo Bird Woman to be "a wonderful old lady, a born story teller with a genius for details." As he persuaded her to share her knowledge of old ways, he found that she "is accuracy itself. I have her measure off on a pole or on the ground any desired lengths and I have again and again tested their amazing accuracy." As he grew to know her, he realized that though she was "conservative, and sighing for the good old times," and "ignorant of English," she nevertheless had "a quick intelligence and a memory that is

BUFFALO BIRD WOMAN MAKING A MODEL CORN STAGE
Photographed by Gilbert Wilson, 1912
MHS photo V-45-1912
Frederick Wilson stood by with a tape measure as Buffalo Bird Woman constructed a scale model of a corn stage.

marvelous" (Wilson 1916e:21, 1913b:[597]; Maxidiwiac 1921:189).

The preservation of her knowledge became an overriding interest to Buffalo Bird Woman, and her energy almost overpowered Wilson's ability to keep up. Her "lore seemed endless and her delight at telling it was almost embarrassing," he said. "In the sweltering heat of an August day she has continued dictation for nine hours, lying down but never flagging in her account, when too weary to sit longer in a chair" (Wilson 1916e:21, 1917:4).

In these marathon sessions, Goodbird translated every word into English and explained obscure concepts. He also acted as diplomat and ambassador when Wilson ran afoul of customs he did not understand. Bargaining for artifacts on the reservation involved a sense of relative values and relationships that Wilson found hard to master. Seeing this, Goodbird "gently made a suggestion . . . that he had adopted me for his brother, and if I would put him on his honor and let him tell the other Indians that he was so put, he would bargain for everything just as if for his own family." If Goodbird's role was merely one of interpreter, his loyalties had to lie with his neighbors. But as Wilson's adopted brother, he could honorably act on his behalf (Wilson 1909c:3).

When he wrote about Goodbird, Wilson was never able to overcome entirely the prejudices of his day that defined the Hidatsa upbringing as "barbarian" and his own as "civilized." Goodbird, he said, was "goodnatured, loyal as steel, generous as he can be under proper handling, and careful and accurate as I can be myself." He acknowledged the "real scholarship, which Goodbird has shown in his help to me. His English is not the best but he is a natural scholar and perfectly trustworthy." In 1913 Wilson was excited to discover Goodbird's artistic talent. "I have a number of drawings by him some of considerable detail and merit," he wrote to the American Museum of Natural History, "and in these he has shown a surprising ability to reproduce scenes by memory. I do not think he was aware that he could draw with perspective, tho he had drawn honor charts for older men years ago" (Wilson 1913c, 1909b:8, 1913b:[594]).

Wolf Chief must have been harder for Wilson to warm to, for their personalities were very different. Wilson, still a Presbyterian minister, was so prim that he recorded beliefs relating to pregnancy in Latin, while Wolf Chief delighted in telling of his sexual conquests. But even they came to respect one another. "We think

you are a very well educated man, Mr. Wilson," Wolf Chief told him once. "Also you are a minister and show that you want to help us and you treat us like a brother. All the people here are not of the best. I think you have done very good." Wilson conscientiously wrote the words down, as he did nearly everything his informants said (Wilson 1914b:316).

Not everyone on the reservation thought so highly of Wilson. Among the more conservative members of the community, there was strong opposition to white men who came to buy and take away sacred or irreplaceable relics of the tribal past. Wilson's reputation was forever tarred when he did such a thing. But he also faced enmity for exactly the opposite reason. When the agent was asked for his opinion of Wilson's activities, he complained bitterly that "some civilized people come among these Indians and gets them to go

GOODBIRD, SIOUX WOMAN, AND BUFFALO BIRD WOMAN CUTTING A HIDE
Photographed by Gilbert Wilson, 1911
MHS photo V-6-1911
The whole family's help was enlisted on particularly challenging projects; "they seemed to take pride in . . . helping me to intelligent interpretation," said Wilson (Wilson 1909a:cover letter, p. 2). This photograph was evidently taken inside Goodbird's home.

through the old notions and tells them, how sad they feel for them, that they have lost or can not recalled some old heathen customs, which are of no benefit to them now, and the sooner they forget the old heathen ways, . . . the faster will be their progress toward civilization" (Hoffman 1911a:2). Wilson acknowledged ruefully that "It has been hard to keep a balance of kindliness between all parties" (Wilson 1909c:7).

Buffalo Bird Woman evidently did not care what the agent thought. Her work with Wilson continued, and she left an indelible mark upon his methods. Wilson realized that his most important contribution was as her transcriber, and he tried to "let the informant interpret her . . . experiences in her own way." The result was an extraordinary series of reminiscences in which individual personalities shone through. "I am quite unwilling to rewrite, on Caucasian method, what is better told in the Indian's own language," Wilson said. "I am equally unwilling to jumble accounts. Let each man tell his own story, then

we have something truthful. The value of this is having on record something that is *Indian*. We have abundance of material upon Indian culture, from white men; but telling us merely what white men think of the subjects treated. It is of no importance that an Indian's war costume struck the Puritan as the Devil's scheme to frighten the heart out of the Lord's annointed. What we want to know is why the Indian donned the costume, and his reasons for doing it" (Wilson 1917:3, 1916d:3).

In the end, Wilson became much more than just the family anthropologist. His friendship and his adoption into the Prairie Chicken clan showed a deeper relationship. Although he struggled to support his own family on his meager $1,200 yearly church salary, he made a point of sending Christmas presents to his adopted family (Wilson 1916d:5, 1911:cover letter, p. 4). They, in turn, welcomed him back each summer, and helped him create a collection that was above all an Indian family's reflections upon itself.

GILBERT WILSON AND MRS. WOLF CHIEF(?) INSPECTING A PLATE OF DRIED MEAT
Collected by Gilbert Wilson, 1915
MHS photo VII-60-15
The schoolteacher at Independence wrote that "I have never seen a man, or a woman either for that matter, who could approach Mr. Wilson in dealing with, or getting what he wants of these Indians. His tact and patience are marvelous, and his success is far greater than that of any one else who has made any overtures to these people" (Shultis 1910:2).

F REDERICK WILSON MAKING A BASKET
Photographed by Gilbert Wilson, 1912
MHS photo V-56-1912

Frederick N. Wilson, a Minneapolis commercial artist, accompanied his brother Gilbert on many expeditions to Fort Berthold. Among his most significant contributions were detailed diagrams of processes like basketry and the construction of an earth lodge.

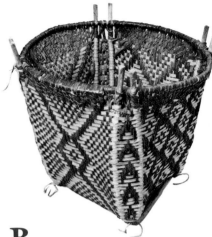

B ASKET
Made by Frederick Wilson, 1912
Collected by Frederick Wilson
Bent willow wood frame. Sides of dyed
*   and undyed willow and box elder*
*   bark strips woven in diamond and*
*   chevron patterns. Rawhide strips*
*   tied to top and base of frame*
H. 40.2 cm, D. 46 cm
MHS 9598.18

Fred Wilson made this basket according to Buffalo Bird Woman's instructions in order to learn her techniques. Unlike most baskets, his featured different designs on each side; he wove them to learn how they were produced. He noted that "As basketry was an art practised only by the women, I was subjected to a good bit of chaffing on the point, by visitors who came in while the weaving was in progress!" (F. Wilson 1912b:[53–54]; see also MHS photos V-56-1912 to V-59-1912).

I LLUSTRATIONS FOR *WAHEENEE*
Drawn by Frederick Wilson, pre-1921
Black ink and pencil on illustration board
H. 28.5 cm, W. 36.5 cm
MHS (Wilson Papers)

Frederick Wilson drew ink sketches, often basing them on photographs, to illustrate his brother's books. These pictures are for Chapter 8, "Training a Dog," of Gilbert's book about Buffalo Bird Woman's early life (Maxidiwiac 1921).

BUFFALO BIRD WOMAN MAKING A MODEL BED
Photographed by Gilbert Wilson, 1910
MHS photo IV-41-1910

"My adopted mother, Buffalo Bird Woman got quite
interested in the project of making a model of a bed,
especially after she learned I wanted a copy of the one her
husband made years ago with his honor marks," said Wilson.
"But when it came to the latter she refused to use anything
but a skin of the first quality and I have long since learned
not to try to move her when her mind is set." He purchased
a fine skin from Mrs. Goodbird for the high price of $11.00,
then photographed and interviewed Buffalo Bird Woman as
she worked (Wilson 1910a:list of items purchased, p. 6,
295-304; see p. 104, 254).

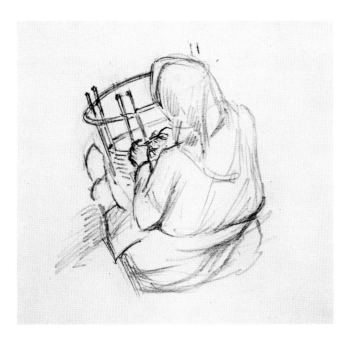

BUFFALO BIRD WOMAN WEAVING A RUSH MAT
Photographed by Gilbert Wilson, 1916
MHS photo VIII-55-1916

The first time Wilson asked Buffalo Bird Woman to make a
rush mat for him, she was reluctant. "She had not woven one
for fifty years, she said and consented only after explanation
that this would probably be the last one ever made and it
would be an honor to be the one who would save a
description of the art for the tribe. It took her about half a
day to experiment and work out the stitches again, as she said
she had not woven one since she was twenty and at first her
memory was at fault. By noon of the first day she had quite
recovered the process. . . . She put in faithful labor, clearing
the tent and getting up at five in the morning so as not to be
bothered at the work." Apparently her interest was revived,
for she was weaving another mat five years later when Wilson
snapped this candid shot of her through a window (Wilson
1910a:list of items purchased, p. 11; see also MHS photos
IV-56-1910 to IV-61-1910 and p. 118).

BUFFALO BIRD WOMAN MAKING A BASKET
Drawn by Frederick Wilson, 1912?
Pencil on paper
L. 21.5 cm, W. 17.7 cm
MHS (Wilson Papers)

For illustrating his brother's books and reports, Frederick
often drew sketches based on photographs or drawings by
Goodbird. This one, however, was probably made from life.

Goodbird Sketching a Hunter's Lodge
Photographed by Gilbert Wilson, 1915
MHS photo VII-49-15

Wilson wrote in 1913 that "The discovery that Goodbird can draw, came as a surprise. I think this should be followed up. He may give us some interesting scenes that he has witnessed himself, that may be valuable." He recommended "developing Goodbird's gift" by supplying him with good linen paper, paints, and other equipment. This was done, and every year thereafter Goodbird supplied a book of illustrations to go with Wilson's reports. Wilson paid him up to $2.50 a day for his efforts (Wilson 1913b:[598], 1915b:[589]).

Goodbird often drew from memory, but in this instance he built a model first and then sketched it.

Shoulder Mouth
Drawn by Goodbird, 1915
Black carbon and pencil on paper
H. 19.2 cm, W. 9.3 cm
MHS (Goodbird 1915:fig. 71)

In addition to drawing traditional life and technology, Goodbird also illustrated Hidatsa stories. Here he portrayed a character from a legend, as he had imagined it as a child. Wilson's note on the sketch comments that Buffalo Bird Woman's conception was different (see also Wilson 1908b:8).

Hunter's Lodge
Drawn by Goodbird, 1915
Black carbon and pencil on paper
H. 7.6 cm, W. 13.5 cm
MHS (Goodbird 1915:fig. 48)

Wilson photographed Goodbird making this sketch from a model. It portrays a lodge used by hunters on an eagle-trapping expedition, and it was reproduced by Wilson in his monograph on the subject (Wilson 1929:122). Wilson kept copies of Goodbird's sketches, traced with carbon paper, and sent the originals to the American Museum of Natural History (Wilson 1913b:[598]). Whether Goodbird or Wilson filled in the pencil shading is unknown.

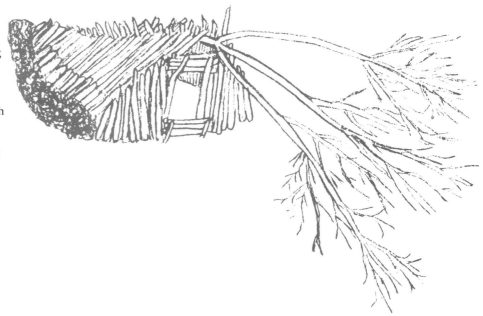

BOAT LOADED FOR CROSSING THE RIVER
Photographed by Gilbert Wilson, 1918
MHS photo X-43-1918

Getting artifacts safely to New York from Independence was a complicated process. The first stage of the trip was made by skiff or ferry. From there the artifacts were taken by wagon to the nearest train station, which by this date was at Van Hook. The artifacts that can be seen in this photograph are, from left to right, a folded bullboat cover, a wooden rake, a bullboat frame, a dog travois, and a bark basket.

Wilson's collections focused on useful, everyday objects. "I did not purchase an article without sitting down with note book and taking down everything I could get concerning the thing," he wrote. "This has proved one of the best sources of information I have yet struck. The notes when completed will be valuable" (Wilson 1909c:6). His efforts made the collection one of the best-documented of the period.

GILBERT WILSON WITH FISH AND BABY
Collected by Gilbert Wilson, 1916
MHS photo VIII-31-16

Wilson occasionally apologized to his sponsors at the American Museum of Natural History for the amount of film he used making snapshots. His camera seems to have been something of a novelty at Independence, since his photographs were valued as gifts (Wilson 1909a:cover letter, p. 2). The child in this picture was Goodbird's son, probably Paul.

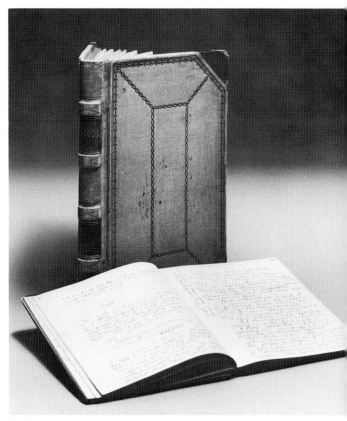

```
                    Elbowoods N.D.
                      Sept. 30, 1908.

Rev. Gilbert L. Wilson,
       Dear Brothers,
             My mother she made 1 large basket and 2 small
baskets so I bought of Mrs. Fighter widow 1 large basket and 1
small basket.  Total 2 large baskets, 3 small baskets.   Then
I look up your order which you left by me this summer I found
your order wanted 1 large basket and 3 small baskets.   Now I
buy 1 large basket too much but I think you will want that one
too?   I will sell you little cheap on larger baskets say $2.00
each instead of $2.50  small baskets $1.25 each.

             2 large baskets $2.00      $4.00
             3 small baskets  1.25       3.75
                                        _____
                                         7.75


    Wolf Chief finished that bone how handle he wanted 50¢  for
his trouble.   I asked Sam Jones make a skin boat and paddle he
said he will made a good one during this month that will be $5.00
boat and paddle.  This man is whom a Skin boat maker.  We are al
well so far.   Please let me hear from you soon also tell me how
I will ship these goods to you.

                      Yours brother,
                        Ed. Goodbird.
```

LETTER
Written by Goodbird, 1908
Black typescript on paper (copy)
H. 27 cm, W. 20.2 cm
AMNH (Goodbird 1908)

Goodbird pursued the work he and Wilson had started after
Wilson had gone home for the season. In this letter he
reported on some purchases Wilson had asked him to make.

NOTEBOOKS
Written by Gilbert Wilson, 1908 (top) and 1906 (bottom)
**Top: ink and pencil on lined paper bound in gray canvas-
covered cardboard covers trimmed with red and black
leather. Bottom: ink and pencil on lined paper bound in
black imitation leather-covered cardboard covers
trimmed with red leather**
**Top: H. 35.7 cm, W. 23.5 cm. Bottom: H. 25 cm, W. 20
cm**
MHS (Wilson 1908a, 1906b)

The diary in the foreground records Wilson's first meeting
with Buffalo Bird Woman and her family. Though he refined
his methods over the years, he always took field notes first by
hand and then brought them home to Minnesota for
transcription into typewritten reports organized by subject.
The words of his informants thus went through several stages:
first they were translated from Hidatsa to English by
Goodbird, then written down by Wilson, then rearranged and
rephrased into better English by Wilson. When he published
his works, Wilson edited them once again.

"I have not the mechanical parts of the work very
satisfactory yet," Wilson said in 1910. "My notes have given
me much trouble. Last season I took a number of convenient
sized note books, using one for each narrator, writing on
alternate pages. The opposite page would hold addenda and
corrections" (Wilson 1909a:cover letter, p. 3). Despite his
doubts, he was a remarkable observer and recorder.

LETTER
Written by Gilbert Wilson, 1910
Black ink on lined paper
H. 20 cm, W. 12.5 cm
AMNH (Wilson 1910b)
Dr. Clark Wissler, to whom this letter was written, was curator of anthropology at the American Museum of Natural History and Wilson's supervisor there. In this letter, Wilson summarized his investigations for 1910 and reported on Dr. Robert Lowie's experiences on the reservation.

GILBERT WILSON WITH NOTEBOOK AND BABY
Collected by Gilbert Wilson, 1914
MHS photo VI-77-14
Wilson's lodging arrangements at Independence gave him much trouble. He rented a house owned by the mission until Goodbird bought and moved into it. "I shall have therefore to live in a tent as far as I can see and probably have to do my own cooking," he said in 1909. After the new chapel was built, he paid the congregation to let him sleep there, though "it was so over run with fleas that life was a torment" (Wilson 1909b:2, 1918c:2). He experimented with insect-proof tents, but it is not known whether the tent shown here was his own or someone else's.

Wilson's pose here reflects one of his anthropological techniques: "The closer I can bind our relation *personally,* the better and more effective the work" (Wilson 1909c:8).

W*AHEENEE: AN INDIAN GIRL'S STORY TOLD BY HERSELF*
Published by Webb Publishing Co., St. Paul, Minn., 1921
Printed paper with engraved illustrations, bound in brown
    cloth with black title and cover design
H. 19.1 cm, W. 13.8 cm
Deborah Swanson

This book, written by Gilbert and illustrated by Frederick
Wilson, was second in a proposed series for children. It told
the story of Buffalo Bird Woman's early life at Like-a-
Fishhook Village. Thinking that her real name, Maxidiwiac
(Mah-chee-dee-WEE-ahsh, with the "ch" given the German
pronunciation), was too difficult for children to say, he
simplified it to Waheenee. "The aim has been not to give a
biography of Waheenee, but a series of stories illustrating the
philosophy, the indian-thinking of her life," Wilson wrote
(Maxidiwiac 1921:189). The book is, in fact, based as much
on Goodbird's and Wolf Chief's accounts as on Buffalo Bird
Woman's. *Waheenee*, much better known than his earlier book
based on Goodbird's story, has been reprinted several times.
In 1925 Wilson noted that his children's books had sold
74,000 copies (Wilson 1925:2). Wilson also intended to
compile a book based on Wolf Chief's life story, but he never
completed it (Wilson 1919).

G*OODBIRD THE INDIAN: HIS STORY*
Published by Fleming H. Revell Co., New York, 1914
Printed paper with engraved illustrations, bound in white
    paper cover printed in red and black
H. 18.7 cm, W. 13 cm
MHS (Goodbird 1914a)

Wilson's original goal in studying Hidatsa culture was
educational. "I am trying to prepare a series, not a large one
perhaps, of books for children between ages of eight and
fifteen, of Indian life. To make them fresh, I have hit on the
plan of getting definite accounts from living Indians of
personal experiences. . . . Simple as this plan would appear to
be, it has I think not been tried by any one so far as I know.
. . . I am ambitious that my work be of a kind that text book
writers, and men preparing books for children may have a
source to go to in after years where they can get a glimpse at
the true Indian" (Wilson 1916d:1, 3).

   This book, an edited version of Goodbird's life story,
was one of the proposed series. It was dictated to Wilson in
1913 (Wilson 1913a); because it was adopted and edited by
the Council for Home Mission Study, it stresses the Christian
aspects of Goodbird's life.

E ATING STEER RIBS
Collected by Gilbert Wilson, 1916
MHS photo IX-14-1916

"Wilson is a painstaking, conscientious worker," wrote anthropologist Robert Lowie. Wilson conscientiously tried Hidatsa foods in order to comment upon them in his notes. "The taking of cooking recipes for strange messes . . . is about the most trying task an anthropological collector ever has put to him," he commented, adding that his notes provided material for "the most unique cook book that ever [a] Ladies Aid Society published for a down-at-the-heel church!" Here Wilson ate with an unidentified man named Hale and Wolf Chief (Lowie 1910; Wilson 1916e: 22).

Wolf Chief sells the shrine

In 1907 Wolf Chief made a decision that would raise a storm of controversy, set his neighbors against him, and make it impossible for him to go back to the traditions and beliefs of his forefathers.

When Wolf Chief's father, Small Ankle, died in 1888, he was still the keeper of the sacred bundle of the Waterbuster or Midipadi clan. It was the same bundle that Missouri River had borne on the tribe's pilgrimage to Like-a-Fishhook Village. Before Missouri River, generations of earlier keepers had owned it, ever since its origin as a gift from a supernatural being who had joined the human race. "No one knows how long the skulls have passed down from keeper to keeper," said Wolf Chief. "When a keeper got too old to care for the mysteries longer he sold it . . . to another who gave rich gifts for the privilege. . . . The skull shrine was the property of the Midipadi [clan]. That is, when a keeper got old he passed the shrine to one of his own [clan] only" (Wilson 1907c:52).

But when Small Ankle died, no member of the Waterbuster clan had come forward to buy the bundle. It remained standing in its wooden shrine in Small Ankle's earth lodge at Independence, where Wolf Chief's mother lived until 1901. After her death, Wolf Chief realized that, without wanting to, he had become responsible for it (Wilson 1906b:141).

The responsibility preyed upon his mind, for he knew how much power lay in the sacred relic. Its most potent force was linked to the terrifying thunderstorms that could sweep the North Dakota plains. In the summer of Wolf Chief's 17th year, drought had threatened the crops, and the people had brought offerings to the shrine, entreating Small Ankle to pray for rain. The old men of the Waterbuster clan had assembled to see Small Ankle perform the ceremony. All day they watched as Small Ankle sang and prayed. That afternoon, black clouds began to gather, until the village was dark. "The clouds hung till midnight," said Wolf Chief, "then came [a] gentle shower, heavier and harder till afternoon next day when it ceased. After [the] rain [was] over – some men came in and thanked my father and measured the earth and it was wet one foot so they said, 'The fields will grow'" (Wilson 1906b:142, 144-45).

Wolf Chief had also seen the bundle bring the buffalo, cure the sick, and grant success in war (Wilson 1906b:139, 142-150). But there was another side to the bundle's power. "Once some Indians did not believe that the shrine could bring rain," Wolf Chief

WOLF CHIEF
Photographed by Gilbert Wilson, 1907
MHS photo II-60
This photograph was taken the year Wolf Chief sold the shrine. He was 58 years old.

said. "They laughed at it and went up on the earth lodge where the skulls were kept and smoked and a rain came up and lightning struck two of them dead" (Wilson 1907c:13).

The keeper had grave responsibilities, for the bundle could not be treated with disrespect. It had to be stored in a certain way, and certain ceremonies had to be performed for it. Failure to do so could be disastrous.

Yet Wolf Chief was not in a position to perform the duties of a keeper. To begin with, he was not a Waterbuster, but a Prairie Chicken, because clans were inherited through the mother's side. The traditional ceremonies required of a keeper were outlawed by the agent, and anyone who performed them risked jail. In addition, as misfortune plagued his family, Wolf Chief had begun to resent the gods he had always served. His numerous marriages had resulted in many children, but one by one they all died. "When we worshiped the old gods and when we were sick, they never helped us, and the people all died, and when they prayed, were never answered," he protested. "All my children died but one little boy and one little girl. So I have left the old way and now I intend to travel the Christian way as long as I live" (Wilson 1913a:120-21).

His conversion to Christianity did not mean cutting himself off entirely from his former beliefs. The missionaries encouraged their converts to destroy sacred bundles as relics of paganism. Wolf Chief sincerely wished to be a good Christian, but he could not bring himself to harm the Waterbuster bundle. He rationalized that he kept it only out of nostalgia, not belief: "I know my parents want me to keep these medicines. When young I made presents, offerings of clouts and other things. I am now Christian & don't care to pray to the old gods but want to keep the things in respect to my parents" (Wilson 1906b:141).

In 1902, his son Frank, a promising young man who had gone to Fargo to attend a business college, unexpectedly died (Wolf Chief 1905:2; Watkins 1902). Perhaps thinking that his own treatment of the sacred bundle had been responsible, Wolf Chief started making efforts to get someone else to take it. He first approached members of the Waterbuster clan. Many of them later testified that he had tried to get them to take the bundle. One by one, they all refused. Sam Jones and Scattered Village wanted nothing to do with the bundle; Foolish Bear's wife did not want it in her house; Butterfly said that he traveled so much he would not be able to take proper care of it. Hairy Coat advised Wolf Chief to leave it alone until its earth lodge fell down around it, but others disagreed. Wolf Chief thought of burying it, but was told such an action would not be appropriate (Meyer 1975:2; Waterbuster Clan Bundle File).

Wolf Chief's uneasiness with his situation had grown acute by 1906, when Gilbert Wilson showed up at Independence. When other white men had asked to see the bundle, Wolf Chief had always refused because "the spirits might be made angry." Convinced of Wilson's sincerity, however, Wolf Chief allowed him to enter. In the empty, silent earth lodge the old shrine must have exuded a powerful aura of mystery. When the anthropologist reached out, intending to touch it, a mouse scuttled out of the bundle and Wilson jerked back, startled. Wolf Chief, looking on, later observed that "something frightened him so that he did not look [at the bundle] & I am sure it was because he was afraid" (Wilson 1907c:7, 13).

When Wilson returned the next year, he was determined to buy the shrine, along with its attendant songs and stories. He came to Wolf Chief's house on July 9. "I must confess that I approached this morning's work with grave anxiety," he wrote in his diary. "It was . . . with some fears of failure that I made appointment this morning with Goodbird to proceed with me to

WOLF CHIEF'S EARTH LODGE
Collected by Gilbert Wilson, 1908
MHS photo III-33
Wolf Chief used this earth lodge, built about 1900, to keep the Waterbuster clan shrine (Wilson 1907c:7). By 1906 it was in poor repair. Gilbert Wilson stood inside in the light from the smoke hole.

Wolf Chief's house and open negotiation for the sale of the shrine and medicine bag. . . .

"A gentle rain was falling as we went into Wolf Chief's cabin. We found him sitting looking at the painting of the shrine which my brother made & which I had delivered but a day or two before. I began speaking thru Goodbird as interpreter.

"'You will remember a year ago that I spoke to you about your selling the shrine and the medicine bag which is in the earth lodge. I tried to get the North Dakota Historical Society to buy them but I failed. Then I tried in other places, for I did not want the shrine and its story to be lost. At last only a week or two before I left Minneapolis a man wrote me from New York. He is wealthy and is interested in the Indians. He told me to buy the shrine if I could – so I came up to see you. If you will sell and will name a price, if it is within my means I will buy it now; if not then I will write to the man in New York and tell him what you want for the shrine and ask him if he wants to buy. The man's name is Mr. [George] Heye. He is going to build a big house with fine floors and windows where Indian things can be kept and shown and where they can't be destroyed by fire or moths.'

"Wolf Chief looked very grave.

"'While all that Mr. Wilson says is true,' he answered, addressing Goodbird, 'since I saw him last year I have been changing my mind. While I believe in one God and pray to Him yet these things were my father's and I like to keep them in honor of him. I have thought I would maybe roof over the earth lodge again & make it strong and dry. . . .'

"'I can quite understand,' I answered him, 'why you may wish to keep the things. But . . . you know that as late even as 50 years ago there were many white people who said it was of no use to try to teach the Indians anything, that the only good Indian was a dead Indian, and for us to pay out money to send schoolteachers among them would only be a waste of our means. . . . Then there arose some men who said, "Maybe the reason we haven't been able to civilize the Indian and get him to live in houses and plant farms is because we don't understand him. Let us send men who will make a study of his ways of living – find out what he thinks, how he elects his chiefs and how he looks on us. Perhaps the reason we are not able to make him understand us is because we do not understand him."

"'So for this reason learned men formed the Ethnological Bureau, and sent students to the different

Indian tribes to see what they could find. And everybody was astonished to find out how much more the Indian knew than we were aware and that his myths and beliefs and government and religion were all interesting.

"'Now this is why I am out here working among you Indians. Mr. Heye is not a trader. He does not do these things for money and neither do I. All I get for my buying is about half my expenses of my month on the Reservation. But I want to buy the shrine for Mr. Heye so he can put it in a big fireproof house where it will be safe and where people can come in to see it. And I want to get the story of the shrine and your picture and the story of your life and hang them up in a frame or else print them in a little book so that when white people see the shrine they can read the story and know what it all means. Then when their congressman at Washington votes for money to send teachers among the Indians they won't call him a fool but will say, "That is the right thing to do. I have seen the shrine and read what it means and those Indians can think and can tell real interesting stories. They are worth civilizing."'

"It was evident that Wolf Chief was impressed somewhat but I was hardly prepared for the honest confession of old belief which followed. He spoke:

"'Well maybe after all the *spirits* want to be taken to New York and be put into that big house where they will be kept nice and dry and not have to stay in the damp earth lodge. Perhaps it is the spirits which put it into Mr. Wilson's mind to come and ask to buy the shrine. Besides everything that Mr. Wilson promised has come true. He promised us pictures and other things last year and everything he said he would do he has done. . . . Then too I have not dreamed of my father for a long time until last night when I dreamed he came to me and told me I was going to get something today. Perhaps what I get is what Mr. Wilson will pay me.'

"I was hardly prepared to close the bargain without consulting Mr. Heye but asked, 'How much do you ask for them?'

"'I want a great deal of money. I want more than a hundred dollars! . . . But I want the money today. For if Mr. Wilson pays me today I will think it is what my father wishes me to do. But if he does not, I will think I ought to keep the things.'

"'That is right, Wolf Chief,' I answered. 'But [Mr. Heye] . . . would not want me to [buy it] until I had seen the shrine and seen everything is in order for that is the way white people do business. But that won't take long. We can go down to the lodge in a few moments and decide on the sale at once.'

"Meanwhile the rain had increased and it was evident that Wolf Chief was uneasy about something.

"'What you say is true,' he said, 'and I believe now in one true God and pray to Him, who is over all spirits. But the shrine was used mostly to get rain and I have seen it come true many many times. It is raining now. . . .'

"[I answered] 'I am sure I can give no disrespect to anything if I go down to the lodge with no wish to mock at the things. . . . I don't think any harm will come if I go down to the lodge with right motive.'

"This seemed to convince Wolf Chief, especially as the sun was now shining. We went down & as among the offerings on the shrine were two prime buffalo

robes I closed at once paying part down & the rest later in the evening. As I made final payment Wolf Chief said,

"'I am glad to get so much money today and I am glad I have sold the shrine for another thing. These were my father's medicines and altho I believe in one true God & pray to Him for I used to pray to these things and they did me no good, yet sometimes I get to thinking of old times and of these medicines. Perhaps now when they are gone I will not think of them so much'" (Wilson 1907c:6-14).

True to tradition, Wolf Chief passed on to Wilson the stories and instructions that went along with each item in the bundle, as he had heard his father tell them. But if he thought he could get the bundle off his mind by selling it, he was mistaken.

When the members of the Waterbuster clan heard

WOLF CHIEF IN ATTITUDE OF PRAYER
Photographed by Gilbert Wilson, 1907
MHS photo II-39
Among the traditions that Wolf Chief passed on to Wilson with the shrine were instructions on how to pray to it. Here he stood as one might have in praying for rain. The calico offerings were folded back to show the wrapped-up bundle.

that Wolf Chief had sold their birthright, they were outraged. He had had no right to sell it, they said, for it was the property of the clan, not of any individual keeper. They were anguished to think that, after all the generations the bundle had been kept and cared for, it now should lie on a museum shelf in a strange city amid people with no understanding and no respect for it.

Their distress reached the ears of officials in Washington, who suspended Wilson's permit to enter the reservation and launched an investigation. But throughout the storm Wolf Chief stood his ground. "Supt. Hoffmen received letters from Washington D.C. about the shrines or the skulls," he wrote Wilson in

1911, "so we have great talks but after all I am right [and] that is all settle now. You can come on reservation again and we do the best we can for you" (Meyer 1975:9-18; Wolf Chief 1911b).

Despite his undaunted attitude, it must have pained Wolf Chief to know of his neighbors' disapproval. As if he had a premonition of what was in store, he told Wilson in 1906 that "I want to be like Christian men and pray God & live right & lead them to church. But my people turn against me – still I keep doing for it is God's work" (Wilson 1906b:151). Yet he could not help having doubts. Shortly after he sold the bundle, he had several close brushes with lightning, and he remained afraid of it for the rest of his life. In 1911 his house and store burned, and he lost everything he owned (Bowers 1965:6; Wolf Chief 1911b). Members of his family did not regain their health. Of the numerous children he fathered, not a single one outlived him. It was as if he had tried once too often to outwit the forces around him.

"INTERIOR OF AN EARTH LODGE"
Painted by Frederick Wilson, 1906
Watercolor on paper. See color page 177
H. 23.4 cm, W. 26.5 cm
MHS
This painting of the Waterbuster clan shrine is one of two Frederick Wilson executed after his and his brother's visit in 1906. The other one was given to Wolf Chief. The bundle itself is not shown; it was placed on a shelf at the top of the wooden stand and covered by offerings of calico. The hat on the buffalo skull at the base was another offering. Beside the shrine stood a pole on which was hung the personal bundle that belonged to Wolf Chief's father, Small Ankle, and grandfather (Wilson 1907c:7). It also was covered by calico offerings. The painting was evidently done from the nearly identical photograph taken in 1906; Frederick added the drum and drumstick at right (Wilson [1903-18]:58).

INTERIOR OF WOLF CHIEF'S EARTH LODGE (DETAIL)
Photographed by Gilbert Wilson, 1906
MHS (Wilson [1903-18]:41)
The Waterbuster shrine stood in the left rear area of Wolf Chief's earth lodge, as it had in Small Ankle's when Wolf Chief was growing up. Among the duties he performed for it were keeping the area around it clean and covering it during rain (Meyer 1975:2). The pieces of calico on the earth lodge pillars are offerings.

200

Point Independance.
Fort Berthold reservation N.D
July 9, 1907.

Received of Mr. George
G. Heye, by Rev. G. L. Wilson
agent, One Hundred Sixty
$160.00/ Dollars, payment
in full for the shrine
containing two skulls and
my hereditary Medicine
Bag with all contents of
both. And I further promise
to give full information con-
cerning them and to tell
in full the stories connected
with each and to answer
all questions asked in ex-
planation of them by Mr.
Wilson while he remains
on the Reservation.
Henry Wolf chief

Attest-
Ed Goodbird.

As Wolf Chief signed above he said [thru in-
terpreter "I am glad to receive so much
money tonight and I am glad for
another thing. I believe in God and
pray to him but some times I
get to thinking of old things and these
are my father's medicines and
I get sometimes to thinking of him.
I think it is a good thing they are
taken away where I will see them no
more.

RECEIPT
Written by Gilbert Wilson and signed by Wolf Chief, 1907
Ink on lined notebook paper
H. 30 cm, W. 19 cm
MHS (Wilson 1907c:200)

Having no receipt forms available, Wilson wrote out this
makeshift receipt for the shrine in his diary. Wolf Chief signed
it and Goodbird was witness. Wilson later regretted getting
involved in the extensive controversy this purchase aroused
(Waterbuster Bundle Files 1909, 1935).

Copy

Elbowoods N.D.

R. Gilbert L. Wilson,

        Minneapolis Minn

Dear Brother.

        I received your two letters and was very glad to hear
from you. I lose lots of things in fire but my good peoples help
me out. they gave me more than what I lose. but it is gain. They
gave me as follows. 100 house logs
9 pony's $135.00 2 stoves 2 guns 1 trunks few dishes Pails corn
beans. calico (calico) I stay at Mr. Goodbird's. I stored right
along doing trade. I make more money than the other years. I am
sure my medicines are stronger than Prof. Libby medicine. The
Supt Hoffmen received letters from Washington D.C. about the shrines or the skulls so we have great talks but after all I am right
that is all settle now. You can come on reservation again and we do
the best we can for you. I understand a photograph of shrine will
next may.

        Yours Brother

            (signed) Henry Wolf Chief

Per
  Ed.

LETTER
Written by Wolf Chief, 1911
Typewritten copy. Purple carbon on paper
H. 28 cm, W. 21.5 cm
AMNH (Wolf Chief 1911b)

The American Museum of Natural History got embroiled in
the controversy surrounding the sale of the Waterbuster shrine
when Orin G. Libby, secretary of the State Historical Society
of North Dakota, charged publically that Wilson had
"induced" Wolf Chief to sell the bundle contents "for a
considerable sum of money, and he thereupon immediately
shipped them from the nearest railroad point and escaped
from the state before the other Indians of the [clan] could
intervene to prevent the loss of their most sacred possessions"
(Meyer 1975:11). Libby did not think, however, that the
bundle should be returned to the tribe, but rather that it
should go to his own museum, and he continued to agitate
to get it. In this letter Wolf Chief reports to Wilson on the
"great talks" that had occurred on the reservation, but says
wryly that "my medicines are stronger than Prof. Libby['s]
medicine."

Independence Day

Once a year, all across Fort Berthold Reservation, people set aside their worries and gathered for a celebration. It was the only occasion when the agent did not mind if people danced or sang to a drum or wore traditional costumes. It was the Fourth of July, the time to rejoice in independence (Meyer 1977:152).

In 1907 Goodbird and Wolf Chief went to celebrate the Fourth of July at the Mandan village across from Elbowoods on the south side of the Missouri River. It was a gala week-long gathering. Gilbert Wilson went along and took notes on everything he saw.

People had come from all over. They camped in

SINGERS
Photographed by Gilbert Wilson, 1908
MHS photo III-40

This double-exposed photograph was taken during the Fourth of July celebration at Elbowoods in 1908. Men were the principal singers, but not the only ones. Wilson noted that "In all the songs where women dance they join the chant in such a way that tho they all use the same tune an effect like harmony is produced." The songs were apparently a mixture of old and new, since some of the words referred to the rivalries of various dancing societies on the reservation (Wilson 1907b: 21, 42).

tents and tipis arranged in a circle around a large dance hall where most of the action took place. As at Like-a-Fishhook Village, events were announced by a crier. Each morning he roused the sleepers near sunrise. "The camp was soon a scene of action. Indian women were making fires and putting on kettles. The older men naked to clout and with a blanket wrapped about them were making their way to the river and women were going down to the watering place with their buckets" (Wilson 1907b:35).

Some mornings started with a church service for the Christians, but more often the schedule was relaxed until afternoon, when people participated in field sports, including foot and horse races. A lively round of the moccasin game drew a crowd one day. But when the dancing started at about 7:00 P.M., things got really lively (Wilson 1907b:38, 40, 41).

Music was provided by a bass drum and "nine young men who sang in a strong falsetto voice." The older men were "gorgeously dressed," and their faces were painted. Men's and women's dances alternated. Men's dances stressed symbolic pantomimes of achievements in war. In one, "the men imitated the charge on horse back against the enemy. Lashing their suppositious steeds with their dancing fans the while, the drums kept up a spirited undertone interrupted by hard but irregular beating as an imitation of gun shots." For the women's dance, people formed a circle around the dancing area: "The men formed one half the circle and the women the other half. They danced standing very close shoulder to shoulder, the women often in groups of four or more, lock armed. They circled to the left by a short jerky side step, the body dropping an inch or two on the right leg as the left foot was advanced two or three inches side wise for the step" (Wilson 1907b:18-20, 33).

As the evening wore on, another old tradition asserted itself. "About 10:30 P.M. gifts began to be made. Following old custom, the Indians made presents to visiting friends and societies. . . . The various givers came forward and made speeches, naming their gifts. Before the evening was over 20 horses had been given away. As each donor concluded his speech loud applause of 'Hau! hau!' were heard. Men and women vibrated palm over mouth to express pleasure or joy. Old women chanted and the warriors danced furiously to express their approbation" (Wilson 1907b:23-24).

As in former days, the gift exchanges often followed the lines of social organizations. In place of the old age-grade societies were dancing societies –

organizations that Goodbird compared to Democrats and Republicans among the whites. One group was called the Hot Thistles "because they talked bitterly and sharply about some other of the bands." The Wooden Faces got their name from their critics' inability to "shame them [any] more than we could wood." The Antelopes – a group of former Christians and "disgruntled members" of other dancing societies – were said to be of an indecisive nature, like their namesake animals who "run all over the country without any fixed home." A group of women formed the Tea Drinkers' Society (Wilson 1909a:141, 1907b:23, 33).

The dancing went on far into the night. At midnight people paused for a meal of fry bread and coffee. Some nights they kept on until 3:30 in the morning (Wilson 1907b:24, 43).

Although the form of the celebration followed Indian tradition, it was still as expressive of patriotism as any band concert, parade, or fireworks show in the towns that ringed the reservation. If any whites doubted the patriotism of the people of Fort Berthold, their doubts were laid to rest in the years that followed.

In the spring of 1917, people on the reservation learned that the United States had entered a European war. President Woodrow Wilson appealed to all citizens to contribute to the war effort – if they could not enlist, by buying Liberty Loan bonds and growing victory gardens. The reservation was galvanized into action.

Young men rushed to enlist, and volunteers from Fort Berthold were among the first American troops to arrive on the battlefields of France. In a single day, the Indians subscribed to more than $6,000 worth of Liberty Loan bonds, and an inspector boasted that "this is a larger amount than has been subscribed by full-blood Indians on any reservation in the country." Reservation land under cultivation doubled to over 11,000 acres in the year after President Wilson's plea to grow crops for freedom (Knight 1917:2, 3; Jermark 1918:20).

"It is believed there are no more loyal people," the agent reported proudly to Washington. "They have certainly taken the war to heart and made every effort to do their part. . . . They have been ready and willing at all times to donate to the Red Cross, Y.M.C.A. etc. In fact it has been necessary in certain cases to refuse gifts in order to prevent want on their part" (Jermark 1918:19).

The Hidatsa men who went to Europe found that warfare among the whites was very different from what their fathers and grandfathers had known. World War I was a war of new technologies. Battles were decided not so much by heroism and tactics as by terrible new weapons like mustard gas and airborne bombs. Back home, the agent struggled to explain to the older men. He drew diagrams to show where the different armies were located, and described "the different kinds of arms used, the part which the aeroplane and submarines are taking in the war, different modes of defense, as the trenches, wire entanglements, etc., all of which is in such great contrast to the kinds of warfare known to them in the early days" (Jermark 1918:19).

Wolf Chief did not like this new kind of war, where a man's spiritual strength did not stand for much against the mines and machine guns. He was not impressed by the agent's grandiose claims that the war was for "assisting the oppressed, establishing justice for all people and making the world a better place in which to live." To Wolf Chief, it sounded barbarous. "I know that a big war has now broken out in Europe and that many are being killed on both sides," he said. "What do they do when enemies have been killed? Do they rejoice as Indians did when an enemy was slain, or do they just get angry and act like wild beasts? This white man's war in Europe is absolutely wrong. In old times when we Indians went to war we fought tribes who were different in speech and customs. You white men fight those of like customs and speech. You fight men who speak the same language as yourselves. All that is wrong" (Jermark 1918:19; Wilson 1914b:194-95).

Whatever they may have thought about the whites' methods of war, the people of Fort Berthold showed no hesitation about honoring the new generation of soldiers, as they had once honored warriors who counted coup upon the enemy. "We were overwhelmed with requests for singing," said the agent, "or a small dance for various boys who enlisted, were drafted, or were going across." Recognizing the power of traditional ceremonies to express a new kind of patriotism, the agent relaxed the rules against dancing. Other barriers broke down as Indian and white soldiers fought side-by-side in Europe (Jermark 1919).

Although white Americans fought for freedom in Europe, it would be years before they would tolerate minority freedoms in their own country. To the Hidatsa, it did not seem strange to honor their country and its veterans in ways harmonious with their own culture. Wolf Chief also used the symbols of white society to express pride in his accomplishments and his country. He erected a flagpole in front of his cabin at Independence in order to fly the Stars and Stripes.

When Goodbird asked him why he flew the flag, he answered, "I have good meals to eat and I feel contented and happy, and I try to observe white customs, so I put that flag up in the air because I see that soldiers put a flag up in the air.

"My [clan] son once came to me and said, 'Wolf Chief, how is this? Are you a soldier?'

"I answered, 'Yes, I am a soldier. I am better than any white soldier'" (Wilson 1913a:153).

DANCE ARBOR, ELBOWOODS
Photographed by Gilbert Wilson, 1907
MHS photo I-55
The Fourth of July celebration at Elbowoods was large but subdued by the nearby presence of the agency. In 1907, the agent forbade any dancing after dark. Instead of using a dance hall, the people set up this shady, open-air booth to dance in. The central flagpole was decorated with a necklace of feathers (Wilson 1907b:35-36).

AMERICAN FLAG
Made by Theresa Erickson, 1907–12
Loosely woven wool strips sewn together
with double rows of machine
stitching
L. 150.5 cm, W. 87.5 cm
MHS 7946.1, Theresa Ericksen

The people of Fort Berthold appreciated the symbolism of the American flag and made it part of their celebrations, especially on the Fourth of July (MHS photos I-29, I-47, I-55, I-71, III-44). Today powwows often open with a flag ceremony that honors both the flag and the veterans entitled to carry it.

LIBERTY LOAN BOND POSTER
Printed by Edwards & Deutsch Litho Co., Chicago, c.
1918
Color lithograph on paper in black, white, yellow, and red
L. 74.5 cm, W. 50.5 cm
MHS poster collection

Government bonds were one method used to finance World War I. The people of Fort Berthold were enthusiastic subscribers, according to the agent: "There was purchased many thousand dollars of Liberty Bonds in the three loans, and it is pleasing to state that in each instance the quota was over-subscribed by adults and minors" (Jermark 1918:19).

As this poster shows, American propagandists vilified Germans – especially the Kaiser – throughout the war. In 1918 Wolf Chief dreamed he was on a war party that caught the Kaiser, whom he shot with a bow and arrow (Wilson 1918b:371). The Sioux at Fort Yates, however, suggested another punishment for the Kaiser: to be given an allotment and to be told, "Now you lazy bad man, you farm and make your living by farming, rain or no rain; and if you do not make your own living, don't come to the Agency whining when you have no food in your stomach and no money, but stay here on your farm and grow fat till you starve" (Robinson 1966:362).

HALT the HUN!

BUY U.S. GOVERNMENT BONDS
THIRD LIBERTY LOAN

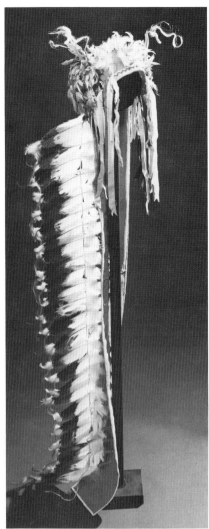

Eagle Wing Fan

Hidatsa style

*Collected by Frederick Wilson,
pre-1918?*

*Eagle wing containing seven long and
numerous short gray and white
feathers. Handle end wrapped in
tanned hide beaded in blue and
green, with fringe*

L. 61 cm, W. 14.2 cm

MHS 9598.1

The eagle was considered a sacred bird
with great powers. Buffalo Bird Woman
recalled that women never carried
feather fans: "Old men used fans of
eagle wings, young men fans made of
eagle tail feathers" (Wilson 1916b:190).
Gilbert Wilson described men using fans
while dancing in 1907, and he later
photographed men carrying ones similar
to this (Wilson 1907b:33; MHS photos
I-88, IV-37). Today such fans are
treasured family heirlooms.

Headdress

*Hidatsa. Made by Wolf Chief as a present for Sam, Gilbert Wilson's son
Collected by Gilbert Wilson, pre-1918?*

*Gray felt cap decorated with a brow band of loom-woven glass beads in zigzag
design; ermine fur strips; silk ribbons; owl feathers tipped with red- and
purple-dyed down; and clumps of yellow-dyed down. Two curved sections of
bison horn are tipped with yellow dyed horsehair, dyed feathers, and ermine
fur bound on with silk ribbon. Trail of red wool with canvas backing has 26
bald eagle tail feathers attached with rawhide and tipped with down and
orange dyed horsehair. See color page 174*

H. 172 cm, W. 48 cm across horns

MHS 9598.23A

This headdress is of the style worn for dances and other special occasions during the
early 20th century (Wilson [1903-18]:46, 63). Its modern materials mimic an older
style. Bonnets made with eagle feathers were very valuable; Buffalo Bird Woman said
that one was worth a horse at the time of her marriage (Wilson 1914b:323).
Accordingly, they were often given as gifts during dances.

In traditional Hidatsa society, successful warriors were allowed to decorate their
hair or a headdress with symbols of their exploits. These headdresses, once restricted
to the bravest men, eventually came into more general use, being worn during
society performances and dances. Wolf Chief said that "In old days only brave men
wore an eagle tail cap. If one killed an enemy wearing such a cap, when the man
danced he would raise his gun and cry, 'I killed a war bonnet wearer!'

"In very old times, as I understand, it was not our custom to wear war
bonnets in the dance. But in my time, when I was a young man, the custom had
come in pretty generally of wearing them in the dance.

"In very old times, when a man had worn a war bonnet in a battle, afterwards
when he danced he showed that war bonnet. But he would be shamed to carry a
war bonnet in the dance that he had not worn in battle.

"A war bonnet, however, was not itself an honor mark. But only very brave
men would wear it because all the enemies would be eager to kill the wearer, so that
they could afterwards say, 'I struck a good enemy – he wore an eagle tail cap.'

"I have never heard that in very old times the wearer of a war bonnet was
leader of a society, and that the feathers on the cap represented the collective honor
strikes of all the members of a society. You say a white man told you this; I never
heard of such a thing" (Wilson 1916b:31-32).

RATTLE

Northern Plains
Collected by Gilbert Wilson, pre-1918?
Carved animal hoofs dyed blue, attached by thong loops to a wooden stick covered
with tanned hide and beaded in white and green. Decorated on top end with
tin cones and blue-dyed feathers; on bottom end with a triangular hide tab,
fringed and beaded in lazy-stitched white, blue, brown, and pink glass seed
beads
L. 58.3 cm, W. 4.5 cm
MHS 7059.64b

Dancers shook rattles made by attaching deer dew claws or cut animal hoofs to a
stick. Ethnomusicologist Frances Densmore, working in the early 20th century,
observed such rattles in use among the Teton Sioux (Densmore 1918:329). The
Hidatsa had them as early as the 1830s (Bodmer 1984:319).

HEADDRESS

Mandan/Hidatsa style
Collected by Harold Case, post-1922
Naturally colored porcupine hair and
deer hair dyed green, pink, purple,
and red, wrapped and sewn around
a base of cotton (?) string. See color
page 174
L. 38 cm, W. 8.5 cm
University of Colorado Museum at
Boulder 33,231, Case

Roach headdresses of deer hair were
introduced to the Northern Plains along
with the Grass Dance. They were still
popular in dances at the turn of the
century (MHS photos I-44, I-47, I-62).
In the Grass Dance, they were worn
with feathers to indicate that the wearer
had struck an enemy; but later, young
men who had not been to war began to
wear them, too (Wilson 1914b:46-47).

TUG OF WAR
Photographed by Gilbert Wilson, 1916
MHS photo IX-29-1916
Gatherings of all kinds were the setting for athletic competitions. This one may have been at a Fourth of July celebration, an agricultural fair, or a rodeo.

MOCCASIN GAME
Photographed by Gilbert Wilson, 1907
MHS photo I-48

This photograph was taken just outside the dance hall on July 4, 1907. Two teams of men – one Hidatsa and one Arikara – were playing. "Originally the game was to hide a stone in a moccasin and make the other side guess which moccasin it was in," Wilson wrote. "Today the stone is held in the hand, two men passing it back and forth. . . . Each side was accompanied by three or four musicians and a drum. There were four players to a side and the sides took turns – tho apparently by some set rule – in hiding the pebble. While the players on one side hid the stone they contorted their bodies, threw out their arms or got up and danced, the drummers beating furiously and all chanting hai-yáh hai-yáh hai-yáh. The object of this was to confuse the other side – the latter remaining silent while their opponents chanted and played. Tally was kept by a number of white sticks in the middle – between the two rows of players. When all the sticks were won by one side they took the stakes. It was surprisingly exciting" (Wilson 1907b:41–42).

PACKS WOLF
Photographed by Gilbert Wilson, 1907
MHS photo I-97

In 1907, Packs Wolf celebrated Independence Day in an embroidered hide shirt of traditional Mandan / Hidatsa style and an eagle feather headdress. The two headdresses in his hands were probably gifts. The women with him were dressed in elk-tooth dresses with ribbon applique skirts, hair pipe breastplates, and shawls. They held paper fans. One of the two women was Nora Smith, Packs Wolf's wife.

WOMEN PLAYING BALL
Photographed by Gilbert Wilson, 1916
MHS photo IX-49-[1916]

Men and boys were not the only ones who played field sports. Here, women play "shinny," a traditional ball game played with sticks.

CHILDREN'S DANCE
Photographed by Gilbert Wilson, 1908
MHS photo III-44

At Elbowoods in 1908, the Fourth of July dance was held outside. These musicians knelt around the drum while a group of boys danced.

Drum and Drumstick

Mandan/Hidatsa style
Collected by Harold Case, post-1922
Drum frame made from hoop of wood.
Cover of rawhide nailed on under
side of rim and painted in brown,
gold, red, blue, and white. Handle
in back formed of two double
strands of string. Drumstick of
wood with head of tanned hide
gathered around stick with string.
See color page 165
Drum: D. 39.7 cm, W. 6.5 cm.
Stick: L. 24.4 cm
University of Colorado Museum at
Boulder 33,247a, b, Case

In 1907, drummers used three kinds of
drums: single-headed hand drums like
this; the large, native-made, double-
headed bass drums introduced by the
Grass Dance; and commercially made
bass drums. Wilson noted that "When
the men danced alone – the orchestra sat
over in a corner to the right of the door
as one entered. They used a large drum
of white man's make placed on the
ground. When the women's dance was
on a large native drum was brought in
. . . besides several of the smaller [hand
drums]" (Wilson 1907b:20). The
decoration of artifacts in patriotic motifs
like this was common at the turn of the
century. The design on this drum has
been partly worn away from use.

Shirt

Hidatsa. Used by Wolf Chief
Collected by Harold Case, post-1922
Tanned hide, hand sewn with thread,
with open sides, set-in sleeves (one
with an added cuff), and patches
in several places. Strips of blue,
red, white, and yellow lazy-stitched
glass seed beads on a canvas
backing sewn down the sleeves and
on front and back over the
shoulders. Tanned hide fringe
attached to canvas
L. 67.5 cm, W. 51 cm across
shoulders
University of Colorado Museum at
Boulder 32,972, Case

This shirt is constructed and decorated
in a traditional style, but beadwork on
canvas has replaced quilled strips, and
the old style of neck flap is missing
altogether. Wolf Chief may have used it
at powwows and dances toward the end
of his life.

WOLF CHIEF'S GRANDSON
Photographed by Gilbert Wilson, 1907
MHS photo II-70
The headdress being modeled here was used by the Tea
Drinkers' Society. The shirt and drum are traditional. All were
among the articles purchased by Wilson for George Heye
(Museum of the American Indian, Heye Foundation 1/3796,
3797, 3798).

MOTHER AND CHILD
Photographed by Gilbert Wilson, 1907
MHS photo I-82
At Fourth of July celebrations, parents dressed their children
in traditional clothing – sometimes elaborate and sometimes
casual. This little boy wore only a shirt and leggings.

Looking forward

As the 1920s grew near, Buffalo Bird Woman, Wolf Chief, and Goodbird looked to the future with different feelings.

Buffalo Bird Woman felt a poignant sense of regret about all she had lost. "I am an old woman now," she said. "The buffaloes and black-tail deer are gone, and our Indian ways are almost gone.

"But for me, I cannot forget our old ways.

"Often in summer I rise at daybreak and steal out to the cornfields; and as I hoe the corn I sing to it, as we did when I was young. No one cares for our corn songs now" (Maxidiwiac 1921:175).

Wolf Chief, isolated by his own actions from the culture of his childhood, spent the rest of his days in his cabin on the hill, where the steeple of the Christian church cast a long shadow over his yard at sunset (Hall 1929:12). But he still had his old fighting spirit. "My people often talk against me & laugh & say 'That man wants to be a white man.' . . . [But] I want to be strong & go forward. . . .

"I belong to [the Prairie] Chicken [clan]. In old times I fight in war. Now war is over, but another war is on. I try to fight evil, but try to change & learn to read and do white ways so you see the Chicken [clan] spirit is not over" (Wilson 1907c:87, 1908b:87).

Goodbird, who had found contentment in his own blend of Christian and Hidatsa values, was known by his neighbors as a truly kind-hearted man. "I think God made all peoples to help one another," he said. "We Indians have helped you white people. All over this country are corn fields; we Indians gave you the seeds for your corn, and we gave you squashes and beans. . . . We Indians think you are but paying us back, when you give us schools and books, and teach us the new way.

"For myself, my family and I own four thousand acres of land; and we have money coming to us from the government. I own cattle and horses. I can read English, and my children are in school. . . .

"I am not afraid" (Goodbird 1914a:73-74).

BUFFALO BIRD WOMAN AND SON OF A STAR
Photographed by Gilbert Wilson, 1906
MHS (Wilson [1903–18]:65)

WOLF CHIEF AND WIFE
Collected by Charles Hall, c. 1920
SHSND, Hall Collection

GOODBIRD AND SON
Photographed by Gilbert Wilson, 1916
MHS photo VIII-30-1916

Afterwards

The village of Independence no longer exists. Its disappearance marked yet another change that awaited the Mandan, Hidatsa, and Arikara in the 20th century – a change more difficult and devastating than any that had come before. Smallpox and allotment they had faced and weathered. Still ahead was the Army Corps of Engineers.*

In the 1950s a huge dam, constructed near Garrison, N.Dak., flooded virtually all the usable land on the Fort Berthold Reservation, including the farms, communities, churches, and schools the Three Tribes had built up over the previous 70 years. Today Buffalo Bird Woman's corn fields and the Independence churchyard lie at the bottom of Lake Sakakawea. Only the tip of Independence Hill still pushes above the waters, and when the lake is low the ruined foundations of Wolf Chief's store can still be seen.

Buffalo Bird Woman, Wolf Chief, and Goodbird were to know nothing of what lay in store for their people. Buffalo Bird Woman lived into the 1920s. Old people today, who were children then, still speak of her in grave, respectful tones. Wolf Chief continued writing letters until his death in 1934. His last letter to Washington described the drought of the dust bowl years to the commissioner of Indian affairs under President Franklin D. Roosevelt (Wolf Chief 1931). Goodbird died in 1938, leaving a large family (Case 1938). His children and grandchildren still live on Fort Berthold Reservation. Gilbert Wilson died in 1930 with a Ph.D. in anthropology but no job in the field. Like Wolf Chief, he had no children who survived him (*St. Paul Pioneer Press 1930)*.

Although Independence is physically gone, it is still present in the memories and stories of those who grew up there. The children and grandchildren of those who lived through the difficult years of allotment now view those days as happy times.

"I was born and raised in the Independence community," said Anson Baker, now of New Town. "It was a very close-knit community – families were self-sufficient, industrious, and loyal to one another and trusting. . . . The members of the community in Independence had their own livestock association. They'd work their own farms and ranches, they raised money to have their own community tractor, their threshing machine, their annual branding. . . . We had a close community network there. In social functions, all of it was designed around our customs. It was not taken out of any textbooks. They

lived close to nature, clanship responsibilities, in other words the people lived much according to their tradition. . . . They never left anybody hungry in the community; they always took care of each others' basic needs" (A. Baker 1985).

"In those days it was very difficult for us here in Independence," said Mercy Walker. "We were isolated and far away from the nearest trading post. We did not have money in those days – we depended entirely on products from our gardens. We had large gardens and we gathered fruit such as chokecherries, Juneberries, and we often dug raw turnips and dried them. . . . It was well over a mile I had to walk to school. I remember the days when the older girls at the school used to do the cooking and it seems I remember eating corn bread a lot. That was our main menu, corn bread. . . . In them years we weren't taught very much except to cook and sew and things like this – household work" (Walker 1978).

By the 1930s, many of the agent's oppressive powers over Indian life had faded. Franklin D. Roosevelt's administration turned federal Indian policy away from the assimilationist approach it had taken for decades. The Indian Reorganization Act of 1934 abolished allotment, which had caused the loss of so much Indian land and lifestyle. It also provided for a degree of tribal self-government. Indians were allowed to adopt constitutions and elect representatives to a tribal council along the lines of a Euro-American democracy. Some people opposed this system, because it ran counter to traditional political structures; but the people of Fort Berthold Reservation took advantage of it. In 1936 they officially organized themselves as a political entity – the Three Affiliated Tribes of the Fort Berthold Indian Reservation. Benjamin Goodbird, Edward's son, was vice-chair of the first tribal council (Meyer 1977:194-96).

Another aspect of the about-face of government policy in the 1930s was a pulling back from the attempt to stamp out Indian languages and customs. Throughout the nation, there was interest in defining and revitalizing American craft, art, and cultural traditions, and the government led the way. Indian Office employees were instructed to encourage expressions of tribal culture – within certain limits. The moment the Hidatsa felt free to speak of their heritage again, their minds turned toward the Waterbuster Bundle.

Wolf Chief had died in the midst of one of the worst droughts ever recorded in the western United States. Almost immediately after his death, the

*This essay is based on research performed by Ann Kubes.

Waterbuster clan petitioned the Museum of the American Indian to return the sacred bundle, citing the obvious imbalance of natural forces in the west. At first the museum was reluctant, but the Bureau of Indian Affairs supported the clan's request. In 1938 three Waterbuster representatives traveled to New York to take back the bundle. The highly publicized case was one of the first successful repatriations of Indian sacred objects. Abundant rainfall returned the first summer the bundle was back on the reservation (Meyer 1977:206-8; Waterbuster Clan Bundle Files). Today the bundle remains in the hands of the clan.

"During that Depression, somehow we had plenty to eat," said Cora Baker, who grew up at Lucky Mound and Independence. "Everybody had cattle, maybe not too many, but everybody had cattle. And they had pigs, chickens, turkeys, everything. And we had our gardens" (C. Baker 1984). Also helping people through the Depression was a favorable judgment in a land claims case. In 1930 the Three Tribes were compensated for the 1871 and 1880 reductions in the reservation, providing members with more than $1,000 apiece in reparation (Meyer 1977:188). In addition, the Civilian Conservation Corps and other works projects improved roads and schools and built some modest irrigation projects.

By the early 1940s the problem was not too little water, but too much. The cities, towns, and farms on the Missouri bottomlands downstream from the reservation experienced floods in those years, and there was pressure on the government to do something about it. People looked to the example of the Tennessee Valley Authority and other huge new water projects that created jobs and power – and wreaked ecological havoc – elsewhere in the nation's river systems.

The Garrison Dam was conceived in 90 days of planning by Col. Lewis A. Pick of the U.S. Army Corps of Engineers. Other government agencies judged

SITE OF LIKE-A-FISHHOOK VILLAGE WITH RISING WATERS OF LAKE SAKAKAWEA
Photographed by Alan R. Woolworth, July 7, 1954
SHSND 32ML/2
In 1954 the waters of the Missouri River, held back by the new Garrison Dam, began to fill the valley and cover the site of Like-a-Fishhook Village. Before the flood, the site was partially excavated by archaeologists from the State Historical Society of North Dakota and the Missouri River Basin Project of the Smithsonian Institution (Smith 1972). This view is to the west.

it to be unnecessary. W. Glenn Sloan, who had drawn up a water control program in the area for the U.S. Bureau of Reclamation (and whose name was later to be attached to Pick's in the bill that authorized the dam), argued that the massive project served no useful purpose. The Bureau of Indian Affairs suspected that the site had been selected mainly because "a large proportion of the inundated area would be comprised of Indian lands." Nevertheless, in 1944 Congress funded both Pick's and Sloan's plans in one massive appropriation (Meyer 1977: 211–12).

To the Three Tribes, the passage of the dam bill seemed like a farce. "Right after World War II, the Corps was a big, big autonomous federal agency," said Anson Baker. "They had all of this manpower, they built the Burma Road over in China, and they had all these engineers with nothing to do, so some bureaucrat in Washington said, 'How about this Pick-Sloan Plan?' . . . Nobody really told anybody, you could just see how these guys planned in Washington" (Baker 1985).

The Indians raised the only effective opposition to the plan at the time. A year before passage of the bill, the Fort Berthold tribal council recorded its formal opposition to the dam. Council members later sent delegations, drew up petitions, and testified before Congress. They offered an alternate dam site that would flood less of the reservation. "We have permanently located on these lands," they said in a memorial to Congress. "Our forefathers also have lived on these grounds and it is the hopes and plans to have our children and their children to occupy this land continually forever; and money or exchange for other land will not compensate us." True to this principle, they refused to consider an offer of alternate land below the dam. After many delays, Congress made a take-it-or-leave-it offer: $5,105,625 or nothing. In an emotion-packed meeting in 1948, the tribal council agreed to take the money. Chairman George Gillette said, "Our Treaty of Fort Laramie, made in 1851 and our tribal constitution are being torn into shreds by this contract" (Meyer 1977: 212–17).

The ordinary people on the reservation knew much less of what was happening than the tribal council. They reactioned with disbelief. "I was fifteen years old living on the Little Missouri River bottomlands ranch that my father, John Fredericks, had built when I first became aware of the pending dam," said Kenneth Fredericks. "At that time it seemed totally impossible that a dam so far away could flood all the beautiful bottoms the Little Missouri created. . . . I was in the U.S. Air Force serving in Germany when I

received a large envelope from the War Department. . . . I opened the envelope and in it was a form letter with several forms filled out with a description of my land and a price of $2600 they had appraised for the sixty-six and two-thirds acres of farm land and they had also noted this included minerals and coal.

"After review of the documents I tore them in half and pitched them in the wastebasket. My roommate was awed by my action but I reassured him saying they are trying to steal from me what we are supposed to be protecting – my homeland. . . .

"About two months later I received another large envelope this time accompanied by a letter from my mother who said that the chief clerk at the agency said I should accept the offer the Corps of Engineers was making for the land. My mother further stated that the proceeds of their flood payment was being held up and they needed funds to start relocating the ranch to higher ground. . . . I signed the papers and sent them back" (JTAC 1986a: 135–36).

"Why is it that such a thing happened?" asked Louella Young Bear at a 1986 government hearing to determine whether the tribes had been sufficiently compensated for the disruption caused by the dam. "When I want to sell my land today there is a big law that says no Indian land can be sold, not yours. You have to call Washington, D.C. You have to call Aberdeen to get your okay first. What are you going to use it for? All these things are said to me.

"Why is it that these Army engineers came right in here and did such a thing to us? . . . This land was not sold. If the Army engineers say that they bought this land they didn't buy it. They condemned it. . . . When you condemn something you throw it away. You don't do anything with it" (JTAC 1986a: 194–95).

The dam was to flood 156,000 acres of the reservation – all of it the wooded bottomland and bench lands where 90% of the tribal population lived. The land was heavily used for agriculture and grazing by the 1940s, and all of the reservation villages with their attendant facilities were located there. The land left over would be the high, arid range land. Its potential for agriculture was unknown at the time, as soil studies had never been performed (JTAC 1986a: 8–11). Members of the Three Tribes saw it as "a treeless, farmless, waterless foreign land" (JTAC 1986a: 26).

The relocation of the people of Fort Berthold proceeded slowly between 1951 and 1954, even as the dam was being completed. "It was a sad day for everyone, especially the older people," said Myra Snow. "Some of the old Indians didn't want to move. They wanted to just go with the water and get drowned" (JTAC 1986a:120).

"We were about the first to move out of that valley, I think," said Cora Baker. "We had no choice, I guess. Just like a gopher, you know, when [they] pour water in your house you better get out or drown. That's how it was. It was very hard leaving the place" (Baker 1984).

"I remember the water was already rising when we were still refusing to move and take any kind of money, compensation, for our homeland," said Adam Mandan. "Even we kids knew that. Our council members tried very hard to salvage what they could because the dam was already going on at Riverdale and the people had the choice to take whatever compensation was offered [and] move or to stay and drown" (JTAC 1986a:91).

The reservation was changed drastically by the flood. Where creeks had been, huge arms of the lake now formed, dividing the land into five isolated segments. Homes were scattered even more widely than during allotment. School districts were reshuffled. The timber resources were gone, as were many of the natural coal outcroppings where the people had mined fuel. The upland proved not only poor for agriculture, but difficult for ranching as well: "Where we got along real well with about one-half ton of riverbottom hay, we found that we needed two tons of upland hay as well as manmade shelter to winter [each cow]. The horses, which fended for themselves in the bottomlands, now required feed and shelter also. Our fuel supply of coal and wood no longer existed so we were compelled to resort to fuel oil and propane for heating and cooking, and this meant new dollar costs that had to come out of ranch production" (JTAC 1986a:138). While the dam produced thousands of kilowatts of hydroelectric power, energy costs paradoxically soared.

Another $7,000,000 appropriated by Congress to compensate reservation residents did not reach far enough to replace all the facilities destroyed by the flood, and there were deep divisions in the tribe over how the money was to be spent (Meyer 1977:229-33). Reservation residents have not forgotten what they have lost: their community hospital, the bridge that united the two shores at Elbowoods, and the many religious and burial sites in the valley. A sense of loss, anger, and regret pervades the reservation.

"I would like to address the things that cannot be measured statistically by the taking act," testified Dani Sue Deane at recent government hearings. "A self-sufficient supporting society changed radically. The

economic heartland was taken away leaving deeper poverty, social dysfunction, further complicated by separating the communities. This separation caused a breakdown of families, communities, clan culture, tribal government and left many feeling totally defeated. Our self-confidence was shattered" (JTAC 1986a:15).

"We should really be used to these broken promises," said Carl Whitman, who served as tribal chair through some of those difficult years, "but it seems like each broken promise never loses its punch. . . . In the cultural-anthropological field sociologists have concluded that when you impose a change on any group of people there are three consequences that occur. One is hostility, one is apathy and the other is self-destruction. These are good theories. They have all come to pass. I have witnessed these" (JTAC 1986a:45, 47).

"It sure hurted us because when we moved up here nothing is the same," said Florence White. "I guess we are going the white man's way. Before we used to just go to anybody's home, just visit, and now you have to knock on the door and somebody peeps through that little hole and says who is there. If they

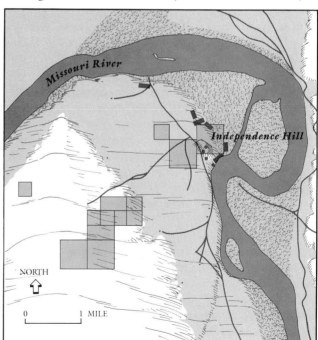

INDEPENDENCE, 1980s
Based on United States Geological Survey maps for New Town SE and Saddle Butte Quadrangles, North Dakota 7.5 Minute Series (Topographic), 1967, 1970
The shaded area is covered by the waters of Lake Sakakawea today.

don't want you to come in, why, they won't answer your knock. . . . These are some of things I wanted to bring up because that dam is sure hurting us, that damn dam" (JTAC 1986a: 189).

"Today the welfare and unemployment rate among the people of the reservation is among the highest in the nation," said Evadne Baker Gillette. "The environmentalists have raised a huge uproar about damaging the ducks and migration areas. What about the Indian people? Who speaks for the negative effects on the Indian people while everyone is worrying about the ducks? . . . Maybe we should send a duck to Congress this month. If the duck can get Congress to take a hard look at the effects on his habitat maybe we can hire him to get us a better place to live" (JTAC 1986a: 51-52, 56).

"I tell my grandchildren about how we used to live on the reservation at Independence," said Bernice Three Irons. "Not too long ago, they came back, and said, 'Grandma, we need some pennies.' I said, 'For what?' . . . 'For the lady.' I said, 'What lady?' They said, 'The Statue of Liberty.' I said, 'What has that ever done for us Indian people?' And I sat and thought to myself, you know, we have lost a lot of shrines and a lot of historical places on this reservation by that water. Did they ever think of restoring anything for us? Did they pay us for anything that we lost down there?" (JTAC 1986b: 35).

"Because of my age I can only listen to the stories of my mother, father and other older relatives when they tell me about the area," said Gerard Baker. "Today I can only go to Independence Point, look over the thousand acres of feet of water and try to imagine what it was like. My thoughts are usually interrupted by speedboats, pleasure boats and fishermen who are usually non-Indian enjoying the lake, not knowing or caring about the history that lay underneath the waters. . . .

"I know the older people feel cheated because of the dam and the flooding of the valley. I, too, feel cheated also when I see the lake and every time I drive across the dam at Pick City. I also feel cheated when I see the roads to my relatives' homes or when I hear about some older person getting sick and not being able to go to a medical facility because it's too far from the reservation or too expensive to get there. . . .

"I guess to steal a phrase from the treaties we will be concerned about these things as long as the grass grows and the water flows" (JTAC 1986a: 27-29).

The history of the Three Tribes has moved in cycles of disruption and stability for two hundred years. On Fort Berthold Reservation today, there is both a sense of past tragedy and a determination not to give in. "It seems that when we Indians progress to a point where we can be self-sustaining they move us again," said Adam Mandan. "The non-Indians seem to think we are lazy and don't want to work, but it comes right back to the fact that when we do learn to cope with a different style of living into which we are forced, they change it again. . . . The needs of the tribe are great but the tribal people can make it even up here in the harsh hilltops given a fair chance. Our homeland can never be replaced and what we lost can never be regained, but we want to make a new start. We did it before and we can do it again" (JTAC 1986a: 100-1).

When people speak of the next generation, the tone is hopeful. "I believe we are in the process of healing," said Catherine Fox Harmon. "My sons, both teenagers, are encouraged by myself to return to their land and people. . . . My objective now is to plan for my children and my grandchildren. They in turn will continue to negotiate the return of our lands" (JTAC 1986a: 78).

"Today," said Hazel Blake, "our only tradition that we're carrying is that dancing ceremony. If you come to these celebrations, you'll see all our young boys and girls with their feathers on. They are proud. They are proud to be Indians. And they are proud to be wearing the eagle feather. And to us, that is very sacred" (JTAC 1986b: 29).

"I'm sure all of us sitting here, we have been in jams," said Anson Baker. "We have pulled ourselves together and a couple of months later [said], 'How did I get out of that?' And you can look back and somewhere you stopped and prayed and you humbled yourself and you *found* a way. . . .

"I am proud of the people from this area here to live and be productive and still stand tall with what they went through. . . . You can't operate independently, you know. . . . We always had a saying in our language, Hidatsa. . . . You could translate [it] to English words, 'People determine your destiny.' And what that there is saying to us is, 'You treat people right, they'll treat you right, they'll take care of you. They're the ones who make or break you.' . . . I have got a lot of faith in the human race. Try to tell that to your kids. It's hard, but you got to keep repeating it. That's an old saying, you know. Keep talking, keep talking because some day down the line, even when you are not there, something is going to come up, and that child or grandkid will say, 'Jeez, I remember, I heard this before somewhere.' It will ring some bells" (Baker 1985).

THE HIDATSA WORLD

The Hidatsa World

Gilbert Wilson was neither the first nor the last scholar to be fascinated with the Mandan, Hidatsa, and Arikara Indians. From David Thompson to George Catlin to Karl Bodmer to Alfred Bowers, the Three Tribes have held a mysterious fascination for the fur traders, artists, explorers, ethnologists, and archaeologists who came across them. The work of these white observers in turn needs to be seen against the background of a much older oral and pictographic record, through which the Three Tribes understood and recorded their own history and relations to the forces around them.

The lives of Buffalo Bird Woman and her family cover only a short segment of the long history of their tribe. The Hidatsa's relationship to their land and each other changed many times over the 200 years of their recorded history – and the centuries before. The essays in this section give a deeper perspective on a people with a rich history and a vital present.

Why is it that the Hidatsa, Mandan, and Arikara have attracted such devoted study over the years? A present-day Hidatsa elder, Anson Baker, asked the same question in talking with the authors of this book: "I try to tell why, why, why things [are] so focused on Indian reservations, Indian people [and] their ways, why are we looked at all the time by microscope? Is it because we are unique? I really don't think it is. I think it is [because] way back when I don't know when, our forefathers, or elders beyond elders, had an insight into this universe in a manner that if you took care of that universe it would take care of you, and some of these mystic things that blow the mind out of the anthropologist and the sociologist, and that's what they are really trying to uncover, I think: how did the Indians, or our people, use those mystic powers?

"You know," he added, "when they say we are losing our tradition, I don't believe we are. . . . It gets back to this, when you take something just take enough; don't get greedy and waste it. . . . Do in your own mind what you think is right and, you know, . . . you can still continue to do these wonderful things" (Baker 1985).

T HE MISSOURI RIVER NEAR FORT CLARK, N.DAK.
Photographed by Sheldon Green, 1986
MHS

Origins and settlements of the Hidatsa

W. Raymond Wood

For nearly a millennium before the arrival of Euro-Americans, Native Americans living in the Northern Plains followed two contrastive ways of life. The Mandan, Hidatsa, and Arikara were hunters and gardeners who occupied settled villages in the Missouri Valley; the Sioux, Assiniboin, Crow, and other nomadic groups lived in tipis and hunted bison on the High Plains.

About 1780, at the beginning of the historic period, the Mandan and Hidatsa lived along the Missouri River in what is now west-central North Dakota. The two tribes were usually on good terms with one another; both were Siouan speakers, although their languages were not mutually intelligible. The traditional homeland of the Mandan was in the vicinity of the mouth of the Heart River, near present Bismarck, while the Hidatsa lived about sixty miles above them, near the junction of the Knife and Missouri rivers (see maps p. ix, 7). After the smallpox epidemic of 1781 the Mandan moved upriver to live near the Hidatsa, because their numbers had been so reduced they were no longer able to defend their villages. Farther downriver, near the mouth of the Grand River, lived a third group of village Indians, the Arikara. Although they spoke a different language (they were related to the Pawnee of Nebraska), their villages and general way of life were much the same as those of the Mandan and Hidatsa.

Members of the three tribes occupied substantial earth-covered lodges clustered in villages of several hundred to more than a thousand individuals. These stable communities were perched on the rims of terraces overlooking the Missouri River floodplain. In the lowlands the Indians grew corn, beans, squash, and sunflowers and hunted white-tailed deer and other woodland animals. Behind their villages were the river bluffs that separated the valley from the rolling, upland plains, where they hunted pronghorn and the massive herds of bison.

Numerous travelers and artists have left us rich accounts of what life was like in these villages. The fur trader Alexander Henry, the younger, visiting the Mandan and Hidatsa in the summer of 1805, left a vivid word-picture of the villages and their environs: "These villages at a distance appear like a cluster of molehills or muskrat cabins. The nearly circular huts are placed very irregularly; some so close to each other as scarcely to leave a foot-passage, others again at a distance of 20 to 30 feet apart. . . . [The road between the villages is] very pleasant, running through an open level country, with corn-fields in sight, in which were numbers of people at work; beyond them we saw several hundred horses, feeding upon the hills and along the banks of Knife river" (Henry and Thompson 1897, 1:337-38, 345).

The lifeway of these sedentary agricultural peoples contrasts sharply with that of their nomadic neighbors. These tipi-dwelling, horse-mounted, bison-hunting nomads have been so celebrated in literature and motion pictures that they serve as a stereotype not only for Plains Indians, but for American Indians in general. Yet their culture was neither more colorful nor more romantic than that of the village Indians, and the nomads lacked the architectural and agricultural traditions of their more settled neighbors. Although they grew no corn, they were quite fond of it and traded with the villagers to obtain the grain. This is revealed in the sign language symbol for the Hidatsa: "The left hand is lightly clenched," Wolf Chief told Gilbert Wilson, "with the thumb lying outside the palm and lightly upon the fore finger. The thumb now represents an ear of corn. With the thumb of the right hand make motion as of shelling the ear. The meaning is 'Corn shelling people'; for the other tribes of the prairies were not corn raising people as we have always been. If these tribes wanted corn they came to us to buy it and so we were thus called in the sign language, 'Corn people'" (Wilson 1909a:16; Wood 1986:94).

Although there were well-established trading relations between the villagers and the nomads, the normal state of affairs between the two groups was one of conflict. It was not possible for a young man to rise to a position of prominence in Plains Indian culture unless he had first attained military honors. To fulfill their ambitions, young men conducted raids and horse-stealing expeditions against other tribes – raids that consistently strained intertribal relations, sometimes resulting in short but intensive wars. The Sioux were the most persistent of their enemies, and their attacks against the villagers became so severe in historic times that they were "classed with the smallpox, the drought, and the grasshopper, as one of the great plagues of existence" by the villagers (Will and Hyde 1917:45).

When Euro-Americans first visited them in the 1780s, the Hidatsa Indians were clustered in three separate earth lodge villages (now known to archaeologists as Big Hidatsa, Sakakawea, and Amahami) near the confluence of the Knife and Missouri rivers. The residents of these villages consisted of three closely related subgroups: the Hidatsa-proper, the Awatixa, and the Awaxawi. The three villages shared a common culture and one language (Bowers 1965:2, 77). Although the residents thought of themselves as distinct from other tribes in the Northern Plains, there was no common name for them before the arrival of Euro-Americans. The three must, however, be considered as separate groups, for their histories, traditions, and customs differ and, before their way of life disintegrated under the impact of Euro-American culture, residents normally married within the village, so that each village group was a distinctive cultural unit. In 1845, after a major smallpox epidemic, the three Hidatsa subgroups moved up the Missouri River and founded Like-a-Fishhook Village. This was to be their last native village before being allotted land on the Fort Berthold Reservation.

Early travelers and scientists agreed unanimously that there were significant differences in the dialects of the three Hidatsa villages. Buffalo Bird Woman said the dialects of the three subgroups "differed a little· bit and there is a story that quarrels sometimes arose through

misunderstanding of one another's language" (Wilson 1913a:194). Another related dialect was spoken by the River and Mountain Crow Indians, who split away from the Hidatsa-proper and Awatixa, respectively, in late prehistoric times and moved into central and western Montana (Lowie 1935:3; Wood and Downer 1977).

The lifeways of the three Hidatsa villages were relatively uniform, so that without written documentation it is impossible to identify any given village as having been occupied by one or another of the subgroups. The architecture and layout of their villages were much the same and, except for rare artifacts, the tools and weapons they made were virtually indistinguishable from village to village. Furthermore, the Hidatsa were so intimately involved with the Mandan for so long that it is usually not possible to differentiate – at least on the basis of archaeological data alone – between Mandan and Hidatsa communities. Very early references to the Mandan, in fact, usually also tacitly included the Hidatsa as well.

BIG HIDATSA VILLAGE SITE
c. 1968
North Dakota State Highway Department
The village at Big Hidatsa was known to its occupants as Hidatsa. This view looks to the northeast; the band of trees marks the terrace above the Missouri River floodplain, which is visible in the background. Snow highlights the remains of the lodges.

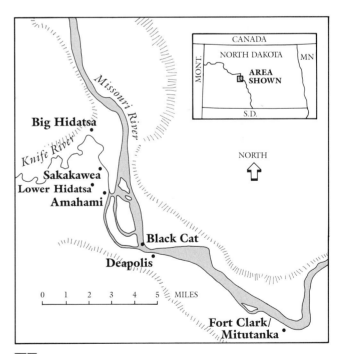

KNIFE RIVER VILLAGE SITES
(Based on Wood and Thiessen 1985)
Archaeologists have located sites of most of these Hidatsa and Mandan villages at Knife River. The remains of Black Cat village have never been found and were probably washed away by the Missouri River.

George Catlin exaggerated the relationship between the two tribes when he said that the Hidatsa's close association with the Mandan had led to "the complete adoption of most of their customs" (1841, 1:186). In spite of the long history of interaction between the two tribes, the Hidatsa clearly have not lost their own culture, although anthropologist Alfred W. Bowers argues that the Mandan dominated the two-way exchange between the two groups (1965:489).

Like all other American Indian groups, the Hidatsa suffered terribly from European diseases from which they had no natural immunity. Their population before the first outbreaks is a matter only for speculation, although it has been estimated at 4,000 to 5,500 (Bowers 1965:486; Lehmer 1977:107). The Hidatsa were undoubtedly subjected to several severe epidemics even before 1781, when smallpox sharply reduced their population, according to native testimony. By 1804 only about 2,700 Hidatsa remained (Lewis and Clark 1904-05, 6:90-91).

The three Hidatsa communities of the late 1700s survive today as archaeological sites (see map p. 323). The Hidatsa-proper occupied Big Hidatsa, the Awatixa lived at Sakakawea, and the Awaxawi were residents of Amahami, all of which were near the mouth of the Knife River. Big Hidatsa and Sakakawea villages are now preserved within the National Park Service's Knife River Indian Villages National Historic Site, but Amahami has been nearly destroyed by construction within the town of Stanton. A few miles downriver were two Mandan villages, Deapolis and Black Cat, built after the Mandan abandoned their villages at the mouth of Heart River. Both villages have since vanished; Deapolis was destroyed by the construction of a power plant, and Black Cat was washed away by the Missouri River. These three Hidatsa and two Mandan communities were collectively known as "The Five Villages."

Although we do not know when the villages were established, it is possible that most of them were occupied by 1787 (Nasatir 1952, 2:492-93). By 1798 two separate travelers – John Thomas Evans, working for Spanish traders in St. Louis, and David Thompson, an employee of the British North West Company – had mapped and described the exact locations of each of the five villages (Wood 1983:pls. 3d and 7). Lewis and Clark also visited and mapped the villages in the winter of 1804-05, when their expedition was encamped at Fort Mandan, a few miles below the mouth of the Knife River (Moulton 1983:map 29).

Hidatsa origin traditions

The origins and migrations of the Hidatsa people can be studied in their oral traditions and in the remains of their many villages. Euro-American travelers and scientists have collected traditional accounts of Hidatsa origins from native informants for nearly two hundred years. These stories vary somewhat in detail, but, as Bowers comments, "these apparent contradictions tend to disappear if one examines each village group as an independent social unit" (1965:476).

Our present rudimentary understanding of Hidatsa and Crow archaeology in present-day North Dakota and Montana adds more pieces to the puzzle. Archaeological work was carried out from 1976 to 1983 at Big Hidatsa, Sakakawea, Lower Hidatsa, and other sites within the Knife River Indian Villages National Historic Site, as well as at several other nearby sites that are believed to be of Hidatsa origin. The studies necessary to document the relationships among these sites, however, have yet to be made on the pottery, trade goods, and other tools and weapons from these excavations. There is, nevertheless, a high degree of over-all consistency between the oral traditions and the archaeological remains.

Two of the Hidatsa subgroups, the Awaxawi and the Hidatsa-proper, believe they came to the Missouri Valley from what is now eastern North Dakota. Some early historic sites on the James River near Jamestown, North Dakota, date to the late 1700s and appear to be the best candidates for such ancestral homes, but their relationship with the Missouri Valley communities has yet to be clarified (Wheeler 1963:212, 229). The Awatixa subgroup, on the other hand, claims to have lived always on the Missouri River.

The fur trader David Thompson was the first white man to collect information on Hidatsa origins. Thompson's sketchy account was based on information he obtained in 1797-98 from a French trader named Menard, whose wife was Hidatsa. "The inhabitants of these Villages," Thompson wrote, "have not been many years on the banks of the Missisourie River." They had formerly lived as farmers on the Red River, he said, but had been forced west by the Ojibway after the latter had obtained firearms (Thompson 1962:171, 174). Thompson's generalization appears to be true only for the Awaxawi and Hidatsa-proper.

More than a century later, between 1906 and 1918, the anthropologist Gilbert L. Wilson compiled massive field notes on the Hidatsa on the Fort Berthold

Reservation. These are only partially published, and the following narrative leans heavily on the origin traditions he collected, especially the accounts of four of his informants. The accounts by Wolf Chief (Wilson 1909a:1-20, 70-72; 1913a:195-201) are in large part consistent with the one by Butterfly (Wilson 1910a:72-88); Buffalo Bird Woman's narratives (1911:303-4, 1913a:188-94) and the one by Wounded Face, a Mandan (1910a:190-98), are much shorter but deviate little from the general picture offered by the others (all are collected in Wood 1986:93-115). During the 1930s Wolf Chief was also an informant for Alfred Bowers, so there are understandable parallels between the studies written by Wilson and Bowers.

Awatixa traditions. The Awatixa claim to have always lived on the Missouri River, having once been the most northerly village Indians on that stream (Bowers 1965:19-20), and they say they were in the area well before the arrival of the other two Hidatsa subgroups. They believe they descended from the sky under the leadership of the great leader, Charred Body. They first settled some thirty miles below the mouth of the Knife River near Turtle Creek, north of Painted Woods Lake and just below the modern town of Washburn. Several of the important ceremonies of the Hidatsa, including the *Naxpike* or Hide Beating ceremony (also known as the Sun Dance), are thought to have originated here (Bowers 1965:308-23). The Awatixa are said to have once moved to the Heart River before the Mountain Crow separated from them and moved west into Montana.

Their earliest known village near the mouth of the Knife River is Lower Hidatsa. Bowers's native informants say the Awatixa lived at this village until about 1781, when its occupants moved upriver. They moved back downriver sometime between 1787 and 1796 and they are said to have founded Sakakawea village (Bowers 1965:17-18). This settlement endured until the spring of 1834, when the Sioux launched a massive attack on the villages at the mouth of the Knife River and burned Sakakawea and Amahami to the ground (Stewart 1974:296). In 1845 the Awatixa survivors joined the other Hidatsa at Like-a-Fishhook Village.

Awaxawi traditions. Traditions of the Awaxawi place their origin beneath the earth and assert that they came to the surface by climbing a vine which had penetrated their underground home. Two culture heroes, First Creator and Only Man, had already created the earth's surface. The Awaxawi, Hidatsa-proper, and River Crow then moved north to Devils Lake. At Devils Lake there was a "celestial fire," when a fire came down from the sky, killing most of the trees east of the Missouri River and many of the people. After this fire the Hidatsa-proper and the River Crow moved farther north, away from the Awaxawi. When a great flood approached, some of the Awaxawi escaped and fled to the Missouri River, settling near Square Buttes, a prominent landmark about thirty miles upriver from the Mandan settlement at the Heart River (now near the town of Bismarck) and about thirty miles below the mouth of the Knife River. The Awaxawi found the Awatixa already living on the Missouri above them (Bowers 1897:298-301; Wilson 1910a:72-88).

The Awaxawi later left the Square Buttes area and tried to build a village on the Missouri upriver from the Hidatsa-proper, who had arrived after the Awaxawi and settled near Knife River. The Hidatsa-proper, however, attacked and drove the Awaxawi back downriver, firmly resisting this and other attempts by village Indians to occupy the territory that the Hidatsa-proper considered their hunting grounds (Henry and Thompson 1897:343; Bowers 1965:21, 214, 486). The Awaxawi are said to have lived for a time near the Cheyenne Indians near the present North Dakota-South Dakota boundary and then to have returned to the Square Buttes area, where they suffered the smallpox epidemic of 1781 (Bowers 1965:5, 20-21, 24). (The Mandan, in a somewhat different version of these events, say the Awaxawi once lived south of them on the Missouri River, and then moved north to join them near the Heart River; see Jackson 1962:524; Wilson 1909a:14-20, 70-72, 1913a:195-201).

One of the earliest historical accounts, recorded by William Clark, may refer to this later Awaxawi settlement near Square Buttes. An Awaxawi chief, White Buffalo Robe Unfolded (Lewis and Clark 1965, 1:143), told Clark that his "little nation formerley lived about 30 miles below" Fort Mandan (Lewis and Clark 1904-05, 1:271). Clark's field notes say the village was occupied "40 year ago" – that is, about 1764 (Clark 1964:164). A copy of Lewis and Clark's map of the area shows this community on the west bank of the Missouri River in a locale corresponding to the village in Molander State Historic Site (Moulton 1983:map 29; Wood and Moulton 1981:384-85). White Buffalo Robe Unfolded told Clark that this village was so oppressed by the Assiniboin and Sioux that its occupants were forced to move on to the mouth of the

Knife River (Lewis and Clark 1904-05, 1:271). By the 1790s the Awaxawi had built Amahami, their historic village, at the Knife River, where they lived until its sacking by the Sioux in 1834. Some of the survivors then undoubtedly joined the Hidatsa-proper at Big Hidatsa and moved with that group to Like-a-Fishhook Village in 1845.

Hidatsa-proper traditions. The first portions of the legendary history of the Hidatsa-proper largely parallels that of the Awaxawi. The group ascended to the earth's surface near Devils Lake and parted company with the Awaxawi. Then they migrated to the north, thus avoiding the flood that pushed the Awaxawi west to the Missouri River. After the flood they returned to Devils Lake, and somewhat later a war party is said to have discovered the Mandan living on the Missouri River. "The [Mandan] villagers saw the Hidatsas," Buffalo Bird Woman explained to Gilbert Wilson, "but like them, feared to cross over, lest the strangers prove to be enemies. It was autumn, and the Missouri River was running low so that an arrow could be shot from shore to shore. The Mandans parched some ears of ripe corn with the grain on the cob; they broke the ears in pieces, thrust the pieces on the points of arrows, and shot them across the river. 'Eat!' they said, whether by voice or signs, I do not know. The word for 'eat' is the same in the Hidatsa and Mandan languages.

"The warriors ate of the parched corn, and liked it. They returned to their village and said, 'We have found a people living by the Missouri River who have a strange kind of grain, which we ate and found good!'" (Wilson 1917:6-7, 1909a:14-20).

The Hidatsa-proper and the River Crow then moved to the Missouri and settled near the Mandan on the Heart River. Mandan leaders, however, told them that "It would be better if you went upstream and built your own village, for our customs are somewhat different from yours. Not knowing each other's ways the young men might have differences and there would be wars. Do not go too far away for people who live far apart are like strangers and wars break out between them. Travel north only until you cannot see the smoke from our lodges and there build your village. Then we will be close enough to be friends and not far enough away to be enemies" (Crows Heart, in Bowers 1965:15). About this time the River Crow moved farther west, into what is today Montana. The Hidatsa-proper, unlike the other two Hidatsa village groups, are still considered a band of the Crow (Bowers 1965:13).

Oral traditions gathered by Prince Maximilian von Wied-Neuwied in 1833-34 (Wied 1905-06, 23:315-17) and by the ethnologist Washington Matthews between 1865 and 1872 (1877:36-37) largely parallel the accounts collected by Wilson in the twentieth century. Wolf Chief told Wilson of the arrival of one group of Hidatsa at the mouth of Knife River, where they were met by a great god, Itsikamahidish. "'I want to show you where you shall build your village,' the god said. He stood up on a hill a little way to the north and looked toward the south. His eyes also viewed the north side of the mouth of the Knife River.

"He raised one foot and rested it upon a stone. He raised his head. 'Now I see the place which shall be your village,' he said. 'You people shall increase and become many. They shall become as willows; therefore I will call you willow people and you shall become numerous and your generations shall be long. . . .'

"The word for willows is Mida-hátsi, the red willows that come up on sand bars. This word afterwards became corrupted into Hidatsa" (Wilson 1913a:200-1; Wood 1986:115).

Two major villages that appear to be of Hidatsa-proper affiliation – at least in part – are a few miles upstream from Big Hidatsa: Rock Village and Nightwalker's Butte. Both villages are thought to date from about the time of the 1781 smallpox epidemic. The Awatixa appear to have been permitted to settle Rock Village because some Hidatsa-proper lived there with them, but rivalries between different subgroups in the community seem to have led to its abandonment (Bowers 1965:17-18, 27). Nightwalker's Butte, a fortified butte-top village, was established under the leadership of Nightwalker, a chief who had a reputation for breaking away and living apart from the rest of the group (Lehmer, Wood, and Dill 1978:66-67).

Two other butte-top sites on the Fort Berthold Reservation may have been occupied by Nightwalker. These are Midipadi Butte, across the Missouri from the old town of Elbowoods, and the Jacobsen site, in the badlands on the lower reaches of the Little Missouri River (Kuehn, Falk, and Drybred 1982; Lehmer, Wood, and Dill 1978:66).

When historic documentation begins, the Hidatsa-proper were living at Big Hidatsa, the largest and most conspicuous of the village sites in the Knife River Indian Villages National Historic Site. It appears to have been occupied almost continuously until 1845, when its residents moved to Like-a-Fishhook Village with the other Hidatsa.

NIGHTWALKER'S BUTTE VILLAGE SITE
Photographed by Nathaniel Dewell, 1952
National Anthropological Archives, National Museum of
*   Natural History, Smithsonian Institution,*
*   Washington, D.C.*
The 27 houses on Nightwalker's Butte (see map p. 7) were
protected by a palisade around the edge of the bluff. In 1952
the site was excavated by a field party from the Smithsonian
Institution's Missouri River Basin Project. The archaeologists'
camp (visible at upper left) was at the foot of the butte.

Like-a-Fishhook Village

In 1845 the three Hidatsa subgroups abandoned the
mouth of the Knife River, moved to a new location
nearly fifty miles upstream from their traditional
homeland, and founded Like-a-Fishhook Village. Later,
they were joined by those Mandan from the village at
Fort Clark who had survived the devastating smallpox
epidemic of 1837. In 1862 the Arikara Indians also
moved upriver to Like-a-Fishhook Village and built
their lodges on the north edge of the Mandan-Hidatsa
community (Smith 1972:9-10).

Life in a village consisting of the remnants of
three separate tribes had its difficulties because of
vested and conflicting interests. In addition, the three
Hidatsa subgroups were thrown into more intimate
relations than they had ever experienced in the past.
Disagreements among members of the same Hidatsa
village, in fact, sometimes led to schisms that resulted
in the dissident group moving away. In the most
prominent example, Crow Flies High, one of the
leaders of the Hidatsa-proper, left Like-a-Fishhook

Village about 1871 and moved up the Missouri River
with a group of his followers. They first lived in a
village (now known as the Garden Coulee site) just east
of Fort Union, near the modern Montana-North
Dakota boundary; then they built a village on a high
bluff overlooking the Missouri River opposite the
mouth of the Little Knife River, not far from the
present town of New Sanish (Fox 1982; Malouf
1963:152-58).

The twilight of traditional native lifeways was now
at hand; at Like-a-Fishhook the three village tribes
occupied their last earth lodge village in the Northern
Plains. Their close association was soon to lead to their
designation as the Three Affiliated Tribes. Like-a-
Fishhook remained their home until reservation lands
were allotted in severalty. The impact of the white
man's ways had been rapidly accelerating, particularly
since there were several trading posts directly associated
with the village. With allotment, the fabric of their
lives was to be torn even further apart. As the
allotments were filled the residents of Like-a-Fishhook
gradually moved away from the communal village onto
isolated farmsteads scattered over the Fort Berthold
Reservation. By about 1885 the old village was all
but abandoned.

Life on the new reservation demanded many
adjustments in their centuries-old traditions. Like-a-
Fishhook had been an urban setting, a compact village
of nearly 1,500 Hidatsa, Mandan, and Arikara living in
close proximity. When they moved away from the
village onto reservation lands they were encouraged to
settle on isolated 160-acre tracts. These former villagers
resisted this breakup of their social networks, however,
and they settled in small communities, such as Shell
Creek, Nishu, and Independence, scattered along the
river. Few people lived in the upland allotments, which
came to be used for ranching.

The Hidatsa continued to cultivate the river
bottomlands, albeit using farm equipment new to
them. In spite of massive population losses in the past
and the pressures of white missionaries and Indian
agents, ceremonial life continued and the people made
every effort to continue their old marriage and kinship
systems. The old village way of life became a thing of
the past, but the Hidatsa clung to as many of their old
ways as they could. These ways were changing rapidly,
however, and many of them were but memories. The
Hidatsa people can be grateful to Gilbert Wilson for the
meticulous record he obtained of their vanishing history
and customs.

The Hidatsa religious experience

Gerard Baker

The Hidatsa religious experience was a part of the everyday activities of the three sub-groups of the Hidatsa, the Hidatsa-proper, the Awatixa, and the Awaxawi. Although they lived close to one another, the groups varied a little in their language, clans, and societies, and in their beliefs about their creation. But the members of all the groups, referred to as Hidatsa in this essay, believed that everything on the earth and in the sky and waters had a spirit. The people had to learn from these spirits, and they had to learn how to respect the spirits through praying, sacrificing, vision questing, stories, and ceremonies.*

According to the Hidatsa, every aspect of every ceremony was given to the people by the spirits through vision questing. This information was passed down through the generations, either given by one family member to another or sold to another member of the tribe. The process was very complicated. The person receiving the information had to learn all there was to know about that ceremony. Many of the ceremonies had prayers and songs that were known only to the individual who had the right or the medicine for the ceremony. Others did not or could not use that prayer or song without this right, or medicine.

The term "medicine" encompasses many physical and spiritual items. The Hidatsa phrase for these sacred items, including bundles, songs, and prayers, is *neupax-eta xhue boady* – translated by this author as "people that are holy." Many versions of the sacred stories, such as parts of the creation story, that early white visitors wrote down are incomplete because the one who was telling the story did not have the medicine or right to tell the parts of the story that were sacred. Today, as in the past, respect is still shown for the sacred songs, stories, and ceremonies, so that much of this information is impossible to tell here without violating the rules of the Indian religion. If it is told, respect for the story, song, or ceremony will be lost and the spirits will lose their respect for the person telling it.

Through vision questing, or fasting, an individual, usually a man, called to the spirits for help in his day-to-day life and in his spiritual life. Wives, sisters, or close female relatives assisted the fasting men by praying in their earth lodges, but they usually did not go out to fast themselves. The women who did fast were considered very holy and were highly respected.

A child, usually male, might make his first vision quest at the age of five or six. The child had a teacher whose responsibility was to educate him in the religion and to interpret visions he might have. Usually this teacher was a grandfather from the mother's clan. The teacher told the child about various spirits and how to pray. Hidatsa children were taught much about respect, for themselves and especially for the Grandmother Earth, the Grandfather River (the Missouri), and every living plant and animal.

A boy usually started his vision quest by taking a sweat bath. There were two different types of sweat lodge. One was for a social sweat, in which, after the first prayer, the men could visit or tell stories and not perform a ceremony. The second type was a ceremonial sweat lodge, where even the direction of the door opening had a meaning. For example, if one had eagle medicine or prayed to the eagle he should place his sweat lodge door opening to the west, because the Hidatsa believed the eagle lived in the mountains to the west. There were rules and regulations one had to follow, such as always entering and moving in the sweat "as the sun goes" or in a clockwise direction. The Hidatsa did not all have the same religious practices. Each had his personal helper, usually in the form of an animal spirit, and he tried to express the characteristics of that particular animal somehow in the sweat.

The sweat lodge, made from willow and covered with hides, looked like an upside-down bowl. Hot sandstone rocks were placed in a pit in the middle of the lodge. Water was poured over the red-hot rocks, creating steam that, it was believed, cleansed the body, mind, and spirit.

Although it was not common, females sometimes went into the sweat. The sweat lodge was prepared for them by men who had the medicine to build and use a sweat lodge for a ceremony. But only the women went in, and they had to tear the lodge down after the sweat ceremony was over.

Following the sweat bath, the young person was accompanied by his grandfather, or teacher, to a hill or area that had some spiritual significance and was left there. If it was the first time the child had fasted, his grandfather would give him an item to help him pray, sometimes even a human skull. He could not eat, sleep, or drink water, but would stay awake and fast, usually for four days and nights, although the period could be longer or shorter. The number four is sacred in the Hidatsa religion, because it represents the four directions of the earth and the four winds. During this

*This essay is based on the author's interviews with Hidatsa and Mandan Indians, many of whom are now deceased. It incorporates information published in Bowers 1965 and Case and Case 1977.

time, the young person prayed to various powers. His prayers began, like most prayers, with the phrase, "I am a man and I am pitiful." He hoped that the spirits would see how much he was suffering and that one would take pity on him and come to him in the form of an animal. This spirit would then direct him throughout his life.

The Hidatsa believe that one must sacrifice through "self-torture" in order to obtain help from the spirits. In the Hidatsa language, there is no word for torture. In fact, this term gives the wrong impression of this aspect of the Indian religion. It was and is still thought that in order to get something, such as a vision, you must give something in return, either something physical or some part of yourself – emotion or suffering. Physical items are usually things of value that could be used in the spirit world, like tobacco or robes. Emotion, on the other hand, is a very personal giving – shedding your blood or tears on the Grandmother Earth and showing the various spirits that you are willing to sacrifice your own bodily needs for food and drink. By crying or maybe cutting yourself and dripping blood on the earth, you show those spirits that you are serious, and you are giving a lot in hopes that the spirits will repay you with a vision.

After a successful vision quest, the young person made a personal medicine bundle, or sacred bundle, on his grandfather's advice. If his vision told him he would be a great warrior, he might include part of a wolf hide to represent that animal's stealth or an eagle head to represent the bird's strength and wisdom. These articles were wrapped in a piece of hide, usually cut from the belly of a deer or a buffalo skin. Other hides were used depending on the type of medicine they contained.

A personal bundle could be owned by only one person. It was usually small enough so the individual could have it in his possession or close to him at all times. Even when he was sleeping in an earth lodge, the bundle was kept near his bed, usually up high off the ground. It was used at the discretion of its owner, who alone knew all its contents. A personal bundle could be sold to another member of the tribe. It was not paid for in labor but in materials, such as buffalo robes, meals, horses, and other items. The bundles were very important to the Hidatsa, because they represented various powers the people could call on in order to survive on the earth.

A second type of sacred bundle was the group bundle, used by the members of a clan or society. Clans were matrilineal family groups, responsible for religious

"IDOLS OF THE MANDAN INDIANS"
Based on a watercolor by Karl Bodmer, 1833-34
Copper plate engraving on paper
H. 31.6 cm, W. 26.1 cm
MHS (Wied 1840–43: tableau 25)
Despite the efforts of missionaries, the complex Mandan-Hidatsa religion thrived during the 1870s and 1880s. Votive poles like those shown here were still erected on the reservation as late as 1908 (MHS photos III-16, III-17).

and family matters. A person was born into a clan and remained a member of that clan throughout his life. Societies, however, were made up of members who were usually all of the same sex and approximately the same age. The societies, responsible for the social organization of the village, were the police, hunters, scouts, and other groups. Because the societies were age-graded, a person could change societies at different times in his life. While most societies were for men, a few were for women, like the Skunk, White Buffalo Cow, and Goose societies.

Most of the society and clan bundles were formed during the time of the earth's creation. For example, the Low Hat or Low Cap clan was organized by an individual named Packs Antelope. He saved the Thunder Bird from extinction by killing a large two-headed snake made of sandstone. Because of this, the Thunder Birds gave Packs Antelope objects for a bundle, so he could pray to the Thunder Birds and get their assistance in bringing rain for the village crops. This clan had other responsibilities as well.

Each clan or society bundle had different contents. The objects within a specific bundle were all sacred and cannot even be mentioned without the medicine or the knowledge to mention them. Each object held some degree of responsibility – that is, it had a meaning and function – within the bundle. Some objects were more powerful and therefore could be prayed to and used more than others. Many bundles had a sacred pipe that was used as a direct communication between the person using the pipe and the spirit world. It was believed the pipe was more holy than most other objects within a bundle, and therefore had a greater degree of responsibility. Some bundles had skulls of supernatural beings given to the bundle to help the people in the future. In some cases, individuals gave their own skulls to the bundle. Usually the skulls were taken by a clan member if the person was holy or had strong powers, to keep those powers alive.

A person, usually male, could buy a group bundle and its spiritual values with horses and other items. He got both the physical bundle and the songs and prayers that went along with it – for without the songs, prayers, and ceremonies it would be useless or inactive. If the owner was told specifically, through a vision quest or a dream, to add some items to the bundle, he would do so, but he could not add anything without this consent from the spirits. To do so would bring trouble to the family and clan, in the form of sickness or death.

The buyer also hosted a feast for all members of the organization to which the bundle belonged. Once this was accomplished, the old owner gave up all rights to the bundle, including the ceremonies and special, or mystery, songs. These songs were only known and sung by the new owner of the bundle. He or she was then the one to care for the bundle and to perform the ceremonies associated with it.

Society and clan bundles were kept inside the earth lodge in a special place. They were covered until used, and the children were taught to respect them and stay away from the area where they were placed. Some bundles were opened only at certain times of the year, while others were opened when the owner or the other

"O FFERINGS OF THE MANDAN INDIANS"
Based on a watercolor by Karl Bodmer, 1832–33
Copper plate engraving on paper
H. 14 cm, W. 20.5 cm
MHS (Wied 1840–43: vignette 14)
Skulls of the dead were often removed from burial scaffolds by clan relatives, painted, and placed on a nest of soft sage in a skull circle dedicated to the Sun or to his sister, Woman Above. A circle of buffalo skulls surrounded the human ones. Skull circles were sacred places, used as fasting areas; one in the hills northeast of Elbowoods was maintained until 1932 (Bowers 1965: 170-71, 330-31).

members of a society or clan needed to pray for something, such as gaining success in battle or calling the buffalo closer to the village. Some bundles could be opened by the owner at his own discretion without a ceremony, but he would leave an offering of tobacco, while other bundles could be opened only with a ceremony. It is important to understand that *each* bundle had its own rules and regulations, and one had to know everything about it before he obtained the bundle. A person could own more than one group bundle at a time, but this was very uncommon. There were so many rules that it was impossible to take care of the bundles in the proper way.

In general, prayer was a way of life. The Hidatsa prayed throughout the day, starting at dawn when the sun came up and ending when the sun went down. To survive, the Hidatsa needed nature and all its spirits, so the respect for them was great. The older people often described prayers as talking to the spirits of the earth and asking for assistance in the many different tasks that were to be accomplished that day. The prayers were not memorized but came directly from the heart. This is not to say that people went around in all their waking hours praying. But if, for instance, they happened to pass by a large tree that was healthy and strong they would ask for its strength to guide them.

Individuals also carried items to help them pray. These objects were considered sacred and representative of their medicine bundles. A person would hold the item in his hand and use it as a prayer tool. In this manner, it was expected that this particular object would show a greater power and offer more assistance than the other things in the bundle. If someone were going into battle, for example, he would pray to the spirit of his war shield and ask for its protection.

Stories were also very important to the Hidatsa. The first storytellers learned how to tell the stories from the spirits at the time of creation. Through the legends, passed down from one generation to another, the religion, discipline, and history of the people were kept alive. Most of the stories were associated with the various group bundles. The sacredness of the bundle kept the legend from changing from generation to generation. The person getting the bundle would learn the story that came with it. According to the rules of the bundle, he could not change or add anything at all to the story without going against the bundle, and this would bring bad luck. Other storytellers were elderly men and women who told everything from war stories to humorous stories. But even these people started their stories with a prayer to the spirits, asking to keep their minds clear so they could remember and not add or delete from the story.

The early Hidatsa had many ceremonies. These are too numerous to list, and too complicated to give in detail, but there were ceremonies about every aspect of the culture, from birth to death. Some ceremonies were held at specific times of the year, some more than once a year. For example, the Okipa, an important ceremony adopted from the Mandan and held every summer, was a play celebrating creation and rebirth, and its participants represented virtually everything in the universe – animals, spiritual and celestial beings, emotions, and fertility. There were also ceremonies for hunting and for calling the buffalo closer to the village to secure better success in hunting. Some ceremonies honored certain animals. Others honored places, like those that were offered to the Missouri River, the Grandfather and the blood line of the people. During that ceremony the women would roll corn balls onto the water to feed the spirits of the river.

Besides individual ceremonies, there were clan and society ceremonies where only those who belonged to the group could participate. Other members could attend and look on but could not take part. Some ceremonies, like the Black Bear ceremony, were so sacred that no one except the participants could attend.

Even in and after death there were certain cermonies performed. Survivors would feed the spirit of the one who had died. About a year after the death, the clan or society would have a large ceremonial feast and end the close family's year of mourning.

The women, who owned the earth lodges and the gardens, had ceremonies for the building of the earth lodges and for the planting and growing of the gardens. The women also had to learn all the correct information about the ceremony and to have the medicine or right to perform it. There were sacred songs to the various seeds in the garden and to the earth lodge, and even songs for tearing down an earth lodge to replace it, all of which could be sung only by the women who purchased the medicine.

Many changes have occurred in Hidatsa religion since the time when the people lived in their traditional villages at Knife River. Smallpox epidemics, the arrival of the missionaries, and the loss of traditional hunting grounds and sacred grounds had great effects. Other changes were caused by relocations of the Hidatsa from their traditional homeland along the Missouri River, first to allotments on the Fort Berthold Indian Reservation along the river and then, after the creation of Lake Sakakawea by the Garrison Dam, to the uplands outside of the Missouri Valley.

In Hidatsa oral history, the smallpox epidemic of 1837 is one of the earliest events marking the start of this change. Many of the medicine bundles and their ceremonies were lost, because when the owner of a bundle died in the smallpox epidemic, so did his bundle and the ceremonies that went with it. Even a person who had seen or been in the ceremony could not obtain the right to perform the ceremony or keep the bundle if the original owner died unexpectedly and did not sell him the bundle. No one wanted to risk taking a bundle without a formal transfer and having something tragic happen to him or his family.

Because of these losses, the Hidatsa had to reorganize their religion. The Hidatsa who survived this epidemic still had their personal medicine bundles and their belief in them. Some of the clan and society bundles survived. Personal prayer and fasting continued, but the Hidatsa performed no major ceremonies until 1845, when the three Hidatsa sub-groups moved together to Like-a-Fishhook Village. There they were joined by the Mandan, and the borrowing of beliefs between these tribes accelerated.

The arrival of white missionaries also brought changes. The missionaries considered the Indian religion to be pagan and the Indian religious practices to be the worshiping of idols. The missionaries even used force to spread their teachings. Many "old timers," some alive at the time of this writing, who are over seventy years of age, remember that the missionaries would often go into Indian homes, seize the medicine bundles, and burn them outside the house. They say that this event was like the death of a loved one. The old men and women cried as they watched their religion burn. Some of the bundles were not burned, however. The old timers say that the missionaries bought them and sold them to large museums. The Indian people who sold them still had the respect for the bundles, but they had more or less been brainwashed into not trusting their bundles. The people were even taught that the Hidatsa religion was negative and heathen. The Indian people still had enough respect not to destroy the bundles, but they did agree to give them up. This was a time of religious confusion, and many adapted to both beliefs. Today this is evident in stories where the name "First Creator" is replaced with "Jesus" by some of the elders.

There were other changes happening in the Hidatsa way of life. White settlement and the policies of the United States government forced many adjustments. Warfare lost importance as most of the "enemies" were now on reservations as well. In the 1880s the government outlawed "self-torture" or sacrifice during vision quests. Since there were no more buffalo, grain farming and cattle raising replaced hunting. The Hidatsa, urged by the Indian agent, moved in the 1880s from Like-a-Fishhook to separate land allotments scattered across the reservation. Family members had to travel many miles by horse and wagon to visit and perform ceremonies.

The teachings of many of the elders also changed during this time. Elders who saw the advantages of knowing "the white man's way" encouraged the young to learn English and attend schools. They thought it was nearly impossible to learn and practice the true Hidatsa religion, although many still kept the "feeling" and their respect for the bundles, clans, societies, and the spirits of nature. Many young people were sent away to government boarding schools, sometimes in other states, where Indian languages, dancing, and singing were forbidden.

Most Hidatsa had at first resisted the new religion of the missionaries, but their beliefs and attitudes toward the Indian religion began to change. Because the people who still practiced the Indian religion were often looked down on by whites, missionaries, and Christian Indians, they performed the ceremonies secretly. The community at Independence probably saw the last traditional Hidatsa religion.

The completion of the Garrison Dam on the Missouri River in 1954 caused the Hidatsa to stray even further from their traditional religion. The flooding of the Missouri forced families to move even farther apart, onto the uplands above the valley. This made it almost impossible for those who still carried on the ceremonies to meet because of the length of time it took to reach each other. Many sacred places were also drowned out.

Although traditional Hidatsa religion has been lost for a long time, it is now beginning to come back. The Hidatsa no longer have any major clan or society ceremonies, but the number of individuals who hold the beliefs is growing. The schools are now teaching Hidatsa traditions to young Hidatsa, who are starting to realize that they are responsible for carrying on the religion and culture. The Hidatsa have much to do in order to reestablish the traditional religion, but they are once again starting to build up the societies and clans. Even though many of the songs, prayers, and ceremonies are lost, the attitude of belief and respect is coming back, and more Hidatsa people are now making vision quests. It will take time, but because the spirits gave the Hidatsa many aspects of the true traditional religion, these sacred songs, ceremonies, and bundles can be obtained again in the same manner.

Yet there are many factors that make this difficult today. Population density now makes it hard to find a holy place that is isolated where one might fast and seek a vision. And even if an isolated spot is found, the noise or presence of automobiles, planes, or oil and gas development always interferes.

The Hidatsa religion has faced many setbacks, from the smallpox epidemic of 1837 to the arrival of the missionaries to the construction of the Garrison Dam. Despite these challenges, the traditional religion, pride in the Hidatsa culture, and the belief of the Hidatsa in themselves and their religion are growing. The spirits and nature still live and are there to aid in bringing back the Hidatsa religion.

The Hidatsa natural environment

Jeffery R. Hanson

All forms of life, if they are to survive, must adapt to their natural surroundings, in order to cope with the constraints of nature and to take advantage of its opportunities. The human species, however, through the invention of culture, has made an adaptation that is unprecedented in the animal kingdom. Each human society, from bands of pristine hunters and gatherers to complex industrial states, has blended language, technology, group organization, and belief to create a unique culture representing time-tested adaptations to its environment. From each society's give-and-take struggles with nature, knowledge is created and, as this knowledge is transmitted from generation to generation, tradition is born.

Interaction between human communities and the natural environment may result in long-term stability or disruptive change for nature and culture. The prehistory and history of the Hidatsa Indians illustrates both of these evolutionary possibilities. The environment in central North Dakota is one of striking contrast between the fertile, wooded valley of the Missouri River and the vast semi-arid upland prairie. The aboriginal Hidatsa farming and hunting culture was in equilibrium with this environment before Euro-American contact; during the latter half of the 19th century, after white contact, the culture underwent drastic and irreversible changes that altered its relationship to nature.

The Hidatsa, their cultural cognates the Mandan, and the Arikara – the Three Affiliated Tribes – are historic representatives of a relatively stable farming and hunting lifeway which archaeologists call the Plains Village Tradition. This lifeway, which began in the Knife River-Heart River region of the Missouri River valley about A.D. 1100, was characterized by sedentary village life and a subsistence economy based on corn agriculture and bison hunting (Lehmer 1971:33, 1977:25; see also maps p. ix, 7). Establishing their permanent earth lodge villages on terraces overlooking the Missouri River and its fertile bottomlands, these peoples exploited resources from the valley as well as the upland prairie (Wood 1974:6). They exercised a variety of communal rights concerning resources and land. Garden plots were transmitted through inheritance along the female line within specified clans and households. Possession of garden areas and hunting territory was in terms of use rights rather than strict ownership. Game and timber resources were open to all who could exploit them. In their adaptation, the Missouri Valley became more than just an ecological focal point. It became a cosmological and spiritual focal

"BUFFALO BULL"
Based on a drawing by George Catlin
Colored lithograph on paper
H. 24 cm, W. 35 cm
MHS (Catlin 1844:pl. 2)

point as well; in the philosophical sense, a "Center," from which man and nature could be comprehended, understood, and acted upon.

Members of these societies needed, therefore, to develop an intimate knowledge of the plants, animals, climate, and topography of valley and upland ecosystems. Game animals, such as bison, elk, mule deer, and bighorn sheep, were both food and sources of raw materials for tools, clothing, shelter, weapons, ornamentation, and ritual. The Hidatsa utilized over seventy species of wild plants for food, technology, medicine, and ritual, so it was vital to know characteristics and stages of growth of both riverine and upland plants. Knowledge of high-quality flint beds, particularly the Knife River beds in western North Dakota, was vital for the manufacturing of efficient stone arrow points, spear points, scrapers, and knives. Finally, for people dependent on corn agriculture who also spent weeks on the prairies searching for bison herds, knowledge of the weather and climate of the Northern Plains was essential to survival.

The habitat to which the Hidatsa adapted is one of climatic and geographical contrasts. The climate of North Dakota is characterized by extreme and rapid seasonal changes in temperature and precipitation. During winter, temperatures may plummet to as low as -60° F, and North Dakotans can expect, on the average, between 40 and 65 days of subzero temperatures annually. During the winter of 1935-36, at Devils Lake, the temperature dropped below freezing on November 27, 1935, and did not rise above freezing until March 1, 1936, a period of 96 days. From January 14 to February 19 of that year, there was only one day during which the temperature registered as high as zero, and the *average* temperature for January and February of that year was -13° F (Jensen 1972:2, 5, 9). A century earlier, during the winter of 1833-34, Prince Maximilian described a winter at Fort Clark, a fur-trading post just a few miles south of the Hidatsa villages along the Knife River: "During these cold days, some of our woodcutters had their noses and cheeks frost-bitten. The horizon was hazy; the river smoked; neither man nor animal was to be seen; yet a party of Mandans, with their wives, were in the prairie hunting buffaloes, of which they killed forty. At night the cold was so intense, that we could not venture to put our hands from our bodies, lest they should be frozen. In the morning we could scarcely endure the severity of the weather, till we had a blazing fire, for the bleak north-west wind penetrated through all the seams of the building" (Wied 1905-06, 24:55-56).

To better cope with the cold temperatures and bitter winds of winter, the Hidatsa, Mandan, and Arikara left their summer villages and built winter earth lodge villages in the river bottomlands. There they were sheltered from winds and close to large quantities of fuel. This practice also conserved the timber supplies near the permanent villages that would otherwise have to be relocated (Griffin 1977; Hanson 1983a:67; Hurt 1969; Wilson 1934:395). The prairie uplands were devoid of wood and subject to the full ferocity of unexpected blizzards; during winter the Hidatsa traversed the prairie only when it was necessary to hunt.

By contrast, North Dakota summers are warm, often hot, and frequently pleasant, with temperatures normally ranging into the eighties and nineties. These temperatures, coupled with long daylight hours, present favorable conditions for agriculture, and the natural vegetation in river valleys and on the prairies matures quickly. In the spring and summer the Hidatsa and other village tribes made the most intense use of the natural environment, planting crops in the bottomland soils and harvesting the wild plant foods offered by valley and upland ecosystems. During hot spells, however, the North Dakota prairie can become a furnace; high temperatures turn the lush grasses a dessicated brown and make simple outdoor activities oppressive. In extreme heat waves, temperatures in

North Dakota have reached as high as 121° F (Jensen 1972:5, 6).

Much of North Dakota, including the Missouri River valley, is semi-arid. Normal annual precipitation is from 17 to 13 inches in the central and western regions, respectively (Jensen 1972:41). Of this, approximately 75 per cent falls as rain during the growing season, from April to September. This precipitation is usually sufficient for agriculture on the moist alluvial soils of the Missouri bottomlands. During normal years, agriculture on the prairie is feasible but risky without irrigation. Extended drought, not uncommon in North Dakota, can prove disastrous to prairie agriculture, and can significantly damage crops in the bottomlands, as the history of agriculture at Fort Berthold aptly demonstrates (Meyer 1977:153, 174, 240). The Hidatsa planted their corn in carefully spaced hills and stored seed corn to guard against such disasters. In historic times, major droughts have occurred in North Dakota in the 1890s and in 1912, 1934, and 1953 – approximately every twenty years (Borchert 1971:2).

The striking contrasts of North Dakota's climate are matched by the geographical and ecological extremes of the Missouri River valley and upland prairie. The valley, a trench of water, hardwood forest, and undergrowth vegetation that cuts through a biome of Northern Temperate Grassland, teems with aquatic life, and lush vegetation (Shelford 1963:329; Johnson 1971). The prairie, on the other hand, consists of a virtual sea of grassland and is barren of trees, except for narrow ribbons of cottonwood along occasional streams. However, for those forms of life that can adapt, the prairie constitutes a favorable habitat. Drought-resistant grasses and sedges thrive and provide sustenance to the large, migratory herbivores: bison, pronghorn, and elk. In addition, the ancient badland formations, carved by wind and water from the prairie landscape, were home to the bighorn sheep and golden eagle (Bailey 1926).

The Missouri Valley and the upland prairie highlight and reinforce each other's distinctiveness. The Hidatsa were well acquainted with the opportunities and limitations provided by each of these Northern Plains environments. In developing a deep intimacy with valley and upland, the Hidatsa were able to take advantage of the plant and animal resources that each offered.

River valley and upland prairie: contrasts in life

"I ascended the hills from whence I had a most pleasing view of the country, particularly of the wide and fertile vallies formed by the missouri and the yellowstone rivers . . . the whol face of the country was covered with herds of Buffaloe, Elk, & Antelopes; deer are also abundant, but keep themselves more concealed in the woodland . . . the timber consists principally of Cottonwood, with some small elm, ash and boxalder. The under growth on the sandbars and verge of the river is the small leafed willow; the low bottoms, rose bushes . . . the redburry, servicebury, and the redwood." – Meriwether Lewis, April 25-26, 1805 (Lewis and Clark 1904-06, 2:335, 337, 338)*

Lewis's panoramic and impressionistic description of the natural environment along the Missouri captures the essence of the flora and fauna of traditional Hidatsa territory. At one time that area stretched northeastward to Turtle Mountain, along a line southward to Opposite Butte (a prominent prairie landmark due east of the Knife River's junction with the Missouri), westward almost to the Little Missouri River, and north to the confluence of the Missouri and Yellowstone rivers (Bowers 1965:12; see map p. 272). This expansive territory, most of which is upland prairie, is bisected by the Missouri River valley, which constituted the mythological and spiritual heartland of the Hidatsa and Mandan tribes (Bowers 1950:117, 163). From this heartland, this "Center," the Hidatsa traversed the upland prairie by way of arterial streams such as the Knife, Little Missouri, Heart, and White Earth rivers. Relying on the tributary streams, prominent buttes, and natural formations as points of orientation, the Hidatsa exploited the seasonal bounty of the prairie.

The Missouri Valley. The Missouri Valley, prominent in Hidatsa and Mandan cosmography and religion, also held a special place in the tribes' adaptation to the natural environment. The river channel, bottomlands, terraces, and Missouri "breaks" provided a rich diversity of natural resources that enabled the traditional Hidatsa to carve an effective farming-hunting niche in the Northern Plains. This basic ecological posture toward the Missouri and its resources began to shift during the latter half of the 19th century and was irrevocably altered by the construction of Garrison Dam in the 1950s.

In addition to providing drinking and bathing water, the Missouri River offered important subsistence resources: paddlefish, walleye, sturgeon, channel catfish, goldeye, bullhead, and buffalofish were harvested with traps, drags, and hook-and-line techniques; turtles were captured for food and fresh-water clams were gathered as raw material for spoons and other utensils; and a variety of aquatic birds, including ducks and geese, were hunted for food and feathering for arrows (Weitzner 1979:196-210).

The Missouri River bottomlands were intensively used by the Hidatsa when they were living in their Knife River villages and later at Like-a-Fishhook Village. Using slash-and-burn techniques, the Hidatsa carved agricultural land from hardwood forest and worked the fertile alluvial soil into productive gardens of corn, beans, squash, sunflowers, and tobacco (Wilson 1917:7). Wild plant resources abounded. From the lush stands of timber the Hidatsa harvested cottonwood for firewood and for the construction of summer and winter earth lodges, drying stages, and village palisades (Wilson 1916b:249-50). Peach-leaved willow provided material for basket frames, bullboat frames, saddle stirrups, and wicker baskets. Diamond and sandbar willow were used for earth lodge roofing and mats, respectively. Chokecherries, Juneberries, currants, gooseberries, and plums provided important wild foods during the growing season (Wilson 1916b:253, 291, 293, 218, 210, 258, 260, 261). Finally, from the wetlands, the Hidatsa gathered slough grass for lining their cache pits and cattail down for insulating baby cradles.

BEAVER DENS ON THE BANK OF THE MISSOURI"
Based on a watercolor by Karl Bodmer, 1832–33
Copper plate engraving on paper
H. 14.5 cm, W. 20.5 cm
MHS (Wied 1840–43:vignette 17)

A wide variety of large and small mammals and birds, on which the Hidatsa depended, lived in the Missouri bottomlands. Abundant white-tailed deer, mule deer, and elk were hunted for food, clothing, and raw materials for bone tools (Weitzner 1979:194-96). Grizzly bears, hunted cautiously, were valued for their meat as well as their claws, which were made into necklaces. Small mammals, used for food, fur, ornamentation, and ritual purposes, included fox, kit fox, bobcat, otter, beaver, raccoon, mink, cottontail, and porcupine (quillwork is a traditional art form in which contemporary Hidatsas excel). Finally, a variety of bottomland bird species – including hawks, cowbirds, cranes, crows, magpies, ravens, and swans – were taken by the Hidatsa for their economic, ornamental, and religious value (Smith 1972:57; Weitzner 1979:197-98).

On the terraces of the Missouri River the Hidatsa established their semi-permanent summer earth lodge villages. The terraces, or "benches," were above the floodplain and hence were free from the ravages of yearly flooding. They were relatively level and well-drained, providing excellent conditions for earth lodge construction. Establishing villages on terraces also allowed the Hidatsa to exploit the resources of both prairie and woodland with relatively equal facility (Wood 1974:6). Ideally, villages were adjacent to well-timbered bottomlands with suitable acreage for gardens. Terraces contained stands of ash, elm, and boxelder, which the Hidatsa used intensively. They fashioned mortars and pestles from ash to grind corn; they made bows from elm wood and brewed tea from its bark; they shaped baskets from boxelder bark and drank the tree's sap (Wilson 1916b:264, 267, 268, 300).

The picturesque landscape along the edges of the Missouri Valley is known as the Missouri breaks: a rough, hilly landscape intermittently broken by hardwood draws that form pathways from valley to upland. The breaks were a primary habitat for pronghorn and mule deer, both of which were favored targets of Hidatsa hunting parties. In addition, the hardwood draws offered natural feed and cover for elk, pronghorn, mule deer, and white-tail deer when they moved between prairie and woodland (Brown, Hanson, and Gregg 1983:82-87).

Upland prairie. The upland prairie is majestic, a vast and treeless carpet of rolling grassland. Its expansiveness, its openness, shrinks things of size to toy-like scale by altering perceptions of space and distance. To those

unfamiliar with its subtleness, the prairie can be disorienting, as the untrained eye searches for a reference point and seemingly unique features disappear into the hills and swales that extend in every direction. Being alone on the prairie can bring feelings of isolation and insignificance, as if one had been swallowed by it.

But to those who can adapt to it, the prairie can offer life and a kind of security and confidence that only comes from knowledge of, and respect for, a prairie habitat. The Hidatsa coped well with the difficulties of prairie travel, and they took advantage of its resources. The upland prairie, dominated by numerous varieties of mixed and short grasses, was prime habitat for buffalo, the mainstay of the Hidatsa hunting economy. A social, migratory animal, buffalo often gathered in tremendous herds that were best hunted during prehistoric times through communal techniques such as the drive or surround (Arthur 1978; Frison 1978:243-50; Hanson 1984; McHugh 1972:60-82). This uncertain and delicate operation blended complicated knowledge of buffalo behavior, natural topography, and weather conditions. The drive also required a high degree of coordination and timing. Buffalo were located (not always an easy task) and their movements continuously monitored. A group of "runners" cautiously and unobtrusively approached the animals from downwind to avoid prematurely starting the herd – bison have poor eyesight, but their sense of smell is keen. The runners had to successfully (and often *successively*) stampede the herd through an ever-narrowing "drive line," consisting

MISSOURI RIVER AND UPLAND PRAIRIE
Photographed by Gilbert Wilson, 1916
MHS photo IX-39-1916
The Missouri River cuts a trench through the rolling upland prairie. This photograph is from a series taken near Independence.

of rock alignments or people, which channeled the animals into a constructed enclosure or over a precipice. Conducting a bison drive was so difficult that during the 1700s, when horses became available, most Plains tribes either abandoned it or relegated it to a secondary role, as did the Hidatsa (Ewers 1949; Roe 1955).

To say that the Hidatsa could use virtually every part of the buffalo is not an exaggeration. In addition to the large quantities of fresh and jerked meat obtained, buffalo also provided hides for tipi covers (used by the Hidatsa on their prairie excursions), shields, bullboats, and robes; sinew for bowstrings and other ties; bones for tools such as hoes, knives, awls, fishhooks, chisels, hide fleshers, spatulas, arrow straighteners, flint-knapping tools, and wedges. The Hidatsa made grease from fats, glue from hooves, and spoons from horns. Internal organs, like the stomach or "paunch" and bladder, were used as skin containers. The buffalo skull held a prominent place in Hidatsa religion and ritual.

While the buffalo was of primary importance to the Hidatsa, there were other important resources on the prairie. Herds of pronghorn and elk were hunted communally and individually. Smaller game included the prairie wolf, coyote, prairie dog, ermine, and jackrabbit. Paramount among birds was the golden eagle, which was ceremonially trapped and held a high place in Hidatsa religion and ritual (Wilson 1929). The upland prairie also offered an array of wild plants that were well-known and gathered by the Hidatsa: prairie turnips and wild onions were collected for food, while buffalo grass was used in the construction of drying mats and varieties of sage were important ritual plants (Wilson 1916b:184, 227, 225, 303).

Nature and changes in Hidatsa life

"In old times our tribe knew many plants and ate them, each in its proper season, no one got sick and no harm came of eating them. Such was our custom. In old days also, we had no white men with us and no guns and we often faced scarcity of food. . . . But in my day it was not necessary to do this, and such wild foods fell in comparative disuse." – Buffalo Bird Woman (Wilson 1916b:231)

Hidatsa contact with Euro-American civilization during the nineteenth century brought changes to the Indians' relationship with the natural environment. Some of these innovations, as Buffalo Bird Woman's statement shows, were due more to shifts in Hidatsa

cultural practices than to alterations in their surroundings. There were, however, other changes, much less subtle and of far greater magnitude, that related directly to the natural environment.

Without question, the single most significant change in the relationship of the Hidatsa with nature came with the introduction of life forms invisible to the naked eye: parasitic viruses and bacteria, the causes of terrible infectious diseases that struck down the Hidatsa and other village tribes in epidemic proportions. Without the natural immunities that are built from generations of exposure to infectious disease, part of the selective process in human adaptation, the Hidatsa had little or no biological resistance to these diseases. The Hidatsa, Mandan, and Arikara were "virgin populations" (McNeill 1976:120, 121), and they experienced drastic and continual depopulation, suffering, and disorganization through repeated episodes of smallpox, measles, and cholera. Families were wiped out, clans and villages were destroyed, and social life was disrupted.

In 1781 (and perhaps earlier) the Hidatsa suffered a devastating smallpox epidemic. From an estimated population of about 5,500, the Hidatsa were reduced to approximately 1,750, a mortality rate of almost 70 per cent. In 1837, the somewhat recovered Hidatsa were again hit with smallpox, and their numbers fell from about 2,500 to a little over a thousand. The Mandan were almost exterminated; the few who survived joined the Hidatsa, thus ending the independent existence of one of the most numerous and culturally complex tribes to evolve in the Great Plains (Hanson 1983a, 1983b; Lehmer 1977:107; Meyer 1977:95-97; Trimble 1979). Disease followed the Hidatsa to Like-a-Fishhook Village. In about 1846, when Buffalo Bird Woman was about six years old, her biological mother Weahtee or Want To Be a Woman died of smallpox (Wilson 1917:9; Maxidiwiac 1921:21). Soon after this epidemic came cholera in 1851 and 1853, followed by another wave of smallpox in 1856 (Meyer 1977:104-5). By 1850 the Hidatsa population had been reduced to about 800, and the total number of Hidatsa, Mandan, and Arikara was only between 1,500 and 2,000 (Meyer 1977:105; Hanson 1983a:238). After 1856, the major epidemics appear to have ceased. However, chronic diseases such as whooping cough and tuberculosis contributed to continuing population decline. By 1906 the total population of the Three Affiliated Tribes had reached its nadir, about 1,100 (Meyer 1977:136).

A second significant change in the Hidatsa natural environment came with the extirpation of buffalo from traditional Hidatsa hunting grounds and reservation boundaries in the 1870s and 1880s. The destruction of the herds, caused by whites who hunted for the hide industry and Indians who hunted for subsistence, ended a hunting adaptation that had been basic to Plains Village survival for nearly seven hundred years. The cessation of buffalo hunting left a huge gap in the Hidatsa subsistence economy; there was little to fill it except for woefully inadequate government-issue food. The general decline in health and nutrition caused by this dietary change was noted by Washington Matthews, a surgeon stationed at Fort Berthold during the late 1860s, who wrote, "When subsisting for the most part on fresh meat, these Indians had the soundest gums and teeth; and no flesh when wounded healed more rapidly than theirs. Lately, however, since the increase in the consumption of bacon and flour among them, and the destruction of their game, there have been many cases of scurvy, a disease which was particularly fatal to them in the winter of 1868-'69; and a tendency to abscesses, to suppurative terminations of diseases, and to a sluggish condition of wounds, manifests itself" (Matthews 1877:25). With the disappearance of buffalo and other game, hunting became a sporadic means of supplementing the diet of the Hidatsa, who were under increasing pressure to become "civilized" homesteaders and market farmers in a land that was only marginally equipped for farming.

A third significant change occurred during the 1860s and 1870s with the depletion of the valuable timber resources in the bottomlands near Like-a-Fishhook Village. During the winter of 1865, badly pressed for fuel, the villagers tore down their palisades for firewood (Matthews 1877:10); this happened in spite of chronic warfare with the Sioux. In 1866, as the winter hunts began to require traveling greater distances to find diminishing game, the Hidatsa abandoned the practice of going into winter camps (Matthews 1877:6-7). Those unable to go on the hunt stayed at Like-a-Fishhook; together with the whites who lived year-round at Fort Berthold, they drew heavily on timber resources near the village. Besides using wood in construction and for domestic fuel, many Indians were cutting timber to provide fuel for the steamboats (Kauffman 1881). One cannot help but think that the depletion of timber resources contributed to the decay and eventual abandonment of Like-a-Fishhook Village in the late 1880s (Meyer 1977:135).

Movement away from the center

By the mid-1880s the formulators of American Indian policy strongly urged the breakup of traditional tribal structures and communalism as necessary means of "civilizing" Indian people. Thus the program of assimilation, the melting of Indian identity into the mainstream of rural America, became the new solution to the "Indian Problem" – the continuing conflict between the various Native American cultures and Euro-American society that had plagued colonial governments and the United States alike.

At Fort Berthold, agency personnel created economic incentives for Hidatsa, Mandan, and Arikara families to leave Like-a-Fishhook Village. Offered log cabins, plowed land, and wagon teams, Arikara families began to leave Like-a-Fishhook in 1885, followed soon by the Hidatsa and Mandan. By 1888 the village was nearly deserted. The people scattered over a wide area along both sides of the Missouri, but still tended to settle along clan and tribal lines (Meyer 1977:134-35). However, from the standpoint of the assimilationist, the problems of changing such institutions as communal land tenure, matrilineal inheritance of land, reciprocal food and resource sharing within clan and tribe, and religious beliefs still remained. In short, Indian policy-makers sought to force the Hidatsa, Mandan, and Arikara to make radical cultural adaptations literally overnight.

The Dawes Act or General Allotment Act, passed in 1887, was highly touted as the solution to these problems (Meyer 1977:136-37). Reservation lands at Fort Berthold were parceled into individually owned tracts of 160, 80, and 40 acres. This new system of land tenure and ownership forced the Hidatsa and Mandan to change their traditional economic, political, and kinship structures (Bruner 1961).

The formal allotment of these lands began in 1894, with most families selecting tracts along the Missouri bottomlands, some taking the lands on which they had already settled (Meyer 1977:137-38). The closeness of village life was replaced by dispersement of people over the reservation and the establishment of a number of small communities (Bruner 1961:250). Homestead farming and the breaking up of original tracts through inheritance (now passed through male heads of households) produced a fundamental shift in the relation of the Hidatsa to the land: their system of communal rights (held by clan, village, or tribe) over nature's resources became one of individual right and title.

For the most part, Hidatsa women continued their traditional activities: gardening in the bottomlands, domestic manufactures, and collecting wild foods. Although men continued to do some hunting, they experienced an abrupt shift in roles as they were now expected to become farmers, ranchers, or entrepreneurs rather than hunters, warriors, society leaders, and chiefs. It was not an easy adjustment, socially or spiritually. In a philosophical sense, the Hidatsa still retained their "Center," but it was slowly and inexorably slipping away from them through changes in land tenure and federal policies that forced educational and religious

OWL WOMAN HARVESTING SQUASH
Photographed by Gilbert Wilson, 1914
MHS photo VII-7-14
Owl Woman's traditional garden near Independence was on the terrace or bench land rather than in the Missouri River bottomlands, where Hidatsa women had gardened for centuries. When the people were moved to allotments, the government urged Hidatsa men to become wheat farmers on the terrace prairie, visible behind her.

assimilation. The fluctuating climatic conditions in a land marginally suited to large-scale agriculture played havoc with federal economic policy at Fort Berthold as drought during the late 1880s discouraged Hidatsa efforts to become market farmers of wheat (Meyer 1977:136, 152-54).

In historical context, the allotment of Hidatsa-Mandan lands can be viewed as a transitional episode in their relationship to the valley when compared with what occurred during the 1950s. The construction of Garrison Dam and the relocation of Fort Berthold Indians between 1947 and 1954 ended an 800-year relationship between Northern Plains Village Indians and the Missouri Valley. It also destroyed many of the gains the Fort Berthold people had made in agriculture. About one-fourth of all reservation land, over 150,000 acres, was covered by the new Lake Sakakawea; no new lands were added in compensation. Of the 370 families that lived on the reservation at the time the Garrison Dam project was initiated, 289 or 78 percent lived in the "taking area" and had to be relocated (U.S. Bureau of Indian Affairs 1954:46). This land had been the heart and soul of Hidatsa agriculture, traditional and modern. Nearly all the bottomlands were gone (Meyer 1977:220). Gone was the floodplain timber that had built earth lodge and cabin, palisade and fence post. Gone was the natural habitat for countless species of mammals and birds and the natural winter cover for deer and livestock. Gone too were the wild plant foods that had thrived in the bottomlands.

Relocation scattered the Fort Berthold people over the upland prairie that remained as reservation land, and the creation of Lake Sakakawea further isolated them. To those who can adapt, however, the prairie can offer life. While economic problems at Fort Berthold have been significant, studies in the 1960s showed that Indian people were increasing their use and management (through operating and leasing) of grazing lands, which now constituted the most substantial land type on the reservation (Meyer 1968:339-40). Despite the severe winters and hot summers, grazing is well suited to the reservation's prairie biome. Out of new interactions with the natural environment, based on traditional and modern knowledge, prairies can be crossed, waters can be bridged, and new "Centers" can be created.

Contributions of the Wilsons to the study of the Hidatsa

Alan R. Woolworth

Gilbert L. Wilson, a Presbyterian minister, and his brother Frederick N. Wilson, an artist, began working with the Hidatsa Indians of the Upper Missouri River in 1906. Like many white people before them and after them, they became interested in an Indian people and began to study them: to ask questions, to record answers, and to collect artifacts of their culture. But more than most white observers, the brothers realized that whites were apt to write about Indian peoples as if they *were* white. Gilbert Wilson attempted instead to help the Hidatsa describe themselves in their own terms. By transcribing the words of his consultants and carefully indicating which observations were his own, he allowed the Hidatsa to speak for themselves. His brother's careful sketches provided accurate depictions of Hidatsa objects and processes of manufacture. By recording the creation, uses, and significance of many of the objects they collected, the two men amassed an amazingly rich and valuable body of information on the Hidatsa.

The Wilson collections are particularly impressive because of their focus on Hidatsa life at a crucial time and place. The Indian world on the Great Plains of North America experienced swift and massive changes in the late nineteenth century. The bison were almost exterminated; Indian peoples were assigned to reservations; much of their land was taken from them and occupied by hordes of white settlers; and inevitably many aspects of white culture were imposed upon them.

The Wilson brothers were two among many people who have observed and studied the Hidatsa. This essay will first discuss those other students, in order to place the work of the Wilsons in perspective; it will then address the brothers' own studies.

Ethnographic and historical studies of the Hidatsa

The body of work on the Hidatsa Indians can be conveniently divided into two parts. Early observers, recording in the 18th and 19th centuries, for the most part visited the region for reasons other than meeting the Hidatsa. In 1906, as Gilbert and Frederick Wilson began their studies of the rapidly changing Hidatsa, the way white people wrote about Indians was also undergoing change. By the beginning of the 20th century, anthropology was becoming a formal discipline, and professionally trained observers began to record what they saw as a vanishing way of life.

G ILBERT L. WILSON (DETAIL)
Painted by Frederick N. Wilson, c. 1916
Oil on canvas
H. 96.7 cm, W. 76.4 cm
MHS AV1987.55.8

Early observers. The earliest contacts between the Hidatsa and white visitors probably took place in the 1780s, when the first French and English fur traders traveled to the Northern Plains from posts on the Souris or Saskatchewan rivers in what is now the Canadian province of Manitoba. French trader and explorer Pierre Gaultier de Varennes, Sieur de la Vérendrye, and his sons traveled from a post on the Assiniboine River to visit the Mandan and Hidatsa villages in the 1730s and 1740s; their descriptions of these journeys are of limited use because they had no interpreter and it is unclear which villages they visited (Wood and Thiessen 1985:21-23). More formal explorations of the Upper Missouri River, made by fur traders, explorers, and army officers who visited from the 1790s to the 1870s, produced notes, letters, and other records of the meetings. Although these men usually worked under adverse conditions, many were required to make detailed observations on the region and its inhabitants as an important part of their official duties. In addition, some unofficial travelers who visited the plains planned to publish their accounts, and some early ethnologists began to study the tribe.

One of the first visitors to note his impressions was David Thompson, who was exploring the region for the North West Company in the winter of 1797-98 and hoping to establish trade with the Mandans. Thompson was the first white person to note the differences between the Mandan and Hidatsa peoples, and he collected data on the history, subsistence patterns, material culture, customs, and population of the Hidatsa (Thompson 1962:169, 172-73, 177-78).

The American explorers Lewis and Clark and their party ascended the winding Missouri River six years later, and in October 1804 they built a simple wooden fort a few miles downstream from the Knife River villages. Members of the party lived there through the long harsh winter, making many contacts with local Indians, including the Hidatsa; they gathered fundamentally important information on the area, its resources, and its native peoples (Lewis and Clark 1904-05, 1:196-200). It was at the Knife River villages that Lewis and Clark met the Shoshoni woman Sakakawea (or Sacajawea), who had been captured by the Hidatsa when she was a girl. She later provided assistance as a guide that was crucial to the expedition's success (Chuinard 1976:18-29).

British trader Charles Mackenzie, who visited the Hidatsa four times between 1804 and 1806, recorded a description of the Hidatsa Sun Dance (Masson 1889-90, 1:354-57). Alexander Henry, the younger, another British trader and a keen observer of nature and native Indian peoples, kept a priceless record of his trip in the summer of 1806; he gathered information on the populations, political organization, subsistence strategies, and customs of the Hidatsa (Henry and Thompson 1897, 1:334-35, 348-52).

For the two decades after Henry's visit, comparatively little first-hand data was gathered on the region. In 1825 another group representing the United States government, the Atkinson-O'Fallon Expedition, was sent up the Missouri with pomp and a military escort. In addition to pursuing its formal objectives – to negotiate treaties, overawe hostile Indian tribes, and increase trade – the expedition also gathered useful information on villages, populations, and relations among tribes (*American State Papers* 1834, 2:601, 1832).

Especially valuable in the study of the Hidatsa are the materials created by artists. George Catlin, a popular American artist, visited the Hidatsa villages on his first

visit to the Upper Missouri country in 1832. Although he was more interested in the nearby Mandan, then reputed to be descended from "lost Welsh explorers," he sketched Hidatsa villages, prominent members of the tribe, and a "green corn ceremony," as well as a Plains Indian "surround" of a bison herd. These were published in his *Letters and Notes on the Manners, Customs, and Condition of the North American Indians* (1841, 1:185-201), which – along with his other illustrated books – captivated Britons and Americans.

The first planned, formal ethnography among the tribes of the Upper Missouri was carried out by the German ethnographer Prince Maximilian von Wied-Neuwied, who was accompanied by a small retinue, including artist Karl Bodmer. The group lived in 1833 and 1834 at Fort Clark, a Missouri River fur post a few miles below the Knife River. Maximilian interviewed such experienced fur traders as James Kipp and Edwin T. Denig, gathering information obtainable nowhere

T HE TRAVELLERS MEETING WITH MINATARRE [HIDATSA] INDIANS NEAR FORT CLARK"
Based on an artwork by Karl Bodmer, 1832–33
Copper plate engraving on paper
H. 15.5 cm, W. 23 cm
MHS (Wied 1840–43: vignette 26)
On June 18, 1833, Prince Maximilian von Wied-Neuwied and his party arrived by steamboat at Fort Clark, where Indians and whites inspected each other. "The view of the prairie around Fort Clarke was at this time highly interesting," Maximilian noted. "A great number of horses were grazing all round; Indians of both sexes and all ages were in motion; we were, every moment, stopped by them, obliged to shake hands, and let them examine us on all sides" (Wied 1905-06, 22:350). In this view, Maximilian is introduced to Hidatsa leaders; Karl Bodmer, the artist, is on the right.

else; he and Bodmer attended ceremonies and the two meticulously recorded their observations in written and graphic forms. They also collected specimens of native costumes and crafts. Their labors soon became even more valuable, for the tragic smallpox epidemic of 1837 made permanent changes in the Hidatsa way of life. Their records simply could not be duplicated after this epidemic (Wied 1905-06, 22:357-66, 23:252-385, 24:24-35, 67-68, 261-76; Bodmer 1984).

Daily life among the American traders on the Missouri has also generated records that provide valuable data on the Hidatsa, although they were generally written for personal use. A wealth of highly detailed information on daily life among the Hidatsa was recorded in the diary of Francis A. Chardon, the hard-bitten, cynical trader at Fort Clark from 1834 to 1839. Many of his journal entries deal with prosaic topics like buffalo hunting, horses, agriculture, and warfare. But he also provided gripping word-pictures of the 1837 smallpox epidemic, which cut the Hidatsa population nearly in half and almost destroyed the Mandan (Chardon 1932:3-19, 93-144).

A Swiss artist, the enthusiastic and romantic-minded Rudolph F. Kurz, spent about six weeks with the traders at Fort Berthold in 1851. Before coming to America, he had sought advice from Bodmer. His journal gives insights into life in a fur post and sketches show Hidatsa costumes, crafts, ornaments, and activities (Kurz 1937:73-107; Bodmer 1984:370).

Life in Like-a-Fishhook Village from 1858 to 1860 is graphically described in letters written by Henry A. Boller, a young, enthusiastic fur trader, to his family in Philadelphia. Boller sent vivid descriptions of his life as clerk at Fort Atkinson, at the southern edge of the village. Influenced by Catlin's books, he wrote of his travels in *Among the Indians: Eight Years in the Far West* (1868 and 1959). His letters give readers unusually immediate accounts of the daily lives of the Hidatsa and the traders (Boller 1966a).

During the last half of the 19th century, ethnology and anthropology were being developed as formal sciences. Several early American ethnologists – some attached to the military – helped create these disciplines through their work with the Hidatsa. In 1862 pioneering ethnologist Lewis Henry Morgan gathered information on kinship, linguistics, ceremonial life, and housing (1959:155, 159-66, 192-96). Dr. Washington Matthews, an Army surgeon stationed at Like-a-Fishhook Village in 1865, collected a substantial body of material and later published a classic ethnography; the volume also included the first

dictionary of the Hidatsa language, which has been used by virtually all students of the Hidatsa to follow him (1877). Two years later, General Philippe Régis de Trobriand, stationed at nearby Fort Stevenson, also visited Like-a-Fishhook Village. He talked with Hidatsa and other tribal leaders, recorded his impressions, and drew sketches of the Indian community (Trobriand 1951:79-119).

The U.S. Army also officially encouraged the collection of ethnological information on Plains tribes. Lieutenant William P. Clark visited Like-a-Fishhook Village in June 1881 to study Plains sign language. His work was one of the early comparative studies of regional ethnology. Aided by the leader Poor Wolf, Clark learned that most Hidatsa men understood and used several languages, including Plains sign language (1885:193-97).

Other early ethnologists gathered information on the Hidatsa in order to pursue comparative studies of Plains tribes. Colonel Garrick Mallery included Hidatsa drawings and information in his study of North American Indian pictographs (1886:158-59, 168, 172, 1893:342, 424-25). The Rev. George L. Curtis of Hampton Institute in Hampton, Va., described and photographed the almost deserted site of Like-a-Fishhook in 1889 (1889:246-47, 249; Yale University 1918:649-51). J. Owen Dorsey compared Hidatsa and other Siouan peoples in his studies of Northern Plains tribes (1894:508-18, 1897:242-43).

Professionally trained observers. By the beginning of the 20th century, when the Wilsons were starting their work in North Dakota, a few of the first generation of professionally trained American ethnologists were starting to do studies among the Hidatsa. Other stimuli brought more attention to the tribe. The centennial of the Lewis and Clark Expedition raised new interest in natural features and historic sites along the Missouri River. Antiquarianism, which usually involved the unsystematic digging of archaeological sites, was developing into the science of archaeology. In addition, soon after the turn of the century most of the plains states were forming historical societies that were beginning to build their own collections. Charles E. DeLand of the South Dakota State Historical Society made invaluable notes and observations at the site of Like-a-Fishhook Village early in September 1905 (1906:572-78).

The first formal archaeological investigations of the Upper Missouri were made by George F. Will and Herbert J. Spinden, young and enthusiastic Harvard undergraduates who were backed by the University's

Peabody Museum. Like the Wilsons and most other ethnologists of the time, they had close contacts with the family of Charles L. Hall, the missionary on the Fort Berthold Reservation at Elbowoods from 1876 to 1922, and with the Hidatsa living around Shell Creek and Independence. Will and Spinden excavated a Mandan village site in 1905 and studied earth lodge village sites on the Fort Berthold Reservation in 1911 (Will and Spinden 1906; Will 1924:291-92). Will's father, who owned the state's oldest nursery and seed firm, had developed commercial seed corn from strains collected on the Fort Berthold Reservation in the 1880s. The son developed a special interest in corn and collaborated with Nebraska ethnologist George E. Hyde in a study of its uses among the Indians of the Upper Missouri. Will, whose work summarized the gradually accruing knowledge of regional Indian peoples, was profuse in his credits to Gilbert Wilson (Will and Hyde 1917:16).

But fieldwork by Will and Spinden aroused the belligerent nature of Orin G. Libby, editor and secretary of the State Historical Society of North Dakota. Libby, who was trained as a historian at the University of Wisconsin under Frederick Jackson Turner, was furious at this "invasion" by outsiders. He wrote many critical letters to local newspapers and immediately began making his own studies and publishing those of others on the Knife River Indian villages and their people (Libby 1906b; Poor Wolf 1906a, 1906b). The publication of Libby's own work on these villages and on La Vérendrye (1906a, 1906b, 1908a, 1908b) exposed him to criticism (Dixon 1909:498-503; Will 1910:473-76). His heated replies (Libby 1910) damaged his reputation and clouded some of his significant work on Mandan and Hidatsa ethnography. In spite of Libby's hostility, other easterners were sent to North Dakota to study the Indians. Edward S. Curtis, a professional photographer interested in Indians, worked for many years with the financial backing of J. P. Morgan to record Indian cultures; he visited the Hidatsa in about 1908 and published his materials the following year (Curtis 1970:129-72, 180-96, 210-11).

At about that time, a more serious competitor for Libby was beginning work in North Dakota. Clark Wissler, curator of ethnology at the American Museum of Natural History in New York City, sponsored the work both of the Wilsons and of Robert H. Lowie, who was Wissler's assistant curator at the museum from 1907 to 1921. Lowie met Wilson on his trips to North Dakota in 1910, 1911, and 1913. Lowie studied the social organization, societies, and linguistics of the

Hidatsa and the allied Crow tribe (Lowie 1912, 1916, 1924a, 1935; Murphy 1972:20).

Frances Densmore, the pioneering ethnomusicologist from Minnesota, recorded Mandan and Hidatsa music at Fort Berthold Reservation in 1912, 1915, and 1918. Many of the songs that she recorded dealt with Hidatsa and Mandan men's societies, although she did gather some women's music as well (1923).

The author of perhaps the most important books on the Hidatsa and Mandan Indians, Alfred W. Bowers, conducted archaeological studies of earth lodge village sites along the Upper Missouri River for the Logan Museum of Beloit College in 1929. Goodbird, Wolf Chief, and Crow's Heart were among his consultants for ethnological studies made from 1929 to 1933 and in 1947. Bowers's *Mandan Social and Ceremonial Organization* (1950) and *Hidatsa Social and Ceremonial Organization* (1965), have both become standard works, integrating archaeology, ethnology, and history in comprehensive and balanced studies.

Martha Warren Beckwith, an experienced folklorist from Vassar College, published the Mandan and Hidatsa materials she had collected at Fort Berthold from 1929 to 1932; they are a significant addition to the body of Hidatsa language texts and literature (1930, 1932, 1934, 1938). Her interpreter, Arthur Mandan, had also worked for Francis Densmore (1938:xviii).

Because of the lack of money and personnel during the Great Depression and World War II, comparatively little other ethnological and archaeological research was done on the Hidatsa in the 1930s and 1940s. Traditional ethnological studies of the Indians of the Northern Plains largely ceased during the 1930s. In part this was caused by the gradual deaths of Indian informants who knew the traditional lifeways of their people first-hand; in addition, the research emphasis of ethnologists was changing. The interest in the historical reconstruction of cultures, inspired by the teaching of anthropologist Franz Boas at Columbia University, led to studies of kinship, social organization, political structure, and so forth (Hoebel 1980:20).

Immediately after the war, archaeologists and historical administrators were faced with the enormous impact to result from the proposed construction of a series of giant dams to be built along the Missouri River in North and South Dakota. The new reservoirs would cover hundreds of historic and prehistoric sites containing the material remains of almost a millennium of village-dwelling horticultural Indian peoples. Dozens of fur trade posts, military sites, missions, and white settlement sites would also be inundated forever.

Hidatsa sites were among those surveyed by an archaeological salvage program, organized in 1946 by the National Park Service and the Smithsonian Institution. The work was carried out by archaeologists working for the Missouri River Basin Project, a subdivision of the River Basin Surveys Project of the Bureau of American Ethnology, Smithsonian Institution. By the early 1950s excavations were underway at many Hidatsa sites, including Rock Village, Like-a-Fishhook Village, Night Walker's Butte, Grandmother's Lodge, and Crow Flies High Village. Various reports were published on the work through the next two decades (Hartle 1960; Smith 1972; Woolworth 1956; Malouf 1963). Archaeologist Donald J. Lehmer published an overview of the salvage program in 1971.

Another relatively recent anthropological study of the Hidatsa was carried out by ethnologist Edward M. Bruner, who made field investigations at Fort Berthold in the early 1950s to study ongoing cultural changes on this reservation (1953, 1955, 1956). Important historical treatments of the Hidatsa and Mandan have been produced by Roy W. Meyer (1977); Gregory L. Fox (1982); W. Raymond Wood (1986); and Wood and Thomas D. Theissen (1985).

The Wilson brothers and their work

The work of Gilbert Wilson, who was aided by his younger brother Frederick, took place at Fort Berthold from 1906 to 1918. Their research and collections represent an important transition between the early amateur recorders of Hidatsa life and later highly trained professionals. The brothers approached the study of the Hidatsa with the zeal of missionaries and the enthusiasm of antiquarian collectors. But Gilbert also became a trained anthropologist, which allowed him to make his careful records of observation known to the scholarly community. The Wilsons began their work free of the blinders that theoretical training can impose. Thus they collected information on the major components of Hidatsa culture, such as life style, subsistence activities, and material culture, and integrated it into an appropriate cultural context, often by using an informant's life story as a connecting link. They also recorded a wealth of information on contemporary life and ongoing cultural changes often ignored by trained anthropologists of the period. As collectors of material culture, they frequently hired people to make traditional objects no longer in use.

The brothers were perhaps as interested in the raw materials, process, and circumstances of an object's manufacture, and in its cultural significance, as they were in the object itself. This "Gestalt approach" greatly enriched the products of their labors.

The Wilson brothers continued their research among the Hidatsa for a decade, using the same informants. This furnished a continuity which is often absent in ethnological studies. The Wilsons characteristically approached the Hidatsa with sympathy and humanism, aware of the Indians' struggle to keep an identity when surrounded by a larger, dominant culture.

Gilbert Wilson was born in Springfield, Ohio, in 1869. His interest in Indians was aroused when he read about them and collected arrowheads from nearby sites as a boy; he wanted to learn more about their lives and cultures when he grew up. He graduated from Wittenberg College in 1896 and entered Princeton Theological Seminary. After earning his B.D. degree in June 1899 he earned a Master's degree from Wittenberg in 1900. He moved to Moorhead, Minnesota, in the fall of 1899 and was ordained as a Presbyterian minister in October. In 1902, when he received a call to serve as pastor at the First Presbyterian Church of Mandan, North Dakota, he gladly accepted the opportunity to be near Indians "in their native haunts" (Wilson 1894-1928). He hoped to study them without neglecting his pastoral duties.

Advised by a doctor to spend time outdoors for his health, Wilson soon met Jacob V. Brower, a Minnesota antiquarian digging in Mandan villages nearby. Brower enthusiastically encouraged him to become a corresponding member of the Minnesota Historical Society and to work with the infant State Historical Society of North Dakota. During this period, Orin Libby supported his interest (Upham 1902; SHSND 1906:[15]).

Perhaps remembering his own boyhood interest, Wilson decided to write accurate and sympathetic books about American Indians for children. He wanted to produce publications for children that combined literature, art, and ethnology. Wilson believed that too many "Indian books" paid little attention to ethnology, and that Indians were often shown thinking and reasoning as white men. It was his hope to do for Indian folklore what the brothers Grimm did for German folklore. He wished to preserve Indian history, traditions, material culture, and – most important of all – Indian ways of thinking and reasoning. He also wanted all of his depictions of Indian life to be in harmony with and true to the people who gave him the information – and to be told in their own words (*St. Paul Pioneer Press* 1914).

Wilson's first book, *Little Ugly Boy and the Bear and the Rainbow Snake*, was published in 1903. In the summer of 1905 he traveled to the Standing Rock Reservation, where he collected Sioux myths and ethnological data for another book, *Myths of the Red Children* (1907a). He planned to have his brother Frederick illustrate this book, and those to follow, with drawings based on artifacts the brothers collected.

Throughout their collaboration, Frederick shared Gilbert's attitudes toward and respect for the culture he was recording. Born at Xenia, Ohio, in 1876, he attended Wittenberg College for a few years and then moved to New York City in 1899 to study at the Art Students' League. For several years in the early 1900s he was an illustrator for the *Women's Home Companion*. He accompanied his brother to Fort Berthold in the summers of 1906 and 1907; in about 1908, at Gilbert's urging, he moved to Minneapolis, where he was employed by an advertising agency and later established his own studio (*Minneapolis Tribune* 1913; *St. Paul Pioneer Press* 1914; G. M. Wilson 1971; *Davison's Minneapolis City Directory* 1908-22).

In 1906 Gilbert and Frederick traveled up the Missouri River with Ernst R. Steinbreuck, curator of the State Historical Society of North Dakota, to the community of Independence on the remote Fort Berthold Reservation. There they met an elderly Hidatsa woman, Buffalo Bird Woman, her brother Henry Wolf Chief, and her son Edward Goodbird, all of whom were well informed on traditional Hidatsa beliefs and customs. The Wilsons and Buffalo Bird Woman's family became friends.

Although Gilbert moved the next spring to Minneapolis and became pastor of Shiloh Presbyterian Church (where he would serve until 1917), he and Frederick returned to Independence in the summer of 1907. Gilbert had written to George Heye, a wealthy New York collector of Indian artifacts. While it is not clear whether Heye actually funded the Wilsons' trip, the brothers did sell him many of the artifacts they collected. Most controversial among these acquisitions was the Waterbuster clan bundle, which Gilbert purchased from Wolf Chief. Wolf Chief no longer wished to carry the expensive ceremonial obligations of custodian and had been unable to find a qualified Hidatsa buyer.

Wilson and George E. Pepper wrote a description of the bundle that was published by the American Museum of Natural History (Pepper and Wilson 1908).

Libby, incensed at Wilson's actions, argued that the bundle was clan property and not Wolf Chief's to sell; in 1910 he tried unsuccessfully to have Wilson barred from the reservation (*Bismarck Tribune* [1907]; Meyer 1977:206).

Wilson's publication on the bundle probably also brought him to the attention of Clark Wissler, then the Museum's curator of anthropology. Wissler was at that time sending ethnologists into the Northern Plains to collect information on the 19th century "flowering" of Plains Indian culture.

The Wilsons' work offered Wissler an ideal means by which to obtain priceless ethnographic information and collections for the American Museum at a low cost for travel, living and collecting expenses, and wages for Frederick; Gilbert, paid by his congregation during his summer vacations, was allowed to use the data for his own studies. Wissler sponsored the Wilsons' field work at Fort Berthold during the summers from 1908 to 1918.

Much of the brothers' work focused on Hidatsa subsistence and material culture. This led logically to the collection of traditional Hidatsa tools and equipment and of the native plants they used. The brothers amassed a unique collection of field notes, autobiographies, photographs, sketches, and objects for the Museum. The Wilsons also obtained an impressive personal collection of duplicate ethnological materials.

About 1909 Gilbert Wilson was adopted into the Hidatsa Prairie Chicken clan. Buffalo Bird Woman became his adopted mother; her son, Goodbird, who was about his age, became his brother. The family ties proved enormously helpful for Wilson's work. The ethnologist transcribed and edited Goodbird's life story for children. True to his goal of telling Indian stories straighforwardly, he included details of the self-torture involved in vision quests; to his dismay, the home mission society that published the book deleted that section (Wilson 1913a:105, 1914a; Goodbird 1914a:25). *Goodbird, the Indian* (Goodbird 1914a) was one of the earliest anthropological uses of biographical writing about an American Indian, but it was largely overlooked by scholars. Wilson also published Buffalo Bird Woman's autobiography, *Waheenee: An Indian Girl's Story, Told by Herself* (Maxidiwiac 1921) and used information from Wolf Chief's biography in his other writings (Wilson 1924).

In 1910 Wilson also became a Ph.D. candidate in anthropology at the University of Minnesota, with Albert E. Jenks as his advisor. Jenks, interested in "primitive agriculture," encouraged Wilson to study Hidatsa horticultural practices. Wilson gathered quantities of fascinating information from 1912 to 1915 and wrote his dissertation, "Agriculture of the Hidatsa Indians: An Indian Interpretation," mostly in the words of Buffalo Bird Woman. Approaching his subject with rare insight and humanism, he combined portions of an informant's life story and philosophy with more technical information to produce "an Indian woman's interpretation of economics; the thoughts she gave to her fields; the philosophy of her labors." The dissertation is written in Buffalo Bird Woman's own words, as translated by Goodbird and recorded by Wilson. "In the sweltering heat of an August day," he noted, "she has continued dictation for nine hours, lying down but never flagging in her account, when too weary to sit longer in a chair." Wilson received his doctoral degree in June 1916 – one of the first awarded by the university in anthropology, and among the earliest in the U.S. – and his dissertation was published by the university the next year (Wilson 1917: 2-3).

In addition to the works discussed above, Wilson produced an impressive series of pieces based on his studies of the Hidatsa: another children's book, *Indian Hero Tales* (1916a); articles in *The Farmer* (Maxidiwiac 1916-17, 1918; Wolf Chief 1919); and monographs on "The Horse and Dog in Hidatsa Culture" (1924) and "Hidatsa Eagle Trapping" (1929). Most of these were illustrated by Frederick. Two posthumous publications edited by Bella Weitzner were based on Wilson's notes: "The Hidatsa Earthlodge" (Wilson 1934) and "Notes on the Hidatsa Indians Based on Data Recorded by the Late Gilbert L. Wilson" (Weitzner 1979).

Wilson's ethnological monographs characteristically preserved original data from native informants little altered by his recording; they were usually presented in the form of ethnological narratives that dealt with some aspect of Hidatsa material culture. Autobiographical narratives such as *Goodbird* and *Waheenee* covered traditional Hidatsa life and the transition to reservation life and adjustment with the white man's world. His two major children's books, *Myths of the Red Children* and *Indian Hero Tales*, introduced their readers to real Indians and were unusual in their presentation of authentic ethnological data.

The brothers' collaboration was auspicious. Each possessed talents that contributed towards common goals. Gilbert was an accomplished observer and he allowed his native informants to talk freely about their lives, tribal beliefs, and customs. Of course, he gently steered them to talk about specific themes until they had told him what they remembered on a topic.

Gilbert once explained his technique in a letter to Clark Wissler: "My chief criticism of anthropological material is that it is gathered too much by deductive methods. A collector approaches an Indian informant; takes up a special subject, say the corn dance. He asks the Indian to tell him all about the corn dance, what were its special features, what things in it are to be emphasized etc.; but this is making the Indian generalize, a work to which he is totally untrained. And in essential method, it is reasoning from *a priori*, for it assumes that the Indian has a clear and general idea of the subject, whereas if he is a good informant, he is too ignorant of English ways to even be able to judge what it is you want. The proper and essential way, in my mind, in the study of primitive cultures, is to take a typical and intelligent informant and use him for a type representative on the chief subject. Get from him your major account, out of his own experiences. Then follow with corroborative accounts, also from personal experience, preferably from other members of the same family. Then add miscellaneous corroborating evidences from any source at hand" (Wilson 1916d).

GILBERT WILSON
Collected by Gilbert Wilson, 1913
MHS photo IV-86-13
Wilson wrapped himself in a blanket to demonstrate how Small Ankle carried a nest of young grouse.

Ethnologist Robert Lowie, who met Wilson in 1910, stated frankly, "Among the Hidatsa I was taken down another peg. The Reverend Gilbert L. Wilson was neither particularly cultivated nor in any sense intellectual, but he was a superb observer. In the recording of ethnographic detail – about house building or pottery making or farming customs or the care of infants, for example – I, the trained ethnologist, could not begin to compete with him" (Lowie 1959:104).

Wilson's informants also drew simple sketches to explain how things appeared or were built; they made models to interpret complex items of the material culture. The Wilsons collected objects to explain processes or native technology and as museum exhibit materials.

The Wilsons generally used "state of the art" field methods and equipment for 1908-18. They relied on notebooks and pencils to record an informant's data. Although photographic equipment and films of the era were primitive when compared to later technology, they were simple enough to be used by amateurs. After a few seasons Gilbert had learned to buy film in large quantities and to take multiple exposures of a subject to be sure that he would obtain at least one good negative. He also made sequential photographs of various stages of a process or demonstration. Prints were then carefully mounted in albums with notes to interpret them. He used a sound recording apparatus to record music on wax cylinders. Frederick used drafting equipment for his carefully measured drawings of complex objects, such as earth lodges, and he supplemented the sketches with photographs. The Wilsons collected botanical specimens in the flowering stage, if at all possible, and then preserved them with presses and absorbent papers (1916e, 1916f).

Their ready access to well-informed native consultants was of course critical. Gilbert frankly stated that he had many difficulties collecting data from the Hidatsa until after he and his brother were adopted. Goodbird, said Wilson, "immediately took a great interest in my work and I only had to make him understand what I wanted and why I wanted it in order to get it" (*Minneapolis Tribune* 1913).

After the summer of 1918, Gilbert Wilson, suffering from poor health and once again busy with his work as a minister, ceased his field work at Fort Berthold Reservation. In June 1909 he had married Ada Myers of Springfield, Ohio; their only child was born the next year and lived to be an undergraduate at a local college when he died unexpectedly. Gilbert's later career alternated between the ministry and the teaching of anthropology. In May 1917 he had become pastor of

the First Presbyterian Church in Stillwater, Minn., where he remained until 1920, when he was hired by Macalester College in St. Paul. After heading a successful endowment campaign, he was appointed professor of anthropology and sociology in 1921. He taught and published monographs until his resignation six years later to seek freedom from administrative work and a pending endowment drive. From May 1927 into early 1930 he was pastor of the Lexington Parkway Presbyterian Church in St. Paul. Illness forced his resignation and he died June 8, 1930. After her husband's death, Mrs. Wilson generously donated his papers and extensive collection of ethnological materials to the Minnesota Historical Society (Wilson 1894-1928; Edwards 1930:546-47; MHS 1932).

Frederick Wilson, who had established his own commercial art studio in Minneapolis, worked there all his life. He was married in the early 1920s and led a quiet life until his death on May 10, 1961 (*Davison's Minneapolis City Directory* 1908-22; G. M. Wilson 1971; *Minneapolis Tribune* 1961).

The significance of the Wilsons' work

The Wilson collections of Hidatsa Indian ethnographic materials, described elsewhere in this volume, are unusual among U.S. museum collections for Plains Indian tribes in terms of size, comprehensiveness, and documentation. Gilbert's writing has also received praise; the famed French anthropologist Claude Lévi-Strauss called "Hidatsa Eagle Trapping" "one of the finest masterpieces in all anthropological literature." Wilson, wrote Lévi-Strauss, "had the inspired idea of allowing his informants to talk freely, and of respecting the harmonious and spontaneous fusion, in their stories, of anecdote and meditation, humble technological actions and intricate liturgical ritual; of hunting, cooking and fishing, on the one hand, and rites and myths on the other" (Lévi-Strauss 1979:288).

The Wilson brothers' collections and publications can be used to interpret this world and educate ourselves about it. Their collections provide scholars with information for highly specialized studies of Indian culture or for large-scale comparative research on many Indian tribes from the Northern Plains. Contemporary Hidatsa Indians, who view these materials as a treasury of information on their cultural heritage, can better know and share in the world of their ancestors; some may use it to guide the revival of portions of traditional Hidatsa culture.

A Guide to the Wilson Collections

Mary Jane Schneider

During the preparation for *The Way to Independence*, the authors realized that the nature and extent of Gilbert and Frederick Wilson's collections were, unlike their publications, unknown and unrecognized outside a small circle of curators. The brothers' vast collection of artifacts, photographs, drawings, and manuscripts, assembled while working with the Hidatsa from 1906 to 1918, is divided among four institutions: the Museum of the American Indian, Heye Foundation (MAI); the American Museum of Natural History (AMNH); the Minnesota Historical Society (MHS); and the Science Museum of Minnesota (SMM). This description of the collections is intended to help other researchers to use them.

The major collections of ethnographic material are held by the AMNH and the MHS; the original correlations among artifacts, photographs, sketches, and written records in these two institutions are fairly simple for researchers to reconstruct. Gilbert, who was responsible for the bulk of the collections, kept his manuscripts and photographs in chronological order and generally worked with one museum at a time, so researchers can often – by using the dates given with the materials – reassemble from the various collections the artifacts, field notes and reports, photographs, and sketches collected at one time. But since each of the four museums' collections represents a different stage in Wilson's career, there are some basic differences among them.

Museum of the American Indian, Heye Foundation, New York.

Gilbert Wilson first began professionally collecting in 1906 when he contacted George Heye, a wealthy New York businessman who was acquiring artifacts for what would become the Museum of the American Indian, Heye Foundation in New York City. In July 1907 he made 29 purchases for Heye (Wilson 1907b: 194), who apparently selected from them the artifacts he wanted to add to his collection. A few items – for example, two brooms bought from Mrs. Walks – were apparently returned to Wilson, because there is no record of them in the Museum. One other item, the Waterbuster Clan's sacred bundle, was returned to the Hidatsa in 1938, after the deaths of Wilson and Wolf Chief. While a few items appear to have been purchased from Wilson at a later date, the 1907 collection remains essentially intact at the Museum. Wilson's 1907 diary (now in the collections of the MHS) describes the events surrounding some of the purchases and includes information not presently in the museum catalog. The MAI collection represents a wide range of objects, including household items, clothing, and sacred objects. The Wilsons' later collections are almost entirely Mandan/Hidatsa, but a few items at the MAI were purchased from Arikara men and women.

American Museum of Natural History, New York.

In 1908 Wilson began working for the American Museum of Natural History. He arranged with Dr. Clark Wissler, the Museum's curator of anthropology, to collect information on tribal life styles, especially technology and material culture, and to acquire illustrative specimens. Wilson collected most of the information in interviews; his transcripts identify speakers and at least some of the time reproduce exact wording. He then typed his handwritten field notes (1908-16, 1918) into more formal reports (1908-16, 1918); before mailing the typed reports to the AMNH, he appended detailed lists of the artifacts collected. Goodbird, who was the translator for most of the interviews, also produced sketchbooks (1913-16, 1918) to illustrate Wilson's Indian stories and to explain processes and events that could no longer be photographed. Wilson sent these materials to the AMNH, with the exception of the 1908 handwritten field notes and Goodbird's original 1913 sketchbook (both now at the MHS). In the 1930s Bella Weitzner, a curator at the Museum, began editing the typed reports for a proposed publication. Researchers should be aware that most of the handwritten editing on the AMNH copies of those reports is Weitzner's rather than Wilson's.

The typewritten reports also include about 375 photographic prints, which Wilson identified and pasted into the volumes (in many cases also supplying the negatives to the Museum). He evidently chose these photos from the many he took each year; the bulk of his photographic collection is at the MHS (described below). In some cases, Wilson selected shots for the AMNH that were better focused, had fewer distracting elements, or showed a scene more exactly as he wished; in other cases his reasoning is a mystery. A series of his photographs on a single process may be split between the AMNH and the MHS. Wilson's careful numbering system, which gives year and sequence to each negative, has been retained by the Museum's Photographic Department, although access is found through AMNH negative numbers subsequently assigned to the collection.

Through Gilbert, the Museum hired Frederick Wilson as an artist. The AMNH holds the original artworks that were used in Gilbert's 1924, 1928, and 1934 publications.

Wilson's professional association with the AMNH lasted from 1908 to 1918, although other Wilson artifacts were added to the Museum's collection after that date. He collected most actively from 1908 to 1912; by 1914, when he began his studies in anthropology at the University of Minnesota, he stopped regularly collecting artifacts for the AMNH (although he continued to make field reports). While Gilbert was working for the Museum, the items that Frederick collected were attributed to Gilbert. After Gilbert's death in 1930 Frederick offered additional objects to the Museum, and the one that was accepted by Wissler is attributed to Frederick.

The Wilson collection at AMNH suffers from Gilbert's lack of a collector's eye – it is not what Indian art experts would consider glamorous – but it is a triumph of his skill as an ethnographer. He sought out mundane examples of material culture or reproductions made to illustrate the process of construction, rather than making purchases for aesthetic value or novelty. (Wilson knew that not all the specimens were of great interest; on an item acquired from Wounded Face, he commented that "The ox-bone [club] he had made at some trouble and I purchased mainly to keep him from getting disappointed" [Wilson 1910a: list of purchases, p. 3].)

As a result of Wilson's own interest in traditional technology and his attempts to get items at good prices, the collection has many duplicates and many gaps. Baskets and agricultural implements are numerous, while there are few examples of clothing or items with sacred significance. Wilson also neglected examples of society paraphernalia, which Robert H. Lowie purchased for the AMNH during his visit to the reservation in 1910, and items documenting contemporary reservation culture.

Wilson also went beyond the collecting methods of his day to learn and record who made the item, where it was acquired, and how it was used. In contrast, Lowie often neglected to record even the name of the person from whom he acquired an object.

When Wilson shipped items to the AMNH, he attached a numbered tag on which he wrote one or two words describing the object. Under separate cover – usually with his typed reports – he sent a detailed list providing extensive documentation for the items. The Museum's catalog includes only the information from the tag. The researcher must read the detailed collection lists in Wilson's reports to obtain the more accurate information. This problem has occasionally led to the publication of misleading information. For example, parfleches attributed to the Mandan and Hidatsa by Spier (1931: 302) may be Sioux; they are described in Wilson's detailed list as having come from Standing Rock, a Sioux reservation (Wilson 1910a: list of items purchased, p. 5).

Using a bulky, imperfect machine and wax cylinders, Wilson also tried his hand at recording Mandan/Hidatsa songs. He made approximately sixty cylinders, keeping about thirty for himself and sending the rest to the AMNH. This was perhaps the least successful and most short-lived of Wilson's collections. The cylinders from the AMNH were turned over to the Archives of Traditional Music at Indiana University, where they were transferred to tape and made available to researchers; Wilson's problems with the machine and the circumstances of recording make them of use only to dedicated specialists.

Minnesota Historical Society, St. Paul. The personal collections of Gilbert and Frederick Wilson eventually found a home at the Minnesota Historical Society. Following Gilbert's death in 1930, his widow Ada M. Wilson gave his manuscripts, books, artifacts, and photographs to the Society; Gladys M. Wilson, Frederick's widow, donated her husband's personal collection after his death in 1961. The two collections, kept separate in the Society's record books, are similar.

The Wilson manuscript collections at the MHS complement those at the AMNH. They contain diaries and notebooks (1905-07), carbon copies of the typewritten reports sent to the AMNH (1908-16, 1918), Goodbird's original 1913 sketchbook and carbon copies of all but one of his other sketchbooks (1915-16, 1918; 1914 is missing), and miscellaneous notebooks (1909-29). The latter contain notes Wilson evidently made for his own use in looking over his various reports to the AMNH, as well as lecture notes, collections of Indian legends, and sermons. This manuscript collection has been used as the primary source for the references given in this volume; it is available to researchers on microfilm.

Wilson's personal artifact collections, begun in 1902 when he moved to Mandan, North Dakota, to serve as pastor at the First Presbyterian Church, are his most varied, containing archaeological and ethnographic specimens collected throughout his life. With a few easily recognized exceptions, the prehistoric materials Wilson gathered can be found in the Archaeological Collection of the MHS Museum Department. Although these materials are not well identified, most of the artifacts were evidently collected from village sites along the Missouri River; they are like those excavated from other village archaeological sites, and his field notes support that conclusion. Other archaeological artifacts appear to have been collected during his travels in Mexico in the 1920s.

The larger share of the personal artifact collection consists of ethnographic specimens, many of them apparently acquired for use as models for Frederick's illustrations of Gilbert's children's books and monographs. Wilson collected these objects on his trips to the Standing Rock and Fort Berthold reservations; he also purchased some items from J. D. Allen, a Bismarck dealer in Indian arts and crafts.

The documentation on the artifacts at the MHS varies from highly specific information to none at all. In August of 1915 Gilbert offered his collection to Wissler and the AMNH, stating that he knew the source of every piece and was willing to write it all down (Wilson 1915b:599). It is not known how Wissler responded; at any rate, Wilson died without passing on his knowledge. There are, however, a number of ways of demonstrating that most of the MHS items came from the Mandan and Hidatsa. Since many of the objects are duplicated in the AMNH, a Fort Berthold provenance can be deduced by comparison. Buried in Wilson's field notes is much information concerning artifacts; this can often, by a process of elimination, be used to assign an origin to a specimen. Finally, Wilson's photographs enable us to document some items.

In terms of focus and quality, the collection at the MHS resembles the one Wilson made for the AMNH. The strength of the collection is in the everyday household goods, tools, agricultural implements, and similar items that would have been used by most Hidatsa people before the incursion of non-Indian technology. Like the artifact collection at the AMNH, the MHS holdings generally lack items used by age societies and those having religious significance.

Another valuable part of the Wilson collection at the MHS consists of Wilson's personal collection of photographs. Many of these are obviously personal pictures taken for his own interest, while others are the result of his field work. The collection contains a large photograph album (Wilson [1903-18]) as well as about

1,200 negatives. The album begins with photographs of Indians around Mandan and Wilson's 1905 trip to the Standing Rock Sioux Reservation. Wilson's captions provide provenance for some artifacts and biographical information that is used in this book. The trips to Fort Berthold from 1906 to 1918 are also documented. Approximately 185 of the photographs in the album are prints from negatives Wilson sent to the AMNH; the rest are from the negatives he kept or prints he collected from others. Thus the MHS photo collection, between album and negatives, represents all but about 190 of the photos known to have been taken by Wilson.

Wilson's photographs, like his artifact collection, show he was more interested in recording information than in composition or aesthetics. He complained about technical difficulties with the camera and the developing process. Many of the pictures, while posed, appear to be snapshots because of imperfect lighting, distance from the subject, or camera angle. Wilson was not always successful in coercing his models; he complained to Wissler that people sometimes preferred to sit in the shade rather than pose in the sun (Wilson 1918c:2-3). He elected to use more unobtrusive methods to get pictures of others (like Buffalo Bird Woman) who were not enthusiastic about posing (see p. 289).

Despite the problems Wilson's photographs provide to the editor or illustrator, they contain valuable information that is not present in other sources. Wilson did not collect artifacts representing Hidatsa reservation life in the early 1900s, but his camera caught many reflections of that life in his subjects' dress, housing, and activities. For instance, a glass water pitcher sat by Wolf Chief as he made a scapular hoe, and a metal basin held prairie turnips that Buffalo Bird Woman was peeling with her teeth (MHS photos III-13, III-2).

The photographs, like the artifacts, served as models for Frederick's sketches and paintings, but Frederick removed intrusive white cultural elements that show in the photographs. The MHS has ten paintings (in oil or water color) as well as about 350 drawings (in charcoal, pencil, ink, or wash); many of the latter were used in Gilbert's publications not printed by the AMNH. A comparison of these illustrations with the photographic sources provides interesting insights into the brothers' work by showing which elements they chose to ignore. (In addition, the Society holds over 60 examples of Frederick's commercial art work.)

The MHS also received about thirty of Gilbert's

wax cylinder recordings. Unfortunately, the labels on the cylinders do not always bear a relationship to the contents, and the quality of the recording is so poor as to make it difficult to discern the words and tune. Some are evidently duplicates of those he sent to the AMNH, but others appear to contain different songs. The cylinders were transferred to tape by the American Folklife Center of the Library of Congress.

Science Museum of Minnesota, St. Paul. Wilson changed his collection orientation in 1914, when he began to study anthropology at the University of Minnesota. His reports to the AMNH became more directed toward his personal goals; the information he collected for the Museum on Hidatsa agriculture in 1912 and 1915 was developed into his doctoral dissertation (1917).

After 1914 Wilson also began to develop an artifact collection for the University of Minnesota. Although the University has no known records of the items he collected, references in his field reports and in the manuscripts at the MHS permit a reconstruction of the collection. In 1916 he assisted the University of Minnesota in a study of Hidatsa botany (1916f). Although the specimens and artifacts were to become part of the University's collections, the data he obtained also became part of his report to the AMNH. No complete account of items collected during the

botanical expedition is available, but a document in the MHS manuscript collection (Wilson 1916e) lists many of the items referred to in the 1916 field report and mentions specific objects collected for the University. The final dispensation of the botanical specimens is unknown; the artifacts collected by Wilson eventually were deposited in the University's department of anthropology, where some were used by Robert F. Spencer and Jesse D. Jennings to illustrate their book *The Native Americans* (1965:343-45). In 1976 all of the department's collections were moved to the SMM for study and storage. Eleven of these items can be identified as Wilson's, either because they have his tags or because they appear on both the 1916 list and Wilson's field report.

Other Collections. Because the Wilsons were well known to scholars interested in Northern Plains Indian history and culture, it is very likely that other items collected by them are held in other museums. For example, the State Historical Society of North Dakota has some of Frederick's paintings amd a small Wilson file consisting mainly of reports, letters, and some notes. Gilbert also apparently sent some corn samples to M. L. Wilson of the University of Montana, and he may also have sent some agricultural implements. This catalog may stimulate other museums to publicize the presence of Wilson items in their collections.

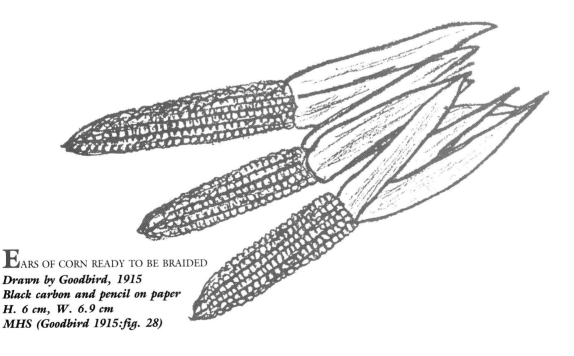

Ears of corn ready to be braided
Drawn by Goodbird, 1915
Black carbon and pencil on paper
H. 6 cm, W. 6.9 cm
MHS (Goodbird 1915:fig. 28)

A note to readers

About the authors.

Gerard Baker, a Mandan-Hidatsa, is north unit district ranger for the National Park Service at Theodore Roosevelt National Park, North Dakota.

Carolyn Gilman is senior project curator at the Minnesota Historical Society. She has curated two MHS exhibitions dealing with how objects form the language of bi-cultural communication: *Chippewa Customs: The Collections of Frances Densmore* (1979) and *Where Two Worlds Meet: The Great Lakes Fur Trade* (1982). Her published works include the catalog for the latter exhibition.

Jeffery R. Hanson, assistant professor of anthropology at the University of Texas at Arlington, is author of *Hidatsa Culture Change: A Cultural Ecological Approach* (1987). He has taught the history of the Three Affiliated Tribes at the University of North Dakota.

Mary Jane Schneider is associate professor of Indian studies at the University of North Dakota. She is the author of *North Dakota Indians: An Introduction* (1986).

W. Raymond Wood, professor of anthropology at the University of Missouri-Columbia, is an expert in Mandan-Hidatsa archaeology and ethnohistory. He has carried out extensive field work with the Village Indians of North Dakota and has published widely on Northern Plains ethnohistory, including *The Origins of the Hidatsa Indians: A Review of Ethnohistorical and Traditional Data* (1986).

Alan R. Woolworth, research fellow at the Minnesota Historical Society, was an archaeologist at Like-a-Fishhook Village in 1952. He acted as principal investigator at Grandmother's Lodge in 1953 and at Fort Berthold I and Like-a-Fishhook Village in 1954. In the 1960s he was a consultant on Mandan-Hidatsa land claims.

Key to captions. Captions in this volume generally give the following information:

OBJECT NAME OR TITLE
Tribe/maker/manufacturer, date of manufacture
Collector, date of collection
Materials and construction
Dimensions (H. – Height; L. – Length; W. – Width;
*   D. – Diameter; C. – Circumference)*
Present owner, accession or catalog number, donor

If a caption does not supply information, that data was not available or applicable. Captions for Wilson artifacts at the AMNH and the MHS do not list donor. Those at the AMNH were given by Gilbert Wilson. Those at the MHS that were collected by Gilbert Wilson were donated by his widow, Ada M. Wilson (accessions 7059, 7857, 8027, and 9661); items collected by Frederick N. Wilson were donated by Frederick (accession 9598) or by his widow, Gladys M. Wilson (accession 9999).

A note on the Wilson materials cited. References in this volume to the Wilson Papers are to the microfilmed edition of the collection at the MHS. For a discussion of the differences between this collection and the Wilson papers at the AMNH, see pages 348-51. Some of Wilson's errors in spelling and punctuation have been silently corrected in passages in which he quotes his informants directly.

Photographic citations are to negatives, not prints, whenever those have been located. Although Wilson varied his cataloging system over the years, he generally used a date and a sequential number, sometimes preceded by a Roman numeral. Wilson's own system has been used for photos at the MHS. Photographs at the AMNH have been assigned sequential negative numbers by the Museum, but Wilson's own numbers are still written on the negatives. Wilson numbered the negatives now at the two institutions in overlapping chronological sequence; for example, two separate photos have the numbers "39-1912." It is therefore essential to distinguish the two series.

Many prints from each series of negatives can be found in the Wilson photograph album, volume 44 in the Wilson Papers, MHS (cited here as Wilson [1903-18]). When the location of a negative is not known, the Album is cited by page number. Several idiocyncratic numbering systems found in the Album alone have not been used.

Researchers should note that there are some negatives in both the MHS and the AMNH that are not reproduced in the Album.

A note on Hidatsa orthography. This volume follows the orthography used in Wilson's notes, which Wilson himself admitted was inconsistent and idiosyncratic. Constraints of typesetting have dictated that short curved lines over and under letters be represented in this volume by straight lines. Researchers wishing to learn pronounciations as interpreted by Wilson are advised to consult Wilson 1918a:[376].

Abbreviations.

AMNH	American Museum of Natural History, New York, N.Y.
CCF	Central Consolidated Files
FB	Fort Berthold
GPO	Government Printing Office
JTAC	Joint Tribal Advisory Committee
Longfellow Papers	Daniel Webster Longfellow Papers, SHSND
M	Microfilm
MHS	Minnesota Historical Society, St. Paul, Minn.
NA	National Archives, Washington, D.C.
NA, Kansas City	National Archives, Kansas City, Mo.
NMNH	National Musuem of Natural History, Smithsonian Institution
RG	Record Group
SHSND	State Historical Society of North Dakota, Bismarck, N.Dak.
USOIA	U.S. Office of Indian Affairs
Wilson Papers	Gilbert L. Wilson Papers, MHS
Word Carrier	Published in Santee, Nebr., as *Word Carrier* (1884-1903), *Word Carrier of Santee Normal Training School* (1903-36), and *Word Carrier of the Santee Normal Training School* (1936-37) by Dakota Mission Training School (1884-1936) and Santee Press (1936-37)

Bibliography

Abbott, F. H.
1911   Speech in "Report of Council Held September 22, 1911
            at Elbowoods, North Dakota, Between Indians of the
            Fort Berthold Reservation and Assistant Commissioner F.
            H. Abbott and Congressman L. B. Hanna." FB. USOIA.
            RG 75. NA, Kansas City.
1913a   Letter to Ernest W. Jermark. Apr. 17. File 36971/13 FB
            751. CCF. USOIA. RG 75. NA.
1913b   Letter to P. D. Norton. July 10. File 83989/13 FB 272.
            CCF. USOIA. RG 75. NA.
Alden, E. H.
1879   Estimate for supplies . . . for the fiscal year ending June
            30, 1880. Jan. 25. FB Agency. Letters Received,
            1824-81. USOIA. RG 75. M234, roll 297, frames
            545-48.
Allen, Edgar A.
1909   Report. Aug. 11. File 65981-3/09 FB 916. CCF.
            USOIA. RG 75. NA.
American Museum Journal
1913   "Museum Notes" about Gilbert L. Wilson (Mar., Oct.):
            149; 288.
1917   "Museum Notes" about Wilson (May, Nov.): 357; 500.
American State Papers: Indian Affairs, vol. 2
1834   Washington, D.C.: Gales and Seaton.
Appleton, Carolyn M.
1985   "Indians Taxed and Indians Not Taxed: Walter Shirlaw,
            Gilbert Gaul and the 1890 Census." *Gilcrease Magazine of
            American History and Art* 7 (Jan.): 28-32.
Arthur, George W.
1978   "A Re-Analysis of the Early Historic Plains Indian Bison
            Drives." *Plains Anthropologist: Journal of the Plains
            Conference* 23, no. 82, pt. 2, Memoir 14 (Nov.): 236-42.
Bailey, Vernon
1926   *A Biological Survey of North Dakota: I. Physiography and Life
            Zones, II. The Mammals.* U.S. Department of Agriculture,
            Bureau of Biological Survey, North American Fauna, no.
            49. Washington, D.C.: GPO.
Baker, Anson
1985   Interview with Carolyn Gilman and Mary Jane Schnieder.
            Mandaree, N.Dak. July 21.
Baker, Cora
1984   Interview with Carolyn Gilman and Mary Jane Schneider.
            Mandaree, N.Dak. July 11.
Bear, Stella
1896   "Band of King's Daughters." *Word Carrier* 25 (June-
            July): 23.
Beckwith, Martha Warren, collector
1930   *Myths and Hunting Stories of the Mandan and Hidatsa
            Sioux.* Publications of the Folk-Lore Foundation, no. 10.
            Poughkeepsie, N.Y.: Vassar College.
1932   *Myths and Ceremonies of the Mandan and Hidatsa: Second
            Series.* Publications of the Folk-Lore Foundation, no. 12.
            Poughkeepsie, N.Y.: Vassar College.
1934   *Mandan and Hidatsa Tales: Third Series.* Publications of the
            Folk-Lore Foundation, no. 14. Poughkeepsie, N.Y.:
            Vassar College.
1938   *Mandan-Hidatsa Myths and Ceremonies.* Memoirs of the
            American Folk-Lore Society, vol. 32. New York: J. J.
            Augustin.
Bismarck Tribune
[1907]   "Fine Exhibits for State Museum: Secretary Libby of the
            State Historical Society, Returns from Fort Berthold
            Laden With Valuable Indian Relics, Including the
            Hoffman Collection." Undated clipping, in Wilson
            1894-1928.
Bobtailed Bull
1906   "A Grosventre Indian Legend." Trans. C[harles] W.
            Hoffman. *Collections of the State Historical Society of North
            Dakota* 1:455.
Bodmer, Karl
1984   *Karl Bodmer's America.* Introduction by William H.
            Goetzmann, annotations by David C. Hunt and Marsha
            V. Gallagher, artist's biography by William J. Orr.
            Omaha, Nebr.: Joslyn Art Museum; Lincoln: University
            of Nebraska Press.
Boller, Henry A.
1959   *Among the Indians: Eight Years in the Far West: 1858-1866.*
            1868. Reprint. Ed. Milo Milton Quaife. The Lakeside
            Classics, no. 57. Chicago: R. R. Donnelley & Sons Co.,
            Lakeside Press. Partial reprint, as *Among the Indians: Four
            Years on the Upper Missouri, 1858-1862.* Ed. Milo Milton
            Quaife. Bison Books. Lincoln: University of Nebraska
            Press, 1972.
1966a   "Henry A. Boller: Upper Missouri River Fur Trader." Ed.
            Ray H. Mattison. *North Dakota History: Journal of the
            Northern Plains* 33 (Spring): 106-219.
1966b   "Journal of a Trip to, and Residence in, the Indian
            Country." Introduction and notes by Ray H. Mattison.
            North Dakota History: Journal of the Northern Plains 33
            (Summer): 260-315.
Borchert, John R.
1971   "The Dust Bowl in the 1970s." *Annals of the Association of
            American Geographers* 61 (Mar.): 1-22.
Bowers, Alfred W.
1948   "A History of the Mandan and Hidatsa." Ph.D. diss.,
            University of Chicago.
1950   *Mandan Social and Ceremonial Organization.* Social
            Anthropological Series. Chicago: University of Chicago
            Press.
1965   *Hidatsa Social and Ceremonial Organization.* Smithsonian
            Institution, Bureau of American Ethnology, Bulletin no.
            194. Washington, D.C.: GPO.
Brasser, Ted J.
1972   "Plains Indian Art." In *American Indian Art: Form and
            Tradition: An Exhibition Organized by: Walker Art Center,
            Indian Art Association, The Minneapolis Institute of Arts: 22
            October-31 December 1972,* 55-61. Minneapolis: Walker Art
            Center and Minneapolis Institute of Arts.
Brickett, Annette P.
1896   "The School Room at Fort Berthold." *Word Carrier* 25
            (May): 20.
Brown, S. Loretta, Jeffery R. Hanson, and Michael L. Gregg
1983   "Environmental Background for the Northern Border
            Project." In *Archeology of the Northern Border Pipeline,
            North Dakota: Survey and Background Information,* ed.
            Matthew J. Root and Michael L. Gregg, 50-134. Vol. 2,
            pt. 1 of *Archeology of the Northern Border Pipeline, North
            Dakota.* University of North Dakota, Department of
            Anthropology and Archaeology, Contribution 194.
Bruner, Edward M.
1953   "Assimilation among Fort Berthold Indians." *American
            Indian* 6 (Summer): 21-29.

1955   "Two Processes of Change in Mandan-Hidatsa Kinship Terminology." *American Anthropologist* 57:840-50.

1956   "Cultural Transmission and Cultural Change." *Southwestern Journal of Anthropology* 12 (Summer): 191-99.

1961   "Mandan." In *Perspectives in American Indian Culture Change*, ed. Edward H. Spicer, 187-277. Chicago: University of Chicago Press.

Buffalo Bird Woman. *See* Maxidiwiac

Butler, David F.

1971   *United States Firearms: The First Century, 1776-1875.* New York: Winchester Press.

Case, Harold W.

1925a   "Rev. Edward Goodbird 25 years in the Ministry," attached to "News Letter." Sept. n.d. Harold W. Case Papers, SHSND.

[1925b] "Goodbird Ordained." Unidentified newspaper clipping. N.d. In scrapbook 3, Case Papers, SHSND.

1932   *The Fort Berthold Indian Mission and Its Work: 1876-1932: With the Gros Ventre, Ree and Mandan Indians: On the Fort Berthold Indian Reservation: Elbowoods, North Dakota.* N.p. Pamphlet in Charles L. Hall Papers, SHSND.

1938   "Noted Indian, Rev. Ed. Goodbird, Died at Elbowoods Mon." *McLean County* (N.Dak.) *Independent.* Sept. 4.

n.d.   Scrapbook 3, Case Papers, SHSND.

Case, Harold W.?

1930s   "Freedom & Simplicity in the cost of Dying With the Indian And the white Man's influence upon him." Typescript, Case Papers, SHSND.

1936   Letter to Fred L. Brownlee. Nov. 17. Case Papers, SHSND.

Case, Harold W., and Eva Case, comps.

1977   *100 Years at Ft. Berthold: The History of the Fort Berthold Indian Mission: 1876-1976.* N.p.: H. W. Case. *See also* Maxfield 1986

Catlin, George

1841   *Letters and Notes on the Manners, Customs, and Condition of the North American Indians: Written during Eight Years' Travel amongst the Wildest Tribes of Indians in North America: In 1832, 33, 34, 35, 36, 37, 38, and 39.* 2 vols. London: G. Catlin. Reprint. Minneapolis: Ross & Haines, 1965.

1844   *North American Indian Portfolio: Hunting Scenes and Amusements of the Rocky Mountains and Prairies of America.* London: n.p.

Chappell, Gordon

1972   *The Search for the Well-dressed Soldier, 1865-1890: Developments and Innovations in United States Army Uniforms on the Western Frontier.* Museum Monograph, no. 5. Tucson: Arizona Historical Society.

Chardon, Francis A.

1932   *Chardon's Journal at Fort Clark: 1834-1839: Descriptive of Life on the Upper Missouri: Of a Fur Trader's Experiences among the Mandans, Gros Ventres, and Their Neighbors: Of the Ravages of the Small-pox Epidemic of 1837.* Ed. Annie Heloise Abel. Pierre, S.Dak.: Under the auspices of Lawrence K. Fox, Superintendent, Department of History, State of South Dakota.

Chuinard, E. G.

1976   "The Actual Role of the Bird Woman: Purposeful Member of the Corps or Casual 'Tag Along'?" *Montana: The Magazine of Western History* 26 (July): 18-29.

Clark, William

1964   *The Field Notes of Captain William Clark: 1803-1805.* Ed. Ernest Staples Osgood. Yale Western Americana Series, 5. New Haven: Yale University Press.

Clark, William P.

1885   *The Indian Sign Language, with Brief Explanatory Notes of the Gestures Taught Deaf-Mutes in Our Institutions for Their Instruction, and a Description of Some of the Peculiar Laws, Customs, Myths, Superstitions, Ways of Living, Code of Peace and War Signals of Our Aboriginies.* Philadelphia: L. R. Hamersly & Co.

Congregational Christian Churches, Missions Council

1947   *Ho-Washte: A Story of the Fort Berthold Mission.* New York: Congregational Christian Churches, Missions Council. Pamphlet in Harold W. Case Papers, SHSND.

Conn, Richard

1982   *Circles of the World: Traditional Art of the Plains Indians.* Denver, Colo.: Denver Art Museum.

Courtenay, William

1879a   Letter to E. J. Brooks, Acting Commissioner. May 27. FB Agency. Letters Received, 1824-81. USOIA. RG 75. M234, roll 299, frame 1071.

1879b   Estimate for stationery. Nov. 21. FB Agency. Letters Received, 1824-81. USOIA. RG 75. M234, roll 299, frames 67-71.

1879c   Order form submitted to Commissioner of Indian Affairs. Dec. 31. FB Agency. Letters Received, 1824-81. USOIA. RG 75. M234, roll 299, frames 72-74.

Cram, George F.

1907   *Cram's Superior Reference Atlas of Minnesota and the World.* New York: F. G. Cram, 1907.

Creighton, Annie R.

1896   "Saving the Body." *Word Carrier* 25 (May): 19.

Crows Heart et al.

1908   Letter to Commissioner of Indian Affairs. Apr. 10. File 26136/08 FB 321. CCF. USOIA. RG 75. NA.

Curtis, Edward S.

1970   *The North American Indian: Being a Series of Volumes Picturing and Describing the Indians of the United States and Alaska.* Ed. Frederick Webb Hodge. Vol. 4. 1909. Reprint. Landmarks in Anthropology, ed. Weston La Barre. New York: Johnson Reprint Corp.

Curtis, George Louis

1889   "The Last Lodges of the Mandans." *Harper's Weekly*, Mar. 30, p. 246-47, 249.

Davis, Charles L.

1911   Inspection report. July 25. File 68170-2/11 FB 916. CCF. USOIA. RG 75. NA.

Davison's Minneapolis City Directory

1908-22 Minneapolis: Minneapolis Directory Co.

Dawson, Anna R.

1901   Annual report. Aug. 13. Attached to Thomas Richards's annual report, Aug. 17. FB. Commissioner's Letters, 1901. USOIA. RG 75. NA, Kansas City.

DeLand, Charles E.

1906   "The Aborigines of South Dakota." Pt. 1. *South Dakota Historical Collections* 3:267-586.

1908   "The Aborigines of South Dakota." Pt. 2, "The Mandan Indians." *South Dakota Historical Collections* 4:275-730.

Densmore, Frances

1918   *Teton Sioux Music.* Smithsonian Institution, Bureau of American Ethnology, Bulletin no. 61. Washington, D.C.: GPO.

1923   *Mandan and Hidatsa Music.* Smithsonian Institution, Bureau of American Ethnology, Bulletin no. 80. Washington, D.C.: GPO.

Dixon, R. B.

1909   Review of *Collections of the State Historical Society of North Dakota*, vol. 2. *American Anthropologist*, n.s. 11:498-503.

Dorsey, James Owen

1894   "A Study of Siouan Cults." In U.S. Bureau of Ethnology, *Eleventh Annual Report of the Bureau of Ethnology to the Secretary of the Smithsonian Institution: 1889-'90*, 351-544. Washington, D.C.: GPO.

1897   "Siouan Sociology: A Posthumous Paper." In U.S.

Bureau of Ethnology, *Fifteenth Annual Report of the Bureau of Ethnology to the Secretary of the Smithsonian Institution: 1893-'94*, 205-44. Washington, D.C.: GPO.

Edwards, Maurice D.
1930   "Gilbert L. Wilson." In Presbyterian Church in the U.S.A., Minnesota Synod, *Minutes of the Synod of Minnesota: 1930*, 546-47. Obituary.

Ellis, Thomas P.
1879   Letter to E. A. Hayt; supply checks enclosed. Apr. 1. FB Agency. Letters Received, 1824-81. USOIA. RG 75. M234, roll 297, frame 834.

Ewers, John Canfield
1939   *Plains Indian Painting: A Description of an Aboriginal American Art.* Stanford University, Calif.: Stanford University Press; London: Humphrey Milford, Oxford University Press.
1949   "The Last Bison Drives of the Blackfoot Indians." *Journal of the Washington Academy of Sciences* 39:355-60.
1957   "Hair Pipes in Plains Indian Adornment: A Study in Indian and White Ingenuity." In *Anthropological Papers*, no. 50, p. 29-85. Smithsonian Institution, Bureau of American Ethnology, Bulletin no. 164. Washington, D.C.: GPO.

Ewers, John Canfield, Royal B. Hassrick, and Anne E. Walton
1985   "Arts and Crafts of the Blackfeet and their Neighbors." In *After the Buffalo Were Gone: The Louis Warren Hill, Sr., Collection of Indian Art*, by Ann T. Walton, John Canfield Ewers, and Royal B. Hassrick, 86-253. St. Paul: Northwest Area Foundation.

Ferguson, James C.
1954   "Reminiscences of Dr. James C. Ferguson of St. Paul, Minnesota." James C. Ferguson Reminiscences, MHS.

Field, Mary E.
1896   "Our Girls' Home Life." *Word Carrier* 25 (May): 20.

Fort Berthold Agency
1917-19   Record of brands/Indian stock ("brand book"). FB. USOIA. RG 75. NA, Kansas City.

Fox, Gregory L.
1982   *The Garden Coulee Site (32WI18): A Late Nineteenth Century Village of a Band of Dissident Hidatsa.* Lincoln, Nebr.: U.S. Department of the Interior, National Park Service, Midwest Archeological Center.

Frison, George C.
1978   *Prehistoric Hunters of the High Plains.* New World Archaeological Record, ed. James Bennett Griffin, vol. 1. New York: Academic Press.

Gardner, Robert S.
1880   Letter to Commissioner of Indian Affairs. Mar. 20. FB Agency. Letters Received, 1824-81. USOIA. RG 75. M234, roll 299, frames 261-62.

Garrison (N.Dak.) *Times*
1913   "Delegation of Indians Return from Wash." Mar. 26, p. 1.

Geiger, Louis G.
1958   *University of the Northern Plains: A History of the University of North Dakota: 1883-1958.* Grand Forks: University of North Dakota Press.

Gifford, Abram J.
1885   Letter to John D. C. Atkins, Commissioner of Indian Affairs. Apr. 14. File 8541/1885. Letters Received. USOIA. RG 75. NA.
1886   Letter to Commissioner of Indian Affairs. Oct. 11. File 27790/1886. Letters Received. USOIA. RG 75. NA.

Gilmore, Melvin R.
1926   "Being an Account of an Hidatsa Shrine and the Beliefs Respecting It." Review of Pepper and Wilson 1908. *American Anthropologist*, n.s. 28 (July-Sept.): 572-78.

Goodall, Anow
1912   Letter to Commissioner of Indian Affairs. Oct. 10. File

108375/11 FB 916. CCF. USOIA. RG 75. NA.

Goodbird, Edward (Tsakakis-sakis)
1906   "The Myth of Packs Antelope." Recorded by Charles L. Hall. *Collections of the State Historical Society of North Dakota* 1:446-54.
1907   Oath of office. Oct. 11. File 83686 FB. CCF. USOIA. RG 75. NA.
1908   Letter to Gilbert Wilson. Sept. 30. Copy in Anthropology Dept., AMNH.
1909a   Letter to C[harles] W. Hoffman. Apr. 13. FB. USOIA. RG 75. NA, Kansas City.
1909b   Letter to C[harles] W. Hoffman. May 19. FB. USOIA. RG 75. NA, Kansas City.
1913   Sketches, vol. 15, Wilson Papers, MHS.
1914a   *Goodbird the Indian: His Story: Told by Himself to Gilbert L. Wilson.* Illus. Frederick N. Wilson. New York: Fleming H. Revell. References are to pages in reprint, *Goodbird the Indian: His Story.* Introduction by Mary Jane Schneider. Borealis Books. St. Paul: Minnesota Historical Society Press, 1985.
1914b   Sketches, Anthropology Dept., AMNH.
1915   Sketches, vol. 19, Wilson Papers, MHS.
1916   Sketches, vol. 21, Wilson Papers, MHS.
1918   Sketches, vol. 23, Wilson Papers, MHS.
        See also H. Wolf Chief 1919; *Word Carrier* 1915, 1925

Grand, W. Joseph
1896   *Illustrated History of the Union Stockyards: A Sketch-book of Familiar Faces and Places at the Yards: Not Forgetting Reminiscences of the Yards . . .* Chicago: Thos. Knapp Pgt. & Bdg. Co.

Griffin, David E.
1977   "Timber Procurement and Village Location in the Middle Missouri Subarea." *Plains Anthropologist: Journal of the Plains Conference* 22, no. 78, pt. 2, Memoir 13 (Nov.): 177-85.

Hagen, Olaf T., and Ray H. Mattison
1952   "Pyramid Park – Where Roosevelt Came to Hunt." *North Dakota History* 19 (Oct.): 215-39.

Hail, Barbara A.
1983   *Hau, Kóla!: The Plains Indian Collection of the Haffenreffer Museum of Anthropology.* Rev. prtg. Studies in Anthropology and Material Culture, vol. 3. Providence, R.I.: The Museum, Brown University.

Hall, Charles L.
[1881-86]   "Records of the Mission of the A.B.C.F.M. at Ft. Berthold D.T." Typescript in Hall Papers, SHSND.
1883   Letter to One Who Stands on Top. Apr. 11. Hall Papers, SHSND.
1888a   "The Mission Home School: Fort Berthold, Dakota." *Word Carrier* 17 (May): 19.
1888b   "Winter Itinerancy: A Graphic Description of a Missionary's Visits to the Out-Posts." *Word Carrier* 17 (May): 18.
1888c   "Fort Berthold Notes." *Word Carrier* 17 (Sept.): 29.
1896   "The Beginning." *Word Carrier* 25 (May): 17.
1897   "Fort Berthold Notes." *Word Carrier* 26 (Oct.-Nov.): 31.
1900   "Report of Superintendent of Mission Home School." In U.S. Office of Indian Affairs, *Report . . . .* , 316-17. Washington, D.C.: GPO.
1902   Marriage license for Charles Goodbird and Nellie Old Mouse. Oct. 5. Marriage License, p. 27. FB. USOIA. RG 75. NA, Kansas City.
1923?   *The Fort Berthold Mission: Elbowoods, North Dakota.* New York: American Missionary Association. Pamphlet in Daniel W. Longfellow Papers, SHSND.
1929   "Hidatsa Sheep." *Word Carrier* 58 (May-June): 12.
1937a-s   "The Story of Fort Berthold." *McLean County Independent* (Garrison, N.Dak.), a, Jan. 14; b, Jan. 21; c, Jan. 28; d,

Feb. 4; e, Feb. 11; f, Feb. 18; g, Feb. 25; h, Mar. 4; i, Mar. 11; j, Mar. 25; k, Apr. 1; l, Apr. 8; m, Apr. 15; n, Apr. 22; o, Apr. 29; p, May 6; q, May 13; r, May 20; s, May 27 – all p. 11.

n.d.   *Fifty Years among the Dakota Indians.* N.p. Pamphlet in Longfellow Papers, SHSND.

Hall, Charles L., and Mrs. Robert D. (Lois J. Halverstadt) Hall
n.d.   *Indians Who Have Made Good: The Story of Sitting Crow and Poor Wolf.* New York: American Missionary Association. Pamphlet in Longfellow Papers, SHSND.

Hamilton, T. M.
1982   *Native American Bows.* 2d ed. Special Publications, no. 5. Columbia, Mo.: Missouri Archaeological Society.

Hanson, Jeffery R.
1983a   "Hidatsa Culture Change, 1780-1845: A Cultural Ecological Approach." Ph.D. diss., University of Missouri-Columbia.
1983b   "Changes in Hidatsa Residence Patterns: A Cross-Cultural Interpretation." *Plains Anthropologist: Journal of the Plains Anthropological Society* 28, no. 99 (Feb.): 69-75.
1984   "Bison Ecology in the Northern Plains and a Reconstruction of Bison Patterns for the North Dakota Region." *Plains Anthropologist: Journal of the Plains Anthropological Society* 29, no. 104 (May): 93-114. *See also* Brown, Hanson, and Gregg 1983; Wood 1986

Harding, A. R.
1907   *Steel Traps: Describes the Various Makes and Tells How to Use Them: Also Chapters on Care of Pelts, Etc.* Columbus, Ohio: A. R. Harding Pub. Co.

Harkness, James
1896   "Diary of James Harkness of the Firm of LaBarge, Harkness and Company: St. Louis to Fort Benton by the Missouri River and to the Deer Lodge Valley and Return in 1862." *Contributions to the Historical Society of Montana* . . . 2:343-61.

Hartle, Donald D.
1960   "Rock Village: An Ethnohistorical Approach to Hidatsa Archaeology." Ph.D. diss., Columbia University.

[Hauke, Charles F.]
1910   Letter to Charles W. Hoffman. Oct. 19. File 80616/10 FB 062. CCF. USOIA. RG 75. NA.

Haynes, John J.
1987   *The Forgotten People – The Story of the Fort Berthold Indian Mission, 1876-1985.* Exeter, England: J. J. Haynes.

Hayt, E. A.
1878   Circular, Department of the Interior, Office of Indian Affairs. Nov. 15. FB Agency. Letters Received, 1824-81. USOIA. RG 75. M234, roll 297, frame 50.

Henry, Alexander, d. 1814, and David Thompson
1897   *New Light on the Early History of the Greater Northwest: The Manuscript Journals of Alexander Henry, Fur Trader of the Northwest Company, and of David Thompson, Official Geographer and Explorer of the Same Company, 1799-1814: Exploration and Adventure among the Indians on the Red, Saskatchewan, Missouri, and Columbia Rivers.* Ed. Elliott Coues. 3 vols. New York: Francis P. Harper. Reprint (3 vols. in 2; same continuous pagination). Minneapolis: Ross & Haines, 1965.

Hiller, Wesley R.
1948a   "Hidatsa Soft Tanning of Hides: As Demonstrated by Uta Wiaś (Weasel Woman)." *Minnesota Archaeologist* 14 (Jan.): 4-23.
1948b   "The Making of Ma-pí or Corn Balls: As Told by Uta Wiaś (Weasel Woman)." *Minnesota Archaeologist* 14 (Jan.): 25-27.

Hoebel, E. Adamson
1980   "The Influence of Plains Ethnography on the Development of Anthropological Theory." In *Anthropology*

on the Great Plains, ed. W. Raymond Wood and Margot Liberty, 16-22. Lincoln: University of Nebraska Press.

Hoffman, Charles W.
1907-12   Daybook ("diary"). References are to entries for June 12, 1909, and Aug. 26, 1910. FB. USOIA. RG 75. NA, Kansas City.
1909a   Letter to Commissioner of Indian Affairs. Mar. 29. File 25287/09 FB 063. CCF. USOIA. RG 75. NA.
1909b   Letter to Commissioner of Indian Affairs. July 26. File 61164/09 FB 916. CCF. USOIA. RG 75. NA.
1909c   Letter to Commissioner of Indian Affairs. Dec. 8. File 99238/09 FB 806. CCF. USOIA. RG 75. NA.
1910   Letter to Commissioner of Indian Affairs. Mar. 29. FB. Letters to Commissioner, June 14, 1909-Aug. 25, 1910, vol. 2. USOIA. RG 75. NA, Kansas City.
1911a   Letter to Commissioner of Indian Affairs. Feb. 9. FB. Letters to Commissioner, Aug. 10, 1910-July 8, 1911, vol. 3. USOIA. RG 75. NA, Kansas City.
1911b   Letter to Commissioner of Indian Affairs. Dec. 11. File 108375/11 FB 916. CCF. USOIA. RG 75. NA.
1912   Circular, "To Returned Students." Jan. 12. File 95714/11 FB 752. CCF. USOIA. RG 75. NA.

Howard, James H.
1953   "The Like-a-Fishhook Village Site, Old Fort Berthold." James H. Howard Papers, SHSND.
1960   "Butterfly's Mandan Winter Count: 1833-1876." *Ethnohistory* 7 (Winter): 28-43.

Hoxie, Frederick E.
1984   *A Final Promise: The Campaign to Assimilate the Indians, 1880-1920.* Lincoln: University of Nebraska Press.

Hurt, Wesley R.
1969   "Seasonal Economic and Settlement Patterns of the Arikara." *Plains Anthropologist: Journal of the Plains Conference* 14, no. 43 (Feb.): 32-37.

Hurt, Wesley R., and William E. Lass
1956   *Frontier Photographer: Stanley J. Morrow's Dakota Years.* Vermillion: University of South Dakota; Lincoln: University of Nebraska Press.

Ilsley, Harriet B.
1895   "From Elbowoods." *Word Carrier* 24 (Nov.-Dec.): 31.
1896a   "From Elbowoods." *Word Carrier* 25 (Jan.): 3.
1896b   "Elbowoods in Winter." *Word Carrier* 25 (May): 19.

Jacknis, Ira
1985   "Franz Boas and Exhibits: On the Limitations of the Museum Method of Anthropology." In *Objects and Others: Essays on Museums and Material Culture,* ed. George W. Stocking, Jr., 75-111. History of Anthropology, vol. 3. Madison: University of Wisconsin Press.

Jackson, Donald, ed.
1962   *Letters of the Lewis and Clark Expedition: With Related Documents: 1783-1854.* Urbana: University of Illinois Press.

Jefferson, Thomas
1955   *Notes on the State of Virginia.* Ed. William Peden. Chapel Hill: University of North Carolina Press.

Jenks, Albert Ernest
1916   Review of *Agriculture of the Hidatsa Indians: An Indian Interpretation,* by Gilbert L. Wilson. *Science,* n.s. 44 (Dec. 15): 864-66.

Jensen, Ray E.
1972   *Climate of North Dakota.* Bismarck: North Dakota State Water Commission.

Jermark, Ernest W.
1913   Letter to Commissioner of Indian Affairs. Mar. 14. File 36971/13. FB 751. CCF. USOIA. RG 75. NA.
1914   Letter to Commissioner of Indian Affairs. July 25. File 64154/14. FB 301. CCF. USOIA. RG 75. NA.

1916   Letter to Commissioner of Indian Affairs. May 17. File 65031/15. FB 113.1. CCF. RG 75. NA.

1918   Annual report to Commissioner of Indian Affairs. N.d. FB. Miscellaneous Correspondence, 1914–1917. USOIA. RG 75. NA, Kansas City.

1919   Letter to Commissioner of Indian Affairs. July 30. File 11796/18 FB 063. CCF. RG 75. NA.

1922   Circular, "To Whom It May Concern." Jan. 30. Fort Berthold Indian Agency Records, SHSND.

Johnson, Warren Carter
1971   "The Forest Overstory Vegetation on the Missouri River Floodplain in North Dakota." Ph.D. diss., North Dakota State University.

Joint Tribal Advisory Committee, Three Affiliated Tribes, Fort Berthold Reservation (JTAC)
1986a   Testimony before committee by tribal members about impact of Garrison Dam. New Town, N.Dak. Jan. 10. Transcript in Legal Dept. files, Three Affiliated Tribes.

1986b   Testimony, Jan. 11.

Kauffman, Jacob
1880a   Bond and oath. Apr. 24. FB Agency. Letters Received, 1824–81. USOIA. RG 75. NA. M234, roll 299, frames 376–77.

1880b   Letter to R. E. Trowbridge. Aug. 5. FB Agency. Letters Received, 1824–81. USOIA. RG 75. NA. M234, roll 299, frames 547–48.

1880c   Letter to R. E. Trowbridge. Dec. 10. FB Agency. Letters Received, 1824–81. USOIA. RG 75. NA. M234, roll 299, frames 817–18.

1881   Letter to H. Price. Oct. 12. File 18388/1881. Letters Received. USOIA. RG 75. NA.

Kehoe, Elizabeth
1896   "Independence Station." *Word Carrier* 25 (May): 19.

Kläy, Ernst J., and Hans Läng
1984   *Das romantische Leben der Indianer malerisch darzustellen: Leben und Werk von Rudolf Friedrich Kurz.* Solothurn, Switz.: AARE.

Knight, Clark M.
1917   "Report on Conditions on the Fort Berthold Reservation." July 5. File 70729/17 FB 916. CCF. USOIA. RG 75. NA. P. 14–15 of this report are contained in File 70731/17 FB 806.

Kuehn, David D., Carl R. Falk, and Amy Drybred
1982   *Archaeological Data Recovery at Midipadi Butte, 32DU2, Dunn County, North Dakota.* University of North Dakota, Department of Anthropology, Contribution no. 181. Grand Forks: University of North Dakota.

Kunstmuseum Bern
1976   *Berner Maler in Amerika: Beitras zur Ausstelluns, Zwei Berner Maler in Amerika: Friedrich Kurz um 1850, Victor Surbek um 1950, Kunstmuseum Bern, 11.11.76–23.1.77.* Essays by Sandor Kuthy and Ernst J. Kläy. Bern: Kunstmuseum Bern.

Kurz, Rudolph Friederich
1937   *Journal of Rudolph Friederich Kurz: An Account of His Experiences among Fur Traders and American Indians on the Mississippi and the Upper Missouri Rivers during the Years 1846 to 1852.* Trans. Myrtis Jarrell. Ed. J. N. B. Hewitt. Smithsonian Institution, Bureau of American Ethnology, Bulletin no. 115. Washington, D.C.: GPO. See also Kläy and Läng 1984; Kunstmuseum Bern 1976.

Ladner, Mildred D.
1984   *William de la Montagne Cary: Artist on the Missouri River.* Norman: University of Oklahoma Press; Tulsa: Thomas Gilcrease Institute of American History and Art.

Larpenteur, Charles
1898   *Forty Years a Fur Trader on the Upper Missouri: The Personal Narrative of Charles Larpenteur: 1833–1892.* Ed. Elliott Coues. American Explorers Series, 2. 2 vols. New York: Francis P. Harper. Reprint (2 vols in 1; same continuous pagination). Minneapolis: Ross & Haines, 1962.

Lee, Walter
1900   Letter to Edward G. Bird [Goodbird]. Sept. 27. FB. Miscellaneous Letters 1900. USOIA. RG 75. NA, Kansas City.

Lehmer, Donald J.
1971   *Introduction to Middle Missouri Archeology.* U.S. Department of the Interior, National Park Service, Anthropological Papers 1. Washington, D.C.: GPO.

1977   "Epidemics among the Indians of the Upper Missouri." In *Selected Writings of Donald J. Lehmer,* 105–11. Reprints in Anthropology, vol. 8. Lincoln, Nebr.: J & L Reprint Co.

Lehmer, Donald J., W. Raymond Wood, and C. L. Dill
1978   *The Knife River Phase.* With contributions by Arnold R. Pilling and Carlyle S. Smith. Blair, Nebr.: Dana College.

Leupp, F. E.
1907   Letter to H. C. Hansbrough. Dec. 19. File 96497/07 FB 916. CCF. USOIA. RG 75. NA.

Lévi-Strauss, Claude
1979   *The Origin of Table Manners.* Trans. John and Doreen Weightman. Introduction to a Science of Mythology, 3. New York: Harper & Row, Harper Colophon Books.

Lewis, Meriwether, and William Clark
1893   *History of the Expedition under the Command of Lewis and Clark, To the Sources of the Missouri River, thence across the Rocky Mountains and down the Columbia River to the Pacific Ocean, Performed during the Years 1804-5-6, by Order of the Government of the United States . . . .* Ed. Elliott Coues. 4 vols. New York: Francis P. Harper. Reprint (4 vols. in 3; same continuous pagination). As *The History of the Lewis and Clark Expedition.* New York: Dover Publications, 1965?

1904–05   *Original Journals of the Lewis and Clark Expedition: 1804–1806 . . .* Ed. Reuben Gold Thwaites. 8 vols. New York: Dodd, Mead & Co.

Libby, O. G.
1906a   "The Mandans and Grosventres." *Collections of the State Historical Society of North Dakota* 1:433.

1906b   "The Five Knife River Villages." With drawings of the villages by Sitting Rabbit. *Collections of the State Historical Society of North Dakota* 1:433–36. *See also* Thiessen, Wood, and Jones 1979

1908a   "La Verendrye's Visit to the Mandans in 1738–39." *Collections of the State Historical Society of North Dakota* 2:502–8.

1908b   "Typical Villages of the Mandans, Arikara and Hidatsa in the Missouri Valley, North Dakota." *Collections of the State Historical Society of North Dakota* 2:498–502.

1910   "The Proper Identification of Indian Village Sites in North Dakota: A Reply to Dr Dixon." *American Anthropologist,* n.s. 12:123–28.

Longfellow, Daniel Webster
1877   "Inventory of Stock at the Traders Store, Ft. Berthold, D. T., March 25th, 1877." Longfellow Papers, SHSND.

1938   "A Brief Sketch of Experiences in the Life of Daniel Webster Longfellow." Longfellow Papers, SHSND.

Lowie, Robert H.
1910   Letter to Clark Wissler. Aug. 30. Anthropology Dept., AMNH.

1912   "Some Problems in the Ethnology of the Crow and Village Indians." *American Anthropologist,* n.s. 14:60–71.

1916   "Societies of the Hidatsa and Mandan Indians." *Anthropological Papers of the American Museum of Natural History* 11:219–358.

1921   "The Hidatsa Sun Dance." *Anthropological Papers of the*

American Museum of Natural History 16:411-31.

1924a   "Notes on the Social Organization and Customs of the Mandan, Hidatsa, and Crow Indians." *Anthropological Papers of the American Museum of Natural History* 21:1-99.

1924b   "Minor Ceremonies of the Crow Indians." *Anthropological Papers of the American Museum of Natural History* 21:323-65.

1924c   "The Material Culture of the Crow Indians." *Anthropological Papers of the American Museum of Natural History* 21:201-70.

1924d   "Crow Indian Art." *Anthropological Papers of the American Museum of Natural History* 21:271-322.

1935   *The Crow Indians.* New York: Farrar & Rinehart.

1959   *Robert H. Lowie: Ethnologist: A Personal Record.* Berkeley: University of California Press.

Lowie, Robert H., Zellig Harris, and C. F. Voegelin

1939   *Hidatsa Texts.* Collected by Robert H. Lowie, with grammatical notes and phonograph transcriptions by Zellig Harris and C. F. Voegelin. Prehistory Research Series, vol. 1, no. 6. Indianapolis: Indiana Historical Society.

McHugh, Tom

1972   *The Time of the Buffalo.* With the assistance of Victoria Hobson. New York: Alfred A. Knopf.

McNeill, William H.

1976   *Plagues and Peoples.* Garden City, N.Y.: Anchor Press/Doubleday.

Mallery, Garrick

1886   "Pictographs of the North American Indians. A Preliminary Paper." In U.S. Bureau of American Ethnology, *Fourth Annual Report of the Bureau of Ethnology to the Secretary of the Smithsonian Institution: 1882-'83,* 3-256. Washington, D.C.: GPO.

1893   "Picture-Writing of the American Indians." In U.S. Bureau of American Ethnology, *Tenth Annual Report of the Bureau of Ethnology to the Secretary of the Smithsonian Institution: 1888-'89,* 1-807. Washington, D.C.: GPO.

Malouf, Carling

1963   "Crow-Flies-High (32MZ1), a Historic Hidatsa Village in the Garrison Reservoir Area, North Dakota." In *River Basin Surveys Papers,* ed. Frank H. H. Roberts, Jr., no. 29, p. 133-66. Smithsonian Institution, Bureau of American Ethnology, Bulletin no. 185. Washington, D.C.: GPO.

Masson, L. R.

1889-90   *Les Bourgeois de la Compagnie du Nord-Ouest: Récits de Voyages, Lettres et Rapports Inédits Relatifs au Nord-Ouest Canadien.* 2 vols. Quebec: A. Coté et Cie.

Matthews, Washington

1877   *Ethnography and Philology of the Hidatsa Indians.* U.S. Department of the Interior, United States Geological and Geographical Survey, Miscellaneous Publications no. 7. Washington, D.C.: GPO. Reprint. University of Minnesota, Program in American Studies, Series in American Studies, ed. Joseph J. Kwiat. New York: Johnson Reprint Corp., 1971.

Mattison, Ray H.

1951   "Old Fort Stevenson – A Typical Missouri River Military Post." *North Dakota History* 18 (Apr.-July): 53-91.

1955   "Report on Historic Sites in the Garrison Reservoir Area, Missouri River." *North Dakota History* 22 (Jan.-Apr.): 5-73.

1957   "Indian Missions and Missionaries on the Upper Missouri to 1900." *Nebraska History* 38 (June): 127-54.

Maxfield, Christyann Ranck

1986   *Goodbye to Elbowoods: The Story of Harold and Eva Case.* North Dakota Mini-Biography Series. Bismarck: State Historical Society of North Dakota.

Maxidiwiac (Buffalo Bird Woman, Waheenee)

1916-17   "'Buffalo Bird Woman' – Her Own Life Story." Pt. 1. Continued as "Buffalo Bird Woman's Story." Pts. 2-8. Told to Gilbert L. Wilson. Illus. Frederick N. Wilson and with photographs. *The Farmer* (St. Paul, Minn.), Dec. 2, 9, 16, 23, 30, 1916, p. 1655, 1662; 1704, 1708; 1732, 1740; 1764, 1767; 1788, 1791; Jan. 6, 13, 20, 1917, p. 6, 14-15; 46; 86, 95.

1918   "Buffalo-Bird-Woman Tales." Told to Gilbert L. Wilson. Illus. Frederick N. Wilson and with photographs. 4 pts. *The Farmer* (St. Paul, Minn.), Feb. 9, 23, Mar. 9, Apr. 6, p. 273-75; 369-71; 486-88; 665-66.

1921   *Waheenee: An Indian Girl's Story: Told by Herself to Gilbert L. Wilson, Ph.D.* Illus. Frederick N. Wilson. St. Paul: Webb Publishing Co. Reprints. *North Dakota History: Journal of the Northern Plains* 38 (Winter-Spring 1971): iii-189. Occasional publication no. 4. Bismarck: State Historical Society of North Dakota, 1981. Introduction by Jeffery R. Hanson. Bison Books. Lincoln: University of Nebraska Press, 1981.

Maximilian. *See* Wied, Maximilian, prinz von

Meyer, Roy W.

1968   "Fort Berthold and the Garrison Dam." *North Dakota History: Journal of the Northern Plains* 35 (Summer-Fall): 217-355.

1977   *The Village Indians of the Upper Missouri: The Mandans, Hidatsas, and Arikaras.* Lincoln: University of Nebraska Press.

Michael, L. F.

1915   "Inspection Report. Fort Berthold Reservation and Schools." Oct. 17. File 113333/15 FB 910. CCF. USOIA. RG 75. NA.

Minneapolis Tribune

1913   "Minneapolis Pastor Recognized as Authority on Mandan Indian Lore; Researchs of G. L. Wilson Applied on Credits for Ph.D. Degree at 'U'." Dec. 14, sec. 3, p. 9.

1961   "Frederick N. Wilson"; "Wilson – Frederick N." May 12, p. 26; 27. Obituaries.

Minnesota Historical Society

1932   "Accessions." *Minnesota History* 13 (Mar.): 102-3.

Missions Council. *See* Congregational Christian Churches. Missions Council

Missouri River Basin Project. *See* U.S. Bureau of Indian Affairs, Missouri River Basin Investigations Project

Montclair, Nellie

1888   "Girls' Compositions, June, 1888: What We Have Learned." *Word Carrier* 17 (July-Aug.): 27.

Mooney, James

1912   "Hidatsa." In *Handbook of American Indians: North of Mexico,* pt. 1, ed. Frederick Webb Hodge, 547-49. Smithsonian Institution, Bureau of American Ethnology, Bulletin no. 30. Washington, D.C.: GPO.

Morgan, Lewis Henry

1959   *The Indian Journals: 1859-62.* Ed. Leslie A. White. Ann Arbor: University of Michigan Press.

Moulton, Gary E., ed.

1983   *Atlas of the Lewis & Clark Expedition.* Vol. 1 of *The Journals of the Lewis and Clark Expedition.* Lincoln: University of Nebraska Press.
        See also Wood and Moulton 1981

Murdock, George Peter, and Timothy J. O'Leary

1975   "09-10 Hidatsa." In *Plains and Southwest,* 85-88. Vol. 5 of *Ethnographic Bibliography of North America.* 4th ed. Behavior Science Bibliographies. New Haven, Conn.: Human Relations Area Files Press.

Murphy, John S.

1890a   Letter to Commissioner of Indian Affairs. Feb. 8. File 4586/1890. Letters Received. USOIA. RG 75. NA.

1890b   Letter to Commissioner of Indian Affairs. Feb. 25. File 6676/1890. Letters Received. USOIA. RG 75. NA.

1891a   "Descriptive Statement of Proposed Changes in the Indian Police Force at Fort Berthold, N.D. Agency." July 13. File 25857/1891. Letters Received. USOIA. RG 75. NA.

1891b   "Descriptive Statement of Proposed Changes in the Indian Police Force at Fort Berthold, N.D. Agency." Sept. 14. File 34165/1891. Letters Received. USOIA. RG 75. NA.

1891c   Letter to Commissioner of Indian Affairs. July 31. File 28862/1891. Letters Received. USOIA. RG 75. NA.

1891d   Letter to Commissioner of Indian Affairs. Nov. 16. File 42068/1891. Letters Received. USOIA. RG 75. NA.

1893a   Letter to Commissioner of Indian Affairs. Feb. 24. FB. Letters to Commissioner, May 31, 1892–May 4, 1893, p. 368-76. USOIA. RG 75. NA, Kansas City.

1893b   Letter to Commissioner of Indian Affairs. Mar. 10. FB. Letters to Commissioner, May 31, 1892–May 4, 1893, p. 387-88. USOIA. RG 75. NA, Kansas City.

Murphy, Robert F.
1972   *Robert H. Lowie.* Leaders of Modern Anthropology. New York: Columbia University Press.

Nasatir, A. P., ed.
1952   *Before Lewis and Clark: Documents Illustrating the History of the Missouri: 1785-1804.* 2 vols. St. Louis: St. Louis Historical Documents Foundation.

New York Times
1917   "The Rev. George L. Curtis." July 12, p. 11. Obituary.

Newton, Elsie E.
1911   Report on field matrons. Oct. 9. File 87310-1/11 FB 160. CCF. USOIA. RG 75. NA.

Nolan, Edward W.
1983   *Northern Pacific Views: The Railroad Photography of F. Jay Haynes, 1876-1905.* Helena: Montana Historical Society Press.

Pepper, George H., and Gilbert L. Wilson
1908   "An Hidatsa Shrine and the Beliefs Respecting It." *Memoirs of the American Anthropological Association* 2, pt. 4:275-328. Reprints. New York: Kraus Reprint Corp., 1964. Millwood, N.Y.: Kraus, 1974.

Poor Wolf
1906a   "Autobiography of Poor Wolf, Head Soldier of the Hidatsa or Grosventre Tribe." Recorded by C[harles] L. Hall. *Collections of the State Historical Society of North Dakota* 1:439-43.

1906b   "Survivors in the Three Grosventre Villages." Pt. 2 of "Names of the Survivors of the Smallpox Scourge of 1837. Five Villages, North Dakota." *Collections of the State Historical Society of North Dakota* 1:437-39.

Powell, Addie Z.
1896   "Boys' Cottage." *Word Carrier* 25 (May): 20.

Presbyterian Church in the U.S.A.
1918   "Ministerial Necrology." *Minutes of the General Assembly of the Presbyterian Church in the United States of America,* n.s. 18 (Aug.): 285-87. Death notice of George L. Curtis.

Quick, Graeme R., and Wesley F. Buchele
1978   *The Grain Harvesters.* St. Joseph, Mich.: American Society of Agricultural Engineers.

Red Bear et al.
1911   Transcript of interview with Commissioner of Indian Affairs. Apr. 5. File 30800/11 FB 060. CCF. USOIA. RG 75. NA.

Richards, Thomas
1901a   Annual report to Commissioner of Indian Affairs. Aug. 17. FB. Letters to Commissioner, p. 157-73. USOIA. RG 75. NA, Kansas City.

1901b   Letter to Commissioner of Indian Affairs. Feb. 6. FB. "Commissioner's Letters Jany 1. 1901." USOIA. RG 75. NA, Kansas City.

1901c   Letter to Edward Goodbird. Sept. 12. FB. Miscellaneous Letters, 1901, p. 209. USOIA. RG 75. NA, Kansas City.

1901d   Letter to Hollis Montclair. Nov. 26. FB. Miscellaneous Letters, 1900, p. 285. USOIA. RG 75. NA, Kansas City.

Rickey, Don, Jr.
1976   *$10 Horse, $40 Saddle: Cowboy Clothing, Arms, Tools and Horse Gear of the 1880's.* Fort Collins, Colo.: Old Army Press.

Roberts, Thomas P.
1875   *Report of a Reconnaissance of the Missouri River in 1872.* Washington, D.C.: GPO.

Robinson, Elwyn B.
1966   *History of North Dakota.* Lincoln: University of Nebraska Press.

Roe, Frank Gilbert
1955   *The Indian and the Horse.* Norman: University of Oklahoma Press.

Rued, O. J.
1910   Invoice. Dec. 9. FB. Letters regarding accounts. USOIA. RG 75. NA, Kansas City.

Russell, Carl P.
1967   *Firearms, Traps, & Tools of the Mountain Men.* New York: Alfred A. Knopf.

St. Paul Pioneer Press
1914   "Being an Indian for Two Months: When G. L. Wilson Isn't Preaching in Minneapolis or in North Dakota He Spends His Time among the Redskins at Fort Berthold Learning Their Traditions and Customs." Oct. 4, feature sec., 4.

Samuels, Peggy, and Harold Samuels
1976   *The Illustrated Biographical Encyclopedia of Artists of the American West.* Garden City, N.Y.: Doubleday & Co.

Schindel, J. P.
1879a   Letter to Assistant Adjutant General, Headquarters, Department of Dakota, St. Paul, Minn. Feb. 27. FB Agency. Letters Received, 1824-81. USOIA. RG 75. M234, roll 298, frames 526-29.

1879b   Letter to Assistant Adjutant General, Headquarters, Department of Dakota, St. Paul, Minn. June 11. FB Agency. Letters Received, 1824-81. USOIA. RG 75. M234, roll 298, frames 534-36.

Schneider, Mary Jane
1986   *North Dakota Indians: An Introduction.* Dubuque, Iowa: Kendall/Hunt Pub. Co.
    See also Goodbird 1914a

Shafer, George F.
1945   "Dr. Orin Grant Libby." *North Dakota History.* 12 (July): 107-10.

Shelford, Victor Ernest
1963   *The Ecology of North America.* Urbana: University of Illinois Press.

Shultis, Charles A.
1901   "Record of Scholars' Attendance and Punctuality." Apr. 1-June 18. FB. Attendance Record, April 1901. USOIA. RG 75. NA, Kansas City.

1910   Letter to Clark Wissler. Mar. 4. Anthropology Dept., AMNH.

Sitting Bear et al.
1913   Petition to Commissioner of Indian Affairs. Received Mar. 21. File 36971/13 FB 751. CCF. USOIA. RG 75. NA.

Smith, G. Hubert
1948   "Wilson's Studies of the Hidatsa." *Minnesota Archaeologist* 14 (Jan.): 33-34.

1960   "Archeological Investigations at the Site of Fort Stevenson (32ML1), Garrison Reservoir, North Dakota." Appendix by Carlyle S. Smith. In *River Basin Surveys Papers,* ed. Frank H. H. Roberts, Jr., no. 19, p. 159-238.

Smithsonian Institution, Bureau of American Ethnology, Bulletin no. 176. Washington, D.C.: GPO.

1972   *Like-a-Fishhook Village and Fort Berthold, Garrison Reservoir, North Dakota.* U.S. Department of the Interior, National Park Service, Anthropological Papers 2. Washington, D.C.: GPO.

Spencer, Robert F., Jesse D. Jennings, et al.
1965   *The Native Americans: Prehistory and Ethnology of the North American Indians.* New York: Harper & Row.

Spier, Leslie
1931   *Plains Indian Parfleche Designs.* University of Washington Publications in Anthropology, vol. 4, no. 3. Seattle: University of Washington Press.

State Historical Society of North Dakota
1906   "Officers and Directors." *Collections of the State Historical Society of North Dakota* 1:15.

Steffen, Randy
1978   *The Frontier, the Mexican War, the Civil War, the Indian Wars: 1851-1880.* Vol. 2 of *The Horse Soldier: 1776-1943: The United States Cavalryman: His Uniforms, Arms, Accoutrements, and Equipments.* Norman: University of Oklahoma Press.

Stewart, Frank H.
1974   "Mandan and Hidatsa Villages in the Eighteenth and Nineteenth Centuries." *Plains Anthropologist: Journal of the Plains Conference* 19, no. 66, pt. 1 (Nov.): 287-302.

Stocking, George W., Jr.
1973   "Wissler, Clark." In *Dictionary of American Biography,* supp. 3, 1941-45, ed. Edward T. James, 906-9. New York: Charles Scribner's Sons.

Stoelting, Benjamin
1909   Letter to L. B. Hanna. Dec. 13. File 36323/08 FB 320. CCF. USOIA. RG 75. NA.

Thiessen, Thomas D., W. Raymond Wood, and A. Wesley Jones
1979   "The Sitting Rabbit 1907 Map of the Missouri River in North Dakota." *Plains Anthropologist: Journal of the Plains Conference* 24, no. 84, pt. 1 (May): 145-67. *See also* Libby 1906b

Thomas, Amzi W.
1903   Letter to Commissioner of Indian Affairs. Apr. 9. FB. Miscellaneous Letters to Commissioner, p. 221. USOIA. RG 75. NA, Kansas City.

1904   Letter to Commissioner of Indian Affairs. July 28. FB. Letters to Commissioner, 1904-06, p. 13. USOIA. RG 75. NA, Kansas City.

1908   Letter to Commissioner of Indian Affairs. July 20. FB. May 1, 1908-June 14, 1909, vol. 1, p. 129-31. USOIA. RG 75. NA, Kansas City.

Thompson, David
1962   *David Thompson's Narrative: 1784-1812.* Ed. Richard Glover. The Publications of The Champlain Society, no. 40. Toronto: Champlain Society. *See also* Wood and Thiessen 1985

Thwaites, Reuben Gold, ed.
1966   *Travels in the Interior of North America,* by Maximilian, prinz von Wied. Trans. Hannibal Evans Lloyd. Atlas. Vol. 25 of *Early Western Travels: 1748-1846,* ed. Reuben Gold Thwaites. Cleveland, Ohio: Arthur H. Clark Co., 1905-06. Reprint. New York: AMS Press. *See also* Lewis and Clark 1904-05; Wied 1905-06

Trimble, Michael K.
1979   "An Ethnohistorical Interpretation of the Spread of Smallpox in the Northern Plains Utilizing Concepts of Disease Ecology." Master's thesis, University of Missouri-Columbia.

Trobriand, Philippe Régis de
1951   *Military Life in Dakota: The Journal of Philippe Régis de Trobriand.* Ed. and trans. Lucile M. Kane. St. Paul:

Alvord Memorial Commission.

Tsakakis-sakis. *See* Goodbird, Edward

Tsĕ-ca ma-tse-ítsic. *See* Wolf Chief, Henry

U.S. Bureau of Indian Affairs, Missouri River Basin Investigations Project
1954   *Comparison of Appraised Values of Indian Properties and of Estimated Costs of Re-establishing Displaced Families, Timber, Wildlife, and Wild Product Losses, and Potential and Intangible Damages to Indians at Fort Berthold, Cheyenne River, Standing Rock, Crow Creek, and Lower Brule Reservations from Garrison, Oahe, and Fort Randall Reservoir Takings, North Dakota and South Dakota.* Report no. 138. Billings, Mont.: The Project.

U.S. Census Office
1894   *Report on Indians Taxed and Indians Not Taxed in the United States (Except Alaska) at the Eleventh Census: 1890.* Washington, D.C.: GPO.

U.S. Office of Indian Affairs (USOIA)
1868-1923 *Report of the Commissioner of Indian Affairs to the Secretary of the Interior.* Washington, D.C.: GPO. Includes 1904a. Fort Berthold section in 1909 report, see "Reports Concerning Indians in North Dakota," 2-7.

1904b   *Regulations of the Indian Office. Effective April 1, 1904.* Washington, D.C.: GPO.

U.S. Office of Indian Affairs, Superintendent of Indian Schools
1893-96 *Report of the Superintendent of Indian Schools.* Washington, D.C.: GPO.

Upham, Warren
1902   Letter to Gilbert L. Wilson. May 13. Wilson Papers, MHS.

Van Dersal, Samuel
1902   *Van Dersal's Stock Growers Directory of Marks and Brands for the State of North Dakota, 1902* . . . Bismarck, N.Dak.: Sam'l Van Dersal.

Van Ostrand, Ferdinand A.
1942-43 "Diary of Ferdinand A. Van Ostrand." Ed. Russell Reid. Pts. 1-3. *North Dakota Historical Quarterly* 9 (July 1942): 219-42; 10 (Jan., Apr. 1943): 3-46; 83-124.

Vennum, Thomas, Jr.
1982   *The Ojibwa Dance Drum: Its History and Construction.* Smithsonian Folklife Studies, 2. Washington: Smithsonian Institution Press.

Wacker, Christ
1910   Invoice. May 14. FB. Letters regarding accounts. USOIA. RG 75. NA, Kansas City.

Waheenee. *See* Maxidiwiac

Walker, James F.
1953   "Old Fort Berthold as I Knew It." *North Dakota History* 20 (Jan.): 25-46.

Walker, Mercy
1978   Interview with Gerard Baker. Independence Point, N.Dak.

Waterbuster Bundle File
1909, 1935 Documents related to controversy. Files 59863/09 FB 113.1 and 1069/35 FB 042. CCF. USOIA. RG 75. NA.

Watkins, F. Leland
1902   Letter to FB Agency. July n.d. FB. USOIA. RG 75. NA, Kansas City.

Weinberger, Caspar W., Jr.
1977   "Curtis, Edward Sheriff." In *Dictionary of American Biography,* supp. 5, 1951-55, ed. John A. Garraty, 148-49. New York: Charles Scribner's Sons.

Weitzner, Bella
1979   "Notes on the Hidatsa Indians Based on Data Recorded by the Late Gilbert L. Wilson." *Anthropological Papers of the American Museum of Natural History* 56:181-322.

Wheeler, Olin D.
1905?   *The Lewis & Clark Exposition: Portland, Oregon: June 1 to*

October 15, 1905. St. Paul: Northern Pacific Railway.

Wheeler, R. P.

1963   "The Stutsman Focus: An Aboriginal Culture Complex in the Jamestown Reservoir Area, North Dakota." In *River Basin Surveys Papers*, ed. Frank H. H. Roberts, Jr., no. 30, p. 167-230. Smithsonian Institution, Bureau of American Ethnology, Bulletin no. 185. Washington, D.C.: GPO.

Wiebe, Robert H.

1967   *The Search for Order: 1877-1920.* The Making of America, ed. David Donald. New York: Hill and Wang.

Wied, Maximilian, prinz von

1840-43   *Voyage dans l'Intérieur de l'Amérique du Nord, Exécuté pendant les Années 1832, 1833 et 1834.* Atlas. Paris: A. Bertrand.

1905-06   *Travels in the Interior of North America.* Trans. Hannibal Evans Lloyd. Vols. 22-24 of *Early Western Travels: 1748-1846*, ed. Reuben Gold Thwaites. Cleveland, Ohio: Arthur H. Clark Co. *See also* Thwaites 1966

Wik, Reynold M.

1953   *Steam Power on the American Farm.* Prepared and published under the direction of the American Historical Association from the income of the Albert J. Beveridge Memorial Fund. Philadelphia: University of Pennsylvania Press.

Will, George F.

1910   "The Bourgeois Village Site." *American Anthropologist*, n.s. 12:473-76.

1924   "Archaeology of the Missouri Valley." *Anthropological Papers of the American Museum of Natural History* 22:285-356.

Will, George F., and George E. Hyde

1917   *Corn among the Indians of the Upper Missouri.* Little Histories of North American Indians, no. 5. St. Louis: William Harvey Miner Co.

Will, George F., and H. J. Spinden

1906   "The Mandans: A Study of Their Culture, Archaeology and Language." *Papers of the Peabody Museum of American Archaeology and Ethnology, Harvard University* 3 (Aug.): 81-219.

Wilson, Frederick N.

1908   Letter to Clark Wissler. July 28. Anthropology Dept., AMNH.

1912a   Field Report, vol. 31 (handwritten copy), Wilson Papers, MHS. Pagination varies; bracketed citations are actual pages.

1912b   Field Report, vol. 12a (typewritten "2d copy"), Wilson Papers, MHS.

1912c   Field Report, vol. 12b (typewritten "3d copy"), Wilson Papers, MHS.
         See also Goodbird 1914a; Maxidiwiac 1916-17, 1918, 1921; G. M. Wilson 1971

Wilson, Gilbert L.

1894-1928   Wilson family scrapbook, vol. 45, Wilson Papers, MHS.

[1903-18]   Photograph album, vol. 44, Wilson Papers, MHS.

1903   *Little Ugly Boy and the Bear; and, The Rainbow Snake.* Mandan, N.Dak.: G. L. Wilson.

1904   "Indian Legends." *Woman's Home Companion* 31 (Oct.): 47-48.

1905   "Glooskap and the Winter Giant." *Woman's Home Companion* 32 (Apr.): 45.

1906a   "The Iktomi Myth." *Collections of the State Historical Society of North Dakota* 1:474-75.

1906b   Diary, vol. 3, Wilson Papers, MHS.

1907a   *Myths of the Red Children.* Illus. Frederick N. Wilson. Boston: Ginn & Co.

1907b   Diary, vol. 4, Wilson Papers, MHS.

1907c   Diary, vol. 5, Wilson Papers, MHS.

[1907d]   Manuscript notes attached to copy of 1907 diaries in Wilson Papers, SHSND.

1908a   Diary, vol. 6, Wilson Papers, MHS.

1908b   Field Report, vol. 7, Wilson Papers, MHS.

1909a   Field Report, vol. 8, Wilson Papers, MHS.

1909b   Letter to Clark Wissler. June 3. Anthropology Dept., AMNH.

1909c   Letter to Clark Wissler. Nov. 6. Anthropology Dept., AMNH.

1909-18   Notebook, vol. 27, Wilson Papers, MHS.

1910a   Field Report, vol. 9, Wilson Papers, MHS.

1910b   Letter to Clark Wissler. Sept. 7. Anthropology Dept., AMNH.

1911   Field Report, vol. 10, Wilson Papers, MHS.

1911a   Letter to Clark Wissler. Jan. 7. Anthropology Dept., AMNH.

1912   Field Report, vol. 11, Wilson Papers, MHS.

1913a   Field Report, vol. 13, Wilson Papers, MHS.

1913b   Field Report, vol. 14, Wilson Papers, MHS.

1913c   Letter to Robert Lowie. Nov. 14. Anthropology Dept., AMNH.

1914a   Letter to Robert Lowie. May 28. Anthropology Dept., AMNH.

1914b   Field Report, vol. 16, Wilson Papers, MHS.

1915a   Field Report, vol. 17, Wilson Papers, MHS.

1915b   Field Report, vol. 18, Wilson Papers, MHS.

1915c   Letter to Clark Wissler. Aug. 30. Anthropology Dept., AMNH.

1916a   *Indian Hero Tales.* Illus. Frederick N. Wilson. New York: American Book Co.

1916b   Field Report, vol. 20, Wilson Papers, MHS.

1916c   Notebook, vol. 35, Wilson Papers, MHS. Wilson did not rewrite these notes in a formal report, so his quoting of Wolf Chief's words is less polished.

1916d   Letter to Clark Wissler. June 14. Anthropology Dept., AMNH.

1916e   "A collection of museum exhibits made by Hidatsa Indians from Wild Plants: Collected by Dr. Gilbert L. Wilson, August 1916." Wilson Papers, MHS.

1916f   "Five Weeks with the Hidatsa Indians." *The Minnesotan* 2 (Oct.): 20-22, 42.

1917   *Agriculture of the Hidatsa Indians: An Indian Interpretation.* Studies in the Social Sciences, no. 9. Minneapolis: University of Minnesota. Reprints. Reprints in Anthropology, vol. 5. Lincoln, Nebr.: J & L Reprint Co., 1977. New York: AMS Press, 1979. Borealis Books. St. Paul: Minnesota Historical Society Press, 1987 forthcoming.

1918a   Field Report, vol. 22, Wilson Papers, MHS.

1918b   Letter to Clark Wissler. Aug. 9. Anthropology Dept., AMNH.

1918c   Letter to Clark Wissler. Oct. 8. Anthropology Dept., AMNH.

1919   Letter to Clark Wissler. July 3. Anthropology Dept., AMNH.

1924   "The Horse and the Dog in Hidatsa Culture." *Anthropological Papers of the American Museum of Natural History* 15:125-311. Reprints. Reprints in Anthropology, vol. 10. Lincoln, Nebr.: J & L Reprint Co., 1978. New York: AMS Press, 1980?. *See also* H. Wolf Chief 1919

1925   Letter to Clark Wissler. Sept. 30. Anthropology Dept., AMNH.

1926   "The Ordeal of Getting Civilized: Troubles of an Indian Treading the White Man's Path." *Natural History* 26 (Jan.-Feb.): 85-89. Reprint. *Minnesota Archaeologist* 37 (May 1978): 79-83. Although informant is called "Wolf-eye," material was evidently gathered from Wolf Chief.

1929   "Hidatsa Eagle Trapping." *Anthropological Papers of the*

American Museum of Natural History 30:99-245. Reprint. Reprints in Anthropology, vol. 13. Lincoln, Nebr.: J & L Reprint Co., 1978.

1934   "The Hidatsa Earthlodge." Ed. Bella Weitzner. *Anthropological Papers of the American Museum of Natural History* 33:341-420. Reprint. Reprints in Anthropology, vol. 11. Lincoln, Nebr.: J & L Reprint Co., 1978.

     See also Goodbird; Maxidiwiac; Pepper and Wilson 1908

Wilson, Gladys M.

1971   Letter to James E. Sperry. Apr. 26. SHSND files.

Wissler, Clark

1916   "General Discussion of Shamanistic and Dancing Societies." *Anthropological Papers of the American Museum of Natural History* 11:853-76.

Wolf Chief, Frank

1898   Letter to Secretary of the Interior. Feb. 12. File 9743/1898. Letters Received. USOIA. RG 75. NA.

Wolf Chief, Henry (Tsé-ca ma-tse-ítsic)

1881a   Letter to Rutherford B. Hayes. Received Jan. 25. File 1792/1881. Letters Received. USOIA. RG 75. NA.

1881b   Letter [to Commissioner of Indian Affairs?]. Received Jan. 28. File 1792/1881. USOIA. RG 75. NA.

1881c   Letter to James A. Garfield. N.d. Enclosure in file 18388/1881. Letters Received. USOIA. RG 75. NA.

1882a   Letter to Commissioner of Indian Affairs. Jan. 14. File 1563/1882. Letters Received. USOIA. RG 75. NA.

1882b   Letter to "Great Father." Mar. 4. File 4980/1882. Letters Received. USOIA. RG 75. NA.

1884   Letter to "Great Father" and Hiram Price. Apr. 10. File 7559/1884. Letters Received. USOIA. RG 75. NA.

1886   Letter to "Great Father" and Commissioner of Indian Affairs. Mar. 11. File 7979/1886. Letters Received. USOIA. RG 75. NA.

1888a   Letter to J. D. C. Atkins, Commissioner of Indian Affairs. Apr. 7. File 9959/1888. Letters Received. USOIA. RG 75. NA.

1888b   Letter to "Great Father" and Commissioner of Indian Affairs. Dec. n.d. File 30060/1888. Letters Received. USOIA. RG 75. NA.

1889a   Letter to John H. Oberly, Commissioner of Indian Affairs. May 30. File 14582/1889. Letters Received. USOIA. RG 75. NA.

1889b   Letter to Commissioner of Indian Affairs. Aug. 10. File 23002/1889. Letters Received. USOIA. RG 75. NA.

1890a   Letter to Commissioner of Indian Affairs. Mar. n.d. File 8999/1890. Letters Received. USOIA. RG 75. NA.

1890b   Letter to Commissioner of Indian Affairs. Sept. 3. File 27936/1890. Letters Received. USOIA. RG 75. NA.

1891a   Letter to "Great Father" and T. J. Morgan, Commissioner of Indian Affairs. Feb. 17. File 7158/1891. Letters Received. USOIA. RG 75. NA.

1891b   Letter to President [Benjamin] Harrison. Apr. n.d. File 15374/1891. Letters Received. USOIA. RG 75. NA.

1891c   Letter to T. J. Morgan, Commissioner of Indian Affairs. Sept. 30. File 36723/1891. Letters Received. USOIA. RG 75. NA.

1892   Letter to "Great Father" and T. J. Morgan, Commissioner of Indian Affairs. May 10. File 19395/1892. Letters Received. USOIA. RG 75. NA.

1894   Letter to Commissioner of Indian Affairs. Dec. 31. File 943/1895. Letters Received. USOIA. RG 75. NA.

1895   Letter to Hake Smith, Secretary of the Interior. Feb. 3. File 8848/1895. Letters Received. USOIA. RG 75. NA.

1899   "Oath of Wolf Chief as Judge Indian Court." July 14. File 49907/1899. Letters Received. USOIA. RG 75. NA.

1905   Letter to F. E. Leupp, Commissioner of Indian Affairs. Dec. 14. File 102416/1905. Letters Received. USOIA. RG 75. NA.

1911a   "Application for a Patent in Fee." Jan. 23. FB. USOIA. RG 75. NA, Kansas City.

1911b   Letter to Gilbert L. Wilson. N.d. Copy in Anthropology Dept., AMNH.

1919   "Indian Lore on the Rearing of Horses." Pt. 1. Continued as "The Indian and His Horse." Pts. 2-5. Told to Gilbert L. Wilson. Illus. Edward Goodbird and with photographs. *The Farmer* (St. Paul, Minn.), Jan. 4, 11, 18, 25, Feb. 1, p. 8, 19; 68, 72; 118; 174, 189; 240, 256. *See also* Wilson 1924

1927   Letter to L. W. Page. May 3. File 161 Personnel – Wolf Chief. FB. USOIA. RG 75. NA, Kansas City.

1931   Letter to Commissioner of Indian Affairs. May 26. File 28436/31 FB 059. CCF. USOIA. RG 75. NA.

Wood, W. Raymond

1974   "Northern Plains Village Cultures: Internal Stability and External Relationships." *Journal of Anthropological Research* 30 (Spring): 1-16.

1983   *An Atlas of Early Maps of the American Midwest*. Scientific Papers, vol. 18. Springfield: Illinois State Museum.

1986   *The Origins of the Hidatsa Indians: A Review of Ethnohistorical and Traditional Data*. With a chapter by Jeffery R. Hanson. Study conducted for the National Park Service, Midwest Region. Lincoln, Nebr.: Midwest Archeological Center, 1980. Reprint. Reprints in Anthropology, vol. 32. Lincoln, Nebr.: J & L Reprint Co.

Wood, W. Raymond, and Alan S. Downer

1977   "Notes on the Crow-Hidatsa Schism." *Plains Anthropologist: Journal of the Plains Conference* 22, no. 78, pt. 2, Memoir 13 (Nov.): 83-100.

Wood, W. Raymond, and Gary E. Moulton

1981   "Prince Maximilian and New Maps of the Missouri and Yellowstone Rivers by William Clark." *Western Historical Quarterly* 12 (Oct.): 373-86.

Wood, W. Raymond, and Thomas D. Thiessen, eds.

1985   *Early Fur Trade on the Northern Plains: Canadian Traders among the Mandan and Hidatsa Indians, 1738-1818: The Narratives of John Macdonell, David Thompson, François-Antoine Larocque, and Charles McKenzie*. The American Exploration and Travel Series, vol. 68. Norman: University of Oklahoma Press. *See also* Thompson 1962

Woolworth, Alan R.

1956   "Archeological Investigations at Site 32ME59 (Grandmother's Lodge)." *North Dakota History* 23 (Apr.): 79-102.

Word Carrier

1888a   "Social Gatherings." Vol. 17 (May): 19.

1888b   "Decoration Day at Berthold." Vol. 17 (June): 24.

1915   "Good Bird the Indian." Review of Goodbird 1914a. Vol. 44 (Jan.-Feb.): 1.

1925   "Goodbird, the Indian, Ordained." Vol. 54 (Sept.-Oct.): 19.

1927a   "Fort Berthold Indians Win at North Dakota Corn Show." Vol. 56 (May-June): 12.

1927b   "Indian Girls Received Prizes." Vol. 56 (Sept.-Oct.): 28.

Yale University

1918   "George Louis Curtis, B.A. 1878." In *Obituary Record of Graduates of Yale University Deceased during the Year Ending July 1, 1918. . . .*, 649-51. New Haven, Conn.: Yale University.

Index

Note: Numbers in italics refer to pictures.

Abbott, F. H., assistant commissioner, 202
Above Woman, sacred being, 13
Adams, Charles P., army officer, 137
Adoptive relationships, described, 20;
    examples, 163, 286
Africans, at Like-a-Fishhook, 128
Agents, characterized, 129-30, 210; goals,
    140, 141, 182, 194, 201, 209; powers,
    140, 209-10, 214-16, 249; bond and
    oath, *141;* training, 141; relations with
    Indian Office, 209-10, *142-43;* handbook,
    210; contradictions in responsibilities,
    210; relations with Wolf Chief, 226-27.
    See also United States Office of Indian
    Affairs, individual agents
Agriculture, traditional methods, 5, 11,
    32-37, 187, 202, *206-8,* 331, 335;
    taught, 33, 149, 233, 237; crops, 33,
    200-204, *206-8,* 312; harvest, 34-36,
    208; produce marketed, 129, 200, 205;
    new methods, 187, *200-205,* 208, 227,
    267, 314; machinery, *200-202, 203, 205,*
    314; impact of weather, 201-2, 227, 334;
    symbolism, 201, 216; fair, 202;
    government farmer, 209-13, 214; affected
    by dam, 317, 339; Wilson's studies, 346.
    See also Allotment, Ranching, specific
    crops and tools
Alden, E. H., agent, 141, 142. *See also*
    Agents
Allen, J. D., merchant, 350
Allotment, system described, 181-82, 210,
    264; impact of, 230, 231, 242-43, 272,
    327, 332, 338-39; Sioux story, 305;
    abolished, 314. *See also* Land
Altar cloth, *284*
Amahami, Hidatsa village, 7, 322-24, 325,
    326
American Board of Commissioners for
    Foreign Missions, 144
American Folklife Center, Library of
    Congress, 351
American Fur Company, posts, 5, 24
American Museum of Natural History,
    collects objects, 73, 74; sponsors Wilson,
    285, 291, 293, 310, 345, 348-49
Ammunition, cartridges, *46,* 229, 230;
    scarcity, 70, 76; bullets, 76; shot, *76, 77,*
    86; powder, 76, 77, *86,* 130; percussion
    caps, *86;* sales, 219, 229, 230. *See also*
    Arrows, Guns
Annuities, delivered, 130, 139-40; defined,
    140. *See also* Issue goods, Rations
Antelopes, dance society, 303
Antelopes (pronghorns), hair used, 19, 29,
    84; hunted, 70, 78, *132,* 336; powers,
    111; hides traded, 153, 217
Anthropology, intellectual development, viii,
    x; studies on reservation, 224. *See also*

individual anthropologists
Anvil, stone, 64, *75, 261*
Archaeology, items collected, xi; sites, *7,*
    315, 323-*24,* 326, 327, 343-44; pursued
    by Wilson, 350
Architecture, *see* Booths, Cabins, Earth
    lodges, Dance arbor
Archives of American Music, Indiana
    University, 349
Arikara, relations with Hidatsa and Mandan,
    2, 28, 140; move to Like-a-Fishhook, 4,
    9, 327; winter villages, 23; craft
    traditions, 51, 118; language, 145, 146,
    147, 150, 322; leave Like-a-Fishhook,
    182, 338; religion prohibited, 223;
    population, 265, 337; patriotism, 303;
    studied, 320. *See also* Three Affiliated
    Tribes
Ark of the First Man, 225
Arm bands, metal, *115, 160. See also* Bracelets
Armstrong, N.Dak, 217
Arrows, *69, 103, 173;* types described, 70,
    71, *74,* 132; used, *70-71,* 80, 132, 197,
    199; tools for construction, *74-75;* metal
    tipped, 74, 75, *132;* case, *173*
Ash, used for tools, 16, 37; used for travois,
    55; used for weapons, 69, 76, *103;* other
    uses, 336
Assiniboine, craft traditions, 51, 89; lifeway,
    322; warfare, 325
Atkins, J. D. C., commissioner, 228
Atkinson-O'Fallon Expedition, military
    expedition, 341
Automobiles, introduced, 264, *269;* impact,
    266, 268, *269;* maintained, 268; licensed,
    268
Awatixa, Hidatsa subgroup, 322; villages, *7,*
    324-25; origin traditions, 325
Awatixa, Hidatsa village, *7*
Awaxawi, Hidatsa subgroup, 322; villages, *7,*
    324-26; origin traditions, 324, 325-26
Awls, *46, 47, 107;* case, *47*
Axes, used in cooking, 16, 58, 63, 258; used
    in construction, 22, 192, *194;* other uses,
    43, 198. *See also* Hatchets

Bad Gun, Henry, markets cattle, 243
Bad Horn, Indian leader, 4
Badge, Indian policeman's, *215*
Bags, storage, *39, 40, 164;* woman's, *48;*
    flint, *50;* uses, 50; paint, *107, 108;*
    bandolier, 132; grain, *205;* purse, *262. See
    also* Boxes, Parfleches
Baker, Anson, quoted, 314, 316, 318, 320
Baker, Cora, quoted, 315, 317
Baker, Gerard, quoted, 318; essay, 328-32;
    identified, 352
Baker, James, policeman, *214;* markets cattle,
    244
Baker, Mrs. James, *263*

Baker, Louis, markets cattle, 243, *244*
Baker, Percy, policeman, *214*
Bale tag, used by traders, *133*
Bandana, *247*
Bandolier bag, 132
Baskets, *16, 170, 288, 291;* construction, 16,
    34, 46, *117, 118,* 133, 288, *289;* types,
    34; uses, 34, *207;* sacred knowledge, 116,
    117
Bassett, Mike, sells charm, 111
Beads, trade goods, *46, 133*
Beadwork, examples, *29, 39, 47-50, 52, 90,*
    91, 93, 162, 163, 169, 176, 262, 306, 307,
    310; girls taught, 38, 262
Beaks, Crosby, markets cattle, 244
Beamer, bone, *45*
Beans, food, 58, 79, 81, *207;* harvested, *190*
Bear, sacred being, 4; gut used, 96; hunted,
    336
Bear Tail, family tree, *21*
Bears Arm, Martin, artwork, *12*
Bear's Ghost, quoted, 272
Beaver, *335;* hunted, 336
"Beaver Dens on the Bank of the Missouri,"
    335
Beaver grass, cord, 62
Beckwith, Martha Warren, folklorist, 343
Beds, 13, 18; canopies, 19, 51; described,
    19, 192; bedding, 19, 256; model, 48,
    104, 289; for childbirth, 122
Beef, rationed, 213. *See also* Cattle
Beef paunch buckets, *17, 41*
Bell, Burton, policeman, *214*
Bells, hoof, 13; sleigh, *132;* hawk, *132;*
    school, *153;* church, 281
Belts, women's, 29; beaded, *50, 176, 262;*
    honor mark, 53; girls', *57;* as gifts, 109;
    leather, *160*
Benson, Ben, sells object, 161; policeman,
    214
Bent Enemy Killed Village, 22
Berries, food, 58; preserved, *64-65. See also*
    specific types
Berry-mashing hide, *64*
Bibles, used, 144, *145,* 280
Big Cloud, Indian leader, 4, 9, 106; Wolf
    Chief's grandfather, 21, *104,* 128; earth
    lodge, 22
Big Grass Dance Society, 157
Big Hidatsa, Hidatsa village, *7,* 322-24, 326
Bighorn sheep, *see* Sheep
Birds, sacred beings, 4, 13, *104,* 330;
    hunted, 70-73, *74,* 336, 337, 346
Bird Woman, Magpie's mother, 109
"Bird's-Eye View of the Mandan Village,
    1800 Miles above St. Louis," painting, *5*
Bismarck, transportation center, 134, 149
Bits, horse, *84, 136*
Black Cat, Mandan village, *7,* 323, 324
Black Chest, scout, 275
Black Hawk, quoted, 102

Black Horn, leads hunt, 80-82

Black Mouth Society, *see* Societies, Black Mouth

Blacksmithing, tools, 194; at agency, 219; taught, 233, 237

Blake, Hazel, quoted, 318

Blankets, as gifts, 90, 108, 109, *277;* as clothing, *115*

Boarding schools, *see* Schools

Boas, Franz, anthropologist, x, 343

Bobcat, hunted, 336

Bodmer, Karl, artist, 6, 26, 51, 52, 82, 94, 341-42; artworks, *6, 14, 23, 80, 83, 88, 93, 106, 122, 169, 329, 330, 333, 341*

Boller, Henry A., fur trader, 8-9, 11, 66, 82, 140, 342; sells goods, 26, *112,* 132

Bonds, agent's, *141;* traders', 218; Liberty Loan, 303, 304

Books, for church, 144, *145,* 280, *283;* for school, *155, 234;* by Wilson, *294, 344-47*

Booths, construction, 275

Boots, *248*

Bottles, glass, *26,* 61

Bowers, Alfred W., anthropologist, 207, 324, 325, 343

Bowls, *see* Dishes

Bows, *69, 70, 76, 173;* used on hunt, 80, 132; elk horn, *103, 132, 198;* case, *103, 173*

Box elder, used for dishes, 16, 60; used in baskets, 16, 116, 207, 288; used for snares, 73; other uses, 336

Boxes, hide, *23, 42, 177. See also* Bags, Parfleches

Boys, *see* Men and boys

Bracelets, as honor marks, 53, *56;* metal, *56, 115, 133;* bone, 133. *See also* Arm bands

Bracer, archer's, *69,* 98

Brands, *249;* system, 242, 249; techniques, 243, *250*

Brave Woman, gives object, 82

Bread, introduced, 128, 233, 236; fry, 255; corn, 314

Breastplates, *see* Necklaces

Bridge, at Elbowoods, *271,* 317

Bridles, *248;* as gifts, 108

Brooms, *38, 39;* construction, 39

Brower, Jacob V., antiquarian, 344

Brown, C. B., photographer, 152

Browning Boarding School, Elbowoods, 262

Brunner, Edward M., anthropologist, 344

Brush, porcupine skin, *107*

Buckbrush, wood used, 39, 69

Buckets, paunch, *17, 41;* heart skin, 17, 41, *101. See also* Pails

Buffalo, *80-81, 87, 333;* hunted, 7, 70, 80-87, 122, 124, 132, 336-37; hoofs used, *13, 93;* organs used, *17, 41, 101;* robes, 19, 56, 104, 109, 122, 129; medicinal uses, 23; flesh used, 27, 66, 82, *87,* 96; traditional beliefs, 27, 80, 82-83, 242, 296; bones used, 30, 32, 62, 74, 238, 266, 337; horn used, 31, *59, 77,* 306, 337; hide used, 34, 55, 64, 75, 82, *84, 85,* 184, 337; calfskin used, 40, 123, 127; albino, 82; disappearance, 140, 338; skull used, 192, *193. See also* Hides, Meat

Buffalo Bird Woman (Maxidiwiac), depicted, *ii, 43, 53, 60, 125, 252, 274, 278, 285, 286, 289, 312;* girlhood, 2, 4, 27, 29, 32-35; work with Wilson, 2, 245-46, 285-89, 294, 325, 345, 346, 350; homes, 4, 13, 192, 218, 252-54; makes objects, 16, 29, 104, 116-17, 118, 119, 133, 289; sells objects, 16, 48; family tree, 20-21; adoptive relationships, 21, 285, 286, 345; name, 23, 294; characterized, 43, 53, 285, 289, 314, 340; clothing, 57, *252;* society member, 92, 106, 223; marriages, 107-10, 113, 116, *287;* shows conservatism, 108, 201-2, 208, 233, 312, 337; sacred knowledge, 116-17, 120-21, 123, 254; gives birth, 122; as farmer, 187, 201-2, 312; wins prize, 202; story published, 294

"Buffalo Bull," engraving, *333*

Bullboats, *291;* used, 13, *53,* 123, 124, *125,* 182; paddle, 135, *198;* construction, *184*

Burden baskets, *see* Baskets

Burden straps (carrying straps), used, 53, 56, 127

Burnt Arrow, culture hero, 74, 199

Bustle, feather, *160*

Butchering, *79, 87*

Butterfly, *219;* informant, 10, 41, 325; sells objects, 34, 55, 163; society member, 91; debts, 134; quoted, 154, 232; refuses to buy bundle, 297

Buttons, military, *136*

Cabins, furnishings, xii, 192, *193,* 194, *263,* 283; at Like-a-Fishhook, 9, 12; etiquette, 183, 192, 193; described, 183, 253; construction, 192, 194, 195, 258; housekeeping, 253-54, 255

Cache pits, described, *19;* used, 22

Calf Woman, sells objects, 39, 42, 82; makes object, 52; votive poles, *222*

Calico, as gift, 108, 109, *277;* traded, 217; in dresses, *252,* 254; offerings, 299, *300*

Canfield, Andrew N., army officer, 137

Cans, for food, *58,* 61; as rattles, 97

Canteen, army, *137*

Cards, playing, *149;* Sunday school, *283*

Carlisle Indian School, Pa., 231

Carnival, depicted, *271*

Carpentry, tools, *194, 237;* taught, 233, 237

Carrying strap, *see* Burden strap

Cartridges, *see* Ammunition

Cary, William de la Montagne, paintings, *12, 26, 128, 171, 180*

Case, Harold W., identified, 29

Catholic church, mission school, 211, 233. *See also* Christianity, Missions and missionaries

Catlin, George, artist, 7, 341; artworks, *5, 7, 28, 168, 333*

Catlinite, *see* Pipestone

Cattails, down used, 123, *124,* 335

Cattle, organs used, 17, 41; hide used, 39; horns used, 91; bones used, 162, 238; raised, 209-10, 214, 242-51, 339; barter forbidden, 210, 230; marketed, 210, 243-46; origin story, 242; meat preserved, *251;* dairy, 259. *See also* Beef, Hides, Meat, Ranching

Cedar, medicinal and sacred uses, 23, 24, 282; used for bows, 103

Cedar Woman, makes object, 16

Ceremonies, Okipa, 10, 331; for healing, 23, 24; purchased, 90-91, 296-97, 328, 330, 331; forbidden, 97, 182, 183, 297; in warfare, 99, 102, 106; Corn, 122; Buffaloes', 122; River, 122, 123; Wolves', 122, 192; skull symbol, 192, 193; include giveaways, 282; for Waterbuster bundle, 296-97; Hide Beating, 325; origins, 328. *See also* Religion, Societies

Chains, logging, *66*

Chaps, depicted, *247*

Chardon, Francis A., trader, 342

Charging, Francis, markets cattle, *244*

Charging Eagle, N.Dak., 182

Charging Enemy, *181;* family tree, 21; donation, 281

Charred Body, culture hero, 325

Chicago, Ill., 244-46

Childbirth, traditions, 122, 123

Children, at play, 27-31, *148-49,* 238-39; at work, 33, 38, 53, 54, 69-73, 233-34, 236-37, 257; clothing, *57, 60, 126, 234, 311;* care of, 92, 107-8, 111-12, 122, 127, 148, 149, 232, 233; at dances, 106, 159, *309, 311,* 318; depicted, *126, 144, 148, 150, 240-41, 311. See also* Men and boys, Schools, Women and girls

Chippewa, *see* Ojibway

Chokecherries, preserved, *64-65, 261;* wood used, 69, 103; gathered, 314, 335

Chouteau, Pierre, Jr., and Co. ("American Fur Company"), fur trading company, 10, 129

Christianity, Indians adopt, 3, 145, 151, 222, 279-80, 332; values, 183, 201, 222-23, 280; funeral customs, 274-75. *See also* Catholic church, Congregational church, Missions and missionaries, Religion

Christmas, at Independence, 186, 282

Churn, depicted, *259*

Circle of the King's Daughters, club, 253-54

Citizenship, Indians granted, 181, 266

Civil War, surplus gear, 136-37

Clans, system described, 20, 297, 329; ceremonial aspects, 58, 329-30, 331; duties of relatives, 125, 274-77, 280, 314

Clapp, William H., agent, 209. *See also* Agents

Clark, William, visits Hidatsa, 4, 324, 325, 341

Clark, William P., studies Hidatsa, 342

Clifford, Walter, agent, 138. *See also* Agents

Clothing, stored, 13, 40, 42; dresses, 29, *57, 167, 178, 257, 309;* sewn, 29, 133, 150, 233, 234, 252, 257; as gift, 43, 90, 109; shirts, *52, 137, 180, 309, 310;* children's, *57, 60, 126, 234, 311;* vest, *60;* in winter, *77,* 124; leggings, 90, 98, 105, *109,* 126, *172, 252, 257, 311;* sashes, 92, 93, 137, *180;* for warfare, 98, 99, 133, *135-37;* robes, *99;* for courting, 114; blankets, *115;* at dances, 132, *159, 160,* 162, *254,*

303; coats, 133, *135;* uniforms, *135, 178,
216, 257; issue goods, 140, 218, 234,
247; white styles adopted, 144, 145, 223,
234, 246, 252-53, *254;* traded, 185, 218,
220-21; breech clout, 245, 303;
cowboy's, *247;* at funerals, 274, 275. *See
also* Boots, Moccasins
Clubs, ceremonial, *95. See also* Hammers,
Mauls
Coal, used, 75, 210, 217; mined, 209, 265;
resources flooded, 317
Coal Harbor, N.Dak., 217
Coffee, 58, 61; preparation, 66, *142, 259,*
260; pots, *66, 260;* grinders, *142, 259;*
traded, 217, 218; medicinal use, 252
Cold Medicine, Buffalo Bird Woman's sister,
21, 53
Collier, John, commissioner, 224
Colton Cottage, mission boardinghouse, *148*
Combs, rubber, *112*
Congregational church, at Like-a-Fishhook,
144-51, 152; at Elbowoods, 152, 211,
233, 283; at Independence, 186, 211,
279-84. *See also* Christianity, Missions and
missionaries
Cooking, traditional methods, 13, 58-60, *79;*
new methods, 236, 252, 260. *See also*
Feasts, Foods, specific foods
Corn, *207,* 351; ceremonies, 7, 331;
preserved, 19, 36, 68, *208;* culture, *33,*
202, 208, 312, 334; cooked, 58, 66, 67,
68, 81; balls, *79,* 331; used in making
pots, 118; recommended by government,
201; bread, 314
Corn husk bag, *164*
Corn People, Hidatsa name, 322
Corn stage, 65, *208, 285. See also* Drying
stage
Corn Stalk, family tree, 21
Corral, in earth lodge, 19; in roundup, 243
Cosmetics, *see* Face paint, Perfume
Cottonwood, used for bowls, 16, 60; bark
used, 74, 77, *118, 119;* used in
construction, 335
Council for Home Mission Study, 294
Courtenay, William, acting agent, 143, 155.
See also Agents
Courtship, opportunities for, 30, 34-35, 38,
65, 82; customs, 107-13
Cowboys, wages, 242; Indian, *242, 250;*
gear, *246-49. See also* Ranching
Coyote Necklace, ration ticket, *213*
Cradle bundle, construction, *123;* use, 124;
toy, *238*
Cradles, 29
Crafts, sacred, *see* Sacred knowledge
Cree Indians, trade, 59
Crow, helps with vision quest, 197-98
Crow Flies High, leader, 49, 137; founds
villages, 327
Crow Flies High Village, 344
Crow Indians, hideworking, 48, 49, 51;
trade, 164; lifeway, 322; Mountain, 323,
325; River, 323, 325, 326; archaeology,
324
Crow's Heart, leader, 225, 343
Crows Heart, Edgar, markets cattle, *244*
Crow's Paunch, quoted, 226

Cups, enamelware, *39;* metal, *68. See also*
Dishes
Currants, used, 335
Curtis, George L., photographer, 342

Dakota Indians, *see* Sioux Indians
Dance arbor, depicted, *304*
"Dance of the Mandan Indians," engraving,
88
Dances, *223, 309;* society, 88, 90-91; for
warfare, 100, 304; clothing, 132, *159,*
160, 162, 254, 303; described, 161, 303; body
painting, 197; dance societies, 281, 303,
311. *See also* Grass Dance, Sun Dance
Dawes, Henry, congressman, 181
Dawes Act, *see* General Allotment Act
Dawson, Anna, field matron, *253*
Deane, Dani Sue, quoted, 317
Deapolis, Mandan village, 7, 324
Decoration Day (Memorial Day), observed,
275, 277
Deer, hide used, 29, 39; antlers used, 37,
85; hides tanned, 45; hunted, 70, 72, 76,
78, 132, 336; call, *78;* butchered, *79;*
other uses, 93, *160, 161,* 307; powers,
111; hides traded, 153, 217
Deer's Head, gives feathers, 104
Deland, Charles E., studies Hidatsa, 342
Denig, Edwin T., trader, 341
Densmore, Frances, ethnomusicologist, 94,
151, 343
Desk, school, *234*
Devils Lake, N.Dak., origin site, 325-26. *See
also* Sioux, at Devils Lake
Digging stick, used, 32, *35,* 204
Dishes, wooden, *16,* 58, 59, *60;* storage, 19;
metal, 58; crockery, *67, 255. See also*
Kettles, Pans, Pots and pottery
Dogs, in village life, 8-9, 13; in lodges, 14,
19; at work, 22, *26,* 53, *54,* 55, *288;* toy,
31; meat eaten, 159, 160
Doors, uses, xii, 192, 317; skin, 13, *19*-20;
board, 192, 194
Dorsey, J. Owen, studies Hidatsa, 342
Dreaming, gives power, 25. *See also* Visions
and vision quests
Drum, society member, 91
Drums, *94, 165, 310, 311;* at dances, 159-60,
302, 303; types, 310
Drumsticks, *94, 165, 310;* at dances, 160,
162
Drying stage, *8,* 34, *36,* 62. *See also* Corn
stage
Duck, beak used, 33
Dyes, used, 49

Eagle, James, policeman, *214*
Eagle trapping, 78, 337; bundles, 35; rattles,
151; lodge, *290*
Eagles, feathers, 75, *82,* 90, *97, 104, 160,*
306, 309, 318
Earth lodges, exteriors depicted, *5-15, 18-19,*
195, 297; described, 9, 13-19, 336;
ownership, 13; etiquette, 13, *18-19;*
housekeeping, 13, 38-39, 40, 42, 118;

activities on, 13, 91, 107, 110, 112;
smoke hole, 13, 113; interiors depicted,
14, 18-19, 177, 263, 300; construction,
22, 116, *120-21,* 194, *195,* 331; in winter
villages, *22,* 334, 338; games in, 27, 29;
for societies, 91, 92
Education, goals, 154, 231; curriculum, 155,
235; standardized, 231, 235; traditional
system disrupted, 254. *See also* Sacred
knowledge, Schools
Egg beater, depicted, *236*
Elbowoods, N.Dak., 187; missions, 144,
152, 211, 232, 283; schools, *152,* 211,
232, 283; fair, 202; agency, *211;* dance,
223, 304; bridge, 264; hospital, 271
Elderly, attitudes toward, 18, 196; diet, 63,
72; affected by dam, 316-17
Elk, bone used, 44; horn used, 44, 45, 46,
111, 112; teeth used, *57,* 60, *167, 309;*
powers, 111; hunted, 336
Elm, used, 103, 336
Enemy, Arikara, *282*
Enemy, Susie, depicted, *150*
Enemy Heart, Arikara spokesman, 264, 265
English, language learned, 152, 226;
interpreters, 212; singing, 283. *See also*
Goodbird, interpreter
"Enroute to Winter Camp, Indian Dog Sleds
Crossing the Ice," painting, *26, 171*
Ermine, fur used, 97, 306; hunted, 337
Evans, John Thomas, trader, 324
Everett, Clair, policeman, *214*
Everlasting Grandmother, culture hero, 37

Face paint, 90, 154; methods, 96, 106, 108,
197; materials, *96, 197;* bags, *107, 108.*
See also Paints
Fairs, agricultural, 202
Fans, scented, 107; eagle wing, *306*
Farmers, government, 209-13, *214*
Farming, *see* Agriculture
Feasts, 197; harvest, 35; society, 88, 90-91,
94, 160; wedding, 109; for lodge
building, 120; dog meat, 159, 160; at
Christmas, 186; at giveaways, 282; at
bundle transfer, 330. *See also* Food
Feathers, on arrows, 75; on headdress, *82;*
protective, *104;* used in bustle, 160. *See
also* specific birds
Female Coyote, depicted, *182*
Ferguson, James B., doctor, 24
Ferry, at Independence, *3,* 187, 264, 291
Field, Miss ———, depicted, *150*
Field matron, office, 253-54
"Fire Canoe at Fort Berthold," painting, *12,*
180
Fireplaces, location, 18; drying pole, 18. *See
also* Stoves
Fire screen, depicted, *19*
Fire steel, depicted, *131*
Fires, built, 48, 131; wood gathered, 53
First Creator, culture hero, 242, 325
Fishing, 335
Five Villages, Knife River settlement, 4, 7,
324
Flag, *305;* flown, 6, 11, 304; at ceremonies,
160, 275

Flax, price, 200

Fleshers, used, *44*

Flies Low, Goodbird's clan uncle, 21, 60, 124–26

Flint, carrying cases, *48, 50,* 131, *176*

Flowers, silk, *277*

Flute, depicted, *110*

Foods, mealtime etiquette, 13, 58–60, 255; stored, 19, 40–42; introduced by whites, 58, 61, 142, 150, 204, 236, 252, 255, 259; shared, 144–45, 245; sold, 220–21; Wilson tests, 295. *See also* Cooking, Feasts, specific foods

Foolish Bear, policeman, *214;* wife, 297

Foolish Woman, markets cattle, *244*

Foolish Woman, Mrs., 25, 139; gives gift, 95

Fork, depicted, *58*

Fort Atkinson, 342; identified, 11; block house, *129;* map, *138. See also* Fort Berthold II

Fort Benton, supplies farm equipment, 200–201, 203–4

Fort Berthold I (Old Fort Berthold), trading post, 10; depicted, *129, 138. See also* Like-a-Fishhook Village

Fort Berthold II, trading post, 11; depicted, *12, 129, 130, 135, 138, 139;* army post, 135–37, 141. *See also* Fort Atkinson, Like-a-Fishhook Village

Fort Berthold Agency, map, *138;* communications, *138, 143,* 212; established, 139–40; described, *141,* 210, *211;* moved, 141, *211;* clinic, 266, 271; financial support, 272

Fort Berthold Indian Reservation, maps, *ix, 273;* farm equipment, 200–201; fair, 202; described, 228; lands, 265, 273, 314; hospital, 271, 314, 317; tribal council, 316

Fort Buford, military post, 23, 136

Fort Clark, fur post, 5, 24, 341, 342; described, 6; Indian village, 6, 7, 28; dances at, 83, 106

Fort Laramie Treaty of *1851,* provisions, 139, 142, 272, 316

Fort Stevenson, army post, 129, 130, 135–36, 139, 154, 342; boarding school, 154, 217, 231–34, 257

Fort Union, trading post, 130

Four Bears, leaders, 52, 139, 271; bridge, 271

Fox, Gregory L., historian, 344

Fox, skin used, 93; hunted, 336

Fredericks, John, rancher, 316

Fredericks, Kenneth, quoted, 316

French, traders, 59, 128, 340

Frosted, Thomas, policeman, 216

Fruits, canned, 58, 61

Fry bread, made, *255*

Full House, Goodbird's relative, 21, 60, 70

Funeral customs, clan responsibilities, xii, 20, 274–77; mourning, 9, *278,* 331; prayers, 20, 274; gift giving, 274–77

Fur trade, at Like-a-Fishhook, 9, 10–11, 340. *See also* Trade and traders

Games, ice slides, *23;* hoop and stick, *27;* ball and stick (shinny), *27,* 28, *309;* mudball fights, *28;* follow-the-leader, 28; throw stick ("sticks"), 28, 38, *239;* cards, *149;* parlor, 233; football, 239; races, 303; moccasin, 303, *308;* tug of war, *308*

Gardens, map, *36. See also* Agriculture

Garfield, James A., president, 158

Garrison, N.Dak., *264,* 314

Garrison Dam, impact, 264, 316–18, 332, 339; built, 315–17. *See also* Lake Sakakawea

Garter Snake, in mudball fight, 28

Garters, dance, *160, 161*

Gas station, depicted, *269*

Geese, bones used, 95

General Allotment Act of *1877* (Indian Severalty Act, Dawes Act), vi, 181, 272, 338

Generosity, on hunt, 70, 82; cultural concepts, 144–45; food sharing, 245. *See also* Gift giving, Giveaways

Geography, taught, 154, *155, 235*

Gerard, Frederic F., trader, 138

Germans, immigrants, 267

Gift giving, 58, 164, 251; system described, 43, 140; in society transfer, 89; in marriage, 107–10, 112–13; in transfer of sacred knowledge, 116; in naming, 123; at dance, 160, 161, 303; in adoptions, 163; at Christmas, 186, 282, 287; effect on raising livestock, 242; at death, 275, 277; in bundle transfer, 296. *See also* Generosity, Giveaways

Gillette, Evadne Baker, quoted, 318

Gillette, George, tribal chairman, 316

Gillette, Maude, at sewing meeting, *150*

Gilman, Carolyn, identified, 352

Gilmore, Melvin R., anthropologist, 207

Girls, *see* Women and girls

Giveaways, system described, 102, 282; U.S. government holds, 140; prohibited, 222, 224

Glue, used, 48; made, *75,* 337

Gods, *see* Religion

Goes Back to Big Bunch, Wolf Chief's sweetheart, 110–13

Goff, O. S., photographer, 11; photographs, *114, 148*

Good Voice, relative of Buffalo Bird Woman, 83

Good Worker, quoted, 232

Goodall, John, Indian Office employee, *244*

Goodbird (Tsakáka-sakis, Edward Goodbird), *ii, 198, 199, 219, 274, 279, 282, 284, 290, 313;* works with Wilson, 2, 20, 71, 285, 292, 294, 345, 348; family tree, 21; sketches, *22, 28, 30, 33, 36, 38, 40, 42, 53, 54, 60, 70–74, 77, 79, 87, 98, 99, 101, 109, 111, 120–21, 125–27, 155, 159, 160, 175, 192, 199, 199, 276, 289, 290;* boyhood, 27, 28, 30, 122–27; clothing, *60;* hunts, 69–71, 80; birth, 122; naming, 123, 209; education, 152, 154, 155, 159; ceremonies, 160; allotment, 187; children, 187, 299, 282, *291,* 225, 314; homes, 192, 195, 293; at dances, 196; vision quest, 196–99; government farmer,

205, 209–13; relations with agent, 209, 215–16, 265; interpreter, 212, 279, 280, 283, 286, 298, 301, 343, 345, 348; policeman, 215–16; rancher, 242, 246, 312; minister, 268, 280–84; speech, 275; converts to Christianity, 279; characterized, 280, 286, 312; as artist, 286, 290, 348, 349; adoptive relationships, 286, 345; death, 314

Goodbird, Alfred, baptized, 279

Goodbird, Benjamin, translator, 282; tribal official, 314

Goodbird, Charles, married, 225; baptized, 279

Goodbird, Mrs. Edward, *see* Sioux Woman

Goodbird, Paul, depicted, *291*

Goodbird the Indian: His Story, book, *294,* 345

Good-furred Robe, culture hero, 33

Goose Society, *see* Societies, Goose

Gooseberries, used, 335. *See also* Berries

Grain, bagged, *205*

Grand Portage Reservation, Minn., 66

Grandfather River, 328

Grandmother Earth, 328

Grandmother's Lodge, village, 344

Grandson, culture hero, 37

Grass Dance, food, 67, 160, 258; drumstick, 94; clothing, 132, *159, 160, 161, 162,* 307; society leaders, 160, 275

Great Depression, 315, 343

Great Northern Railway Company, impact of line, 264; snowplow, *266*

Gristmill, at agency, 210

Gros Ventre, *see* Hidatsa

Guns, barrels reused, 44, 95; in hunting, 72, 86, 100; flintlock, *76,* 132; transition to, 80, 103, 132; rifles, *86, 100,* 132; as gifts, 90, 108; in warfare, 98, 99, 100; carbine, *136. See also* Ammunition

Guts, warrior, 106

Had Many Antelopes, 185; quoted, 226

Hair, brush, *107;* length, 144, 145, 278; decorations, 159, 162

Hairpipes, ornaments, *160, 162, 238*

Hairy Coat, sells objects, 27, 40, 85; lodge, 42, 113, *213;* informant, 93, 151; ration ticket, *213;* gives advice, 297

Hairy Coat, Mrs., *263*

Hale, Mr. ———, *295*

Hale, William, paints robe, 119

Hall, Mr. ———, markets cattle, *244*

Hall, Charles L., Congregational minister, 144–50, 279; opposes traditional ways, 145, 183, 223; quoted, 182; performs wedding, 225; preaches at Independence, 279; publications, 282; helps anthropologists, 285, 343

Hall, Emma Calhoun, missionary, 144, 145, 146

Hall, Robert, missionary, 280

Hall, Susan Webb, missionary, *144, 145*

Hammers, secular, *64, 194;* society, *90;* used, 192, *194*

Hampton Institute, Va., 231, 253, 342

Hanging Stone, Crow, 108–9

Hanson, Jeffery, essay, 333-39; identified, 352

Harmon, Catherine Fox, quoted, 318

Harness making, taught at boarding school, 233, 237

Has Game Stick, Indian leader, 4

Has Much Sweet Grass, sacred knowledge, 116

Has Red Shield, quoted, 232

Hat, cowboy, *247. See also* Headdresses

Hatchets, shingling, *77;* used, 192. *See also* Axes

Hawks, feathers used, *82, 90, 96;* in medicine bundle, 99

Hawk's Nest Bluff, N.Dak., 188

Hay, cut, 205, 209, *250*

Hayes, Rutherford B., president, 158

Hayfork, depicted, *205*

Haynes, F. Jay, photographer, 135; photograph, *135*

Hayt, E. A., commissioner, 143

Headdresses, hunting cap, 29; feather war bonnet, 42, 109, 126, *174, 282, 306, 309;* society, *82,* 91, 93, *96, 170;* weasel skin, 109; as gifts, 109, 161, 282; roach, *161, 174, 307. See also* Hat

Health and health care, diseases, 23, 337; doctor, 25, 266, *271;* in earth lodges, 121; clinics and hospitals, 210, 266, 271, 317; effects of diet, 252, 337, 338. *See also* Medicine, Smallpox

Heart River, boundary, 272; villages at, 322, 325-26

Hebron, N.Dak., shipping point, 200, 243

Henry, Alexander the younger, trader, 5, 322, 341

Herbs, medicinal, *23, 25, 177;* teas, 66

Heron, bones used, 95

Heye, George, collector, 298, 311, 345, 348

Hidatsa, Hidatsa village, 7, 323

Hidatsa (Gros Ventre, Minitaree) Indians, identified, viii, 4; relations with Arikara, 2, 28, 140; relations with Mandan, 2, 28, 140, 322, 323-24, 326; earth lodge villages, 4, *7,* 8-12, 23, 322-27; move to Like-a-Fishhook, 4, 327; relations with Sioux, 129, 164; language, 145, 146, 147, 150, 283, 314, 318, 322, 323, 342; leave Like-a-Fishhook, 182, 338; visit other reservations, 202; work ethic, 209; tribal income, 210; population, 265, 324, 337; traditional territory, *272-73,* 333, 335; patriotism, 303; trade with other tribes, 322; subgroups explained, 322-23; name, 322, 326; relations with Ojibway, 324

"Hidatsa Village, Earth-covered Lodges, on the Knife River, 1810 Miles above St. Louis," painting, *7, 168*

Hidatsa-proper, Hidatsa subgroup, 322; villages, 324-26; origin traditions, 324, 325, 326

Hides, techniques of working, 43-49; painted, 51, *166;* berry mashing, *64. See also* specific animals

Hides and Eats, pot maker, 17, 41, 118

High Back Bone, owns pipe, 49

High Eagle, scout, 275

Hoes, 192, 202; metal, *32, 78, 206;* bone, *32, 206*

Hoffman, Charles W., agent, 286-87, 300. *See also* Agents

Holding Eagle, LeRoy, translator, 147

Holidays, Decoration Day, 275, 277; Christmas, 282; Fourth of July, 302-3

Honor marks, 92, 161, 163, 196; earned, 52, 56, 82, 100; examples, *95, 101, 104, 105, 198, 274, 276;* defined, 102

Hoofs, bells, 13; on rattles, *93, 307. See also* specific animals

Horn, utensils, 17; toys, *31;* for powder, *76. See also* specific animals

Horse mint, perfume, *107*

Horses, care, 9, 10, 19; other uses, 22, 28, 35, 97; in warfare, 28, 84, 102, 104; hair used, *39, 47, 52, 57, 89, 90, 91, 97, 105, 107, 162, 163, 306;* as gifts, 43, 108, 109, 110, 112-13, 160, 282; value, 56; in hunting, 70-71, *79,* 80-82, 109, 337; equipment, *84-85, 136, 237;* in agriculture, *200-201, 203,* 243

Hospital, at Elbowoods, 210, 317. *See also* Health and health care

Hot Thistles, dance society, 303

Howard, James H., archaeologist, 62

Howling Wolf, Arikara, 282

Howlingwolf, Mrs., depicted, *150*

Huber, Fred, teacher, 153

Hunting, methods, 69-73, 78, 81-92; locations, 196, 336; lodge, *239, 290;* supplements rations, 338

Hunts Along, policeman, *214*

Hyde, George E., anthropologist, 343

Hymns, *see* Songs

Hypodermic kit, *24*

Immigration, railroad encourages, 265

Independence, N.Dak., ferry, *2-3,* 187, 264, 291; region described, 2, 22, 196, 198; founded, 182; maps, *186-87, 317;* issue house, 186, *189;* school, 186, *189,* 268, 314; church, 186, *189, 279-84;* name, 196; community described, 203, 314-15; holidays celebrated, 275, 277, 282; flooded, 314

Independence Hill, N.Dak., 182, 314

Indian Office, *see* United States Office of Indian Affairs

Indian Reorganization Act of *1934,* 314

Indian Severalty Act, *see* General Allotment Act

"Indians Hunting the Bison," engraving, *80*

Inheritance, system of, 13, 338

Inkwells, depicted, *157, 227*

"The Interior of the Hut of a Mandan Chief," engraving, *14*

Iron Woman, Sioux, sells object, 23

Irrigation, projects built, 315

Issue goods (annuities), tools, 45, 200, 203, 204, 248, 258; sundries, 46, 112; household items, 58, 59, 67, 256; blankets, 115; defined, 140; cloth and clothing, 140, 218, 234, 247, 257; seeds, 204; stored, 219. *See also* Annuities, Rations

Issue house, at Independence, 186, *189*

Itsikamahidish, culture hero, 154, 326

Jacobs, Johann, immigrant family, *267*

Jacobsen site, village, 326

James River, N.Dak., villages, 324

Jefferson, Thomas, quoted, 201

Jenks, Albert E., anthropologist, 345

Jermark, Ernest W., agent, 224. *See also* Agents

Jones, Sam, refuses to buy bundle, 297

Juneberries, preserved, *64-65;* gathered, 65, 314, 335; wood used, 74, 77, *197*

June Berry Blossoms, makes object, 85

Kauffman, Jacob, agent, 141, 158. *See also* Agents

Kehoe, Elizabeth, mission worker, 189

Kettles, iron, *59;* gift, 90; for tea, *260. See also* Dishes, Pans, Pots and pottery

Kinship, types, 20. *See also* Adoptive relationships, Clans, Societies

Kipp, James, trader, 341

Knife River, Indian villages, 4, *5-7,* 322, 324-26, 341

Knife River Indian Villages National Historic Site, 324

Knives, metal, 16, *62, 87;* sheath, *50;* bone, *58, 62;* issue goods, *142*

Knowledge, sacred, *see* Sacred knowledge

Kurz, Rudolph F., artist, 48, 128, 342; watercolor, *129*

Ladles, *see* Spoons

Lake Sakakawea, *315;* map, *ix, 317;* impact, 332, 339. *See also* Garrison Dam

Lamps, kerosene, *149, 160*

Lance, ceremonial, *103*

Lance Owner, quoted, 105; sells objects, 108

Land, patterns of ownership, x, 181, 272; leased, 212, 265-66, 339; sold, 227, 228, 264-65, 272, 316; claims case, 315; condemned, 316. *See also* Allotment

"Landscape with Herd of Buffalo on the Upper Missouri," painting, *81, 169*

Larpenteur, Charles, fur trader, 129

Latta, Samuel, Indian agent, 129. *See also* Agents

Laundry, at boarding school, 233, 234, *236;* traditional methods, 253; at home, 253, *256*

Law enforcement, controls on traders, 218-19, 229; Indian courts, 222. *See also* Police; Societies, Black Mouth

Leader, quoted, 46; makes leggings, 105

Lee, Walter, agent, 212. *See also* Agents

Lehmer, Donald J., archaeologist, 344

Levings, Gertrude, makes objects, 57

Lévi-Strauss, Claude, anthropologist, 347

Lewis, Meriwether, visits Hidatsa, 4, 324, 335, 341

Libby, Orin G., secretary, 301, 344, 345

Liberty Loan, bond sales, 303, 304

Like-a-Fishhook Village, founded, 4, 327; described, *8-12,* 129, 225, 327, 342;

maps, *10–11, 36;* white influence, 128–30;
army post, 135–38; Indian agency,
139–40; schools, 152; abandoned, 182,
183, 327, 338; story about, 294; site
flooded, *315;* excavated, 344. *See also* Fort
Berthold I, Fort Berthold II
Lincoln, Rev. Robert, depicted, *282*
Liquor, used, 217; sold, 219
Little Bear, makes object, 97
Little Bear, Mrs., sells object, 45
Little Missouri River, N.Dak., 124, 275, 316
Little Owl, Mandan, *282*
Livestock, *see* Ranching
Log cabins, *see* Cabins
Lone Fight, Theodore, sells object, 52;
drum, 94
Long Fox, Sioux, 163
Longfellow, Daniel W., trader, 11, 134, 138
Love charm, horn, *111. See also* Courting
Low Hat clan, origin, 330
Lower Hidatsa, Hidatsa village, 325
Lowie, Robert H., anthropologist, 49, 151,
238, 293; collector, 96, 97, 162, 349;
makes donation, 281; quoted on Wilson,
295, 347
Lucky Mound, N.Dak., 182, 187

Macalester College, St. Paul, Minn., 347
Mackenzie, Charles, trader, 341
McKenzie, Jessie, missionary, 285
McLean County, N.Dak., 267
Magpie, marriage, 21, 108–10; death, 113
Magpie, hunted, *73;* feathers used, 93
Mallery, Garrick, studies Hidatsa, 342
Mandan, Adam, quoted, 317, 318
Mandan, Arthur, at dedication, 281;
interpreter, 343
Mandan, Howard, debts, 134; hired, 277
Mandan Indians, relations with Hidatsa, 2,
4, 28, 140, 322, 323–24, 326; relations
with Arikara, 2, 28, 140; move to Like-a-
Fishhook, 4, 327; villages, *5, 8–12, 23,*
322; religion, 10, 225, 329, 330;
quillwork, 51; generosity, 58; traditional
stories, 83; societies, 88, 97; language,
145, 146, 147, 150, 322; leave Like-a-
Fishhook, 182, 338; population, 265,
337; patriotism, 303; studied, 320;
origins, 341
Many Growths, Goodbird's clan relative, 277
Many Growths, Small Bull's mother, 113
Maps, of village sites, *7, 323;* of Like-a-
Fishhook, *10–11, 12, 138;* of an earth
lodge, *18–19;* of Fort Berthold, *138;* of
Independence, *186–87, 317*
Marriage, story about, 27; customs, 107–13,
233; with whites, 128; new ways, 222,
225, 233. *See also* Courting
Mason, Thad, ration ticket, *213*
Mats, rush, 116, *118,* 289
Matthews, Washington, ethnologist, 326,
338, 342
Mauls, stone, *64, 261. See also* Clubs,
Hammers
Maximilian, Prince of Wied-Neuwied, studies
Hidatsa, 6, 88, 89, 326, *341–42;* quoted,
31, 334, 341

Meat, cooked, 44, 58–60, 63, *79,* 82;
canned, 58, 61; dried, *63,* 257, 261;
transported, 79, 85; smoked, *190. See also*
specific animals
Medicine bundles, *see* Sacred bundles
"Medicine lodge," depicted, *8*
Medicine poles, *see* Votive Poles
Medicines, 266, 271, 296; vaccines, 23, 24;
herb cures, *23, 25, 177;* powers
purchased, 25, 122, 123; prohibited, 25,
222, 224; patent remedies, *26;* for
childbirth, 122, *123;* defined, 328. *See also*
Health and health care, Religion, Sacred
bundles
Melons, *207*
Men and boys, inheritance, 13, 296; games,
27–31, 239; ways to success, 38, 95, 98,
101, 102, 154, 196, 328; traditional
tasks, 69–87, 98–106, 192; cosmetics,
107, 108; new tasks, 192, 194, 200–205,
233, 237, 242–50, 339; dances, 203. *See
also* Children, Courting, Marriage, specific
tasks
Menard, ——, trader, 324
Metal, in arrow points, 74
Meyer, Roy W., historian, 344
Mice, in earth lodges, 40, 69
Midipadi Butte, village, 326
Midipadi clan, *see* Waterbuster clan
Midwives, 122; medicines, *123*
Mih-tutta-hang-kusch, Mandan village, *6, 7.*
See also Fort Clark
"Mih-Tutta-Hang-Kusch, Mandan Village,"
watercolor, *6*
Minitarees, *see* Hidatsa
Mink, hunted, 336
Minneapolis, St. Paul and Sault Ste. Marie
Railroad (Soo Line), impact, 265, 266
Minnesota Historical Society, St. Paul,
Wilson collections, 347–51
Mirror, depicted, *108*
Missions and missionaries, Sunday school,
129; impact on religious life, 196, 332;
relations with Wolf Chief, 210; clinic,
266; financial support, 272. *See also*
Catholic church; Christianity;
Congregational church; Schools, mission
Missouri River, Hidatsa leader, 4; owns
bundle, 4, 13, 296
Missouri River, Indian villages, 3, 4, *7,* 22,
128, 322–27; in games, *7, 9,* 27, 29;
bottomlands, 36, 187, 188, 189, 334,
335–36; water source, 38; sewer, 38;
depicted, *122, 188, 191, 320–21;* at
Independence, 196, 197; boundary, 272;
dammed, 315–18; sacred nature, 328. *See
also* Ferry, Garrison Dam, Lake Sakakawea
Missouri River Basin Investigations Project,
315, 327, 344
Mitchell, David D., fur trader, 24
Mitutanka, *see* Mih-Tutta-Hang-Kusch
Moccasins, 81, 98, 102, 118, 248; quilled,
51, 115, 126, 168, 276; beaded, *52;*
children's, *126;* dogskin, *160*
Molander State Historic Site, N.Dak., 325
Montclair, Hollis, baptized, 279
Moose, tail used, 161
Morgan, Lewis Henry, ethnologist, 342

Morrow, Stanley J., photographer, 52;
photographs, *8–9, 130, 140*
Mortar and pestle, depicted, *16, 63*
Murphy, John S., agent, 215, 216; relations
with Wolf Chief, 214–15, 218–19, 227.
See also Agents
Museum of the American Indian, Heye
Foundation, works with Wilson, 298,
348; returns bundle, 315
Music, *see* Songs, specific musical instruments
Mussels, shell spoons, 68

Nails, used, *194*
Naming, customs, 102, 123
Napkin rings, *262*
Naxpike, see Sun Dance
Necklaces, bead, *115;* hairpipe, *160, 162, 254*
New Town, N.Dak., bridge, 271
Newspapers, advertisements, *270*
Nez Percé Indians, trade with, 164
Night Grass Dance Society, 157
Nightwalker, leader, 326
Nightwalker's Butte, village, 326, *327,* 343
Nishu, N.Dak., 182
No Tears, makes object, 85
North Dakota, map, *ix;* population, 265;
licenses automobiles, 268; State Fair, 202
North Dakota, State Historical Society of,
344; collections, 11, 351; reacts to
bundle sale, 298, 301; conducts
archaeology, 315
North West Company, fur traders, 324, 341
Northern Pacific Railway Company, ships
goods, 134, 135, 200; impact, 264, 265,
272; advertisement, *265*
Not-Woman, makes toy, 27

Oats, price, 200
Oil, used, 205; can, *268*
Ojibway (Chippewa) Indians, relations with
Hidatsa, 142, 324; Drum Dance, 159
Okipa, ceremony, 10, 331
Old Mouse, Nellie, marriage, 225
Olsen, Fred, photographer, 214
Only Man, culture hero, 80, 242, 324
Otter, Buffalo Bird Woman's grandmother,
21, 25, 32
Otter, skins used, 88, 91, 132, 160; hunted,
336
Otter Goes Out, sells object, 50
Owl, feathers used, 93, 306; used to frighten
children, 125, 126
Owl Woman, *206, 261, 339;* sells object, 44,
50; photographed, 62, 65

Packineau, Frank, markets cattle, 243
Packineau, Joseph, quoted, 223; weaves
hatband, 247
Packs Antelope, culture hero, 330
Packs Wolf, depicted, *309*
Paddles, for bullboat, 125
Pails, metal, 109, 190, *259. See also* Buckets
Painted Woods Lake, N.Dak., 325
Paints, *108, 197;* on hides, *23, 42, 48, 51,*
104, 105, 166; tools, *47;* used on bodies,

93, *102, 160,* 197; used in hair, *160. See also* Face paint

Pankratz, J. J., photographer, 200-201

Pans, frying, *67, 260;* muffin, *236;* basin, *258. See also* Dishes, Kettles, Pots and pottery

Paper, stationery, 157

Parfleches, *40, 42, 164. See also* Bags, Boxes

Parshall, N.Dak., founded, 265

Pawnee Indians, make mats, 118

Peabody Museum, Cambridge, Mass., 343

Péhriska-rúhpa, Hidatsa, 51, *93*

"Pehriska-Ruhpa / Mennitarre in the Dog Danse," engraving, *93*

Pelicans, bones used, 95

Pencils, slate, *156;* graphite, *156*

Pens, depicted, *157, 227*

Pepper, George E., anthropologist, 345

Perfumes, depicted, *107*

Pick, Lewis A., plans dams, 315

Pick City, N.Dak., 318

Pigs, raised, 242, 244

Pine, used, 35

Pipes, sacred, *25,* 98-99, 330; bags, *49, 163;* everyday, *78, 81, 131;* tamper, *89;* society, *89, 160, 163, 176*

Pipestone (catlinite), pipes, *25, 78, 89, 163, 176;* mined, 163

Plain Color, quoted, 232

Plenty Chiefs, Walter, finds hoe, 78

Plows, used, 192, *200, 203;* symbolism, 201, 216

Plums, tree used, 103; as food, 335

Police, Black Mouths, xii, 38, 80-82, 88, 214, 215; Indian, xii, 214-16, 219, 230

Poor Wolf, informant, 89, 342; Christian convert, 144, 145; tattoos, 145, *151*

Porcupine, Francis, quoted, 275

Porcupine, hunted, 70, 78, 336; tail used, *107;* roach headdresses, *160, 161, 307. See also* Quillwork

"Portrait of Good Bird," painting, *173, 196*

Poster, religious, *283*

Potatoes, grown, 201, 204; sold, 215

Pots and pottery, *17, 41,* 118; tools, *118, 119;* care for, *17,* 34, 119; used, *41,* 59; iron, 41, 59; stands, *41, 119;* coffee, *66, 260;* sacred knowledge, 116, 118. *See also* Dishes, Kettles, Pans

Powder horn, depicted, *76*

Prairie Chicken (Tsistska) clan, 20, 287, 297, 312

Prairie chickens, sketched, *72;* hunted, 76

Prairie turnips, food, 206-7, 278, 337

Pronghorn, *see* Antelopes

Purse, change, *262*

Quillwork, 33; examples, *31, 39,* 47-52, *57, 61, 64, 89, 161, 163, 168, 169, 238, 276;* value, 43; techniques, 46, 49, 131; tools, *47, 131;* earns honor mark, 53, 56

Quilts, *171, 256;* in funeral customs, 277

Quirt, depicted, *246*

Rabbit Head, society leader, 78, 275

Rabbits, hunted, 73, 336; fur used, 95

Raccoons, hunted, 336

Railroads, *266;* Hidatsa name, 244; impact, 264-65; advertisement, *265. See also* specific railroad companies

Raise Heart, makes hammers, 64

Rakes, antler, *37;* wood, *37,* 219

Ranching, livestock, 202, 242-46; taught, 237; range land, 242-43, 265-66; markets, 243-46; methods, 243, *250-51;* equipment, 246-50, 314; affected by dam, 317. *See also* Cattle; Land, leased

Rations, system described, 140, 141, 213; issued, 186, *213;* tickets, *213;* withheld, 222, 231; insufficient, 227, 229. *See also* Annuities

Rattles, ceremonial uses, *24, 93, 97,* 151, 307

Rattlesnakes, bones used, 123

Raymond, J. W., merchant, 134

"The Real Site of Fish Hook Village, 1834-1886," painting, *12*

Red Bear, debts, 134; Arikara spokesman, 266

Red Blossom, Buffalo Bird Woman's mother, 21, 109-10; sacred knowledge, 116

Red Butte, N.Dak., 182

Red Kettle, Wolf Chief's brother, 21, 60, *181*

Red River, Hidatsa villages, 324

Red Stone, Son of a Star's brother, 56, 82, 122

Religion, 102, 328-32; prayers, 100, 122, 328-31; sacred places, 196, 317, 332; prohibited, 198, 222-25; Mandan, 225, 331, 332; resurgence, 332. *See also* Catholic church, Ceremonies, Christianity, Congregational church, Missions and missionaries, Sacred bundles, Sacred knowledge, Songs, Stories, Visions and vision quests

Republican party, on reservation, 266

Riggs, Alfred L., missionary, 144, 145

Riggs, Stephen R., missionary, 145

Rings, *114;* as honor marks, 53, *56*

Roaches, *see* Headdresses

Road Maker, tattoo artist, 151

Roads, constructed, 266

Robes, quilled, 43. *See also* specific animals

Robinson, George L., merchant, 217-18, 219

Rock Village, Hidatsa village, 326, 344

Rocky Mountain sheep, *see* Sheep

Roosevelt, Franklin D., president, 314

Rope, leather, *84;* rawhide, *197,* 198

Roseglen, N.Dak., 203

Rough Arm, gets vaccine, 23

Rued, O. J., merchant, 221

Russians, immigrants, 267

Sacajawea, Shoshone woman, 341

Sacred bundles (sacred objects), care of, 19, 330; used for curing, 23, 25, 296; Sacred Woman's, 35; used in warfare, 98, 99, 102, *104,* 246; prohibited, 145, 223, 297, 332; system described, 296, 329-30, 331; effects of diseases, 331. *See also* Religion, Waterbuster clan bundle

Sacred Woman, sacred being, 13; bundle, 35

Saddle Butte, N.Dak., 188

Saddles, depicted, *84, 85*

Sage, Buffalo Bird Woman's aunt, 53

St. Paul, Minn., stockyards, 243

Sakakawea, Shoshone woman, 341

Sakakawea, Hidatsa village, 7, 322-24, *325*

Sakakawea, Lake, *see* Lake Sakakawea

Salt, shaker, *68*

Sanish, N.Dak., 265

Santee, Nebr., mission, 144, 147

Santee Normal Training School, Santee, Nebr., 147, 231, 253

Sawmill, agency, 194, 195, 210

Saws, used, 192, *194,* 237

"Scalp Dance of the Minatarees," engraving, *106*

Scandinavians, immigrants, 267

Scattered Village, makes bucket, 101; debts, 134; refuses to buy bundle, 297

Schneider, Mary Jane, identified, 352

Schools, 159; Sunday, 129, 283; boarding, 138, 147, 148, 150, *152,* 154, 211, 217, 227, 231-39, 253, 257, 262; mission, 138, 147, 148, 150, *152,* 211, 231, 232-33, 235, 239, 262; teach Victorian aesthetic, 144, *148,* 149, *232,* 262; classroom etiquette, 152; government, 152, 186, *189,* 227, 231-34, 236-38, 314; day, 152, 186, *189,* 314; financial support, 272; improved, 315; affected by dam, 317

Science Museum of Minnesota, St. Paul, Wilson collections, 351

Scissors, in kit, 107; used, *133*

Scoria, stone, 75

Scott, Julian, artist, *196,* 173

Scripture Selections and Hymns, book, 283

Scythes, issue goods, *45;* used, 205

"Self-torture," in funeral customs, 278; discussed, 329. *See also* Visions and vision quests

Service berries, *see* Juneberries

Sewing, 29, 133; societies, *150,* 252, 256; exhibited, 202; classes, 234, 257; products sold, *262*

"Sham Fight by Mandan Boys," sketch, *28*

Shaw, W. B., trader, 156

Sheep (Bighorn sheep, Rocky Mountain sheep), horn used, *17, 46, 59, 61;* skin used, 131

Shell Creek, N.Dak., 182, 187, 275

Shells, dentalium, *47;* mussel, *68*

Shoemaking, taught at boarding school, 237

Shoes, *see* Boots, Moccasins

Shoulder Mouth, traditional story, *290*

Shovel, used, 192. *See also* Spade

Sinew, *47;* thread, 107

Sioux (Dakota) Indians, craft traditions, 39, 42, 51; at Standing Rock, 51, 142, 164, 215, 216, 345, 350; warfare, 100, 102, 106, 129, 137, 164, 322, 325, 326; at Devils Lake, 100, 132, 159, 162, 164; language, 145, 146, 147, 150; tell story, 305

Sioux Woman (daughter of Hides and Eats), sells object, 40

Sioux Woman (Goodbird's wife), *206, 278;* sells object, 48; makes object, 276; hires clan relative, 277

Sioux Woman (otherwise unidentified), sells object, 56; ration ticket, 213

Sitting Bear, Arikara, quoted, 265

Sitting Crow, quoted, 279

Sixth Iowa Cavalry, at Fort Berthold, 135

Slate, for school, *156;* pencils, *156*

Sleighs, in winter, 187

Sloan, W. Glenn, government official, 316

Small Ankle, Buffalo Bird Woman's father, 60; earth lodge, 11, 12, 13, 18-19, 75; makes object, 16; family tree, 21; generosity, 58; hunting, 69, 77, 79; teaches warfare, 102; advises Buffalo Bird Woman, 108-10, 116; sacred bundles, 122, 296, 300; opinion of education, 152, 226; honor marks, *159;* death, 181; vision quests, 246

Small Bull, marries, 113

Smallpox, 26, 342; effects, 4, 20, 322, 323, 324, 331-32, 337; vaccine, 23, 24

Smith, Hake, secretary, 230

Smith, John, quoted, 226

Smith, Nora, at celebration, *309*

Smith, Tom, markets cattle, *244;* helps build chapel, 280-81

Smoke hole, in earth lodges, 13, 113; in cabins, 192

Snakes, powers, 123

Snare plant, used, 73

Snares, for birds, 72, *73;* for rabbits, *73*

Snow, Myra, quoted, 316-17

Societies, Black Mouth, xii, 38, 80-82, 88, 89, 95, 214-15; boys' stealing, 19, 91; described, 21, 88, 329; Goose, 33, 88, 94, 329; help in harvest, 34; White Buffalo, *82-83,* 329; Kit Fox, 82, 97; Half-Shaved Head, 88; Crow, 88; sale of, 88-89; Stone Hammer, 88-92, 94, 98, 104; Skunk, 88, 92, 106, 329; Grass Crown, 89; Dog, 89, 95; Lumpwood, 89, 96; Crazy (Reckless) Dog, 92, 95; Cheyenne, 95; Horse, 97; Rough Wood, 101, 113; Fox, 103; Raven Imitator, 103; Enemy-Imitates-Woman, 103; Older Women's, 108; prayers, 122; sewing, 150, 252, 256; prohibited, 222; Enemy Woman, 223; dance, 281, 303; ceremonies, 303, 331; bundles, 329-30

Soft White Corn, family tree, 21

Son of a Star, Goodbird's father, 21, 30, *60,* 122, 124, *125,* 215, *274, 312;* as warrior, 103, 104, 126; honor marks, *104, 274, 276;* cosmetic kit, 107, 108; marriage, 113; clothing, 133, *274, 276;* debts, 134; society member, 145, 159; religious beliefs, 145, 274; allotment, 187; cabin, *192;* owns ceremonies, 192, 193; helps in vision quest, 196-98; death, 274, 278

Songs, in curing, 24; corn, 34, 312; society, 81, 89-91, 94, 106, 160, 161; for warfare, 100; sacred, 104, 122, 298, 328, 330; in courtship, 107; for children, 124; prohibited, 145, 222, 224; Christian, 146, 147, 184, 283; at boarding schools, 233; at dance, *302;* recorded, 349, 351

Souris River, boundary, 272

South St. Paul, Minn., stockyards, 243

Spade, used, 192, *204*

Sperry, Lyman B., agent, 138, 204. *See also* Agents

Spinden, Herbert J., ethnologist, 342-43

Spoons, horn, *17, 59, 61,* 66; metal, *58;* shell, *68. See also* Utensils

Spurs, depicted, *136, 248*

Square Buttes, 325

Squash, eaten, 58, 79, 81; dried, *61;* knives, *62;* cultivated, *206, 207;* harvested, *339*

Standing Bear, quoted, 232

Standing Rock Indian Reservation, Wilson visits, 51, 345, 350; issue goods, 142; attacked, 164; police, 215, 216

Stanton, N.Dak., 324

Steamboats, 6, 11, *188;* fuel, 53, 128; transport goods, 128, 134, 139-40; in vision, 182-83

Stockyards, South St. Paul, 243; Chicago, 244-46

Stomach pusher, depicted, *24*

Storage swings, depicted, *40*

Stories, 27, 199, 290; about buffalo, 27, 80, 242; about agriculture, 33, 37; about origins, 80, 242, 324-26, 328; about cattle, 242; about whites, 242, 305; transmitted, 299, 331. *See also* Religion

Stoves, replace fireplaces, 192; issued, 260

Strikes Many Women, Wolf Chief's mother, 21; owns dog, 53; cook, 58-60, 68; sacred knowledge, 122, 123

Strikes Many Women, Wolf Chief's wife, makes object, 41. *See also* Wolf Chief, Mrs.

Studebaker wagon, 181, 185

Sugar, traded, 66, 217, 218

Sun, Hidatsa concept, 154, *155*

Sun Dance, rattles, 24, 151; observed, 196-97, 341; prohibited, 198, 222; origin, 325

Sunday schools, *see* Schools, Sunday

Sunflowers, seeds eaten, 79, 81

Sunset Woman, god, 4

Supply check, *141*

Sweat baths, 328

Sweetgrass, medicinal uses, *25;* perfume, 107

Swift & Co., Chicago stockyard, 244

Swimming, in Missouri River, *7, 9*

Swings, storage, *40;* carrying strap, *127;* child's, *127*

Tailoring, taught at boarding school, 237

Tattooing, process described, *151*

Tea, herbal, 66; kettle, *260*

Tea Drinkers, dance society, 303, 311

Telegraph, at Like-a-Fishhook, 138

Telephone, reaches Independence, 264, *266;* company employs Indians, 266

Tents, in hunting camp, 77, 81

Thiessen, Thomas D., historian, 344

Thirteenth United States Infantry, at Fort Berthold, 137

Thomas, Amzi, agent, 209. *See also* Agents

Thompson, David, trader, 324, 341

Three Affiliated Tribes of the Fort Berthold Reservation (Three Tribes), identified, viii, 140; organized, 314; oppose dam, 316

Three Irons, Bernice, quoted, 318

Thresher, depicted, *203*

Thunder Birds, *see* Birds, sacred beings

Time, measured, 13

Tipis, used, 4, 192, 337; right to make, 117

Tobacco, used, 49, 131, 160; traded, 131, 217. *See also* Pipes

Torture, *see* "'Self-torture," Visions and vision quests

Toys, dolls, *29, 239;* sleds, *30, 239;* ball, *31;* travois, *31;* top, *31, 239;* bow and arrow, 69; swing, *127;* dominoes, *238;* wagon, *239;* boat, *239. See also* Games

Trade and traders, goods, 68, 75, 132-33, 153, 156-57, *179,* 220; supplied, *128;* stores, 128-30, *135,* 217-21; role, 129; competition, 130, 218-19; paperwork, *134;* among tribes, 142, 159, 164; language barrier, 154; prices, 217-19, 227; regulated, 218-19, 229. *See also* Fur trade

"Traders Departing from Ft. Berthold," painting, *129*

"The Trading Post," painting, *128*

Travois, *291;* toy, *31;* dog, 53, *54, 55;* used, 53, *55,* 85; construction, 55

Treaties, payments, 182. *See also* United States, Indian policy; individual treaties

Trobriand, Philippe Régis de, army officer, 130, 342; sketch, *139*

Tsistska clan, *see* Prairie Chicken clan

Turnips, prairie, 35, 58, *63,* 314

Turtle, Buffalo Bird Woman's grandmother, 20, 21; makes doll, 29; at work, 32, 33

Turtle No Head, self-sacrifice, 196

Turtle River, boundary, 272

Tweezers, metal, *112, 131*

Uniforms, army, *135-37;* police, *178,* 214-16

United States, Indian policy, 2, 181-82, 198, 222-25, 228, 264, 314. *See also* Treaties

United States Army, supplies medicine, 24; at Fort Stevenson, 129; at Like-a-Fishhook, 129, 135; uniforms, *135-37;* weapons, *136-37;* departmental district headquarters, 139. *See also* specific posts

United States Army Corps of Engineers, builds dam, 315-16

United States Bureau of Indian Affairs, supports return of bundle, 315; opposes dam, 316. *See also* United States Office of Indian Affairs

United States Bureau of Reclamation, 316

United States Census, *1894* report, 196

United States Congress, funds dam, 316; payments to Three Tribes, 316, 317; lobbied, 316, 318

United States Office of Indian Affairs (Indian Office, USOIA), policies, 25, 222-25, 243, 248; dispenses drugs, 26; described, 143; relations with Wolf Chief, 158, 226-30; relations with agents, 209-10; inspectors, 215, 219, 226. *See also* Allotment; Annuities; Treaties; Religion prohibited; United States Bureau of Indian Affairs

University of Minnesota, Minneapolis, Wilson collections, 73, 351

Utensils, ladles, *17, 41;* stirring paddle, *66.* See also Forks, Knives, Spoons

Van Hook, N.Dak., 265; carnival, 271
Vérendrye, Pierre Gaultier de Varennes, Sieur de la, trader, 340
Visions and vision quests, symbols, 90; Wolf Chief's, 102, 154; among Christians, 144; purpose, 154, 196, 328; fasting, 154, 328-29; Goodbird's, 196-99; method, 196-99, 328-29; prohibited, 198, 332; Small Ankle's, 246; modern difficulties, 333; Wilson's description, 345. See also Dreaming
Votive poles (medicine poles), described, 9; depicted, *13, 222, 329*

Wages, supply checks, *141;* Indian police, 214, 216; cowboy's, 242; Wilson pays, 290
Wagons, requested, 158; used, 181, 182, 192, 205, 208; issued, *185*
Waheenee, book, 294, 345; sketches, *288*
War bonnet, *see* Headdress
War Eagle, steamboat, 139
Warfare, methods, 28, 92, 95, 98-102, 184, 303-4; ended, 97, 159, 332; spies, 99, 100, 101, 104; ceremonies, 99, 100, *106,* 159-60, 197, 303-4; weapons, *100, 103, 104,* 304; sacred powers used, *104,* 296; with Sioux, 164; symbolism of headdresses, 306, 307; purposes, 322. *See also* Ammunition, Arrows, Bows, Guns, Honor marks, United States Army, World War I
[Wa]shboard, depicted, *236*
[Wa]shburn, N.Dak., *267,* 325
[Wa]ter, supply, 9, 38, 245; fetched, 17, 34, 38, 41, *101,* 110, *190;* stored, 17, 41, *137*
[Wa]ter Chief, markets cattle, 243; society leader, 281
[Wa]ter Drop, smallpox victim, 23
[Wa]terbuster (Midipadi) clan bundle, *299, 300;* powers, 4, 296-97; care of, 13, 19, 296-97, 298; sold, 296-301, 345; returned, 314-15
[W]eahtee, Buffalo Bird Woman's mother, 21; death, 20, 337
[W]easels, skin used, 91, *96,* 162
[W]eather, summer, 9, 195, 334; affects earth lodge construction, 13, 19; storms, 124-25, 296; effects on agriculture, 201, 227, 234; droughts, 296, 314-15, 339; described, 333-34. See also Winter
[W]egel, Charlie, livestock dealer, 243-46
[W]eitzner, Bella, anthropologist, 348
[Whe]at, price, 200; crop, 267
[Whet]stone, *45;* flint, 48
[Whi]stles, in hunting, *78;* in dances, 95; in courting, *110,* 111
[...], Florence, quoted, 317-18

White Buffalo Robe Unfolded, quoted, 325
White Calf, Frank, quoted, 280
White Calf, Mrs., donation, 281
White Neck, child of Wolf Chief, 127
White Shield, Arikara, 150
White Woman, summer kitchen, *195*
Whitebull, Arikara, *282*
Whitewolf, Mrs., depicted, *150*
Whitman, Carl, quoted, 317
Will, George F., anthropologist, 207, 342-43
Will, Oscar H., anthropologist, 207
Williamson, John P., missionary, 145, 146
Williamson, Thomas S., missionary, 145
Willow, used in baskets, 16, *116,* 207, 288, 335; used in pottery stands, 17, 119; used in toys, 27, 28, 31; other uses, 41, 62, 73, 86, 328, 335; used in construction, 192, 195, 335
Wilson, Ada Meyers, *217,* 347; donates collection, 349
Wilson, Frederick N., *288;* maps, *10-11, 18, 36;* artworks, 60, 61, *177, 285, 288, 289, 294, 300,* 349-50; weaves basket, 117, 288; work characterized, 340; biographical sketch, 345, 347; collections, 349-50; techniques, 350
Wilson, Gilbert L., *291, 293, 295, 297, 340, 346;* collections, vi, viii, 291, 344, 347, 348-50; techniques, vi, 285-87, 290-95, 344-52; work at Independence, 2, 281, 284, 285-95, 324-35, 344-51; relations with Lowie, 151, 238, 293, 295; adoption, 285, 286, 345; biographical sketches, 285, 344-51; prejudices, 286; relations with agent, 286-87; salary, 287; work characterized, 287, 295, 340, 344, 347; work as photographer, 291, 348-50, 352; goals, 294; author, 294, 344-47; buys bundle, 297-301, 345; death, 314, 347
Wilson, Gladys M., donates collection, 349
Wilson, M. L., professor, 351
Wilson, Sam, war bonnet, 306
Windows, used, 148, 192
Winter, 333-34; in earth lodges, 9, 12, *22, 23, 120-21;* dangers, 23, 82, 83, *190,* 252; snowstorms, 77, 78, 82, 83, 198, 266; clothing, 77, 124; effect on railroads, 266
"Winter Village of the Minatarres," engraving, *23*
Wissler, Clark, anthropologist, 293, 345, 348, 350
Wolf Chief (Kuahawi, Tsé-ka ma-tse-ítsic, Wolf C. Chief, Henry Wolf Chief), depicted, *ii, 72, 98, 101, 111, 114, 135, 181, 217, 219, 282, 295, 296, 299, 313;* boyhood, 2, 27, 28, 31, 128; works with Wilson, 2, 285, 286, 294, 296-301, 325, 326, 345; family tree, 21; illness, 23; makes objects, 35, 41, 77, 78, 101, 103, 306; sells object, 44; bag, 48; on hunts, 48, 69-73, 77, 79, 80-82, 86, 100; clothing, 56, *98, 114,* 133, *310;* society

memberships, 67, 157, 160; in war, 98-102, 104; on vision quest, 102; love life, 110-13, *114,* 154, 222, 246, 286; family, 127, *182, 183,* 218, 297, 300, *311, 313;* debts, 134; letters, 135, 153, 157, *158,* 219, 220, *226-30,* 232, 301, 314; Christianity, 145, 151, 222, 280, 297; education, 153-54, 156, 157; vision quests, 182; allotment, 182, 187, 188; store, 186, 217-21, 229, 230, 300, 314; cabin, 194, *263;* competency, 210-11; land sale, 210-11, 281; relations with agents, 210, 214-15, 218-19, 226-27, 265; policeman, 214-15; relations with neighbors, 214, 300, 312; name, 221; judge, 222; farmer, 227; supports education, 231; markets cattle, 243-46; brand, *249;* opinion of leases, 265-66; opinion of cars, 269; opinion of funeral customs, 275; helps build chapel, 280-81; gives gifts, 282; gives speech, 284; opinion of modern warfare, 304; dream, 305; death, 314; helps Bowers, 343
Wolf Chief, Mrs., *287.* See also Strikes Many Women
Wolf Chief, Frank, *182;* letter, 227; death, 297
Wolf Eyes, *99;* leads war party, 98-102
Wolf Ghost, Hidatsa, 105; sells objects, 24, 68, 131
Wolves, skins, 88; immitated, 99, 100
Women and girls, mourning, 9, 278; inheritance, 13, 338; traditional tasks, 22, 32-68, 116-21, 123, 202, 206-8, 251, 261, 288, 339; games, 27-29, 31, 238, 309; ways to success, 38, 43, 53, 116, 338; new tasks, 192, 196, 233-34, 236, 252-58, 262; dances, 303; religious life, 328, 329, 331. See also Children, Courting, Marriage, various specific tasks
Wood, W. Raymond, 344; essay, 322-37; identified, 352
Wood, gathered, 9, 38, *53,* 55, 128, 338; lumber, 194, 195; sold, 217; resources flooded, 317
Wooden Faces, dance society, 303
Woolworth, Alan R., photographer, 315; essay, 340-47; identified, 352
Word Carrier, described, *147,* 352
World War I, 303, 304
Wounded Face, Mandan, 105, 275, 325; quoted, 33; sells objects, 164, 349
Wounded Face, Joseph, makes objects, 69, 239
Wrench, monkey, 182, *185;* auto, 268

Yellow Elk, family tree, 21
Yellow Hair, sells objects, 57
Yellowstone River, *122;* hunting near, 30, 81; boundary, 272
Young Bear, Louella, quoted, 316
Young Snake, policeman, *214*